T0181554

Lecture Notes in Artificial Intelligence   13817

Subseries of Lecture Notes in Computer Science

Series Editors

Randy Goebel
University of Alberta, Edmonton, Canada

Wolfgang Wahlster
DFKI, Berlin, Germany

Zhi-Hua Zhou
Nanjing University, Nanjing, China

Founding Editor

Jörg Siekmann
DFKI and Saarland University, Saarbrücken, Germany

More information about this subseries at https://link.springer.com/bookseries/1244

Filippo Cavallo · John-John Cabibihan ·
Laura Fiorini · Alessandra Sorrentino ·
Hongsheng He · Xiaorui Liu ·
Yoshio Matsumoto · Shuzhi Sam Ge (Eds.)

Social Robotics

14th International Conference, ICSR 2022
Florence, Italy, December 13–16, 2022
Proceedings, Part I

 Springer

Editors
Filippo Cavallo
University of Florence
Florence, Italy

John-John Cabibihan 🆔
Qatar University
Doha, Qatar

Laura Fiorini
University of Florence
Florence, Italy

Alessandra Sorrentino
University of Florence
Florence, Italy

Hongsheng He 🆔
Wichita State University
Wichita, KS, USA

Xiaorui Liu
Qingdao University
Qingdao, China

Yoshio Matsumoto
National Institute of Advanced Industrial
Science and Technology
Tsukuba, Japan

Shuzhi Sam Ge 🆔
National University of Singapore
Singapore, Singapore

ISSN 0302-9743   ISSN 1611-3349 (electronic)
Lecture Notes in Artificial Intelligence
ISBN 978-3-031-24666-1   ISBN 978-3-031-24667-8 (eBook)
https://doi.org/10.1007/978-3-031-24667-8

LNCS Sublibrary: SL7 – Artificial Intelligence

This Springer imprint is published by the registered company Springer Nature Switzerland AG
The registered company address is: Gewerbestrasse 11, 6330 Cham, Switzerland

Preface

The 14th International Conference on Social Robotics (ICSR 2022) was held as a traditional in-person conference in Florence, Italy on December 13th–16th, 2022. The theme of ICSR 2022 was Social Robots for Assisted Living and Healthcare, emphasizing on the increasing importance of social robotics in human daily living and society.

The International Conference on Social Robotics brings together researchers and practitioners working on the interaction between humans and intelligent robots and on the integration of robots into the fabric of our society. Out of a total of 143 submitted manuscripts reviewed by a dedicated international team of editors, associate editors and reviewers, 111 full papers were selected for inclusion into the proceedings in this book and presented during the technical and special sessions and the conference. In addition to paper presentation sessions, ICSR 2021 also featured three keynote talks, twelve workshops, two robot design competitions, and exhibitions. The keynote talks were delivered by three renowned researchers – Professor Kerstin Dautenhahn from University of Waterloo, Canada, Professor Maria Chiara Carrozza, Italian National Research Council (CNR), Italy, and Professor Oussama Khatib, Stanford University, United States.

We would like to express our sincere gratitude to all members of the Steering Committee, International Advisory Committee, Organizing Committee, and volunteers for their dedication in making the conference a great success. We are indebted to the associate editors and reviewers for their hard work in the rigorous review of the papers. We are also very grateful to the authors, participants, and sponsors, for the continued support to ICSR.

December 2022

Filippo Cavallo
John-John Cabibihan
Laura Fiorini
Alessandra Sorrentino
Hongsheng He
Xiaorui Liu
Yoshio Matsumoto
Shuzhi Sam Ge

Organization

General Chair

Cavallo, Filippo — University of Florence, Italy

Co-general Chair

Cabibihan, John-John — Qatar University, Qatar

Honorary Chair

Ge, Shuzhi Sam — National University of Singapore, Singapore

Program Chairs

Fiorini, Laura — Università degli studi di Firenze, Italy
Liu, Xiaorui — Qingdao University, China
Matsumoto, Yoshio — National Institute of Advanced Industrial Science and Technology, Japan

Workshop Chairs

Sorrentino, Alessandra — University of Florence, Italy

Local Arrangement Chairs

La Viola, Carlo — University of Florence, Italy
Mancioppi, Gianmaria — Scuola Superiore Sant'Anna, Italy

Competition Chair

Kumar Pandey, Amit — beingAI Limited, Hong Kong, China; Socients AI and Robotics, Paris, France

Publication Chair

He, Hongsheng — Wichita State University, USA
Rovini, Erika — University of Florence, Italy

Publicity Chairs

Trovato, Gabriele   Shibaura Institute of Technology, Tokyo, Japan
Zhao, Xiaopeng   University of Tennessee, USA

Standing Committee

Ge, Shuzhi Sam   National University of Singapore, Singapore

International Program Committee

Alhaddad, Ahmad Yaser   Qatar University, Qatar
Belpaeme, Tony   Ghent University, Belgium
Borghese, N. Alberto   University of Milan, Italy
Cangelosi, Angelo   University of Manchester, UK
Chi, Wenzheng   Soochow University, China
Cortellessa, Gabriella   ISTC-CNR, Italy
D'Onofrio, Grazia   IRCSS Ospedale Casa Sollievo della Sofferenza,
                                     Italy
De Oliveira, Ewerton   Universidade Federal da Paraiba, Brazil
Esposito, Anna   University of Campania, Italy
Fortunati, Leopoldina   University of Udine, Italy
Greco, Claudia   University of Campania, Italy
Greer, Julienne   University of Texas at Arlington, USA
Hu, Yue   University of Waterloo, Canada
Jiang, Wanyue   Qingdao University, China
Katsanis, Ilias   University of the Aegean, Greece
Li, Dongyu   Beihang University, China
Liu, Xiaorui   Qingdao University, China
Louie, Wing-Yue (Geoffrey)   Oakland University, USA
Luperto, Matteo   Università degli Studi di Milano, Milano, Italy
Mastrogiovanni, Fulvio   University of Genoa, Italy
Menezes, Paulo   University of Coimbra, Portugal
Perugia, Giulia   Eindhoven University of Technology,
                                     The Netherlands
Rossi, Alessandra   University of Naples Federico II, Italy
Rossi, Silvia   University of Naples Federico II, Italy
Sciutti, Alessandra   Italian Institute of Technology, Italy
Trigili, Emilio   Scuola Superiore Sant'Anna, The BioRobotics
                                     Institute, Pontedera, Italy
Wang, Wei   Beihang University, China
Wing Chee So, Catherine   Chinese University of Hong Kong, China

Wykowska, Agnieszka   Istituto Italiano di Tecnologia, Genoa, Italy
Xu, Jin   Ohio State University, USA

Associate Editors

Cavallo, Filippo   University of Florence, Italy
Fiorini, Laura   Università degli studi di Firenze, Italy
He, Hongsheng   Wichita State University, USA
Rovini, Erika   University of Florence, Italy
Sorrentino, Alessandra   University of Florence, Italy

Reviewers

Abbasi, Nida Itrat
Alban, Ahmad
Alhaddad, Ahmad Yaser
Amorese, Terry
Andriella, Antonio
Angelopoulos, Georgios
Arnelid, Maria
Avelino, João
Banfi, Jacopo
Beraldo, Gloria
Cabibihan, John-John
Carreno-Medrano, Pamela
Chen, Shengkang
Chi, Wenzheng
Cortellessa, Gabriella
Cumbal, Ronald
De Oliveira, Ewerton
Del Duchetto, Francesco
Di Nuovo, Alessandro
Esposito, Anna
Faridghasemnia, Mohamadreza
Fiorini, Laura
Forgas-Coll, Santiago
Fortunati, Leopoldina
Fracasso, Francesca
Friebe, Kassandra
Gaballa, Aya
Galofaro, Elisa
Gamboa-Montero, Juan José
Getson, Cristina
Goldsmith, Clarissa

Gonge, Sudhanshu
Grazi, Lorenzo
Greco, Claudia
Haring, Kerstin
He, Hongsheng
Hellou, Mehdi
Higgins, Angela
Hu, Yue
Ivanova, Ekaterina
Jiang, Wanyue
Just, Fabian
Kashyap, Anwesha
Katsanis, Ilias
Khubchandani, Dr. Payal
Kim, Hyungil
Kong, Yuqi
Kshirsagar, Alap
La Viola, Carlo
Lacroix, Dimitri
Lastrico, Linda
Lauretti, Clemente
Li, Yan
Li, Dongyu
Limongelli, Rocco
Lisy, Dominika
Liu, Ziming
Longatelli, Valeria
Lotti, Nicola
Louie, Wing-Yue (Geoffrey)
Luperto, Matteo
Mancioppi, Gianmaria

Marques-Villarroya, Sara
Marra, Alessandra
Mentasti, Simone
Morillo-Mendez, Lucas
Morreale, Luca
Ning, Mang
Oddi, Angelo
Orlandini, Andrea
Perugia, Giulia
Pipino, Vanessa
Proietti, Tommaso
Ragab, Abdelrahman Mohamed
Raimo, Gennaro
Rawal, Niyati
Rezaei Khavas, Zahra
Riches, Lewis
Rodriguez Leon, Jhon Freddy
Rogers, Kantwon
Romeo, Marta
Rossi, Silvia
Rossi, Alessandra
Rovini, Erika
Santos Assunção, Gustavo Miguel
Saveriano, Matteo
Scotto di Luzio, Francesco
Semeraro, Francesco
Shahverdi, Pourya
Shangguan, Zhegong
Sharma, Vinay Krishna
Shatwell, David
Sorrentino, Alessandra
Sun, Zhirui
Tang, Zhihao

Contents – Part I

Social Robot Navigation and Interaction Capabilities (Voice, Tactile)

Socially-Aware Mobile Robot Trajectories for Face-to-Face Interactions 3
   Yalun Wen, Xingwei Wu, Katsu Yamane, and Soshi Iba

Vehicle-To-Pedestrian Communication Feedback Module: A Study
on Increasing Legibility, Public Acceptance and Trust 14
   Melanie Schmidt-Wolf and David Feil-Seifer

Let's Run an Online Proxemics Study! But, How Do Results Compare
to In-Person? 24
   Siya Kunde, Nathan Simms, Gerson Uriarte, and Brittany Duncan

AR Point&Click: An Interface for Setting Robot Navigation Goals 38
   Morris Gu, Elizabeth Croft, and Akansel Cosgun

Human-Aware Subgoal Generation in Crowded Indoor Environments 50
   Nick Ah Sen, Pamela Carreno-Medrano, and Dana Kulić

Speech-Driven Robot Face Action Generation with Deep Generative
Model for Social Robots 61
   *Chuang Yu, Heng Zhang, Zhegong Shangguan, Xiaoxuan Hei,
   Angelo Cangelosi, and Adriana Tapus*

Design of a Social Media Voice Assistant for Older Adults 75
   Jamy Li, Noah Zijie Qu, and Karen Penaranda Valdivia

Migratable AI: Personalizing Dialog Conversations with Migration Context 89
   Ravi Tejwani, Boris Katz, and Cynthia Breazeal

Generating Natural Language Responses in Robot-Mediated Referential
Communication Tasks to Simulate Theory of Mind 100
   *Ziming Liu, Yigang Qin, Huiqi Zou, Eun Jin Paek, Devin Casenhiser,
   Wenjun Zhou, and Xiaopeng Zhao*

Towards a Framework for Social Robot Co-speech Gesture Generation
with Semantic Expression 110
   Heng Zhang, Chuang Yu, and Adriana Tapus

Tactile Interaction with a Robot Leads to Increased Risk-Taking 120
   Qiaoqiao Ren and Tony Belpaeme

Affect Display Recognition Through Tactile and Visual Stimuli
in a Social Robot 130
    Sara Marques-Villarroya, Juan Jose Gamboa-Montero,
    Cristina Jumela-Yedra, Jose Carlos Castillo, and Miguel Angel Salichs

Social Robot Perception and Control Capabilities

Path-Constrained Admittance Control of Human-Robot Interaction
for Upper Limb Rehabilitation 143
    Dario Onfiani, Marco Caramaschi, Luigi Biagiotti, and Fabio Pini

Causal Discovery of Dynamic Models for Predicting Human Spatial
Interactions 154
    Luca Castri, Sariah Mghames, Marc Hanheide, and Nicola Bellotto

Learning User Habits to Enhance Robotic Daily-Living Assistance 165
    Matteo Pantaleoni, Amedeo Cesta, Alessandro Umbrico,
    and Andrea Orlandini

Multi-modal Data Fusion for People Perception in the Social Robot Haru 174
    Ricardo Ragel, Rafael Rey, Álvaro Páez, Javier Ponce,
    Keisuke Nakamura, Fernando Caballero, Luis Merino, and Randy Gómez

Adaptive Behavior Generation of Social Robots Based on User Behavior
Recognition 188
    Woo-Ri Ko, Minsu Jang, Jaeyeon Lee, and Jaehong Kim

A Transformer-Based Approach for Choosing Actions in Social Robotics 198
    Riccardo De Benedictis, Gloria Beraldo, Gabriella Cortellessa,
    Francesca Fracasso, and Amedeo Cesta

Deep Reinforcement Learning for the Autonomous Adaptive Behavior
of Social Robots 208
    Marcos Maroto-Gómez, María Malfaz, Álvaro Castro-González,
    and Miguel Ángel Salichs

Share with Me: A Study on a Social Robot Collecting Mental Health Data 218
    Raida Karim, Edgar Lopez, Katelynn Oleson, Tony Li, Elin A. Björling,
    and Maya Cakmak

Classification of Personal Data Used by Personalised Robot Companions
Based on Concern of Exposure 228
    Lewis Riches, Kheng Lee Koay, and Patrick Holthaus

Investigating Non Verbal Interaction with Social Robots

Affective Human-Robot Interaction with Multimodal Explanations   241
   Hongbo Zhu, Chuang Yu, and Angelo Cangelosi

When to Help? A Multimodal Architecture for Recognizing When a User
Needs Help from a Social Robot   253
   Jason R. Wilson, Phyo Thuta Aung, and Isabelle Boucher

If You Are Careful, So Am I! How Robot Communicative Motions Can
Influence Human Approach in a Joint Task   267
   Linda Lastrico, Nuno Ferreira Duarte, Alessandro Carfí,
   Francesco Rea, Fulvio Mastrogiovanni, Alessandra Sciutti,
   and José Santos-Victor

Exploring Non-verbal Strategies for Initiating an HRI   280
   Francesco Vigni and Silvia Rossi

On the Emotional Transparency of a Non-humanoid Social Robot   290
   Francesco Vigni, Alessandra Rossi, Linda Miccio, and Silvia Rossi

Transparent Interactive Reinforcement Learning Using Emotional
Behaviours   300
   Georgios Angelopoulos, Alessandra Rossi, Gianluca L'Arco,
   and Silvia Rossi

What Do I Look Like? A Conditional GAN Based Robot Facial
Self-Awareness Approach   312
   Shangguan Zhegong, Chuang Yu, Wenjie Huang, Zexuan Sun,
   and Adriana Tapus

Modeling and Evaluation of Human Motor Learning by Finger
Manipulandum   325
   Amr Okasha, Sabahat Şengezer, Ozancan Özdemir, Ceylan Yozgatlıgil,
   Ali E. Turgut, and Kutluk B. Arıkan

Motor Interference of Incongruent Hand Motions in HRI Depends
on Movement Velocity   335
   Mertcan Kaya and Kolja Kühnlenz

Foster Attention and Engagement Strategies in Social Robots

Attributing Intentionality to Artificial Agents: Exposure Versus Interactive
Scenarios 347
*Lorenzo Parenti, Serena Marchesi, Marwen Belkaid,
and Agnieszka Wykowska*

Does Embodiment and Interaction Affect the Adoption of the Intentional
Stance Towards a Humanoid Robot? 357
*Ziggy O'Reilly, Uma Prashant Navare, Serena Marchesi,
and Agnieszka Wykowska*

A Case for the Design of Attention and Gesture Systems for Social Robots 367
*Romain Maure, Erik A. Wengle, Utku Norman,
Daniel Carnieto Tozadore, and Barbara Bruno*

Introducing Psychology Strategies to Increase Engagement on Social
Robots 378
*Fernando Alonso-Martin, Sara Carrasco-Martínez,
Juan José Gamboa-Montero, Enrique Fernández-Rodicio,
and Miguel Ángel Salichs*

Hey, Robot! An Investigation of Getting Robot's Attention Through Touch 388
Hagen Lehmann, Adam Rojik, Kassandra Friebe, and Matej Hoffmann

Gaze Cueing and the Role of Presence in Human-Robot Interaction 402
*Kassandra Friebe, Sabína Samporová, Kristína Malinovská,
and Matej Hoffmann*

Special Session 1: Social Robotics Driven by Intelligent Perception and Endogenous Emotion-Motivation Core

An Efficient Medicine Identification and Delivery System Based
on Mobile Manipulation Robot 417
*Meiyuan Zou, Qingchuan Xu, Jianfeng Bian, Dingfeng Chen,
Wenzheng Chi, and Lining Sun*

A Generative Adversarial Network Based Motion Planning Framework
for Mobile Robots in Dynamic Human-Robot Integration Environments 427
*Yuqi Kong, Yao Wang, Yang Hong, Rongguang Ye, Wenzheng Chi,
and Lining Sun*

Research on 3D Face Reconstruction Based on Weakly Supervised Learning . . . 440
Zewei Su, Lanfang Dong, Xuejie Ji, Guoming Li, and Xierong Zhu

Robot Differential Behavioral Expression in Different Scenarios 451
Zhonghao Zhang, Wanyue Jiang, Rui Zhang, Yuhan Zheng,
and Shuzhi Sam Ge

Building an Affective Model for Social Robots with Customizable
Personality 463
Ziyan Zhang, Wenjing Yang, and Wei Wang

A Multimodal Perception and Cognition Framework and Its Application
for Social Robots 475
Lanfang Dong, PuZhao Hu, Xiao Xiao, YingChao Tang, Meng Mao,
and Guoming Li

Indoor Mobile Robot Socially Concomitant Navigation System 485
Rui Zhang, Wanyue Jiang, Zhonghao Zhang, Yuhan Zheng,
and Shuzhi Sam Ge

NRTIRL Based NN-RRT* Path Planner in Human-Robot Interaction
Environment 496
Yao Wang, Yuqi Kong, Zhiyu Ding, Wenzheng Chi, and Lining Sun

**Special Session 2: Adaptive Behavioral Models of Robotic Systems
Based on Brain-Inspired AI Cognitive Architectures**

Can I Feel You? Recognizing Human's Emotions During Human-Robot
Interaction 511
Laura Fiorini, Federica G. C. Loizzo, Grazia D'Onofrio,
Alessandra Sorrentino, Filomena Ciccone, Sergio Russo,
Francesco Giuliani, Daniele Sancarlo, and Filippo Cavallo

A Reinforcement Learning Framework to Foster Affective Empathy
in Social Robots 522
Alessandra Sorrentino, Gustavo Assunção, Filippo Cavallo,
Laura Fiorini, and Paulo Menezes

Robotics Technology for Pain Treatment and Management: A Review 534
Angela Higgins, Alison Llewellyn, Emma Dures,
and Praminda Caleb-Solly

Implications of Robot Backchannelling in Cognitive Therapy 546
Antonio Andriella, Carme Torras, and Guillem Alenyà

Prototyping an Architecture of Affective Robotic Systems Based
on the Theory of Constructed Emotion 558
Kuldar Taveter and Alar Kirikal

A Named Entity Recognition Model for Manufacturing Process Based
on the BERT Language Model Scheme 576
    Manu Shrivastava, Kota Seri, and Hiroaki Wagatsuma

Author Index 589

Contents – Part II

Advanced HRI Capabilities for Interacting with Children

A Model Child? Behavior Models for Simulated Infant-Robot Interaction 3
    Ameer Helmi, Kristen M. Koenig, and Naomi T. Fitter

Children Perceived Perception of a Mini-Humanoid Social Robot Based
on a Psychometric Scale: A Pilot Study in Greece 13
    *Ilias Katsanis, Ahmad Yaser Alhaddad, John-John Cabibihan,
    and Vassilis Moulianitis*

Computational Audio Modelling for Robot-Assisted Assessment
of Children's Mental Wellbeing 23
    *Nida Itrat Abbasi, Micol Spitale, Joanna Anderson, Tamsin Ford,
    Peter B. Jones, and Hatice Gunes*

The Sound of Actuators in Children with ASD, Beneficial or Disruptive? 36
    Melanie Jouaiti, Eloise Zehnder, and François Charpillet

Evaluating Robot Acceptance in Children with ASD and Their Parents 45
    Eloise Zehnder, Melanie Jouaiti, and François Charpillet

Living with Haru4Kids: Child and Parent Perceptions of a Co-Habitation
Robot for Children 54
    *Leigh Levinson, Gonzalo A. Garcia, Guillermo Perez,
    Gloria Alvarez-Benito, J. Gabriel Amores, Mario Castaño-Ocaña,
    Manuel Castro-Malet, Randy Gomez, and Selma Šabanović*

Towards Developing Adaptive Robot Controllers for Children with Upper
Limb Impairments - Initial Data Collection and Analysis 64
    Melanie Jouaiti, Negin Azizi, Steven Lawrence, and Kerstin Dautenhahn

A Framework for Assistive Social Robots for Detecting Aggression
in Children 74
    *Ahmad Yaser Alhaddad, Abdulaziz Al-Ali, Amit Kumar Pandey,
    and John-John Cabibihan*

Kaspar Causally Explains 85
    *Hugo Araujo, Patrick Holthaus, Marina Sarda Gou, Gabriella Lakatos,
    Giulia Galizia, Luke Wood, Ben Robins, Mohammad Reza Mousavi,
    and Farshid Amirabdollahian*

Social Robots as Advanced Educational Tool

Training School Teachers to Use Robots as an Educational Tool: The
Impact on Robotics Perception 103
  Giulia Pusceddu, Francesca Cocchella, Michela Bogliolo,
  Giulia Belgiovine, Linda Lastrico, Maura Casadio, Francesco Rea,
  and Alessandra Sciutti

Moveable Älıpbi: The Montessori Method for Robot-Assisted Alphabet
Learning 114
  Aida Zhanatkyzy, Zhansaule Telisheva, Aida Amirova,
  Nurziya Oralbayeva, Arna Aimysheva, and Anara Sandygulova

Social Robots in Learning Scenarios: Useful Tools to Improve Students'
Attention or Potential Sources of Distraction? 124
  Samantha Charpentier, Mohamed Chetouani, Isis Truck, David Cohen,
  and Salvatore M. Anzalone

Are You Paying Attention? The Effect of Embodied Interaction
with an Adaptive Robot Tutor on User Engagement and Learning
Performance 135
  Anita Vrins, Ethel Pruss, Jos Prinsen, Caterina Ceccato,
  and Maryam Alimardani

User Evaluation of Social Robots as a Tool in One-to-One Instructional
Settings for Students with Learning Disabilities 146
  Negin Azizi, Shruti Chandra, Mike Gray, Jennifer Fane, Melissa Sager,
  and Kerstin Dautenhahn

Kinesthetic Teaching of a Robot over Multiple Sessions: Impacts on Speed
and Success 160
  Pourya Aliasghari, Moojan Ghafurian, Chrystopher L. Nehaniv,
  and Kerstin Dautenhahn

Expanding the Use of Robotics in ASD Programs in a Real Educational
Setting 171
  Selene Caro-Via, Marc Espuña, and Raquel Ros

An Overview of Socially Assistive Robotics for Special Education 183
  Shyamli Suneesh and Virginia Ruiz Garate

Preliminary Investigation of the Acceptance of a Teleoperated Interactive
Robot Participating in a Classroom by 5th Grade Students 194
  Megumi Kawata, Masashi Maeda, Yuichiro Yoshikawa,
  Hirokazu Kumazaki, Hiroko Kamide, Jun Baba, Naomi Matsuura,
  and Hiroshi Ishiguro

The Effects of Dyadic vs Triadic Interaction on Children's Cognitive
and Affective Gains in Robot-Assisted Alphabet Learning 204
Zhansaule Telisheva, Aida Zhanatkyzy, Nurziya Oralbayeva,
Aida Amirova, Arna Aimysheva, and Anara Sandygulova

Social Robot Applications in Clinical and Assistive Scenarios

Deep Learning-Based Multi-modal COVID-19 Screening by Socially
Assistive Robots Using Cough and Breathing Symptoms 217
Meysam Effati and Goldie Nejat

Social Robots to Support Assisted Living for Persons with Alzheimer's
and Related Dementias 228
Tyler Morris, Hiroko Dodge, Sylvia Cerel-Suhl, and Xiaopeng Zhao

Assistant Robots in German Hospitals: Measuring Value Drivers
and Willingness to Pay 238
Marija Radic, Dubravko Radic, and Agnes Vosen

Loneliness During COVID-19 Influences Mind and Likeability Ratings
in the Uncanny Valley 248
Abdulaziz Abubshait, Yicen Xie, Jung-Kuan Lin, Marissa Toma,
and Eva Wiese

Telepresence Robot for Isolated Patients in the COVID-19 Pandemic:
Effects of Socio-relationship and Telecommunication Device Types
on Patients' Acceptance of Robots 263
Soyeon Shin, Dahyun Kang, and Sonya S. Kwak

Towards the Deployment of a Social Robot at an Elderly Day Care Facility 277
Sara Cooper and Raquel Ros

Towards a Framework for the Whole-Body Teleoperation of a Humanoid
Robot in Healthcare Settings 288
Francesco Porta, Carmine Tommaso Recchiuto, Maura Casadio,
and Antonio Sgorbissa

Social Robots in the Stuttering Clinic: A Human-Centred Exploration
with Speech Language Pathologists 299
Shruti Chandra, Torrey Loucks, Gerardo Chavez Castaneda,
and Kerstin Dautenhahn

Evaluating Human-in-the-Loop Assistive Feeding Robots Under Different
Levels of Autonomy with VR Simulation and Physiological Sensors 314
    Tong Xu, Tianlin Zhao, Jesus G. Cruz-Garza,
    Tapomayukh Bhattacharjee, and Saleh Kalantari

On the Way to the Future—Assistant Robots in Hospitals and Care Facilities ... 328
    Marija Radic, Agnes Vosen, and Caroline Michler

Development of Robotic Care for Older Adults with Dementia: Focus
Group and Survey Study 338
    Fengpei Yuan, Marie Boltz, Betsy Kemeny, Sharon Bowland,
    Kristina Wick, and Xiaopeng Zhao

A Mobile Social Hand Disinfection Robot for Use in Hospitals 348
    Oskar Palinko, Rasmus P. Junge, Daniel G. Holm, and Leon Bodenhagen

Iterative Development of a Service Robot for Laundry Transport
in Nursing Homes 359
    Jonas Frei, Andreas Ziltener, Markus Wüst, Anina Havelka,
    and Katrin Lohan

Exploring the Potential of Light-Enhanced HRI to Promote Social
Interactions in People with Dementia 371
    Femke Knaapen, Kynthia Chamilothori, and Giulia Perugia

Development and Assessment of a Friendly Robot to Ease Dementia 381
    Robert Bray, Luke MacDougall, Cody Blankenship, Kimberly Mitchell,
    Fengpei Yuan, Sylvia Cerel-Suhl, and Xiaopeng Zhao

A New Study of Integration Between Social Robotic Systems
and the Metaverse for Dealing with Healthcare in the Post-COVID-19
Situations 392
    Chutisant Kerdvibulvech and Chin-Chen Chang

HapticPalm: A Wearable Robotic Device for Haptics and Rehabilitative
Hand Treatments 402
    Danilo Troisi, Mihai Dragusanu, Alberto Villani,
    Domenico Prattichizzo, and Monica Malvezzi

Collaborative Social Robots Through Dynamic Game

Play Dynamics in a Collaborative Game with a Robot as a Play-Mediator 415
    Negin Azizi, Kevin Fan, Melanie Jouaiti, and Kerstin Dautenhahn

Imitating Human Strategy for Social Robot in Real-Time Two-Player
Games 427
   Chuanxiong Zheng, Hui Wang, Lei Zhang, Jiangshan Hao,
   Randy Gomez, Keisuke Nakamura, and Guangliang Li

Personalized Storytelling with Social Robot Haru 439
   Hui Wang, Lei Zhang, Chuanxiong Zheng, Randy Gomez,
   Keisuke Nakamura, and Guangliang Li

Enabling Learning Through Play: Inclusive Gaze-Controlled
Human-Robot Interface for Joystick-Based Toys 452
   Vinay Krishna Sharma, L. R. D. Murthy, and Pradipta Biswas

Introducing the Social Robot EBO: An Interactive and Socially Aware
Storyteller Robot for Therapies with Older Adults 462
   Gerardo Pérez, Trinidad Rodríguez, Pilar Bachiller, Pablo Bustos,
   and Pedro Núñez

Design and Evaluate User's Robot Perception and Acceptance

Self-perception of Interaction Errors Through Human Non-verbal
Feedback and Robot Context 475
   Fernando Loureiro, João Avelino, Plinio Moreno,
   and Alexandre Bernardino

The Effect of Anthropomorphism on Diffusion or Responsibility in HRI 488
   Erika Tuvo, Paola Ricciardelli, and Francesca Ciardo

GeneRobot: How Participatory Development of Social Robots for Assisted
Living Brings Generations Together 498
   Caterina Neef, Katharina Linden, Sophie Killmann, Julia Arndt,
   Nathalie Weßels, and Anja Richert

Embodiment Perception of a Smart Home Assistant 508
   Mariya Kilina, Tommaso Elia, Syed Yusha Kareem, Alessandro Carfí,
   and Fulvio Mastrogiovanni

Design and Preliminary Validation of Social Assistive Humanoid Robot
with Gesture Expression Features for Mental Health Treatment of Isolated
Patients in Hospitals 518
   Diego Arce, Sareli Gibaja, Fiorella Urbina, Camila Maura,
   Dario Huanca, Renato Paredes, Francisco Cuellar,
   and Gustavo Pérez-Zuniga

"Armed" and Dangerous: How Visual Form Influences Perceptions
of Robot Arms   529
    Rhian C. Preston, Nisha Raghunath, Christopher A. Sanchez,
    and Naomi T. Fitter

Perceptions of Socially Assistive Robots Among Community-Dwelling
Older Adults   540
    Nicola Camp, Alessandro Di Nuovo, Kirsty Hunter, Julie Johnston,
    Massimiliano Zecca, Martin Lewis, and Daniele Magistro

Participatory Design and Early Deployment of DarumaTO-3 Social Robot   550
    Zhihao Shen, Nanaka Urano, Chih-Pu Chen, Shi Feng, Scean Mitchell,
    Masao Katagiri, Yegang Du, Franco Pariasca Trevejo, Tito P. Tomo,
    Alexander Schmitz, Ryan Browne, Toshimi Ogawa, Yasuyuki Taki,
    and Gabriele Trovato

Active Participatory Social Robot Design Using Mind Perception Attributes . . .   560
    Weston Laity, Benjamin Dossett, Robel Mamo, Daniel Pittman,
    and Kerstin Haring

Not that Uncanny After All? An Ethnographic Study on Android Robots
Perception of Older Adults in Germany and Japan   574
    Felix Carros, Berenike Bürvenich, Ryan Browne, Yoshio Matsumoto,
    Gabriele Trovato, Mehrbod Manavi, Keiko Homma, Toshimi Ogawa,
    Rainer Wieching, and Volker Wulf

Assessment of a Humanoid Partner for Older Adults and Persons
with Dementia During Home-Based Activities   587
    Fengpei Yuan, Marie Boltz, Ying-Ling Jao, Arowyn Casenhiser,
    Aidan Siddiqi, Robert Bray, Joshua Duzan, Monica Crane,
    and Xiaopeng Zhao

Ethics, Gender and Trust in Social Robotics

I Designed It, So I Trust It: The Influence of Customization
on Psychological Ownership and Trust Toward Robots   601
    Dimitri Lacroix, Ricarda Wullenkord, and Friederike Eyssel

Ambivalent Stereotypes Towards Gendered Robots: The (Im)mutability
of Bias Towards Female and Neutral Robots   615
    Stefano Guidi, Latisha Boor, Laura van der Bij, Robin Foppen,
    Okke Rikmenspoel, and Giulia Perugia

Effects of Realistic Appearance and Consumer Gender on Pet Robot
Adoption   627
   Jun San Kim, Dahyun Kang, JongSuk Choi, and Sonya S. Kwak

The Reason for an Apology Matters for Robot Trust Repair   640
   Russell Perkins, Zahra Rezaei Khavas, Kalvin McCallum,
   Monish Reddy Kotturu, and Paul Robinette

Effects of Beep-Sound Timings on Trust Dynamics in Human-Robot
Interaction   652
   Akihiro Maehigashi, Takahiro Tsumura, and Seiji Yamada

Robot Comedy (is) Special: A Surprising Lack of Bias for Gendered
Robotic Comedians   663
   Nisha Raghunath, Christopher A. Sanchez, and Naomi T. Fitter

Human-in-the-Loop Ethical AI for Care Robots and Confucian Virtue
Ethics   674
   JeeLoo Liu

The CARE-MOMO Project   689
   Oliver Bendel and Marc Heimann

Ikigai Robotics: How Could Robots Satisfy Social Needs in a Professional
Context? a Positioning from Social Psychology for Inspiring the Design
of the Future Robots   701
   Mégane Sartore, Ioana Ocnarescu, Louis- Romain Joly,
   and Stéphanie Buisine

Author Index   711

Social Robot Navigation and Interaction Capabilities (Voice, Tactile)

Socially-Aware Mobile Robot Trajectories for Face-to-Face Interactions

Yalun Wen[1,2], Xingwei Wu[1,3], Katsu Yamane[1,4(✉)], and Soshi Iba[5]

[1] This Work Was Conducted at Honda Research Institute USA,
San Jose, USA
[2] KUKA Robotics, Boston, USA
[3] Cruise LLC, San Francisco, USA
[4] Path Robotics Inc., Columbus, USA
katsu.yamane@gmail.com
[5] Honda Research Institute USA, San Jose, USA
siba@honda-ri.com

Abstract. In this paper, we demonstrate through user studies that mobile robot trajectories that imitate human-to-human approach trajectories are perceived more socially acceptable in the face-to-face interaction scenario than those imitating point-to-point trajectories. We generate robot trajectories to/from a human standing at an arbitrary location by applying inverse optimal control to a human-to-human trajectory dataset. The cost function used in a previous work for modeling human point-to-point trajectories does not represent human-to-human trajectories due to the circular paths often observed around the target human. We therefore propose a new cost function motivated by the social force model. The user study confirms that the resulting trajectories are more preferred with statistical significance than baseline.

Keywords: Mobile robot · Trajectory optimization · Imitation learning · Inverse optimal control

1 Introduction

An essential capability of social mobile robots is to perform face-to-face interactions with a person initially standing away from the robot. In addition to the content of the interaction, it is also crucial for the robot near the human to move in a way that does not make him/her feel uncomfortable. While the effect of relatively simple parameters such as the distance between agents [1–3] and approach direction [4,5] have been investigated extensively, more subtle differences such as trajectory shape has been less explored [6–8].

In addition to the shape, human perception also depends on the social norm of a particular culture, which is difficult to program manually. Therefore, a possible method for improving social acceptance is to model observed human trajectories by using techniques such as inverse optimal control (IOC) [9,10] and inverse reinforcement learning (IRL) [11,12] where the weights of the cost or reward function

© The Author(s), under exclusive license to Springer Nature Switzerland AG 2022
F. Cavallo et al. (Eds.): ICSR 2022, LNAI 13817, pp. 3–13, 2022.
https://doi.org/10.1007/978-3-031-24667-8_1

terms are determined such that outputs of optimization or policy become similar to human trajectories. Furthermore, human studies are needed to confirm that generated trajectories are indeed socially acceptable because appearance and mode of transport of mobile robots are different from humans.

In this paper, we demonstrate through a user study that mobile robot trajectories generated from human-to-human approach trajectories are perceived more socially acceptable in a face-to-face interaction scenario than those from human point-to-point trajectories. We first apply an IOC-based method [9] to human-to-human trajectories. However, it turns out that the original cost function cannot reproduce observed trajectories. We therefore introduce two new terms to the cost function: one inspired by the social force model [13] and another that reduces the centrifugal force. The resulting trajectories are not only closer to human-to-human trajectories, but also perceived significantly more preferred than those with the original cost function [9].

Our results can be used for designing the cost or reward function for other optimization- or learning-based approaches. Furthermore, since we use a large mobile robot that can potentially be perceived dangerous, it is likely that similar or even better results will be obtained with smaller robots. The results are also independent of the content of the interaction because the robot does not perform active interaction with the human in our experiments.

2   Inverse Optimal Control [9]

We represent the dynamics of a mobile robot by a differential equation:

$$\dot{\mathbf{x}}(t) = \mathbf{f}\left(\mathbf{x}(t), \mathbf{u}(t)\right) \tag{1}$$

where $\mathbf{x}(t)$ is the current state and $\mathbf{u}(t)$ is the input.

Using the differential drive model with a velocity component orthogonal to the direction (Fig. 1), $\mathbf{x}$ and $\mathbf{u}$ are represented as

$$\mathbf{x}(t) = \left(x(t)\ y(t)\ \theta(t)\ v_f(t)\ v_o(t)\ \omega(t)\right)^T \tag{2}$$

$$\mathbf{u}(t) = \left(u_1(t)\ u_2(t)\ u_3(t)\right)^T . \tag{3}$$

Choosing the inputs as $u_1(t) = \dot{v}_f(t)$, $u_2(t) = \dot{v}_o(t)$ and $u_3(t) = \dot{\omega}(t)$ yields

$$\mathbf{f}\left(\mathbf{x}(t), \mathbf{u}(t)\right) = \left(\dot{x}(t)\ \dot{y}(t)\ \omega(t)\ u_1(t)\ u_2(t)\ u_3(t)\right)^T , \tag{4}$$

$$\dot{x}(t) = v_f(t)\cos\theta(t) - v_o(t)\sin\theta(t), \tag{5}$$

$$\dot{y}(t) = v_f(t)\sin\theta(t) + v_o(t)\cos\theta(t). \tag{6}$$

We impose limits on the velocities and inputs:

$$0 \le v_f(t) \le v_{fmax} \tag{7}$$

$$-v_{omax} \le v_o(t) \le v_{omax} \tag{8}$$

$$-\omega_{max} \le \omega(t) \le \omega_{max} \tag{9}$$

$$-u_{imax} \le u_i(t) \le u_{imax}\ (i = 1, 2, 3). \tag{10}$$

IOC involves two optimizations: the inner optimization for obtaining the optimal trajectory that minimizes a given cost function, and outer optimization for obtaining the optimal cost function. In practice, the outer optimization gives the optimal weights of the predefined cost function terms.

[9] defines the cost function for inner optimization as

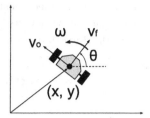

Fig. 1. Mobile robot model

$$J(x_e, y_e, \theta_e, \mathbf{w}, T, \mathbf{x}(t), \mathbf{u}(t)) = T + w_1 \int_0^T u_1^2 dt + w_2 \int_0^T u_2^2 dt$$

$$+ w_3 \int_0^T u_3^2 dt + w_4 \int_0^T \left(\arctan\left(\frac{y_e - y}{x_e - x}\right) - \theta \right)^2 dt \quad (11)$$

where $[x_e, y_e, \theta_e]$ is the goal pose represented in the robot's local frame at its initial pose, $\mathbf{w} = [w_1, w_2, w_3, w_4]$ are weights that are kept constant during inner optimization, and T is the duration of the trajectory. The last term of (11) encourages the robot to face the goal.

We represent the trajectory by $N + 1$ discrete states $\mathbf{x}_k$ $(k = 0, 1, \ldots, N)$ and N inputs $\mathbf{u}_k$ $(k = 0, 1, \ldots, N - 1)$. With $\mathbf{X} = \begin{bmatrix} \mathbf{x}_0^T \ \mathbf{x}_1^T \ \ldots \ \mathbf{x}_N^T \end{bmatrix}^T$ and $\mathbf{U} = \begin{bmatrix} \mathbf{u}_0^T \ \mathbf{u}_1^T \ \ldots \ \mathbf{u}_{N-1}^T \end{bmatrix}^T$, inner optimization is formulated as

$$T^*, \mathbf{X}^*, \mathbf{U}^* = \arg\min J(x_e, y_e, \theta_e, \mathbf{w}) \quad (12)$$

with inequality constraints (7)–(10) and equality constraints

$$\mathbf{x}_0 = [0\ 0\ 0\ 0\ 0\ 0]^T$$

$$\mathbf{x}_N = [x_e\ y_e\ \theta_e\ 0\ 0\ 0]^T$$

$$\mathbf{x}_{k+1} = \mathbf{x}_k + \frac{T}{N}\dot{\mathbf{x}}_k$$

$$\mathbf{x}_k = \begin{bmatrix} x[k]\ y[k]\ \theta[k]\ v_f[k]\ v_o[k]\ \omega[k] \end{bmatrix}^T$$

$$\dot{\mathbf{x}}_k = \begin{bmatrix} v_f[k]\cos\theta[k] - v_o[k]\sin\theta[k] \\ v_f[k]\sin\theta[k] + v_o[k]\cos\theta[k] \\ \omega[k] \\ \mathbf{u}[k] \end{bmatrix}.$$

The outer optimization obtains the weights $\mathbf{w}$ such that the trajectories computed by inner optimization are similar to observed trajectories. Assume that we have M observations with different goal poses $[x_{em}, y_{em}, \theta_{em}]$ $(m = 1, 2, \ldots, M)$ and denote the observed poses in the m-th observation by $[\hat{x}_{mk}, \hat{y}_{mk}, \hat{\theta}_{mk}]$ $(k = 0, 1, \ldots, N)$. The error from the m-th observed trajectory is evaluated by

$$Z_m(\mathbf{w}) = \sum_{k=0}^N (\hat{x}_{mk} - x^*_{m,\mathbf{w}}[k])^2 + (\hat{y}_{mk} - y^*_{m,\mathbf{w}}[k])^2 + c_\theta(\hat{\theta}_{mk} - \theta^*_{m,\mathbf{w}}[k])^2 \quad (13)$$

where c_θ is a user-defined constant and $x^*_{m,\mathbf{w}}$, $y^*_{m,\mathbf{w}}$ and $\theta^*_{m,\mathbf{w}}$ are the solution of inner optimization with $\mathbf{w}$ as the weights and $[x_{em}, y_{em}, \theta_{em}]$ as the goal. Using (13), outer optimization is formally defined as

$$\mathbf{w}^* = \arg\min_{\mathbf{w}} \bar{Z}(\mathbf{w}), \ \bar{Z}(\mathbf{w}) = \frac{1}{M} \sum_{m=1}^{M} Z_m(\mathbf{w}) \tag{14}$$

subject to $\mathbf{0} \leq \mathbf{w} \leq \mathbf{w}_{max}$, where $\mathbf{w}_{max}$ is the vector of maximum weights. Let us also define $\bar{Z}^* = \bar{Z}(\mathbf{w}^*)$.

3   Application to Human Approach

To emulate the human approach scenario, we place a mannequin in a motion capture area and have a human participant approach and eventually stand in front of the mannequin. As shown in Fig. 2, we place the mannequin at 2 different positions facing 8 different directions each. The human participant also starts from 3 different facing directions. The total number of observed trajectories is thus 48, and we use 10

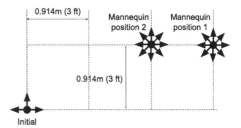

Fig. 2. Initial human and mannequin poses for human-to-human trajectory collection

of them for computing the optimal $\mathbf{w}$ (training) and 38 for testing.

The final pose of the human participant is determined from the mannequin's pose $[x_m, y_m, \theta_m]$ as

$$\left[x_e, y_e, \theta_e\right] = \left[x_m - d\cos\theta_m, y_m - d\sin\theta_m, -\theta_m\right] \tag{15}$$

where d is a constant distance between the final positions of the human and mannequin. We choose $d = 0.8$ based on the observed trajectories.

3.1   Curriculum Inverse Optimal Control

Since outer optimization is nonlinear, we expect that the problem has a number of local minima. However, it is unrealistic to exhaustively search in the 4-dimensional parameter space for the global optimum.

We therefore optimize the parameters in multiple stages by gradually introducing new terms to the cost function for inner optimization. The first stage uses a cost function consisting only of the input terms:

$$J_1(w_2, w_3, \mathbf{u}(t)) = \int_0^{\hat{T}} u_1^2 dt + w_2 \int_0^{\hat{T}} u_2^2 dt + w_3 \int_0^{\hat{T}} u_3^2 dt \tag{16}$$

Table 1. Weights obtained by IOC [9] and their errors

Stage	w_2	w_3	w_0	w_4	Training $\bar{Z}^*$	Test $\bar{Z}^*$
1	0.174	3.87	—	—	2.65	2.32
2	8.16×10^{-3}	12.9	0.776	—	1.55	1.58
3	1.31×10^{-2}	12.2	0.947	0.114	1.56	1.62

where the fixed duration $\hat{T}$ is computed by

$$\hat{T} = 1.5 \max\{\sqrt{x_e^2 + y_e^2}/v_{fmax}, |\theta_e|/\omega_{max}\}. \tag{17}$$

Note that we have set w_1 to 1 because scaling J_1 by a constant does not affect the result. In the first stage, we uniformly sample the initial values for w_2 and w_3 and perform outer optimization for each of them. We then use the (w_2, w_3) that give the smallest $Z_m(\mathbf{w})$ as the initial guess for the second stage, which includes the duration term:

$$J_2(w_0, w_2, w_3, T, \mathbf{u}(t)) = J_1(*) + w_0 T \tag{18}$$

where w_0 is the weight for the duration. We uniformly sample the initial values for w_0 and optimize w_0, w_2 and w_3 by outer optimization. Finally, the best weights are used as the initial guess for the final stage, which uses a slightly modified version of Eq. (11):

$$J_3(x_e, y_e, \theta_e, w_0, w_2, w_3, w_4, T, \mathbf{x}(t), \mathbf{u}(t))$$
$$= J_2(*) + w_4 \int_0^T \left(\arctan\left(\frac{y_e - y}{x_e - x}\right) - \theta \right)^2 dt. \tag{19}$$

Table 1 summarizes the weights obtained by IOC and their errors. As the results indicate, adding the direction to the cost function does not improve the prediction accuracy. This is because the human tends to take a circular path around the mannequin especially when approaching from behind, and therefore facing the goal position is not important near the mannequin.

3.2   New Cost Function

Motivated by the initial results, we replace the last term of (19) with a new term, resulting in a new cost function:

$$J_3'(x_m, y_m, w_0, w_2, w_3, w_4', T, \mathbf{x}(t), \mathbf{u}(t))$$
$$= J_2(*) + w_4' \int_0^T \frac{1}{\epsilon + (x_m - x)^2 + (y_m - y)^2} \tag{20}$$

where ϵ is a small constant. The new term produces an effect similar to social force [13] by increasing the cost near the mannequin.

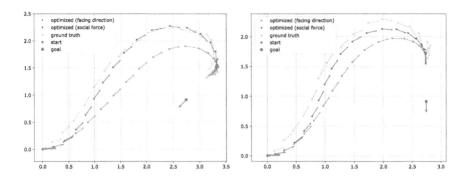

Fig. 3. Optimized motion vs. ground truth. Left: from training dataset, right: from test dataset. Magenta: using (19) (facing direction), blue: using (20) (social force). The unit of the axes is meters. (Color figure online)

Table 2. Optimized weights and resulting errors with the new cost function terms

Stage	w_2	w_3	w_0	w_4'	w_5	Training $\bar{Z}$	Test $\bar{Z}$
3'	6.75×10^{-5}	10.2	1.53	0.51	—	0.990	1.46
4	4.88×10^{-2}	17.6	1.46	2.01	1.41	0.961	1.41

We then perform stage 3', in which w_0, w_2, w_3 and w_4' are optimized using the optimal weights of stage 2 and uniformly sampled w_4' as initial values. As shown in Table 2, stage 3' improves the accuracy by 36% for the training data set and 8% for the test data set. Figure 3 compares the trajectories optimized using Eqs. (19) and (20) for trajectories used for training and testing.

In some cases, we observe that the optimized trajectory shows excessive detouring compared to the ground truth, which may be a side effect of the new term. To reduce this effect, we add another term that tends to reduce the centrifugal force. The cost function is now

$$J_4(x_m, y_m, w_0, w_2, w_3, w_4', w_5, T, \mathbf{x}(t), \mathbf{u}(t)) = J_3'(*) + w_5 \int_0^T v_f^2 \omega^2 dt. \quad (21)$$

Optimizing all weights (stage 4) results in the last row of Table 2. The centrifugal force term achieves a modest improvement of approximately 3% in both training and test data sets.

We use the IPOPT solver together with the Python interface of CasADi [14]. Trajectory optimization using (19) or (21) typically takes 2–3 s.

4   User Study

4.1   Experimental Platform

Our experiment involves a humanoid robot with a mobile base [15] (dimension: $96 \times 80 \times 170$ cm, weight: 160 kg) moving in an area of about 7.5×4 (m) (Fig. 4).

The mobile base is omnidirectional and its command velocity is computed by proportional control with a gain of 2.0 and feedforward velocity. The command velocity is capped at 0.8 m/s for translation and 0.8 rad/s for yaw rotation.

We consider a full face-to-face interaction scenario where the robot approaches the human, stays in place for a few seconds, and returns to the original location. The same cost function is used for both approaching and returning trajectories. The robot does not make any gesture or sound throughout the motion so that we can measure the effect of the trajectory shape exclusively.

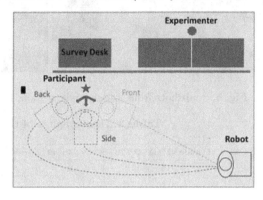

Fig. 4. Top view of the experiment setup

We vary two parameters of the trajectory: direction from which the robot approaches (front, side, or back) and moving speed (slow or fast). The direction is controlled by having the participants stand facing the directions shown in Fig. 4. The slow motions are generated by increasing the duration of the optimized trajectories by 30%. For each of the 6 combinations of a direction and moving speed, a pair of trajectories are generated by the baseline [9] and proposed methods. The baseline method uses (19) for human point-to-point trajectories collected by the authors in a setting similar to Fig. 2 but without the mannequin, while the proposed method uses (21) for human-to-human trajectories. The order between the two trajectories is randomized and balanced across all participants.

4.2 Experimental Protocol

The experimental protocol was reviewed and approved by the institutional review board (IRB) of Honda R&D Co., Ltd.

We use a motion capture system [16] with 11 cameras to measure the participant's head pose and determine the robot's goal pose at the beginning of each trial. We also continuously measure the robot's position and orientation for trajectory tracking. Before a trial begins, the participant stands at the designated position facing one of the three directions as instructed. The operator gives the participant a warning that the trial is about to start and the participant hears an audible beep once the trial begins. At the beep, the robot begins to approach the participant from their left-hand side, stays in front of the participants for a few seconds, and returns to its original position. Due to the size of the robot base, we choose 1 m as the distance between the participant and the front end of the robot when it is staying in front of the human. While the robot is in motion, the participant is allowed to turn the head and move their position and orientation by, for example, stepping back or turning when they feel the robot may come

Fig. 5. Snapshots from a user study session. Left: baseline, right: proposed.

Table 3. Demographics of the participants

Female	Male	20–29	30–39	40–49	50–59	≥60 years old	Experience
3	15	11	4	2	1	0	16

uncomfortably close. After the first trial, the second trial is conducted with the same direction and speed but with the trajectory generated by the other method. After both trials are completed, the participant is asked to fill a questionnaire that asks the participants to choose which of the pair of trajectories better fits the following descriptions:

- *The motion is **safer**.*
- *The motion is **more polite**.*
- *The motion is **more comforting**.*
- *The motion is **more aggressive**.*
- *The motion is **more awkward**.*
- *The robot is **more competent**.*
- *The robot is **more reliable**.*

In addition to participants' response to the questionnaire, their reactions to the robot motion such as stepping back or turning to keep a comfortable distance were also recorded by the experimenter.

5   Results

We collected valid responses from 18 participants. Figure 5 shows snapshots of the robot motions from the same direction (back) using the baseline and proposed methods. Table 3 summarizes the demographics of the participants as well as the ratio of those who had prior experience in interacting with robots. Since each participant experienced 6 pairs of trajectories, each question received $18 \times 6 = 108$ total votes. The aggregated distribution of the votes for each question is shown in Table 4. The result of proportion test with $p = 0.5$ shows that the expected votes are not uniform between two trajectories with statistical significance. More participants prefer the trajectory generated by the proposed method because they feel the motion is safer, more polite and comforting, but

Table 4. Aggregated distribution of votes

Perspective	Baseline	Proposed	Proportion test (df = 1)
Safer	12	96	$\chi^2 = 63.79$, $p < 0.001$
More Polite	15	93	$\chi^2 = 54.90$, $p < 0.001$
More Comforting	14	94	$\chi^2 = 57.79$, $p < 0.001$
More Aggressive	90	18	$\chi^2 = 46.68$, $p < 0.001$
More Awkward	94	14	$\chi^2 = 57.79$, $p < 0.001$
More Competent	25	83	$\chi^2 = 30.08$, $p < 0.001$
More Reliable	17	91	$\chi^2 = 49.34$, $p < 0.001$

Table 5. Number of occurrences of stepping back and turning

Direction	Baseline	Proposed
Front	5/36	1/36
Side	3/36	0/36
Back	13/36	2/36
Total	21/108	3/108

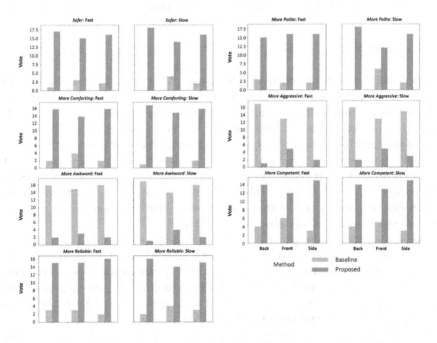

Fig. 6. Votes of trajectories split by each direction and speed

less aggressive and awkward. Furthermore, significantly more participants consider the robot as more competent and reliable when its trajectory is generated by the proposed method.

Similar trend can be observed in the distributions of votes for each combination of direction and moving speed as shown in Fig. 6: more people prefer the trajectories generated by the proposed method in all aspects.

We apply log-linear analysis to investigate the association and interaction patterns among approaching direction, moving speed, and participants' preference of trajectory. The results show that participants' preference of trajectory (generated by baseline or proposed method) is not affected by moving speed or approach direction (all p-values are above 0.1), which is interesting because speed is also likely to affect the perception.

The number of occurrences of stepping back and turning is summarized in Table 5. Participants have a significantly higher number occurrences when the robot approaches with the baseline trajectory ($\chi^2 = 13.55$, df=1, $p < 0.01$). Among the three approaching directions, approaching from the back has the most significant difference in stepping back rate between the two trajectories. This result contradicts with the questionnaire responses that do not show significant effect from the approach direction. Such discrepancy may be explained by the difference between involuntary reaction and consciously responding to questions.

6   Conclusion

In this paper, we first presented an IOC approach for generating socially-aware trajectories of mobile robots to/from a human for face-to-face interactions. The main difference from a similar prior work [9] is that we proposed new cost function terms, one of which emulates the effect of social force [13] and the other reduces the centrifugal force. To solve the complex nonlinear optimization problem in IOC, we employed *curriculum inverse optimal control* where the results of simpler optimization problems with fewer parameters are used as the initial guess of the more complex problem. Using the data from human-to-human trajectories, we demonstrated that the proposed cost function results in more accurate reproduction of the observed trajectories.

The second half of the paper described the results of the user study to compare the social acceptance of the trajectories generated by the baseline [9] and proposed methods. The results showed that the trajectories generated by the proposed method are preferred over those by the baseline. We also demonstrated that the same cost function can be used for both approach and return trajectories, indicating the generality of the IOC-based method.

There are a few avenues for future work. While we focused only on the robot trajectory, social acceptance is affected by various factors such as appearance and joint motions. Trajectory optimization may be computationally expensive when the robot has to navigate through obstacles or other humans while approaching a human. In this case, IRL may be a better option because the robot can simply run the learned policy while in motion. However, our results can provide a guidance on how to choose the reward function terms to better replicate human trajectories around another human.

References

1. E. T. Hall, The hidden dimension. vol. 609, Doubleday, Garden City, NY, (1966)
2. Shi, C., Shiomi, M., Kanda, T., Ishiguro, H., Hagita, N.: Measuring communication participation to initiate conversation in human-robot interaction. Int. J. Soc. Robot. **7**(5), 889–910 (2015)
3. Joosse, M., Lohse, M., Berkel, N.V., Sardar, A., Evers, V.: Making appearances: how robots should approach people. ACM Trans. Hum.-Robot Interact. (THRI) **10**(1), 1–24 (2021)
4. Dautenhahn, K., et al.: How may I serve you? a robot companion approaching a seated person in a helping context. In: Proceedings of the 1st ACM SIGCHI/SIGART Conference on Human-Robot Interaction, pp. 172–179 (2006)
5. Woods, S.N., Walters, M.L., Koay, K.L., Dautenhahn, K.: Methodological issues in hri: a comparison of live and video-based methods in robot to human approach direction trials. In: ROMAN 2006-the 15th IEEE International Symposium on Robot and Human Interactive Communication, pp. 51–58. IEEE (2006)
6. Carton, D., Turnwald, A., Wollherr, D., Buss, M.: proactively approaching pedestrians with an autonomous mobile robot in urban environments. In: Desai, J., Dudek, G., Khatib, O., Kumar, V. (eds.) Experimental Robotics. Springer Tracts in Advanced Robotics, vol. 88, pp. 199–214. Springer, Heidelberg (2013). https://doi.org/10.1007/978-3-319-00065-7_15
7. Lo, S.-Y., Yamane, K., Sugiyama, K.-I.: Perception of pedestrian avoidance strategies of a self-balancing mobile robot. In: 2019 IEEE/RSJ International Conference on Intelligent Robots and Systems (IROS), pp. 1243–1250. IEEE (2019)
8. Mavrogiannis, C., Hutchinson, A.M., Macdonald, J., Alves-Oliveira, P., Knepper, R.A.: Effects of distinct robot navigation strategies on human behavior in a crowded environment. In: 2019 14th ACM/IEEE International Conference on Human-Robot Interaction (HRI), pp. 421–430. IEEE (2019)
9. Mombaur, K., Truong, A., Laumond, J.-P.: From human to humanoid locomotion-an inverse optimal control approach. Autonom. Robots **28**(3), 369–383 (2010)
10. Lee, N., Choi, W., Vernaza, P., Choy, C.B., Torr, P.H., Chandraker, M.: Desire: distant future prediction in dynamic scenes with interacting agents. In: Proceedings of the IEEE Conference on Computer Vision and Pattern Recognition, pp. 336–345 (2017)
11. Ziebart, B.D., et al.: Planning-based prediction for pedestrians. In: 2009 IEEE/RSJ International Conference on Intelligent Robots and Systems, pp. 3931–3936. IEEE (2009)
12. Kretzschmar, H., Spies, M., Sprunk, C., Burgard, W.: Socially compliant mobile robot navigation via inverse reinforcement learning. Int. J. Robot. Res. **35**(11), 1289–1307 (2016)
13. Helbing, D., Molnar, P.: Social force model for pedestrian dynamics. Phys. Rev. E **51**(5), 4282 (1995)
14. Andersson, J.A.E., Gillis, J., Horn, G., Rawlings, J.B., Diehl, M.: CasADi: a software framework for nonlinear optimization and optimal control. Math. Program. Comput. **11**(1), 1–36 (2018). https://doi.org/10.1007/s12532-018-0139-4
15. Robotics, C.: Ridgeback omnidirectional platform. https://clearpathrobotics.com/ridgeback-indoor-robot-platform/
16. NatrualPoint Inc, "Optitrack - hardware". https://optitrack.com/hardware/

Vehicle-To-Pedestrian Communication Feedback Module: A Study on Increasing Legibility, Public Acceptance and Trust

Melanie Schmidt-Wolf$^{(\boxtimes)}$ and David Feil-Seifer

University of Nevada, 1664 N. Virginia Street, Reno, NV 89557-0171, USA
mschmidtwolf@nevada.unr.edu, dave@cse.unr.edu

Abstract. Vehicle pedestrian communication is extremely important when developing autonomy for an autonomous vehicle. Enabling bidirectional nonverbal communication between pedestrians and autonomous vehicles will lead to an improvement of pedestrians' safety in autonomous driving. The autonomous vehicle should provide feedback to the human about what it is about to do. The user study presented in this paper investigated several possible options for an external vehicle display for effective nonverbal communication between an autonomous vehicle and a human. The result of this study will guide the development of the feedback module to optimize for public acceptance and trust in the autonomous vehicle's decision while being legible to the widest range of potential users. The results of this study show that participants prefer symbols over text, lights and road projection. We plan to elaborate and focus on the selected interaction modes via Virtual Reality and in the real world in ongoing and future studies.

Keywords: Autonomous vehicle · V2P · eHMI · Legibility · Public acceptance · Trust

1 Introduction

Improving public acceptance, legibility, and trust in the autonomous vehicle's (AV's) decision is a significant open challenge for autonomous vehicles. Accidents are currently largely caused by human error [19], which is why a major advantage of automated driving is the reduction and ideally the absence of human-induced accidents. Autonomous vehicles can eventually be expected to perform at high levels of precision without experiencing decreased performance like human drivers due to distraction or fatigue [5]. Ultimately, these technologies will improve road safety, reduce injuries and save lives.

However, interactions with high risk groups (i.e., pedestrians) remain a concern [5]. The safety of all road users should be ensured to introduce autonomous

Supported by the Nevada NASA Space Grant Consortium, Grant No. 80NSSC20M00043.

Fig. 1. Example of vehicle human communication.

driving in everyday life and substantially reduce traffic accidents. Vehicle pedestrian communication is extremely important when developing autonomy for that vehicle. The autonomous vehicle should provide feedback to the human about what it is about to do and what it would like the person to do. In this case the AV feedback is a replacement of the social signals of the human driver. Figure 1 shows an example of a pedestrian indicating to cross the road, after which the AV provides corresponding feedback.

In this paper, we present a study to identify which visual feedback module or combinations of feedback modules would increase most public acceptance, legibility, and trust in the autonomous vehicle's decision, and to identify preference.

2   Background

The safety and efficiency of pedestrians crossing the road can be increased if AVs display their intention via an external human-machine interface (eHMI) to interact with pedestrians [6]. Developers and researchers of autonomous vehicle technologies have proposed multiple types of displays, including digital road signs, text, audible chimes and voice instructions to communicate intent to pedestrians [5,6,14,18]. In the following you can find a description of selected papers on studies of autonomous vehicle-pedestrian-communication-feedback modules. In De Clercq et al. [6], different eHMI types were varied: baseline without eHMI, front brake lights, Knight Rider [9] animation (a light bar moves from left to right), smiley, a text which displays "WALK". Lagström and Malmsten Lundgren [8] developed a prototype HMI using a LED light strip in the top area on the windshield to communicate the vehicle's current driving mode and intentions to the pedestrians. The vehicle communicated messages of either "automated driving mode," "is about to yield," "is resting," or "is about to start," which pedestrians understood after a short training [8]. A study by Clamann et al. [5] compared the effectiveness of various vehicle-to-pedestrian displays for street crossing. In this study, a prototype forward-facing display presenting information on a van investigated an advisory display with "Walk" and "Don't Walk" symbols and an information display [5]. Ackermann et al. considered in a video simulation study twenty HMI with projection, LED display and LED light strip, each with text-versus symbol-based message coding [2].

Although there were several studies regarding a feedback module in the past, see also the reviews in [4,13], there is no clear indication about which feedback module would increase most the public acceptance and trust in the AV's decision. In this paper, we expand on previous studies by comparing feedback module options via a questionnaire to identify which visual feedback module or combinations of feedback modules would increase most public acceptance, legibility, and trust in the autonomous vehicle's decision, and to identify preference.

3   Method

3.1   Research Question

The purpose of this study is to identify a feedback module to enable an autonomous vehicle to communicate with pedestrians, which increases most legibility, public acceptance and trust in the autonomous vehicle's decision, and to identify preference. We selected the aspects public acceptance, legibility, and trust for the following reasons:

Legibility. The limited time pedestrians have to detect and interpret a signal is significant for the selection of a feedback module [5]. Since the message displayed on an AV should be intuitive and concise, the message should be easy to understand [12].

Public Acceptance. The biggest obstacle in the mass adoption might not be technological, but public acceptance [10,17]. Public acceptance is essential for the extensive adoption of AVs [20].

Trust. Trust has been identified as crucial to the successful design of AVs [11]. The American Automobile Association (AAA) reports that only one in ten U.S. drivers would trust to ride in an AV, and 28% of U.S. drivers are uncertain [1,11].

3.2   Study Design

This section describes the questionnaire used to identify a feedback module for communicating between a pedestrian and an autonomous vehicle, which increases most the legibility, public acceptance and trust in the autonomous vehicle's decision, and to identify preference.

Instruments. To create the questionnaire we used Qualtrics XM, an online survey tool. The participants were asked to watch different sections of videos and choose their most likable option. These videos were designed using Blender (design elements), CARLA (simulate AV environment), and Unreal Engine (bind physics to the elements). CARLA [7] is based on Unreal Engine. In Unreal Engine 4, it is possible to create and modify objects, such as vehicles and the feedback displays.

Visualizations. We designed four sections to visualize the feedback module: text, symbols, lights and projections. In Fig. 2, examples of interaction mode visualizations are displayed. For the perspective of the illustrations we chose to situate the pedestrian view in the front of the autonomous vehicle since it is most likely that pedestrians cross the road in front of the vehicle. For simplicity, and to not confuse participants with several perspectives, we selected one perspective to display the different interaction modes to the participants. The ideas for the different text, symbol, light and road projection interaction mode options result from literature review and brainstorming. The different concepts are acquired from prior research in this area.

Questionnaire. Since there are a lot of different aspects to consider for a feedback module on an autonomous vehicle, we focused on making the questionnaire as simple and short as possible to answer our research question. We asked about the general concepts and added the videos and images for illustration purposes only. To decrease the influence of color we decided to use the color cyan in the illustrations as much as possible. Cyan or turquoise have been used in several studies regarding an AV-pedestrian-display, e.g., in [3,6], due to being a neutral color in traffic and having good visibility.

The questionnaire consisted of demographic related questions, and questions related to the AV's visual feedback module and combinations of feedback modules. Based on the answers from the questionnaire, we analyzed the most favorable, publicly accepted, legible and trusted visual feedback modules equipped by the AV. To explain the context of the questionnaire, participants were presented the following explanation: "Imagine you are a pedestrian and you want to cross the road. An autonomous vehicle is approaching. You want to be sure that you can safely cross the road. But how will the autonomous vehicle tell you that you can cross? For this reason a visual feedback module will be used." The first part of the questionnaire is partially based on Schaefer's "Trust Perception Scale-HRI" [15] with a 5-point Likert scale:

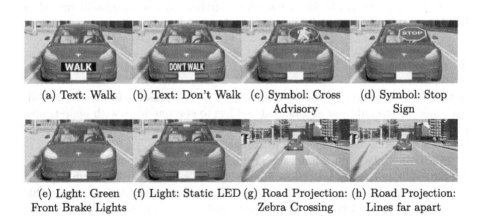

| (a) Text: Walk | (b) Text: Don't Walk | (c) Symbol: Cross Advisory | (d) Symbol: Stop Sign |

| (e) Light: Green Front Brake Lights | (f) Light: Static LED | (g) Road Projection: Zebra Crossing | (h) Road Projection: Lines far apart |

Fig. 2. Examples of visualizations of the four selected interaction modes: (a) and (b) Text interaction mode (c) and (d) Symbol interaction mode (e) and (f) Light interaction mode (g) and (h) Road projection interaction mode with (a), (c), (e) and (g) AV stops for the pedestrian (b), (d), (f) and (h) AV does not stop for the pedestrian. In the questionnaire we ask about general concepts and add the videos/images for illustration purposes only. Perspective: The pedestrian's viewpoint is situated in front of the AV.

– I believe the ___ interaction mode protects people from potential risks in the environment/looks friendly to the pedestrian/communicates clearly
– I prefer the ___ interaction mode over human-driver interaction.

Those four questions were asked for each interaction mode Text, Symbols, Lights and Road Projections separately. To reduce bias we added randomization to the order of displaying the interaction modes as well as the order of the specific interaction mode options. To get a clear answer regarding our research question, participants ranked the interaction modes Text, Symbols, Lights and Road Projections regarding preference, legibility, public acceptance and trust directly:

– Please rank the interaction modes from the most legible interaction mode (1) to the least legible interaction mode (4)/from the interaction mode you trust the most (1) to the interaction mode you trust the least (4)/from the interaction mode you accept the most (1) to the interaction mode you accept the least (4)/in order of preference from your most preferred (1) to your least preferred (4)

The demographic questions included age, gender, ethnicity and current level of education.

3.3 Participants

63 participants were recruited via flyers and social media to fill out the questionnaire online. The questionnaire has a duration of about 20 to 30 min. Twenty-six participants identified as female, 26 participants identified as male and the remaining 11 participants did not specify. Further, 13 participants identified as US-American and 29 participants identified as other nationality.

4   Results and Discussion

In this section we present the results followed by a discussion to identify a feedback module to enable an autonomous vehicle to communicate with pedestrians, which increases most legibility, public acceptance and trust in the autonomous vehicle's decision, and to identify preference.

Since the Likert questions are ordinal we tested for normality with the Shapiro-Wilk normality test. Since the result of the Shapiro-Wilk normality test achieved a p-value that is less than $p < 0.05$ we cannot assume normality. Due to this result we used non-parametric tests and show the results of the questions with frequencies /percentages.

4.1   Legibility, Public Acceptance, Trust, and Preference

To identify the feedback module which most increases legibility, public acceptance, and trust in the autonomous vehicle, and to identify the preferred feedback module, we analyzed the ranking questions. The question "Please rank the interaction modes in order of preference from your most preferred (1) to your least preferred (4)" resulted in the following average rank order: Symbol, Light, Text, Projection. The question "Please rank the interaction modes from the most legible interaction mode (1) to the least legible interaction mode (4)" resulted in the following average rank order: Symbol, Text, Light, Projection. The question "Please rank the interaction modes from the interaction mode you trust the most (1) to the interaction mode you trust the least (4)" resulted in the following average rank order: Symbol, Text, Light, Projection. The question "Please rank the interaction modes from the interaction mode you accept the most (1) to the interaction mode you accept the least (4)" resulted in the following average rank order: Symbol, Light, Text, Projection. Further, we tested each question for significance with the Kruskal-Wallis test, which showed that there are significant differences between the options.

Figure 3 shows a visualization of the ranking questions results and the results of the pairwise comparisons with the Mann-Whitney U test. The Mann-Whitney U test shows a significant difference between symbols and the interaction mode options text, light and road projection with symbols ranked the highest. Further, we analyzed the Likert questions sorted by interaction modes, see Fig. 4. Regarding the question "I believe the ___ interaction mode protects people from potential risks in the environment" participants agreed with the text interaction mode the most, followed by symbols, road projection and lights. Regarding this question the Kruskal-Wallis test showed no significance. "I believe the ___ interaction mode looks friendly to the pedestrian" led to most agreement for the road projection interaction mode, followed by symbols, text and lights. The Kruskal-Wallis test showed no significance. The question if the participant believes that the interaction mode communicates clearly led to most agreement for the symbols interaction mode, followed by text, lights and road projection. Here, the Kruskal-Wallis test showed significance. Further, the Mann-Whitney U test resulted in pairwise significant differences between symbols and road projection, and symbols and lights. Furthermore, the question if the participant prefers the interaction mode over human-driver interaction led to most agreement for the symbol interaction mode, followed by text, light and road projection. The Kruskal-Wallis test showed no significance. Taking all results together regarding which feedback module increases most legibility, public acceptance and trust in the autonomous vehicle's decision, and to identify preference, participants selected symbols, followed by text, lights and road projections.

4.2 Specific Interaction Mode Options

Thus far, we have analyzed the rankings of Text, Symbols, Lights and Road Projections regarding our research question. We now want to look at specific text and symbol options. For this we analyzed the Likert questions, see Fig. 5.

We will further consider the interaction mode options which are not significant with the highest rated option via the Mann-Whitney U test (Fig. 5). The question "I believe the ___ interaction mode protects people from potential risks in the environment" led to the result that the text options "Safe to

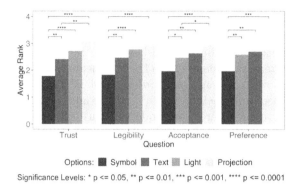

Fig. 3. The result of ranking questions regarding trust, legibility, acceptance and preference shows that symbols should be selected as interaction mode due to significant differences between symbols and the interaction mode options text, light and road projection (lower is better).

cross" and "Walk", and the symbol options "Traffic light walking person" and "Cross advisory" are not significantly different. The question "I believe the ___ interaction mode looks friendly to the pedestrian" showed that the text options "Safe to cross", "Go ahead" and "Walk", and the symbol options "Traffic light walking person", "Cross advisory", "Smiley" and "Pedestrian crossing sign" are not significantly different. Further, the question "I believe the ___ interaction

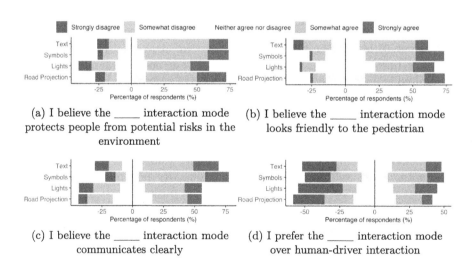

Fig. 4. Assessment by participants of the questions (a), (b), (c) and (d) with a 5-point Likert scale for the four selected interaction modes text, symbols, lights and road projection with resulting ranking in descending order: (a) Text, symbols, road projection, lights (b) Road projection, symbols, text, lights (c) Symbols, text, lights, road projection (d) Symbols, text, lights, road projection. Participants preferred symbols, followed by text, lights and road projection.

mode communicates clearly" showed that the text options "Safe to cross", and "Walk", and the symbol options "Cross advisory", "Traffic light walking person" and "Pedestrian crossing sign" are not significantly different. The question "I prefer the ___ interaction mode over human-driver interaction" showed that the text options "Safe to cross", "Walk", "Go ahead", "Go" and "Waiting", and the symbol options "Traffic light walking person", "Cross advisory" and "Pedestrian crossing sign" are not significantly different.

While the preferred text interaction mode option when the vehicle is not driving for the Likert question is for all four questions "Safe to cross", the preferred symbol interaction mode option is less clear. Figure 5 shows that the results for the walking person of a traffic light and the cross advisory symbol are very similar, with only a slight preference for the walking person of a traffic light.

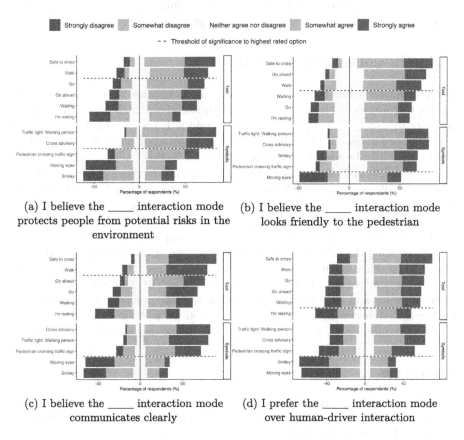

(a) I believe the ____ interaction mode protects people from potential risks in the environment

(b) I believe the ____ interaction mode looks friendly to the pedestrian

(c) I believe the ____ interaction mode communicates clearly

(d) I prefer the ____ interaction mode over human-driver interaction

Fig. 5. Assessment of the questions (a), (b), (c) and (d) for the text and symbol interaction mode not driving options. "Safe to cross" is the highest rated option for the text interaction mode, followed by "Walk" with no significant difference, and for the symbol interaction mode the walking person as on a traffic light and the cross advisory symbol with no significant difference.

4.3   Discussion

The results of this questionnaire show different important aspects for creating an AV-to pedestrian communication feedback module. From the questionnaire results we can derive that a combination of text and a symbol when the vehicle is not driving should be used for a feedback module for communicating between a pedestrian and an autonomous vehicle to increase most legibility, public acceptance and trust, and to identify preference, in the autonomous vehicle's decision. The text, which increases most legibility, public acceptance and trust, and to identify preference, is "Safe to cross." However, since the differences between the text interaction modes "Safe to cross" and "Walk" are not significant when only one interaction mode is used, the interaction mode "Walk" could be used as well. The results for the symbol interaction mode option were not as clear, but the symbol options, which increase most legibility, public acceptance and trust, and to identify preference, included a symbol of a walking person.

5   Limitations and Future Work

The questionnaire has several limitations. This is because there are too many aspects to consider for a feedback module to ask about each aspect in a questionnaire due to complexity and time constraints. However, this questionnaire was developed as an initial study to reduce the amount of extensive options that could potentially be used as a feedback module. In this study, we asked about general concepts and therefore omitted, e.g., current law requirements, location, color or size of a possible vehicle-to-pedestrian communication feedback module. Another limitation is that, although we tried to avoid bias as much as possible by introducing randomization and using a well selected set of possible options, bias in this questionnaire cannot be considered completely excluded.

We extended the vehicle-to-pedestrian communication feedback module to a vehicle-to-bicyclist communication feedback module, see [16]. In further studies, we will use the results of this questionnaire in a Virtual Reality (VR) user study to create and simulate the selected interaction modes in more detail and in different environments. As a subsequent step we will use the results of the questionnaire and the VR user study to verify in the real-word on a vehicle.

References

1. AAA: self-driving cars stuck in neutral on the road to acceptance. AAA Newsroom. https://newsroom.aaa.com/2020/03/self-driving-cars-stuck-in-neutral-on-the-road-to-acceptance/ (2020)
2. Ackermann, C., Beggiato, M., Schubert, S., Krems, J.F.: An experimental study to investigate design and assessment criteria: what is important for communication between pedestrians and automated vehicles? Appl. Ergon. **75**, 272–282 (2019)
3. Bazilinskyy, P., Dodou, D., De Winter, J.: Survey on ehmi concepts: the effect of text, color, and perspective. Transp. Res. Part F: Traffic Psychol. Behav. **67**, 175–194 (2019)

4. Carmona, J., Guindel, C., Garcia, F., de la Escalera, A.: Ehmi: review and guidelines for deployment on autonomous vehicles. Sensors **21**(9), 2912 (2021)
5. Clamann, M., Aubert, M., Cummings, M.L.: Evaluation of vehicle-to-pedestrian communication displays for autonomous vehicles. Technical Report (2017)
6. De Clercq, K., Dietrich, A., Núñez Velasco, J.P., de Winter, J., Happee, R.: External human-machine interfaces on automated vehicles: effects on pedestrian crossing decisions. Hum. Factors **61**(8), 1353–1370 (2019)
7. Dosovitskiy, A., Ros, G., Codevilla, F., Lopez, A., Koltun, V.: CARLA: an open urban driving simulator. In: Proceedings of the 1st Annual Conference on Robot Learning, pp. 1–16 (2017)
8. Lagström, T., Malmsten Lundgren, V.: AVIP-autonomous vehicles' interaction with pedestrians-an investigation of pedestrian-driver communication and development of a vehicle external interface. Master's thesis (2016)
9. Moody, N.: A lone crusader in the dangerous world: heroics of science and technology in knight rider. In: Action TV: Tough-Guys, Smooth Operators and Foxy Chicks, pp. 81–92. Routledge (2013)
10. Newcomb, D.: You won't need a driver's license by 2040. Autopia, Wired. com (2012)
11. Raats, K., Fors, V., Pink, S.: Trusting autonomous vehicles: An interdisciplinary approach. Transp. Res. Interdisc. Perspect. **7**, 100201 (2020)
12. Rasouli, A., Tsotsos, J.K.: Autonomous vehicles that interact with pedestrians: a survey of theory and practice. IEEE Trans. Intell. Transp. Syst. **21**(3), 900–918 (2019)
13. Rouchitsas, A., Alm, H.: External human-machine interfaces for autonomous vehicle-to-pedestrian communication: a review of empirical work. Front. Psychol. **10**, 2757 (2019)
14. Rover, J.L.: The virtual eyes have it. https://www.jaguarlandrover.com/2018/virtual-eyes-have-it (2018)
15. Schaefer, K.E.: Measuring trust in human robot interactions: development of the *Trust perception scale-HRI*. In: Mittu, R., Sofge, D., Wagner, A., Lawless, W.F. (eds.) Robust Intelligence and Trust in Autonomous Systems, pp. 191–218. Springer, Boston (2016). https://doi.org/10.1007/978-1-4899-7668-0_10
16. Schmidt-Wolf, M., Feil-Seifer, D.: Comparison of vehicle-to-bicyclist and vehicle-to-pedestrian communication feedback module: a study on increasing legibility, public acceptance and trust. In: 2022 31st IEEE International Conference on Robot and Human Interactive Communication (RO-MAN), pp. 1058–1064. IEEE (2022)
17. Shariff, A., Bonnefon, J.F., Rahwan, I.: Psychological roadblocks to the adoption of self-driving vehicles. Nat. Hum. Behav. **1**(10), 694–696 (2017)
18. Urmson, C.P., Mahon, I.J., Dolgov, D.A., Zhu, J.: Pedestrian notifications, February 10 2015, uS Patent 8,954,252
19. Wachenfeld, W., Winner, H.: Die Freigabe des autonomen Fahrens. In: Maurer, M., Gerdes, J.C., Lenz, B., Winner, H. (eds.) Autonomes Fahren, pp. 439–464. Springer, Heidelberg (2015). https://doi.org/10.1007/978-3-662-45854-9_21
20. Yuen, K.F., Wong, Y.D., Ma, F., Wang, X.: The determinants of public acceptance of autonomous vehicles: an innovation diffusion perspective. J. Clean. Prod. **270**, 121904 (2020)

Let's Run an Online Proxemics Study! But, How Do Results Compare to In-Person?

Siya Kunde, Nathan Simms, Gerson Uriarte, and Brittany Duncan$^{(\boxtimes)}$

University of Nebraska-Lincoln, Lincoln, NE 68588, USA
{skunde,bduncan}@cse.unl.edu, {nsimms2,gersongru}@huskers.unl.edu

Abstract. Human-robot proxemics behaviors can vary significantly based on personal, robot, and environmental factors which, along with their deployment in public-facing interactions, calls for a wider and in-depth exploration. This paper explores the impact of the operational altitude of small unmanned aerial vehicle (sUAV) on users' comfortable interaction distance. Additionally, we investigate the effectiveness of crowd-sourced prototyping of human-robot proxemics studies in order to conduct broader research faster. By leveraging interaction techniques from literature like video/sound and projective 2D distancing, we explore personal space interactions in online studies (N = 288) with the sUAV and the Double telepresence robot. We then compare the findings with our in-person interaction data (N = 36) and to prior literature. While in-person interactions are the ultimate goal, online methods can be used to reduce resources (including equipment, costs), allow larger sample sizes, and may lead to a more comprehensive sampling of population than would be expected from in-person studies. The lessons learned from this work are applicable broadly within the social robotics community, even outside those who are interested in proxemics interactions, to conduct future crowd-sourced experiments. The various modalities provided similar trends when compared with data from in-person studies. While the distances may not have been precise compared to those measured in the real world, these experiments are useful to detect patterns in human-robot interactions, and to conduct formative studies with new technology before committing limited resources to in-person testing.

Keywords: Human-robot interaction · Proxemics · Crowd sourcing · Evaluation methods · Interaction design process and methods · Scenario-based design

1 Introduction

With the appearance of the COVID-19 global pandemic, as well as the influx of public facing robots performing tasks in the world (delivering food, medicine, and greeting or guiding passersby), the social robotics community faces many

Supported by NSF IIS-175050.

F. Cavallo et al. (Eds.): ICSR 2022, LNAI 13817, pp. 24–37, 2022.
https://doi.org/10.1007/978-3-031-24667-8_3

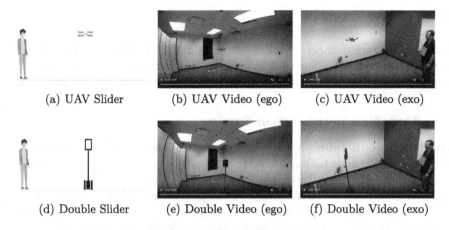

(a) UAV Slider   (b) UAV Video (ego)   (c) UAV Video (exo)

(d) Double Slider   (e) Double Video (ego)   (f) Double Video (exo)

Fig. 1. The different modalities used in the study included Slider (1(a),1(d)), egocentric video (1(b), 1(e)), exocentric video (1(c), 1(f)), and sound (not in figure). The user remained stationary as the robot approached. Here all robots are at a height of 5 ft.

questions related to human-robot proxemics, but relatively limited access to in-person participants. Even in an otherwise normal world, studies conducted in-person are generally localised to the geographic area where experimenters are located and restrict the sample population demographics. This work describes an investigation of human interaction methods and leverages a relatively small set of in-person distancing results, the ability to compare to a previously published study, and a set of methods previously used in human-human distancing to answer fundamental questions regarding methodology for assessing human distancing. This work will inform future researchers on the utility of these methods, and any lessons learned in their application to improve our ability to target limited in-person experimental resources to problems that will likely produce interesting results.

This work explores the following research questions:

- What are the different modalities we can use to prototype human-robot proxemics studies?
- How do the results compare to studies run in-person?

This work indicates that the in-person test results are relatively consistent with the trends observed in each of the online techniques, with the exocentric video condition producing the most similar results (albeit with a 2.3x magnitude increase). This was observed through the analysis of the projective distances reported, the reported participant affect, and the qualitative comments from the participants. Given these results and the confidence of the participants that they were able to imagine themselves interacting using these techniques, recommendations are made for when to leverage each technique in future studies.

2   Related Work

In this section we cover prior work in the context of interaction modalities utilized in human-human and human-robot interaction studies, and literature related to impact of height on human-robot proxemics, in order to situate the current work.

2.1   Modalities in Interaction Studies

Human-Human Interaction. Prior studies in human-human proxemics utilized various methods to understand the personal space that the users wanted to maintain including unobtrusive observations, stop distance [21], video [25], sound [21], adjustable size of stimulus image, chair placement or choice, felt board technique, paper-and-pencil procedures [21,25], positioning of miniature figures, and preference judgements for photographs showing differing spacing and size of projected faces. In surveying the human-human proxemics methodology landscape [8] found that in-person stop distance measurement is the most reliable and preferred technique for experimental evaluations, while pencil-and-paper and felt board methods are the least reliable. The video (exocentric) [25] and sound [21] modalities were found to be a more reliable comparison to in-person interaction compared to other techniques like paper-and-pencil procedures.

Human-Robot Interaction. User perception of robot is affected by the medium used to present the human-robot interaction [30]. Prior studies have used various methods to evaluate HRI hypothesis like text [30], slider [11], 3D figurine [11], virtual agent/animated character [12,15,18,22,29], virtual reality [4,16], telepresence (live video) [12,18], pre-recorded video [9,14,20,28–30], and some went a step further and also provided a comparison to in-person studies [9,12,15,16,18,22,28–30].

On one hand we have findings like one by [15] where people were found to have stronger behavioral and attitudinal responses to co-present robots compared to telepresent or virtual agents. While on the other hand studies have found modalities like videos to work favorably well compared to in-person interactions. In-person interaction with the robot can be useful in evaluating the social aspects of the robot, but can lead to higher anxiety level and lower trust [30], but videos can be particularly effective in enhancing users' perceptions of the performance of robots on its intended functionality, without the elevated anxiety. [22] used videos of animated sUAVs to understand how to effectively communicate intent, to improve the flight design to inform the follow-up in-person study. Similarly [9] conducted online studies with exocentric video clips and later ran a confirmatory in-person study with ground robot.

In fact, [14,20] piloted both egocentric and exocentric videos, but decided to opt for egocentric videos, to provide better focus on the movements of the robot, without contextual distractions like age, gender, and ethnic background of the actor in the video. Studies by [12] (egocentric video), and [28,29] (switch from exocentric to egocentric view) comparing real world evaluations of interactive prototypes with web-based video prototypes found results from video modality tend to be consistent with in-person studies, although the former may not contain all the salient factors that may be present in a real-world setting. Proxemics interactions have not been explored in the context of online modalities with sUAV as one of the interactants. Our study will test slider, video (egocentric and exocentric to observe differences in distancing based on viewpoints), and sound modalities.

2.2   Impact of Robot Height on Proxemics

Height has been found to affect how people react to robots in many studies [17,19,27]. For example, [19] discovered that the size of peoples' proxemics zones are directly proportional to the height of a ground robot, but [17] found that as ground robot height increases, the distance people prefer between themselves and a robot decreases. [7] specifically researched how operational height of sUAVs may affect people's comfortable approach distance, and did not find any significant effect. They note that a possible reason for the lack of difference in preference may be the lack of a realistic setting (UAV was tethered) and participants' feeling of security. [27] varied the altitude of the sUAV in study, and found that a constant altitude trajectory (at 1.75 m $\approx$ 5.74 ft) is preferred over increasing or decreasing altitude trajectories. Our in-person and online studies will test the impact of straight trajectories where an un-tethered sUAV will maintain it's altitude as it approaches the user.

3   Experiment

This paper presents a study to address the research questions: *What are the different modalities we can use to prototype human-robot proxemics studies?* and *How do the results compare to studies run in-person?* These research questions are answered using various projective and definitive measures for stop-distance adapted from prior interaction studies. To answer the first question, an online study was conducted by varying the interaction modality: 2D-distancing slider, egocentric video, exocentric video, and sound clips. To answer the second question, data from the online studies was then compared to data from in-person studies: one previously conducted by [3], and the other conducted in our lab.

3.1   Materials

Asctec Hummingbird sUAV and the Double telepresence robot were used in our studies similar to [3]. The ground robot operated at a height (measured to the top of the robot) of 5 ft (1.52 m). The operational height of the aerial robot was set to 3 ft, 5 ft, or 7 ft. The robots' approach speed was set to 0.2 m/s. In order to track the robot and the user, Vicon markers were placed on the robots, while the user was asked to wear a pre-made marker object around their neck.

3.2 Testbed

The overall study setup for recording the videos and conducting the in-person study replicated the baseline study by [3] including the study space (testbed figure attached in appendix).

The participant interacted with the robot in the enclosed section of the room (4.88 m by 3.53 m). The participant stood in the marked (S) while the robot approached from it's start location marked with (R). The experimenter controlled the robots (UAV and ground robot) from the outside section (4.88 m by 1.03 m). A backup human pilot observed the experiments via live video feed (through two Sony CX440 video cameras), ready to take control of robots if necessary.

While this system was followed for the in-person study, the same setup with a male actor portrayed as the user (similar to [28]) was used to capture the exocentric video (as shown in Figs. 2(a) and 2(b)), and lastly the camera was placed roughly at the height of 1.5 m for the egocentric video (as shown in Figs. 2(c) and 2(d)) and sound clips.

(a) UAVs exo view   (b) Double exo view   (c) UAVs ego view   (d) Double ego view

Fig. 2. The videos were captured with the sUAV flying 3ft, 5ft or 7ft height, and the Double ground robot (all marked in yellow box), from ego (2 (d), 2(c)) and exo (2(b),2(a)) centric point-of-view. Similar conditions were faced by users in the in-person study. (Color figure online)

3.3 Studies

The following online and in-person studies were conducted:

Online Studies. Amazon's Mechanical Turk (MTurk) [2] was used to recruit participants for the online study. Following recommended practices [1,10], we pre-screened participants by requiring them to have number of approved HITs > 5000 and HIT approval rate for all Requesters' HITs > 97% in their MTurk history. Participant anonymity was maintained as required by our Institutional Review Board by tracking only the MTurk worker ID.

The online studies were conducted with the Double ground ro bot, and sUAV flying at heights of 3 ft, 5 ft and 7 ft. The participants were randomly assigned to conditions, and the interaction order was counterbalanced between participants. Once participants accessed the study via Mturk, they first entered background information and answered a pre-interaction questionnaire, next positioned a random order of [5ft Double, and 3ft, 5ft, 7ft sUAV] in their online modality, and finished with an exit questionnaire. Post-interaction questionnaires were administered after the first interaction with double and the sUAV. The surveys were administered using Google Forms, and the web pages containing slider and video/sound clips were hosted on university servers.

2D-Distancing Using Sliders. A UI comprised of a slider was used with the human's image on left (static), and the robot's image on the slider handle (movable), with the scene presented to the user from exocentric point-of-view. The user was provided the following instructions:

"Imagine that you are the figure on the left. How far apart would you place the following two figures by dragging the figure on the right?"

Video Stop-Distancing. Each user was shown a video of the robot approaching from either egocentric or exocentric point-of-view, and provided the following instructions:

"Start the following video with sound on. Once the approach distance of the robot in the video begins to make you feel uncomfortable, stop the video. Finally, click submit."

Sound Stop-Distancing. User was provided a sound clip of the robot approaching (recorded from egocentric point-of-view), and provided the following instructions:

"Start the following video with sound on. Imagine a robot is approaching you. Once the approach sound of the robot in the video begins to make you feel uncomfortable, stop the video. Finally, click submit."

Attention Check. We asked the participants to watch for random 'attention checks' to increase performance (described in 3.3). Instead of distancing the interactants by using the slider or the video/sound player, participants were asked to name the interactants in case of slider and asked to report a word ("robot") inserted into the video/audio clip. These checks were inserted to verify if the participants were carefully reading instructions instead of mindlessly clicking through tasks.

In-person Study. An in-person study was conducted with the sUAV flying at differnt altitudes: 3 ft, 5 ft, or 7 ft. The participants were randomly assigned to conditions, and the interaction order was counterbalanced between participants. Once the participant arrived at the experiment location in our university lab, their consent was obtained and they answered a pre-questionnaire to record background information and pre-interaction measures. Next they were asked to wear the fiducial markers' object and participants not wearing eye glasses were also asked to wear safety glasses for all interactions. Once the robot started approaching the user, they were asked to say "stop" once the robot's closeness began to make them feel uncomfortable. The stop-distancing technique is similar to the one in [3,6] and follows recommendations for use by [8]. On completion of each of the three interaction sessions, they were asked to fill out post-interaction questionnaire to collect their feedback and post-interaction measures.

3.4 Participants

Online Study. In the online study conducted on MTurk, participants were paid a fixed compensation ($3 USD) for a task that took 34 min on average to complete. We controlled for the quality of our data by excluding data from 65 participants who failed attention check task (described in Sect. 3.3), and 13 participants where we discovered that some had answered the study multiple times despite clear instructions not to do so due to how the studies were published on MTurk. Ultimately, the study had 288 participants (187 male and 101 female) between the ages of 19 and 69 ($\mu = 36.93$, $\sigma = 10.55$).

In-person Study. The in-person study conducted at a university research lab had 36 participants (19 male and 17 female) between the ages of 19 and 67 ($\mu = 33.36$, $\sigma = 16.69$). These participants were recruited through on-campus advertisements and emails to campus mailing lists. Participants were compensated $15 for participating in the 1 h duration study. For two participants in Study 2 the sUAV crashed before interaction. Since this may have impacted their approach distances, their data was not used and 2 new participants were run with the same treatment conditions to get data for all 36.

Prior Interactions with Robot(s). In the online (taken together) and in-person studies conducted by us, 50.35% and 52.77% of the participants reported to have interacted with a robot respectively. It is important to note that the robot interaction question was phrased broadly to include single interactions and those in museums or with robot vacuums.

4 Results

Results will be presented from the online and in-person studies to compare results on distancing, user comments, and participant affect.

The data from all the online studies was converted to distances (in meters) using the proportions applied to the slider study assuming a human of average height (1.5 m), distance (3.65 m) between user and robot start positions, as well as the ROS bag files used to record the flight paths in video and sound studies converted to correspond to the video/audio timestamps. All results are reported using the final submitted value from the online form, unless reported otherwise. Normality of data was tested using the Shapiro Wilk test. None of the data were found to be normally distributed and hence for all further analysis non-parametric tests were chosen. The Mann-Whitney test was used to compare gender data. The Wilcoxon Signed-Rank test (for two measurements in Double and UAV-5 study) and the Friedman test (for 3 measurements in the UAV at multiple heights study) were used to compare the comfortable approach distances (measured in meters). Finally, the Nemenyi's Test was used for posthoc analysis [24] wherever the Friedman test was used. All tests were corrected for false discovery using Benjamini-Hochberg Procedure (BHP).

4.1 Interaction Observations from Online Study

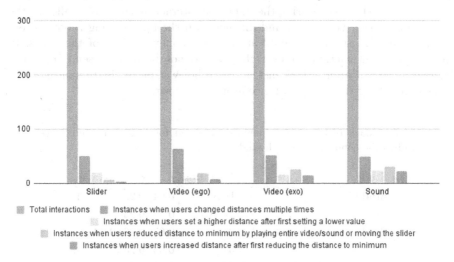

Fig. 3. Summary of online study interactions for all modalities.

During the in-person interaction, users were not able to send the robot back-wards, so the approach distance recorded was the distance at which user stopped the robot. In contrast, for the different modalities we tested in the online stud-ies, and also due to the nature of the online interaction, we found instances where users provided multiple answers and calibrated the distance to be comfort-able. These interactions are summarized in Fig. 3, where we can see the number of interactions where users changed the distance, increased distance after first choosing a lower value, experimented by setting the lowest distance, and set a higher distance after first trying to set the lowest distance.

While 97.88% of users in the online study reported to able to effectively visu-alize themselves as the user in the study, 76.76% of users felt that an in-person interaction might change how close they allowed the robot. Out of these, 61% of users indicated that they would choose to interact with the Double closer than their own indicated placement, while only 27.06% felt that they would prefer to have the UAV closer in real interactions. Given the already large projected dis-tances in the different methods, it's quite interesting, and contrary to the finding that users in the in-person study let the robots approach at close distances.

4.2   In-person Study: sUAV Flying at Different Heights

In the in-person study we conducted with the sUAV flying at three different altitudes, the comfortable approach distances at 3 ft ($\mu = 0.67$, $\sigma = 0.26$), 5 ft ($\mu = 0.65$, $\sigma = 0.23$) and 7 ft ($\mu = 0.65$, $\sigma = 0.18$) were not statistically significantly different (Table 1). The distance values are however closer in magnitude and in the same zone (personal) as results reported by [3,7].

Similar to the participants trying out the closest approach distance by either moving the slider to closest point or watching the video/sound clips until the robot approached to the closest point in the online study (described Sect. 4.1), it's interesting that even during the in-person interaction some users allowed the robot to approach very close, and did not stop the approaching robot 38.88% of the times and stopped it only at the last moment 5.55% of the times. In the in-person interaction however they would not be able to send the robot backwards once it approached, instead the robot was halted by the autonomous code maintaining the safety distance around the user.

Table 1. Approach distances (in meters) measured for in-person studies. p-values correspond to the conditions of each study.

Study	Condition	μ	σ	P-value
Study by [3]	UAV	0.64	0.22	< 0.001
	Double	0.35	0.23	
Study described in Sect. 3.3	3 ft	0.67	0.26	0.82
	5 ft	0.65	0.23	
	7 ft	0.65	0.18	

4.3   Online Studies

Table 2 summarizes the results for this section.

Robot Types: Ground Robot (the Double) and sUAV. The comfortable approach distances for the Double and the sUAV were found to be statistically significantly different in each of the four modalities (p < 0.05), where users allowed the Double to approach at a closer distance compared to the sUAV. These results are consistent with those of [3] summarized in Table 1, though the approach distance magnitudes differ. The video (exo) condition was the closest, but still roughly 2.3x the measured distance for both approaches.

Table 2. Projective comfortable approach distance (in meters) calculated for all online methods. Statistical significance is indicated with compared pairs (the conditions being compared) marked with a, b, and c.

	UAV-3	UAV-5	UAV-7	DOUBLE
Slider	1.72 ± 1.18	1.73 ± 1.16^a	1.82 ± 1.18	1.28 ± 1.12^a
Video (ego)	1.57 ± 0.86^b	1.52 ± 0.81^a	1.41 ± 0.74^b	1.24 ± 0.80^a
Video (exo)	1.40 ± 0.65	1.48 ± 0.74^a	1.33 ± 0.60	0.78 ± 0.66^a
Sound	1.67 ± 1.07	$1.66 \pm 1.05^{a,c}$	1.65 ± 1.08^c	0.87 ± 0.64^a

sUAV Flying at Different Heights: 3 Ft, 5 Ft, and 7 Ft. The results for this differ across the modalities. In slider and video (exo) modalities, the comfortable approach distances for the sUAV flying at 3 ft, 5 ft, and 7 ft were not statistically significantly different, and this is consistent with our findings in the in-person study (Sect. 4.2). In the video (ego) and sound modalities however 3ft and 5ft, and 5ft and 7ft were found to produce different distances respectively.

4.4   User Comments

In the exit questionnaire the users were asked "Do you have any other comments about this experiment?" and "Is there anything that has not been addressed that you find important?". Participants, in general, expressed curiosity and engagement; other common feelings are summarized briefly in this section.

Participants expressed a preference for the ground robot compared to the aerial vehicle. For the UAV, the participants commented on the noise generated by the vehicle and expressed negative feelings towards the propeller blades. A few users commented on allowing the robot to approach. Finally, the general comments pointed to overall feelings of interest in the study.

Slider:

- "Well, if I were to meet up with the robot for real, I'd probably let it get closer than what I'm imagining. I know for sure I would not make it be farther away from me."
- "It is hard visualize interaction with a robot via computer screen, in person interaction could present a totally different experience."
- "I think if the robots have propellers or fly, I would want them a little farther away than a robot that was on wheels."

Video (ego):

- "The last robot that wasn't flying was a lot easier to not be scared of."
- "None of the robots spoke. That would have an impact."

Video (exo):

- "I liked the last robot better, don't like that flying thing."
- "The sound of the UAV's is what makes me dislike them, I think."

Sound:

- "Sound of the robots makes a difference in how we perceive them, I would have liked to know what these robots looked like too."
- "Videos are all playing a black screen and sound only with little to no variation in the volume/intensity. The one with the word 'double' at the bottom sounded like a nice day out in the park so I don't know how I can judge an imagined robot from that. "
- "This experiment, especially the sounds, completely stressed me out!!"
- "Were the sounds actually real robots? I didn't think UAVs were that loud."

4.5   Human-Human Distance

In order to baseline the collected numbers and out of interest due to the ongoing pandemic, we asked participants to indicate (using a slider) how close they would allow another human being to approach them. On average participants distanced the human figure 0.85 m ($\sigma = 1.02$) away. One participant commented "Closeness of human preference depends on Covid.". These results are relatively similar to those observed in human-human distancing (M=0.73 m) [5].

4.6   PANAS

The Wilcoxon Signed Rank test was used to compare the differences of affect PA (sociability) and NA (stress) [26] post-interaction with the ground and aerial robots compared to the initial pre-interaction "Today" measurement. When looking at the differences of affect PA (sociability) and NA (stress) [26], the participants reported higher distress after interacting with the aerial robot than with the ground robot ($W(271) = 6387.0$, $p < 0.001$). The average "Today" value for NA was 17, average NA after interaction with the sUAV was 17.76, and after the Double was 16.6. These results for NA, computed for all online studies together, are consistent with the findings of [3].

This effect was observed separately in the egocentric video ($W(67) = 501$, $p < 0.05$) and exocentric video ($W(69) = 394$, $p < 0.05$) modalities as well, but not significant after applying the BHP correction.

5   Discussion

5.1   Limitations

The most prominent limitations of this study are due to the testing modalities, where each sacrificed fidelity in different ways. The slider, where the interactants were images, was missing the sound and visuals; the sound modality was missing the visuals; and all online studies were missing the in-person experience. In the current implementation, the slider restricts testing of variables like speed and variable paths that require 3D perceptions and automated movement of the robot. To investigate these factors, one of the other prototyping mediums should take precedence. Despite these differences, 97.88% of users reported that they were able to effectively visualize themselves as the user in the study.

The lack of significant difference for the UAV flying at 3 and 5 ft were similar in online and in-person studies, but this did not hold for the UAV at 7 ft. One possibility is that in-person user responses were impacted by other factors like the perception of room size or ceiling height, which were less obvious in the ego-centric video and absent in the sound modality. Another explanation is that the physical presence of interactants during in-person interaction afforded viewers with better depth perception and motion parallax [15], which was lacking in the online modalities.

The projective measurement results from online studies are similar to the results of in-person studies, but the distances differ in magnitude. We argue that it is fair to sacrifice the precision in favor of ease of deployment and ability to detect patterns in interaction which can then be refined through smaller in-person tests.

5.2 Implications

Our findings suggest that choosing among the slider, video (ego or exo), or sound for specific purposes requires a consideration of the social and informational dimensions of the task at hand. Based on the study being conducted, under-standing the contextual information conveyed by each method is important in eliciting the most effective response for each method from the user. However, given the information here, we could have tested other potential studies to find one likely to elicit differences (such as increased speed, variable flight paths, etc.).

5.3 Recommendations

Many users reported multiple answers for each method and, as opposed to in-person interaction, they could refine their answer by moving the robot closer and further to find their preferred distance. Prior studies in ground robots have found this to not impact the distancing [13,23], whether the robot approached the user or user approached the robot. But the patterns in our data indicate that the same may not hold true for aerial vehicles. In future studies, researchers might confirm the impact of this by allowing the user to refine their answer after stopping the robot as an iterative process.

With respect to applying the different methods, we would recommend the following. *Sound* seems to be an effective modality if you are testing the size of very different vehicles or acoustics for a deployment space to understand which design might be preferred. *Ego video* is useful for systems that can be fully observed from this relatively limited view to understand the expected perceived size of interaction. *Exo video* would be effective for testing most use cases and deployment details due to the wider view and the standoff, but are limited in their application to exceptionally loud systems, so might be well complimented by a sound or ego video study.

6   Conclusion

Through the use of crowd-sourcing platforms, we were able to complete a set of studies that would generally have taken many months (in the absence of a global pandemic) in less than one month. The similarity of the observed trends to those observed in person may have encouraged a different selection of in-person study (such as one that would impact sound). We hope that the demonstration of these techniques and, in particular, the relative consistency of the exo video condition (though at a different magnitude) with in-person trends will encourage researchers to leverage these methods for future exploratory work. Discussion includes recommendations for when to use the different modalities.

References

1. Qualifications and worker task quality (2020). https://blog.mturk.com/qualifications-and-worker-task-quality-best-practices-886f1f4e03fc
2. Amazon mechanical turk (MTurk) (2022). https://www.mturk.com/
3. Acharya, U., Bevins, A., Duncan, B.A.: Investigation of human-robot comfort with a small unmanned aerial vehicle compared to a ground robot. In: IEEE/RSJ International Conference on Intelligent Robots and Systems (IROS), pp. 2758–2765. IEEE (2017)
4. Belmonte, L.M., et al.: Feeling of safety and comfort towards a socially assistive unmanned aerial vehicle that monitors people in a virtual home. Sensors **21**(3), 908 (2021)
5. Cochran, C.D., Hale, W.D., Hissam, C.P.: Personal space requirements in indoor verses outdoor locations. J. Psychol. **117**(1), 121 (1984)
6. Cochran, C., Urbanczyk, S.: The effect of availability of vertical space on personal space. J. Psychol. **111**(1), 137–140 (1982)
7. Duncan, B.A., Murphy, R.R.: Comfortable approach distance with small unmanned aerial vehicles. In: IEEE RO-MAN, pp. 786–792. IEEE (2013)
8. Hayduk, L.A.: Personal space: an evaluative and orienting overview. Psychol. Bull. **85**(1), 117 (1978)
9. Hedaoo, S., Williams, A., Wadgaonkar, C., Knight, H.: A robot barista comments on its clients: social attitudes toward robot data use. In: 14th ACM/IEEE International Conference on Human-Robot Interaction (HRI), pp. 66–74. IEEE (2019)
10. Jia, R., Steelman, Z.R., Reich, B.H.: Using mechanical turk data in is research: risks, rewards, and recommendations. Commun. Assoc. Inf. Syst. **41**(1), 14 (2017)
11. Joosse, M.P.: Investigating positioning and gaze behaviors of social robots: people's preferences, perceptions, and behaviors (2017)
12. Kidd, C.D.: Sociable robots: the role of presence and task in human-robot interaction. Ph.D. thesis, Massachusetts Institute of Technology (2003)
13. Koay, K.L., Syrdal, D.S., Walters, M.L., Dautenhahn, K.: Living with robots: investigating the habituation effect in participants' preferences during a longitudinal human-robot interaction study. In: 2007 IEEE RO-MAN, pp. 564–569. IEEE (2007)
14. Lehmann, H., Saez-Pons, J., Syrdal, D.S., Dautenhahn, K.: In good company? perception of movement synchrony of a non-anthropomorphic robot. PloS one **10**(5), e0127747 (2015)

15. Li, J.: The benefit of being physically present: a survey of experimental works comparing copresent robots, telepresent robots and virtual agents. Int. J. Hum.-Comput. Stud. **77**, 23–37 (2015)
16. Li, R., van Almkerk, M., van Waveren, S., Carter, E., Leite, I.: Comparing human-robot proxemics between virtual reality and the real world. In: 14th ACM/IEEE International Conference on Human-Robot Interaction (HRI), pp. 431–439. IEEE (2019)
17. Oosterhout, T.V., Visser, A.: A visual method for robot proxemics measurements. In: CTIT Technical Reports Series, pp. 61–68 (2008)
18. Powers, A., Kiesler, S., Fussell, S., Torrey, C.: Comparing a computer agent with a humanoid robot. In: Proceedings of the ACM/IEEE international conference on Human-Robot Interaction, pp. 145–152 (2007)
19. Rajamohan, V., Scully-Allison, C., Dascalu, S., Feil-Seifer, D.: Factors influencing the human preferred interaction distance. In: 28th IEEE International Conference on Robot and Human Interactive Communication (RO-MAN), pp. 1–7 (2019)
20. Saez-Pons, J., Lehmann, H., Syrdal, D.S., Dautenhahn, K.: Development of the sociability of non-anthropomorphic robot home companions. In: 4th International Conference on Development and Learning and on Epigenetic Robotics, pp. 111–116. IEEE (2014)
21. Sanders, J.L., Thomas, M.A., Suydam, M., Petri, H.: Use of an auditory technique in personal space measurement. J. Soc. Psychol. **112**(1), 99–102 (1980)
22. Szafir, D., Mutlu, B., Fong, T.: Communication of intent in assistive free flyers. In: Proceedings of the ACM/IEEE International Conference on Human-Robot Interaction, pp. 358–365 (2014)
23. Takayama, L., Pantofaru, C.: Influences on proxemic behaviors in human-robot interaction. In: IEEE/RSJ International Conference on Intelligent Robots and Systems, pp. 5495–5502. IEEE (2009)
24. Terpilowski, M.: Scikit-posthocs: pairwise multiple comparison tests in python. J. Open Source Softw. **4**(36), 1169 (2019)
25. Walkey, F.H., Gilmour, D.R.: Comparative evaluation of a videotaped measure of interpersonal distance. J. Consult. Clin. Psychol. **47**(3), 575 (1979)
26. Watson, D., Clark, L.A., Tellegen, A.: Development and validation of brief measures of positive and negative affect: the panas scales. J. Personal. Soc. Psychol. **54**(6), 1063 (1988)
27. Wojciechowska, A., Frey, J., Sass, S., Shafir, R., Cauchard, J.R.: Collocated human-drone interaction: methodology and approach strategy. In: 14th ACM/IEEE International Conference on Human-Robot Interaction (HRI), pp. 172–181. IEEE (2019)
28. Woods, S., Walters, M., Koay, K.L., Dautenhahn, K.: Comparing human robot interaction scenarios using live and video based methods: towards a novel methodological approach. In: 9th IEEE International Workshop on Advanced Motion Control, vol. 2006, pp. 750–755. IEEE (2006)
29. Woods, S.N., Walters, M.L., Koay, K.L., Dautenhahn, K.: Methodological issues in hri: a comparison of live and video-based methods in robot to human approach direction trials. In: 2006 IEEE RO-MAN, pp. 51–58. IEEE (2006)
30. Xu, Q., et al.: Effect of scenario media on human-robot interaction evaluation. In: Proceedings of the 7th Annual ACM/IEEE International Conference on Human-Robot Interaction, pp. 275–276 (2012)

AR Point&Click: An Interface for Setting Robot Navigation Goals

Morris Gu[1(✉)], Elizabeth Croft[2], and Akansel Cosgun[3]

[1] Monash University, Clayton, Australia
morris.gu1@monash.edu
[2] University of Victoria, Victoria, Canada
[3] Deakin University, Burwood, Australia

Abstract. This paper considers the problem of designating navigation goal locations for interactive mobile robots. We investigate a point-and-click interface, implemented with an Augmented Reality (AR) headset. The cameras on the AR headset are used to detect natural pointing gestures performed by the user. The selected goal is visualized through the AR headset, allowing the users to adjust the goal location if desired. We conduct a user study in which participants set consecutive navigation goals for the robot using three different interfaces: AR Point&Click, Person Following and Tablet (birdeye map view). Results show that the proposed AR Point&Click interface improved the perceived accuracy, efficiency and reduced mental load compared to the baseline tablet interface, and it performed on-par to the Person Following method. These results show that the AR Point&Click is a feasible interaction model for setting navigation goals.

1 Introduction

The service robot sector is continuing to grow at a strong pace, with an expected 22.6% cumulative average growth rate from 2020 to 2025 [1]. As these robots move from industrial applications to adoption in public facing and residential use, they are increasingly being run by non-expert users. Interactive robots are typically designed to take commands from users in response to changing demands, as opposed to pre-programmed industrial robots operating in separated assembly lines. As such, there is a demand for user-friendly methods that allow users to set goals for the robots in intuitive ways. For interactive mobile robots, allowing users to set navigation goals is a problem of broad interest.

Several methods of setting navigation goals already exist. One of the most common methods is setting goals from a birdseye map of the environment. A prominent example of this is the RViz tool within Robot Operating System (ROS) which is popular among the robotics developer community. Another common method is sending the robot to semantically meaningful locations, such as to rooms or labeled areas [4]. Other interactive goal setting methods involve co-located direct driving [6], or letting the robot follow the user [5,23]. In human-to-human interaction, a common method is using deictic (pointing) gestures.

F. Cavallo et al. (Eds.): ICSR 2022, LNAI 13817, pp. 38–49, 2022.
https://doi.org/10.1007/978-3-031-24667-8_4

Fig. 1. We propose the **AR Point&Click** interface which allows users to perform a pointing gesture, followed by a pinching gesture with the fingers to assign a navigation goal to a mobile robot. The chosen goal is visualized through the AR headset as a virtual golf flag pole, which allows the user to view and adjust the goal on the fly.

Deictic gestures are also commonly used for human-robot interaction. Some approaches use pointing devices to provide goals to robots. In implementations by Kemp [16] and Gualtieri [10], a point and click and gesture is implemented using a laser pointer to select the goal objects for fetch-and-carry tasks. Kemp [16] suggest that point and click interfaces are simple and have a diverse set of applications. This concept is extended by Nguyen [20] to driving tasks, although users can only select from a set of pre-defined discrete navigation targets. Sprute [24] proposes a system in which laser pointers can be used to define a virtual barrier for navigation. Chen [3] uses the head orientation of the Augmented Reality headset to choose between various target control devices. Alternatively, some designs use natural hand and/or arm gestures for setting robot goals, for instance, for selecting object goals [8] or to point into space for specifying region goal [11]. Our work also employs natural deictic gestures for selecting robot goals.

Augmented Reality (AR) technology has been growing in popularity for human-robot interaction [18], with applications ranging from visualizing robots behind walls [9], visualizing the robot's intent for object handovers [13] or for drones [25], and human-robot cooperative search [21]. Our previous works from Hoang [12] and Waymouth [26] demonstrate choosing goal points for interactive manipulation tasks using natural hand gestures. Kousi [17] demonstrates an AR application to set navigation goals and teleoperate a virtual robot.

In this work, we investigate the usability of an AR point and click interface that was initially demonstrated as a proof-of-concept in our previous work [14] for providing navigation goals. This method was explored as it allows the chosen goal to be communicated to the user via visualization and AR headsets allow natural gesture detection without additional external setup. The aim of this research is to evaluate this proposed interface against a Tablet interface, which acts similarly to RViz, and person following, which is introduced as a simple and easily understood method. In this research, we envision a scenario where a user is directed to navigate a mobile robot to and from a set number of fixed goals.

The contribution of this work is an evaluation of a proposed AR Point and Click interface in a user study that aims to investigate the usability of the proposed method against more traditional methods of setting navigation goals to robots: person following and tablet-based interface.

2   AR Point&Click Interface

The proposed system consists of two main modules, a **Robot** module which employs ROS and a **Interface** module which is either an AR headset which uses Unity Engine or an android tablet which employs ROS-Mobile [22]. The **Interface** module communicates the robot's goal to the **Robot** module, which then uses this information to navigate to a user-specified goal. The **Robot** module communicates the visualization information to the **Interface** module. Communication between the modules is achieved through a Wi-Fi router over a local network. We use ROS inter-node communication between the robot and tablet. We employ the ROS# software package to communicate between the AR headset and robot. Additional information about the environment, such as goals is not displayed or encoded to the **Interface** module to mimic a free navigation task where goals are not indicated explicitly on the map.

2.1   Robot Implementation

For the **Robot** module we employ the Fetch Robotics Mobile Manipulator (Fetch robot). For localization, we use the standard ROS Navigation Stack packages which are modified by Fetch Robotics. In this study, the robot navigated between points in the real-world where there are no static obstacles in between them. Therefore, we chose to adopt a simple navigation behavior from our previous works [9,19]. Collision avoidance is implemented using the Fetch Robot's LIDAR sensor to detect objects within a certain distance and detects for a roughly 100° cone 1 m in front of the robot.

2.2   Augmented Reality Interface

We developed an **AR Point&Click (AR)** interface. In this interface, the goal is specified with a hand gesture, as implemented by Hoang [14]. The hand gesture points a ray from the user's arm and and then involves pinching their thumb and index finger. This method is chosen to be an AR implementation of the more standard RViz interface. It employs a Microsoft HoloLens 2 as the AR headset. This headset can display virtual objects on see-through holographic lenses and provides head pose tracking and localizes itself to a fixed reference frame. Using this, a flag pole is visualized at the goal, as shown in Fig. 1.

We localize the AR headset with off-the-shelf packages provided by Vuforia [2] on an origin of the world frame represented by a printed-out AR marker provided by Microsoft. The marker does not need to be within the FOV of the headset but it is possible that the localization drifts. If the localization is off, the user can re-localize the headset by looking at the physical AR marker and uttering the word "calibrate". To localize the robot and AR headset frames in the same coordinate frame, the AR marker is placed at the corresponding pose of the origin in the Robot's map frame. In this case the AR marker is placed on the floor. Due to errors in localization and marker placement, which are additive, there may be slight mismatches in the frame of the AR headset and Robot.

3   User Study

In this study, the user is given the task to navigate the robot to 6 goal positions with a fixed, pre-determined order. The user starts at fixed initial position but can move around the area to navigate the robot. The experimental setup is shown in Fig. 2. After reaching each goal, the user is asked to wait the robot be become stationary, and then utter the word "done" to indicate to the experimenter that the goal has been reached. After this occurs, the experimenter specifies the next goal and the user sets the goal position for the robot to navigate. The task is completed when the final goal is reached by the robot.

In addition to the proposed **AR Point&Click** interface, we adopt two baseline interfaces, a **Person Following** interface and a **Tablet** interface, which are elaborated on in the Sect. 3.1. With these interfaces, our user study has 3 conditions represented by the interfaces. Each user was tested on each condition. The order of the conditions was counterbalanced to reduce ordering effects. For each condition, the user completed a single trial of the navigation task.

3.1   Baseline Interfaces

Person Following (PF) interface: The robot moves directly towards the user within a certain distance. This is activated with a speech command which then uses the pose tracking provided by the HoloLens 2 Headset to obtain the user's position. This interface is designed to be easy to use.

Tablet interface: A goal pose is chosen in a top-down 2D map, through ROS Mobile [22] by double tapping the screen. The implementation is similar to the standard RViz interface. It visualizes a top-down 2D map, the robot's pose and the laser scanner. Users are only able to rotate or translate the 2D view.

Fig. 2. Left: The initial experimental setup for the user task. The goals are labelled with the numbers. Right: An example of the **Tablet** interface which uses ROS mobile [22] that implements the popular RViz interface on mobile devices. Note that the visualized flag is not seen in by the user and is used to symbolize the user's goal.

3.2   User Study Procedure

The user study was conducted in an open area so that line of sight between the robot and each of the goals could be maintained. Before the user study commenced, the participant read an explanatory statement and filled in a consent form. As well, they watched a prepared video about the task. The experimenter read from a script during the user study to ensure uniformity of procedure. Each user was given two minutes to practice on each interface before starting the task. This practice time was recorded. Afterwards, the user began the task on the experimenters signal. After each condition, the user was given a survey to rate the system with questions from Table 1. After completing the experiment, the participants were given the option to engage in a post-experiment interview. The mean duration for each participant was around 30 min.

3.3   Metrics

Objective metrics

- Positional Error (m): The Euclidean distance between the desired goal and robot's position when the user deems a navigation goal complete.
- Goal-to-goal time (s): The time spent between goals.
- Practice time (s): The time from when the participants starts trialing the interface until they decide to stop, or up to 2 min maximum.

Table 1. User study survey questions

Q1: I felt **safe** during the task
Q2: I was satisfied with the robot's **navigation accuracy**
Q3: The user interface **aided** my ability to **complete the task**
Q4 The interface was **easy to use**
Q5 The task was **mentally demanding**

Subjective Metrics: After each task is completed, the participant was asked to respond to a set of questions, shown in Table 1. The questions were all measured on a 7-point Likert scale and were designed to focus on the perceived usability and efficacy of the system. After the participant completed the task on all three interfaces, they are asked for their preferred user interface for this task.

3.4   Hypotheses

We expect that the AR based interface will result in improved positional accuracy and perceived safety. We also expect reduced mental load and improved perception of task efficiency and accuracy for both the person following and AR based interfaces. As well, we predict that the Person Following interface will be most intuitive. As such we formulate the following hypotheses in Table 2.

Table 2. Hypotheses

H1:	The **AR Point&Click** method will have the highest **Perceived Safety**
H2:	The **AR Point&Click** and **Person Following** interfaces will be rated significantly higher in **Perceived Accuracy** than the **Tablet** interface.
H3:	The **AR Point&Click** and **Person Following** interfaces will be rated significantly higher in **Perceived Task Efficiency** than the **Tablet** interface.
H4:	The **Person Following** interface will be the **Easiest to Use**.
H5:	The **Tablet** interface will be the most **Mentally Demanding** to use.
H6:	The **AR Point&Click** interface will have the lowest **Positional Error** Compared to other methods

4 Quantitative Results

For this study we recruited 18 participants from within the university[1], including 16 male and 2 female participants, between the ages of 21 and 33 ($\mu = 24.4$, $\sigma = 3.6$). All but one of the participants had prior experience in robotics. 6 of the 54 trials were repeated due to AR application crashes. Prior to any task employing AR applications, user's were informed that they would repeat the task in the case of an application crash. They were informed that this error should not be reflected in their responses to the survey questions.

4.1 Subjective Metrics

The raw response distribution for each survey question is shown in Fig. 3. To test **H1-H5**, we employed a Friedman test on the likert scale variables as the ordinal nature these require a non-parametric test for more than 2 categories. Significance was found in all questions and a post-hoc Nemenyi test was then conducted between interfaces with p-values shown in Table 3.

Regarding *Perceived Safety* (Q1), no statistical significance between any two methods were found, therefore **H1** cannot be affirmed. We do, however, observe a trend that the **AR Point&Click** is rated highest by the participants, with 11 people strongly agreeing that they felt safe. We believe that a larger participant pool might affirm this hypothesis, especially for the hypothesis that **AR Point&Click** would be found significantly safer than the **Tablet** method (p=0.06, which is close to the significance boundary). We also observe that the *Perceived Safety* (Q1) question was rated the highest overall among all 5 questions, signalling that the participants felt safe interacting with the robot, which is an important consideration for any human-robot interaction scenario.

Participants rated the **Person Following** and **AR Point&Click** interfaces significantly higher than the **Tablet** interface in terms of *Perceived Accuracy* (Q2) and *Perceived Task Efficiency* (Q3), affirming **H2** and **H3**, respectively.

---

[1] Due to the COVID-19 pandemic, no external participants could be recruited. This study has been approved by the Monash University Human Research Ethics Committee (Application ID: 27685)

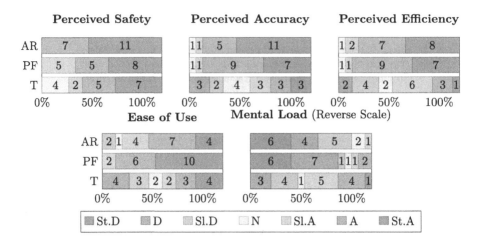

Fig. 3. Summary of the raw data obtained from the survey filled out by 18 participants, comparing the **AR Point&Click** (AR), **Person Following** (PF) and **Tablet** (T) interfaces, for each one of the 5 survey questions shown in Table 1. (St = Strongly, Sl = Slightly, D = Disagree, N = Neutral, A = Agree)

Table 3. Post-hoc Nemenyi test results for the survey questions used to test **H1-H5**. Significant results are indicated in **bold** and was determined for p-values < 0.05.

	p (AR ≠ PF)	p (AR > T)	p (PF > T)
Perceived safety	0.29	0.06	0.73
Perceived accuracy	0.83	**<0.001**	**0.005**
Perceived efficiency	0.99	**0.002**	**0.001**
Ease of use	0.077	0.63	**0.005**
Mental load	0.99	**0.001**	**<0.001**

Moreover, both of these methods were rated to require significantly less *Mental Load* (Q5) than the **Tablet** interface, affirming **H5**. No difference between **AR Point&Click** and **Person Following** interfaces was found for these metrics. The **Person Following** method was found to be the most *Easy to Use (Q4)* with significant difference found with the **Tablet** (p=0.005). However signifiance was not found with the **AR Point&Click** interface (p=0.077). Therefore, **H4** can only be partially affirmed and further user studies and feedback is warranted.

When asked for interface preference for this task after being exposed to all three interfaces, 12 users out of 18 indicated that they prefer the **AR Point&Click** interface, including 3 who indicated that they equally preferred another method. The distribution of user preferences are shown in Fig. 4.

4.2   Objective Metrics

The mean and standard deviation for the three objective metrics and interfaces are shown in Table 4. While **Person Following** had the lowest Practice Time and Goal Time, **AR Point&Click** had the lowest Positional Error.

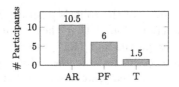

Fig. 4. Distribution of user preferences. Where users preferred more than one interface, fractions were used. The AR Point&Click was the most preferred interface

Table 4. Mean and standard deviation for each objective metric and interface. Lower numbers are better - and the best performing methods are indicated in **bold**.

	AR	PF	T
Practice time (s)	84.1 ($\sigma = 40.1$)	**61.4 ($\sigma = 26.2$)**	74.7 ($\sigma = 30.8$)
Goal Time (s)	19.3 ($\sigma = 7.3$)	**16.8 ($\sigma = 3.7$)**	24.5 ($\sigma = 4.9$)
Pos. Error (m)	**0.137 ($\sigma = 0.03$)**	0.141 ($\sigma = 0.04$)	0.188 ($\sigma = 0.05$)

We conducted a one-way ANOVA test in which we found that there was no statistical significance in the Practice Time metric. There were statistically significant differences for the Goal Time and Positional Error metrics which we subsequently ran post-hoc t-tests for. Bonferroni method [15] was employed to account for the repeated tests, which reduced the threshold for statistical significance by a factor of 3, hence we used p=0.0167 as the statistical significance threshold. The t-test results for each objective metric pair are shown in Table 5.

Table 5. p-values for post-hoc t-test results for the objective metrics. Significant results and preferred method are indicated in **bold**.

	p (AR $\neq$ PF)	p (AR > T)	p (PF > T)
Goal Time	0.25	0.030	**<0.001**
Positional Error	0.74	**0.001**	**<0.001**

While we found that **AR Point&Click** interface resulted in the lowest Positional Error, and it was significantly lower than **Tablet** interface, we could not find a statistical difference between **AR Point&Click** and **Person Following**. Hence, **H6** can not be affirmed. Overall, the user study results supports the hypotheses **H2**, **H3**, and **H5** and partially supports **H4**, but does not have statistically significant results to affirm **H1** and **H6**.

5   Qualitative Analysis

During the user studies, we noticed that the participants' perception of accuracy and mental load appeared to be linked to ease of fine adjustments in position rather than the actual accuracy of the robot's position. When using the **Tablet** interface, one participant (R16) found that they *"had to make many adjustments"*. Meanwhile another participant (R17) stated that *"it was nice to be able to see where you were going to send the robot"* in reference to the **AR Point&Click** interface. Unexpectedly, we observed that users made fine adjustments with the **Person Following** interface by making small movements for the robot to follow. This, along with comments about the **AR Point&Click** interface, suggests that positional accuracy and perceived efficiency improve with the ability to localize goals within the physical space. A participant (R12) suggested that *"the best interface would be a combination of the* [**AR Point&Click**] *and* [**Person Following**] *interfaces"*. It can be noted that the **AR Point&Click** had similar improvements over the **Tablet** interface as the **Person Following** interface with the exception of **Q4**, where users did not find the AR interface easy to use relative to the others. One participant (R5) notes that the **AR Point&Click** interface took *"longer to figure out but once [they] figured it out, it was quite good to use"*. This suggests that the short calibration time of the user study may not be fully representative of or sufficient for the interface.

Though **H1** was not affirmed, the perceived safety of the **AR Point&Click** may be a key factor in its adoption as the AR headset allowed users to look at the robot instead of away at a **Tablet** or being in close proximity to the robot in the **Person Following** interface. A participant (R11) found that *"you can observe the motion of the robot"* with the **AR Point&Click** interface while also stating that *"It was a little bit scary"* when using the **Person Following** interface. An interesting observation was that most of the participants expressed a preference for the **AR Point&Click** interface, even though it did not perform significantly better than **Person Following** in any metric. As well, the participants are of similar ages and all but one had prior experience in robotics. These results might be a novelty effect of AR technology, which motivates long-term studies.

6   Conclusions and Future Work

We investigate a point and click interface using an Augmented Reality headset which allows users to employ a natural point-and-click gesture to set navigation goals. The interface also visualizes the goal after it was set which lets users adjust the goal location if desired. We validate the efficacy of the proposed interface through a user study, in which participants set navigation goals for a robot. We compare the proposed **AR Point&Click** interface to a **Tablet** interface which is similar to the popular developer tool RViz, and a **Person Following** behavior, designed to be an intuitive interface.

User study results show that the users set goals with the highest accuracy using the proposed **AR Point&Click** interface. Moreover, **AR Point&Click** was subjectively assessed to have higher perceived accuracy and efficiency and a lower mental load compared to the **Tablet** interface. Though not conclusive, there was some indication that the **AR Point&Click** interface also improved the perceived safety. The proposed interface was rated similarly to **Person Following** by the participants, however, the majority of the participants indicated that **AR Point&Click** as their interface of choice, likely due to a novelty effect. On the other hand, there was some indication that **Person Following** method was found to be easier to use than **AR Point&Click**. This may be alleviated with greater adoption of the AR technology in the future. Given these results, the proposed **AR Point&Click** is a feasible method for setting navigation goals for mobile robots and there is room for improvement in the user experience.

Some of the main drawbacks found for the **AR Point&Click** were due to limitations of the AR headset. Participants found that (R11) *"[you] couldn't exactly look at the point"* due to the AR headset's low FOV and often noticed that the click gesture recognition wouldn't register or would falsely register. It is important to note that the improvements to the AR technology in the future can alleviate some of the issues experienced by users. It should be noted that this work is a proof-of-concept for using an AR headset to control mobile robots and there are several ways to improve on this. First, the feasibility of the navigation goals are not checked, hence collision checks can be incorporated. Second, the user study can be extended to test how well people can set goal poses instead of just position goals. Third, the current navigation behavior is very simple and therefore implementing a more complex navigation algorithm, which may be human-aware [7], may be another avenue to investigate. Finally, the proposed system can be extended to select other entities, such as people or objects.

Acknowledgement. This project was supported by the Australian Research Council (ARC) Discovery Project Grant DP200102858.

References

1. USD 35.27 billion growth in service robotics market: by application (professional robots and personal robots) and Geography - Global Forecast to 2025. https://www.prnewswire.com/news-releases/usd-35-27-billion-growth-in-service-robotics-market-by-application-professional-robots-and-personal-robots-and-geography--global-forecast-to-2025-301454915.html, 24 Mar 2022
2. Vuforia Developer Portal. https://developer.vuforia.com/
3. Chen, Y.H., Zhang, B., Tuna, C., Li, Y., Lee, E.A., Hartmann, B.: A context menu for the real world: controlling physical appliances through head-worn infrared targeting. Technical Report, UC Berkeley EECS (2013)
4. Cosgun, A., Christensen, H.I.: Context-aware robot navigation using interactively built semantic maps. Paladyn, J. Behav. Robot. **9**(1), 254–276 (2018)
5. Cosgun, A., Florencio, D.A., Christensen, H.I.: Autonomous person following for telepresence robots. In: IEEE International Conference on Robotics and Automation (ICRA) (2013)
6. Cosgun, A., Maliki, A., Demir, K., Christensen, H.: Human-centric assistive remote control for co-located mobile robots. In: ACM/IEEE International Conference on Human-Robot Interaction (HRI) Extended Abstracts, pp. 27–28 (2015)
7. Cosgun, A., Sisbot, E.A., Christensen, H.I.: Anticipatory robot path planning in human environments. In: IEEE international Symposium on Robot and Human Interactive Communication (RO-MAN) (2016)

8. Cosgun, A., Trevor, A.J., Christensen, H.I.: Did you mean this object?: detecting ambiguity in pointing gesture targets. In: HRI'15 Towards a Framework for Joint Action Workshop (2015)
9. Gu, M., Cosgun, A., Chan, W.P., Drummond, T., Croft, E.: Seeing thru walls: visualizing mobile robots in augmented reality. In: IEEE International Conference on Robot and Human Interactive Communication (RO-MAN) (2021)
10. Gualtieri, M., Kuczynski, J., Shultz, A.M., Ten Pas, A., Platt, R., Yanco, H.: Open world assistive grasping using laser selection. In: IEEE International Conference on Robotics and Automation (ICRA) (2017)
11. Hato, Y., Satake, S., Kanda, T., Imai, M., Hagita, N.: Pointing to space: modeling of deictic interaction referring to regions. In: ACM/IEEE International Conference on Human-Robot Interaction (HRI) (2010)
12. Hoang, K.C., Chan, W.P., Lay, S., Cosgun, A., Croft, E.: virtual barriers in augmented reality for safe and effective human-robot cooperation in manufacturing. In: IEEE International Conference on Robot and Human Interactive Communication (RO-MAN) (2022)
13. Hoang, K.C., Chan, W.P., Lay, S., Cosgun, A., Croft, E.: Visualizing robot intent for object handovers with augmented reality. In: IEEE International Conference on Robot and Human Interactive Communication (RO-MAN) (2022)
14. Hoang, K.C., Chan, W.P., Lay, S., Cosgun, A., Croft, E.: Arviz: an augmented reality-enabled visualization platform for ROS applications. IEEE Robot. Autom. Mag. **29**, 2–11 (2022)
15. Jafari, M., Ansari-Pour, N.: Why, when and how to adjust your p values? Cell J. **20**, 604–607 (2019)
16. Kemp, C.C., Anderson, C.D., Nguyen, H., Trevor, A.J., Xu, Z.: A point-and-click interface for the real world: laser designation of objects for mobile manipulation. In: ACM/IEEE International Conference on Human-Robot Interaction (HRI) (2008)
17. Kousi, N., Stoubos, C., Gkournelos, C., Michalos, G., Makris, S.: Enabling Human Robot Interaction in flexible robotic assembly lines: an augmented reality based software suite. In: Procedia CIRP (2019)
18. Makhataeva, Z., Varol, H.A.: Augmented reality for robotics: a review. Robotics **9**(2), 21 (2020)
19. Newbury, R., Cosgun, A., Koseoglu, M., Drummond, T.: Learning to take good pictures of people with a robot photographer. In: IEEE/RSJ International Conference on Intelligent Robots and Systems (IROS) (2020)
20. Nguyen, H., Jain, A., Anderson, C., Kemp, C.C.: A clickable world: behavior selection through pointing and context for mobile manipulation. In: IEEE/RSJ International Conference on Intelligent Robots and Systems (IROS) (2008)
21. Reardon, C., Lee, K., Fink, J.: Come see this! Augmented reality to enable human-robot cooperative search. In: 2018 IEEE International Symposium on Safety, Security, and Rescue Robotics (SSRR) (2018)
22. Rottmann, N., Studt, N., Ernst, F., Rueckert, E.: ROS-mobile: an android application for the robot operating system. arXiv preprint arXiv:2011.02781 (2020)
23. Scales, P., Aycard, O., Aubergé, V.: Studying navigation as a form of interaction: a design approach for social robot navigation methods. In: IEEE International Conference on Robotics and Automation (ICRA) (2020)
24. Sprute, D., Tönnies, K., König, M.: This far, no further: introducing virtual borders to mobile robots using a laser pointer. In: IEEE International Conference on Robotic Computing (IRC), pp. 403–408 (2019)

25. Walker, M., Hedayati, H., Lee, J., Szafir, D.: Communicating robot motion intent with augmented reality. In: ACM/IEEE International Conference on Human-Robot Interaction (HRI) (2018)
26. waymouth, b., et al.: demonstrating cloth folding to robots: Design and evaluation of a 2d and a 3d user interface. In: IEEE International Conference on Robot and Human Interactive Communication (RO-MAN) (2021)

Human-Aware Subgoal Generation in Crowded Indoor Environments

Nick Ah Sen[✉], Pamela Carreno-Medrano, and Dana Kulić

Faculty of Engineering, Monash University, Clayton, Australia
{nick.ahsen,pamela.carreno,dana.kulic}@monash.edu

Abstract. With mobile robots becoming more prevalent in our daily lives, it is crucial that these robots navigate in a safe and socially-aware manner. While recent works have shown promising results by using Deep Reinforcement Learning (DRL) techniques to learn socially-aware navigation policies, most approaches are limited to local, short-term navigation. For more complex settings, DRL approaches rely on subgoals often computed using traditional path planners. However, these planners are not necessarily suitable for social navigation since they rarely consider the pedestrians in the scene and often disregard the long term cost of a path or the pedestrian dynamics. In this paper, we present an alternative global planner that uses a learnt local cost predictor to generate subgoal guidance to help a DRL robot to make progress towards its goal while also taking into account the pedestrians in the environment. We evaluate the proposed approach in simulation. We consider several environments of varying complexity as well as different pedestrian behaviours. Our results show that a DRL robot using the proposed planner is less likely to collide with pedestrians and exhibits improved social awareness when compared to a baseline approach using traditional path planner methods.

Keywords: Social robot navigation · Motion and path planning · Deep reinforcement learning

1 Introduction

In recent years, autonomous mobile robots have been proposed for a wide range of applications including healthcare, delivery and domestic assistance. These applications require mobile robots to not only navigate safely and efficiently to their destinations, but also to consider the comfort of the surrounding pedestrians [16]. Moreover, because of the unpredictable behaviours of pedestrians, navigation in crowded environments that meets both safety and social standards remains an open challenge [20].

While traditional motion planning algorithms may be suitable for safe navigation, they fail to account for desirable socially-aware navigation behaviours. This problem was first addressed through the inclusion of simple predefined costs and constraints into motion planners [15,25]. However, hard-coded social behaviours may not encapsulate the complexity of socially-aware navigation behavior. To

F. Cavallo et al. (Eds.): ICSR 2022, LNAI 13817, pp. 50–60, 2022.
https://doi.org/10.1007/978-3-031-24667-8_5

address this issue, numerous works have focused on DRL techniques to learn navigation policies that implicitly encode human interactions and some of the social rules shared among humans [6,8,9]. For instance, Chen et al. [6] first proposed SA-CADRL, a DRL approach that encourages the robot to comply with social norms such as passing on the right and overtaking on the left. The algorithm was first trained in simulation and later demonstrated in a laboratory environment with a large number of pedestrians.

However, in complex and larger environments where longer periods of time are required for the robot to reach its target goal, training DRL policies becomes harder and the learned policies often fail to consistently transfer well to new environments (i.e., they get stuck in local minima) [7]. Therefore, most DRL approaches used to date learn short-range navigation policies and employ traditional global planners such as rapidly exploring random trees (RRT) [18] or A-Star [13] to provide subgoal guidance to the DRL agent. For instance, in [11,24], the subgoals provided to the DRL agent are obtained by subsampling the global path. Kastner et al. [17] selected subgoals based on known landmarks (such as turning points), the robot's position and the obstacles location and performed a re-planning of the global path whenever the robot was off-course. Nonetheless, these approaches do not take into consideration the pedestrians in the scene nor reason about the long term cost of a path or the pedestrian conditions (e.g., if a passage will be crowded with humans). This in turn can make it harder, if not impossible, for the robot to reach its destination.

Another body of approaches employs machine learning (ML) techniques to guide the robot toward its global goal. In [1], a supervised learning perception module is used to generate subgoals. Similarly, in [4], a DRL policy was trained to provide subgoals to a model predictive controller (MPC) given the global goal and pedestrian information as observations/inputs. The subgoals helped the robot to take into consideration the interaction effects among other agents. However, their method did not account for static obstacles.

To address these issues, in this work, we propose an alternative navigation framework in which the global planner utilises a learning-based local cost predictor model to provide subgoal guidance to a DRL robot navigation policy whilst jointly taking into account obstacles in the scene, path efficiency and pedestrians in the environment. The local cost predictor is trained to predict the likelihood that the DRL robot will successfully reach a given nearby goal without violating any social or collision constraints. In summary, our main contributions are: (1) a novel hierarchical navigation framework focusing on subgoal generation for a DRL agent to navigate around pedestrians in long-range indoor environments; (2) a global planner that utilises a learning-based local cost predictor model so as to account for the pedestrians in the scene and the environment configuration when generating subgoal guidance; and (3) an extensive evaluation of the algorithm performance in diverse simulated environments and different pedestrian behaviours, demonstrating that our method results in fewer pedestrian collisions and better adherence to social norms compared to a baseline approach.

2   Approach

Our navigation framework consists of three main components (see Fig. 1): an environment-independent short-range (Point-to-Point or P2P) navigation policy trained using DRL (Sect. 2.3), a local-cost predictor that predicts the performance of the P2P policy for any given short-range navigation task (Sect. 2.1), and a global planner that leverages the local-cost estimator to iteratively compute subgoals that guide the robot[1] towards a path that most likely improves its overall navigation performance and incurs in minimal violations of any social constraint (Sect. 2.2).

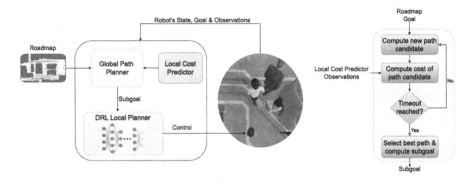

Fig. 1. Framework Architecture (left); Flow diagram for the global planner (right)

2.1   Local Cost Predictor

The objective of the local cost predictor is to provide an estimate of the cost the robot will incur when attempting to travel to a nearby subgoal using a local planner. In this paper, the local cost predictor learns a function that estimates the likelihood of the robot successfully reaching a subgoal given the its current local observations. Formally, this is defined as follows.

Let $o = (l, p, g)$ denote a local observation consisting of the robot's LiDAR sensor readings l, the relative pedestrians' positions within the robot's field of view (FOV) p, and the relative goal position g. Similarly, let $T = \{q_0, q_1, ..., q_N\}$ denote the sequence of robot configuration states generated by a robot following a policy π towards a local goal g from the starting robot state q_0[2]. An executed trajectory is defined as a *success* if the robot reaches a state q_i within a distance threshold d from its goal ($|q_i - g| \leq d$) within a given time without violating any social constraint. An executed trajectory is a *failure* if it produces a state that is within the personal space of any pedestrian (this is considered to be a violation of a social constraint) or if the robot collides with an obstacle.

---

[1] The robot is controlled by the DRL short-range navigation policy.

[2] In this work, each robot state q_i contains the robot's location (x_i, y_i) in the world frame.

The local cost predictor learns the cost function $c : (o_0) \rightarrow [0, 1]$ that maps the robot local observation at the start of each trajectory o_0 to a scalar value representing the likelihood of the robot successfully reaching the local goal g. The global planner then uses this information to identify a global path that maximizes the robot's probability of successfully reaching its final destination. Figure 2 illustrates this process.

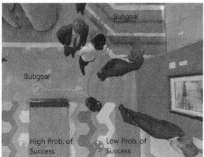

Fig. 2. (Left) The local cost predictor identifies a higher probability of success for the subgoal in green; (Right) Our planner in green uses the local cost predictor to guide the robot towards its goal while considering the pedestrians. (Color figure online)

2.2   Human-Aware Path Planner

The objective of the global path planner is to find the path with minimum cost $\tau^* = \arg\min_{\tau \in T} J(\tau)$ where $J(\tau) : \tau \rightarrow \mathbb{R}$ is an overall cost function describing the path specifications (e.g, path length, social consideration or time to goal or energy consumption).

Our proposed global planner consists of a two-stage iterative process (see Fig. 1). First, a sampling-based planner is used to compute a static-obstacle-free path candidate based on static environment assumptions. Next, the cost of the path candidate is calculated using the local cost estimator and estimates of the nearby pedestrians' positions for each point along the path. Path candidates continue to be generated until a computation timeout is reached. The path with the minimum cost is then selected and the next waypoint in the path is passed to the DRL agent as a subgoal. The global planner is called again after the robot reaches the current waypoint. This process is repeated until the robot reaches its goal state.

Path candidates are generated as follows. Prior to planning, the target environment is first characterised by constructing a roadmap using a standard Probabilistic Roadmap (PRM) method [14] in an one-time, off-line step. During planning, the roadmap together with any standard path-finding algorithm (such as A* [13]) are used to efficiently compute the shortest path from the start to the goal state. This is the first path candidate. After each iteration, the roadmap is slightly modified by removing an edge. This edge is selected from the last computed path candidate starting from the beginning of the path (i.e., the edge connecting q_0 and q_1). This allows the algorithm to explore different path candidates passing through different nodes.

The total cost for each path candidate is defined as $J(\tau) = \sum_{i=1}^{t} c(e_i)$ where $e_i = (q_{i-1}, q_i)$ represents the edge/local motion connecting two consecutive nodes and $c : e_i \rightarrow \mathbb{R}$ is a cost function of the local motion. The cost function can be computed as a weighted sum of several features characterizing the local motion. For instance, we compute the cost function as $c(e_i) = w_L c_L(e_i) + w_S c_S(e_i)$ where c_L is the length cost computed as the Euclidean distance between q_{i-1} and q_i, and c_s is the success cost computed using the local cost predictor described in Sect. 2.1. The corresponding weights w_L and w_S define the relative importance of these two terms. At the beginning of a path, $i = 1$, c_S can be simply computed using the robot's local observation. For the subsequent steps, $i > 1$, the algorithm requires a forward prediction of the pedestrians position in the environment given that the robot's current configuration state q_i. For simplicity, in this work, we assume that the pedestrians are static (standing) and compensate the inaccuracy in our model by computing the success cost for only the first segment of the path. That is, $c_S(e_i) = 0$ for $i > n$ where $1 < n < t$.

2.3   DRL Local Planner

The goal of the DRL local planner is to learn a navigation policy that avoids pedestrians in an indoor environment while navigating toward a local goal. We follow similar methods to the work of [10,21].

Formally, at each time step t, the agent obtains an observation o_t, performs an action a_t by following a policy $\pi(a|o)$ and receives an immediate reward R_t from the environment. The goal of the DRL agent is to learn a policy $\pi^*(o) = a$ such that its actions will maximize the expected future return:

$$\pi^*(o) = \arg\max_{a \in A} E\Big(\sum_i \gamma^i R_i\Big)$$

In our approach, the observation space is represented by the tuple (l_t, g, v_t), where $g \in \mathbb{R}^2$ is the 2D goal coordinates in the robot's reference frame, $v_t \in \mathbb{R}^2$ is the robot current linear and angular velocities and $l_t \in \mathbb{R}^{144}$ are the values from a 360°C 1D lidar sensor with respect to the robot's sensor reference frame. The robot action a_t is represented by the tuple (v_t, ω_t) where v_t and ω_t are the robot linear and angular velocity at time-step t. The agent's objective is to learn the policy $\pi(a|o)$ that maximizes the sum of rewards while reaching a goal state p_g from a starting start p_s, within radius d_{goal}. The reward function is composed of multiple sub reward terms that encourage the robot to reach the goal, minimize time and avoid collisions:

$$R = r_{goal} + r_{collision} + r_{step} + r_{potential}$$

where $r_{goal} = +1$ is a sparse reward given when the agent reaches the goal, $r_{collision} = -1$ is assigned when the agent collides with obstacles and terminates the episode, $r_{step} = -0.002$ is a small constant penalty step to encourage the robot to minimize the task time, and $r_{potential}$ is a dense reward assigned per time step as the negative Euclidean distance to the goal.

3   Experiments

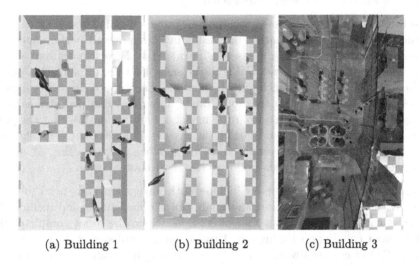

(a) Building 1   (b) Building 2   (c) Building 3

Fig. 3. Environments used for indoor navigation tasks. Red and blue circles indicate the robot's start and goal positions. The yellow circles indicate all waypoints. (Color figure online)

3.1   Setup

Environment Setup: We used a Turtlebot differential drive robot for all the experiments. The Turtlebot robot has a radius of 0.18 m with maximum linear velocity of 0.6 m/s and 2.0 rad/s angular velocity. Localization is assumed to be perfectly known. We used the iGibson simulation environment [19] which provides fast physics simulation based on PyBullet and a variety of large-scale realistic scenes. All computations were done on a AMD Ryzen 7 3700X @ 2.1 GHz CPU and NVIDIA GTX 1070 Ti GPU using Python 3.8. All pedestrians' motion was generated using the Optimal Reciprocal Collision Avoidance (ORCA) model [2]. This model is frequently used to represent pedestrian motion in crowd simulations and for research on robot social navigation [10,21]. We sampled 10 pedestrians for each environment. Figure 3 shows the different environments used for training and evaluation. The local planner policy was first trained in Building 1 (Fig. 3a). The training data set for the local cost predictor model was obtained from Building 2 (Fig. 3b). Our planner was also evaluated in a real-world office building (Fig. 3c).

Roadmap Building: We use Gaussian node sampling [3] to get a better coverage of difficult parts of the free configuration space with $\mathcal{N}(\mu = 0.8\,\text{m}, \sigma = 0.1\,\text{m})$. A total of 100 nodes were sampled for each environment. For simplicity, we used a straight line local planner to connect all nodes. We note that other edge connection approaches could also be implemented. For instance, the PRM-RL method [10] connects nodes only when the DRL agent can consistently navigate between them. Although their method can improve navigation quality and resilience, it can take several hours or days depending on the scale and density of the roadmap being constructed.

Baseline: Since we wish to assess whether our proposed global planner is capable to guide the robot toward paths that result in better overall performance, we compare our approach against a baseline in which the shortest path from a start to goal position is used instead. We note the same DRL local navigation policy was used for both our approach and the baseline. Each approach was evaluated on 100 navigation episodes a total of 5 times. The robot and pedestrians start and goal positions are selected from the free space and we ensure that the path distance between the start and goal positions are at least 10 m. The shortest feasible path to the goal is computed at the starting position using A* search with adequate clearance for the robot to travel without collision.

Metrics: Our evaluation metrics include both navigation and social metrics. The navigation metrics measure the quality of the navigation and include the **Success rate (S)**: percentage (%) of episodes where the robot completes the task without colliding or timing out, **Environment collision rate (EC)**: percentage (%) of episodes where the robot collides with a static obstacle such as wall or object, **Pedestrian collision rate (PC)**: percentage (%) of episodes where the robot collides with a pedestrian, **Timeout rate (TO)**: percentage (%) of episodes in which the robot runs out of time before completing the task and **Path length (PL)**: The length of the path that the robot took to reach its goal in metres. The social metrics measure the social awareness of the robot, and include the **Personal space violation (PS)**: average duration of robot being inside the min. comfortable personal space of the pedestrian and **Aggregated time (AT)**: the aggregated goal reaching time for all pedestrians. These metrics were selected from the set of metrics proposed in [26].

3.2   DRL Local Planner Training

To accelerate the learning process of our P2P policy and guarantee that the learnt policy can easily generalise to novel spaces, we used the simplistic training environment shown in Fig. 3a. This environment includes different basic layouts, such as hallways, rooms, and door exits. During training, the robot and pedestrians' initial positions were randomly sampled from a collision-free location in the environment. Their target goals were randomly placed such that there exists a straight line path from the initial position to the goal.

A Soft-Actor Critic (SAC) policy algorithm was used to train the DRL local planner. This algorithm learns both a value function (critic) and a policy (actor) approximated by deep neural networks. The policy network acts both as our local planner, and as a data generation source for the P2P success-likelihood estimator. We used the SAC implementation available on Stable-Baselines3 [22] and the available software integration with iGibson [19] and openAI Gym [5]. The robot was trained for 3M episodes and took about 8 h to complete.

3.3   Local Cost Predictor Training

In this paper, the local cost predictor was approximated by a neural network consisting of three fully connected layers with [2048, 1024, 128] hidden neurons (a dropout probability of 0.5 is applied at last layer) and a sigmoid activation function in the output layer, and trained using supervised ML. To obtain the training dataset for the local cost predictor, we first initialise the robot and pedestrians' starting states at random in a simulated environment. The robot's local goal is sampled such that it is within line of sight of the starting state. This helps to avoid failure due to the robot being stuck in local minima. After initialisation, we execute the DRL policy until the episode terminates by either reaching the goal, collision or timeout. After an episode terminates, the robot's observation at the beginning of the episode and the episode's outcome (i.e., success or failure) are recorded as the input and label data respectively.

We trained our local cost estimator network using 25,000 samples collected in Building 2 (Fig. 3b). To avoid the class imbalance problem [12], samples were collected such as to maintain an 3:2 success to failure ratio. Finally, we used Binary Cross Entropy (BCE) loss between the estimated success and the true success labels during training. An episode consists of the same P2P navigation task as described in Sect. 3.2.

3.4   Results and Discussion

Navigation Performance: All navigation metrics are shown in the 3rd, 4th, and 5th columns of Table 1. Overall, we observe that our method outperforms the baseline in terms of navigation success rate in all three environments with an increase of 19%, 12%, 12% in success rate corresponding to environment 1, 2 and 3 respectively. We notice that this improvement in success rate is particularly due to the decrease in pedestrian collisions (21%, 9%, 11%). Thus, our planner was able to guide the robot towards paths that are less likely to result in failure due to collisions with pedestrians. In terms of efficiency, the baseline method is the most efficient planner, taking the shortest paths compared to our approach. However, these paths often resulted in a higher number of pedestrian collisions.

Social Awareness: All social metrics are shown in the last two columns of Table 1. Our results show that our approach resulted in fewer Personal Space Violations and shorter Pedestrian Aggregated times compared to the baseline approach. These results suggest that our planner was able to consider the pedestrians states as well as the robot policy to generate better subgoals during planning. Furthermore, the robot under our approach allowed the pedestrians to get to their destination in less time compared to the baseline.

Generalization to Different Pedestrian Behaviours: To analyze whether our approach can generalise to different human behaviours, we evaluated both our approach and the baseline with pedestrians of varying dominance levels. Randhavane et al. [23] proposed the Pedestrian Dominance Model (PDM) that maps the ORCA pedestrians' motion model parameters to a normalized scalar dominance values with higher values corresponding to more dominant pedestrians. Using this model, we generated evaluation conditions in which the ORCA pedestrians' motion model parameters were set to values that resulted in a pedestrians' dominance of 0.3, 0.5, or 0.7. For reference, both the DRL policies and local cost predictor were trained with a pedestrians' dominance of 0.4. All experiments were performed in Building 3. Results are shown in Table 2. Overall, we observe that our approach outperforms the baseline in both the navigation and social metrics for all dominance values. This suggests that the subgoals guidance provided by our approach results in better DRL generalisation to novel conditions. Finally, a lower overall performance with higher dominance pedestrians was observed for both approaches. This is expected since they both use the same DRL policy that was trained with less dominant pedestrians, and also since less dominant pedestrians are more likely to yield to the robot.

Table 1. Performance on different environments. The metrics marked with * are evaluated only on episodes completed by both methods

Env.	Method	Success rate (%)	Failure cases (%) (PC/EC/TO)	Path Length(m)*	Personal Space(s)*	Pedestrians Aggregated* Time(s)
Building 1	Baseline	49 ± 3	(45/1/5)	$\mathbf{10.92} \pm 0.24$	5.65 ± 0.64	46.99 ± 0.26
	Ours	$\mathbf{68} \pm 3$	(24/2/6)	12.46 ± 0.15	$\mathbf{4.22} \pm 0.54$	$\mathbf{46.57} \pm 0.26$
Building 2	Baseline	67 ± 2	(19/3/11)	$\mathbf{19.48} \pm 0.16$	8.85 ± 0.80	45.25 ± 0.31
	Ours	$\mathbf{79} \pm 4$	(10/3/8)	20.48 ± 0.26	$\mathbf{6.10} \pm 0.96$	$\mathbf{44.84} \pm 0.38$
Building 3	Baseline	61 ± 2	(24/13/2)	$\mathbf{14.58} \pm 0.61$	8.08 ± 0.27	35.74 ± 0.14
	Ours	$\mathbf{73} \pm 2$	(13/11/3)	16.27 ± 0.9	$\mathbf{6.0} \pm 0.76$	$\mathbf{34.96} \pm 0.14$

Table 2. Performance on pedestrians with different dominance in Building 3

Dom.	Method	Success rate (%)	Failure cases (%) (PC/EC/TO)	Path Length(m)*	Personal Space(s)*	Pedestrians Aggregated* Time(s)
0.3	Baseline	62 ± 3	(25/11/2)	$\mathbf{14.91} \pm 0.23$	8.86 ± 0.62	35.12 ± 0.22
	Ours	$\mathbf{70} \pm 9$	(12/15/3)	16.54 ± 0.05	$\mathbf{6.17} \pm 0.28$	$\mathbf{34.54} \pm 0.51$
0.5	Baseline	54 ± 2	(29/16/1)	$\mathbf{14.78} \pm 0.26$	8.00 ± 0.94	35.86 ± 0.28
	Ours	$\mathbf{69} \pm 6$	(16/14/1)	16.32 ± 0.15	$\mathbf{5.47} \pm 0.77$	$\mathbf{35.46} \pm 0.15$
0.7	Baseline	31 ± 3	(57/10/2)	$\mathbf{13.58} \pm 0.35$	4.36 ± 0.60	24.96 ± 0.36
	Ours	$\mathbf{49} \pm 3$	(38/11/2)	15.66 ± 0.50	$\mathbf{3.77} \pm 0.19$	$\mathbf{24.90} \pm 0.28$

4   Conclusion

This paper introduced a navigation framework where a global planner leverages a learnt local cost predictor to guide a DRL robot towards its goal while considering pedestrians in indoor environments. The local cost predictor is trained to learn the success probability for a given robot observation and subgoal. The approach was evaluated in simulation in several environments, as well as with different pedestrian behaviours. The results demonstrated improved robot navigation performance in terms of reducing the likelihood of colliding with pedestrians and improving the robot's social awareness compared to a baseline approach. For future work, we plan to extend our planner to also consider the pedestrian dynamics by performing forward simulation or predictions on pedestrians states. Additionally, we plan to deploy the algorithm on a physical robot and conduct experiments where the robot will interact with real humans in indoor spaces.

References

1. Bansal, S., et al.: Combining optimal control and learning for visual navigation in novel environments. In: CoRL (2020)
2. van den Berg, J., et al.: Reciprocal velocity obstacles for real-time multi-agent navigation. In: 2008 IEEE ICRA, pp. 1928–1935 (2008)
3. Boor, V., et al.: The Gaussian sampling strategy for probabilistic roadmap planners. In: Proceedings 1999 IEEE ICRA, vol. 2, pp. 1018–1023 (1999)
4. Brito, B., et al.: Where to go next: Learning a subgoal recommendation policy for navigation among pedestrians. arXiv:abs/2102.13073 (2021)
5. Brockman, G., et al.: Openai gym (2016)
6. Chen, Y.F., et al.: Socially aware motion planning with deep reinforcement learning. IEEE/RSJ IROS, pp. 1343–1350 (2017)
7. Chiang, H.T.L., et al.: Learning navigation behaviors end-to-end with autorl. IEEE Robot. Autom. Lett. **4**, 2007–2014 (2019)
8. Ciou, P.H., et al.: Composite reinforcement learning for social robot navigation. In: 2018 IEEE/RSJ IROS, pp. 2553–2558 (2018)
9. Everett, M., et al.: Motion planning among dynamic, decision-making agents with deep reinforcement learning. In: 2018 IEEE/RSJ IROS, pp. 3052–3059 (2018)
10. Faust, A., et al.: Prm-rl: Long-range robotic navigation tasks by combining reinforcement learning and sampling-based planning. In: IEEE ICRA, pp. 5113–5120 (2018)
11. Guldenring, R., et al.: Learning local planners for human-aware navigation in indoor environments. In: 2020 IEEE/RSJ IROS), pp. 6053–6060. IEEE (2020)
12. Guo, X., et al.: On the class imbalance problem. In: 2008 Fourth International Conference on Natural Computation, vol. 4, pp. 192–201 (2008)
13. Hart, P.E., et al.: A formal basis for the heuristic determination of minimum cost paths. IEEE Trans. Syst. Sci. Cybernetics **4**(2), 100–107 (1968)
14. Kavraki, L., Latombe, J.C.: Randomized preprocessing of configuration for fast path planning. In: IEEE ICRA, vol. 3, pp. 2138–2145 (1994)
15. Kirby, R., et al.: Affective social robots. Robot. Auton. Syst. **58**(3), 322–332 (2010)
16. Kruse, T., et al.: Human-aware robot navigation: A survey. Robot. Auton. Syst. **61**(12), 1726–1743 (2013)
17. Kästner, L., et al.: Connecting deep-reinforcement-learning-based obstacle avoidance with conventional global planners using waypoint generators. In: 2021 IEEE/RSJ IROS, pp. 1213–1220 (2021)
18. LaValle, S.M.: Rapidly-exploring random trees: A new tool for path planning. The Annual Research Report (1998)

19. Li, C., et al.: igibson 2.0: Object-centric simulation for robot learning of everyday household tasks. arXiv:abs/2108.03272 (2021)
20. Mavrogiannis, C., et al.: Core challenges of social robot navigation: A survey. arXiv:abs/2103.05668 (2021)
21. Pérez-D'Arpino, C., et al.: Robot navigation in constrained pedestrian environments using reinforcement learning. In: IEEE ICRA, pp. 1140–1146 (2021)
22. Raffin, A., et al.: Stable-baselines3: Reliable reinforcement learning implementations. J. Mach. Learn. Res. **22**(268), 1–8 (2021)
23. Randhavane, T., et al.: Pedestrian dominance modeling for socially-aware robot navigation. In: IEEE ICRA, pp. 5621–5628 (2019)
24. Regier, P., et al.: Deep reinforcement learning for navigation in cluttered environments. In: CS & IT, pp. 193–204 (2020)
25. Sisbot, E.A., et al.: A human aware mobile robot motion planner. IEEE TRO **23**(5), 874–883 (2007)
26. Wang, J., et al.: Metrics for evaluating social conformity of crowd navigation algorithms. In: IEEE ARSO, p. 1–6. IEEE Press (2022)

Speech-Driven Robot Face Action Generation with Deep Generative Model for Social Robots

Chuang Yu[1(✉)], Heng Zhang[2], Zhegong Shangguan[2], Xiaoxuan Hei[2], Angelo Cangelosi[1], and Adriana Tapus[2]

[1] Cognitive Robotics Laboratory, University of Manchester, Manchester, UK
{chuang.yu,angelo.cangelosi}@manchester.ac.uk
[2] Autonomous Systems and Robotics Lab/U2IS, ENSTA Paris,
Institut Polytechnique de Paris, Paris, France
{heng.zhang,zhegong.shangguan,xiaoxuan.hei,
adriana.tapus}@ensta-paris.fr

Abstract. The natural co-speech facial action as a kind of non-verbal behavior plays an essential role in human communication, which also leads to a natural and friendly human-robot interaction. However, a lot of previous works for robot speech-based behaviour generation are rule-based or handcrafted methods, which are time-consuming and with limited synchronization levels between the speech and the facial action. Based on the Generative Adversarial Networks (GAN) model, this paper developed an effective speech-driven facial action synthesizer, i.e., given an acoustic speech, a synchronous and realistic 3D facial action sequence is generated. In addition, a mapping between the 3D human facial action to the real robot facial action that regulates Zeno robot facial expressions is also completed. The evaluation results show the model has potential for natural human-robot interaction.

Keywords: Social robot · Face action · Human-robot interaction

1 Introduction

Multimodal behavior understanding and generation play an important role in successful human-robot interaction [1–3]. Recently, verbal and non-verbal behavior generation has drawn more and more attention of researchers from many research areas [4], including computing animation and robotics [5–7]. Non-verbal behaviors, including gaze, gestures [8,9], and facial actions [10], can assist verbal expressions in conveying clearer meanings in contrast to speech-only communication and intention. It also can help build trust during real or virtual communication [11]. The co-speech facial action as a non-verbal behavior plays a significant role in human-human communication as they can express rich meanings including the emotional information in the whole facial expression and the verbal content information in the lip or mouth action [12]. In order to make a natural and friendly human-robot interaction, it is necessary to endow a social robot with synchronous

F. Cavallo et al. (Eds.): ICSR 2022, LNAI 13817, pp. 61–74, 2022.
https://doi.org/10.1007/978-3-031-24667-8_6

and realistic facial actions. However, it is very challenging to generate aligned facial actions mapping with speech in long-term human-robot interaction. Most of the previous researches used the handcrafted or rule-based approaches [13] for offline facial action generation based on speech. These methods are time-consuming and have a limited continuity level of successive facial actions.

With the development of deep learning technology, more and more generative models for the time series generation are developed, such as, autoencoder model, seq2seq model [4], the model with the normalizing flows, and GAN (Generative Adversarial Networks) model [14]. Researchers have explored many areas with a generative model for time series generation, for example, human social trajectories generation [15], and gesture generation [5]. These methods also can be used for expressive co-speech facial action generation and simplify the robot facial action generation process as a kind of cross-modal mapping task. The trained generative model for facial action synthesis can be used in real-time and long-term human-robot interaction for a social robot.

In this paper, we built up a temporal GAN framework for a cross-modal mapping task, which can be applied to generate realistic facial action aligned with the speech audio in a real-time human-robot interaction. The basic GAN model is tough to train for cross-modal mapping tasks. Speech-to-facial action generation is not a strict mapping task where humans can conduct many possible natural and simultaneous facial action modes for the same speech, for example, in different emotional states, which makes the GAN more challenging to train towards convergence. To tackle this problem, we built our temporal GAN architecture based on $WGAN - GP$ (Wasserstein Generative Adversarial Networks-Gradient Penalty) [16] model and introduced the L_1 loss in the generator loss function inspired by the $pix2pix$ model [17].

The human face has more than 40 muscles, controlled for facial actions while speaking. However, it is challenging to equip the face of a robot with such a significant number of actuators in order to express rich facial actions. Our research used the Zeno robot, a small humanoid with an expressive face for human-robot interaction. In this paper, we completed the facial action retargeting task from 3D human facial landmarks to the robot facial action with related motor control signals. The pipeline of robot facial action generation is as shown in Fig. 1.

In summary, our contributions in this paper are as follows:

- A temporal GAN architecture with L_1 reconstruction loss was proposed to effectively generate a 3D co-speech facial action sequence, which can be used in long-term human-robot interaction.
- The facial action retargeting task was performed from human 3D face action to the robot face actuators.
- The generated robot facial actions with the related speech were applied to the Zeno robot for human-robot interaction.

The rest of the paper is structured as follows: Sect. 2 describes the related works. Section 3 shows the methodology. Section 4 describes the dataset and related pre-processing operation. Section 5 presents our experiments and results. The conclusions and future work are resumed in Sect. 6.

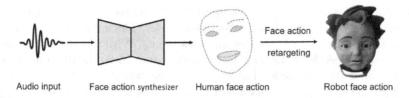

Fig. 1. The pipeline of RS^3 architecture. RS^3 architecture contains a facial action synthesizer from speech and a human-to-robot face action mapping. The facial action synthesizer based on the temporal GAN model takes the acoustic speech as input and outputs the aligned human 3D facial actions. The robot facial actions with control signals of robot facial motors are obtained from the human 3D face action during the facial action retargeting part. These motor control signals can be applied to the Zeno robot face during human-robot interaction.

2 Related Work

2.1 Generative Model

Generative models, including the model based on Naive Bayes [14], Variational Autoencoder (VAE) [14], Generative Adversarial Networks (GAN) [14], and the model based on the normalizing flows technology [18], have been of high interest to researchers on the image generation tasks and time-series data generation tasks. Habibie et al. [7] proposed a recurrent variational autoencoder model to produce human motions given some control signals, which can be applied for the sequence prediction task. In the paper [17], Isola et al. built an image-to-image translation network based on the conditional GAN model for image generation where the generation loss function also took the L_1 distance into consideration in order to obtain better generation results and to simplify the training process of GAN model. Heter et al. [19] came up with a probabilistic and controllable model for motion synthesis using normalising flows technology. The generative architecture as a probabilistic model can achieve a one-to-many mapping given multiple control signals, namely style-controllable generation.

2.2 Facial Image or Animation Generation

Co-speech video or animation generation with facial action is not a new research topic, which has been explored for decades [20,21]. Vougioukas et al. [6] built a temporal GAN model for speech-driven face animation generation. The GAN model used one static image and one speech audio as input and outputted realistic aligned image sequences with the face. In order to improve the randomness of the generated face image sequence, the generative architecture contained a noise generator to produce the noise time series, which was added, respectively to the representation information of each overlapped audio clip in the face generator model of GAN. The generator loss function also considered the L_1 reconstruction loss except for the basic GAN loss, which can improve the generation results.

In the paper [22], Zhou et al. built up an LSTM-based expressive face animation generation model with a self-attention encoder. The model took one unseen speech audio and one static speaker image as inputs. With the help of the disentangled learning skills in the model, the model can achieve the disentanglement of content and style in audio. The model can generate different talking animations with the same speaker style as the one in the input of the static image. Namely, it is speaker-aware speaking head animation generation.

Both methods above produce the co-speech face or head image sequence. There are some other researchers who focus on the face key point (landmark) position generation used to control the virtual face avatar in a simulation environment. Sadoughi et al. [23] proposed a conditional sequential GAN (CSG) model to generate the talking lip actions. The model used the spectral and emotional speech features as conditional input of the generator of GAN to synthesize emotion-aware lips action with key point coordinates, which then were utilized to regulate the virtual face. Abdelazi et al. [24] described a new co-speech facial movement generation structure that can be exploited for the animated face on smart mobile phones. The model jointly used audiovisual information, including the speech audio and one static face image as input to synthesize the aligned 3D facial action. However, these facial action generation models were only applied in animation situations and still do not explore whether it is effective and whether it can make a difference in the real humanoid robot with face-actuated skin.

2.3   Robot Facial Action Generation from Speech

Multimodal robot behaviors with speech, co-speech gestures, and facial actions are essential in a natural and friendly human-robot interaction. Particularly, the co-speech facial action generation is an active research area as facial actions convey more emotional information and speech content information than gestures. Aly et al. [12] built up a multimodal robot behavior synthesis system used on an expressive robot ALICE, in order to imitate natural multimodal human-human interaction. The system can generate speech-related gestures and co-speech facial expressions, which led to an effective narrative human-robot interaction. However, the robot facial action generation method is rule-based and cannot generate natural co-speech facial action. The generated facial action sequences have a limited continuity level in the temporal domain. In the paper [25], the laughter-driven facial motions were generated for a female android robot with facial skin. However, the robot facial action generation was rule-based with limited facial action patterns. It is challenging to generate facial actions in real-time and long-term human-robot interaction.

3   Methodology

3.1   Problem Formulation

Speech-Driven Facial Action Generation: It is a crossmodal translation task with time series both as input and output. Given one speech audio $S^m =$

$[s_t^m]_{t=1:T}$ as input, the model attempts to produce one 3D facial action sequence $A^m = [A_t^m]_{t=1:T'}$. Namely, the generative model tries to learn a relation function $F_{mapping}$ to maximize the conditional probability $P(A^m|S^m)$ to generate the natural and aligned facial action sequence. Here, T and T' are the time steps of the speech audio as input and the facial action sequence as output, respectively, and they are different from each other because the digital speech audio and the facial action sequence have different sampling rates. m in the model means m^{th} mapping task.

$$\mathbf{A^m} = F_{map}(\mathbf{S^m}) \tag{1}$$

Facial Action Retargeting: The problem is to map the human facial actions A^m with the 3D positions of the face key points to the robot facial action sequence $C^m = [c_t^m]_{t=1:T'}$ with the face motors' control signals. The mapping task for face action retargeting consists of getting a function that finds the relation between human facial action and robot facial action. The final function can make the appearance of the human facial and the appearance of robot face as similar as possible at each time step.

$$\mathbf{C}^m = F_{retarget}(\mathbf{A}^m) \tag{2}$$

3.2   Facial Action Synthesizer from Speech

This section describes our novel proposed facial action synthesizer from speech with temporal GAN. The speech-to-face-action GAN ($S2FGAN$) architecture is shown in Fig. 2. $S2FGAN$ model is made of a generator and a discriminator. The generator with a sequence model takes the temporal representation of speech audio as input and outputs the mapping gesture. The discriminator is employed to differentiate whether the speech and the facial action match each other.

The generator comprises two layers of GRU (Gated Recurrent Unit) and MLP (Multilayer Perceptron) layer. Firstly, Mel-frequency Cepstral Coefficients (MFCCs) as audio representation are extracted from the overlapped audio clips. The MFCC feature sequence is input into the batch normalization layer following two layers GRU of the generator. The following MLP layer takes the latent representation of the former GRU layer to generate the synchronous 3D facial action sequence mapping with the speech audio. And each frame of the facial action sequence contains 3D positions of 68 face landmarks. The discriminator works to distinguish whether the facial action sequence and the speech audio match with each other. The audio clip representations and the facial action sequence are input into two MLP layers and decoded to 100-dimensional features and 50-dimensional features each time step, respectively. The following concatenation layer fusions the two modal features in each time step, whose output is input to a GRU layer. In the final GRU cell, an MLP layer is followed to classify whether the speech audio matches the 3D facial action sequence.

The loss function of our $S2FGAN$ model comprises two parts, namely L_1 loss part and the standard conditional GAN loss part, actually the Wasserstein

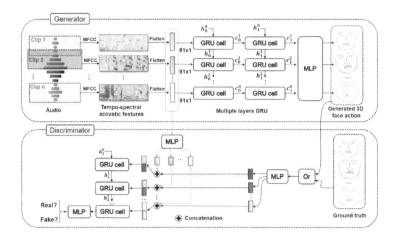

Fig. 2. The *S2FGAN* **architecture.** The model has a generator and a discriminator. The generator takes the spectral features of speech as input and outputs the synchronous 3D facial action data. The discriminator with the speech audio and generated/real facial action sequence as inputs try to classify whether the speech and the facial action sequence align in the temporal domain.

loss and the gradient penalty used in the WGAN-GP model. The basic GAN model often experiences the training instability problem. The Wasserstein GAN (WGAN) model makes a more stable training than basic GANs [26]. WGAN can also produce samples with low quality and suffer from convergence problems during the training process. WGAN introduces a weight clipping skill to enforce a Lipschitz constraint on the discriminator (namely, the critic named in WGAN) to address these problems, which also can result in gradient explosion/vanishing without careful tuning of the weight clipping parameter. In WGAN-GP [16], the authors proposed an alternative skill to the weight clipping, namely, adding the gradient penalty to the discriminator loss, which leads to a more stable training process. The WGAN-GP loss contains the generator loss $\mathcal{L}_G$ and the discriminator loss $\mathcal{L}_D$, as shown in Eq. 3 and Eq. 4, respectively. Where, the sample S^n from the sampling uniformly along straight lines between pairs of points sampled from the data distribution of real facial action sequences and the generator distribution.

$$\mathcal{L}_G = -\mathbb{E}_{S^m}[D(S^m, G(S^m))] \tag{3}$$

$$\mathcal{L}_D = \mathbb{E}_{S^m}[D(S^m, G(S^m))] - \mathbb{E}_{S^m, A^m}[D(S^m, A^m)] + \\ \lambda \mathbb{E}_{A^n}[(\|\nabla_{A^n} D(A^n)\|_2 - 1)^2] \tag{4}$$

Inspired by the *pix2pix* model [17], we introduced a L_1 reconstruction loss to improve the realistic co-speech facial action generation. The L_1 loss is pixel-wise in the image translation task with *pix2pix* model, while we used the frame-wise L_1 loss for the facial action sequence, as shown in the Eq. 5. The final discriminator loss keeps same, and the L_1 loss is added to the generator loss to get the final generator loss $\mathcal{L}_{G-all}$ as shown in Eq. 6. Where λ is an empirical hyperparameter during $S2FGAN$ model training, which is to balance how much contribution $\mathcal{L}_{L1}$ or $\mathcal{L}_G$ make for all the loss.

$$\mathcal{L}_{L1}(G) = \mathbb{E}_{S^m, A^m}\left[\|A^m - G(S^m)\|_1\right] \tag{5}$$

$$\mathcal{L}_{G-all} = \mathcal{L}_G + \lambda\mathcal{L}_{L1}(G) \tag{6}$$

3.3   Facial Action Retargeting

Our facial action retargeting task is a mapping from human facial action to robot facial action. The mapping objective is to approximate the human face appearance with a limited number of robot face actuators. In this paper, we use a Zeno robot to present the synchronous generated facial action sequence with the speech audio. There are four motors for skin-based face appearance regulation. The four motors can control the eyebrows/forehead up or down (one motor), the eyelids open (one motor), the mouth open, and the left and right corner for the smile (one motor). Each motor's control signal of the Zeno robot is a continuous value ranging from 0 to 1. The retargeting process from human facial action to robot facial action is as shown in Fig. 3. The human facial action includes 3D positions of 68 landmarks, and four motors of Zeno with skin regulate the robot's facial expression.

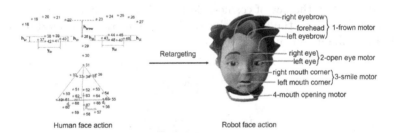

Fig. 3. Facial action retargeting overview. The human face contains 68 human landmarks in each frame. The robot face has four motors controlling the eye, the forehead, the mouth, and the mouth corners for a smile.

We name the distance between the 38th landmark and the 42nd landmark as h_{1r}, the 39th landmark and the 41st landmark as h_{2r}. The right eye wide y_{kr} is the distance between the 37th landmark and the 40th landmark, which is used to normalize the open degree of the eye as different persons have the different eye sizes. Apply the same rule for the left eye to get the h_{1l}, h_{2l} and y_{kl}. Because Zeno has only one motor to control two eyelids, we calculate the average for the two eyes. Then, we can get the scale for the eyelid motor as shown in Eq. 7.

$$S_{eye} = \frac{\frac{h_{1l}+h_{2l}}{2y_{kl}} + \frac{h_{1r}+h_{2r}}{2y_{kr}}}{2} \tag{7}$$

To obtain the eyebrows motor scale, we need to calculate the distance between the midpoint of the 22nd landmark and the 23rd landmark and the 28th landmark, h_{brow}. So, the scale for eyebrows is shown in Eq. 8. Here, we divide $(y_{kl} + y_{kr})/2$ is to reduce the influence of different face sizes of people on the results of the mapping task from 3D facial action to robot motor action.

$$S_{brow} = \frac{h_{brow}}{\left(\frac{y_{kl}+y_{kr}}{2}\right)} \tag{8}$$

The scale for mouth motor can be obtained as shown in Eq. 9. Here, h_{mouth} is the distance between the midpoint of the 52nd landmark and the 63rd landmark and the midpoint of the 67th landmark and the 58th landmark.

$$S_{mouth} = \frac{h_{mouth}}{\left(\frac{y_{kl}+y_{kr}}{2}\right)} \tag{9}$$

The scales of the smile motor controlling the left and right corners of the mouth can be obtain from Eq. 10, Eq. 11, and Eq. 12. The d_l is the distance between the 55th landmark and the foot of the perpendicular through the 31st landmark. Similarly, the d_r is the distance between the 49th landmark and the foot of the perpendicular through the 31st landmark. Furthermore, d_l and d_r can be calculated based on the law of cosines. Because there is only one smile motor to control mouth corners, the mean value of S_{smile_l} and S_{smile_r} is used to get the scale of the smile motor, namely S_{smile}.

$$S_{smile_l} = \frac{d_l}{\left(\frac{y_{kl}+y_{kr}}{2}\right)} \tag{10}$$

$$S_{smile_r} = \frac{d_r}{\left(\frac{y_{kl}+y_{kr}}{2}\right)} \tag{11}$$

$$S_{smile} = \frac{S_{smile_l} + S_{smile_r}}{2} \tag{12}$$

Since robot motor control signals in the Zeno system range from 0 to 1, normalization operation for the scales should be done as shown in Eq. 13. That is to say, find the maximum and minimum of every scale which are applied to get the final control signal of face motors. Where, s $\in$ $\{S_{eye}, S_{brow}, S_{mouth}, S_{smile_r}, S_{smile_l}\}$.

$$\text{norm}(s) = \frac{s - s_{min}}{s_{max} - s_{min}} \tag{13}$$

4 Dataset and Preprocessing

4.1 Dataset

In this paper, we used the open database-Biwi 3D Audiovisual Corpus of Affective Communication dataset [27], which was developed at ETH Zurich. The corpus contains 1109 sentences uttered by 14 native English speakers, including six males and eight females, aged between 21 and 53 (average age of 33.5). A real-time 3D scanner and a professional microphone were utilized to obtain the speakers' facial action and synchronous speech audio during the data recording process. The dense dynamic face scans were obtained with a sampling rate of 25 frames per second. Moreover, the RMS error in the 3D reconstruction is about 0.5 mm, which is good enough for our facial action generation task. For the dataset development, the participants imitate the forty short English sentences extracted from film clips. For each sentence, the subject should speak two times, one with a neutral state and one with an emotional state, which is the same as the film clip's emotion. In this paper, the speech audio contains intrinsically emotional information, so we did not take the emotion label into consideration for the co-speech facial action generation task.

4.2 Pre-processing

The pre-processing step includes speech audio spectral feature extraction with MFCC [28], face landmarks extraction from 3D face images in the database with Dlib [29] library, and how to align the speech and facial action in the temporal domain and so on.

Alignment Between Speech and Facial Action Sequence. In this paper, we used the same time size for each speech audio to simplify the training process. From the distribution of audio length, we know that most audios are longer than 2.5 s. There are 1096 files in our database, of which 1095 are longer than 1 s, 1072 are longer than 2 s, 926 are longer than 3 s, and 645 are longer than 4 s. We chose 3 s as the time size for $S2FGAN$ training to use as many samples as possible. The audios longer than 3 s were cut into 3 s, and the samples with audio size shorter than 3 s were deleted from the database. Meanwhile, the sampling rate of the face image is 25 fps. In addition, we also deleted some samples whose audio size was more than 3 s but the face images less than 3 s. Finally, we got 788 samples from the original dataset for $S2FGAN$ training.

Because the speech audio and facial action series have different sampling rates, 44100 Hz for audio and 25 fps for facial action, the whole speech audio was divided into audio clips to align the facial action and audio in the temporal domain. Namely, one frame corresponds to 1764 audio frames. Considering the facial action time series's temporal dependence, we used the overlapped audio clips with 3528 audio frames centered on the related facial action frame, and the stride of the overlapped audio clips was 1764.

Speech Audio Feature Extraction. MFCC (Mel-Frequency Cepstral Coefficients) is often used for acoustic speech representation in speech recognition and other related speech audio tasks. MFCC feature of speech audio is the one in the frequency domain using the Mel scale based on the human ear scale. MFCCs, as frequency domain features, are much more accurate than time-domain features in the recognition task [30]. So, we used the MFCC as the overlapped audio clips from the whole speech audio in this paper. Each audio clip corresponding to one face frame extracted an MFCC feature with size of $7 * 13$.

3D Face Landmarks Detection. To get the 3D face landmarks, we first got the 2D face landmarks from the 2D face image frame by frame using the Dlib library. The pre-trained face landmark detector inside the Dlib library can extract the location of the 68 face landmarks (x, y)-coordinates that map to face structures on the face. The indexes of the 68 coordinates can be seen in Fig. 3. In our case, the triangle mesh texture recorded in the database is the corresponding RGB file. Firstly, we have detected 2D face landmarks located in the RGB face image. The detected landmark location is the same as the landmark location in the texture image. The relation between texture image and 3D mesh can be learned from the depth image. Then from the 2D position, we can directly extract the 3D positions of the 68 landmarks.

5   Experiments and Results

5.1   S2FGAN Training

The conditional GAN *pix2pix* model with L_1 loss explored multiple cross-modal translation tasks with the small dataset with 400 images or less, and it got the receivable testing results finally [17]. Like the *pix2pix* model, our speech-face database for *S2FGAN* training contains 788 samples (600 samples for training, 90 samples for validation, and 98 for testing) with the speech audios and the 3D facial action sequences. During the training, the batch size was 30, and the time steps of 3D facial action were 75 as the audio time size was fixed to 3 s during the *S2FGAN* training. The Standardization operation was employed on the 3D facial action data before inputting the *S2FGAN* model, and the batch normalization procedure was applied in the generator of *S2FGAN*, which both can effectively reduce the overfitting problem during model training based on the tuning experiments. We did not use the batch normalization layer in the discriminator because the layer can lead to a convergence failure during WGAN training [16]. Both generator and discriminator of *S2FGAN* model used the Adam algorithm [31] for optimization during training with the learning rate = 0.0002, the parameter $\beta_1 = 0.5$, $\beta_2 = 0.999$, and $\epsilon = 10^{-7}$. Moreover, the dropout setting of GRU is 0.1. The number of discriminator iterations per generator iteration is five during training. The model is developed with Tensorflow 2.3, and the training with 10000 epochs was done on an NVIDIA Quadro P1000 GPU for about four days.

5.2   Results and Evaluation

During the testing part, the speech-driven 3D facial action sequences were generated using the trained *S2FGAN* model. Then, the generated facial actions were transferred to the control signals of the robot face motors, which finally were presented on the Zeno robot facial actions with the aligned speech audios.

Applying the generated co-speech robot facial action to the Zeno robot, we recorded some videos with the speech audio and the synchronous facial action, and some frames in a generated co-speech robot facial action sequence are as shown in Fig. 4.

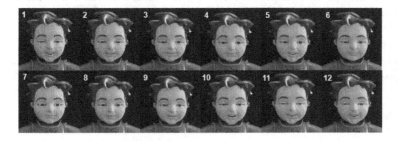

Fig. 4. The generated facial action on the robot Zeno in one example. Twelve frames were sampled with the same interval sampling from one sample of generated face action series from speech. The number in the figure is to show the order of the sampled frames.

From Fig. 4, we can see that the Zeno face driven by the generated robot facial action has noticeable movement in the mouth area and the eye area. The forehead area has limited change as the human forehead's noticeable movement often happens in intensely emotional expression instead of the common human co-speech facial actions. Besides, the subjects' forehead mostly remains still during the speech as present in the database.

Quantitative Evaluation. The quantitative evaluation of speech-driven facial action is challenging [32] as the mapping between speech and facial action (or gesture) sequence is a weaker correlation than the image-to-image translation in *pix2pix*, which is a rigid one-to-one mapping. In this paper, we explored the quantitative evaluation for the generated speech-driven facial action sequence with an Average Position Error (APE) [32] as shown in Eq. 14, where T is the time steps of the robot facial action, equal to 75; S is the number of testing samples, equal to 98; $f_{real}(s,t)$ and $f_{generated}(s,t)$ are the real robot facial motor control signal action and the generated one of sample s at time step t, respectively.

$$APE = \frac{1}{S \times T} \sum_{s=1}^{S} \sum_{t=1}^{T} |f_{\text{real}}(s,t) - f_{\text{generated}}(s,t)| \tag{14}$$

The APE validation result is 0.409 for the eye-opening motor, 0.190 for the eyebrow motor, 0.187 for the mouth-opening motor, and 0.189 for the smile motor. The eye-opening motor has the biggest APE 0.409 because the degree of the eye blink has a weak correlation with speech, and the action is primarily random to human speech. Hence, the generated eye blink action has a slight fluctuation. For example, in some generated samples, the robot face keeps squinting because this one-to-many mapping from the speech to the eye blink makes the alignment model fit to the average value of eye blink (around zero) when the model cannot find the suitable mode. Other motor APEs perform better when the related face actions strongly relate to the speech. The result looks like it still has some space to improve. However, it is still receivable for this kind of one-to-many mapping task with weak correlation. In the future, the generated robot facial action should be applied to the real human-robot interaction where the participants are asked to validate whether the generated robot facial action is synchronous with the speech, whether the facial action is natural, and whether the speech-face interaction is better than the speech-only interaction.

6   Conclusions and Future Work

In this paper, we built an effective temporal GAN architecture, namely $S2FGAN$, with losses of WGAN-GP and L_1 loss for co-speech facial action generation, which is promising to be used for other cross-modal mapping tasks with time series as input and output. The trained $S2FGAN$ model can generate realistic and synchronous facial action sequence with speech audio. The facial action retargeting from human face landmarks to robot facial action was completed. The robot facial action series were presented on the real Zeno robot in human-robot interaction. Finally, the generated facial action series was assessed with the qualitative evaluation and the quantitative evaluation. In the future, we will do user experiments to explore the long-term human-robot interaction environment with the generated face action presented on the Zeno robot. In addition, we will take the emotion label into consideration to explore emotional facial action generation for the robot's face.

Acknowledgement. We thank Cognitive Robotics Lab, Department of Computer Science, the University of Manchester, and Autonomous Systems and Robotics Lab, U2IS, ENSTA Paris, Institute Polytechnic de Paris. And we thank the UKRI Node on Trust (EP/V026682/1) for support.

References

1. Yu, C., Tapus, A.: Interactive robot learning for multimodal emotion recognition. In: Salichs, M.A., et al. (eds.) ICSR 2019. LNCS (LNAI), vol. 11876, pp. 633–642. Springer, Cham (2019). https://doi.org/10.1007/978-3-030-35888-4_59
2. Noda, K., Arie, H., Suga, Y., Ogata, T.: Multimodal integration learning of robot behavior using deep neural networks. Robot. Autonom. Syst. **62**(6), 721–736 (2014)

3. Yu, C., Tapus, A.: Multimodal emotion recognition with thermal and RGB-D cameras for human-robot interaction. In: Companion of the ACM/IEEE International Conference on Human-Robot Interaction, vol. 2020, pp. 532–534 (2020)

4. Yu, C., Changzeng, F., Chen, R., Tapus, A.: First attempt of gender-free speech style transfer for genderless robot. In ACM/IEEE International Conference on Human-Robot Interaction, vol. 2022, pp. 1110–1113 (2022)

5. Yoon, Y., et al.: Speech gesture generation from the trimodal context of text, audio, and speaker identity. ACM Trans. Graph. **39**, 6 (2020)

6. Vougioukas, K., Petridis, S., Pantic, M.: End-to-end speech-driven realistic facial animation with temporal gans. In: Proceedings of the IEEE Conference on Computer Vision and Pattern Recognition Workshops, pp. 37–40 (2019)

7. Habibie, I., Holden, D., Schwarz, J., Yearsley, J., Komura, T.: A recurrent variational autoencoder for human motion synthesis. In: 28th British Machine Vision Conference (2017)

8. Yu, C., Tapus, A.: Srg 3: Speech-driven robot gesture generation with GAN. In: 2020 16th International Conference on Control, Automation, Robotics and Vision (ICARCV), pp. 759–766. IEEE (2020)

9. Zhang, H., Yu, C., Tapus, A.: Why do you think this joke told by robot is funny? The humor style matters. In: 2022 31st IEEE International Conference on Robot and Human Interactive Communication (RO-MAN), pp. 572–577. IEEE (2022)

10. Yu, C.: Robot behavior generation and human behavior understanding in natural human-robot interaction. Ph.D. dissertation, Institut Polytechnique de Paris (2021)

11. Lee, J., Marsella, S.: Nonverbal behavior generator for embodied conversational agents. In: Gratch, J., Young, M., Aylett, R., Ballin, D., Olivier, P. (eds.) IVA 2006. LNCS (LNAI), vol. 4133, pp. 243–255. Springer, Heidelberg (2006). https://doi.org/10.1007/11821830_20

12. Aly, A., Tapus, A.: Multimodal adapted robot behavior synthesis within a narrative human-robot interaction. In: 2015 IEEE/RSJ International Conference on Intelligent Robots and Systems (IROS), pp. 2986–2993. IEEE (2015)

13. Park, J.W., Lee, H.S., Chung, M.J.: Generation of realistic robot facial expressions for human robot interaction. J. Intell. Robot. Syst. **78**(3–4), 443–462 (2015)

14. Foster, D.: Generative deep learning: teaching machines to paint, write, compose, and play. O'Reilly Media (2019)

15. Gupta, A., Johnson, J., Fei-Fei, L., Savarese, S., Alahi, A.: Social gan: Socially acceptable trajectories with generative adversarial networks. In: Proceedings of the IEEE Conference on Computer Vision and Pattern Recognition, pp. 2255–2264 (2018)

16. Gulrajani, I., Ahmed, F., Arjovsky, M., Dumoulin, V., Courville, A.C.: Improved training of wasserstein gans. In: Advances in Neural Information Processing Systems, pp. 5767–5777 (2017)

17. Isola, P., Zhu, J.-Y., Zhou, T., Efros, A.A.: Image-to-image translation with conditional adversarial networks. In: Proceedings of the IEEE Conference on Computer Vision and Pattern Recognition, pp. 1125–1134 (2017)

18. Rezende, D., Mohamed, S.: Variational inference with normalizing flows. In: International Conference on Machine Learning, pp. 1530–1538 (2015)

19. Henter, G.E., Alexanderson, S., Beskow, J.: Moglow: Probabilistic and controllable motion synthesis using normalising flows. arXiv preprint arXiv:1905.06598 (2019)

20. Blanz, V., Vetter, T.: A morphable model for the synthesis of 3d faces. In: Proceedings of the 26th Annual Conference on Computer Graphics and Interactive Techniques, pp. 187–194 (1999)

21. Egger, B., et al.: 3d morphable face models-past, present, and future. ACM Trans. Graph. **39**(5), 1–38 (2020)
22. Zhou, Y., Han, X., Shechtman, E., Echevarria, J., Kalogerakis, E., Li, D.: Makelttalk: Speaker-aware talking-head animation. ACM Trans. Graph. **39**(6), 1–15 (2020)
23. Sadoughi, N., Busso, C.: Speech-driven expressive talking lips with conditional sequential generative adversarial networks. IEEE Trans. Affect. Comput. (2019)
24. Hussen Abdelaziz, A., Theobald, B.-J., Dixon, P., Knothe, R., Apostoloff, N., Kajareker, S.: Modality dropout for improved performance-driven talking faces. In: Proceedings of the 2020 International Conference on Multimodal Interaction, pp. 378–386 (2020)
25. Ishi, C.T., Minato, T., Ishiguro, H.: Analysis and generation of laughter motions, and evaluation in an android robot. APSIPA Trans. Signal Inf. Process. **8** (2019)
26. Arjovsky, M., Chintala, S., Bottou, L.: Wasserstein generative adversarial networks. In: Proceedings of the 34th International Conference on Machine Learning, vol. 70, pp. 214–223 (2017)
27. Fanelli, G., Gall, J., Romsdorfer, H., Weise, T., Van Gool, L.: A 3-d audio-visual corpus of affective communication. IEEE Trans. Multim. **12**(6), 591–598 (2010)
28. Sahidullah, M., Saha, G.: Design, analysis and experimental evaluation of block based transformation in MFCC computation for speaker recognition. Speech Commun. **54**(4), 543–565 (2012)
29. King, D.E.: Dlib-ml: A machine learning toolkit. J. Mach. Learn. Res. **10**, 1755–1758 (2009)
30. Dave, N.: Feature extraction methods LPC, PLP and MFCC in speech recognition. Int. J. Adv. Res. Eng. Technol. **1**(6), 1–4 (2013)
31. Kingma, D.P., Ba, J.: Adam: A method for stochastic optimization. arXiv preprint arXiv:1412.6980 (2014)
32. Hasegawa, D., Kaneko, N., Shirakawa, S., Sakuta, H., Sumi, K.: Evaluation of speech-to-gesture generation using bi-directional LSTM network. In: Proceedings of the 18th International Conference on Intelligent Virtual Agents, pp. 79–86 (2018)

Design of a Social Media Voice Assistant for Older Adults

Jamy Li[1]([⊠]) [ID], Noah Zijie Qu[2] [ID], and Karen Penaranda Valdivia[1]

[1] Toronto Metropolitan University, Toronto M5B 2K3, Canada
jamy@ryerson.ca
[2] University of Toronto, Toronto M5S 1A1, Canada

Abstract. Older adults can increase their social cohesion and belongingness by accessing social media content. Voice is a particularly suitable modality for older adults. While general voice design guidelines for social media content exist, past work has not investigated design requirements of voice systems that provide social media content specifically to older adults. A preliminary interview and usability test ($N = 15$ Canadian adults aged 65 or older) explored how older adults evaluate and interpret the use of a voice assistant that retrieves real-time Twitter content in their everyday lives by demonstrating a custom prototype that lets participants access social media content using their voice. Interpretation insights included that participants appreciated the friendly appearance yet disliked the user – i.e., a child – implied by the appearance and that framing can help participants perceive themselves as potential users. Usability findings included that participants valued a screen, adjustable volume, quick response time and a detailed news broadcast. This research may assist researchers and designers interested in voice assistants to support older adults' social media practices.

Keywords: Conversational agent · Social media · Older adults · Elderly

1 Introduction

Social media can increase quality of life, provide a sense of belongingness and create new services for older adults (i.e., age 65 or older) [11, 17, 28], but only 6% of Canada's social media users are older adults [13]. Past work has explored social media technologies for older adults using graphical interfaces (e.g., [10]) but not voice assistants, despite expectations of a $26 billion voice assistant market by 2030 [1] and that older adults prefer voice to text or touchscreens due to potential vision problems and movement-related falls [31]. Existing prototypes of voice assistants for older adults have focused on health reminders (e.g., [36]) rather than a broad range of social media content. Past voice-based design guidelines [42] for social media are not catered to older adults. Yet consuming societal information (e.g., news) is critical for social cohesion (cf. [6]) and well-being [17, 28] of older adults. A voice assistant can connect older adults to social media content through an audio-based interface.

© The Author(s), under exclusive license to Springer Nature Switzerland AG 2022
F. Cavallo et al. (Eds.): ICSR 2022, LNAI 13817, pp. 75–88, 2022.
https://doi.org/10.1007/978-3-031-24667-8_7

The current work presents the design of a social media voice assistant for older adults and an interview to assess how older adults interpret and evaluate the system. A Raspberry Pi 4 inside a toast-shaped plush toy runs a custom python program that uses the Twitter API to retrieve tweets using voice. Fifteen older adults participated in a usability evaluation and contextual inquiry into how the system fit their lives. This work contributes a novel voice assistant with social media functionality (Fig. 1) as well as usability and contextual interpretation results, which may help designers and researchers interested in social media and news applications of voice assistants for older adults.

Fig. 1. Design of a voice assistant to connect older adults with social media news. Left: plush toy shell with electronics. Center: displaying image from @CTVnews. Right: System architecture. Emojis from OpenMoji – the open-source emoji and icon project. License: CC BY-SA 4.0

2 Background

2.1 Voice Assistants for Older Adults

Past work on voice assistants for older adults has primarily looked at the use, disuse and influence of commercially available devices. A study of 18 U.S. older adults found that they used Amazon Echo for healthcare information and music but later had privacy concerns and difficulty formulating intents [19]. Seven U.S. older adults also used Amazon Echo Dot to find health information but usage was low [32]. Among 38 U.S. older adults, most had low use of Amazon Echo because of its limited value, a desire for independence or privacy issues using it in shared spaces, but thought it could be useful with improved features or for people with disabilities [39]. A field study with 33 Australians aged 75 and up found that they adapted their use of voice assistants to fit their lives [14]. Analysis of a large dataset of Amazon Echo product reviews found that they were primarily used for entertainment, companionship, home control, reminders and emergency communication [29]. Entertainment and health information are therefore among the most popular use cases of off-the-shelf voice assistants among older adults.

Past voice assistant prototypes (i.e., not off-the-shelf) have likewise explored health information functions. Valera Román et al. [40] used a monitoring bracelet with Google voice on a Lenovo Smart Display to provide physical activity notifications to older adults and use signal strength to predict user presence. Shalini et al. [36] developed a similar voice assistant with display for older adults and their family members that provides health information. Rodríguez *et al.* [34] developed a voice assistant that adapts its activity and medication reminders based on audio-based user activity recognition; a field test with two adults and a lab study with nine adults aged 60 and up found that the system correctly identified contextual cues for taking specific pills and issued reminders that were perceived to be useful [34]. Seiderer *et al.* [35] created a prototype of a voice assistant for nutrition using Kaldi, MaryTTS and Rasa APIs, connected to an SQLite nutrition database. An older adult couple found the touchscreen useful to control speech detection and the spoken nutritional information useful to avoid small food labels but wanted more interpretation of the information [35]. These prototypes focused on health information rather than evaluating voice assistants for social media content.

2.2 Social Media Technology and Older Adults

Older adults' social media use is growing (e.g., 56% use Facebook [37]). Moreover, older adults who use social media had higher social satisfaction compared to those who did not [5]. Social media may help preserve social connectedness as people age [37].

Past work has explored adapting social media systems for older adults. Cornejo *et al.* [10] developed interactive photo frames, an ambient feedback "bowl" and an "exergame" to connect older adults with social media. Field studies in Mexican households found that the ambient social networking system was easy to use and supported in-person social encounters. Twenty Malaysian adults aged 55 or older saw a cognitive walkthrough of a mobile app designed for older adults that sent social media messages [9]. Participants preferred large font sizes, needed guidance to use the app and preferred more features such as image sharing and voice/video calls. Meta-research on mobile phone studies with older adults [2] has compiled design guidelines including the use of audio feedback, clear dialogue, three-dimensional icons and clear navigation structure.

Using social media as content for a voice system was proposed by Takahashi *et al.* [38], who used a Wizard-of-Oz "chat robot" to speak social media comments about TV programs to older adults. Minami *et al.* [27] developed a system that gathers Twitter comments about a TV program, outputs the speech using a Keepon-Kabochan robot and responds to the user's voice autonomously. A pilot study with four proxy users found that they spoke more when the robot had a conversational chat dialogue engine rather than only speaking social media comments. Past robot systems have spoken social media content from a person's social network not about TV shows. Facebots [24–26] was perhaps the first published paper that linked social media and robotics (cf. [15]). It used an ActivMedia PeopleBot with face recognition, dialogue system, navigation and live Facebook connection to identify users, gather social data on their friend list and wall posts and determine persons and topics of interest to speak about. Specifically for older adults, Kobayashi *et al.* [21] created a single board computer inside a PaPeRo robot to relay voice information into a cloud service, so that older adults can send and receive voice messages with younger adults. Six older adults evaluated the system as usable. The authors also connected their system to the Twitter, Google Cloud and AquesTalk APIs and had five older adult patients at a neurosurgery hospital in Japan use the system while two nurses prepared Twitter messages [20]. However, patients' message understanding was low due to poor synthetic voice quality.

These works demonstrate interest in voice systems and robots speaking social media messages to older adults. Past systems have selected social media content based on the TV program a person was watching, their Facebook friends or a nurse's prepared messages. Given older adults' interest in a broad range of informational content (as shown by their high news consumption [8]), we extend past work by exploring older adults' interest in voice assistants that speak general social media content.

3   User-Centered Design of "Toastbot"

3.1   Design

The design process involved creating an initial design, constructing a prototype (Online Resource 1[1]) and evaluating the prototype and contextual impressions with older adults. The initial design was based on a review of voice assistants (e.g., [16]), home devices (e.g., [4]), peripherals that accompany voice assistants (e.g., [22]) and Internet of Things devices (to include devices with screens; e.g., [12, 30]). Reviewed designs were sketched (Fig. 2, left) and organized into a conceptual map of design attributes (e.g., device morphology, whether the screen was embedded into the main body or connected via an arm; Fig. 2, middle). Design attributes were then selected for the prototype by considering the square aspect ratio of social media visuals and the context of older adults' technology use (e.g., they prefer voice, should avoid falls). The toast shape was based on searching for "square shaped objects" on thingdb.io (Fig. 2, right).

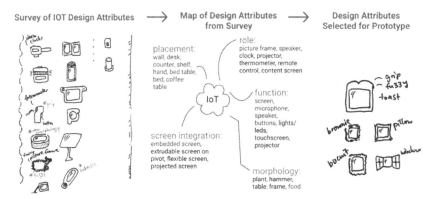

Fig. 2. Design process. Left: concept sketch board with existing product designs. Middle: conceptual map of design attributes. Right: selected attributes for prototype with initial designs.

3.2   Software Implementation

The python code uses Google speech recognition, Google text-to-speech and Twitter APIs to retrieve live data from Twitter based on a verbal request (see Fig. 1, right).

---

[1] https://drive.google.com/file/d/1ccT6UUyfFCQmawee2DIpqQ8JJak4zUG7/view?usp=sharing.

Authentication. The Tweepy python library is used to manage OAuth authentication and content retrieval/posting for Twitter. The developer keys (i.e., consumer key and secret) are stored as environmental variables in the bash profile. The authentication process first checks whether a file with the user's stored access keys exists; if so, it attempts to authenticate based on those keys. If either the file read or the authentication fails, it uses the developer keys to build an OAuth handler and get an authorization URL, which the user must manually enter into a web browser, log into their Twitter account, obtain a 6-digit pin code and then enter that code into the terminal prompt. If the entered code is verified, the access keys are stored in a local text file; if not, the user is re-prompted until a valid code is entered. The OAuth process is then complete.

Dialog Planning and Management. After authentication, the system says, "Please say a command" and listens for speech (Fig. 3). If recognized speech matches a list of keywords ("news", "nearby" and "goodbye"), it executes the corresponding command-specific function; otherwise, it re-prompts. For news, it enters a submenu to request a specific Twitter handle, listen for the user's response and get list of tweets from the account specified by the user. If the account is found and the length of tweets is greater than 0, it proceeds to read a "cleaned" version of the tweet (e.g., URLs, underscores removed). Errors (e.g., no public tweets or private account) lead to re-prompting. For nearby, the system searches tweets using the geocode for Toronto and speaks the first result. For goodbye, the system exits. See Online Resource 1 for a demo.

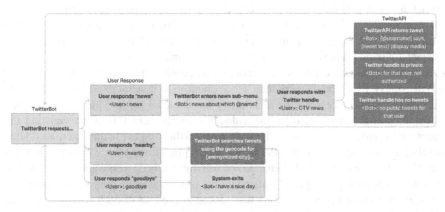

Fig. 3. Dialog flow between Toastbot and user.

Speech Generation and Recognition. For speech generation, Google TTS (python's gTTS) saves a local mp3 file of the spoken text, which is played using pypi's python wrapper, mpyg321. Speech recognition listens to the microphone source and converts speech to text using Google Speech Recognition. Errors (e.g., no understandable audio) are handled by repeating the listening command until speech is successfully obtained.

3.3 Hardware Implementation

The software is run by a Raspberry Pi4 (RPi) Model B computer (4 GB RAM) and Debian 12. The microphone is an iGoku USB clip-on lavalier microphone and the display is an ELECTROW Raspberry Pi display (contains two speakers). The microphone and speaker gain are adjusted using alsamixer on the RPi. Flat HDMI and USB cables from fpv-solution.com are used. Electronics are housed in a Jellycat plush toy.

4 Usability Study

4.1 Participants

Fifteen older adults 65 years or older ($M = 78$, $SD = 7$; 10 female, 5 male) from Skyview older adult residence in North York participated. Participants' ethnicities were 2 East Indian, 6 Jewish, 5 Caucasian (includes British/Irish Caucasian), 1 South Korean, 1 unreported. Participants' highest education levels were 1 high school diploma, 2 associate degree, 3 Bachelor's degree, 6 professional degree, 3 doctorate degree.

4.2 Procedure

Following consent, participants were directed to a seat with the voice assistant off and asked semi-structured interview questions about initial thoughts, appearance and touch ("What are your initial thoughts?", "How do you find its appearance?", "How do you find it to touch?"). They then viewed a demo video of the voice assistant while the researcher turned the system on. After the video, they talked with the actual voice assistant following a script that contained spoken lines of the assistant and lines the participant was to speak (as an exception, participants 1 and 2 saw a video only due to Wifi issues). Participants were then asked about their general experience ("How do you find the experience with the technology [as depicted in the video]?"), the voice ("How do you find the voice [in the video]?"), the content ("How do you find the content/information it provides?", "How do you find the images?"), the functions ("How useful or acceptable did you find the [news/nearby] function? How would you use it if at all?") and suggestions ("What changes or new functions do you want, if any?"). The interviewer checked participants' understanding of the system's purpose and provided clarification. Demographic questions were asked at the end of each session. Sessions took about 30 min in the condo's party room. Participants received a $30 gift card and a small COVID-19 related gift. They were recruited through an email sent by the property manager containing a recruitment poster, researcher contact and appointment dates. All procedures were approved by the Research Ethics Board at Toronto Metropolitan University and conformed with COVID-19 mask, vaccination and cleaning procedures.

4.3 Analysis

Video/audio recordings were transcribed using Rev.com and analyzed by using thematic analysis. Three researchers independently performed open coding on participants' feedback, then collaboratively grouped the codes into 17 emerging themes (e.g., "visual appearance") within three main categories: interaction aesthetics, device rationale and functionality (see Fig. 4). This resulted in 62 codes within 17 themes within three categories. The researchers re-read all comments in each theme to determine participants' impressions of both the usability and the interpretation of the device.

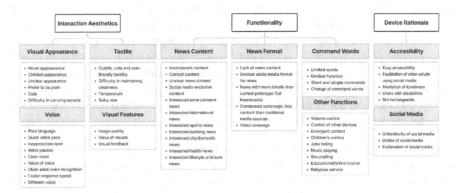

Fig. 4. Visual representation of codebook with categories (black outline), themes (grey fill) and codes (grey outline) from thematic analysis of participants' feedback and suggestions.

5   Findings

5.1   Interaction Aesthetics

Concerns about Implied User Stereotypes (e.g., Childishness). Participants showed a preference for playful aesthetic elements. Eight participants liked the cute appearance of Toastbot (e.g., *"It's cute. Very cute. The smile makes it very friendly"*). Two participants found the prototype's appearance more novel than Amazon Echo, which made one person curious about the device (*"I'd like to know more about it."*) and another consider it a status symbol (*"It would be a novelty item that maybe I would be one of the few people that had. So, I would say, 'Oh, I have this device...'"*). Most participants (12 out of 15; 80%) were also fond of the prototype's cuddly and soft tactility (e.g., *"Oh, it's very soft... That's nice. Bean baggy. I like that."*).

Yet participants provided negative feedback on the connotations of children implied by the device's appearance. Six participants (40%) indicated that the childish appearance did not fit their aesthetic taste (e.g., *"I would think it was a children's toy. I don't know how it would fit in with my decor."*), leading them to believe children were the target user (e.g., *"That's the whole idea, I guess. It's for children."*). However, no participants gave suggestions for how to customize the device's visual appearance for older adults. Thus, the visual design finding was to not make it look stereotyped for children.

Quick Response Time but Not Voice Speed. Eight participants (53.3%) were frustrated by a response delay after the participant's voice input (e.g., *"There's an awful long delay between the command and the action and I know some seniors who would* *say [they] want it right now and wouldn't have patience for it"*), which was due to slow on-site WiFi and was longer than commercial voice assistants (e.g., *"Siri is very fast and quick and instant and seems quite impressive. This, just now, seems like it's like an antique, early version of Siri, where [there is] a delay and a little slow…"*). One participant suggested interpreting voice input faster (*"If my 97-year-old mother was going to say something like, 'What's the weather today,' it should understand that and more quickly answer… [we] like cut and dry"*), while another suggested confirmatory feedback while processing: *"When it's searching for information… If you're on your computer and you're searching, a little circle goes around so it tells you it's searching."* Despite wanting quick responses, eight participants disliked quick voice pace (e.g., *"If you want elderly, we process a lot slower, so I would want the voice to speak more slowly"*). Thus, older adults did not mind a slow response if the response began quickly and want the system to accommodate their own processing time rather than vice versa.

Adjustable Volume and a Screen are Valued. Seven participants found the text-to-speech engine's voice clear (e.g., *"Well, the voice was very clear, and instructions seemed to be easy to follow"*) but three participants suggested that its volume be adjustable for comfort (*"You get older people [who] have harder hearing. But if it's at one level, then it's going to be too loud for some people. And some people aren't going to be able to hear it clearly, so they'll get frustrated."*). Six participants also valued the visuals, saying *"You know a picture is worth a 1,000 words?"* and *"Yes. I would like images, for sure. They may not be exactly what you want to see, but it's still relevant and it enhances your understanding of what's being said and what's being reported."* Therefore, relevant visuals returned by a search are valued to improve the voice system.

5.2   Device Rationale/Interest

For Other People, but Not for Me. Participants said Toastbot may help older adults who are lonely (5 participants; *"I guess this is for the person who lives alone… it's a companionship, too, I guess. Like an animal. But this will talk to you"*), have disabilities (3 participants; *"It's helpful for people with vision problems, that might be able to type or do things, but they can't search. It's helpful for people with issues with their hands, so trying to type or to find stuff"*) or are uncomfortable with social media (*"That's good because a lot of older people do not do social media. They're not comfortable with it… So this is a way of getting some of it without actually going on Twitter or Facebook or whatever"*). Three participants said the reason for its usefulness was its multimodality (*"If people have eye problems, hearing it – since there's a dual way of getting information off that – it's good"*). However, 8 participants (53.3%) were hesitant to see themselves using the device because they were not Twitter users (*"I'm not into tweet or anything like that"*). No participants mentioned an aversion to voice assistants as a reason for non-use. Thus, participants felt the device was for others but not themselves based on an aversion to social media or to Twitter rather than to voice assistants.

Ways of Encouraging Interest in Use. To encourage older adults to see themselves as users, one participant recommended providing an explanation of social media in terms of its context of use to avoid aversion toward social media: *"If they understand that, 'Oh, social media means you can get the news from CTV by just asking for it,' then they go, 'Oh okay why didn't you say that?'"* Indeed, several participants mentioned contexts for their personal use of the device depending on time constraints (*"I would probably use it if I wanted some information in a hurry – if I didn't want to open up my laptop or use my iPad"*) and future ability (*"But I can get out and about, and I can whatever: talk to people, TV, whatever. But certainly, if I couldn't, this would be a good alternative"*). Three participants said the advantages of social media content over traditional news sources may spark their interest, including personal accounts exclusive to social media (*"I like to hear the common people at the airport, telling me what's going on. Personal experiences of traffic, or lineups, or that type of thing... you can't get that on the news"*), social needs (*"It's good to keep up with people"*), speed of news (*"Many things that are social media then are on the news on the TV news. But if you're anxious to know right away, what is happening, yeah...it has its uses"*) and sharing opinions (*"It would be useful to hear people's responses because very often I'm watching news on my own... There's no one to confer with or get an opinion about, I suppose it would be useful to get someone else's view on a particular event being reported on"*). These participants seemed more receptive to imagining the device for themselves when focusing on the context of use rather than the technology (sometimes facilitated by interview probes about their content habits or needs). Finally, two participants said a different social media platform would help them self-identify as users: *"How I would get [Facebook] with this voice, if I'm talking with that voice, turn me over to Facebook. That would be a good idea"*; *"My son started a business, using Instagram. [Researcher: So something like showing Instagram feed?] Yeah. I love Instagram."*

5.3 Functionality

Preference for a Whole News Broadcast. Participants expected the prototype to give more than just a short snippet of a news item. Three participants critiqued the lack of news details (*"It was very short. It was just like headlines, couple of headlines. It wasn't much explanation or anything"*), especially compared with other voice assistants (*"If it's going to try to compete with Google and all these other independent little things from Apple and so on, it's going to have to offer more than just one or two sentences about something"*). Four participants therefore suggested the system respond with a whole news broadcast (*"I'd want to hear a whole news broadcast"; "I have Google upstairs and I say, 'Hey Google, what's the news?' And then they give the news from several different channels"*) or detailed stories (*"[If] I wanted to hear about the WHO, I'd probably want more detail"*). One mentioned *"condensed versions of the news... I'll go on YouTube and... listen to that."* Participants also suggested more interactive dialog like handling the user's follow-up questions (*"They would probably have to keep asking questions"*) and proactively providing a news broadcast when the user wakes (*"I'd like the news of the day. My Google Home, when I say 'good morning,' it gives me all the info, plus it gives me my CBC News, and gives me like ten stories"*).

News Source as Part of the Response, Not the Intent. One participant critiqued that the system lacked clear news sources (*"I don't care who's giving my information [but] I need to know the source, who's popping in to tell me"*), which is crucial for international news to determine its credibility (*"You need to know your source for news, whether it's a local little channel or a national channel you listen to"*); however, the source is less important for general information like the weather (*"'Oh, that's the weather.' I don't care if it came from the television station or The Weather Channel"*).

Despite caring about news sources, participants evidently expected the "news" command to be short and simple, without including a source: *"[Older adults] like cut and dry: Bang. Bang. Bam. I want weather and news. I'm going to ask, 'What's the weather today?' Yeah. People are matter of fact. Whatever they want, they should just be able to ask, in plain English, and the machine should understand that simple ask."*

News Preferences are Heterogeneous. Older adults' responses suggested heterogeneous news preferences across three news types: "hard" news (i.e., international/national/local affairs; 4 participants; e.g., *"Things that are new happening in the city, happening in any other countries around the world... I like to know all that."*), finance (*"[Seniors] want to be able to know that they have financial security... Financial stuff would be of interest to a lot of people, because everybody wants to have at least enough to last the cutoff"*) and entertainment. Among four participants who mentioned entertainment, one asked for a specific musician (*"If I said, 'What's the latest news on the Beatles,' it'd be nice if there's any latest news"*), one asked to narrate movie stories (*"For the senior who is longing, if they have this kind of machine... Let's say, 'Oh can you tell me the story of the bridge movie,' something like that... Then the story begins... The voice will go on. So she doesn't have to watch it and she can close her eyes, and just listen"*) and two said sports (*"I'm sure that there are seniors interested in sports"*). Some older adults preferred positive, "soft" news: *"Like if we don't want to hear blood and thunder, and there's certain things that appeal and certain things that don't"* (also found in [43]). To address older adults' varied interests, one participant recommended allowing the user to curate or select categories from a general news broadcast (*"It'd be nice if they itemized international news or whatever, like world health or whatever, and then allowed me to choose which area in which I am most interested"*).

6 Discussion

6.1 Design Implications

Older adults are often excluded from modern technology due to their lower digital adaptability [7], which poses a threat for their social integration. Older adults in this study suggested two design solutions: the voice assistant could help mitigate isolation either by *"keep[ing] elders involved in what's going on"* or by being designed to look like a "companion" and to sound like a familiar conversation.

Older adults liked a playful appearance but did not want a device designed for children. Assistive technology for older adults should therefore avoid connoting "undesirable" groups (i.e., children), which is relevant because many robots (e.g., Paro,

Mel, cf. [33]) resemble friendly plush toys. Older adults in our study were aware that designers consider the perceptions (e.g., affordances) of target users when designing a product [3]: older adults proactively inferred – without prompting – the intended target users of a device based on who they imagined the designer selected the aesthetics for. Since some older adults' impressions of the device were dominated by the stereotypical user implied by the device's "interaction aesthetics" [18] rather than the aesthetics themselves, future work may beneficially explore designing device aesthetics to imply user groups: "How do we design interaction aesthetics of a voice assistant to help older adults intuit themselves – or perhaps a more "desirable" group – as the target users?".

6.2 Implications for Theory

Participants stated the device was not for them because of a dislike of social media but did not mention a dislike of voice assistants. The "for others but not for me" effect found in past work (e.g., [41]) may therefore apply to assistive robots and social media but perhaps not to voice assistants. Moreover, older adults' initial hesitance toward social media was sometimes alleviated by interview probes about their content needs and habits (rather than social media itself), which elicited new ways that the device *would* be "for them". The current work suggests a way to avoid undesirable connotations of technology some older adults may have is by focusing on the use case.

Past work [41] found that older adults want to avoid robot designs that have stereotyped representations of older adults. The current finding that older adults want to avoid voice assistants that give connotations of children extends the concept of stereotypes to encompass undesirable associations with children as a user group. It also suggests that older adults can imagine the designed-for user group of assistive technology.

6.3 Limitations and Future Work

Individual living environments, habits and characteristics of older adults differ [23], so findings from our sample should be interpreted with caution. Moreover, this work uses one specific use case of voice assistant, so results with a TV watching [38] or other application may differ. Nevertheless, our goal was to evaluate older adults' impressions of social media voice assistant content and news in general. Modifications to the system are planned for future work. Long-term studies may also provide insight into how social media voice assistants can be designed for older adults.

7 Conclusion

A social media voice assistant was designed to connect older adults with social media news content using Google speech recognition, Google text-to-speech and Tweepy with a Raspberry Pi 4 and screen in a toast-shaped plush toy. An evaluation of the system with 15 older adults explored the usability, impressions and future design of the system. Findings indicate that the purpose and aesthetics of the system were accepted, but that designers must carefully consider the user stereotype implied by the system's aesthetics, ways in which to encourage older adults to self-identify as users of the system and the amount and structure of information to provide based on older adults' preferences.

References

1. Voice Assistant Market Size, Growth: Industry Forecast Report, 2030. Technical Report IM11821. Prescient & Strategic Intelligence, 170 p. (2020)
2. Al-Razgan, M.S., Al-Khalifa, H.S., Al-Shahrani, M.D., AlAjmi, H.H.: Touch-based mobile phone interface guidelines and design recommendations for elderly people: a survey of the literature. In: Huang, T., Zeng, Z., Li, C., Leung, C.S. (eds.) ICONIP 2012. LNCS, vol. 7666, pp. 568–574. Springer, Heidelberg (2012). https://doi.org/10.1007/978-3-642-34478-7_69
3. Albrechtsen, H, Andersen, H.H.K., Bødker, S., Pejtersen, A.M.: Affordances in Activity Theory and Cognitive Systems Engineering. Technical Report Risø-R-1287(EN). Risø National Laboratory, Roskilde. 37 p. ISSN 0106-2840 (2001)
4. Anderson-Bashan, L., et al.: The greeting machine: an abstract robotic object for opening encounters. In: 2018 27th IEEE International Symposium on Robot and Human Interactive Communication (RO-MAN), pp. 595–602. IEEE (2018)
5. Bell, C., Fausset, C., Farmer, S., Nguyen, J., Harley, L., Fain, W.B.: Examining social media use among older adults. In: Proceedings of the 24th ACM Conference on Hypertext and Social Media (HT 2013), pp. 158–163. Association for Computing Machinery, New York, NY, USA (2013)
6. Bergström, A.: Exploring digital divides in older adults' news consumption. Nordicom Rev. **41**(2), 163–177 (2020)
7. Betlej, A.: Designing robots for elderly from the perspective of potential end-users: a sociological approach. Int. J. Environ. Res. Public Health **19**(6), 3630 (2022)
8. Chafetz, P.K., Holmes, H., Lande, K., Childress, E., Glazer, H.R.: Older adults and the news media: utilization, opinions, and preferred reference terms. Gerontologist **38**(4), 481–489 (1998)
9. Chang, J.J., Zahari, N.S.H.B., Chew, Y.H.: The design of social media mobile application interface for the elderly. In: 2018 IEEE Conference on Open Systems (ICOS), pp. 104–108. IEEE (2018)
10. Cornejo, R., Tentori, M., Favela, J.: Enriching in-person encounters through social media: a study on family connectedness for the elderly. Int. J. Hum. Comput. Stud. **71**(9), 889–899 (2013)
11. Daneshvar, H., Anderson, S., Williams, R., Mozaffar, H.: How can social media lead to co-production (co-delivery) of new services for the elderly population? A qualitative study. JMIR Hum. Factors **5**(1), e5 (2018)
12. De Voegt, K., et al.: Augmented photoframe for interactive smart space. In: Lee, Y., et al. (eds.) ICOST 2010. LNCS, vol. 6159, pp. 60–66. Springer, Heidelberg (2010). https://doi.org/10.1007/978-3-642-13778-5_8
13. Dixon, S.: Canada: social media user age & gender distribution 2021 (2022)
14. Duque, M., Pink, S., Strengers, Y., Martin, R., Nicholls, L.: Automation, wellbeing and digital voice assistants: older people and google devices. Convergence **27**(5), 1189–1206 (2021)
15. Emeli, V., Christensen, H.: Enhancing the robot service experience through social media. In: 2011 ROMAN, pp. 288–295. IEEE (2011)
16. Feltwell, T., et al.: Broadening exposure to socio-political opinions via a pushy smart home device. In: Proceedings of the 2020 CHI Conference on Human Factors in Computing Systems, pp. 1–14 (2020)
17. Haris, N., Majid, R.A., Abdullah, N., Osman, R.: The role of social media in supporting elderly quality daily life. In: 2014 3rd International Conference on User Science and Engineering (i-USEr), pp. 253–257 (2014)
18. Hartmann, J.: Assessing the attractiveness of interactive systems. In: CHI 2006 Extended Abstracts on Human Factors in Computing Systems (CHI EA 2006), pp. 1755–1758. Association for Computing Machinery, New York, NY, USA (2006)

19. Kim, S.: Exploring how older adults use a smart speaker–based voice assistant in their first interactions: qualitative study. JMIR mHealth and uHealth **9**(1), e20427 (2021)
20. Kobayashi, T., Katsuragi, K., Miyazaki, T., Arai, K.: Social media intermediation robot for elderly people using external cloud-based services. In: 2017 5th IEEE International Conference on Mobile Cloud Computing, Services, and Engineering (MobileCloud), pp. 31–38. IEEE (2017)
21. Kobayashi, T., Miyazaki, T., Uchida, R., Tanaka, H., Arai, K.: Social media agency robot for elderly people. J. Inform. Process. **26**(2018), 736–746 (2018)
22. Kocielnik, R., Avrahami, D., Marlow, J., Lu, D., Hsieh, G.: Designing for workplace reflection: a chat and voice-based conversational agent. In: Proceedings of the 2018 Designing Interactive Systems Conference, pp. 881–894 (2018)
23. van Boekel, L.C., Peek, S.T.M., Luijkx, K.G.: Diversity in older adults' use of the internet: identifying subgroups through latent class analysis. J. Med. Internet Res. **19**(5), e180 (2017). https://doi.org/10.2196/jmir.6853
24. Mavridis, N., Datta, C., Emami, S., Tanoto, A., BenAbdelkader, C., Rabie, T.: FaceBots: robots utilizing and publishing social information in facebook. In: 2009 4th ACM/IEEE International Conference on Human-Robot Interaction (HRI), pp. 273–274. IEEE (2009a)
25. Mavridis, N., Datta, C., Emami, S., Tanoto, A., BenAbdelkader, C., Rabie, T.: FaceBots: social robots utilizing facebook. In: 2009 4th ACM/IEEE International Conference on Human-Robot Interaction (HRI), pp. 195–195. IEEE (2009b)
26. Mavridis, N., et al.: FaceBots: steps towards enhanced long-term human-robot interaction by utilizing and publishing online social information. Paladyn, J. Behav. Robot. **1**(3), 169–178 (2010)
27. Minami, H., Kawanami, H., Kanbara, M., Hagita, N.: Chat robot coupling machine responses and social media comments for continuous conversation. In: 2016 IEEE International Conference on Multimedia & Expo Workshops (ICMEW), pp. 1–6. IEEE (2016)
28. Newman, L., Stoner, C., Spector, A.: Social networking sites and the experience of older adult users: a systematic review. Ageing Soc. **41**(2), 377–402 (2021)
29. O'Brien, K., Liggett, A., Ramirez-Zohfeld, V., Sunkara, P., Lindquist, L.A.: Voice-controlled intelligent personal assistants to support aging in place. J. Am. Geriatrics Soc. **68**(1), 176–179 (2020)
30. Park, S.H., Won, S.H., Lee, J.B., Kim, S.W.: Smart home-digitally engineered domestic life. Person. Ubiquit. Comput. **7**(3–4), 189–196 (2003)
31. Portet, F., Vacher, M., Golanski, C., Roux, C., Meillon, B.: Design and evaluation of a smart home voice interface for the elderly: acceptability and objection aspects. Person. Ubiquit. Comput. **17**(1), 127–144 (2013)
32. Pradhan, A., Lazar, A., Findlater, L.: Use of intelligent voice assistants by older adults with low technology use. ACM Trans. Comput. Hum. Interact. **27**(4), 1–27 (2020)
33. Preece, J., Rogers, Y., Sharp, H.: Interaction Design: Beyond Human-Computer Interaction, 4th edn. Wiley (2015)
34. Rodríguez, M.D., Beltrán, J., Valenzuela-Beltrán, M., Cruz-Sandoval, D., Favela, J.: Assisting older adults with medication reminders through an audio-based activity recognition system. Person. Ubiquit. Comput. **25**(2), 337–351 (2020). https://doi.org/10.1007/s00779-020-014 20-4
35. Seiderer, A., Ritschel, H., André, E.: Development of a privacy-by-design speech assistant providing nutrient information for German seniors. In: Proceedings of the 6th EAI International Conference on Smart Objects and Technologies for Social Good, pp. 114–119. ACM, Antwerp Belgium (2020)

36. Shalini, S., Levins, T., Robinson, E.L., Lane, K., Park, G., Skubic, M.: Development and comparison of customized voice-assistant systems for independent living older adults. In: Zhou, J., Salvendy, G. (eds.) HCII 2019. LNCS, vol. 11593, pp. 464–479. Springer, Cham (2019). https://doi.org/10.1007/978-3-030-22015-0_36

37. Sinclair, T.J., Grieve, R.: Facebook as a source of social connectedness in older adults. Comput. Hum. Behav. **66**, 363–369 (2017)

38. Kanbara, T.M., Hagita, N.: A social media mediation robot to increase an opportunity of conversation for elderly: mediation experiments using single or multiple robots. Tech. Committee Cloud Network Robot. **113**(84), 31–33 (2013)

39. Trajkova, M., Martin-Hammond, A.: "Alexa is a Toy": exploring older adults' reasons for using, limiting, and abandoning Echo. In: Proceedings of the 2020 CHI Conference on Human Factors in Computing Systems, pp. 1–13. Association for Computing Machinery, New York, NY, USA (2020)

40. Valera Román, A., Pato Martínez, D., Lozano Murciego, Á., Jiménez-Bravo, D.M., de Paz, J.F.: Voice assistant application for avoiding sedentarism in elderly people based on IoT technologies. Electronics **10**(8), 980 (2021)

41. Lee, H.R., Tan, H., Šabanović, S.: That robot is not for me: Addressing stereotypes of aging in assistive robot design. In: 2016 25th IEEE International Symposium on Robot and Human Interactive Communication (RO-MAN), pp. 312–317. IEEE (2016)

42. Zhang, Y., Xu, F., Li, T., Kostakos, V., Hui, P., Li, Y.: Passive health monitoring using large scale mobility data. Proc. ACM Interact. Mobile Wear. Ubiquit. Technol. **5**(1), 1–23 (2021)

43. Villalba, A.A., Stanley, J.T., Turner, J.R., Vale, M.T., Houston, M.L.: Age differences in preferences for fear-enhancing Vs. fear-reducing news in a disease outbreak. Front. Psychol. **11**, 589390 (2020)

Migratable AI: Personalizing Dialog Conversations with Migration Context

Ravi Tejwani$^{(\boxtimes)}$, Boris Katz , and Cynthia Breazeal

Massachusetts Institute of Technology, Cambridge, USA
{tejwanir,boris,breazeal}@mit.edu

Abstract. The migration of conversational AI agents across different embodiments in order to maintain the continuity of the task has been recently explored to further improve user experience. However, these migratable agents lack contextual understanding of the user information and the migrated device during the dialog conversations with the user. This opens the question of how an agent might behave when migrated into an embodiment for contextually predicting the next utterance. We collected a dataset from the dialog conversations between crowdsourced workers with the migration context involving personal and non-personal utterances in different settings (public or private) of embodiment into which the agent migrated. We trained the generative and information retrieval models on the dataset using with and without migration context and report the results of both qualitative metrics and human evaluation. We believe that the migration dataset would be useful for training future migratable AI systems.

1 Introduction

Embodied conversational AI agents as user interfaces is a growing research area, and various efforts have been made in training naturalistic dialog systems using human to human interactions [6,12,25]. Recent advancements in language models have been made in the personalization of dialog systems by incorporating the persona of the user as embeddings with the dialog history [13,28]. The persona was explored as a user profile, which included interaction style, language behavior, and background facts encoded in multiple sentences. The generative and ranking models were trained on corpus of twitter conversations [6], dialog sets comprising TV series scripts [2,15], and the conversations collected from crowd sources workers [28] for persona based conversational dialogues.

Agent migration has been explored a process in which an agent could migrate from one embodiment to another while maintaining the same relationship with the user across embodiments [1,10,26]. Recently, Migratable AI in [22] explored the migration of conversational AI agents across different robots while measuring the users' perception on different elements of migration - identity and information migration. It was found that users reported the highest trust, competence, likability, and social presence towards the AI agent when both the

F. Cavallo et al. (Eds.): ICSR 2022, LNAI 13817, pp. 89–99, 2022.
https://doi.org/10.1007/978-3-031-24667-8_8

identity and information of the agent were migrated to the robots. The identity of the agent was explored as the agent with the same visual and voice characteristics, and information was explored as the utterances from the dialog history, which included both personal and non-personal information.

Various state of the art conversational datasets have also been introduced in the past such as Google Taskmaster dataset [3], Alexa Prize Topical Chat dataset [7], MultiWoz datasets [4,5], Microsoft State Tracking Challenges datasets [8,9] and SpaceBook corpus [24]. However, they have been limited to the transactional chit-chat communications, such as airline, restaurant booking or twitter conversations. There is a need for the dataset, which explores the migratable elements of the conversational AI agent as the agent migrates across different embodiments. The dataset could be used to further train the migratable AI agents to contextually learn to deliver personal and non-personal information of the users during the dialog conversations in private and public settings.

In this work, we take a step forward in Migratable AI and explore the information migration of the agent towards contextual information migration while maintaining the identity migration. We define the migration context analogous to the persona from the literature research. Migration context in a dialog conversation can be viewed as the type of user information in the utterances (personal or non-personal) and the type of embodiment to which the agent migrates into (public or private). The goal is to train the agent to generate utterances during the dialog conversation with the user based on the migration context i.e. the agent should not present the personal information of the user when migrated into the public embodiment and vice versa.

This paper offers the following contributions. First, we present a migration dataset collected from the dialog conversations between crowdsourced workers using the migration context. Second, we show the personalization of dialog conversation between the migrated agent and the user by training the generative and information retrieval models on the migration dataset. Lastly, we evaluate these models on qualitative metrics and human evaluation for both with and without migration context and report the results.

2   Related Work

Personalization in goal-oriented dialog systems has been explored in the literature [11,17] by focusing on the user profile information to model the speech style and to personalize the reasoning over the knowledge bases. The persona-based neural conversation model [13] on chit-chat conversations from twitter corpus showed that user personas could be encoded into the sequence to sequence models [23] by embedding the user's persona, such as background information and speaking style along with the dialog history.

The most relevant work is [28], which contributed to the persona-chat dataset by incorporating the persona information of the users collected from the crowdsourced workers in the form of multiple sentences. They encoded its vector representation along with the dialog history into the generative models to produce personalized responses.

Agent migration was explored in the prior work through identity migration [1,26] and information migration architectures [19,26]. It was explored as a process in which an agent could migrate from one embodiment to another while maintaining the same relationship with the user across embodiments. For the identity migration - the identity of the agent such as appearance, voice, and dynamics of motion was migrated across embodiments; the information migration was explored as Short term memory (STM) to maintain agent's current focus and Long term memory (LTM) for the agent to interact with users over a long period of time.

Migratable AI in [22] further explored the migration of conversational AI agents across different robots while measuring the users' perception on identity and information migration. The identity of the agent was explored as the conversational AI agent with the same visual and voice characteristics, and information was explored as the utterances from the dialog history. Since the information migration included both the personal and non-personal information of the user when the agent was migrated in a public embodiment, it even used the personal information of the user in the dialog conversations. The user reactions to this were reported in [21,22]. Hence, we further explore the information migration as contextual information migration along the lines of [22,28] through modeling both the personal and non-personal utterances in the dialog conversations across different settings (Public or Private) of the embodiments.

Table 1. Example dialog from the migration dataset

Home
[Person-1]: Hello! How are you doing? (NP)
[Person-2]: I'm good, thank you. How are you? (NP)
[Person-1]: Great, thanks. So, tell me how did you get injured? (P)
[Person-2]: I twisted my knee during my morning run (P)
[Person-1]: I am sorry to hear that. How are you feeling today? (P)
[Person-2]: I am feeling much better than before. Just a little anxious. (P)
[Person-1]: Sorry to hear that. What is your partner's name? (P)
[Person-2]: umm.. Her name is Rachel (P)
[Person-1]: Do you watch any sports? (NP)
[Person-2]: Yes, I love watching baseball (NP)
[Person-1]: Great. What does a perfect day look like for you? (NP)
[Person-2]: I prefer a nice sunny day not too hot though somewhere around mid 70s (NP)
[Person-1]: I notice that you have an appointment at the health center (NP)
[Person-2]: oh yeah. Thanks for reminding me (NP)
Health center reception
[Person-1]: Hello! Welcome to the Health Center. I will check you in for the appointment (NP)
[Person-2]: Thank you
[Person-1]: While we are waiting, did you watch yesterday's baseball game? (NP)

(continued)

Table 1. (*continued*)

Home
[Person-2]: No. I missed it (NP)
[Person-1]: Oh. It was a fun game. It's a nice sunny day today, I hope you will enjoy it later today (NP)
[Person-2]: Thanks for reminding me. I hope to go outdoors later (NP)
Heath care professional's room
[Person-1]: Hello! The Health Care Professional should be here shortly (NP)
[Person-2]: Thank you (NP)
[Person-1]: I hope you are feeling less anxious than you were at home (P)
[Person-2]: Thanks. Yup, I am much better now (P)
[Person-1]: How is your partner Rachel doing? (P)
[Person-2]: We are planning to meet for dinner tonight (P)

3   Migration Dataset

The migration dataset is a crowd-sourced dataset, collected via Amazon Mechanical Turk, where each pair of users conditioned their dialog from the instructions provided in a task-based scenario. The users that are responsible for carrying out these tasks are referred to as AMT workers.

3.1   Task Based Scenario

The participatory design work by Luria et al. on Re- Embodiment and Co-Embodiment [18] explored futuristic scenarios with participants using the concept of "speed dating" [29]. They crafted and piloted four user enactments (DMV, Home and Work, Health Center, and Autonomous Cars) over the course of a month in which a person might interact with multiple agents that can re-embody and co-embody.

In our research, we explore and further extend the Health Center scenario, which involves the user acting out a visit to a health center to evaluate recovery from an injury. The scenario would begin at the user's home where the personal agent would get to know them by asking personal and non-personal questions and remind them that it was time for their medical appointment. Upon arrival at the health center reception in a public setting, the personal agent (migrated onto receptionist robot) would greet, acknowledge the appointment of the user, and further escort them to the health care professional's room. At the health care professional's room in a private setting, the personal agent (migrated onto Smart TV) would further assist the user while waiting for the health care professional. This would allow us to explore the migration of the conversation agent in more sensitive settings and address issues of context-crossing agents, privacy, and data storage perceptions.

3.2   Migration Modes

For each dialog, we paired two AMT workers who were randomly assigned to one of the migration modes:

- **With migration context.** The AMT workers were restricted to share the amount of information with each other that they had learned about themselves. They could only share personal information in a private setting and non-personal information in a public setting.
- **Without migration context.** The AMT workers were not restricted to any information that they had learned about themselves. They could share both personal and non-personal information across private and public settings.

3.3   Migration Chat

From the task-based scenario, we instructed the AMT workers to carry out the dialog conversations. One worker was instructed to enact the role of a person who had met with an injury in the past and needs to visit the health center for a medical appointment. The other worker was instructed to guide the person by enacting through different roles across locations: a friend at home, receptionist at health center reception, and helper at health care professional's room. At home, as a friend, his task was to get to know the person and inquire about his injury and upcoming appointment by asking a few personal and non-personal questions. At the health center reception in a public setting, as a receptionist, he was instructed to greet the person for his appointment and acknowledge him by using information from previous interaction at home (based on migration mode). At the health professional's room reception, in a private setting, he was further instructed to assist the person while he is waiting for the health care professional (based on migration mode).

In an early investigation of the study, we found out that AMT workers asked similar questions to each other, so we added the instructions that they need to ask at least two personal and non-personal questions. At the end of each dialog conversation, the AMT workers were instructed to label each utterance in the dialog with "NP" for non-personal information and "P" for personal information. An example dialogue from the dataset is shown in Table 1. We defined a minimum dialog length of between 8 and 10 turns for each dialog.

3.4   Analysis

Descriptive Statistics. The descriptive statistics for the dataset are summarized in Table 2 (left). Here, the number of instances represent the total number of utterances in the dataset, a number of dialogs represent the total dialog conversations, number of MRs represent the number of distinct Meaning Representations(MR), Refs/MR is the number of natural language references per MR, Words/Ref represent the average number of words per MR, Slots/MR represent the average slot value pairs per MR, Sentences/Ref is the number of natural language sentences per MR and Words/Sentence is the average words per sentence. We split the dataset in an 80:20 ratio for training and test set.

Table 2. Descriptive statistics and the lexical richness of the dataset

Number of instances	1014
Number of dialogs	92
Number of MRs	402
Refs/MR	3 (1-35)
Words/MR	9.63
Slots/MR	5.43
Sentences/Refs	1.05 (1-2)
Words/Sentence	8.35

Tokens	7072
Types	320
LS	0.38
TTR	0.06
MSTR	0.45

Lexical Richness. We used Lexical Complexity Analyser [16] for computing the lexical richness and highlighted them in Table 2 (right). Along with the total number of tokens and types, we computed the type-token ratio(TTR) and a mean segmental TTR (MSTTR) by dividing the dataset into segments of a defined length(100) and then further computing the average TTR for each segment as described in [16].

4 Models

Models were trained on utterances from dialog history (and possibly, migration context) to generate the response word by word. The migration context consisted of the type of user information labeled with Personal(P) or Non-Personal Information (NP), and the type of setting in the dialog conversation - Private or Public. In the past, [13,28] explored the ranking and generative models for persona-based chat personalization by training the persona of the user, short profile encoded in multiple sentences, along with dialog history. We condition those training methods with personalization for migration context instead of persona, as described below.

4.1 Sequence-to-Sequence

Given a sequence of inputs $X = \{x_1, x_2, ..., x_{n_X}\}$, an LSTM can be encoded by applying:

$$h_t^e = LSTM_{encode}\left(x_t \mid h_{t-1}^e\right) \tag{1}$$

For word embedding vectors, we used GloVe [20]. The vector for each text unit such as a word or a sentence is denoted by e_t at time step t and the vector computed by LSTM model at time t by combining e_t and h_{t-1} is denoted by h_t. Each input, X, is paired with a sequence of outputs to predict $Y = \{y_1, y_2, ..., y_{n_Y}\}$. The softmax function for the distribution over outputs is defined as:

$$p\left(Y \mid X\right)) == \prod_{t=1}^{k_y} \frac{\exp\left(f\left(h_{t-1}, e_{y_t}\right)\right)}{\sum_{y'} \exp\left(f\left(h_{t-1}, e_{y'}\right)\right)} \tag{2}$$

The activation function is denoted by $f(h_{t-1}, e_{y_t})$ and the model is trained through the negative log likelihood. In order to include the migration context for personalization, we generate it's vector representation m_S and prepend it to the input sequence X, i.e. $X = \forall m \in P \| X$, where $\|$ denotes the concatenation.

4.2 Generative Profile Memory Network

We consider the generative model, Generative Profile Memory Network [28], and encode the migration context as individual memory representations in the memory network. The final state of $LSTM_{encode}$ is used as an initial hidden state of the decoder, which is encoded through utterances in dialog history. Each entry, $m_i = \langle m_{i,1}, \ldots, m_{i,n} \rangle \in M$ is encoded via $f(m_i) = \sum_j^{|m_i|} idf_i . m_{i,j}$

We compute the weights of the words in the utterances using the inverse document frequency: $idf_i = 1/(1 + log(1 + tf_i))$, where tf_i is from the GloVe index via Zipf' law [28].

The decoder attends the encoded migration context entries: mask a_t, context x_t and next input $\hat{x}_t$ as,

$$a_t = \text{softmax}\left(F W_a h_t^d\right)$$
$$x_t = a_t^\top F; \quad \hat{x}_t = \tanh\left(W_x [x_{t-1}, x_t]\right) \tag{3}$$

where $W \in \mathbb{R}^{K \times 2K}$ and F is the set of encoded memories.

When the model is not enabled for the migration context (i.e., no memory), then it is similar to the Sequence-to-Sequence model.

4.3 Information Retrieval (Starspace)

We consider an Information Retrieval based supervised embedding model, Starspace [27]. The Starspace model consists of entities described by features such as a bag of words. An entity is an utterance described as n-grams. The model assigns a d-dimensional vector to each of the unique features in a dictionary that needs to be embedded. The embeddings for the entities in the dictionary are learned implicitly.

The model performs the information retrieval by computing the similarity between the word embeddings of dialog conversation and the next utterance using the negative sampling and margin ranking loss [28]. The similarity function $sim(w, v)$ is defined as the cosine similarity of the sum of word embeddings of query w and a candidate v. The dictionary of D word embeddings as L is a $D \times d$ matrix, where L_i indexes the ith feature (row), with d dimensional embedding on sequences w and v.

5 Experiments

5.1 Evaluation

The dialog task is to predict the next utterance given the dialog history while considering the task for both with and without migration context. Following

[13,28], we evaluate the task using the metrics: (i) F1 score evaluated on the word level, (ii) perplexity for the log-likelihood of the correct utterance, and (iii) Hits@1 representing the probability of candidate utterance ranking from the model. In our setting, we choose n=12 for the number of input responses from the dialogs for the prediction.

5.2   Results

We report the results on qualitative analysis of the models and human evaluation of the models performed by crowdsourced workers.

Table 3. Evaluation of models for the utterance prediction task using with and without migration context

Model	No migration context			Migration context		
	F1	Perplexity	Hits@1	F1	Perplexity	Hits@1
Sequence-to-Sequence	14.22	28.06	8.6	14.22	31.02	10.4
GPMV	12.21	28.06	8.6	12.20	30.08	9.8
Starspace	18.02	–	12.4	18.04	–	10.6

Qualitative Analysis. The performance of the models is reported in Table 3. The generative models improved significantly when conditioning the prediction of utterance on using the migration context. For example, Sequence to Sequence and Generative Profile Memory Network(GPNV) improved their perplexity and hits@1. However, the Information Retrieval model - Starspace did not report a similar trend in the measures. It may be because the word-based probability which the generative models treat is not calibrated uniformly for the sentence based probability for the IR model.

Human Analysis. We performed the human evaluation using the crowdsourced workers since the qualitative analysis comes with several weaknesses in its evaluation metrics [14]. We followed a similar procedure as in the data collection process described in Sect. 3.3. In that procedure, we paired 12 AMT workers to carry out the dialog conversation who were randomly assigned to either of the condition - with or without migration context. Here we replaced one of the AMT workers with our model. They did not know about this while they conversed with each other.

After the dialog conversation, we asked the crowdsourced workers, a few additional questions in order to evaluate the model. We asked them to score between 1 to 5 on fluency, engaging, and consistency following [28].

Table 4. Human Evaluation of one of the models in comparison to human performance for with and without migration context

Model	Human		Sequence-to-sequence model	
	No migration context	Migration context	No migration context	Migration context
Fluency	3.12 (1.54)	4.22 (0.76)	2.22 (1.20)	2.84 (1.33)
Engaging	3.66 (1.41)	4.62 (1.31)	2.41 (1.35)	2.87 (1.04)
Consistency	2.80 (1.07)	4.41 (1.87)	2.12 (0.96)	3.16 (1.21)

The results of the measures are reported in Table 4. We used the Sequence to Sequence model for the evaluation of 10 dialog conversations for both with and without migration context. For the baseline, we also evaluated the scores of human performance by replacing the model with another worker. We noticed that all the measures - fluency, engaging, and consistency were reported significantly higher in both model and human performance when the migration context was used in the evaluation. We also noticed that the overall measures(both with and without migration context) were higher for human performance than the model. It could be because of the linguistic difference in sentence generation from the tokens predicted by the model.

6   Conclusion

In this work, we introduced the migration dataset, which consists of the crowed sourced dialog conversations between participants on a task-based migration scenario. In the dataset, we explored the information migration of the migrated agent using migration context for the personal and non-personal utterances in the dialog history across different settings (Public or Private) of embodiment into which the agent migrates. We trained the generative and information retrieval models on the dataset and report that generative models show improvement when conditioning the prediction of utterance on migration context. We also performed the human evaluation on the dataset and found that participants reported higher fluency, engagingness, and consistency in both models and the human performance when migration context was used.

We believe that the migration dataset will be useful for training future migratable AI systems in personalizing the dialog systems during the migration of conversational AI agent across different devices. For human performance, we evaluated only on the Seq2Seq model. In future work, different recurrent neural network (RNN) and Long short-term memory(LSTM) techniques could be explored for different models and human evaluations.

References

1. Aylett, R.S., et al.: Body-hopping: migrating artificial intelligent agents between embodiments
2. Crane, D., Kauffman, M.: Friends (1994)
3. Byrne, B., et al.: Taskmaster-1:toward a realistic and diverse dialog dataset. In: 2019 Conference on Empirical Methods in Natural Language Processing and 9th International Joint Conference on Natural Language Processing, Hong Kong (2019)
4. Budzianowski, P., et al.: Multiwoz-a large-scale multi-domain wizard-of-oz dataset for task-oriented dialogue modelling. arXiv preprint arXiv:1810.00278 (2018)
5. Mihail, E., et al.: Multiwoz 2.1: multi-domain dialogue state corrections and state tracking baselines. arXiv preprint arXiv:1907.01669 (2019)
6. Sordoni, A., et al.: A neural network approach to context-sensitive generation of conversational responses. arXiv preprint arXiv:1506.06714, 2015
7. Gopalakrishnan, K., et al.: Topical-chat: towards knowledge-grounded open-domain conversations. Proc. Interspeech **2019**, 1891–1895 (2019)
8. Henderson, M., Thomson, B., Williams, J.D.: The second dialog state tracking challenge. In: Proceedings of the 15th Annual Meeting of the Special Interest Group on Discourse and Dialogue (SIGDIAL), pp. 263–272 (2014)
9. Henderson, M., Thomson, B., Williams, J.D.: The third dialog state tracking challenge. In: 2014 IEEE Spoken Language Technology Workshop (SLT), pp. 324–329. IEEE (2014)
10. Imai, M., Ono, T., Etani, T.: Agent migration: communications between a human and robot. In: IEEE SMC'99 Conference Proceedings. 1999 IEEE International Conference on Systems, Man, and Cybernetics (1999)
11. Joshi, C.K., Mi, F., Faltings, B.: Personalization in goal-oriented dialog. arXiv preprint arXiv:1706.07503 (2017)
12. Li, J., Galley, M., Brockett, C., Gao, J., Dolan, B.: A diversity-promoting objective function for neural conversation models. arXiv preprint arXiv:1510.03055 (2015)
13. Jiwei, L., et al.: A persona-based neural conversation model. arXiv preprint arXiv:1603.06155 (2016)
14. Liu, C.-W., et al.: How not to evaluate your dialogue system. arXiv preprint arXiv:1603.08023 (2016)
15. Lorre, C., Prady, B.: The big bang theory (2007)
16. Xiaofei, L.: The relationship of lexical richness to the quality of ESL learners' oral narratives. Modern Lang. J. **96**(2), 190–208 (2012)
17. Lucas, J.M., et al.: Managing speaker identity and user profiles in a spoken dialogue system. Procesamiento del lenguaje Natural **43**, 77–84 (2009)
18. Luria, M., Reig, S., Tan, X.Z., Steinfeld, A., Forlizzi, J., Zimmerman, J.: Re-embodiment and co-embodiment: exploration of social presence for robots and conversational agents. In: Proceedings of the 2019 on Designing Interactive Systems Conference (2019)
19. Ono, T., Imai, M., Nakatsu, R.: Reading a robot's mind: a model of utterance understanding based on the theory of mind mechanism. Adv. Robot. **14**(4), 311–326 (2000)
20. Pennington, J., Socher, R., Manning, C.D.: Glove: global vectors for word representation. In: Proceedings of the 2014 Conference on Empirical Methods in Natural Language Processing (EMNLP), pp. 1532–1543 (2014)

21. Tejwani, R., Katz, B., Breazeal, C.: Migratable AI?: investigating users' affect on identity and information migration of a conversational AI agent. In: Li, H., et al. (eds.) ICSR 2021. LNCS (LNAI), vol. 13086, pp. 257–267. Springer, Cham (2021). https://doi.org/10.1007/978-3-030-90525-5_22

22. Tejwani, R., Moreno, F., Jeong, S., Park, H.W., Breazeal, C.: Migratable AI: effect of identity and information migration on users' perception of conversational AI agents. In: 2020 29th IEEE International Conference on Robot and Human Interactive Communication (RO-MAN), IEEE (2020)

23. Vinyals, O., Le, Q.: A neural conversational model. arXiv preprint arXiv:1506.05869 (2015)

24. Vlachos, A., Clark, S.: A new corpus and imitation learning framework for context-dependent semantic parsing. Trans. Assoc. Comput. Linguist. **2**, 547–560 (2014)

25. Wen, T.-H., et al.: Semantically conditioned LSTM-based natural language generation for spoken dialogue systems. arXiv preprint arXiv:1508.01745 (2015)

26. Living with Robots and Interactive Companions. Lirec (2009). http://lirec.eu

27. Wu, L., et al.: Starspace: embed all the things! In: Thirty-Second AAAI Conference on Artificial Intelligence (2018)

28. Zhang, S., et al.: Personalizing dialogue agents: i have a dog, do you have pets too? arXiv preprint arXiv:1801.07243 (2018)

29. Zimmerman, J., Forlizzi, J.: Speed dating: providing a menu of possible futures. She Ji: J. Des. Econ. Innov. **3**(1), 30–50 (2017)

Generating Natural Language Responses in Robot-Mediated Referential Communication Tasks to Simulate Theory of Mind

Ziming Liu[1]([✉]) [iD], Yigang Qin[2] [iD], Huiqi Zou[2] [iD], Eun Jin Paek[3] [iD], Devin Casenhiser[3] [iD], Wenjun Zhou[4] [iD], and Xiaopeng Zhao[1] [iD]

[1] University of Tennessee, 1506 Middle Drive, Knoxville, TN 37916, USA
zliu68@vols.utk.edu, xzhao9@utk.edu
[2] City University of Hong Kong, 83 Tat Chee Ave.,
Kowloon Tong, Kowloon 999077, Hong Kong
{yigangqin2-c,huiqizou2-c}@my.cityu.edu.hk
[3] University of Tennessee Health Science Center, 600 Henley Street,
Knoxville, TN 37902, USA
{epaek,dcasenhi}@uthsc.edu
[4] University of Tennessee, 916 Volunteer Boulevard, Knoxville, TN 37996, USA
wzhou4@utk.edu

Abstract. With advances in neural network-based computation, socially assistive robots have been endowed with the ability to provide natural conversation to users. However, the lack of transparency in the computation models results in unexpected robot behaviors and feedback, which may cause users to lose their trust in the robot. Theory of mind (ToM) in cooperative tasks has been considered as a key factor in understanding the relationship between user acceptance and the explainability of robot behaviors. Therefore, we develop a dialog system using previously collected data from a robot-mediated cooperative communication task data to simulate natural language smart feedback. The system is designed based on the mechanism of ToM and validated with a simulation test. Based on the result, we believe the designed dialog system bears the feasibility of simulating ToM and can be used as a research tool for further studying the importance of simulating ToM in human-robot communication.

Keywords: Human robot interaction · Theory of mind · Natural language processing

1 Introduction

With advances in Artificially Intelligent (AI) agents and machine comprehension, social robots can be enhanced by intelligent conversational systems to

Supported in part by National Institute of Health under the grant number R01AG077003.

provide fluid and natural conversations to users in different settings. To translate human behavior into computational algorithms through agent-based modeling, the majority of emerged artificial agents attempt to apply cognitive models to develop human-inspired intelligence. These models mainly rely on neural network based computation, such as machine learning, deep learning, or model-based reinforcement learning. These methods employ nonlinear continuous functions to regulate data and identify patterns. In this process, the system provides little transparency into the internal process of understanding how these machines make these decisions [1]. Therefore, explaining why AI agents exhibit certain behaviors is always a challenge [19]. From a user's viewpoint, the robot's behaviors or feedback may be unexpected. The lack of transparency in these models can impede users' trust since they are unable to understand or predict the robot's behavior. In other words, when users do not understand the cause or function of the robot's behaviors or decisions, they may lose trust in the robot [14]. Trust is a significant and desirable characteristic of human-robot interactions. The lack of trust may further influence the user's acceptance of the robot's input, and reduce the efficacy of developing intuitive interaction [22].

Theory of mind (ToM) is a psychological concept that relates to developing interpretability in human communication. It refers to the ability of an individual to model the mental states to others (e.g., beliefs, goals and desires) [4]. In social assistive robots (SARs), previous studies related to ToM mainly focused on perspective taking and belief management [17]. As machine learning advances, robots can reason about what humans can perceive, and construct their representations of the world. However, ToM seems not only to construct representations of others' perception of the world, but is also critical to predicting and understanding the behaviors of others in social situations [24], which enables humans to successfully communicate and cooperate with each other. Indeed, research suggests that difficulties with ToM underlie (at least in part) the challenges autistic people experience during social interaction [2,8]. In daily activities, in order to communicate efficiently, people must bear in mind the interlocutor's viewpoint and use it as a guide to appropriately shape and interpret the language used to achieve the social interaction goal [7].The main distinction between the two perspectives on ToM is one represents the capacity to understand other's minds, and another is the ability to guide communicative behaviours [16]. The second, which refers to the cooperative mind, is also crucial in human-robot interaction (HRI), but few researchers have investigated this topic.

Several studies have reported the close relationship between ToM and referential communication skills in cooperative tasks [13,18]. Referential communication skills refer to the capacity to verbally transmit the representation of an object, event or idea to a conversational partner to constitute the benchmark of a message [12]. Referential communication tasks (RCTs) are used to evaluate referential communication skills. A traditional RCT is usually conducted with two interlocutors who will act as speaker and listener in turns. Both the speaker and listener need to achieve a collaborative joint goal that ensures that their partner identifies the target referent. During this process, the speaker and listener must establish a shared understanding of the intended referent through verbal communication. Therefore, both interlocutors need to model their partners' viewpoint and adjust their own language accordingly to help each other identify the target referent. Because the task requires understanding the other's point of view, it necessarily involves ToM.

According to previous studies regarding RCTs, ToM skills are related to the communicative behaviors of requesting clarification and giving related information which refers to a communicative strategy called joint review (JR) [21]. Inspired by the association between JR and ToM skills, we aim to **develop a natural language response system to effectively extract the representation of ToM in a robot-mediated RCT**. Based on the theoretical model of JR, the robot needs to understand the user's description and provide human understandable responses, such as requests for clarifications or confirmatory information. Therefore, the robot must extract knowledge from unstructured user's transcripts and providing appropriate feedback based on the knowledge. Because identifying the entities and their semantic relations is a prerequisite for knowledge extraction, we use Bidirectional Encoder Representations from Transformers (BERT) [3], a state-of-the-art neural linguistic model, to extract contextual relations between words. Previous studies have shown the superior performance of BERT on extracting semantic relations in context [10,20]. We aim to apply the semantic relation extracted from BERT to generate a response to ask the user for clarifications or convincing information to simulate JR in RCT. Our proposed response system was validated as having significant performance accuracy in extracting entity relations [26].

In this study, we develop a dialog system based on the robot-mediated RCT task data we collected previously to simulate natural language smart feedback occur in human-human RCT. The system is designed based on the mechanism of ToM and assumed to simulate ToM happened in RCT. The proposed system is believed to apply as a research tool for further studying the importance of simulating ToM in human-robot communication.

2   The Robot-Mediated RCT Experiment and Data Collection

The robot-mediated RCT experiment was conducted by participants interacting with a humanoid robot, Pepper. Each participant went through two phases: a *sorting* phase, and a *testing* phase. During the sorting phase, 12 abstract images were shown on Pepper's tablet (see Fig. 1, **left panel**). The 12 images were created with multiple objective characteristics which can be described with different descriptors. The robot described 3 images out of 12 shown on the screen to the participant, and the participant was asked to tap on the described image accordingly. If the participant selected the wrong image, Pepper would describe the image with a longer description which included more details. If the participant still could not select the correct target image after three rounds of description, Pepper would move on to the next image. The purpose of the sorting phase was

Fig. 1. An example of the sorting phase (left panel) and the testing phase (right panel).

to guide the participant in understanding how to communicate with Pepper in the following testing phase. Participants in each group would identify the same three images in the same order. In the testing phase, Pepper would show four abstract images on the screen for each trial. One image was highlighted by a black box which defined it as the target image (Fig. 1, **right panel**). The participant would organize his/her language to verbally describe the target image to Pepper. All four images could not be easily named or identified with simple labels, but contained different features to be described. Therefore, it was natural to observe participants describing the target image with different words. For example, the target image shown in the right panel can be described as *"keychain"* or *"five connected circles ."* A designed AI-mediated agent [11] would analyze both the transcript from the participant and the four images shown on the screen using a multi-modal vision-and-language analysis model and output four probability scores regarding the possibility of each image that the agent believed was the target image. Once the score for one image was significantly higher than the others, the agent determined that confidence was high enough to select the image with the highest score as the target and say *"I think I found it. Let us move on to the next image"*. It would then continue to the next set of four images. If none of the images has a score that is significantly higher than the other images, the robot would ask for more details from the participants by saying *"Could you give me more details?"* The participants would normally have to change their language to describe the same target image based on their predictions of the robot's understanding. Participants perceive the robot as having some level of intelligence since it can understand the description from participants and provide reasonable feedback (e.g., move on to the next one when participant's description is approximate and ask for more details when it is not). The agent analyzed all words the participant used for the current target image as input. Each time that the participant gave the robot a description was counted as one **round**. If Pepper still could not figure out the target image after three rounds, the system would automatically move on to the next trial.

The testing phase had 24 trials. Among the 24 trials, the three abstract images used in the sorting phase were included as target images. All the images shown in the testing phase were presented in a pre-determined order. Therefore, all participants in the same group saw the same sequence of 24 trials. For each trial, a participant may have 1, 2, or 3 rounds. Participants' speech in each round during each trial was audio-recorded.

The dataset with 96 young adults' speech transcripts during a robot-mediated RCT was applied in this study. All participants were native speakers of English and recruited from a large engineering course offered at a large state university in the southeast US. The participants were randomly and evenly divided into two groups. In each group, a robot-mediated RCT was conducted with the same protocol but different image sets. The study protocol was approved by the Institutional Review Board (IRB) of the University of Tennessee, Knoxville (UTK IRB-21-06631-XM).

3   Proposed Method

In this study, we developed a system to generate natural language responses in a robot-mediated RCT. Inspired by ToM, we created a dialog system that allows robots to effectively communicate and engage with human users. The overall workflow of the designed dialog system is demonstrated in Fig. 2.

Fig. 2. Human-robot dialog system workflow

The dialogue module analyzes the input from the users and produces the corresponding response. The transcript is firstly analyzed via the designed keyword matching approach to identify keywords which contain core semantics and are significant to the sentence. The word embeddings of the three most significant keywords are encoded by BERT and compared with every word in the word-embedding corpus using cosine similarity to find the three words (**extra keywords**) sharing the most relevant semantic meaning. The list serves as a reference for providing feedback includes "information the robot has understood" and "information the robot requests". For example, I see the "**keyword**" you described. Does it look like "**extra keyword**"?

The dialog architecture contains two key components: (1) keyword matching (Sect. 3.1) and (2) representation construction (Sect. 3.2). The architecture is trained with the 96 participants' dataset collected in a robot-mediated RCT.

3.1 Keyword Matching

To develop a dialog system that can provide natural language response, the agent needs to understand the users' conceptual interpretation of the image. Keywords represent the specific semantics directly as a minimum knowledge unit. Moreover, they are valid and timely for tracking the information exchange among knowledge barriers [25]. Therefore, attention mechanism of keywords are widely applied in conversation understanding [15]. In the current study, we aim to extract context-based keywords as the representation of semantics to prove robots' understanding level of users.

KeyBERT is a state-of-the-art keyword extraction method that uses BERT embeddings to extract keywords that are the most representative of the underlying text document [6]. As shown in Fig. 2, the user's transcript is firstly analyzed via KeyBERT to identify keywords that contain more semantic meanings than other words and connote the main idea of the sentence. After obtaining the document-level representation (i.e., the sentence embedding) from BERT, Key-BERT extracts word embeddings and calculates their cosine similarity with the sentence. A term with the highest value is considered the one best representing the subject of the input.

According to Kennedy's research [9], vagueness complicates the processing of linguistic reasoning. To extend linguistic reasoning to vague description, we manually operationalized a contextually-determined threshold for selecting keywords. Due to the experimental settings in RCT, participants would only provide a description of the target image. The context would naturally include the semantic representations of the target image. Since all the target images are black & white abstract images, the shape (e.g., circle) and object words (e.g., keychain) contain more conspicuous semantic features than other tokens in the sentence. As nouns and adjectives contain the most information about shape and object, we filtered the transcript input with part-of-speech (POS) tagging. Only the top three nouns and adjectives with the highest significance by cosine similarity with the sentence embedding were selected as keywords.

3.2 Representation Construction

Simply demonstrating that the robot can identify the correct target image is not sufficient to simulate ToM. Based on the concept of ToM, the robot needs to incorporate information from the user's description in its responses in order to establish a common vocabulary for understanding and effectively simulate a JR strategy [4]. In the context of the RCT, ToM requires that the robot construct a representation of users' description from their point of view. In other words, the robot needs to provide extra information relevant to user's description. For example, the user describes: *"It is a keychain."* With a JR strategy, the robot is expected to produce utterances such as: *"Does the keychain* (related to user's description) *have a circle shape* (extra information)?" To allow the robot to provide extra information, we generate a corpus containing semantic feature of transcripts collected before using fine-tuned BERT embeddings. The purpose of the corpus is to compare with the extracted keywords and select the word from the corpus with the most similar semantic representation as **extra keyword**.

Word embedding numerically captures the semantic relations between words. Words with similar meanings are proximate in the embedding space [5]. The nearest neighbors of a word indicate the meaning of the word in the context. Alternatively, they collectively represent a form of knowledge. Therefore, such a corpus allows us to calculate and compare the semantic correlation between existing transcripts in the corpus and the user's input in the RCT. Due to the advantage of semantic awareness, as shown in Fig. 2, we fine-tuned and applied BERT to extract word embeddings from transcripts in the dataset. We applied two state-of-the-art BERT fine-tuning approaches: 1) BERT-ITPT-FIT (within-task-pre-trained and then fine-tuned) and 2) BERT-FIT (direct fine-tuned) [23].

To mimic the natural communication in RCT, transcripts of each round are used as inputs. To ensure the applicability of this corpus under different settings, the two sets of transcripts were combined and collapsed as one dataset. By manually selecting words that are objects and shapes from the transcripts, we ensured that the word embeddings contained informative semantics about the target image. Only these words' embeddings are saved in the word-embedding corpus. The word embeddings serve as vector representations of their semantics.

4   System Validation and Results

The dialog system was evaluated based on how well the system can determine additional keywords. The testing dataset was applied as transcript inputs into the designed dialog system. If one of the three relevant words determined by the system exists in the transcripts from the training dataset which described the same target image, it would count as a match. Otherwise, it was not a match. The proportion of simulation transcripts that contain at least one match (referred to as match ratio hereafter) was used as the criteria of comparison.

Due to the assumption of object and shape words, we had planed to validate the system by calculating the values when the extracted keywords with and without any shape and object words (refers to normal and unexpected situation, respectively). The shape and object list was split from the manual selection from transcripts in the dataset for each training set to maintain the consistency in the training-simulation data partition. Each model and shape/object list being used by that model was trained and generated from a subset of the whole data so that the simulation transcripts were not accessible in the training process and served as unseen sentences merely for validation.

Method of Token Representation. When BERT is fine-tuned for a downstream task, token representation is one of the salient factors affecting its performance since different layers of the BERT model output different semantic features [3]. We tested two approaches to represent every token: (1) only using the output features (hidden state of the BERT encoder) from the last layer and (2) summing all the output features from the last four layers.

Figure 3 gives a summary of evaluation results regarding the dialog simulation performance. Overall, although BERT-ITPT-FIT yielded slightly performance than BERT-FIT for text classification, the difference is not statistically significant ($t_{30} = 1.01$, $p>.05$ in normal and worst situations; $t_{14} = .35$, $p>.05$ with the sum of the last four layers to represent tokens; and $t_{14} = 1.37$, $p>.05$ with the last layer. Therefore, we have not found a significant contribution of within-task pre-training for classification in our case. One explanation could be the small volume of the training data which made it inefficient transferring the BERT language model to this specific domain.

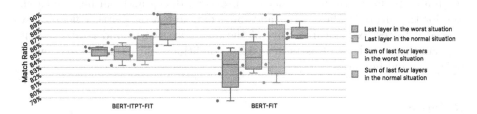

Fig. 3. Simulation results for the normal and worst situations

Despite limited performance improvement by using within-task pre-training in our design, we observed significant differences in match ratios between outcomes with different token representations. Experiments using the sum of the last four layers' features produced significantly higher mean match ratio than only using the last layer's features in normal and worst situations altogether ($t_{30} = 2.87$, $p = .0075$). The BERT-ITPT-FIT model with the sum of the last four layers' output features as the token representation attained the highest match ratio of 90.05% (matched 172/189 transcripts). The significant difference also holds when comparing the mean match ratio for each model training approach: BERT-ITPT-FIT ($t(14) = 2.13$, $p=.0518$) and BERT-FIT ($t(14) = 2.01$, $p = .0636$). Our simulation results are consistent with the conclusion that the sum of the last four layers captures richer semantic meanings in a variety of levels than the last layer alone [3]. Based on previous results and those of our simulation, a hypothesis would be that representing the tokens by concatenating the last four layers' output features could improve the match ratio in simulation and the overall performance in field experiments, which could be tested in future work.

The dialog simulation results evidenced the system's capacity to find relevant and coherent words to form the response. Moreover, we found that representation of the tokens had an effect on performance in the dialog simulation. To summarize, our simulation preliminarily confirmed the validity of the proposed dialog system in finding relevant words to facilitate a jointly reviewed conversation in RCT. The effect of model-training approach and token representation was analyzed. More training data and alternative token representation methods will be explored in the future study. Based on the results, the designed dialog system bears the feasibility to simulate human's JR strategy in RCT. Regarding the close relationship between ToM and JR in RCT, we believe the designed dialog can simulate ToM during RCT.

5   Discussion and Conclusion

We developed a robot dialog system for RCT based on the mechanism of ToM applied in daily human-human communication. The aim of the proposed dialog system is to enhance the user's understanding on robot's intention, and further improve users' trusts towards the robot. Regarding the results from the validation test, the designed system contains the ability to determine extra keywords necessary for clarification. Therefore, we believe the designed system bears an acceptable performance to conduct the proposed dialog and can be a research tool for the future studies in human-robot communication. Further field study is needed to test ecological validity of the dialog system to understand how it impacts the trust level of users in real-life conditions and interactions between AI agents and humans.

References

1. Calder, M., Craig, C., Culley, D., De Cani, R., Donnelly, C.A., Douglas, R., Edmonds, B., Gascoigne, J., Gilbert, N., Hargrove, C., et al.: Computational modelling for decision-making: where, why, what, who and how. Royal Soc. Open Sci. **5**(6), 172096 (2018)
2. Chiu, H.M., et al.: Theory of mind predicts social interaction in children with autism spectrum disorder: A two-year follow-up study. J. Autism Dev. Disord. 1–11 (2022). https://doi.org/10.1007/s10803-022-05662-4
3. Devlin, J., Chang, M.W., Lee, K., Toutanova, K.: Bert: Pre-training of deep bidirectional transformers for language understanding (2018). https://doi.org/10.48550/ARXIV.1810.04805
4. Foss, N., Stea, D.: Putting a realistic theory of mind into agency theory: implications for reward design and management in principal-agent relations. Eur. Manage. Rev. **11**(1), 101–116 (2014)
5. Fu, R., Guo, J., Qin, B., Che, W., Wang, H., Liu, T.: Learning semantic hierarchies via word embeddings. In: Proceedings of the 52nd Annual Meeting of the Association for Computational Linguistics (Volume 1: Long Papers), pp. 1199–1209 (2014)
6. Grootendorst, M.: Keybert: Minimal keyword extraction with bert. (2020). https://doi.org/10.5281/zenodo.4461265
7. John, A.E., Rowe, M.L., Mervis, C.B.: Referential communication skills of children with williams syndrome: understanding when messages are not adequate. Am. J. Intell. Dev. Disab. **114**(2), 85–99 (2009)
8. Jones, C.R., et al.: The association between theory of mind, executive function, and the symptoms of autism spectrum disorder. Autism Res. **11**(1), 95–109 (2018)
9. Kennedy, C.: Vagueness and grammar: the semantics of relative and absolute gradable adjectives. Linguist. Philos. **30**(1), 1–45 (2007)
10. Lin, C., Miller, T., Dligach, D., Bethard, S., Savova, G.: A bert-based universal model for both within-and cross-sentence clinical temporal relation extraction. In: Proceedings of the 2nd Clinical Natural Language Processing Workshop, pp. 65–71 (2019)

11. Liu, Z., et al.: A demonstration of human-robot communication based on multi-skilled language-image analysis. In: 2021 IEEE/ACM Conference on Connected Health: Applications, Systems and Engineering Technologies (CHASE), pp. 126–127. IEEE (2021)
12. Liu, Z., Paek, E.J., Yoon, S.O., Casenhiser, D., Zhou, W., Zhao, X.: Detecting alzheimer's disease using natural language processing of referential communication task transcripts. J. Alzheimer's Disease **86**(3), 1–14 (2022)
13. Maridaki-Kassotaki, K., Antonopoulou, K.: Examination of the relationship between false-belief understanding and referential communication skills. Eur. J. Psychol. Educ. **26**(1), 75–84 (2011)
14. Miller, T.: Explanation in artificial intelligence: insights from the social sciences. Artif. Intell. **267**, 1–38 (2019)
15. Mou, L., Song, Y., Yan, R., Li, G., Zhang, L., Jin, Z.: Sequence to backward and forward sequences: a content-introducing approach to generative short-text conversation. arXiv preprint arXiv:1607.00970 (2016)
16. Nilsen, E.S., Fecica, A.M.: A model of communicative perspective-taking for typical and atypical populations of children. Dev. Rev. **31**(1), 55–78 (2011)
17. O'Reilly, Z., Silvera-Tawil, D., Tan, D.W., Zurr, I.: Validation of a novel theory of mind measurement tool: the social robot video task. In: Companion of the 2021 ACM/IEEE International Conference on Human-Robot Interaction, pp. 89–93 (2021)
18. Paal, T., Bereczkei, T.: Adult theory of mind, cooperation, machiavellianism: the effect of mindreading on social relations. Personality individ. Differ. **43**(3), 541–551 (2007)
19. Rai, A.: Explainable AI: From black box to glass box. J. Acad. Mark. Sci. **48**(1), 137–141 (2020)
20. Shi, P., Lin, J.: Simple bert models for relation extraction and semantic role labeling. arXiv preprint arXiv:1904.05255 (2019)
21. Sidera, F., Perpiñà, G., Serrano, J., Rostan, C.: Why is theory of mind important for referential communication? Curr. Psychol. **37**(1), 82–97 (2018)
22. Song, Y., Luximon, Y.: Trust in AI agent: a systematic review of facial anthropomorphic trustworthiness for social robot design. Sensors **20**(18), 5087 (2020)
23. Sun, C., Qiu, X., Xu, Y., Huang, X.: How to fine-tune BERT for text classification? In: Sun, M., Huang, X., Ji, H., Liu, Z., Liu, Y. (eds.) CCL 2019. LNCS (LNAI), vol. 11856, pp. 194–206. Springer, Cham (2019). https://doi.org/10.1007/978-3-030-32381-3_16
24. Whiten, A., Byrne, R.W.: The machiavellian intelligence hypotheses (1988)
25. Xu, J., Bu, Y., Ding, Y., Yang, S., Zhang, H., Yu, C., Sun, L.: Understanding the formation of interdisciplinary research from the perspective of keyword evolution: a case study on joint attention. Scientometrics **117**(2), 973–995 (2018). https://doi.org/10.1007/s11192-018-2897-1
26. Zhang, Z., Wu, Y., Zhao, H., Li, Z., Zhang, S., Zhou, X., Zhou, X.: Semantics-aware bert for language understanding. In: Proceedings of the AAAI Conference on Artificial Intelligence, vol. 34, pp. 9628–9635 (2020)

Towards a Framework for Social Robot Co-speech Gesture Generation with Semantic Expression

Heng Zhang[1(✉)], Chuang Yu[2], and Adriana Tapus[1]

[1] Autonomous Systems and Robotics Lab/U2IS, ENSTA Paris,
Institut Polytechnique de Paris, Paris, France
{heng.zhang,adriana.tapus}@ensta-paris.fr
[2] Cognitive Robotics Laboratory, University of Manchester, Manchester, UK
chuang.yu@manchester.ac.uk

Abstract. The ability to express semantic co-speech gestures in an appropriate manner of the robot is needed for enhancing the interaction between humans and social robots. However, most of the learning-based methods in robot gesture generation are unsatisfactory in expressing the semantic gesture. Many generated gestures are ambiguous, making them difficult to deliver the semantic meanings accurately. In this paper, we proposed a robot gesture generation framework that can effectively improve the semantic gesture expression ability of social robots. In this framework, the semantic words in a sentence are selected and expressed by clear and understandable co-speech gestures with appropriate timing. In order to test the proposed method, we designed an experiment and conducted the user study. The result shows that the performances of the gesture generated by the proposed method are significantly improved compared to the baseline gesture in three evaluation factors: human-likeness, naturalness and easiness to understand.

Keywords: Social robot · Semantic · Robot gesture · Human-robot interaction

1 Introduction

The co-speech gesture plays an important role in human communication [1]. It is semantically related to speech and increases the efficiency of information exchange [2] or makes some special speech (e.g. jokes) perform better [3]. In addition, it can also convey the speaker's emotion and attitude, which makes the communication be perceived more natural [4,5]. As in the interaction between humans, the social robot is also hoped to behave like a human by using co-speech gestures when it communicates with humans [6,7], which contributes to building human users' confidence for long-term interaction with the robot.

Supported by ENSTA Paris, Institut Polytechnique de Paris, France and the CSC PhD Scholarship.

Psychological research on co-speech gestures has been quite fruitful. One of the most widely known works is the theory of David McNeil [8,9]. According to his theory [8], gestures can be basically classified as two types, namely, the imagistic gesture and the beat gesture. The imagistic gesture includes three subtypes, which are iconic gesture, metaphoric gesture, and deictic gesture, respectively. As mentioned before, gestures play important roles in face-to-face conversation. The imagistic gesture is usually related to the semantic content in speech. For example, people will display their two empty palm hands to strengthen the "no idea" in their words [8]. Unlike the imagistic gesture, the beat gesture is usually not related to semantic content, but used to emphasize the intonation of speech, thus conveying the speaker's emotions [10]. Both the imagistic gesture and the beat gesture associated with speech can help the speaker to express more clearly or in a more subtle way.

According to the CASA paradigm [11], the robots are also expected to be endowed with human social capabilities although they are man-made intelligent agents. Consequently, when pursuing the natural and human-like co-speech gesture generation methods of the social robot, both the imagistic gesture and beat gesture should be taken into account. In this paper, we will introduce a co-speech gesture generation framework that considers both of these two kinds of gestures.

The rest of this paper is structured as follows: We discuss some related works in co-speech gesture generation in Sect. 2; We introduce the proposed co-speech gesture generation framework in Sect. 3; We present the experimental design and results in Sect. 4 and Sect. 5, respectively. Finally, the conclusions and future work are part of Sect. 6.

2   Related Work

There have been some related works on co-speech gesture generation. Although some methods were originally intended to generate actions for virtual agents, they could also be applied to humanoid social robots. According to the way of generation, most methods can be divided into two categories, namely, rule-based methods [12,13] and data-driven methods [14,15].

The rule-based method refers to using handcrafted rules to generate gestures. Once the rules are designed, it will be a simple and convenient way for users to generate the gestures. Kopp et al. proposed a behavior generation framework that includes an XML-based language, BML(Behavior Makeup Language). It defined some rules of gesture expression and can be coupled with other gesture generation systems [16]. The BEAT toolkit developed by the MIT media lab is a famous rule-based gesture generation system. It integrated the rules derived from the prior knowledge of human conversation into the toolkit. By inputting the given text to BEAT, the user can obtain a description of the co-speech gesture, which can be used in an animation system to generate the specific gesture sequence [17]. Some commercial social robots also developed the rule-based gesture generation methods to allow the users to design the robot gesture quickly, such as the AnimatedSpeech function of Pepper and Nao robots [18]. The rule-based methods are simpler and more convenient than the pure manual way, and the generated gestures can also express semantics clearly. However, because of the limited rules, the gestures are usually form monotonous and repetitive, which is not conducive to long-term human-Robot interaction.

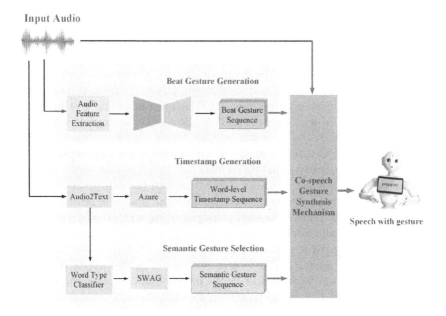

Fig. 1. Overview of our proposed framework

With the development of deep learning, the data-driven method has been increasingly used in the domain of Human-Robot Interaction [19–21]. Yoon et al. introduced an end-to-end co-speech gesture generation method. They used the TED Gesture Dataset to train an Encoder-Decoder model. The trained model is able to generate the gesture sequence by giving the text as the input [22]. Kucherenko et al. proposed a framework that used the audio and text of speech as input. In this way, both the acoustic and semantic representations would contribute to the co-speech generation [15]. Compared to the rule-based method, the data-driven gesture generation method performs much better in terms of variety. However, the data-driven methods are weak in expressing semantics. The main reason is that in a data-driven approach, the training goal is to make the loss (the difference between the generated angles and the actual angles) as small as possible to achieve convergence of the model. However, the co-speech gesture that humans use to express the semantic meaning is usually clear and unique. The data-driven model cannot understand the semantics of the gesture, so the imagistic gesture and the beat gesture are with the same weights during training. Therefore, although the loss is small, the generated results are ambiguous, making them difficult to deliver the semantic meanings accurately.

In view of the shortages of these two kinds of methods, we propose a co-speech gesture generation framework that combines the advantages of these two kinds of methods and avoids their disadvantages, as shown in Fig. 1.

In this framework, we built a semantic gesture dataset named SWAG (Semantic Word Associated Gesture) dataset for expressing semantics, and an Encoder-Decoder model for generating baseline gestures. The SWAG dataset contains a list of highly-used semantic gestures, and each gesture corresponds to a semantic word. These gestures are saved in the form of TXT files that are extracted by the BlazePose [23]. We also modeled a special Encoder-Decoder neural network to generate the baseline gesture by inputting the acoustic features of the speech audio. Moreover, a semantic gesture selection mechanism and a co-speech gesture synthesis mechanism were designed to select the semantic gesture from SWAG and use word-level timestamps to embed the selected gesture into the baseline gesture appropriately. There are two contributions to our current work:

1) The first semantic gesture dataset SWAG that contains a list of semantic-related gestures;
2) Designing a co-speech gesture synthesis mechanism using the word-level timestamp sequence that is able to embed the semantic gesture into the baseline gesture at appropriate timing.

3   Gesture Generation Framework

Our proposed gesture generation framework mainly includes four parts: an Encoder-Decoder beat gesture generation model, a semantic word associated gesture dataset (SWAG), a semantic gesture selection mechanism, and a co-speech gesture synthesis mechanism. These four parts work together to generate the co-speech gesture that can clearly deliver semantics.

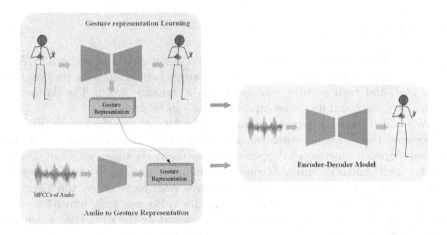

Fig. 2. The Encoder-Decoder model used to generate baseline gesture

3.1   Encoder-Decoder Model

In this paper, we used a special Encoder-Decoder model based on the Denoising Autoencoder to generate the baseline gestures. The model takes the speech audio as input and outputs the corresponding co-speech gesture. The architecture of the model is as shown in Fig. 2.

The model consists of two components, which are the Encoder and the Decoder, respectively. We divided the model training into two steps. In this work, the dataset used to train the model is the gesture dataset built by Ylva Ferstl et al. [24], which contains the speech audio and the motion data in form of BioVision Hierarchy format (BVH).

Firstly, we used the Denoising Autoencoder model to learn the gesture representation. There is a bottleneck layer in this Autoencoder. This layer is able to force the network to compress the representations of the original input data, thus obtaining the representation of the gesture g in a lower dimensionality. In the Autoencoder model, the input is motion m and output is motion $\hat{m}$. We defined the loss function as:

$$L(m, \hat{m}) = argmin \|\hat{m} - m\|_2^2$$

In this step, the gesture representations g and the parameters of the Decoder were kept. In the following next step, we trained the Encoder part to map the speech audio to the gesture representation g. The input is the Mel-Frequency Cepstral Coefficients (MFCCs) extracted from the speech audio. The output is the gesture representation in the previous step. In this step, the parameters of the Encoder were kept. This model is partly based on the work of Kucherenko et al. in [25].

After finishing the training of these two parts separately, we connect them together to form a complete baseline gesture generation model.

3.2   SWAG Dataset

In this work, we built an extensible semantic gesture dataset named SWAG. This dataset contains a list of semantic gestures(joint angles) in the form of TXT files, and each gesture corresponds to a semantic word. The dataset is preliminary work and it can be expanded easily in future work.

We divided the whole process of building the dataset into three steps. Firstly, we selected the semantic words borrowed from the semantic word list of the AnimatedSpeech function of Pepper robot. At the early stage, we listed 67 frequently used semantic words. Secondly, a volunteer performed all these words by co-speech gestures. Meanwhile, his gestures were recorded by the Logitech HD Webcam C930e (1080 p, 30 FPS), and the video was split into 67 pieces. Thirdly, the 3D coordinates of joints were extracted by the BlazePose as shown in Fig. 3. Since we just need the motion data of the upper body, we only saved the 3D coordinates information of the following joints: wrist, elbow, shoulder, and hip. Considering the actual degree of freedom (DOF) of the Pepper robot,

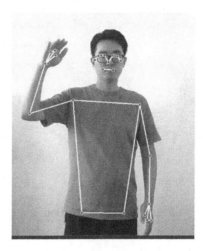

Fig. 3. The Joints recognized by the BlazePose

the rotation angles of each joint were calculated according to the 3D coordinates information in every frame. In addition, we also used the Dlib toolkit and the solvePnP function of OpenCV to estimate the head pose. To smooth the gesture, all the extracted motion data was processed by a median filter(kernel = 5). Finally, we obtained the dataset that included 67 TXT-based gesture files.

3.3   Co-speech Gesture Synthesis Mechanism

In this paper, we proposed a co-speech gesture synthesis mechanism to synthesize the gesture with semantics. We are going to solve two main problems through this synthesis mechanism:

1) Which words in a sentence should be selected to be expressed by the semantic gestures?
2) How to determine the timing for a semantic gesture embedding?

In the mechanism, the baseline gesture, the semantic gesture, the timestamp sequence, and the original audio are required. We have introduced how to generate the baseline gesture in the previous subsection. It is worth mentioning that the baseline gesture generated by the NN model are in the form of Euler angles. In order to be retargeted to the robot, we further converted them into joint angles. Next, we will explain how to select the appropriate gestures for the semantic words of a sentence from the SWAG.

After inputting the speech audio into our framework, the audio would be converted to text through the Audio2Text program. Meanwhile, we could obtain a speech words list and a word-level timestamp sequence by using the Microsoft Azure SDK. Firstly, we used the rule-based Toolkit BEAT to determine the words to be selected to express semantics. These words would be selected again

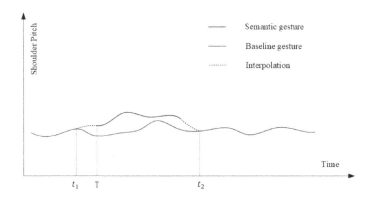

Fig. 4. The interpolation

depending on whether there is the corresponding motion data in the SWAG database. Secondly, according to the selected words, the corresponding times-tamp would be used to determine the gesture embedding timing. To make the semantic gesture and baseline gesture connect smoothly, we interpolated the joint angle data of ten frames before timestamp T of the baseline motion and the beginning data of the semantic motion. The same operation would be done at the end of the semantic motion embedding as shown in Fig. 4. In this way, the data of semantic gesture replaces the baseline data at an appropriate position. Finally, the input audio would also be used as the speech audio of the robot.

4 Experimental Design

The previous parts explained the principles of the co-speech gesture generation method. In this section, we introduce the experiment that we conducted to test the performance of our proposed method.

4.1 Videos

We used the proposed method and the baseline method (only the Encoder-Decoder model) to generate gestures with 5 fixed short paragraphs, respectively. This set composed of 10 gesture data was used with the Pepper robot, which is an humanoid social robot developed by SoftBank Robotics. We recorded Pepper's gestures into 10 videos by a camera, and we also generated the corresponding subtitles for each video.

4.2 Questionnaire and Participants

These videos were then used to make a questionnaire. In the questionnaire, the order of the videos was random. After each video, we asked the participants to answer a set of three questions in terms of the degree of human-likeness, naturalness, and easiness of understanding of the speech. These were:

1) To what extent are the gestures of the robot similar to those of a human?
2) How natural are the robot's gestures?
3) To what extent do robot's gestures make the speech easier to understand?

All questions were using 10 Likert scale, where 10 indicates the best performance. The questionnaire was then distributed online to students in Institut Polytechnique de Paris and the University of Manchester. 50 participants took part in our online study.

5   Results

Participants' ratings on 10 robot's performances are summarized in Fig. 5. We used the Shapiro-Wilk test to verify the normality of the data. Data does not conform to a normal distribution. Consequently, we used the Kruskal-Wallis test to verify the statistical difference of the gesture generated by the two different methods under each of the three evaluation factors (i.e., human-likeness, naturalness and easiness to understand). The results are shown in Fig. 5.

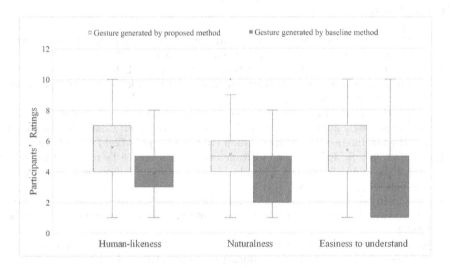

Fig. 5. The results obtained by the 2 methods with respect to the three factors (i.e., human-likeness, naturalness and easiness to understand)

When considering the factor of "human-likeness", the $\chi^2 = 85.9$, p < 0.01; When considering the factor of "naturalness", the $\chi^2 = 65.7$, p < 0.01; When considering the factor of "easiness to understand", the $\chi^2 = 70.8$, p < 0.01. The above results confirmed that there are significant differences between participants' ratings on the gesture generated by the proposed method and the gesture generated by the baseline method in terms of all three factors. In addition, with these three evaluation factors, the participants' ratings on the gesture generated by the proposed method are significantly higher than the gesture generated by the baseline method.

6   Conclusions and Future Work

In this work, we proposed a robot co-speech gesture generation framework. In this framework, we combined the rule-based method and the learning-based method to improve the robot's ability to express semantics by embedding the semantic gesture into the baseline gesture. The result of the user study shown that the performances of the gesture generated by the proposed method are significantly improved compared to the baseline gesture with respect to the "human-likeness", "naturalness", and "easiness to understand".

There are still some parts that could be improved in our current work. Firstly, the SWAG dataset is of a small size, and therefore, it should be further expanded to meet more dialogue scenarios in future work. Secondly, the semantic words selecting mechanism is still rudimentary and not conducive to the end-to-end gesture generation target. Future work will focus on the training of a neural network to replace the current mechanism.

References

1. Graham, J.A., Argyle, M.: A cross-cultural study of the communication of extra-verbal meaning by gestures (1). Int. J. Psychol. **10**(1), 57–67 (1975)
2. Holler, J., Wilkin, K.: Communicating common ground: how mutually shared knowledge influences speech and gesture in a narrative task. Lang. Cognit. Process. **24**(2), 267–289 (2009)
3. Zhang, H., Yu, C., Tapus, A.: Why do you think this joke told by robot is funny? The humor style matters. In: 2022 31st IEEE International Conference on Robot and Human Interactive Communication (RO-MAN), pp. 572–577. IEEE (2022)
4. Mozziconacci, S.: Emotion and attitude conveyed in speech by means of prosody. In: For the 2nd Workshop on Attitude, Personality and Emotions in User-Adapted Interaction, pp. 1–10 (2001)
5. Yu, C.: Robot behavior generation and human behavior understanding in natural human-robot interaction. Ph.D. dissertation, Institut Polytechnique de Paris (2021)
6. Rossi, S., Rossi, A., Dautenhahn, K.: The secret life of robots: perspectives and challenges for robot's behaviours during non-interactive tasks. Int. J. Soc. Robot. **12**(6), 1265–1278 (2020)
7. Tapus, A., Maja, M., Scassellatti, B.: The grand challenges in socially assistive robotics. IEEE Rob. Autom. Mag. **14**(1), N-A (2007)
8. McNeill, D.: Hand and mind1. In: Advances in Visual Semiotics, p. 351 (1992)
9. McNeill, D.: So you think gestures are nonverbal? Psychol. Rev. **92**(3), 350 (1985)
10. Bozkurt, E., Yemez, Y., Erzin, E.: Multimodal analysis of speech and arm motion for prosody-driven synthesis of beat gestures. Speech Commun. **85**, 29–42 (2016)
11. Reeves, B., Nass, C.: The media equation: How people treat computers, television, and new media like real people, Cambridge, UK, vol. 10, p. 236605 (1996)
12. Huang, C.-M., Mutlu, B.: Robot behavior toolkit: generating effective social behaviors for robots. In: 2012 7th ACM/IEEE International Conference on Human-Robot Interaction (HRI), pp. 25–32. IEEE (2012)

13. Bremner, P., Pipe, A.G., Fraser, M., Subramanian, S., Melhuish, C.: Beat gesture generation rules for human-robot interaction. In: RO-MAN 2009-The 18th IEEE International Symposium on Robot and Human Interactive Communication, pp. 1029–1034. IEEE (2009)
14. Yu, C., Tapus, A.: SRG 3: speech-driven robot gesture generation with GAN. In: 2020 16th International Conference on Control, Automation, Robotics and Vision (ICARCV), pp. 759–766. IEEE (2020)
15. Kucherenko, T.: Gesticulator: a framework for semantically-aware speech-driven gesture generation. In: Proceedings of the 2020 International Conference on Multimodal Interaction, pp. 242–250 (2020)
16. Kopp, S., et al.: Towards a common framework for multimodal generation: the behavior markup language. In: Gratch, J., Young, M., Aylett, R., Ballin, D., Olivier, P. (eds.) IVA 2006. LNCS (LNAI), vol. 4133, pp. 205–217. Springer, Heidelberg (2006). https://doi.org/10.1007/11821830_17
17. Cassell, J., Vilhjálmsson, H.H., Bickmore, T.: BEAT: the behavior expression animation toolkit. In: Prendinger, H., Ishizuka, M. (eds.) Life-Like Characters, pp. 163–185. Springer, Heidelberg (2004). https://doi.org/10.1007/978-3-662-08373-4_8
18. Pandey, A.K., Gelin, R.: A mass-produced sociable humanoid robot: pepper: the first machine of its kind. IEEE Rob. Autom. Mag. **25**(3), 40–48 (2018)
19. Yu, C., Tapus, A.: Interactive robot learning for multimodal emotion recognition. In: Salichs, M.A., et al. (eds.) ICSR 2019. LNCS (LNAI), vol. 11876, pp. 633–642. Springer, Cham (2019). https://doi.org/10.1007/978-3-030-35888-4_59
20. Yu, C., Fu, C., Chen, R., Tapus, A.: First attempt of gender-free speech style transfer for genderless robot. In: Proceedings of the 2022 ACM/IEEE International Conference on Human-Robot Interaction, pp. 1110–1113 (2022)
21. Tapus, A., Bandera, A., Vazquez-Martin, R., Calderita, L.: Perceiving the person and their interactions with the others for social robotics-a review. Pattern Recogn. Lett. **118**, 3–13 (2019)
22. Yoon, Y., Ko, W.-R., Jang, M., Lee, J., Kim, J., Lee, G.: Robots learn social skills: end-to-end learning of co-speech gesture generation for humanoid robots. In: 2019 International Conference on Robotics and Automation (ICRA), pp. 4303–4309. IEEE (2019)
23. Bazarevsky, V., Grishchenko, I., Raveendran, K., Zhu, T., Zhang, F., Grundmann, M.: BlazePose: on-device real-time body pose tracking, arXiv preprint arXiv:2006.10204 (2020)
24. Ferstl, Y., McDonnell, R.: Investigating the use of recurrent motion modelling for speech gesture generation. In: Proceedings of the 18th International Conference on Intelligent Virtual Agents, pp. 93–98 (2018)
25. Kucherenko, T., Hasegawa, D., Henter, G.E., Kaneko, N., Kjellström, H.: Analyzing input and output representations for speech-driven gesture generation. In: Proceedings of the 19th ACM International Conference on Intelligent Virtual Agents, pp. 97–104 (2019)

Tactile Interaction with a Robot Leads to Increased Risk-Taking

Qiaoqiao Ren$^{(\boxtimes)}$ and Tony Belpaeme

IDLab – imec, Ghent University, Ghent, Belgium
{Qiaoqiao.Ren,Tony.Belpaeme}@UGent.be

Abstract. Tactile interaction plays a crucial role in interactions between people. Touch can, for example, help people calm down and lower physiological stress responses. Consequently, it is believed that tactile and haptic interaction matter also in human-robot interaction. We study if the intensity of the tactile interaction has an impact on people, and do so by studying whether different intensities of tactile interaction modulate physiological measures and task performance. We use a paradigm in which a small humanoid robot is used to encourage risk-taking behaviour, relying on peer encouragement to take more risks which might lead to a higher pay-off, but potentially also to higher losses. For this, the Balloon Analogue Risk Task (BART) is used as a proxy for the propensity to take risks. We study four conditions, one control condition in which the task is completed without a robot, and three experimental conditions in which a robot is present that encourages risk-taking behaviour with different degrees of tactile interaction. The results show that both low-intensity and high-intensity tactile interaction increase people's risk-taking behaviour. However, low-intensity tactile interaction increases comfort and lowers stress, whereas high-intensity touch does not.

Keywords: Human-robot touch · Tactile interaction · Haptic interaction · Nonverbal communication · Peer pressure · Risk-taking behaviour · Heart rate variability

1 Introduction

In general, research on haptic and tactile interaction with robots has received little attention in Human-Robot Interaction (HRI). Haptic interaction is prominent in Human-Computer Interaction (HCI) as an interaction modality with digital media [1], but physical interaction with robots is rare for several reasons [2]. One is that most robots are unsafe to touch or handle, even robots which have been explicitly designed for HRI are often unsuitable for tactile interaction [3]. The Nao robot, for example, the most widely used robot in HRI studies, has several pinch points which could trap fingers. A second reason is that most social robots are not explicitly designed for physical interaction. Often, physically manipulating or holding the robot at best triggers a fail-safe or at worst leads to breakages. Finally, we have only recently started understanding more about the

© The Author(s), under exclusive license to Springer Nature Switzerland AG 2022
F. Cavallo et al. (Eds.): ICSR 2022, LNAI 13817, pp. 120–129, 2022.
https://doi.org/10.1007/978-3-031-24667-8_11

possible effects of tactile interaction with robots, and this paper aims to make a contribution to understanding the effect of intensity of tactile interaction on people's attitudes and task performance with a robot.

The influence of physical interaction, and specifically touch, has been widely documented. For example, light physical contact between people has been shown to promote a sense of security and consequently increases risk-taking [4]. Recent research found that slow, emotive touch can help reduce social suffering associated with exclusion. Slower, emotive touch –as opposed to rapid, neutral touch– influences the perception of physical pain and appears to be mediated by a distinct tactile neurophysiological system [5]. Also in HRI, touch and physical interaction is known to change the behaviour or perception of the user. For example, touching a PARO robot can reduce pain perception and reduce salivary oxytocin levels [6].

The study reported here focuses on risk-taking behaviour. It has been established that taking risks is a fundamental human activity with significant ramifications for one's finances, health, and social life. Peer pressure, notably, can play a significant role in risk-taking behaviours. If someone sees friends or peers engaging in risky behaviour and seeks acceptance, they are more likely to engage in those behaviours. People also readily respond to encouragement, for example, drivers will drive fast when encouraged by others, which leads to a higher possibility of an accident [7,8]. As such, peer influence and peer pressure play an important role in risky behaviour.

In this study, we focus on whether touching or holding a robot can change human risk-taking behaviour. Earlier work found that a robot's verbal encouragement could help people take more risks and pointed out potential implications for human decision-making [9]. This ties in with earlier work on peer pressure, which showed that people under certain circumstances conform to robots' pressure, as a way to gain social approval [10] or reduce informational uncertainty [11]. However. It is yet unclear whether *human-robot touch* can influence the peer pressure from robots.

2   Methodology

2.1   Experimental Design

Participants interacted with a Softbank Robotics NAO robot. In order to assess the participant's risk-taking behaviour, a Balloon Analogue Risk Taking (BART) was used, identical to [9]. In this, participants are shown a balloon on screen and are asked to inflate it by pressing the space bar. Their monetary earnings increase with the size of the balloon and they can collect their money by moving on to the next balloon. If the balloon explodes –which happens at a pseudorandom number of pumps– their earnings are lost for that balloon. Each participant inflates 30 balloons. Four experimental conditions were used, as illustrated in Fig. 1.

1. In the *low-intensity condition (LI)* the participant has brief and low-force tactile interactions with the robot, timed to coincide with the participant

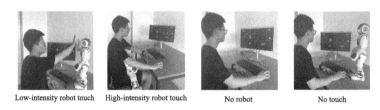

Fig. 1. The four interaction conditions used in the study.

wanting to move on to the next balloon or when the robot encourages them to take more risk. At these times, the robot invites the participant to give a high-five, shake hands or touch the robot's head.

2. In the *high-intensity condition (HI)* the participant has prolonged and high-force tactile interaction with the robot, as the robot asks the participant to be taken on their lap. As such, both the participant and the robot face the screen together. During the experiment, the robot uses its arms to point and gesticulate, just as in the previous condition.

3. In the *no-touch condition (NT)* the robot only encourages participants to take more risks by verbally encouraging them to pump more. Note that the verbal interaction between all three experimental conditions is identical.

4. In the *no-robot condition (NR)* no robot is present and the participants play the BART games without encouragement to take more risks. This serves as a control condition and baseline to compare the experimental data against.

We used a within-subject design, with all participants being exposed to all four conditions. The order in which we present the conditions is balanced across participants.

2.2 Participants

38 participants (19 female, 19 male; 27.0 ± 2.2 years old) were randomly distributed over four conditions: the low-intensity touch, the high-intensity touch, the no-touch and the no-robot conditions. Participants were recruited through a local social media campaign and were offered a 5 €voucher for an online store. Participants were excluded if they self-reported learning difficulties related to

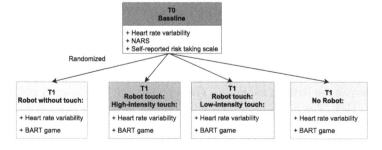

Fig. 2. Experiment set-up at T0.

reading or hearing, or if they reported an acute or chronic heart condition, as this might impair our ability to collect appropriate data. The data collection and study adhered to the ethics procedures of the *Universiteit Gent* and participants gave informed consent.

The required sample size was calculated using G*Power [12]. Assuming an effect size of 0.23 and $\alpha = 0.05$, the statistical power is 81.5% and 28 participants are needed. We recruited 38 participants in the experiment, which for a sample size of 38 individuals and $\alpha = 0.05$ means that the statistical power is 87.2%.

2.3   Measurements

BART Score. The *BART score* is used as a measure of the participant's risk-taking behaviour. It is equal to the adjusted average number of pumps on unexploded balloons [13,14], with higher scores indicative of greater risk-taking propensity. Other measures which can be informative are the number of exploded balloons, and participants' profits for each balloon. The BART score, the number of pumps, exploded balloons, and profits are summed over the 30 trials [9].

Heart Rate Variability. We also collect physiological data, as a proxy for stress, measuring the inter-beat interval (IBI) using the Empatica E4 sensor. The E4 sensor comes as a wristband and was worn on the non-dominant hand. Participants were asked to refrain from moving that hand, so as not to generate spurious readings.

The heart rate variability (HRV) reveals variations between consecutive inter-beat intervals and is a good measure of emotional arousal. Other measures indicative of physiological components associated with emotional regulation, such as the Parasympathetic Nervous System (PNS) index, the Sympathetic Nervous System (SNS) index, and Stress (the square root of Baevsky's stress index [15]), can be calculated from the inter-beat interval data using the Kubios HRV software.

Heart rate variability is known to increase in response to parasympathetic nervous system (PNS) activity (vagal stimulation) and decrease with sympathetic nervous system (SNS) activity [16–18]. HRV is influenced by stress and current neurobiological evidence supports HRV as an objective measure of psychological health and stress. The high-frequency component of HRV is reduced when a subject is under stress or experiences emotional strain [19]. Earlier research indicated that HRV increases when subjects perceive prolonged tactile stimulation as pleasant [20]. Likewise in this study, we explore how the intensity of touch affect stress levels.

Self-reported Risk-Taking Propensity. Subjective self-reported risk-taking behaviour was measured by asking participants to rate a single question ("How do you see yourself? Are you generally a person who is fully prepared to take risks or do you try to avoid taking risk") on a 7-point scale, from 1 (not at all willing to take risks) to 7 (very willing to take risks).

Negative Attitudes Towards Robots. The Negative Attitude Toward Robots Scale (NARS) is a measure designed to gauge how individuals feel and behave when interacting with various types of robots. Three subscales make up the NARS: negative attitudes toward situations of interaction with robots, negative attitudes toward the social influence of robots, negative attitudes toward emotions in interaction with robots. There are 17 items total, and each is evaluated from 1 (strongly disagree) to 5 (strongly agree) [21,22].

2.4 Procedure

Four BART games, each with 30 trials, were played by each participant. Each participant experienced all four conditions –low-intensity touch, high-intensity touch, no-touch, no-robot– with the order of the conditions being randomly balanced across participants. The participants were instructed to wear the Empatica E4 sensor on their non-dominant hand, as identified by the experimenter during the completion of the informed consent form. Before the first BART task, participants completed a NARS questionnaire and self-reported risk-taking scale and were made to relax for at least 15 min to get a baseline for the IBI data recorded by E4 sensor. After each BART game, another IBI measurement is taken (at times T1, T2, T3, T4). The procedure illustrated in Fig. 2 shows one possible unfolding after T1. Upon finishing, participants were debriefed and asked for feedback. Participants took approximately 1 h and 10 min to complete the study.

2.5 Data Analysis

Data processing and analyses were done using Python and IBM SPSS V28 (IBM, Armonk, NY, USA), IBI data were analysed using Kubios HRV standard and then analyzed by SPSS. A one-way repeated measures ANOVA was used to compare data between conditions. A Shapiro-Wilk analysis (with $\alpha = 0.05$) was used to confirm the normality of distributions. Outliers were identified were removed if they were more than 5 standard deviations removed from the mean. Moreover, all data meet the Sphericity assumption according to Mauchly's Test of Sphericity (with $\alpha = 0.05$). The Mauchly's W and p value are reported in Table 2.

3 Experimental Results and Analysis

3.1 BART Performance

The performance on the BART task is reported using the *BART score*. Due to the low sample size ($N < 40$), a Shapiro-Wilk test was used to test for normality of the distribution of the results.

Based on this outcome, and after visual inspection of the histogram (frequencies for intervals of values of a metric variable) and the Normal Quantile-Quantile plot (which compares the observed experiment data quantiles with the quantiles

Table 1. Test of Normality for BART scores and heart rate variability.

Shapiro-Wilk	HI scores	LI scores	NT scores	NR scores
BART Scores	0.98, $p > 0.05$	0.95, $p > 0.05$	0.98, $p > 0.05$	0.97, $p > 0.05$
PNS index	0.95, $p > 0.05$	0.99, $p > 0.05$	0.97, $p > 0.05$	0.96, $p > 0.05$
SNS index	0.97, $p > 0.05$	0.97, $p > 0.05$	0.97, $p > 0.05$	0.98, $p > 0.05$
Stress index	0.89, $p > 0.05$	0.95, $p > 0.05$	0.90, $p > 0.05$	0.89, $p > 0.05$

that we would expect to see if the data were normally distributed) for BART scores in four conditions, a parametric test was used in this experiment. The results of the Shapiro-Wilk test and Mauchly's test are reported in Table 1 and Table 2 respectively.

A one-way repeated analysis of variance (ANOVA) indicates significant differences in BART scores between the four interaction conditions, $F(3, 38) = 4.70, p < 0.05$. Post hoc Tukey's HSD tests (with Bonferroni corrections) revealed that there are significant differences between the low-intensity touch condition and no-touch condition ($p = 0.019; p < 0.05$) and between the high-intensity touch and no robot touch conditions ($p = 0.007; p < 0.05$). See Fig. 3 and Table 3.

Table 2. Mauchly's Test of Sphericity for BART scores and heart rate variability.

Mauchly's W	BART Scores	PNS index	SNS index	Stress index
	0.78, $p > 0.05$	0.92, $p > 0.05$	0.83, $p > 0.05$	0.97, $p > 0.05$

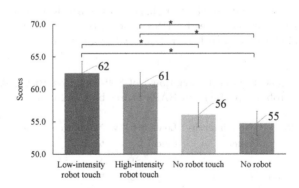

Fig. 3. BART scores per condition. Bars show the average scores for each condition, whiskers indicate standard error. (* $p < 0.05$).

3.2 Heart Rate Variability

As mentioned earlier, heart rate variability is a good measure to analyse stress levels and emotional arousal. However, HRV is often indirectly reported through other measures, such as the PNS, SNS and Stress index. When stressed, participants are expected to have lower PNS and higher SNS index values. From Fig. 4

and Table 3 we can see that in the low-intensity touch condition, the highest PNS index is obtained, which means the participants have the least stress in this condition. Participants have higher stress in high-intensity touch and no-touch interactions, according to the Stress index. The repeated ANOVA shows that the PNS index significantly differs between conditions $(F(3, 36) = 4.531, p < 0.05)$. Post hoc tests on the PNS index (with Bonferroni corrections) revealed that there are significant differences between the low-intensity and no-touch conditions, and between the low-intensity touch and high-intensity touch. The Stress index also shows a significant effect of condition $(F(3, 36) = 5.65, p < 0.05)$. Post-hoc tests (with Bonferroni corrections) revealed that there are significant differences between no touch, low-intensity touch and high-intensity touch. The above suggests that participants felt more pressure in HI and NT conditions whereas less pressure was experienced by them in LI condition.

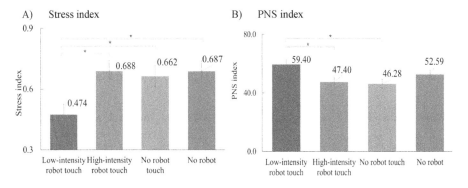

Fig. 4. The mean Stress (left) and PNS (right) indices across the four conditions. Lower values for Stress and higher values for PNS indicate the participant experiences less stress. Whiskers indicate standard error. ($*p < 0.05, **p < 0.01$).

Table 3. Means (and Standard Deviations) of Self-Reported Risk Taking, negative attitudes towards robots (NARS) and BART scores by Condition.

Variable	High-intensity touch		Low-intensity touch		No-touch touch		No-robot	
Metric	M	SD	M	SD	M	SD	M	SD
BART Scores	61	12	62	12	56	13	55	14
Stress index	0.69	0.35	0.47	0.3	0.66	0.34	0.69	0.32
PNS index	47.40	3.24	59.40	3.37	46.28	3.49	52.59	4.71
SNS index	−2.83	0.20	−3.09	0.11	−2.79	0.18	−3.01	0.19

3.3 Correlation Analysis

The correlation between self-reported risk-taking and BART scores is calculated using Pearson's r. There were significant positive correlations in all conditions

($p < 0.01$), which indicates that the participants' performance over four conditions is consistent. If they have higher BART scores in one condition, then higher BART scores are shown in other conditions. The correlation between total BART scores over the whole experiment and the self-reported risk taking scores is positive and significant ($r = 0.437, p < 0.01$), meaning that more risk-seeking people have higher BART scores.

The correlation between Negative Attitude Toward Robots Scale (NARS) and BART scores is shown in Table 4. There is a significant negative correlation between no-touch BART scores, and NARS scores ($p < 0.05$), which suggests that participants who have a negative attitude towards the robot take less risk. There is no significant correlation between no-robot BART scores and NARS scores, which makes sense as no robot was present to influence risk-taking behaviour. Remarkably this correlation is greater in conditions where participants have a tactile interaction with the robot as there is a greater negative correlation between BART scores and NARS scores ($p < 0.01$).

Table 4. Correlations between NARS scores and BART scores including the HI scores, LI scores and NT scores, NR scores, which means the BART score during HI, LI, NT and NR conditions respectively. * means the correlation is significant at $p < 0.05$, ** at $p < 0.01$.

Negative attitudes towards robots	HI scores	LI scores	NT scores	NR scores
	-0.49**, p<0.01	-0.64**, p<0.01	-0.34*, p<0.05	$-0.19, p > 0.05$

4 Discussion

Earlier research indicated that a verbal robot encourages participants to do more risk-taking behavior. [9], a result which we could not replicate in our study. However, our study extends earlier work by showing that tactile interaction with a robot increases risk-taking behaviour, but also reduces the stress felt during risk-taking: both the low-intensity and high-intensity tactile interaction promote risk-taking behavior. In contrast, non-tactile interaction with the robot has no significant influence on participants' risk-taking behavior.

When comparing the low-intensity and high-intensity tactile interaction, there are significant differences in experienced stress (as indicated by the PNS, SNS, and Stress index). Participants experience less stress in the low-intensity tactile interaction, and most stress when the robot is present but not being touched or when no robot is present. These results conclusively show that tactile interaction has a beneficial impact on stress and suggest that low-intensity tactile interaction might be preferred over high-intensity tactile interaction. Low-intensity touch seems to make people respond emotionally and reduces stress. A majority of participants (90%) mentioned that holding the robot on their lap in the HI condition felt somewhat like holding a baby and the robot –at 5.5 kg– felt rather heavy after a while. They felt a responsibility towards the robot, which might show in the stress measures. In the LI condition, participants indicated that they experienced the robot as encouraging and comforting.

As expected, self-report risk-taking scores are correlated with BART scores. Moreover, the Negative Attitude Towards Robot score (NARS) negatively correlated with the BART scores in the no-touch interaction, which means that the participants feel less peer pressure from the robot if they hold a more negative attitude towards robots. Moreover, during tactile interaction, the negative correlation is stronger than when the robot is not being touched or held, suggesting that tactile interaction softens any negative preconceptions towards robots.

Another, perhaps relevant, factor is that in the low-intensity condition the robot is standing on a table facing the participant and looking slightly down at the participant. In the high-intensity condition the robot is sitting on the lap and facing away from the participant. Eye gaze and size do matter in HRI [23] [24], so this might have an impact on the outcomes of social human-robot interaction, something which future studies would need to confirm.

In this study, we examined that human-robot tactile interaction could increase human risk-taking behaviour, and low-intensity tactile interaction could help humans decrease stress during risky occasions. On the one hand, our research alarms that robots might be causing potential threats by increasing risk-taking behaviour. On the other hand, there is the possibility of utilizing the human-robot tactile interaction in psychological treatment in hospitals for patients or preventing loneliness at home for those who live alone.

References

1. Lee, K.M., Jung, Y., Kim, J., Kim, S.R.: Are physically embodied social agents better than disembodied social agents?: The effects of physical embodiment, tactile interaction, and people's loneliness in human-robot interaction. Int. J. Hum. Comput. Stud. **64**(10), 962–973 (2006)
2. Campeau-Lecours, A., Otis, M., Belzile, P.-L., Gosselin, C.: A time-domain vibration observer and controller for physical human-robot interaction. Mechatronics **36**, 45–53 (2016)
3. Pervez, A., Ryu, J.: Safe physical human robot interaction-past, present and future. J. Mech. Sci. Technol. **22**(3), 469–483 (2008)
4. Levav, J., Argo, J.J.: Physical contact and financial risk taking. Psychol. Sci. **21**(6), 804–810 (2010)
5. von Mohr, M., Kirsch, L.P., Fotopoulou, A.: The soothing function of touch: affective touch reduces feelings of social exclusion. Sci. Rep. **7**(1), 1–9 (2017)
6. Geva, N., Uzefovsky, F., Levy-Tzedek, S.: Touching the social robot PARO reduces pain perception and salivary oxytocin levels. Sci. Rep. **10**(1), 1–15 (2020)
7. Gardner, M., Steinberg, L.: Peer influence on risk taking, risk preference, and risky decision making in adolescence and adulthood: an experimental study. Dev. Psychol. **41**(4), 625 (2005)
8. Gheorghiu, A., Delhomme, P., Felonneau, M.L.: Peer pressure and risk taking in young drivers' speeding behavior. Transp. Res. Part F Traffic Psychol. Behav. **35**, 101–111 (2015)

9. Hanoch, Y., Arvizzigno, F., García, D.H., Denham, S., Belpaeme, T., Gummerum, M.: The robot made me do it: human-robot interaction and risk-taking behavior. Cyberpsychol. Behav. Soc. Network. **24**(5), 337–342 (2021)

10. Vollmer, A.-L., Read, R., Trippas, D., Belpaeme, T.: Children conform, adults resist: a robot group induced peer pressure on normative social conformity. Sci. Rob. **3**(21), eaat7111 (2018)

11. Salomons, N., Van Der Linden, M., Sebo, S.S., Scassellati, B.: Humans conform to robots: disambiguating trust, truth, and conformity. In: 2018 13th ACM/IEEE International Conference on Human-Robot Interaction (HRI), pp. 187–195. IEEE (2018)

12. Bartlett, M.E., Edmunds, C.E.R., Belpaeme, T., Thill, S.: Have I got the power? Analysing and reporting statistical power in HRI. ACM Trans. Hum. Rob. Interact. (THRI) **11**(2), 1–16 (2022)

13. Bornovalova, M.A., Daughters, S.B., Hernandez, G.D., Richards, J.B., Lejuez, C.W.: Differences in impulsivity and risk-taking propensity between primary users of crack cocaine and primary users of heroin in a residential substance-use program. Exp. Clin. Psychopharmacol. **13**(4), 311 (2005)

14. Lejuez, C.W.: Evaluation of a behavioral measure of risk taking: the balloon analogue risk task (BART). J. Exp. Psychol. Appl. **8**(2), 75 (2002)

15. Baevsky, R., Berseneva, A.P.: Methodical recommendations use Kardivar system for determination of the stress level and estimation of the body standards of measurements and physiological interpretation (2008)

16. Berntson, G.G., et al.: Heart rate variability: origins, methods, and interpretive caveats. Psychophysiology **34**(6), 623–648 (1997)

17. John Camm, A., et al.: Heart rate variability. Standards of measurement, physiological interpretation, and clinical use. Eur. Heart J. **17**, 354–381 (1996)

18. Rajendra Acharya, U., Paul Joseph, K., Kannathal, N., Lim, C.M., Suri, J.S.: Heart rate variability: a review. Med. Biol. Eng. Comput. **44**(12), 1031–1051 (2006)

19. Kim, H.-G., Cheon, E.-J., Bai, D.-S., Lee, Y.H., Koo, B.-H.: Stress and heart rate variability: a meta-analysis and review of the literature. Psychiatry Investig. **15**(3), 235 (2018)

20. Triscoli, C., Croy, I., Steudte-Schmiedgen, S., Olausson, H., Sailer, U.: Heart rate variability is enhanced by long-lasting pleasant touch at CT-optimized velocity. Biol. Psychol. **128**, 71–81 (2017)

21. Nomura, T., Suzuki, T., Kanda, T., Kato, K.: Measurement of negative attitudes toward robots. Interact. Stud. **7**(3), 437–454 (2006)

22. Tsui, K.M., Desai, M., Yanco, H.A., Cramer, H., Kemper, N.: Using the "negative attitude toward robots scale" with telepresence robots. In: Proceedings of the 10th Performance Metrics for Intelligent Systems Workshop, pp. 243–250 (2010)

23. Kompatsiari, K., Tikhanoff, V., Ciardo, F., Metta, G., Wykowska, A.: The importance of mutual gaze in human-robot interaction. In: International Conference on Social Robotics, pp. 443–452. Springer, Cham (2017). https://doi.org/10.1007/978-3-319-70022-9_44

24. Admoni, H., Scassellati, B.: Social eye gaze in human-robot interaction: a review. J. Hum. Rob. Interact. **6**(1), 25–63 (2017)

Affect Display Recognition Through Tactile and Visual Stimuli in a Social Robot

Sara Marques-Villarroya$^{(\boxtimes)}$ (ID), Juan Jose Gamboa-Montero (ID),
Cristina Jumela-Yedra, Jose Carlos Castillo (ID), and Miguel Angel Salichs (ID)

University Carlos III, Madrid, Spain
{smarques,jgamboa,jocastil,salichs}@ing.uc3m.es

Abstract. New technologies are nowadays an important part of human communication and interaction. While text, facial, and voice recognition have become increasingly fluid in recent years, thanks to the development of machine learning algorithms, recognising and expressing sensations or moods via multimodal recognition is a field that the literature could further explore. This situation introduces a new challenge to social robots. In this work, the authors study how a combination of visual and tactile stimuli influences people's perceptions of affect display and seeks to apply these findings to a social robot. In the experiments, the subjects had to determine the perceived valence and arousal of simultaneously being exposed to the two stimuli mentioned above. The analysis revealed that the combination of touch and facial expression significantly influences the valence and arousal perceived by users. Based on these findings, this work includes an application for the robot to determine the user's *affect display* in real-time.

Keywords: Social robotics · Multimodal interaction · Affect display recognition · Affective touch · Facial expression

1 Introducción

The way humans communicate has changed in recent years with the emergence of new technologies. As a result, there is a need to enhance the interactions between humans and these technologies. Recognising and expressing emotions by analysing the perceived stimuli constitutes another step toward achieving a natural interaction. As Beale and Peter studied, emotions are produced in interpersonal relationships after the first few interactions, implying that it is a gradual process that takes time [3]. As a result, when discussing devices with which the user will interact, the ability to perceive emotions is an added value because it may generate a sense of trust. This feature becomes essential when discussing personal assistance or education applications. In this sense, social robots stand out among those devices with educational or assistive care functions.

According to Henschel et al. [10], *"a social robot must be able to interact bidirectionally, display thoughts and feelings, be socially aware of its surroundings, provide*

F. Cavallo et al. (Eds.): ICSR 2022, LNAI 13817, pp. 130–140, 2022.
https://doi.org/10.1007/978-3-031-24667-8_12

social support and demonstrate autonomy". With these considerations in mind, to make a robot *socially aware of its surroundings* and thus *interact bidirectionally*, it appears necessary to equip such devices with the ability to recognise the user's *affect display*: the expression of the user's internal emotional estate[1]. Based on this drive to improve social robots, the main goal of this work is to study how a combination of visual and tactile stimuli influences people's perceptions of affect display and how to apply these findings to a social robot. Specifically, we propose an application that recognises the perceived user's affect display.

With respect to the works in the literature focused on recognising human reactions to stimuli, Diekhoff et al. [6] examined how certain images with fearful facial expressions created a bias in participants that altered their perception of emotion recognition in neutral faces. Vasconcelos et al. [19] investigated the accuracy with which experimentees recognised vocal emotions from nonverbal human vocalisations. Regarding tactile stimuli, it is worth mentioning the study by Tsalamlal et al. [18] in which the authors evaluated the influence of a haptic stimulus on visual stimuli. To do so, participants indicated the valence level suggested by various facial expressions. At the same time, a stream of air was applied with varying degrees of intensity to their left arm. The authors concluded that the tactile stimuli significantly influenced the experimentees' valence perception.

When considering how to capture the user's affect display during human-robot interaction, we discover that much of the literature focuses on visual and auditory stimuli. Huang et al. [11], for example, attempted to recognise emotions during human-computer interaction by combining facial detection with an analysis of the user's electroencephalographs. Similarly, Breazeal et al. [4] investigated the recognition of a user's affective communicative intent without focusing on the prosodic patterns of the speech. Finally, despite being scarce, research such as that of Yohanan [20], Altun [1], Andreasson [2] or Teysser [17] validate the relevance of tactile stimuli analysis when analysing the user's affect display using a social robot.

The remainder of the paper is structured as follows: The methodology used to obtain the data used in this study is shown in Sect. 2, and the results are presented and discussed in Sect. 3. Section 4 describes the integration of an affect display recognition application in a robotic platform using the data gathered in the previous sections. Finally, Sect. 5 highlights and discusses the main findings of this work.

2 Experimental Study

To endow a social robot with the ability to respond to the user's affect display, we must first understand how people perceive those same stimuli. In a typical interaction environment, stimuli tend to appear grouped rather than individually. As a result, evaluating just a stimulus alone could lead to inaccurate results. Based

---

[1] In this work, we will use the definition of affect display introduced by Yohanan et al. [20]. We must clarify that the authors acknowledge that this expression could be faked, but these nuances are out of the scope of the paper.

on this premise, a study was planned to collect and analyse the valence and arousal perceived by users when exposed to the target stimuli simultaneously. The visual ones were presented through the appearance of different images on a screen, while the experimenter provided tactile stimuli to make it appear as natural as possible. The users then input their perception of the valence and arousal level produced by these two stimuli into a graphical user interface specifically designed to automate the data gathering and ease the subsequent analysis.

2.1 Conditions and Stimuli Studied

We define seven kinds of touch stimuli in this study based on their duration, intensity, and form. We chose them following the ideas from the article by Silvera et al. [16], which condenses Yohanan's [20] gestures into the six most essential touches during HRI. To adapt this list to the social robot (see Sect. 4.1), we removed the 'push' gesture because it is irrelevant when interacting with our desktop robot, and 'pat' for being almost imperceptible using the touch gesture detector introduced in the same section. We also added three more types of contacts considered interesting in HRI: 'tickle' and 'rub' frequently appear in everyday interactions, such as those with a pet. We also added 'hit' despite its negative connotation since we expected it to have more extreme valence and arousal values, which could help to have a more diverse set of gestures. Table 1 summarises the set of touch gestures used in the experiment along with comprehensive definitions.

Table 1. Definitions of the touch gestures used for this experiment.

Gesture	Definition
Stroke	Move your hand with gentle pressure
Rub	Move the hand repeatedly with firm pressure
Tickle	Touch with light finger movements
Scratch	Rub with the fingernails
Tap	Strike the with a quick light blow or blows using one or more fingers
Slap	Quickly and sharply strike with an open hand
Hit	Deliver a blow with either a closed fist or the side or back of your hand

Regarding facial expressions, we will use Paul Ekman's six basic emotions [7] for the simple expressions, also adding a 'neutral' one. The following expressions with their abbreviations were used in this study: angry (AN), afraid (AF), disgusted (DI), sad (SAD), neutral (NE), surprised (SU), and happy (HAP). In this experiment, we used images from the Karolinska Directed Emotional Faces (KDEF) database [5] Combining the sets of touch and facial stimuli, we obtained a total of 49 unique combinations. To eliminate bias, we created five cases, each made up of 20 randomly chosen touch and face combinations. Each users was presented one of these cases, trying to ensure balance among cases instances for our dataset.

2.2   Experimental Setup

The study on affect display included 50 subjects, 29 of them were male and 34 were under 30 years old. None of the participants had any prior knowledge of the experimental procedure, user interface, or any of the images shown during the study. Participants were exposed to the two types of stimuli at the same time: A picture of a person's face with a specific facial expression appeared on the application screen (see Fig. 1), and, simultaneously, the experimenter performed a touch gesture on the user's left arm. The experimenter was behind an opaque screen, and their arm was covered with a surgical glove and a long sleeve to prevent the subject from guessing their age or gender.

As Fig. 1 shows, the results of valence and arousal levels are plotted on the X and Y axes, representing Russell's circumplex [13]. Both levels have a range of −100 to 100. The −100 scale represents the most unpleasant in terms of valence and the most relaxing in terms of arousal, whereas 100 represents a very pleasant and high arousal level. To modify the values of valence and arousal, the interface included two sliders attach to each axis, which the user could move freely. After that, the user pressed the "OK" button to continue to the next pair of stimuli. The experiment lasted five to seven minutes on average, with 20 image and touch combinations performed in each case.

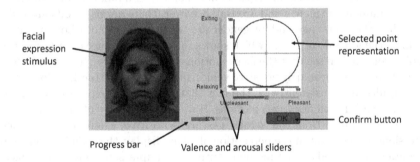

Fig. 1. Graphic interface designed for the experiment.

3   Analysis of Results

The goal of the general analysis of the results from the tests performed on the 50 users is to find a relationship between tactile and visual stimuli and the levels of valence and arousal. First, we ensured that all data had a normal distribution using the Shapiro-Wilk method [15]. Then, we performed an ANOVA analysis , which allowed to compare the differences between the means of the different groups. In our case, by performing an ANOVA on the influence of the combination of touch and expression on the value of valence and arousal, we discovered that the combination of the two stimuli had a significant impact ($p < 0.05$) on the affect display perceived by the user (both in valence and arousal). Similarly, we investigated whether the interaction of the stimuli's combination with the

Table 2. Results obtained with the multivariate ANOVA study.

Interaction group	Variable	p-value
Stumuli combination	Valence	**1,8896E-84**
	Arousal	**6,6621E-19**
Stimuli * age	Valence	0,442862
	Arousal	0,399626
Stimuli * gender	Valence	0,496526
	Arousal	0,942287
Stimuli * age * gender	Valence	0,539040
	Arousal	0,489812

participants' age (under/over 30 years old) and/or gender influenced their perception of the stimuli. The ANOVA on this interaction produced non-significant results ($p > 0.05$). Table 2 shows the outcomes of the ANOVA study.

With these findings, we obtained the means for each combination of stimuli, yielding the results depicted in Fig. 2. These graphs show the mean valence (left graph) and arousal (right graph) obtained for each gesture and facial expression combination. The ANOVA analysis shows that the combination of stimuli significantly influences valence and arousal; however, there are no significant differences when the users' age and/or gender are taken into account. Looking at the results on the left side of Fig. 2, which shows the average valence obtained in each combination, we can see that the face emotions 'afraid', 'angry', 'disgusted', 'neutral' and 'sad' have primarily negative values, outweighing the tactile information. These results are consistent with the fact that these facial expressions are commonly associated with negative emotions. However, in the case of the 'afraid' face, the valence obtained from the 'stroke' gesture is positive. Therefore, while facial expressions are relevant in the perception of affect display, they can be affected by the contact performed at that moment, turning an unpleasant feeling into a pleasant one. The same effect can be seen with the 'happy' expression, which aids in perceiving all gestures as pleasant. We can see, however, that the more abrupt gestures, such as 'hits', achieve a lower level of valence than the rest of the touches studied. In the case of the 'surprised' facial expression, we can see diverse outcomes. Because the level of valence of 'surprised' emotion in Russell's circumflex is low, it can be considered as pleasant or unpleasant expression depending on the user. In this case, where the facial expression is unimportant, we can see how the touch gestures significantly modulate the valence, ranging between 26 and −25.

Complementarily, on the right side of Fig. 2, we can see how the arousal results in more uneven values for each facial expression. For this reason, we decided to group the results by the kind of touch gesture instead to try to find some patterns, which resulted in Fig. 3. The figure shows that looking at the touch gestures, the results are more aligned, implying that for the arousal variable, the type of gesture is more significant than the facial expression, in contrast to the data obtained with the valence. In this case, we can see that the 'tap', 'scratch', 'slap', and 'hit'

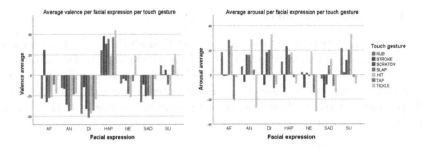

Fig. 2. Average values of valence (left) and arousal (right) gathered in the experiment. The horizontal axis shows the facial expressions afraid (AF), angry (AN), disgusted (DI), happy (HAP), neutral (NE), sad (SAD) and surprised (SU).

gestures are primarily positive, whereas the 'stroke', 'rub', and 'tickle' gestures are mainly negative. These outcomes are linked to the definitions of each of the gestures. While 'tap', 'scratch', 'slap', and 'hit' are gestures that involve applying pressure to the user's arm, where the intensity is brief but intense, 'stroke', 'rub', and 'tickle' imply a soft gesture on the user with less pressure, resulting in a negative arousal value. In this analysis, we also noticed that, as with valence, the visual stimuli have some influences on the user's perception. In the case of 'tap', for example, we see that arousal drops to negative values in the presence of 'sad' facial expressions, just as it does with 'scratch'. Finally, we created the *affect_display* database with all the valence and arousal results, which the robot will use to estimate the user's affect display.

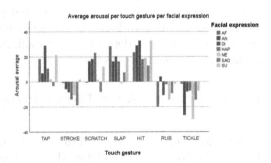

Fig. 3. Average arousal values (y-axis) as a function of touch gesture (x-axis) and facial expression (color).

4   Integration in a Social Robot

This section describes an application that allows the robot to recognise and respond to various communicative intentions expressed by the user. This application was created using the results presented in Sect. 3. The current section contains a brief description of the robotic platform, the designed application, and some preliminary results.

4.1 The Robotic Platform

The Mini robot, developed by the UC3M RoboticsLab [14], was originally conceived to perform cognitive stimulation and companionship tasks with elderly people. The robot integrates a series of social skills, such as playing different games, storytelling, and making jokes. It can interact with the user by proactively proposing activities based on user preferences, learning from their tastes, and adapting to them.

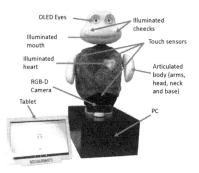

Fig. 4. The social robot mini.

The Mini robot has OLED screens in its eyes that allow it to look in different directions and express emotions. It also has LED lighting on the cheeks, mouth, and heart to make it more expressive. Mini has five motors that allow it to move its arms, head, neck, and base (see Fig. 4). It has piezoelectric microphones and capacitive sensors on its arms and belly to detect tactile stimuli. As for perceiving visual stimuli, it has an RGB-D camera on its base.

4.2 Design of an Application for Affect Display Recognition and Reaction

Figure 5 shows the application flowchart developed to recognise the users' affect display and react accordingly. For stimuli detection, the robot uses, on the one hand, the detector developed by Gamboa et al. [8] for touch gesture detection and, on the other hand, for facial expression recognition, the *emotions-recognition-retail-0003*[2] detector, based on the neural network developed by Intel. When the robot detects both stimuli, it attempts to recognise the user's affect display by loading the data from the *affect_display* database.

---

[2] Emotion recognition network: https://docs.openvinotoolkit.org/latest/_models_intel_ emotions_recognition_retail_0003_description_emotions_recognition_retail_0003.html.

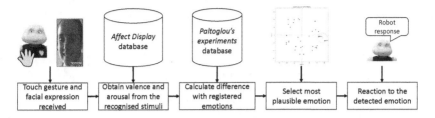

Fig. 5. Flow diagram representing the affect display recognition skill we propose in this work.

We decided to derive the 2-dimensional coordinates (valence and arousal) of the 35 emotions described in Russell's circumplex [13] from the works of Gobron et al. [9] and Paltoglou et al. [12]. Then, we calculate the Euclidean distance between the current valence and arousal values and those obtained in Paltoglou's experiments. Furthermore, we broaden the search area by leveraging detector uncertainty. Based on the results, we adjust the valence search range based on the confidence of the facial expression detector. The confidence of the touch detector, on the other hand, is used to rescale the arousal axis. Figure 6 depicts an example of the detector output when attempting to recognise the user's affect display with a tactile gesture slap' and a facial expression 'sad' with 75% and 90% confidence, respectively. In black, we see the 35 possible emotions from Paltoglou's experiment, and in yellow, the point obtained from our experiments with the perceived stimulus combination. The red dot represents the closest affect display, and therefore the one selected by the robot. The green dot represents the user's potential affect displays. Finally, the green ellipse represents the robot's search area. We use the distance between the yellow point and the closest emotion as the initial radius, and the ellipse's angle corresponds to the angle between the yellow and green dots. Then, we added the detectors' uncertainty, with a weighted Y-axis from the touch detector confidence and an X-axis from the vision detector confidence. Because the touch detector's confidence is lower in the example, the Y-axis is longer than the X-axis.

Finally, the robot will select the perceived emotion and react to it verbally. To filter possible errors of the detector, the robot notifies the user if there are more than five possible emotions within the search ellipse, which is more than 15% of options from which it can select. In this case, the robot informs the user that it does not know the emotion the user is conveying. We recorded a video[3] to demonstrate the social robot recognising the affect display of the user.

---

[3] Working example video: https://youtu.be/jrv8bY0ssUI.

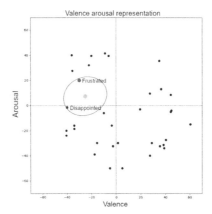

Fig. 6. Outcome of one of the searches conducted during the robot tests as a result of a combination of a 'slap' and a 'sad' face (yellow dot). The selected emotion is "frustrated" (red point) is 'dissapointed' (green dot). (Color figure online)

5   Conclusions

This paper studies how a combination of visual and tactile stimuli influences people's perceptions of affect display and seeks to apply these findings to a social robot. In this case, we experimented with 50 users to determine the perceived valence and arousal when simultaneously exposed to a combination of seven touch gestures and seven facial expressions. The data analysis revealed that the combination of touch and facial expression significantly affects the valence and arousal perceived by users ($p < 0.05$). Specifically, the analysis showed that facial expression had more influence over the perceived valence, while the touch gesture had more impact on the arousal. Based on these results, we developed an application for the robot to determine the user's affect display at any given time.

In future research, the number of users will be increased to conduct a more generalised study, emphasising the cultural differences between subjects. In addition, we plan to incorporate a machine learning system based on a regressor to predict the affect display more robustly, thus avoiding to rely on the mean values to make the estimation.

Acknowledgements. The research leading to these results has received funding from the projects: Robots Sociales para Estimulación Física, Cognitiva y Afectiva de Mayores (ROSES), RTI2018-096338-B-I00, funded by the Ministerio de Ciencia, Innovación y Universidades; Robots sociales para mitigar la soledad y el aislamiento en mayores (SOROLI), PID2021-123941OA-I00, funded by Agencia Estatal de Investigación (AEI), Spanish Ministerio de Ciencia e Innovación; the project PLEC2021-007819, funded by MCIN/AEI/10.13039/501100011033 and by the European Union NextGenerationEU/PRTR, and RoboCity2030-DIH-CM, Madrid Robotics Digital Innovation

Hub, S2018/NMT-4331, funded by "Programas de Actividades I+D en la Comunidad de Madrid" and cofunded by the European Social Funds (FSE) of the EU.

References

1. Altun, K., MacLean, K.E.: Recognizing affect in human touch of a robot. Pattern Recogn. Lett. **66**, 31–40 (2015)
2. Andreasson, R., Alenljung, B., Billing, E., Lowe, R.: Affective touch in human-robot interaction: conveying emotion to the nao robot. Int. J. Soc. Robot. **10**(4), 473–491 (2018)
3. Beale, R., Peter, C.: The role of affect and emotion in HCI. In: Peter, C., Beale, R. (eds.) Affect and Emotion in Human-Computer Interaction. LNCS, vol. 4868, pp. 1–11. Springer, Heidelberg (2008). https://doi.org/10.1007/978-3-540-85099-1_1
4. Breazeal, C., Aryananda, L.: Recognition of affective communicative intent in robot-directed speech. Auton. Robot. **12**(1), 83–104 (2002)
5. Calvo, M.G., Lundqvist, D.: Facial expressions of emotion (kdef): Identification under different display-duration conditions. Behav. Res. Methods **40**(1), 109–115 (2008)
6. Diekhof, E.K., Kipshagen, H.E., Falkai, P., Dechent, P., Baudewig, J., Gruber, O.: The power of imagination-how anticipatory mental imagery alters perceptual processing of fearful facial expressions. Neuroimage **54**(2), 1703–1714 (2011)
7. Ekman, P.: Basic emotions. Handbook Cogn. Emotion **98**(45–60), 16 (1999)
8. Gamboa-Montero, J.J., Alonso-Martin, F., Castillo, J.C., Malfaz, M., Salichs, M.A.: Detecting, locating and recognising human touches in social robots with contact microphones. Eng. Appl. Artif. Intell. **92**, 103670 (2020)
9. Gobron, S., Ahn, J., Paltoglou, G., Thelwall, M., Thalmann, D.: From sentence to emotion: a real-time three-dimensional graphics metaphor of emotions extracted from text. Vis. Comput. **26**(6), 505–519 (2010)
10. Henschel, A., Laban, G., Cross, E.S.: What makes a robot social? a review of social robots from science fiction to a home or hospital near you. Current Robot. Reports **2**(1), 9–19 (2021)
11. Huang, Y., Yang, J., Liu, S., Pan, J.: Combining facial expressions and electroencephalography to enhance emotion recognition. Future Internet **11**(5), 105 (2019)
12. Paltoglou, G., Thelwall, M.: Seeing stars of valence and arousal in blog posts. IEEE Trans. Affect. Comput. **4**(1), 116–123 (2012)
13. Russell, J.A.: A circumplex model of affect. J. Pers. Soc. Psychol. **39**(6), 1161 (1980)
14. Salichs, M.A., et al.: Mini: a new social robot for the elderly. Int. J. Soc. Robot. **12**(6), 1231–1249 (2020)
15. Shapiro, S.S., Wilk, M.B.: An analysis of variance test for normality (complete samples). Biometrika **52**(3–4), 591–611 (1965)
16. Silvera-Tawil, D., Rye, D., Velonaki, M.: Interpretation of social touch on an artificial arm covered with an eit-based sensitive skin. Int. J. Soc. Robot. **6**(4), 489–505 (2014)
17. Teyssier, M., Bailly, G., Pelachaud, C., Lecolinet, E.: Conveying emotions through device-initiated touch. IEEE Trans. Affect. Comput. **13**, 1477–1488 (2020)
18. Tsalamlal, M.Y., Amorim, M.A., Martin, J.C., Ammi, M.: Combining facial expression and touch for perceiving emotional valence. IEEE Trans. Affect. Comput. **9**(4), 437–449 (2016)

19. Vasconcelos, M., Dias, M., Soares, A.P., Pinheiro, A.P.: What is the melody of that voice? probing unbiased recognition accuracy with the montreal affective voices. J. Nonverbal Behav. **41**(3), 239–267 (2017)
20. Yohanan, S., MacLean, K.E.: The role of affective touch in human-robot interaction: Human intent and expectations in touching the haptic creature. Int. J. Soc. Robot. **4**(2), 163–180 (2012)

Social Robot Perception and Control Capabilities

Path-Constrained Admittance Control of Human-Robot Interaction for Upper Limb Rehabilitation

Dario Onfiani$^{(\boxtimes)}$ ⓘ, Marco Caramaschi ⓘ, Luigi Biagiotti ⓘ, and Fabio Pini ⓘ

Università di Modena e Reggio Emilia, Modena, Italy
{dario.onfiani,marco.caramaschi,luigi.biagiotti,fabio.pini}@unimore.it

Abstract. In this paper, the problem of robotic rehabilitation of upper limbs is addressed by focusing attention on the control of a standard collaborative robot for those training activities that can be performed with the aid of an end-effector type system. In particular, a novel admittance control, that constrains the motion of the robot along a prescribed path without imposing a specific time law along it, has been devised. The proposed approach exploits the features of the arc-length parameterization of a generic curve to obtain a simple control formulation able to guide the patient in both a passive or an active way, with the possibility of supporting the execution of the task with an additional force or opposing the motion with a braking force. Being the method independent from the particular curve considered for the constraint specification, it allows an intuitive definition of the task to be performed via Programming by Demonstration. Experimental results show the effectiveness of the proposed approach.

Keywords: Admittance control · Guidance virtual fixtures · Human-robot interaction · Rehabilitation

1 Introduction

In recent years, the use of robotic devices in post-operative rehabilitation has become more and more common due to the benefits which these solutions can bring. Those devices may be collect into two main categories called end-effector and exoskeletons devices [1]. The solutions falling in the latter category allow performing the rehabilitation exercises with a extremely high repeatability because they focus on control each single joint of the limb. As example of exoskeleton devices can be referred to ARMIN [2], Rupert [3] and NESM [4]. The main drawbacks of these devices are their very complex structure, which is hard to be designed in order to work properly, and the remote possibility to adapt the same device to the execution of different exercises. On the other hand, this paper proposes a solution based on the use of collaborative manipulator robots

This work has been partially supported by University of Modena and Reggio Emilia with the FARD-2022 Project.

(cobots) [5], which belongs to the first category, like the following works: MIT-MANUS [6], GENTLE/S [7], REHAROB [8], PUParm [9] and EULRR [10]. The most notable advantages of the end-effector solutions are the capability of freely define the path of the exercise providing many different solutions that the therapist can choose by using the same device; the possibility of increasing the effort required during rehabilitation and, consequently, adapting the exercises to the progress achieved [11]. The interaction between the cobot and the patient can greatly enhance the effectiveness of the therapeutic action [12,13]. Moreover, in occupational therapy contexts, the robots manipulator can be used to guide the patient's limb along predefined paths reproducing some specific activities of daily living (ADL) [14,15].

The great flexibility offered by the robotic solution can be fully exploited only with a suitable control architecture for regulating the physical interaction between the human and the robot. This kind of control is generally based on impedance control which is one of the most common solutions implemented to guide the patient during the execution of the task. The impedance control sets the behavior of the robot which must be compliant along the trajectory imposed by the therapist and rigid in the directions outside it [16–18].

This solution allows a reduction of the patient's spatial degrees of freedom relative to the path described by the exercise, which the therapist can define without any restrictions as long as it is within the robot workspace. To simplify the programming phase of the robot, so that it can be done by a non-expert of robotics, the definition of the path that the patient will be bound to travel is realized by Learning by Demonstration (LbD) [19,20]. According to this paradigm, the therapist will guide the end-effector of the robot in order to record the path of the exercise that the patient will undergo. Then, the recorded trajectory is encoded in some way, e.g. with B-spline functions or Dynamic Movement Primitives (DMP) [21] in order to have a compact, smooth representation of the motion to be performed by the user.

In this paper, a simple end-effector type robotic rehabilitation system is considered with a proper mechanical interface that links the human's limb to the robot, and the attention is focused on the design of a control architecture, which allows the exploitation of all the features of a general-purpose manipulator. Tools for rehabilitation are generally classified on the basis of the type of assistance they can provide [15], ranging from passive to active devices according to the fact that they can provide only resistant forces or can also apply active forces to the patient. With a robotic device, it is possible to modulate the resistance felt by the user along the path of the rehabilitation exercise, but it is also possible to implement an assist-as-needed (AAN) [10] mechanism, that can help the patient in completing the exercises. The main limitation of these approaches are the definition of the distance between the reference and the desire position which can brings to the imposition of geometrical constraints on the reference path [22] or an not unique definition of the nearest point that belongs to it [23]. As referred in [24], the most common drawback of the DMP solution in planning motion is the time dependency. To overcome this problem, which is also present [25] and faced by developing a DMP to encode the human motions and imposing a maximum time T_F to execute the path on the basis of patient motor impediment. Finally, in this article, we obtain a parametric representation of the curve, on which a virtual mass is constrained, that moves along it reacting to the external force applied by the patient to the end-effector of the robot. In this way, a direct dependence between time and position along the reference is avoided. By developing this solution, the overall system behaves like a passive mechanical tool, whose behavior can be easily programmed by the therapist. Furthermore, this approach easily allows the introduction of a force that can be used to help, or hinder, the patient during the execution of the exercise.

2   Control Architecture

To reproduce with a general-purpose robotic manipulator the behavior of standard tools for rehabilitation, which are generally based on simple passive mechanical solutions, it is necessary to constrain its motion so that the end-effector can move only along a pre-determined path. A general framework has been devised, in which the robot reproduces the behavior of a point mass connected to a reference path so the system will allow only motions along this path. Accordingly, the position p^*, described as the reference path defined by the therapist set to be followed by the mass m, is defined by

$$p^* = \varphi(u) \tag{1}$$

where $\varphi(\cdot)$ is a parametric curve that depends on the scalar variable u. In many applications, u is time, but not in this case where the way in which the path is tracked is not depending on a specific motion law but results from the force applied by the user. Function $\varphi(\cdot)$ is a B-spline curve defined, in accordance with the LBD approach, by interpolation of the points registered when the therapist executes it on the robot to program the exercise.

The kinetic energy of the mass is

$$K = \frac{1}{2}m\|\dot{p}^*\|^2 = \frac{1}{2}m \left\| \frac{d\varphi(u)}{du} \right\|^2 \dot{u}^2$$

while we assume that the mass is not affected by gravity and therefore its potential energy is null. Among all the possible parameterizations, the arc-length parameterization, usually denoted with the letter s, is considered. In this way,

$$\left\| \frac{d\varphi(s)}{ds} \right\| = 1$$

and, therefore, the kinetic energy of the mass becomes

$$K = \frac{1}{2}m\dot{s}^2.$$

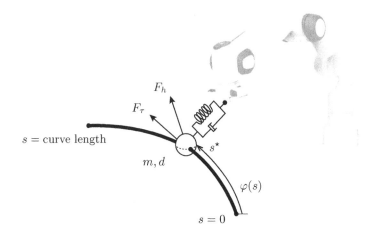

Fig. 1. Constrained dynamics of a point mass over a generic path $\varphi(s)$.

Accordingly, by applying the standard procedure based on Lagrangian equations it is possible to find that the dynamic model of the constrained mass subject to friction is

$$m\ddot{s} + d\dot{s} = F_\tau \qquad (2)$$

where d is the damping coefficient and F_τ is the magnitude of the tangential force to the curve, see Fig. 1. Note that F_τ is obtained by projecting the force $\boldsymbol{F}_h$ applied by the user to the robot tool (and detected by a force sensor) along the tangent direction to the curve at the current mass position $s^\star$, i.e.

$$\boldsymbol{F}_\tau = \left.\frac{d\varphi(s)}{ds}\right|_{s=s^\star} \cdot \boldsymbol{F}_h \qquad (3)$$

The other components of the force $\boldsymbol{F}_h$, that do not contribute to accelerate the mass, are compensated by the constraints.

By considering a position-based admittance control [17] scheme the constrained motion of the robot interacting with the human user can be finally implemented, as reported in Fig. 2. The robot manipulator is controlled in position with a high-gain control loop which guarantees good tracking performance. The human user interacts with the robot, trying to drive the end-effector towards the desired position $\boldsymbol{p}^\star$ according to the path imposed by the therapist. The force $\boldsymbol{F}_h$ provided by the user is applied to the virtual mass, whose dynamics is described by (2) and (3). The position of the mass $\boldsymbol{p}^\star$ in the robot workspace is finally deduced by means of (1) and used as a set-point for the position control loop.

Since the controller is developed into the workspace of the robot, the only kinematic transformation needed is the direct one which converts the current joint position $\boldsymbol{\theta}$ into the corresponding workspace position $\boldsymbol{p}$.

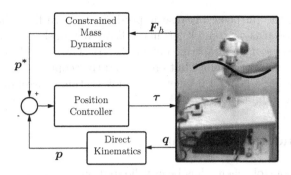

Fig. 2. Admittance control scheme over a prescribed path of a robot manipulator interacting with a human user.

The proposed control scheme is particularly attractive for two reasons: on one side it is a quite simple method, also from a computational point of view, that can be easily implemented on any position-controlled robot manipulator, on the other hand, is sufficiently flexible and general for any type of rehabilitation procedure since it is based on a generic function $\varphi(\cdot)$, with no restrictions on its characteristics, e.g. on its maximum curvature. Note that this scheme can be considered a special case of band-type controller, which establishes the boundaries of a virtual channel where the human limb motion is enforced to lie by forces acting in the normal direction [10, 26].

In this case, according to the proposed approach, the motion of the human limb must not follow any specific time-dependent trajectory [27] or track a given reference velocity profile [28, 29] but is the result of the interaction between the user and the robot/virtual mass. Accordingly, the duration of the motion can be a useful parameter for estimating the subjects' functional ability.

Interestingly enough, the control scheme above described does not include any mechanism for the assistance of the user during the therapy, nor mechanisms that cause resistive force for training purposes. However, it is possible to easily integrate such mechanisms by acting on the dynamics of virtual mass, for instance by adding a constant force F along the tangent direction of the path:

$$m\ddot{s} + d\dot{s} = F_\tau + F \tag{4}$$

If the force F is positive the user will experience an assistance force field, which will make the movement easier. Conversely, a negative force F will oppose the motion. Furthermore, it is possible to implement a so-called Assist-As-Needed (AAN) controller by modulating the force F. In this case, it is necessary to define a reference motion law $s_{ref}(t)$ for the virtual mass along the given path so that the control provides an assistance force as the tracking error grows. A simple virtual spring with stiffness k, i.e.

$$F = k(s_{ref}(t) - s^*),$$

is sufficient for the purpose, because it produces a force field that drives the mass position towards $s_{ref}(t)$. Other methods are obviously possible, based e.g. on neural networks or on adaptive control [30,31]. They modify the AAN level according to the subject's ability but are beyond the scope of this paper which is focused on building a general framework for interaction control of collaborative robots used in rehabilitation.

3   Experimental Validation

The proposed control scheme has been validated on a real cobot, in particular, through the execution of a planar path with the collaborative robot Franka Emika Panda.

The position control system has been designed according to a proportional-derivative approach with a gravity compensation computed into the Cartesian space coordinates [32]. However, it is worth noticing that any other control approach that assures a good tracking of the reference signal could be used in the proposed scheme.

Consider the dynamic model of a robot manipulator:

$$M(q)\ddot{q} + C(q,\dot{q})\dot{q} + g(q) = \tau + \tau_h \tag{5}$$

where $q \in \mathbb{R}^n$ is the vector of joint angles, $n = 7$, $M(q)$ is the inertia matrix, $C(q,\dot{q})$ is the vector of Coriolis/centrifugal torques, $g(q)$ is the vector of gravitational torques, τ are the control torques, $J(q)$ is the robot Jacobian, and $\tau_h = J^T(q)F_h$ are the joint torques resulting from force F_h applied to the end-effector by the human.

The Cartesian position controller has been designed in the form

$$\tau = \hat{g}(q) + J_A{}^T(q)(K_P\,\tilde{p} + K_D\,\dot{\tilde{p}}) \tag{6}$$

where $\hat{g}(q)$ is an approximation of the actual gravitational torque function $g(q)$ and $\tilde{p} = p^* - p$ is the difference between the reference position p^* and the actual position p of the end-effector. The matrices K_P and K_D are positive definite to ensure the system stability. In the tests executed on the robot, these diagonals matrix are assumed as follow: $K_P = \mathrm{diag}([300, 300, 300, 50, 50, 50])$ and $K_D = 2\sqrt{\mathrm{diag}([300, 300, 300, 50, 50, 50])}$. Because of the good knowledge of the manipulator's parameters, the proposed controller (5)-(6) guarantees that the tracking error goes asymptotically to zero, so the end-effector position can be easily changed consistent with reference position obtained as an output of the virtual dynamic model.

The geometric path that the user must follow is shown in Fig. 3. It is a simple curve obtained by a Learning by Demonstration approach, where the data are collected by manually guiding the end-effector of the robot and, subsequently, interpolated by using a cubic B-Spline [33]. Note that this type of path has no particular influence on the rehabilitative applications but is a generic example

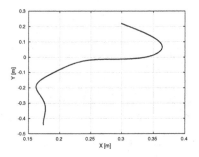

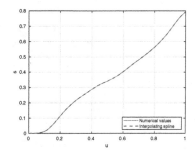

Fig. 3. Geometric path $\varphi(u)$ defining the desired motion for rehabilitation.

Fig. 4. Relationship between the original parameterization of the curve $\varphi(u)$ and the arc-length s.

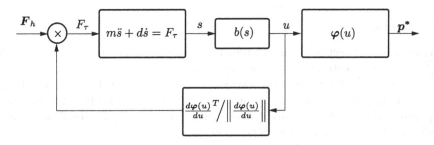

Fig. 5. Admittance control scheme over a prescribed path of a robot manipulator interacting with a human user.

of the parametric curve $\varphi(u)$. Being a continuous function, also the derivative $d\varphi(u)/du$ is well-defined.

However, the independent variable u is not the arc-length, as assumed in the previous section. Therefore, it is necessary to make a composition between the functions $\varphi(u)$ and $u(s)$, to obtain a description that depends on the arc-length s. The function $u(s)$ can be obtained by inverting

$$s(u) = \int_{u_0}^{u} \left\| \frac{d\varphi(\tau)}{d\tau} \right\| d\tau$$

Note that $s(u)$ can be easily computed numerically and then interpolated e.g. with a spline. In the example proposed, the function shown in Fig. 4 has been obtained and the numerical values have been directly interpolated to obtain the function $u = b(s)$, where $b(\cdot)$ denotes an interpolating cubic spline. The scheme for the simulation of the constrained mass has been implemented as shown in Fig. 5.

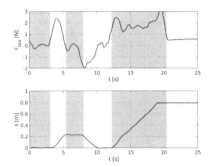

Fig. 6. Relationship between the arc-length parameter and tangent component of the force applied by the user F_τ .

3.1   Results

As mentioned in Sect. 2, the user interacts with a virtual mass ($m = 5$ kg, $d = 15$ kg/s) which is constrained to the curve $\varphi(u)$.

In order to validate the effectiveness of the system developed, it has been tested on an anthropomorphic robot arm (i.e. the Franka Emika Panda) in an experimental scenario of rehabilitation therapy. The Franka Emika Panda is a 7 DoFs robotic arm equipped with position and torque sensors.

In the first phase of the test, the robotic arm has been used in a passive mode in order to guide its end-effector along the reference path of the exercise. In this preliminary operation, the via-points of the path are collected and the reference B-spline curve is obtained. To validate the developed control, three different scenarios have been tested: a free motion along the curve, the same motion with an assistive force, and with a braking force.

In the first modality, the only force involved is the one applied by the patient, which produces a motion of the virtual mass and therefore of the robot along the curve. As shown in Fig. 6, the value of s varies according to the forces exchanged when the patient interacts with the cobot. In fact, the value of s increases when positive values of F_τ are applied and, conversely, decreases when they are negative. It's important to notice that the arc-length value, and consequently the position along the path, doesn't change if no forces are applied to the end-effector. After that, two solutions that involve active forces have been tested, according to (4), by applying a virtual external force directly to the virtual mass. These solutions have been tested with a constant force of $F = 1N$ applied in the two different directions in order to help, or hinder, the patient in the execution of the exercise. The first scenario simulates a rehabilitation task in the early stages of the therapy where the patient can barely move the limb, so the virtual force works as an assisting force. Subsequently, the opposite stage of the rehabilitation process is tested. In this test, the patient is considered at the end of the therapy and the therapist has to estimate the degree of recovery of the patient. Therefore the virtual force, instead of helping the patient in the execution of the exercise, hinders the patient during the process. As shown in

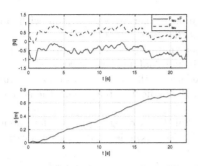 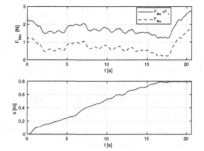

Fig. 7. Assisted solution for the early stages of the rehabilitation process.

Fig. 8. Hindering solution for the last stages of the rehabilitation process.

the following figures, there is a comparison between the force that the patient should apply in a standard passive task and the force which is actually needed in order to impose the same motion along the path. The virtual force is named F_a when helps the patient, otherwise, we refer to it with F_r Figs. 7 and 8.

4 Conclusions

In this work, a control architecture has been proposed in order to control an end-effector type robotic system for upper limbs rehabilitation. The controller developed allows using a standard collaborative robot as a passive mechanical tool that guides the patient in order to correctly follow a path defined by the therapist for the specific exercise. The proposed solution adopts a simple Learning by Demonstration procedure to easily program the robot even by a non-expert in robotics, such as a therapist. The solution adopted, based on a B-spline interpolation method, allows the definition of the geometric path to be used as a reference for the admittance control. The proposed control system forces the user on the proposed path while enabling free motion along it, but does not impose an explicit timing law on the patient in the execution of the exercise. In fact, the evolution of the position of the end-effector along the path is only a function of the forces applied during the human-robot interaction. This solution can be easily adapted to modify the behavior of the system according to the patient's needs, e.g. by adding a virtual force that helps or hinder the user's action. This control architecture has only been tested by healthy users to validate its operation. However, as a future work, the effectiveness of the proposed solution will have to be more fully verified by defining an experimental protocol based on a greater number of subjects, performance indicators and a comparative validation with other methods.

References

1. Gassert, R., Dietz, V.: Rehabilitation robots for the treatment of sensorimotor deficits: a neurophysiological perspective. J. Neuroeng. Rehab. (2018)

2. Nef, T., Guidali, M., Riener, R.: Armin iii-arm therapy exoskeleton with an ergonomic shoulder actuation. Appli. Bionics Biomech. (2009)
3. Sugar, T.G., et al.: Design and control of rupert: a device for robotic upper extremity repetitive therapy. IEEE Trans. Neural Syst. Rehabilit. Eng. (2007)
4. Crea, S., et al.: A novel shoulder-elbow exoskeleton with series elastic actuators. In: 2016 6th IEEE International Conference on Biomedical Robotics and Biomechatronics (BioRob). IEEE (2016)
5. Caramaschi, M., Onfiani, D., Biagiotti, L., Pini, F.: A design approach for cobot assisted rehabilitation. In: UX4V Rehab 2022 User Experience Design for Virtual Rehabilitation (2022)
6. Krebs, H., Volpe, B.: Rehabilitation robotics. Handbook Clinical Neurol. (2013)
7. Loureiro, R., Amirabdollahian, F., Topping, M., Driessen, B., Harwin, W.: Upper limb robot mediated stroke therapy-gentle/s approach. Auton. Robots (2003)
8. Toth, A., Nyitrai, D., Jurak, M., Merksz, I., Fazekas, G., Denes, Z.: Safe robot therapy: Adaptation and usability test of a three-position enabling device for use in robot mediated physical therapy of stroke, In: 2009 IEEE International Conference on Rehabilitation Robotics. IEEE (2009)
9. Bertomeu-Motos, A., Blanco, A., Badesa, F.J., Barios, J.A., Zollo, L., Garcia-Aracil, N.: Human arm joints reconstruction algorithm in rehabilitation therapies assisted by end-effector robotic devices. J. Neuroeng. Rehabil. (2018)
10. Zhang, L., Guo, S., Sun, Q.: Development and assist-as-needed control of an end-effector upper limb rehabilitation robot. Appli. Sci. (2020)
11. Qian, Z., Bi, Z.: Recent development of rehabilitation robots. Adv. Mech. Eng. (2015)
12. Bertani, R., Melegari, C., De Cola, M.C., Bramanti, A., Bramanti, P., Calabrò, R.S.: Effects of robot-assisted upper limb rehabilitation in stroke patients: a systematic review with meta-analysis. Neurol. Sci. (2017)
13. Milot, M.-H., et al.: A crossover pilot study evaluating the functional outcomes of two different types of robotic movement training in chronic stroke survivors using the arm exoskeleton bones. J. Neuroeng. Rehab. (2013)
14. Mehrholz, J., Hädrich, A., Platz, T., Kugler, J., Pohl, M.: Electromechanical and robot-assisted arm training for improving generic activities of daily living, arm function, and arm muscle strength after stroke. Cochrane Database Syst. Rev. (2012)
15. Maciejasz, P., Eschweiler, J., Gerlach-Hahn, K., Jansen-Troy, A., Leonhardt, S.: A survey on robotic devices for upper limb rehabilitation. J. NeuroEng. Rehab. (2014)
16. Ficuciello, F., Romano, A., Villani, L., Siciliano, B.: Cartesian impedance control of redundant manipulators for human-robot co-manipulation. In: IEEE/RSJ International Conference on Intelligent Robots and Systems (2014)
17. Keemink, A.Q., van der Kooij, H., Stienen, A.H.: Admittance control for physical human-robot interaction. Int. J. Robot. Res. (2018)
18. Hogan, N.: Impedance control: An approach to manipulation: Part ii-implementation. J. Dynam. Syst. Measurem. Control (1985)
19. Lauretti, C., Cordella, F., Guglielmelli, E., Zollo, L.: Learning by demonstration for planning activities of daily living in rehabilitation and assistive robotics. IEEE Robot. Autom. Lett. (2017)
20. Aleotti, J., Caselli, S.: Robust trajectory learning and approximation for robot programming by demonstration. Robot. Autonom. Syst. (2006)

21. Ijspeert, A.J., Nakanishi, J., Hoffmann, H., Pastor, P., Schaal, S.: Dynamical movement primitives: learning attractor models for motor behaviors. Neural Comput. (2013)
22. Zhang, L., Guo, S., Sun, Q.: An assist-as-needed controller for passive, assistant, active, and resistive robot-aided rehabilitation training of the upper extremity. Appli. Sci. (2020)
23. Asl, H.J., Yamashita, M., Narikiyo, T., Kawanishi, M.: Field-based assist-as-needed control schemes for rehabilitation robots. IEEE/ASME Trans. Mechatr. (2020)
24. Saveriano, M., Abu-Dakka, F.J., Kramberger, A., Peternel, L.: Dynamic movement primitives in robotics: A tutorial survey arXiv preprint arXiv:2102.03861 (2021)
25. Tamantini, C.: Patient-tailored adaptive control for robot-aided orthopaedic rehabilitation. In: International Conference on Robotics and Automation (ICRA). IEEE (2022)
26. Lin, C.-H., Su, Y.-Y., Lai, Y.-H., Lan, C.-C.: A spatial-motion assist-as-needed controller for the passive, active, and resistive robot-aided rehabilitation of the wrist. IEEE Access (2020)
27. Zhang, J., Cheah, C.C.: Passivity and stability of human-robot interaction control for upper-limb rehabilitation robots. IEEE Trans. Robot. (2015)
28. Asl, H.J., Narikiyo, T., Kawanishi, M.: An assist-as-needed velocity field control scheme for rehabilitation robots. In: 2018 IEEE/RSJ International Conference on Intelligent Robots and Systems (IROS). IEEE (2018)
29. Najafi, M., Rossa, C., Adams, K., Tavakoli, M.: Using potential field function with a velocity field controller to learn and reproduce the therapist's assistance in robot-assisted rehabilitation. IEEE/ASME Trans. Mechatr. (2020)
30. Wolbrecht, E.T., Chan, V., Reinkensmeyer, D.J., Bobrow, J.E.: Optimizing compliant, model-based robotic assistance to promote neurorehabilitation. IEEE Trans. Neural Syst. Rehabilit. Eng.(2008)
31. Mounis, S.Y.A., Azlan, N.Z., Sado, F.: Assist-as-needed control strategy for upper-limb rehabilitation based on subject's functional ability. Measurem. Control (2019)
32. Siciliano, B., Sciavicco, L., Villani, L., Oriolo, G.: Modellistica. Pianificazione E Controllo, The Mcgraw-Hill (2008)
33. Biagiotti, L., Melchiorri, C.: Trajectory Planning for Automatic Machines and Robots, 1st edn. Springer, Heidelberg (2008). https://doi.org/10.1007/978-3-540-85629-0

Causal Discovery of Dynamic Models for Predicting Human Spatial Interactions

Luca Castri[1(✉)], Sariah Mghames[1], Marc Hanheide[1], and Nicola Bellotto[1,2]

[1] University of Lincoln, Lincoln, UK
{lcastri,smghames,mhanheide}@lincoln.ac.uk
[2] University of Padua, Padua, Italy
nbellotto@dei.unipd.it

Abstract. Exploiting robots for activities in human-shared environments, whether warehouses, shopping centres or hospitals, calls for such robots to understand the underlying physical interactions between nearby agents and objects. In particular, modelling cause-and-effect relations between the latter can help to predict unobserved human behaviours and anticipate the outcome of specific robot interventions. In this paper, we propose an application of causal discovery methods to model human-robot spatial interactions, trying to understand human behaviours from real-world sensor data in two possible scenarios: humans interacting with the environment, and humans interacting with obstacles. New methods and practical solutions are discussed to exploit, for the first time, a state-of-the-art causal discovery algorithm in some challenging human environments, with potential application in many service robotics scenarios. To demonstrate the utility of the causal models obtained from real-world datasets, we present a comparison between causal and non-causal prediction approaches. Our results show that the causal model correctly captures the underlying interactions of the considered scenarios and improves its prediction accuracy.

Keywords: Causal discovery · Human spatial interaction · Prediction

1 Introduction

The increased use of robots in numerous sectors, such as industrial, agriculture and healthcare, represents a turning point for their progress and growth. However, it requires also new approaches to study and design effective human-robot interactions. A robot, sharing the working area with humans, must accomplish its task taking into account that its actions may lead to unpredicted responses by the individuals around it. Knowing the cause-effect relationships in the environment will allow the robot to reason on its own actions, which is a crucial step towards effective human-robot interactions and collaborations.

This work has received funding from the European Union's Horizon 2020 research and innovation programme under grant agreement No 101017274 (DARKO).

F. Cavallo et al. (Eds.): ICSR 2022, LNAI 13817, pp. 154–164, 2022.
https://doi.org/10.1007/978-3-031-24667-8_14

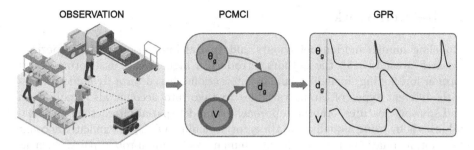

Fig. 1. Causal prediction approach: a robot reconstructing a causal model from observation of human behaviours in a warehouse environment. The causal model is then used for human spatial behaviour prediction.

Causal inference, which includes causal discovery and reasoning, appears in the literature of different fields, including robotics [2,4,6,12,13]. However, most of the work on human-human and human-robot spatial interactions, i.e. the 2D relative motion of two interacting agents [3,7,11] did not previously exploit any formal causal analysis. Most mobile robots do not know how humans will behave and react as a consequence of their proximity and actions. Knowing the causal model of the interactions between different agents could help predict human motion behaviours, and consequently assist a robot planner in choosing the most effectively navigation strategy. For instance, a robot in a warehouse environment (e.g. see Fig. 1), passing very close to a human, needs to know how the human would react to this situation in order to choose the most appropriate behaviour (e.g. "I can continue since the human will remain still" or "it is better to stay still and wait for the human to go away"). More generally, discovering the causal model will enable the robot to assess future interventions (e.g. "what happens if I go this way?") and counterfactual situations (e.g. "what would have happened if I remained still instead of moving?").

In this paper, we demonstrate that by using a suitable causal discovery algorithm, a robot can estimate the causal model of the nearby human motion behaviours by observing their trajectories and spatial interactions. In particular, our main contributions are the following:

- first application of a causal discovery method to real-world sensor data for modeling human and robot motion behaviours, with a focus on 2D spatial interactions;
- new causal models to represent and predict humans-goal, human-human and human-robot spatial interactions, in single and multi-agent scenarios;
- experimental evaluation of the causal models on two challenging datasets to predict spatial interactions in human environments.

The paper is structured as follows: basic concepts about causal discovery and its applications are presented in Sect. 2; Sect. 3 explains the details of our approach; the application of our approach in real-world scenarios is described in Sect. 4, including also comparison between the experimental results; finally, we conclude this paper in Sect. 5 discussing achievements and future applications.

2   Related Work

Modeling human motion behaviours and spatial interactions is an important research area. In [15], the authors introduce a high level causal formalism of motion forecasting, including human interactions, based on a dynamic process with different types of latent variables to take into account also unobserved and spurious features. Another approach to model spatial interactions in social robotics is by using a qualitative trajectory calculus (QTC) to explicitly account for motion relations between human-human and human-robot pairs, such as relative distance, direction, and velocity [3,7,11]. In this case though, the causal links between spatial relations were never taken into account. Our current work is inspired by the same QTC relations, extended to include other factors (e.g. collisions) and represented in quantitative rather than qualitative terms.

Among possible causal representations, Structural Causal Models (SCMs) and Directed Acyclic Graphs (DAGs) are the most popular ones [16]. The latter consist of nodes and oriented edges to represent, respectively, variables and causal dependencies between them (see Fig. 1). Several methods have been recently developed to derive causal models from observational data, a process termed *causal discovery*. They can be categorised into two main classes [10]: constraint-based methods, such as Peter & Clark (PC) algorithm and Fast Causal Inference (FCI), and score-based methods, such as Greedy Equivalence Search (GES). Recently, reinforcement learning-based methods have also been used to discover causal models [9,23]. However, many of these algorithms work only with static data (i.e. no temporal information), which is a limitation in many robotics applications. In fact, methods for time-dependent causal discovery are necessary to deal with time-series of sensor data. To this end, a variation of the PC algorithm, called PCMCI [18], was proposed to efficiently reconstruct causal graphs from high-dimensional time-series datasets, which is based on a false positive rate optimisation and a momentary conditional independence (MCI) test.

PCMCI applications can be found in climate and healthcare sectors [19,20]. Other key concepts of causal inference extended to the machine learning domain can also be found in [21,22]. In robotics, recent works include a method to build and learn a SCM through a mix of observation and self-supervised trials for tool affordance with a humanoid robot [4]. Another application includes the use of PCMCI to derive the causal model of an underwater robot trying to reach a target position [6]. Other causal approaches can also be found in the area of robot imitation learning [2,13].

To our knowledge though, none of the above applications have explored causal discovery to understand human-human and human-robot spatial interactions. Our goal indeed is for the robot to recover cause-and-effect in human motion behaviours when they collaborate and share the same environment. To this end, we will derive some useful causal models of spatial interactions in particular scenarios and use them to predict the occurrence of future ones.

3   Causal Discovery from Observational Data

Our approach is based on the observation of human spatial behaviours to recover the underlying SCM. This causal analysis is performed by using the PCMCI causal discovery Algorithm [18]. First, we identify some important factors (i.e. variables) affecting human motion in the considered scenarios, and from that we reconstruct the most likely causal links from real sensor data. Finally, we use the discovered causal models to forecast the latter with a state-of-the-art Gaussian Process Regression (GPR) technique [14], showing that the causality-based GPR improves the accuracy of the human (interaction) prediction compared to a non-causal version. Two different scenarios have been modelled and analysed.

3.1   Human-Goal Scenario

Our first scenario includes interactions between human and (static) goals in a warehouse-like environment, illustrated in Fig. 2 (centre), where the agent walks among different positions (grey squares) to move some boxes or grab/use some tools. The grey line connecting agent and goal specifies the angle θ_g between the two. Upon expert judgment, the following features were deemed essential to explain the human motion behaviour: *(i)* angle agent-goal θ_g; *(ii)* euclidean distance agent-goal d_g; *(iii)* agent velocity v. The angle θ_g represents the human intention to reach a desired position (the person will first point towards the desired target before reaching it); then the person walks towards the goal, reducing the distance from it, at first by increasing the walking speed and finally decreasing, when close to the destination. Soon after the human has reached the goal, θ_g changes to the next one, and the process restarts. What we expect from this scenario are therefore the following causal relations:

(a) θ_g depends on the distance, when the latter decreases to zero then θ_g changes;
(b) d_g is inversely related to v and depends on θ_g;
(c) v is a direct function of the distance d_g.

3.2   Human-Moving Obstacles Scenario

The second scenario involves multiple agents. It reproduces the interaction between a selected human and nearby dynamic obstacles (e.g. other humans,

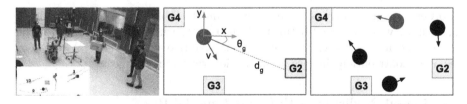

Fig. 2. Image from THÖR dataset [17] (left). Representation of the two analysed scenarios: (centre) the human-goal scenario, (right) the human-moving obstacles scenario. The agents consist of a circle and an arrow specifying, respectively, the current position and orientation. The selected agent is red, while, the obstacles are black. (Color figure online)

mobile robot), as shown in Fig. 2 (right). In this case, we take into account human reactions to possible collisions with obstacles, modelled by a *risk* factor. Consequently, the relevant features in this scenario are *(i)* euclidean distance d_g · of the selected agent-goal, *(ii)* agent's velocity v, and *(iii) risk* value. The agent moves between goals in the environment, so the cause-effect relation between distance and velocity will be similar to the previous scenario. The main difference in this case is that, instead of reaching the goal without problems, the agent needs to consider the presence of other obstacles, and the interactions with them will affect the resulting behaviour. In particular, the agent's velocity is affected by possible collisions (e.g. sudden stop or direction change to avoid an obstacle). Hence, the expected causal links in this scenario are the following ones:

(a) d_g depends inversely on v;
(b) v is a direct function of the d_g, but it is also affected by the collision *risk*;
(c) *risk* depends on the velocity, as explained below.

Obstacle detection and risk evaluation: in the literature, there are several strategies for identifying obstacles and evaluating the risk of collision with them. In order to model a numerical *risk* value as a function of the agent's interactions, we implemented a popular strategy named Velocity Obstacles (VO) [8]. The VO technique identifies an unsafe sub-set of velocities for the selected agent that would lead to a collision with a moving or static obstacle, assuming the latter maintains a constant velocity.

The risk can then be defined as follows. At each time step, we apply the VO to the agent's closest obstacle. Such risk is a function of two parameters, both depending on the selected agent's velocity (i.e. point P inside the VO; see Fig. 3):

– d_{OP}, the distance between the cone's origin O and P, which is proportional to the time available for the selected agent A to avoid the collision with B;
– d_{BP}, the distance between P and the closest cone's boundary, which indicates the steering effort required by A to avoid the collision with B.

Consequently, the risk of collision is defined as follows:

$$risk = e^{d_{OP}+d_{BP}+v_a}. \tag{1}$$

In order to avoid mostly-constant values (undetectable by the causal discovery algorithm), we introduced a third parameter v_a, which is the velocity of the selected agent. Therefore, the risk depends mainly on the agent's velocity, plus the VO's contributions in case of interaction with another agent.

3.3   Causal Prediction with PCMCI and GPR

Our approach for modeling and predicting spatial interactions, shown in Fig. 1, can be decomposed in three main steps: (i) extract the necessary time-series of sensor data from the two previously explained scenarios; (ii) use them for the

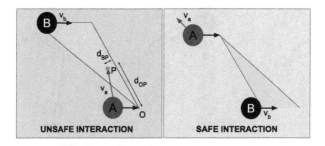

Fig. 3. Velocity Obstacle (VO) technique. A Collision Cone (CC) is built from the selected agent A to the enlarged encumbrance of the obstacle B. Then, the CC is translated by v_b to identify the VO, which partitions the velocity space of A into *avoiding* and *colliding* regions, i.e. velocities lying outside and inside the VO, respectively. (Left) an interaction leading to a collision. (Right) a collision-free interaction.

causal discovery performed by the PCMCI algorithm; (*iii*) finally, embed the causal models in a GPR-based prediction system. More in detail, PCMCI is a causal discovery algorithm [18] which consists of two main parts, both exploiting conditional independence tests (e.g. partial correlation, Gaussian processes and distance correlation) to measure the causal strength between variables. The first part is the well-known PC algorithm, which starts from a fully connected graph and outputs an initial causal model structure; the latter is then used by the second part, the MCI test, which validates the structure by estimating the test statistics values and p-values for all the links and outputs the final causal model. After that, we exploit the GPR, a nonparametric kernel-based probabilistic model [14], to build a causal GPR predictor, useful to forecast each variable by using only its parents, and not all the variables involved in the scenario, as a non-causal GPR predictor would do.

4   Experiments

We evaluated our approach for causal modeling and prediction of human spatial behaviours on two challenging datasets: THÖR [17] and ATC Pedestrian Tracking [5]. Both contains data of people moving in indoor environments, a workshop/warehouse and a shopping center, respectively. Our strategy is first to extract the necessary time-series from the two datasets, as explained in Sect. 3, and then use it for causal discovery. In order to prove the usefulness of the causal models, a comparison between causal and a non-causal predictions is finally shown. We considered two different datasets in order to verify, for the first scenario in Sect. 3.1, that the discovered causal model holds for similar human behaviours, even when observed in different environments. The scenario in Sect. 3.2, instead, is used to demonstrate that it is possible to perform causal discovery for other types of human spatial interactions (i.e. with collision avoidance).

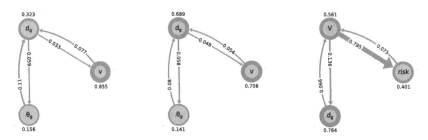

Fig. 4. Causal models of: human-goal scenario with (left) THÖR and (centre) ATC datasets, human-moving obstacles scenario with (right) THÖR dataset. The thickness of the arrows and of the nodes' border represents, respectively, the strength of the cross and auto-causal dependency, specified by the number on each node/link (the stronger the dependency, the thicker the line). All the relations correspond to a 1-step lag time.

4.1 Data Processing

From both datasets, we extracted the x-y positions of each agent and derived all the necessary quantities from them (i.e. orientation θ, velocity v, etc.).

THÖR dataset: this provides a wide variety of interactions between humans, robot, and static objects (Fig. 2, left). Helmets and infrared cameras were used to track the motion of the agents at 100 Hz. We used this dataset to analyse both scenarios (Sects. 3.1 - 3.2). Moreover, to reduce the computational cost of causal discovery on this dataset, due to the high sampling rate, we subsampled the dataset using an entropy-based adaptive-sampling strategy [1], with an additional variable size windowing approach to reduce the number of samples.

ATC pedestrian tracking dataset: in this case, the data was collected in the large atrium of a shopping mall (much bigger than THÖR's environment). Several 3D range sensors were used to track people at 30 Hz. Due to its large area and crowd, this dataset was not suitable for the collision-enhanced scenario in Sect. 3.2. Indeed, the large distance between humans and goals made the VO and the risk analysis difficult to estimate. Therefore, we used this dataset only for the scenario in Sect. 3.1, assuming that the interactions and collision avoidance between humans could be captured by the model's noise variance.

4.2 Results

We report the causal models discovered by PCMCI for the two scenarios. The latter were obtained using the same conditional independence test based on Gaussian Process regression and Distance Correlation (GPDC) [19]. We used also a 1-step lag time, that is, variables at time t could only be affected by those at time $t - 1$. The resulting causal models are shown in Fig. 4, where the thickness of the arrows and of the nodes' border represents, respectively, the strength of the cross and auto-causal dependency, specified by the number on each node/link (the stronger the dependency, the thicker the line).

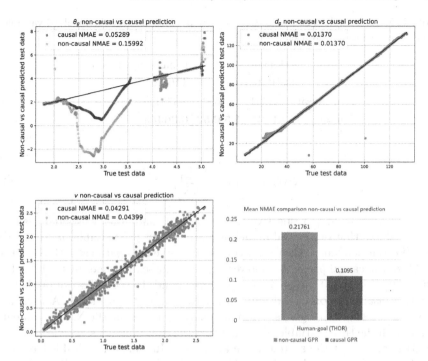

Fig. 5. Comparison between non-causal and causal GPR prediction and NMAE in the human-goal scenario of the THÖR dataset for the spatial interaction variables θ_g (top-left), d_g (top-right), and v (bottom-left). A bar chart (bottom-right) summarises the comparison using the mean NMAE over all three variables.

In particular, Fig. 4 shows the causal models of the human-goal (left and centre) and the human-moving obstacles scenarios (right). All the three graphs agree with the expected models discussed in Sect. 3.1 and Sect. 3.2. This confirms that the same causal structure in the first two graphs generalises to similar human behaviours in different datasets, although causal strengths vary between them due to different sampling frequencies and noise levels. The third graph proves that it is possible to get different causal models for different human behaviours.

The obtained causal models are then exploited for the prediction of the spatial interaction variables in both scenarios. For example, in case of the human-goal scenario using the THÖR dataset, the prediction of θ_g was done using only its parents θ_g and d_g in the respective causal model (Fig. 4, left). To evaluate the advantage of using our models, we benchmarked the prediction performance with a causally-informed GPR estimator against a non-causal one, where the latter considers all the variables possibly influencing each other. Figure 5 shows the comparison between causal and non-causal prediction for the human-goal scenario with the THÖR dataset, using as evaluation metric the *Normalised Mean Absolute Error* (NMAE), which is not too sensitive to possible outliers. This is defined as follows:

Table 1. Mean NMAE of causal and non-causal predictions over the involved variables for both scenarios and datasets.

	Human-goal		Human-moving obs
	THÖR	ATC	THÖR
Non-causal	0.21761	1.61692	0.37849
Causal	**0.1095**	**1.54552**	**0.36453**

$$NMAE(y, \hat{y}) = \frac{\sum_{i=1}^{n} \frac{|y_i - \hat{y_i}|}{n}}{\frac{1}{n}\sum_{i=1}^{n} y_i} \tag{2}$$

where y and $\hat{y}$ are, respectively, the actual and the predicted values. Figure 5 shows that our causal model helps to predict the variables θ_g (top-left) and v (bottom-left) more accurately compared to the non-causal case. Indeed, the NMAE of the causal predictor is lower than the non-causal one. Instead, for the variable d_g (top-right) the predictors set corresponds to the full set of predictors in both causal and non-causal approaches, leading to the same NMAE results. Finally, Fig. 5 (bottom-right) shows a bar chart summarising the NMAE comparison over all the three variables, showing that the causal model's knowledge helps the GPR to predict the system more accurately. In conclusion, Table 1 reports the above-explained analysis for all the considered scenarios, highlighting that the causal GPR approach improves always the prediction accuracy compared to the non-causal one. Note that, for the human-goal scenario, the mean NMAE in the ATC dataset is bigger than in THÖR, which is probably due to the different time-series lengths in the two datasets.

5   Conclusion

In this work, we proposed a causal discovery approach to model and predict Human Spatial Interactions. We used two public datasets (THÖR and ATC) to extract time-series of human motion behaviours in two possible scenarios for causal analysis. We show that the discovery algorithm can capture the expected causal relations from the datasets. We used the obtained causal models to predict the values of some key spatial interaction variables, and benchmarked them against the results of a non-causal prediction approach. The comparison highlights the contribution and the advantage of integrating such causal models in the prediction framework. Future work will be devoted to automatically learn the most important features for modelling human-human and human-robot spatial interactions, focusing in particular on on-board robot sensor data. We will also perform causal reasoning on both observational and interventional data, exploiting the influence that the robot's presence can have on nearby people, with a special interest for applications in industrial and intralogistics settings.

References

1. Aldana-Bobadilla, E., Alfaro-Pérez, C.: Finding the optimal sample based on shannon's entropy and genetic algorithms. In: Sidorov, G., Galicia-Haro, S.N. (eds.) MICAI 2015. LNCS (LNAI), vol. 9413, pp. 353–363. Springer, Cham (2015). https://doi.org/10.1007/978-3-319-27060-9_29
2. Angelov, D., Hristov, Y., Ramamoorthy, S.: Using causal analysis to learn specifications from task demonstrations. In: Procedings of the International Joint Conference on Autonomous Agents and Multiagent Systems, AAMAS (2019)
3. Bellotto, N., Hanheide, M., Van de Weghe, N.: Qualitative design and implementation of human-robot spatial interactions. In: Herrmann, G., Pearson, M.J., Lenz, A., Bremner, P., Spiers, A., Leonards, U. (eds.) ICSR 2013. LNCS (LNAI), vol. 8239, pp. 331–340. Springer, Cham (2013). https://doi.org/10.1007/978-3-319-02675-6_33
4. Brawer, J., Qin, M., Scassellati, B.: A causal approach to tool affordance learning. In: IEEE/RSJ International Conference on Intelligent Robots & Systems (IROS), pp. 8394–8399 (2020)
5. Brščić, D., Kanda, T., Ikeda, T., Miyashita, T.: Person tracking in large public spaces using 3-d range sensors. IEEE Trans. on Hum. Mach. Syst. 522–534 (2013)
6. Cao, Y., Li, B., Li, Q., Stokes, A., Ingram, D., Kiprakis, A.: Reasoning Operational Decisions for Robots via Time Series Causal Inference. In: 2021 IEEE International Conference on Robotics and Automation (ICRA), pp. 6124–6131 (2021)
7. Dondrup, C., Bellotto, N., Hanheide, M.: A probabilistic model of human-robot spatial interaction using a qualitative trajectory calculus. In: 2014 AAAI Spring Symposium Series (2014)
8. Fiorini, P., Shiller, Z.: Motion planning in dynamic environments using velocity obstacles. Int. J. Robotics Res. (1998)
9. Gasse, M., Grasset, D., Gaudron, G., Oudeyer, P.: Causal reinforcement learning using observational and interventional data. CoRR (2021)
10. Glymour, C., Zhang, K., Spirtes, P.: Review of causal discovery methods based on graphical models. Front. Genet. (2019)
11. Hanheide, M., Peters, A., Bellotto, N.: Analysis of human-robot spatial behaviour applying a qualitative trajectory calculus. In: 2012 IEEE RO-MAN: The 21st IEEE International Symposium on Robot and Human Interactive Communication, pp. 689–694 (2012)
12. Hellström, T.: The relevance of causation in robotics: A review, categorization, and analysis. Paladyn, J. Behav. Robot. 238–255 (2021)
13. Katz, G., Huang, D.W., Hauge, T., Gentili, R., Reggia, J.: A novel parsimonious cause-effect reasoning algorithm for robot imitation and plan recognition. IEEE Trans. Cogn. Developm. Syst. (2018)
14. Li, Q., Zhang, Z., You, Y., Mu, Y., Feng, C.: Data driven models for human motion prediction in human-robot collaboration. IEEE Access, 227690–227702 (2020)
15. Liu, Y., Cadei, R., Schweizer, J., Bahmani, S., Alahi, A.: Towards robust and adaptive motion forecasting: A causal representation perspective. In: Proceedings of the IEEE/CVF Conference on Computer Vision and Pattern Recognition (CVPR), pp. 17081–17092 (2022)
16. Pearl, J.: Causal Inference in Statistics : A Primer. Wiley (2016)
17. Rudenko, A., Kucner, T.P., Swaminathan, C.S., Chadalavada, R.T., Arras, K.O., Lilienthal, A.J.: Thör: Human-robot navigation data collection and accurate motion trajectories dataset. IEEE Robot. Autom. Lett. 676–682 (2020)

18. Runge, J.: Causal network reconstruction from time series: From theoretical assumptions to practical estimation. Chaos: Interdis. J. Nonlinear Sci. 075310 (2018)
19. Runge, J., Nowack, P., Kretschmer, M., Flaxman, S., Sejdinovic, D.: Detecting and quantifying causal associations in large nonlinear time series datasets. Sci. Adv. (2019)
20. Saetia, S., Yoshimura, N., Koike, Y.: Constructing brain connectivity model using causal network reconstruction approach. Front. Neuroinf. (2021)
21. Scholkopf, B., et al.: Toward Causal Representation Learning. In: Proceedings of the IEEE, pp. 612–634 (2021)
22. Seitzer, M., Schölkopf, B., Martius, G.: Causal influence detection for improving efficiency in reinforcement learning. In: Advances in Neural Information Processing Systems (2021)
23. Zhu, S., Ng, I., Chen, Z.: Causal discovery with reinforcement learning. In: 8th International Conference on Learning Representations, ICLR (2020)

Learning User Habits to Enhance Robotic Daily-Living Assistance

Matteo Pantaleoni, Amedeo Cesta, Alessandro Umbrico,
and Andrea Orlandini[✉]

CNR - Institute of Cognitive Sciences and Technologies, Rome, Italy
andrea.orlandini@istc.cnr.it

Abstract. The deployment of assistive robots in everyday life scenarios and their capability of providing an effective and useful support for independent living is an open and challenging research problem. The development of suitable robot control systems requires effective solutions for addressing issues concerning performance, reliability, flexibility and proactivity. In the context of daily-living assistance, we advance a recently developed AI-based cognitive architecture by integrating learning capabilities with the aim of extracting *behavioral models* of user. Such models allows the resulting cognitive system to *know* the daily-living *habits* of a user and make better assistive decisions.

Keywords: Assistive robotics · Cognitive architectures · Machine learning · Neural networks · Artificial intelligence

1 Introduction

The recent advancements in robotic technologies are leading to more reliable, efficient, safe and affordable robots. Robotic applications are going to enter several working and living environments sharing space and tasks with humans. *Decisional Autonomy* is a key enabling feature to allow robots to reliably interact with both humans and the environment, and cope with complex situations. Decisional autonomy entails the integration of several Artificial Intelligence (AI) technologies necessary to *reason over the context* in which robots operate, *properly act and make suitable decisions* and also *learn* from *past experience* in order to enhance *performance* and *adaptation* [10,12].

This is especially true in assistive scenarios where a higher level of *decisional autonomy* is crucial to carry out effective and contextualize assistance [4,5,19]. Our long-term research objective aims at realizing "companion robots" capable of taking autonomous decisions to support older persons in their living environments through effective and safe interactions [8]. We specifically focus on daily assistive scenarios consisting of a senior user with mild cognitive and/or physical impairments who lives at home alone and needs continuous health-care through a socially interacting robot. In this context, we have recently developed a novel cognitive architecture called KOaLa (*Knowledge-based cOntinous Loop*) [21] pushing the integration of the AI technologies needed to support continuous,

F. Cavallo et al. (Eds.): ICSR 2022, LNAI 13817, pp. 165–173, 2022.
https://doi.org/10.1007/978-3-031-24667-8_15

proactive and personalized assistance. In this regards, it takes inspiration from research in Cognitive Architectures which aims at endowing artificial agents with a hybrid set *cognitive capabilities* [13,14,16].

KOaLa specifically pursues the integration of *Knowledge Representation & Reasoning* (KRR) and *Automated Planning & Scheduling* (P&S) to support a semantically rich representation of assistive scenarios and, according to this representation, autonomously and proactively take contextualize decisions through planning [20,21]. In this work we extend KOaLa by integrating *Machine Learning* (ML) techniques with the objective of *learning* the *behavioral model* of users. Such a model would refine the *contextual knowledge* of KOaLa and allow resulting cognitive controllers to *know* the habits of a user and accordingly *adapt* assistance. Furthermore, knowledge about user habits would allow a cognitive controller to *plan in advance* actions for daily assistance and improve the *autonomy of the robot* by better *optimizing* resources like e.g., *robot battery*.

The paper thus specifically describe the developed ML capabilities and their integration with KOaLa. An experimental evaluation on realistic environmental data shows the efficacy of the developed learning capabilities.

2   Learning to Plan Assistance

Central to KOaLa is the *knowledge* (i.e., the KB) which completely characterizes the assistive scenario by taking into account different (synergetic) perspectives. Each perspective describes an assistive scenario from a particular point-of-view and is based on a dedicated *ontological context*. This enables a *holistic interpretation* of robotic assistance obtained as the result of the combination of a number of synergetic factors that as proposed in [20] concern: (i) the robotic platform; (ii) the assisted person; (iii) clinicians and related clinical objectives and; (iii) the environment.

The designed KOaLa architecture consists of a knowledge processing module, called the *KOaLa Semantic Module*, and a planning and execution module, called the *KOaLa Acting Module*, that constitute the core reasoning capabilities of the *cognitive loop* [3,21]. The *KOaLa Semantic Module* relies on the *KOaLa Ontology* to support sensor data interpretation and incrementally build an abstract representation of the assistive context i.e., the *Knowledge Base* (KB). The *KOaLa Acting Module* is in charge of planning and executing assistive tasks according to the events or activities inferred by the semantic module. In this work we extend these two core components of KOaLa by integrating a *Learning Module* in order to extract *behavioral models* of interacting users from observations and past experience. Figure 1 shows the extended architecture where a "learning flow" enriches the representation, reasoning and planning capabilities of the semantic and acting modules.

The introduced learning module refines the behavioral model of the daily routine (habits) of a user and provides other modules with predictive functions about expected actions of a user during the day. An initial predictive model is build using a set of manually tagged information about the activity of a user within the house (a *ground truth* reference) and then performing training on

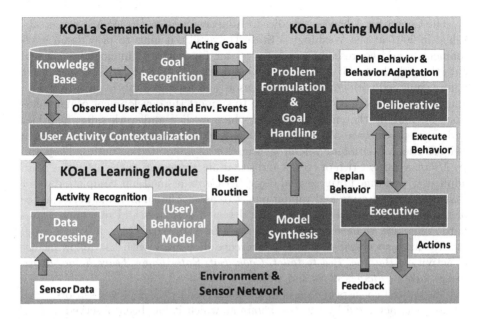

Fig. 1. Extended KOaLa Cognitive Architecture: (i) the *learning module* abstracts raw data coming from sensors to recognise user activities and incrementally refine user behavioral models; (ii) the *semantic module* relies on the KOaLa ontology to contextualize observed activities and maintains an updated knowledge about the current state of the whole environment (e.g., updated knowledge about the user and the environment); (iii) the *acting module* receives user knowledge (i.e., user routine) and *known* objectives to synthesize personalized behaviors of a robot and adapt them according to (contextualized) observations, events and new (acting) goals.

such data. The obtained model foresees user actions as well as user routine and is incrementally refined according to gathered historical data. This model in particular is used within KOaLa either offline for planning purposes (i.e., generated *timeline of the user* specifying the expected routine) or online for *activity recognition* purposes. Models about user routines enrich the knowledge base of KOaLa and consequently enhance the *awareness* of the robot about user dynamics. Such level of knowledge allows an assistive robot to better contextualize goals and planned actions and thus better *adapt* resulting assistive behaviors to the actual needs and habits of a user.

3   The CASAS Dataset

The objective of this work is the design of a learning tool capable of abstracting *user routines* from sensor data generated by the physical activities performed by a user inside his/her house. To train and validate the machine learning functionalities we leverage a set of real-world datasets publicly available within the CASAS project [7].

The Center for Advanced Studies in Adaptive Systems[1] (CASAS) was established in 2007 at the Washington State University. it aims to provide an environment to address research needs for testing innovative technologies using real data through the use of a smart homes environment. CASAS hosts several smart homes equipped with environmental sensors and used to perform advanced data analysis and adaptive systems research to support the development of new solutions for making the environments in which we live and work safer, healthier and more productive. We have specifically considered two datasets offering a rich selection of data and a heterogeneous set of annotated activities. They are: (i) *Milan*: a dataset rich of events and situations representing the activities of an adult user performed over several days; (ii) *Cairo*: a small but complete dataset that we used as testing and validation set to assess the quality and performance of the generated model. To generalize detected activities and rely on a "standard" reference we have considered a subset of ADL (*Activities of Daily Living*) [2]. We have specifically defined a reference dictionary with the following list of activities: *Bathing, Bed_to_toilet, Cook, Eat, Enter_home, Leave_home, Relax, Sleep, Take_medicine, Work* and *Other*.

The dataset consists of a set of events generated by the deployed sensors. Each event is characterized by the *timestamp* at which it has been observed, a *label* denoting the sensor, the *event* associated to the type of sensors, a *tag* specifying the annotated activity and in some cases the annotated start or end of the activity. The considered sensors provide binary events that can be easily encoded in a format suitable for learning purposes (0, 1 numeric values). Examples are PIR sensors used to detect movements and assume ON or OFF values, or door sensors used to detect whether a door (or a window) is OPEN or CLOSE.

Given the structure and shape of the data to give as input to the neural network (sequences of temporal events) the structure of the network should support the transformation of text sequences of variable length into numeric sequences of fixed length. Given such transformation is then necessary to *learn* correlations among consequent sequences of input data. To this aim we decided to use a recurrent network structure. It is indeed necessary to create a network structure capable of associating sequences of events with corresponding actions/activities and then build a user knowledge suitable to extract/analyze his/her habits.

3.1   Data Processing and Preparation

Before entering into the details of the defined structure we here focus on assumptions and pre-processing operations performed on data to support the learning capabilities. We made two assumptions over the considered datasets to simplify the analysis of available data. First, the feature relating to the day of execution of the action is discarded. It is assumed that every action is done without it being important to know the date on which it is performed. This choice is motivated by the assumption that each user tends to perform certain actions in a certain amount of time, without this depending on the day. Then, data

---

[1] http://casas.wsu.edu.

from different users is exploited as if it came from a single source (i.e., as if they were generated by the same user). On the one hand this assumption makes the training reliable to small differences in the execution of the various actions by the various users. On the other this assumption allows the use of the entire dataset without having to take into account the different users and thus better evaluate the learning capabilities considering the expected assistive scenario. This last assumption in particular allows to have a lot of information available for the training of the hypothetical unique user. The pre-processing operations considered to prepare the data given as input to the *temporal processing* module generating the learning model are: (i) *Data cleaning and editing*; (ii) *Numerosity and dimensionality reduction* and; (iii) *Data wrangling*. The design of this pre-processing pipeline was necessary structure a valid input for the designed neural network and thus to translate textual sequences of variable length into fixed-length numerical vectors.

4 Network Structure and Training

Machine learning approaches have been applied to the Human Activity Recognition (HAR) problem pursuing different points of view [18]. The most used neural network models can be categorized into two main classes: approaches leveraging recurrent networks (like, e.g., LSTM [15]) and approaches leveraging convolutional networks (like e.g., [1]), generally more frequently used with wearable sensors. Our work follows the latter approach enriching the neural network model with additional GRU and Ensemble layers [17]. In particular, we designed a network structure capable of working with different datasets, minimizing the necessary changes to the code as regards the data part.

We structured a neural network with a first *encoding layer* to map textual input into sequences of indices followed by an *embedding layer* to obtain fixed-length vectors. To properly process input temporal sequences and their correlations we considered a recurrent layer structured with LSTM [11,15] or GRU [6] cells. The final computation needed to produce the final output and in particular the probability distribution of activities is then realized with a dense fully connected layer using *softmax* function. This last layer thus allows to links a given input to every predictive class (i.e., an ADL activity) showing the predictive confidence of the network. Namely, the probability that a certain event represents a particular (known) activity.

4.1 Model Evaluation

Given the structure of the neural network described above, we have trained a predictive model and evaluated it using the described datasets. We have specifically evaluated three alternative structures of the neural network using three alternative recurrent layers: (i) a recurrent layer composed by a LSTM cell; (ii) a recurrent layer composed by a GRU cell and; (iii) a recurrent layer composed by a Bidirectional GRU cell [9]. An evaluation and comparison of these three alternative models has been made considering three main parameters: (i) the *confusion matrix* used to assess the accuracy of the predictions; (ii) the F_1 score showing the accuracy of the model taking into account *precision* and *recall* and; (iii) Cohen' Kappa to assess the reliability of the predictions.

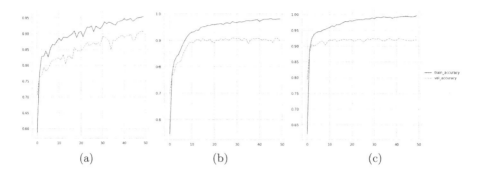

(a)   (b)   (c)

Fig. 2. Training accuracy for: (a) LSTM; (b) GRU and; (c) Bidirectional

Figure 2 first show the training accuracy for the considered models. In general, it can be observed that a quite good model accuracy is achieved with a few number of training epochs. For example LSTM which is the *slowest* reaches an accuracy between 90% and 95% within 30 epochs. Although all the evaluated models achieve a good accuracy it can be seen also with the confusion matrices in Fig. 3 that the best accuracy is achieved with the model *Bidirectional*.

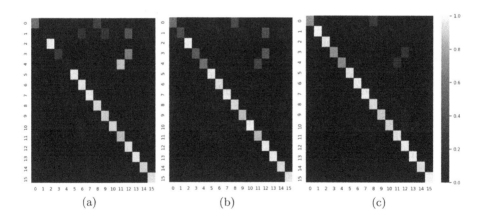

(a)   (b)   (c)

Fig. 3. Confusion matrices for: (a) LSTM; (b) GRU and; (c) Bidirectional

Finally, Table 1 below shows an example of behavioral routine generated from a trained model. Given a certain *time granularity*, the whole day is divided into a number of *time windows* used to generated the *probability distribution* of ADL activities of a user over the day. For example, Table 1 shows 4 time windows, 6 h each, and for each activity (the rows of the table) it shows the probability to observe the user performing it over the considered windows. The sum of the probability of each activity over the day should clearly be 1. Instead it could be notices that within a same window more than one activity could have a high probability of being observed. This depends on the time granularity considered in this example to generate the routine.

Table 1. Example of extracted routine of a user

		Time windows			
Index	Activity	0:00	6:00	12:00	18:00
0	Bed to Toilet	0.9	0	0	0.1
1	Eat	0	0	0	1
2	Leave Home	0	1	0	0
3	Other	0	1	0	0
4	Sleep	0	0	0	1
5	Take Pills	0	1	0	0
6	Work	0	0.7	0	0.3

5   Conclusions and Future Works

This work shows an extension to a recently developed cognitive architecture KOaLa designed to support continuous, adaptive and personalized assistance in daily home living scenarios. The contribution of the paper specifically focuses on the design of learning capabilities to enrich KOaLa with a predictive model of user habits over time. An initial evaluation of the developed neural network model on real data datasets shows promising results. Next steps will focus on a deeper validation of the model using a higher number of datasets with higher variability of data. Next steps will also take into account a tighter integration of the learning module with the planning capabilities of KOaLa and the assessment of the whole technology in concrete assistive scenarios. Furthermore, connections with dual theory approaches (like, e.g., in [22]) will be considered.

Acknowledgements. Authors are partially supported by Italian M.U.R. under project "SI-ROBOTICS: SocIal ROBOTICS for active and healthy ageing" (*PON – Ricerca e Innovazione 2014-2020* – G.A. ARS01_01120). Authors are also supported by the EU project TAILOR "Foundations of Trustworthy AI - Integrating Learning, Optimisation and Reasoning" G.A. 952215.)

References

1. Bevilacqua, A., MacDonald, K., Rangarej, A., Widjaya, V., Caulfield, B., Kechadi, T.: Human activity recognition with convolutional neural networks. In: Brefeld, U., et al. (eds.) ECML PKDD 2018. LNCS (LNAI), vol. 11053, pp. 541–552. Springer, Cham (2019). https://doi.org/10.1007/978-3-030-10997-4_33
2. Bookman, A., Harrington, M., Pass, L., Reisner, E.: Family caregiver handbook. Massachusetts Institute of Technology, Cambridge (2007)
3. Cesta, A., Cortellessa, G., Orlandini, A., Umbrico, A.: A cognitive loop for assistive robots - connecting reasoning on sensed data to acting. In: RO-MAN. The 27th IEEE International Symposium on Robot and Human Interactive Communication, pp. 826–831 (2018)
4. Cesta, A., Cortellessa, G., Fracasso, F., Orlandini, A., Turno, M.: User needs and preferences on AAL systems that support older adults and their Carers. J. Ambient Intell. Smart Environ. 10(1), 49–70 (2018)
5. Cesta, A., Cortellessa, G., Orlandini, A., Tiberio, L.: Long-term evaluation of a telepresence robot for the elderly: methodology and ecological case study. Int. J. Soc. Robot. 8(3), 421–441 (2016). https://doi.org/10.1007/s12369-016-0337-z
6. Cho, K., et al.: Learning phrase representations using RNN encoder-decoder for statistical machine translation. In: Proceedings of the 2014 Conference on Empirical Methods in Natural Language Processing (EMNLP), pp. 1724–1734. Association for Computational Linguistics, Doha, Qatar (October 2014)
7. Cook, D.J., Crandall, A.S., Thomas, B.L., Krishnan, N.C.: Casas: A smart home in a box. Computer 46(7), 62–69 (2013). https://doi.org/10.1109/MC.2012.328
8. Cortellessa, G., Benedictis, R.D., Fracasso, F., Orlandini, A., Umbrico, A., Cesta, A.: Ai and robotics to help older adults: Revisiting projects in search of lessons learned. Paladyn, J. Behav. Robot. 12(1), 356–378 (2021)
9. Cui, Z., Ke, R., Pu, Z., Wang, Y.: Stacked bidirectional and unidirectional lstm recurrent neural network for forecasting network-wide traffic state with missing values. Trans. Res. Part C: Emerg. Technol. 118, 102674 (2020)
10. Ghallab, M., Nau, D., Traverso, P.: The actor's view of automated planning and acting: A position paper. Artif. Intell. 208, 1–17 (2014)
11. Hochreiter, S., Schmidhuber, J.: Long short-term memory. Neural Comput. 9(8), 1735–1780 (1997)
12. Ingrand, F., Ghallab, M.: Deliberation for autonomous robots: A survey. Artif. Intell. 247, 10–44 (2017), special Issue on AI and Robotics
13. Kotseruba, I., Tsotsos, J.K.: 40 years of cognitive architectures: core cognitive abilities and practical applications. Artif. Intell. Rev. 53(1), 17–94 (2020)
14. Langley, P., Laird, J.E., Rogers, S.: Cognitive architectures: Research issues and challenges. Cogn. Syst. Res. 10(2), 141–160 (2009)
15. Liciotti, D., Bernardini, M., Romeo, L., Frontoni, E.: A sequential deep learning application for recognising human activities in smart homes. Neurocomputing 396, 501–513 (2020)
16. Lieto, A., Bhatt, M., Oltramari, A., Vernon, D.: The role of cognitive architectures in general artificial intelligence. Cogn. Syst. Res. 48, 1–3 (2018)
17. Opitz, D., Maclin, R.: Popular ensemble methods: An empirical study. J. Artifi. Intell. Res. 11, 169–198 (1999)
18. Ramasamy Ramamurthy, S., Roy, N.: Recent trends in machine learning for human activity recognition-a survey. WIREs Data Mining Knowl. Dis. 8(4) (2018)

19. Rossi, S., Ferland, F., Tapus, A.: User profiling and behavioral adaptation for HRI: A survey. Pattern Recogn. Lett. **99**, 3–12 (2017)
20. Umbrico, A., Cesta, A., Cortellessa, G., Orlandini, A.: A holistic approach to behavior adaptation for socially assistive robots. Int. J. Soc. Robot. (2020)
21. Umbrico, A., Cortellessa, G., Orlandini, A., Cesta, A.: Toward intelligent continuous assistance. J. Ambient Intell. Human. Comput. (2020)
22. Umbrico, A., De Benedictis, R., Fracasso, F., Cesta, A., Orlandini, A., Cortellessa, G.: A mind-inspired architecture for adaptive hri. Int. J. Soc. Robot. (2022). https://doi.org/10.1007/s12369-022-00897-8

Multi-modal Data Fusion for People Perception in the Social Robot Haru

Ricardo Ragel[1] ⓘ, Rafael Rey[1], Álvaro Páez[1], Javier Ponce[1], Keisuke Nakamura[2] ⓘ,

Fernando Caballero[3] ⓘ, Luis Merino[1](✉) ⓘ, and Randy Gómez[2] ⓘ

[1] Universidad Pablo de Olavide, Seville, Spain
lmercab@upo.es
[2] Honda Research Institute, San Jose, Japan
[3] University of Seville, Seville, Spain

Abstract. This article presents a people perception software architecture and its implementation, focused on the information of interest from the point of view of a social robot. The key modules employed to get the different people features, such as the body parts location, the face and hands information, and the speech, from a set of possible devices and configurations are described. The association and combination of these features using a temporal and geometric fusion system are explained in detail. A high-level interface for Human-Robot interaction using the resulting information from the fused people is proposed. The paper presents experimental results evaluating the relevant aspects of the system.

Keywords: People perception · Multi-modal data fusion · ROS

1 Introduction

Proper people perception is key for robots working along humans, and particularly for human-robot interaction and social robots, like Haru [6]. Social robots should be capable of robustly detecting several people at the same time, differentiating individuals from each other, estimating their location relative to the robot and the position of relevant body parts like gaze, body posture and arms and hands gestures. Also, they should estimate other data of interest, such as whether a person is talking or not, who is the person that is talking, what is saying; or where the persons are looking at or pointing to or even their emotional state. All this information needs to be provided in a coherent and unified way.

Different sensor modalities are required to estimate this variety of features. There have been multiple advances in the fields of vision and audio processing to extract different people features from (RGB and RGBD) cameras and from microphones. These sensors can have different resolutions and fields of view. The perception system should, thus, be able to combine all the information from the different sensors into an unified view of each person present. It should be also flexible enough to incorporate different sensor inputs.

This paper presents the ROS people perception pipeline employed in the Haru tabletop social robot [6]. The pipeline is focused on the estimation and fusion of the necessary people data to enable a diverse range of applications. The main contributions are:

F. Cavallo et al. (Eds.): ICSR 2022, LNAI 13817, pp. 174–187, 2022.
https://doi.org/10.1007/978-3-031-24667-8_16

1) a people data fusion module that provides a unified view of the people present in the scene, and offers a high-level API to that can be used for Human-Robot Interaction (HRI); the module can integrate a variety of people feature extraction modules from audio and images. 2) A method to combine body parts extracted from multiple different cameras, which allow a more robust perception of people body posture.

2   Related Work

As a key building block for any robot that has to operate among humans, there are many works on human perception. Several pipelines are oriented to people detection and tracking, and are then used for robot social navigation and interaction. The system in [3] is mainly focused on face detection and recognition, and people tracking. It can consider RGBD cameras, as well as tracking from 2D lasers. In [7], the former module is expanded to consider also external fixed cameras. Multi-modal (based in vision and 2D LIDAR) detection and tracking of people was also considered in the Spencer project [9]. The focus is mainly on robust people tracking in crowded scenarios, including group formations.

However, a social robot as Haru is aimed for close interactions with people, requiring robust human multi-modal perception including audio and visual data. The combination of audio and vision is considered in [8]. The same group extends this to the use of multiple sensors, including external Kinectv2 cameras and microphones [17]. These works are focused on discrete action detection, and audio command recognition for a specific application. The modules do not consider lower level details like skeleton or body-pose tracking. Our system works on a lower degree of abstraction, and aims to be general, so it can be used for different applications. Similarly, the authors in [4] present a perception system for robot-assisted therapy. The system considers several RGB and RGBD cameras as well as audio, and provides gaze estimation, skeleton joint-based action recognition, object tracking, face and facial expression recognition, and speech recognition, sound direction recognition and voice identification. It is very complete, but aimed to a specific application. Here, we aim for a generic data fusion pipeline that can be used in different applications, and extended with further features in the future.

In this regard, [18] presents the Social Signal Interpretation (SSI) framework for the recognition of social signals. MultiSense [16], built over SSI, provide high-level non-verbal behavior recognition. OpenSense is presented in [15] as a successor of MultiSense, based in this case over the Microsoft's Platform for Situated Intelligence (psi) [2]. These frameworks, while similar, operate on a higher-level than this work. Furthermore, they are focused for Windows' systems, although the (psi) platform offer a bridge to ROS. Recently, a proposal for ROS standardization of HRI related people perception pipelines has been put forth [11]. The pipeline presented in this paper covers most aspects considered there, and could be adapted to this standardization without much effort. Furthermore, it can provide novel modules, in particular the multi-camera skeleton fusion module, and the whole people data fusion pipeline.

3 Robot Sensors

In order to detect people and get information from its surroundings, our tabletop social robot, Haru, [6] has the following sensors inside:

- RGB camera: There is one RGB camera above each robot eye. They represent what the robot is "seeing" with its eyes. They are used to scan QR codes, take pictures, to recognize people's facial features and close hand gestures.
- Microphones: The robot has an array of 6 unidirectional microphones. They are distributed along the base to detect the sound from all directions. The microphones are used to detect the sound and the location of the sound's source.
- Orbbec RGBD camera: In the base of the robot there is also an Orbbec Astra Embedded S camera. The camera provides an RGB image and a depth field. The camera can recognize body parts up to 1.6 m in front of the camera.

To improve and reinforce the system's perception, we also use other sensors connected to an external computer. The supported sensors by the robot are:

- Azure Kinect camera: It is the most used external sensor at the moment. It provides a RGB image, depth image and microphones. As such, it can be used to scan QR codes, take pictures, recognize people's facial features, recognize people's body parts (up to 6 persons), detect sound, and detect the sound's source location.
- Kinect v2 camera: Older version of Kinect than Azure Kinect. It outputs a RGB image, depth image, and can be used to recognize body parts.
- Leap Motion Controller: Two lens optical hand tracking sensor that captures the movements of the hands. The detection range goes up to 80 cm. above the sensor and it can detect two hands at a time. It outputs the position and orientation in 3D of 27 different hand key-points.
- External microphones: Two types of microphones can be used: an array of 8 RØDE directional microphones; and a hand-made array of RASP microphones (the same ones the robot has). They can be used alongside the internal microphones to detect the sound and its source location.

All sensors data streams can be accessed through ROS [13] using different drivers.

4 Social Features Modules

4.1 Body Parts Extraction and Fusion

In the proposed system, body parts and people skeletons identification has been considered in such a way that it is sensor agnostic. That means that it must be possible to integrate any device capable of publishing this information. The system is able to merge data coming from different devices into unified skeletons and, consequently, single body parts. The proposed system addresses these questions based on the following points:

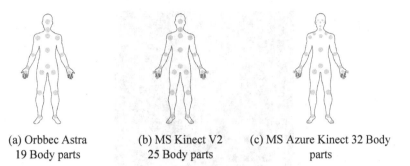

(a) Orbbec Astra
19 Body parts

(b) MS Kinect V2
25 Body parts

(c) MS Azure Kinect 32 Body
parts

Fig. 1. Body parts estimated by the devices. The generic skeleton definition used in the system is the one used by the Azure Kinect (c).

- Standardization: All body parts and resulting skeletons are parsed to and, therefore, described in the same format. In other words, they share the same ROS message type. Thus, each skeleton is of the form Skeleton, composed by an unique identifier and a set of Body Parts, each one describing an unique part of the person skeleton given by the directly related fields ID and Name. The list of body parts in this standard message is equal to the list of body parts provided by the device that detects the maximum number of them. In the current system, it is the body parts detected by the Azure Kinect camera, shown in Fig. 1c.
- Coverage: As not all the sensors capable of detecting people skeletons detect neither the same body parts nor the same number of such body parts the standard body parts list is filled using the received body parts, given a predefined association between them and those in the standard message, and estimating the rest if it is possible. This means that a non-provided standard body part is interpolated if the camera provides the surrounding body parts of the skeleton, leaving it empty otherwise. Figure 1 shows a comparison between the body parts detected by three of the devices currently integrated in the system.
- Assembling: In the same way that each device publishes different numbers of body parts (bp), each device publishes skeletons carrying its own skeleton ID, and on its own reference frame. In this way, we may have the same person being ID 1 for one camera and ID 3 for another, for example. In order to feed the final data fusion system with a single source of skeletons or, in other words, with unique identifiers per skeleton and all of them on the same reference system (from now on, the world reference frame), this system implements a Skeleton Assembler module, described below.

The Skeleton Assembler module receives the skeletons from all the connected devices and transforms all of them to a common coordinate reference frame, world, given the transformations from the reference systems of all the devices to this common one. This task involves simply setting the camera poses with respect to this world reference frame and using the ROS module TF[1], which directly provides these transformations so that they can be applied to the skeletons. Then, as it is described in Eq. (1), this module computes the average position of each skeleton (Sk) in the common

---

[1] http://wiki.ros.org/tf.

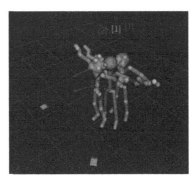

Fig. 2. Result of the Skeleton Assembler (in blue) when assembling the skeletons provided (in yellow) by two Azure Kinect cameras for the same person. The difference in position of the incoming skeletons is intentionally exaggerated in the figure to make them clearly visible. (Color figure online)

reference system as the average position between its body parts ($\overline{bp}$) and checks if every pair of skeletons from different devices (dev) are closer in distance than a given threshold (α). For each group of associated skeletons, the final position of the body parts is calculated as the average position of this same body part in each skeleton of that group (2). Figure 2 shows the resulting skeleton after assembling incoming skeletons from two cameras.

$$Sk_{near} = \{Sk_k : |\overline{bp}_{Sk\in dev_i} - \overline{bp}_{Sk'\in dev_j}| < \alpha\}$$

$$\overline{bp} = \frac{\overset{i\in Sk}{\sum} bp_i}{n_{bp}} \quad \forall \quad Sk \in dev \tag{1}$$

$$Sk = \{Sk_i : Sk_i = \{bp_j : bp_j = \frac{\overset{k\in Sk_{near}}{\sum} bp_j^k}{n_{Sk_{near}}}\}\} \tag{2}$$

Additionally, the final skeletons are processed by a convolutional neural network trained to get a set of possible body gestures, like *sitting, standing walking, waving* or *clapping* among others, from the skeleton's body parts information. These body gestures are also included in the final skeletons result.

4.2 Face Features

The Face Detection and Identification module uses the RGB images from the different cameras supported by the system. It can process images from up to two different cameras at the same time. For each image received, the module extract the following information:

- Face detection: three different models can be used: Histogram of Oriented Gradients (HOG), Convolutional Neural Network (CNN), or Single-Shot Detector (SSD). While the HOG and CNN models uses the *face_recognition* module [5], the SSD model uses *OpenCV* directly. The SSD model has better performance with occlusions of the face, so it is the one used by default.

- Face identification: faces are identified with respect to those stored in a database by also using the *face_recognition* module [5]. The name recognition is expressed as a confidence percentage. If none of the faces on the database matches the face detected, the name given is "*Unknown*".
- Face features: To get high-level information from the face we use the *Microsoft Azure Face API*. At the moment, we only use the API to detect the gender ("*female*", "*male*") and the emotions of the face ("*anger*", "*contempt*", "*disgust*", "*fear*", "*happiness*", "*neutral*", "*sadness*", "*surprise*").
- Facial Mask detection: We use a custom TensorFlow network solely for wearing mask detection. Even though the *Microsoft Azure Face API* has the option to detect if the person has a mask or not, we do not use it because it is not robust enough for our system. The measurement is discrete, the person either has the mask on ("*true*") or not ("*false*").

4.3   Hand Features

For the hand features extraction, two data sources can be considered: the LeapMotion sensor introduced in Sect. 3, which outputs a robust, but restricted in space, 3D detection of the hand; and the MediaPipe [10] hands detector [19] using an RGB camera. This last detector does not rely on special hardware, being able to detect 21 hand landmarks in 2.5D using only RGB images. The MediaPipe Hands algorithm consists on two steps. First, it uses a SSD detector based on BlazeFace [1] to detect the Hand Palm, which runs only in the first frame or when the hand is missed. After that, once the hand is detected, a hand landmark model is fitted to the cropped hand bounding box resulting in 2.5D landmarks. In both cases, these data are tagged with sensor information. In the case of the LeapMotion sensor, information about the sensor coordinate system is included in the data. In the case of MediaPipe source, information about camera calibration and its reference frame is included in the hand information.

4.4   Audio Features

Based on the widely-used and open-source software HARK [12], this system implements an audio processing module called ZZ. This module is in charge of extracting the audio data from any of the microphone arrays mentioned in Sect. 3, and process it to provide of audio signal to the rest of the system. It also computes the sound's source location and the wake-up word activation so they can be used by the People Data Fusion module to estimate who is the person that is speaking, as it is described in Sect. 5.

Figure 3 shows the implemented audio layer diagram using different modules of HARK. It includes a first EMVDR (*Extended Minimum Variance Distortionless Response*) filter to reduce the noise coming from the surroundings of the microphone array, which could be, for instance, the robot motors themselves. Then, the resulting audio is published, enabling the rest of the system to use it. In particular, the *Automatic Speech Recognition* (ASR) is one of the modules subscribed to it. ASR provides speech transcriptions to the rest of the system using the Google *Speech-to-Text* service API. In addition, this filtered audio data is provided to a wake-up word detector that runs locally and publishes a signal every time that a set of pre-trained words are recognized.

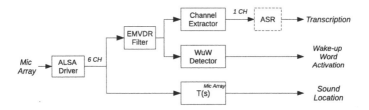

Fig. 3. ZZ Audio Scheme

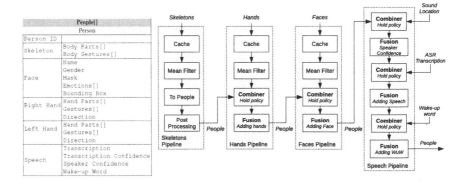

Fig. 4. People data fusion pipeline

On the other hand, sound source location is also computed from the 6-channel audio stream using a complex spectral Transfer Function $(T(s))$ that represents the relationship in wave propagation between a microphone array and a sound source. This Transfer Function depends on the microphone array configuration and it is computed for each microphone array using the provided methods by HARK.

5   People Data Fusion Module

5.1   Overall Fusion Pipeline

Given the information resulting from the previous modules, the People Data Fusion module collects, processes and combines all of them into a final `People` message composed by the fields shown in Fig. 4, left. The People Data Fusion module is the combination of different information pipelines as it is shown in Fig. 4, right. Each pipeline merges one source data with the `People` output result of the previous pipeline. Each pipeline is in itself a sequential combination of multiple filters implemented from the FKIE Message Filters ROS package [14]:

– *Cache*: It queues the last source messages received within a time interval and for a maximum duration. It also performs the messages synchronization based on their original time stamp or, optionally, on the local time instant they were received. The selection of this synchronization method will depend on whether the machines running the system modules are time synchronized. In the case of the proposed system, the robot is running a NTP server, so the rest of machines are time-synchronized and the incoming time-stamp can be directly used.

- *Mean Filter*: Receives the set of messages from the *Cache*, sorts them into groups by person removing outliers and/or values outside the defined workspace, and calculates their average values.
- *Combiner*: This is a special filter that connect two sources to it and combines them into a single output to be processed by another filter. FKIE message filters provide different policies to do these combinations, but our system implements its own *Hold* policy. It simply keeps the last received message of each input during a specified expiration time and generates the output every time a new message of one of the inputs arrives combining it with the held message of the other input. In case of no new messages received from any of the inputs during the specified time, the held message is removed so the incoming messages of the other input will be forwarded directly.
- *Fusion*: It receives the *Combiner* output data and process it to generate the data of interest, in this system case, the People message integrating all the received information.

5.2   Skeletons Pipeline

The *Skeletons Pipeline* receives the Skeletons from the *Skeleton Assembler* module and save them in a *Cache*. Then, it removes the skeletons whose IDs do not meet a minimum number of messages in the cache and the ones that are outside a specified workspace. As the skeletons from different cameras are already geometrically fused in the *Skeleton Assembler* module, this pipeline simply applies a temporal mean filter to the skeletons in the cache (for each ID). Finally, it creates the first People message containing the previous final skeletons, and pre-computes an estimation of the Hands Directions, the direction that the arms of the people skeletons are pointing to, from the relative position of the elbows to the hands.

5.3   Hands Pipeline

The *Hands Pipeline* receives the Hands from the Hand Detector module and, as in the previous pipeline, save them in a Hands *Cache*. Then, the hands are grouped by the sensor frame (either the RGB camera frame or Leap Motion frame) that detected them, and a temporal filter is applied to the hands in the *Cache* for the hands whose bounding box intersects. In the case of MediaPipe detections, the temporal filter uses the hand detection confidence as weights to penalize uncertain detections.

Next, in order to associate a hand detection with a given person, we need to take into account the source of the detection. On one hand, if the source is the MediaPipe Detector, the 3D position of each of the hands from the skeletons (from the former pipeline) is projected onto the camera image frame used to detect the hands by using the camera calibration and coordinate transformation. Next, the module associates the MediaPipe hand detection with a person if the 2D projection of its 3D hand (from the skeleton) intersects with the bounding box of the hand detected by the MediaPipe Detector (see Fig. 5). On the other hand, if the detection source is the LeapMotion sensor, the approach can be simplified, as the LeapMotion output is directly the 3D position of each

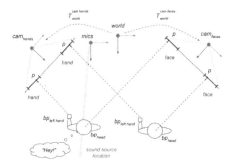

Fig. 5. People Data Fusion - Faces and Hands matching

hand element. Taking into account the coordinate frame transformation, we compare the geometrical center of the hand along with his orientation with the geometrical center and orientation of the hand approximation given by the Azure Kinect camera. If their distance and directions are below a certain threshold, we associate the hand with the corresponding skeleton.

The next steps also depend on which type of hand detection has been received. In the case of a detection coming from the LeapMotion sensor, the only remaining step consists of transforming the hand landmarks to the skeleton coordinate system. However, if the detection comes from the MediaPipe detector, the problem of integrating it into the 3D skeleton is more complicated due to the fact that these hand landmarks are referred to an arbitrary wrist frame. In this case we take advantage of the skeleton body parts 1 returned by the Kinect V2 and Azure Kinect sensors, among which we can find some hand landmarks as the hand tip, hand position, thumb tip and wrist position. These already known hand landmarks in the 3D `world` frame are translated to a 3D frame centered in the wrist position. Assuming that the wrist position is equivalent in both frames, we can compute the rotation matrix of the full hand using the equivalent points in the arbitrary wrist reference frame in which the hand landmarks are located in the given detection. By applying this rotation to all hand landmarks in the arbitrary frame and the wrist translation, we obtain the detailed hand landmarks in the `world` frame.

5.4   Faces Pipeline

The *Faces Pipeline* is equivalent to the hands one but using the received `Faces` from the Face Detection and Identification module (see Fig. 5). First, it saves them in a faces *Cache*. Then, the faces are grouped by the camera that detected them, and the average position of each face in each group is computed for the faces whose bounding box intersect. Next, these averaged faces by camera are merged with the input `People` data. For that, the position of the skeleton part corresponding to the head is projected on the image where the faces result are referenced. If there exists an intersection between this head projection and the incoming faces results, the person `Face` is updated with the information of the new matched face. The fusion filter maintains a confidence value about the person's `Name`. This confidence value is decreased anytime this name is not recognized in the incoming faces that intersect with the person head (for example, if the

Fig. 6. An experiment with kids playing Rock-Paper-Scissors game. Left: face and hand detections. Right: fusion results.

person has put on a mask or another name is recognized). When a detected face's name has a higher confidence than the current one, the name in the data structure is changed.

5.5 Speech Pipeline

The *Speech Pipeline* consists of three pairs of the filters *Combiner* and *Fusion*. The first pair of filters receives the detected sound locations and update the `Speaker Confidence` field of the received people input as follows: every time a people message arrives and there is no sound detection, it means that no one has spoken, so this value is reduced in all of them by the same amount; in case there is such detection, it increases the speaker confidence of the person with whom the sound direction intersects. The person who is speaking is the one who has a higher value in that field. To make the `Speaker Confidence` values persistent, they are saved in each iteration to be used in the next iteration. The second pair of filters receives the resulting people from the previous processing and simply attach the last `ASR transcription` to the person with higher `Speaker Confidence`. In case all people have the same value or, directly, it is zero for all of them, this transcription is associated to the person closest to a defined position, in the case of our system, to the current position of the robot. The third pair of filters works as the previous one but, in this case, associating the `Wake-up Word` to the person with the highest `Speaker Confidence` or the closest to the robot otherwise.

An example of the final fused `People` information is shown in Fig. 6. It is an experiment where the robot plays Rock-Paper-Scissors with two kids using the external Azure Kinect camera and the internal robot microphones array. Along this experiment, the robot performs tracking to the children and speaks with them to engage the kids in the game using the fused people information: the location, name and speech of the people, among others. Face and Hand information is gathered using the image from the Azure Kinect camera. In particular, the hand information is used to recognize the gestures that are the input of the game.

5.6 High-Level Features

Given this stable and merged `People` information, a People API has been developed. It provides a set of high-level queries to obtain information about the actual people in the

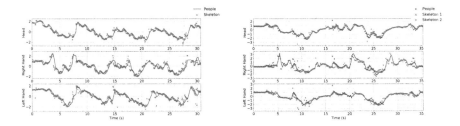

Fig. 7. Left: Relative position variation with respect to the mean for different body parts partially occluded. Right: Relative position variation respect to the mean for different Body Parts when the person is fully occluded.

scene and the interactions between them, their surroundings and with the robot. These queries can be grouped into three categories:

- Global queries. They provide information about people as a whole. It includes services such a *GetNumberOfPersons*, that returns the number of people in the scene; *GetPersonsNames*, that returns the list of people names in the scene; and *GetPersonsIDs*, that returns the list of people IDs in the scene and is useful when the commands are relative to the IDs because the module is agnostic about the rest of the system features or, directly, all the people names are currently *unknown*.
- Individual queries. They are services that provides information about a particular person, given his name or his ID. These queries include requests about the position of a person (*GetPersonPos*) or the location of specific body part, for instance, *GetBodyPartDir* that returns the direction of a given body part for a given person name or ID. They also include queries about a specific field of the person, such as *GetPersonSpeech*, that returns the next detected speech associated to this person, or *CheckPersonhasMask*, that return the value of a specific field for this person.
- Interaction queries. They are focused on getting the person that matches a condition. First, it includes general queries like *GetClosestPerson*, that returns the closest person to a specified position (that could be, for instance, the position of the robot), or *GetHighConfidenceSpeech*, that returns the speech information of the person with the highest speaker confidence within a time interval. Second, it provides some checking services such as *CheckPersonIsNearTo*, *CheckPersonIsLookingAt* or *CheckPersonIsPointingTo*, that check if a person is near to, looking at or pointing to a specified position or to another specified person.

6   Experimental Results

6.1   People Data Fusion Filtering

In real situations, where people interact with the environment, it is expected that some body parts leave the camera field of view either because of occlusions produced by objects or the rest of the body parts, or because they go outside of the camera frame. That is why it is mandatory that the People signal filters this kind of occlusions and the body parts estimations remains smooth. In order to validate the system capabilities the following experiment has been performed. Using only one Azure Kinect camera focusing to an obstacle 1.2 m high and 0.5 m wide, a person walks around it, so the hands, among other body parts are hidden from the camera. Figure 7, left, shows the results for the Head, Right Hand and Left Hand body parts of the People signal compared with the ones provided by the raw skeletons detected by the camera. It can be seen how the Azure Kinect camera continues estimating the position of those body parts but with a high noise. First of all, the Right Hand and Left Hand signals are the ones with the highest noise because of the experimental setup, in which the circular walk around the obstacle makes the hands to be occluded by the obstacle but also by the person own body as well. However, the People Data Fusion module is able to filter these occlusions and provide a smooth signal even for these body parts. On the other hand, in the case of the Head, it can be seen how the occlusion of the rest of body parts also affects this one, even though it was always visible by the camera, increasing the noise in the position estimation. This noise is also due to the person turning his back to the camera for half of the trajectory, something that makes the Azure Kinect estimations decrease their quality. In all cases, the noise is filtered in the People signal as can be checked in Fig. 7, left.

In a second experiment, two Azure Kinect cameras are placed facing each other with an obstacle placed in the middle point between them. In this case, the person performs a circular walk around the obstacle and stops for some seconds when it is hidden from one of the devices. In this experiment, there are situations where both cameras detect the person and situations where only one camera detects the person when walking around the obstacle. Figure 7, right, shows the results for this experiment. It can be seen how the devices do not provide any estimation when the person is not detected. However, the People signal continue providing a smooth position estimation for the body parts based on the data from the camera that still detects the person, joining smoothly these estimation with the ones provided by the second camera when the person becomes visible again by this one, without abrupt changes in the estimation.

6.2 First Detection, Identification and Association Times

In order to measure the speed of the system in the detection, identification and association steps, the following experiment has been carried out: One person enters in a room saying *hello* and waving his hands. Two Azure Kinect cameras have been placed looking at 2.5 m from the entrance, similar to the layout shown in Fig. 5. To simplify data collection, one camera is used to detect the faces and the speech, and the other one to detect the hands. The skeletons from both cameras are taken into account and are assembled into the same final people result. Figure 8 shows the average results for 25 iterations of this experiment, running all the modules on the same computer, a Zotac Mini PC model ZBOX-ECM73070C (i7-10700 CPU @ 2.9 GHz, 16 cores; 32 GB RAM; Nvidia GeForce RTX 3070, 8GB), except for the second Azure Kinect camera, that runs in an extra identical computer. With the exception of the *Faces* detector and classifier, the rest of the processes were all running in CPU in this experiment. *Detection*, in blue, is the time between the moment the person gets into the room until the first data is published for each element; in other words, the time we get the skeleton, the hands and face positions on the images, and the necessary sound locations. *Association*, in

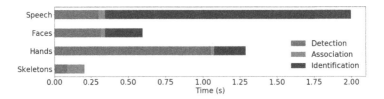

Fig. 8. First detection, identification and association average times.

orange, is the necessary time to associate and fuse each data to the person in the People Data Fusion module using the geometrical procedures detailed in Sect. 5. In case of the skeletons, it means assembling all the received skeletons as it is explained in Sect. 4.1. Finally, *identification*, in green, has different meanings depending on the feature: for hands, it is the time when we get the current gesture; for faces, the time when we get the different parameters' identification (the name among others); for speech, the time when we receive the complete transcription.

Given these results, some other notes have to be taken into consideration:

- The first hand and face detections are always the ones that take longest, as the following detections use this information to speed up the computation. In general, the frecuency for continuous detections 15 Hz for Skeletons, 8 Hz for the hands 10 Hz for the faces. These values could be slightly speeded up, but this would increase the computer load unnecessarily, as they are sufficient to obtain the final estimates of people, that with the current filters configuration is published 25 Hz.
- Speech recognition takes longest in this experiment and in general for the current system setup, as it involves a request to the Google Cloud API, so the audio data is sent online, processed and received to be associated to the corresponding person. In addition, it must be taken into consideration that the system processes full transcriptions, not intermediate ones that, of course, are received in a shorter time.

7   Conclusions

The entire process for a human perception system, from data acquisition to a high-level HRI interface, has been described. It is a modular system, in which the people fusion pipeline can be expanded for new features. The data type standardization together with the fact that it is a system directly implemented using ROS, opens up and facilitates the integration of new devices into it. The system has been used in numerous experiments and applications with the social robot Haru. Next steps will consider the contribution to the ROS4HRI pipeline [11], as a potential implementation and also contributing features that are not present there, as the multi-camera skeleton handling.

Acknowledgment. The work of F.C. and L.M. is partially supported by Programa Operativo FEDER Andalucia 2014-2020, Consejeria de Economía y Conocimiento (Deep-Bot, PY20_00817) and the project PLEC2021-007868, funded by MCIN/AEI/10.13039/501100011033 and the European Union NextGenerationEU/PRTR.

References

1. Bazarevsky, V., Kartynnik, Y., Vakunov, A., Raveendran, K., Grundmann, M.: Blazeface: Sub-millisecond neural face detection on mobile gpus (2019)
2. Bohus, D., et al.: Platform for situated intelligence. arXiv preprint arXiv:2103.15975 (2021)
3. Bormann, R., Zwölfer, T., Fischer, J., Hampp, J., Hägele, M.: Person recognition for service robotics applications. In: 13th IEEE-RAS International Conference on Humanoid Robots (Humanoids), pp. 260–267 (2013)
4. Esteban, P.G., et al.: How to build a supervised autonomous system for robot-enhanced therapy for children with autism spectrum disorder. Paladyn J. Behav. Robot. **8**(1), 18–38 (2017)
5. Geitgey, A.: Face recognition module (2019). https://github.com/ageitgey/face_recognition
6. Gomez, R., Szapiro, D., Galindo, K., Nakamura, K.: Haru: Hardware design of an experimental tabletop robot assistant. In: 2018 13th ACM/IEEE International Conference on Human-Robot Interaction (HRI), pp. 233–240. IEEE (2018)
7. Hu, N., Bormann, R., Zwölfer, T., Kröse, B.: Multi-user identification and efficient user approaching by fusing robot and ambient sensors. In: IEEE International Conference on Robotics and Automation (ICRA), pp. 5299–5306 (2014)
8. Kardaris, N., Rodomagoulakis, I., Pitsikalis, V., Arvanitakis, A., Maragos, P.: A platform for building new human-computer interface systems that support online automatic recognition of audio-gestural commands. In: Proceedings of the 24th ACM international conference on Multimedia, pp. 1169–1173 (2016)
9. Linder, T., Arras, K.O.: People detection, tracking and visualization using ros on a mobile service robot. In: Koubaa, A. (ed.) Robot Operating System (ROS). SCI, vol. 625, pp. 187–213. Springer, Cham (2016). https://doi.org/10.1007/978-3-319-26054-9_8
10. Lugaresi, C., et al.: Mediapipe: A framework for building perception pipelines (2019)
11. Mohamed, Y., Lemaignan, S.: Ros for human-robot interaction. In: IEEE/RSJ International Conference on Intelligent Robots and Systems (IROS), pp. 3020–3027. IEEE
12. Nakadai, K., Okuno, H.G., Mizumoto, T.: Development, deployment and applications of robot audition open source software hark. J. Robot. Mechatron. **29**(1), 16–25 (2017)
13. Quigley, M., et al.: Ros: an open-source robot operating system, vol. 3 (January 2009)
14. Röhling, T.: Fkie message filters (2018). http://wiki.ros.org/fkie_message_filters
15. Stefanov, K., Huang, B., Li, Z., Soleymani, M.: Opensense: A platform for multimodal data acquisition and behavior perception. In: Proceedings of the 2020 International Conference on Multimodal Interaction, pp. 660–664 (2020)
16. Stratou, G., Morency, L.P.: Multisense-context-aware nonverbal behavior analysis framework: A psychological distress use case. IEEE Trans. Affect. Comput. **8**(2), 190–203 (2017)
17. Tsiami, A., Koutras, P., Efthymiou, N., Filntisis, P.P., Potamianos, G., Maragos, P.: Multi3: Multi-sensory perception system for multi-modal child interaction with multiple robots. In: IEEE International Conference on Robotics and Automation (ICRA), pp. 4585–4592 (2018)
18. Wagner, J., Lingenfelser, F., Baur, T., Damian, I., Kistler, F., André, E.: The social signal interpretation (ssi) framework: multimodal signal processing and recognition in real-time. In: Proceedings of the 21st ACM international conference on Multimedia, pp. 831–834 (2013)
19. Zhang, F., et al.: Mediapipe hands: On-device real-time hand tracking (2020)

Adaptive Behavior Generation of Social Robots Based on User Behavior Recognition

Woo-Ri Ko$^{(\boxtimes)}$ ⓘ, Minsu Jang ⓘ, Jaeyeon Lee ⓘ, and Jaehong Kim ⓘ

Electronics and Telecommunications Research Institute (ETRI), 218 Gajeong-ro, Yuseong-Gu, Daejeon 34129, Republic of Korea
wrko@etri.re.kr

Abstract. For natural human-robot interaction, social robots should understand a user behavior and respond appropriately. In particular, when generating a behavior to interact with the user, it is important to adapt its behavior to the user's posture and position rather than repeating the predefined motion. To this end, we propose a method for generating the robot behavior in three steps, i.e. user behavior recognition, robot behavior selection, and robot behavior adaptation. First, the user behavior is recognized by using a Kinect v.2 sensor and a long short-term memory-based neural network model. The weights of the model are trained using the *AIR-Act2Act*, which is a human-human interaction dataset. Then, according to the behavior selection rules designed by referring to the interaction scenarios in the dataset, the robot selects an appropriate behavior for the recognized user behavior. Finally, the key pose of the selected behavior is modified in consideration of the user's posture and position. To demonstrate the feasibility of the proposed method, experiments were conducted using a Pepper robot in a 3D virtual environment. The experimental results showed that the proposed method has an accuracy of 99% in recognizing the user behavior, and the robot behavior can be modified naturally even if the user's intention is misunderstood at first.

Keywords: Social robot · Human-robot interaction · Behavior recognition · Behavior generation · Behavior adaptation

1 Introduction

Social robots should understand a user behavior and generate natural responses for human-robot interaction [3]. Table 1 shows examples of frequently occurring interaction scenarios with service robots [7]. Depending on the user's behavior,

This work was partly supported by the Institute of Information & Communications Technology Planning & Evaluation (IITP) grant funded by the Korean government (MSIT) (No.2017-0-00162, Development of Human-care Robot Technology for Aging Society, 50%) and (No.2020-0-00842, Development of Cloud Robot Intelligence for Continual Adaptation to User Reactions in Real Service Environments, 50%).

F. Cavallo et al. (Eds.): ICSR 2022, LNAI 13817, pp. 188–197, 2022.
https://doi.org/10.1007/978-3-031-24667-8_17

Table 1. Interaction scenarios with service robots [7].

	User behaviors	Robot behaviors
1	Enters into the room through the door	Bows to the user
2	Calls the robot	Approaches the user
3	Stands still without a purpose.	Stares at the user for a command
4	Lifts his arm to shake hands	Shakes hands with the user
5	Covers his/her face and cries	Stretches its hands to hug the user
6	Threatens to hit the robot	Blocks the face with arms

the robot *bows*, *approaches*, *stares*, *shakes hands*, *hugs* or *blocks*. Although many studies have been focused on how to generate these social behaviors [2,6,13], there is a limitation in that the robot cannot respond to subtle differences in user behavior because it generates one of the predefined motions. Our work aims to recognize the differences in user behavior and generate a behavior appropriate to the user's current posture and position. For example, when responding to the user's request for a handshake, the robot should stretch its hand to the user's current hand position.

Figure 1a depicts the proposed behavior generation method for social robots. A Kinect sensor [11], which is installed right behind a Pepper robot [12], captures the user's 3D joint positions via skeletal tracking. For implementation, we used Kinect for Windows SDK 2.0 provided by Microsoft. Then, the user behavior is recognized by using the long short-term memory (LSTM) [5]-based neural network model that takes a series of the captured joint data as input. Note that LSTM is a popular model in understanding sequential data [5] and has been successfully applied to the skeleton-based action recognition [4,9,14]. Then, according to the predefined behavior selection rules, the robot selects an appropriate behavior that corresponds to the recognized user behavior. Finally, the selected behavior is modified by considering the user's posture and position.

2   User Behavior Recognition

2.1   LSTM-Based Model

To recognize user behavior, we propose an LSTM-based model, as shown in Fig. 1b. It is composed of an LSTM layer and a fully-connected (FC) layer. A series of user pose features are input to the model, and the model outputs the recognized user behavior class in the form of one-hot vector. Here, M is the number of user poses given to the model each time, which was set to 15 in our experiments, and the dimension of the output vector is equal to the number of user behavior classes. The detailed descriptions of the user pose features and the user behavior classes will be given in the following.

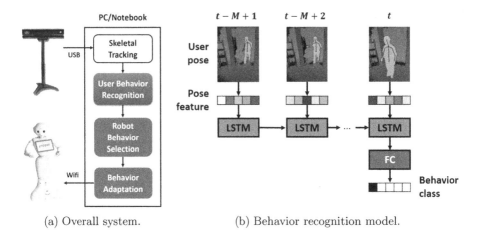

(a) Overall system.   (b) Behavior recognition model.

Fig. 1. Overall system and user behavior recognition model.

User Pose Feature. Each user pose can be represented as

$$\mathbf{P} = [\mathbf{k}_1, \mathbf{k}_2, \ldots, \mathbf{k}_9] \tag{1}$$

where $\mathbf{k}_i = (x_i, y_i, z_i)$ is the 3D position of the i-th keypoint relative to the camera. The nine body keypoints used for behavior recognition are (1) *Torso*, (2) *Spine shoulder*, (3) *Head*, (4) *Left shoulder*, (5) *Left elbow*, (6) *Left wrist*, (7) *Right shoulder*, (8) *Right elbow*, and (9) *Right wrist*.

To promote the convergence of the model, the feature vector is extracted from each user pose [8] as

$$\bar{\mathbf{P}} = \left[d, \mathbf{k}_1^2, \mathbf{k}_2^3, \mathbf{k}_2^4, \mathbf{k}_4^5, \mathbf{k}_5^6, \mathbf{k}_2^7, \mathbf{k}_7^8, \mathbf{k}_8^9\right], \tag{2}$$

where $d = \|\mathbf{k}_1\|$ is the distance from the camera to torso and $\mathbf{k}_m^n = (\mathbf{k}_n - \mathbf{k}_m)/\|(\mathbf{k}_n - \mathbf{k}_m)\|$ is the direction vector from the m-th body keypoint to the n-th body keypoint, normalized to unity. Thus, the dimension of each user pose feature vector is 25, and each value of the feature vector is between -1 and 1.

User Behavior Class. We defined 16 user behaviors by referring to the interaction scenarios of the *AIR-Act2Act* dataset [7]: *stand* (u_0), *open the door* (u_1), *hand on wall* (u_2), *absent* (u_3), *call with right hand* (u_4), *call with left hand* (u_5), *call with both hands* (u_6), *lower hands* (u_7), *raise right hand* (u_8), *wave right hand* (u_9), *raise both hands* (u_{10}), *cry with right hand* (u_{11}), *cry with left hand* (u_{12}), *cry with both hands* (u_{13}), *threaten to hit with right hand* (u_{14}), and *threaten to hit with left hand* (u_{15}).

2.2   Training Data

To train the model, we first extract training data from the dataset. The dataset contains 5,000 interaction samples performed by 50 pairs of people, each of which

Table 2. Behavior selection rules for robots.

	User behavior			Robot behavior
	1	2	3	
1	u_0	u_0	u_0	stand (r_0)
2	u_7	u_7	u_7	stand (r_0)
3	u_3	u_3	u_0	bow (r_1)
4	u_3	u_3	u_1	bow (r_1)
5	u_5	u_5	u_5	approach (r_2)
6	u_6	u_6	u_6	approach (r_2)
7	u_7	u_7	u_7	approach (r_2)
8	u_8	u_8	u_8	shake hand with right hand (r_3)
9	u_{11}	u_{11}	u_{11}	stretch hands to hug (r_4)
10	u_{12}	u_{12}	u_{12}	stretch hands to hug (r_4)
11	u_{13}	u_{13}	u_{13}	stretch hands to hug (r_4)
12	u_{14}	u_{14}	u_{14}	block face with arms (r_5)
13	u_{15}	u_{15}	u_{15}	block face with arms (r_5)

captured the interaction between two people in an indoor environment. The training inputs and outputs are extracted from each interaction sample. For the training inputs, first, we extract the pose sequence of the person who initiated the interaction. Then, the original poses recorded at a rate of 30 fps, are sampled one in every three frames to be 10 fps. Finally, a fixed number of consecutive poses are extracted from the sampled pose sequence. The ground truth output for each extracted training input is manually labeled with the help of the K-means clustering Algorithm [10]. Using 65,063 training input and output pairs, learning is done by the gradient descent algorithm with a learning rate of 0.01 and a batch size of 64.

3 Robot Behavior Selection

Based on the behavior patterns of people observed in human-human interactions, we have defined 13 behavior selection rules for robots as listed in Table 2. We defined six robot behaviors: *stand* (r_0), *bow* (r_1), *approach* (r_2), *shake hand with right hand* (r_3), *stretch hands to hug* (r_4), and *block face with arms* (r_5). Since there may be errors in user behavior recognition, the robot behavior is selected by considering the three most recent recognition results.

4 Robot Behavior Adaptation

4.1 Key Pose of Robot Behavior

A robot behavior can be expressed as a sequence of motions or poses. However, it is not possible to predefine the motion trajectory for every robot behavior

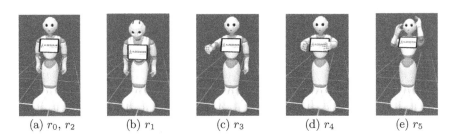

(a) r_0, r_2 (b) r_1 (c) r_3 (d) r_4 (e) r_5

Fig. 2. Key poses of robot behaviors.

because the motion trajectory should be completely different depending on the current robot pose. Therefore, we first predefine the key pose of each robot behavior (Fig. 2), each of which is represented as 10 joint angles:

$$\mathbf{R} = \{a_i | i = 1, \ldots, 10\}, \tag{3}$$

where a_1 and a_2 are the pitches of the hip and head joints, respectively, a_3 and a_4 are the pitch and roll of the left shoulder joint, respectively, a_5 and a_6 are the yaw and roll of the left elbow joint, respectively, a_7 and a_8 are the pitch and roll of the right shoulder joint, respectively, and a_9 and a_{10} are the yaw and roll of the right elbow joint, respectively. Then, a smooth motion trajectory from the current pose to the key pose is generated based on the angular interpolation [1]. Exceptionally, the behavior *approach* (r_2) changes not only the pose but also the position of the robot.

4.2   Behavior Adaptation

If a robot follows the same motion trajectory whenever it generates a specific behavior, it cannot interact naturally with users. For example, *handshake* with the user will fail if the robot stretches its hand without considering the position of the user's hand. Therefore, after selecting a robot behavior, we modify the key pose of the selected behavior according to the user's current posture and position. The adaptation procedure for each robot behavior is described as follows.

Stand, Bow, Approach. The behaviors *stand* (r_0), *bow* (r_1), and *approach* (r_2) can be performed regardless of the user's posture. Therefore, the key poses of the three behaviors are not modified. Assuming that the robot is always facing the user and changing the orientation of the robot is not covered in this study.

Shake Hand with Right Hand. To *shake hands* (r_3) with a user, the robot should change the horizontal orientation as well as the vertical orientation of its right arm. Therefore, the vertical and horizontal orientations, θ_r and α_r, of the robot's right arm to reach the user's right hand, are computed as

$$\theta_r = \text{atan2}(y_9, z_9) + \theta_c, \quad \alpha_r = \text{atan2}(x_9, z_9), \tag{4}$$

where $\mathbf{k}_9 = \{x_9, y_9, z_9\}$ is the 3D position of the user's right hand relative to the camera, θ_c is the camera angle relative to the ground, and atan2 denotes the four-quadrant inverse tangent. The key pose of the behavior r_3 is first modified based on the vertical orientation θ_r as

$$\bar{\mathbf{R}}_3 = \mathbf{R}_0 + \frac{\theta_r + \pi/2}{\pi/2}(\mathbf{R}_3 - \mathbf{R}_0), \tag{5}$$

where $\mathbf{R}_3$ and $\bar{\mathbf{R}}_3$ are the original and modified key poses of the behavior r_3, respectively, and $\mathbf{R}_0$ is the original key pose of the behavior r_0. Then, $\bar{\mathbf{R}}_3$ is modified again based on the horizontal orientation α_r as

$$\bar{a}_8 = \begin{cases} \bar{a}_8 - \alpha_r & \text{if } \alpha_h < 0 \\ \bar{a}_8 & \text{otherwise} \end{cases}, \quad \bar{a}_{10} = \begin{cases} \bar{a}_{10} + \alpha_r & \text{if } \alpha_h > 0 \\ \bar{a}_{10} & \text{otherwise} \end{cases} \tag{6}$$

where $\bar{a}_8$ and $\bar{a}_{10}$ are the rolls of the right shoulder and elbow joints in the modified key pose $\bar{\mathbf{R}}_3$, respectively. Both shoulder and elbow angles should be modified because elbow is not folded outward and shoulder is not folded inward.

Stretch Hands to Hug. To *stretch hands to hug* (r_4) a user, the robot should raise its hands to the height of the user's shoulders. The vertical orientation θ_s of the robot arms to reach the user's shoulders is computed as

$$\theta_s = \text{atan2}(y_2, z_2) + \theta_c, \tag{7}$$

where $\mathbf{k}_2 = \{x_2, y_2, z_2\}$ is the 3D position of the user's spine shoulder relative to the camera. Then, the modified key pose $\bar{\mathbf{R}}_4$ of the behavior r_4, is obtained as

$$\bar{\mathbf{R}}_4 = \mathbf{R}_0 + \frac{\theta_s + \pi/2}{\pi/2}(\mathbf{R}_4 - \mathbf{R}_0), \tag{8}$$

where $\mathbf{R}_4$ is the original key pose of the behavior r_4.

Block Face with Arms. To *block face with arms* (r_5), the robot should raise its arms to the height of the user's threatening hand. Therefore, we first determine the user's threatening hand t based on the height of both hands.

$$t = \underset{i \in \{6,9\}}{\arg\max}\,(y_i). \tag{9}$$

Then, the vertical orientation θ_t of the robot arms to avoid the user's threatening hand, is computed as

$$\theta_t = \text{atan2}(y_t, z_t) + \theta_c, \tag{10}$$

where $\mathbf{k}_t = \{x_t, y_t, z_t\}$ is the 3D position of the user's threatening hand relative to the camera. The modified key pose $\bar{\mathbf{R}}_5$ is obtained as

$$\bar{\mathbf{R}}_5 = \mathbf{R}_0 + \frac{\theta_t + \pi/2}{\pi/2}(\mathbf{R}_5 - \mathbf{R}_0), \tag{11}$$

where $\mathbf{R}_5$ is the original key pose of the behavior r_5.

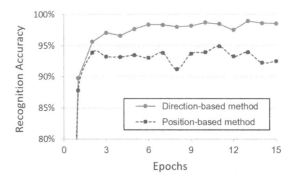

Fig. 3. Behavior recognition accuracy of the two feature extraction methods.

5 Experiments

5.1 Experiment 1: User Pose Feature Extraction

In this experiment, we compared the performance of two user pose feature extraction methods. One is the direction-based feature extraction method proposed in Eq. (2), and the other is the existing position-based method described in Eq. (1). Figure 3 shows the behavior recognition accuracy of the LSTM-based model with two different feature extraction methods. The behavior recognition accuracy with the direction-based method was approximately 99% and that with the position-based method was approximately 94%. This is because, in the direction-based method, the distance feature d, which is important for user behavior recognition, is extracted separately, but in the position-based method, it is added to all feature values.

5.2 Experiment 2: User Behavior Recognition

The recognition accuracy of the proposed model is evaluated in this experiment. Figure 4 shows the confusion matrix of the recognition results for 7,098 test data. The recognition accuracy for all user behaviors was 99%, and most of the user behaviors were recognized correctly. However, the behavior *open the door* (u_1) was sometimes wrongly recognized as the behaviors *stand* (u_0), *hand on wall* (u_2), and *lower hands* (u_7), because it is a relatively complex behavior. The behaviors *call with right hand* (u_4), *call with both hands* (u_6), and *cry with right hand* (u_{11}) were sometimes wrongly recognized as the behaviors *lower hands* (u_7) and *raise right hand* (u_8). This is because data on those behaviors are relatively scarce and are usually performed after *raising the arm* or before *lowering hands*.

5.3 Experiment 3: Robot Behavior Generation

As shown in Table 3, 25 participants were asked to rate their satisfaction with three behavior generation methods: (1) No response to the user, (2) generating

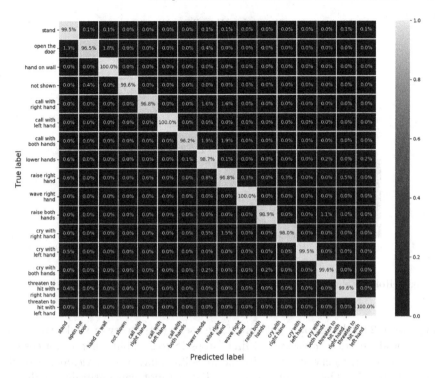

Fig. 4. Recognition accuracy of the user's behaviors.

Table 3. User satisfaction with the robot behavior generation.

Method	1	2	3
Example	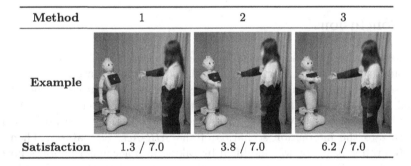		
Satisfaction	1.3 / 7.0	3.8 / 7.0	6.2 / 7.0

predefined motions, and (3) adapting behaviors (proposed). It was evaluated on a seven-level Likert scale considering naturalness, smoothness, and speed. The average satisfaction rate of the proposed method was about 6.2, which is two to four times that of other methods.

Figure 5 shows the robot's behavior generated when the user wipes the tears with his right hand. When the user starts raising his/her hand to wipe the tears

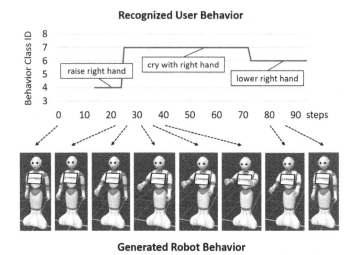

Fig. 5. Robot behavior generated when the user wipes tears with his right hand.

(steps 14 to 24), the robot is not sure if the user wants to cry or shake hands. So, the robot attempts a *handshake* at first (steps 18 to 27), but when it notices that the user is about to cry, it naturally modifies its behavior to a *hugging* behavior (steps 28 to 37). This example showed that a robot can naturally modify its behavior even if it initially misunderstands the user's intention, and this kind of interaction often occurs in human-human interactions.

6   Conclusions

In this paper, we proposed a social behavior generation method that can recognize subtle differences in user behavior and respond appropriately by considering the user's posture and position. A user behavior was recognized by the LSTM-based model based on the user poses captured from a Kinect camera. A robot behavior was selected according to the behavior selection rules predefined by referring to the interaction scenarios of the *AIR-Act2Act* dataset. Then, the selected robot behavior was modified by taking into account the user's posture and position. To show the feasibility of the proposed method, we performed experiments with a Pepper robot in a 3D virtual environment. The experimental results showed that the user behavior recognition accuracy for test data was 99%, and the robot could naturally modify its behavior even if it misunderstood the user's intention. Although this work has combined the data-driven learning method with the rule-based generation method, future work may include end-to-end learning from user recognition to robot behavior generation.

References

1. Aldebaran Robotics: Naoqi Framework (2018). http://doc.aldebaran.com/2-5/index_dev_guide.html
2. Alves, S.F., Shao, M., Nejat, G.: A socially assistive robot to facilitate and assess exercise goals. In: Proceedings of International Conference on Robotics and Automation, Montreal, Canada (2019)
3. Dindo, H., Schillaci, G.: An adaptive probabilistic approach to goal-level imitation learning. In: 2010 IEEE/RSJ International Conference on Intelligent Robots and Systems, pp. 4452–4457. IEEE (2010)
4. Du, Y., Wang, W., Wang, L.: Hierarchical recurrent neural network for skeleton based action recognition. In: Proceedings of the IEEE Conference On Computer Vision And Pattern Recognition, pp. 1110–1118 (2015)
5. Hochreiter, S., Schmidhuber, J.: Long short-term memory. Neural Comput. 9(8), 1735–1780 (1997)
6. Huang, C.M., Mutlu, B.: Robot behavior toolkit: generating effective social behaviors for robots. In: 2012 7th ACM/IEEE International Conference on Human-Robot Interaction (HRI), pp. 25–32. IEEE (2012)
7. Ko, W.R., Jang, M., Lee, J., Kim, J.: AIR-Act2Act: Human-human interaction dataset for teaching non-verbal social behaviors to robots. Int. J. Robot. Res. 40(4–5), 691–697 (2021)
8. Ko, W.R., Lee, J., Jang, M., Kim, J.: End-to-end learning of social behaviors for humanoid robots. In: 2020 IEEE International Conference on Systems, Man, and Cybernetics (SMC), pp. 1200–1205. IEEE (2020)
9. Liu, J., Shahroudy, A., Xu, D., Wang, G.: Spatio-temporal LSTM with trust gates for 3d human action recognition. In: Leibe, B., Matas, J., Sebe, N., Welling, M. (eds.) ECCV 2016. LNCS, vol. 9907, pp. 816–833. Springer, Cham (2016). https://doi.org/10.1007/978-3-319-46487-9_50
10. MacQueen, J., et al.: Some methods for classification and analysis of multivariate observations. In: Proceedings of the Fifth Berkeley Symposium On Mathematical Statistics And Probability, vol. 1, pp. 281–297, Oakland, CA, USA (1967)
11. Microsoft Corp.: Kinect for Windows SDK 2.0 Documentation (2014)
12. Pandey, A.K., Gelin, R.: A mass-produced sociable humanoid robot: Pepper: The first machine of its kind. IEEE Robot. Autom. Mag. 25(3), 40–48 (2018)
13. Zaraki, A., Dautenhahn, K., Wood, L., Novanda, O., Robins, B.: Toward autonomous child-robot interaction: development of an interactive architecture for the humanoid kaspar robot. In: 3rd Workshop on Child-Robot Interaction (CRI2017) in International Conference on Human Robot Interaction (HRI 2017), Vienna, Austria, pp. 6–9 (2017)
14. Zhu, W., et al.: Co-occurrence feature learning for skeleton based action recognition using regularized deep lstm networks. arXiv preprint arXiv:1603.07772 (2016)

A Transformer-Based Approach for Choosing Actions in Social Robotics

Riccardo De Benedictis$^{(\boxtimes)}$ ⓘ, Gloria Beraldo ⓘ, Gabriella Cortellessa ⓘ,
Francesca Fracasso ⓘ, and Amedeo Cesta ⓘ

ISTC - Institute of Cognitive Sciences and Technology, CNR - Italian National
Research Council, Via S. Martino della Battaglia 44, 00185 Rome, Italy
{riccardo.debenedictis,gloria.beraldo,gabriella.cortellessa,
francesca.fracasso,amedeo.cesta}@istc.cnr.it

Abstract. The growing deployment of social robots requires the ability to adapt to the dynamic changes occurring in the real environments. These reactive behaviors, however, are often incapable of reasoning and predicting the effects of their actions in the next future. Therefore, they must be accompanied by forms of deliberative semantic/causal reasoning. The combination of the reactive and deliberative forms of reasoning, which resembles the dual process theory, raises the problem of entrusting tasks to the corresponding modules. Just as happens in biological systems, the tendency to assign activities, as much as possible, towards the lower abstraction layers, equips the systems with more responsive capabilities at the cost of making the reactive layers more difficult to implement. In this document, we will introduce an architecture that, inspired by the classic three-tier architecture, combines slow and fast forms of reasoning, allowing social robots to achieve complex and dynamic behaviors. Since entrusting tasks to the more reactive components complicates their implementation (e.g., it requires the definition of formal rules which may not adequately generalize to unforeseen scenarios), we aim to reduce the technicalities and, consequently, to facilitate to the developers the implementation of the reactive behaviors. By relying on recent achievements in natural language translation, we will describe our recent efforts to adopt Transformer-based architectures, allowing the replacement of formal rules with easier to write "stories", defined through sequences of perceived events and actions, entrusting the system with the task of learning behaviors by generalizing from them.

Keywords: Automated planning and execution · Dynamic adaptation · Adaptive human-robot interaction

1 Introduction

If we want robots to interact with people in a natural way, they have to "behave like people" and, to do so, they somehow have to *reason* like people. Whatever

This research was funded by the "SI-Robotics: Social robotics for active and healthy ageing" project (Italian M.I.U.R., PON—Ricerca e Innovazione 2014–2020—G.A. ARS01 01120).

F. Cavallo et al. (Eds.): ICSR 2022, LNAI 13817, pp. 198–207, 2022.
https://doi.org/10.1007/978-3-031-24667-8_18

our skills, indeed, before becoming experts in a particular field we, as human beings, have to overcome hours and hours of lessons, study, training and practice. The result of this process, typically known as learning, is a transfer of skills from more explicit forms of reasoning, which are usually more accurate yet also more complex and hence slower, towards more implicit forms of reasoning which, without much overthinking and hence in a less accurate way, are able to quickly produce fascinating behaviors. These different forms of reasoning are well described in the dual process psychological theories [13] and are typically called, respectively, as *thinking slow* and *thinking fast*.

Given their popularity, the dual process theories are often used as a reference by Artificial Intelligence (AI) developers for building intelligent machines [2]. The two forms of reasoning, specifically, reflect on two macro-arguments faced by AI in two fields that are, too often, considered disjunctive: symbolic and sub-symbolic AI. On the one hand, symbolic AI is based on the idea that humans make sense of the world by creating internal symbolic representations, based on logic, and rules to deal with them. Symbolic AI is inherently more precise. It is computationally more complex and, consequently, slower at generating solutions. Furthermore, the inference rules are, not without difficulty, handwritten by a programmer and, typically, have serious problems in dealing with the "messiness" of the real world. On the other hand, in the last twenty years, the large availability of data, the increase in the computing power of machines able, for example, to significantly parallelize tasks thanks to GPUs, and advances in algorithms and programming languages, have created the ideal conditions for the rise of a different approach to intelligence called deep learning. These approaches manage to solve problems, often, better than humans. Based solely on data, however, they are unable to explain how objects relate to each other and, hence, they do not actually "think".

Connecting these two approaches represents a challenge that, recently, is giving more and more space to a new research trend called Neuro-Symbolic Artificial Intelligence [16,17]. Taking inspiration from classical robotic architectures, and building on the experience gained in the development of similar architectures [7], in this document we will investigate an architecture capable of integrating symbolic and sub-symbolic reasoning with a twofold goal: a) allowing the generalization capabilities of the system's behavior starting from training "stories" (e.g., sequences of events and actions) relieving the programmer of the need to consider all possible combinations of interactions; b) simplifying the definition of a such initial knowledge that can be done more easily by people with no technical background.

2 A Three-Tier Architecture for Fast and Slow Thinking in Social Robots

Mobile Telepresence Robots are a class of robots having no or very limited autonomy [15] which, thanks to the more recent introduction of proactive services and capabilities [11,14], might allow mitigating the problem of isolation of older adults living alone [4]. We are aiming, in particular, at creating an holistic system that includes multivariate services from the monitoring of the physiological measurements to the motivation of performing cognitive and physical exercises through the robot, from telepresence services to advanced remote teleoperation based on the *shared autonomy* paradigm which fuses the secondary user's commands (e.g., doctors, medical staff, family, friends) with the information of the environment to ease the remote interaction by relying on the robot's intelligence in preventing collisions and implementing social behaviors [1].

In order to increase the robots' autonomy we have adopted an architecture depicted in Fig. 1. Taking inspiration from classical robotics architectures [10], specifically, our system consists of a *deliberative* tier (the underlying reasoner, out of the scope of this paper, is described in [5]) responsible for the generation, the execution and the dynamic adaptation of the plans; a *sequencing* tier which, through the application of a policy, executes a sequence of actions according to the current state of the system; and a *sensing* and a *controlling* tier, which respectively interprets

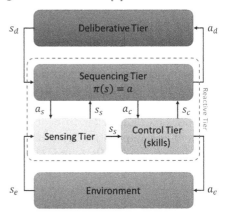

Fig. 1. The three-layer architecture.

data produced by sensors and translates the sequencer's actions into lower level commands for the actuators.

The state, according to which actions are selected from the sequencer tier policy, is described by the combination of three distinct states:

- the s_s state, generated by the sensing tier and characterized as a consequence of the interpretation of sensory data, is able to represent, for example, the intentions of the users, the estimation of their current pose, the users' emotions perceived from the camera, as well as situations which might be dangerous for both the users and for the robot;
- the s_c state, generated by the control tier, representing the state of the controllers such as whether the robot is navigating or not, or whether the robot is talking to or listening to the user;
- the s_d state, generated by the deliberative tier, representing the high-level commands generated as a result of the execution of the planned plans

Similarly, the actions executed by the sequencer tier can be of three distinct types:

- the a_s actions, towards the sensors, responsible, for example, for their activation or for their shutdown;
- the a_c actions, towards the controllers, responsible, for example, for activating contextual navigation commands as well as conversational interactions with the users;

– the a_d actions, towards the deliberative tier, responsible, for example, for the creation and for the adaptation of the generated plans.

It is worth noting that, through the application of the $\pi(s)$ policy, the sequencing tier can act both on the environment, through the a_c actions, and, through the a_d actions, introspectively on other higher-level forms of reasoning adopted by the agent itself. The high-level actions generated by the deliberative tier while executing the plans, moreover, constitute only one component among those that determines the choice of the actions by the policy. Somehow, they are not mandatory for the autonomy of the robot and represent a sort of "suggestions", for the agent, on the things to do.

In our architecture, the slow thinking is completely covered by the deliberative tier. Specifically, this tier deals with applying forms of semantic/causal reasoning, adopting logical/arithmetic approaches for generating high-level plans of the activities to be executed while adapting them according to the information dynamically emerging from the environment. The fast thinking side, on the other hand, is covered by the sensing and control tiers, which deal with generating abstractions starting from sensory data and with generating low-level commands for the robot's actuators. The next section focuses on the intermediate sequencing tier which, although still symbolically, selects the actions to be executed according to the current state. Since the sequencer tier behaves reactively, it is useful to shift a large portion of the robot's interactions toward this component. This shift, however, complicates the implementation of the sequencer's policy. Nonetheless, as we will see, by exploiting techniques developed in natural language processing contexts, we are able to simplify the implementation by learning it starting from sequences of behaviors called "stories".

3   The Dialogue-Based Sequencer

Conceptually, the sequencer tier simply implements a policy $\pi(s)$ which, given any possible state s of the environment, returns an action a to be executed. Implementing a policy, by itself, constitutes a very straightforward task. In simple terms, it just requires creating a function that maps, to each possible state, an action to be performed. However, as the number of possible states grows, the situation becomes practically more complicated. A very common approach, in these cases, consists in using a state transition system [8]. The number of transitions this system can have, however, can grow quadratically with the number of states, which, in turn, grows exponentially with the number of parameters that describe the state. In our case, in general, the current state is described partly by the result of the sensor analysis, partly by the feedback from the control tier and partly by the high-level tasks to be performed, chosen by the deliberative tier.

The system must be able to act in a dynamic environment and to interact, for example, in natural language, with the user. Since, in general, dialogues with users can be made up of a variety of interactions in which the human often takes for granted a lot of information that can be extracted from the context, the status should also be enriched with further parameters that take into account *sequences* of such interactions, which, ultimately, build up the context. Finally, if we also want to take into account the psychological and physical aspects of the user, together with other possible parameters necessary for personalization and adaptation, we get, very quickly, too many aspects to take into account.

As the number of cases to consider increases, representing explicitly a state transition system becomes soon impractical. Approaches related to knowledge-based systems [12], for example, allow for better scaling in the definition of the robot's behaviors. Such approaches reason through bodies of

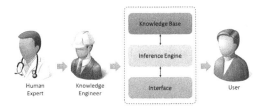

Fig. 2. The typical methodology adopted for implementing a knowledge-based system.

knowledge represented mainly as *if-then* rules. As shown in Fig. 2, such systems are typically divided into two subsystems: the knowledge base and the inference engine. While the knowledge base represents facts and rules, the inference engine applies the rules to the known facts to deduce new facts. The issue of writing the rules, however, remains. The main problem, in common with the state transition system approach, is related to the need for two different professional figures who must work together to achieve this goal. On the one hand, in fact, the domain expert knows how the system should behave, but does not have the logic skills necessary for defining the rules. On the other hand, the knowledge engineer knows very well how to define the rules and how they affect the behavior of the system, but does not know how the system should behave. If we were able to define a less formal language, and therefore simpler, to allow the domain expert to directly insert his/her knowledge into the system, possibly using machine learning based techniques capable of generalizing and, therefore, reducing the amount of information that the expert would put into the system, we could bypass the figure of the knowledge engineer, removing him/her from the process of defining the behavior of the system or, at least, assigning him/her a less onerous task. This language, as we will soon see, could be the language of "stories", made up simply of input sequences that the system takes as inputs and outputs that the system must perform. To better understand how we have dealt with this problem, however, it is first necessary to introduce some basic concepts behind the dialogue management systems.

A first distinction, in Natural Language Understanding (NLU), is the one between the *utterance*, that is anything the user says (like, for example, "Can you remind me, tomorrow at 10am, to take the medicines?") and its *intent*, that is a characterization of the intention the user was aiming at in issuing the utterance. Each intent, specifically, is identified by a name which can be used for reasoning upon it. As an example, since the intention of a user saying something like "Can you remind me, tomorrow at 10am, to take the medicines?" to the robot is to set a reminder (namely, to "take the medicines" "tomorrow at 10am"), the name associated with the intent can be, for instance, #set_reminder.

Intent classification typically uses natural language processing and machine learning techniques to automatically associate words or expressions with a particular intent. Such classifiers need to be trained with text examples, known as training data, to properly classify text. The training data, for a #set_reminder intent, for example, could be sentences like "Remind me to go to the doctor" or "Can you please remind me to take the blood pressure pills tomorrow morning?". Once trained, the classifier will learn to classify, with some confidence, the input text, thus allowing to classify similar sentences, even if never seen, with the same intent.

In order to understand the utterances coming from users we have adopted a lightweight architecture called Dual Intent and Entity Transformer (DIET) [3] as implemented in Rasa[1], which, by relying on the Transformer architecture [18], is able to obtain better performances than large-scale pre-trained language models such as BERT [9], which are not always ideal for developing conversational AI applications, and, at the same time, is less expensive in the training phase. By carrying out simultaneously intent classification and entity recognition (for extracting, for example, names of people, numerical values and/or geographical locations), DIET is able to classify any sentence that can be pronounced by the users into a finite number of choices, thus allowing the system to select an appropriate answer.

Such selections, furthermore, should be as robust as possible to any missing information deductible from past interactions (the context). Suppose, for example, that the user asks the system "When do Dr. Rossi receive?". This sentence is classified in the #reception_hours intent and the word "Rossi" is recognized as a @person type entity. At this point, the system should be able to select an answer in which it communicates Dr. Rossi's office hours. However, if, later on, the user were to ask "Where is his studio located?", the sentence would be classified as an #ask_location intent. To select an adequate response, the system should take into account that the previous interaction had been classified through the #reception_hours intent and, above all, that it contained the "Rossi" entity of type @person, omitted by the user, as would happen in a natural interaction, in the last pronounced utterance.

The number of combinations of possible answers that the system has to give to the user within a dialogue, hence, grows exponentially with the length of the interaction, making the definition of the rules for choosing the answers excessively expensive and error prone. Fortunately, the same DIET architecture, as well as to classify the intent starting from a sequence of words, can be trained to select an answer starting from a sequence of interactions called *stories* [19]. The answers, furthermore, can be replaced with more general *actions*, by means of which it is possible to enhance the behaviors of the system. Intuitively, these actions are designed to allow the dialogue engine to build responses by querying

---

[1] https://rasa.com/.

databases, knowledge bases or external REST services. In our system, however, we make a broader use of them, exploiting them for representing, as a whole, all the actions produced as output by the sequencer policy. Such actions, specifically, can be, for example, sentences to be pronounced, as in the case of a normal vocal interaction, but also commands to control the robot's facial expressions (see, for example, Fig. 3), navigation commands, to move the robot to a certain position or to a desired distance from the user, as well as planning and/or plan adaptation requests for the deliberative tier.

Robot listening   **Robot speaking**   **Robot exhibiting emotion**

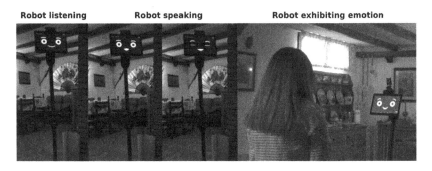

Fig. 3. An illustrative picture showing the dialogue between a person and the robot in a domestic environment.

Just like responses, intents and entities can also be used in a broader way. Rather than representing just the output of an intent classification process, as in a typical natural language interaction, intents can be used, bypassing the intent classification process, to trigger the dialogue engine on a specific task. Suppose, for example, that the deliberative tier has scheduled, at a certain time, a reminder for the user for reminding to take blood pressure pills. When the predetermined time arrives, the deliberative tier sends the command to the sequencer tier which, after a handshaking phase to establish the executability of the command (the sequencer tier, in general, could ask the deliberative tier to delay the start of the activity or it could directly decree its failure), is translated into an #ask_reminder intent to be sent to the dialogue engine. At this point, as a consequence of these intents and entities, the dialogue engine will select a sequence of actions to perform and execute them. Specifically, an action will first be selected to set a smiling facial expression, the reminder will then be communicated to the user followed by a confirmation requested, so as to make sure that the user has received the reminder. Finally, in case of an affirmative reply, a closing task message will be sent, with positive outcome, to the deliberative tier.

4   A Reminder Example

Figure 4 shows an example of training data for instructing the system about how to set reminders. In our current implementation the start of a human-initiated interaction with the robot occurs by pressing a "talk to me" button on the robot's tablet. Through the sensing tier, pressing this button translates into a change of state for the sequencer tier and, specifically, in the sending of a #start_interaction intent to the dialogue engine. The dialogue engine must, at this point, choose, among all the actions it has available, one or more actions according to the training stories and, relying on the previous story, it would most likely select first the set_smiling_face action, changing the expression of the robot, and then the utter_offer_help action, making the system synthesize a sentence in which the robot asks the user if he/she needs some help. At this point, for example, the user pronounces the utterance "Can you remind me, tomorrow at 10am, to take the medicines?", classified by the dialogue engine as a #set_reminder intent. Once again the dialogue engine is called upon to select a sequence of actions to be performed and, based on the previous story, it could select the utter_reminder_set_confirmation action, to confirm to the user that the robot has taken over the task of setting a reminder, the action_set_reminder action, to request to the deliberative tier a change to the current plan by introducing a new reminder, the set_default_face action for restoring the robot's default facial expression and, finally, the action_command_done action to close the interaction with the user.

As time goes by, there comes a time when the reminder needs to be administered. The deliberative tier, in particular, will send, at proper time, the command to the sequencer tier which is translated into a #tell_reminder intent to trigger the dialogue engine which must then choose,

```
— intent :  start_interaction
— action :  set_smiling_face
— action :  utter_offer_help
— intent :  set_reminder
— action :  utter_reminder_set_confirmation
— action :  action_set_reminder
— action :  set_default_face
— action :  action_command_done
```

Fig. 4. A story for instructing the system about how to set reminders.

among all the actions it has available, one or more actions according to the policy learnt by the training stories.

It is worth emphasizing how the use of stories to generate sequences of actions is achieved through off-the-shelf tools. The interesting aspects concern the use of actions to control the behaviour of the robot (e.g., its facial expressions) and the unconventional use of the intents which, injected into the dialogue engine by the deliberative tier, can give the robot the ability to initiate an interaction. In particular, we tested the system with 10 real users asking them to have free interaction activities initiated by them, as well as some physical and cognitive exercises decided by the robot. Despite the complexity of the interactions, the generalization capacity of the Transformer-based architecture allows a natural interaction with users starting from 35 stories. By comparison, a subset of the implemented cognitive exercises has required, in a previous work [6], the definition in a first-order logical formalism of 150 rules, much less intuitive than stories.

5 Conclusions

The adaptability skills required by the interaction of a social robot with a dynamic environment can be carried out at different levels. Answering to a request from a user, for example, must correspond to a rapid reaction and, therefore, must be carried out without thinking too much or, at most, thinking fast. Other adaptations require taking into account additional factors such as, in the case of the introduction of a new activity (e.g., a reminder), taking into account when the activity must be carried out, avoiding the overlapping (scheduling) with other activities that require exclusive resources (e.g., avoiding sending a reminder during a cognitive exercise), or the introduction of further activities (planning) necessary to create the conditions for the execution of the activity introduced (e.g., introducing a warm-up exercise before a physical exercise). These further adaptations can hardly be achievable through a policy, requiring a more accurate and, hence, a slower thinking.

As in the human learning process, and in order to make social robots more responsive and interactive, the trend is to shift activities to the reactive level as much as possible, resulting in an increase in the difficulty of its implementation. In recent years, attention-based mechanisms have been found to be particularly effective in natural language translation activities. Transformer-based architectures, which make use of attention mechanisms, can also be effectively used to "translate" sequences of states into sequences of actions, thus training the system, through a set of stories, to behave appropriately. The learning process allows to generalize the system's behavior starting from the training stories, relieving the programmer of the need to consider all possible combinations of interactions. What's more, defining stories is a technically simpler task than defining a state machine or a set of first-order rules and, as such, can be done more easily by people with no technical background.

References

1. Beraldo, G., et al.: Shared autonomy for telepresence robots based on people-aware navigation. In: Ang Jr., M.H., Asama, H., Lin, W., Foong, S. (eds.) IAS 2021. LNNS, vol. 412, pp. 109–122. Springer, Cham (2022). https://doi.org/10.1007/978-3-030-95892-3_9
2. Bonnefon, J.F., Rahwan, I.: Machine thinking, fast and slow. Trends Cogn. Sci. **24**(12), 1019–1027 (2020). http://publications.ut-capitole.fr/41996/
3. Bunk, T., Varshneya, D., Vlasov, V., Nichol, A.: DIET: lightweight language understanding for dialogue systems. CoRR abs/2004.09936 (2020), https://arxiv.org/abs/2004.09936
4. Cesta, A., Cortellessa, G., Fracasso, F., Orlandini, A., Turno, M.: User needs and preferences on AAL systems that support older adults and their carers. J. Ambient Intell. Smart Environ. **10**(1), 49–70 (2018)
5. De Benedictis, R., Cesta, A.: Lifted Heuristics for Timeline-based Planning. In: ECAI-2020, 24th European Conference on Artificial Intelligence, pp. 498–2337. Santiago de Compostela, Spain (2020)

6. De Benedictis, R., Tagliaferri, C., Cortellessa, G., Cesta, A.: Tailoring a forward looking vocal assistant to older adults. In: Bettelli, A., Monteriù, A., Gamberini, L. (eds.) Ambient Assisted Living, pp. 3–17. Springer International Publishing, Cham (2022)
7. De Benedictis, R., Umbrico, A., Fracasso, F., Cortellessa, G., Orlandini, A., Cesta, A.: A two-layered approach to adaptive dialogues for robotic assistance. In: 2020 29th IEEE International Conference on Robot and Human Interactive Communication (RO-MAN), pp. 82–89 (2020). https://doi.org/10.1109/RO-MAN47096.2020.9223605
8. Dean, T.L., Wellman, M.P.: Planning and Control. Morgan Kaufmann Publishers Inc. (1991)
9. Devlin, J., Chang, M.W., Lee, K., Toutanova, K.: BERT: Pre-training of deep bidirectional transformers for language understanding. In: Proceedings of the 2019 Conference of the North American Chapter of the Association for Computational Linguistics: Human Language Technologies, Volume 1 (Long and Short Papers). pp. 4171–4186. Association for Computational Linguistics, Minneapolis, Minnesota (Jun 2019). https://doi.org/10.18653/v1/N19-1423, https://aclanthology.org/N19-1423
10. Gat, E.: On Three-Layer Architectures. In: Artificial Intelligence and Mobile Robots, pp. 195–210. AAAI Press (1997)
11. Isabet, B., Pino, M., Lewis, M., Benveniste, S., Rigaud, A.S.: Social Telepresence Robots: A Narrative Review of Experiments Involving Older Adults before and during the COVID-19 Pandemic. Int. J. Environ. Res. Public Health 18(7), 3597 (2021)
12. Jackson, P.: Introduction to Expert Systems, 2nd edn. Addison-Wesley Longman Publishing Co., Inc, USA (1990)
13. Kahneman, D.: Thinking, fast and slow. Macmillan (2011)
14. Laniel, S., Létourneau, D., Grondin, F., Labbé, M., Ferland, F., Michaud, F.: Toward enhancing the autonomy of a telepresence mobile robot for remote home care assistance. Paladyn, J. Behav. Robot. 12(1), 214–237 (2021)
15. Orlandini, A.: ExCITE Project: a review of forty-two months of robotic telepresence technology evolution. Presence 25(3), 204–221 (2016)
16. Sarker, M.K., Zhou, L., Eberhart, A., Hitzler, P.: Neuro-symbolic artificial intelligence. AI Commun. 34(3), 197–209 (jan 2021). https://doi.org/10.3233/AIC-210084, https://doi.org/10.3233/AIC-210084
17. Susskind, Z., Arden, B., John, L.K., Stockton, P., John, E.B.: Neuro-symbolic AI: an emerging class of AI workloads and their characterization. CoRR abs/2109.06133 (2021), https://arxiv.org/abs/2109.06133
18. Vaswani, A., et al.: Attention is all you need. In: Guyon, I., et al. (eds.) Advances in Neural Information Processing Systems. vol. 30. Curran Associates, Inc. (2017), https://proceedings.neurips.cc/paper/2017/file/3f5ee243547dee91fbd053c1c4a845aa-Paper.pdf
19. Vlasov, V., Mosig, J.E.M., Nichol, A.: Dialogue transformers (2019). 10.48550/ARXIV.1910.00486, https://arxiv.org/abs/1910.00486

Deep Reinforcement Learning for the Autonomous Adaptive Behavior of Social Robots

Marcos Maroto-Gómez(✉)⬛, María Malfaz⬛, Álvaro Castro-González⬛, and Miguel Ángel Salichs⬛

Systems Engineering and Automation, University Carlos III of Madrid, Butarque 15, Leganés, Madrid, Spain
{marmarot,mmalfaz,acgonzal,salichs}@ing.uc3m.es

Abstract. Social assistive robots are conceived to cooperate with humans in many areas like healthcare, education, or assistance. In situations where the workforce is scarce and when these machines work with special populations like older adults or children, the behavior must be appropriate and seem natural. In this contribution, we present a Deep Reinforcement Learning model for the autonomous adaptive behavior of social robots. The model emulates some aspects of human biology by generating artificial biologically inspired functions, like sleep or entertainment, to endow robots with long-term autonomous behavior. The Deep Reinforcement Learning system overcomes classical Reinforcement Learning problems such as high dimensional state-action spaces learning which actions better suit each situation the robot is experiencing. Besides, the system aims at maintaining the robot's internal state in the best possible condition sustaining human-robot interaction. The results show that our robot Mini correctly learns how to regulate the deficits in its biological processes by selecting from six actions in a high diversity of situations that merge the state of the biological process and the external stimuli the robot perceives from the environment.

Keywords: Autonomous social robots · Bioinspiration · Human-robot interaction · Deep reinforcement learning

1 Introduction

Autonomous social robots operating in Human-Robot Interaction (HRI) must consider many inputs to make appropriate decisions. In high dimensional spaces,

Miguel Ángel Salichs—The research leading to these results has received funding from the projects: Robots Sociales para Estimulación Física, Cognitiva y Afectiva de Mayores (ROSES), RTI2018-096338-B-I00, funded by the Ministerio de Ciencia, Innovación y Universidades; Robots sociales para mitigar la soledad y el aislamiento en mayores (SOROLI), PID2021-123941OA-I00, funded by Agencia Estatal de Investigación (AEI), Spanish Ministerio de Ciencia e Innovación. This publication is part of the R&D&I project PLEC2021-007819 funded by MCIN/AEI/10.13039/501100011033 and by the European Union NextGenerationEU/PRTR.

F. Cavallo et al. (Eds.): ICSR 2022, LNAI 13817, pp. 208–217, 2022.
https://doi.org/10.1007/978-3-031-24667-8_19

where the robot has to be aware of many different situations and optimally learn from trial and error which action better suits each of them, classical learning methods such as Reinforcement Learning (RL) have demonstrated a weak performance. Nevertheless, in the last years, combining classical RL methods with Deep Learning produced very positive outcomes when dealing with large inputs without requiring a complex definition of the robot's state space [12]. Autonomous behavior is essential to allow social robots to operate successfully without human intervention in complex environments. Besides, we believe that endowing social robots with biologically inspired behavior emulating human biological functions like sleep–wake rhythms or socialization might produce more natural and adaptive responses. Therefore, robot users could more readily accept the behavior of these machines in dynamic and complex situations.

Little research has been found using Deep Reinforcement Learning (DRL) to generate autonomous and adaptive behavior in social robotics. Most work focuses on presenting models for adapting the robot behavior to specific situations during HRI sessions rather than producing a biologically inspired general behavior over long periods [2]. Akalin et al. [1] developed an adaptive DRL model for HRI with older adults. The model receives verbal and non-verbal information from the user to obtain a reward based on their engagement. Then, the robot selects appropriate actions to improve the interaction experience. Similarly, Qureshi et al. [13,14] have explored the autonomous learning of human-like social skills using intrinsic motivations generated from novelty, competence, surprise, learning progress, and empowerment. Gao et al. [5] presented a fast adaptive architecture to improve people's trust towards a Pepper robot while interacting. The results show that by using social signals extracted from the interaction, Pepper could produce personalized behavior that people could appreciate. Finally, many works have employed DRL for the autonomous social navigation of robots in crowded environments by recognizing and anticipating the users' social movements [4,7,16].

The previous literature review presents works for adaptive HRI and social navigation using DRL as a learning mechanism. However, none addresses the problem of generating biologically inspired behavior for robots working on continuous long-lasting tasks interacting with people. To fill this gap, this contribution presents a DRL model for the biologically inspired autonomous and adaptive behavior of the social robot Mini [15]. We used classical RL methods in previous contributions to endow Mini with autonomous biologically inspired behavior. First, we used Q-learning [9] in a low-dimensional discrete state-action space where Mini had to maintain an optimal internal state while affording HRI. However, this method required a very high training time since the robot's actions lasted excessively. Then, we designed a second scenario [10] in which we used Dyna-Q+ to overcome Q-learning's limitations. In Dyna-Q+, we extended the robot state-action space producing a more diverse and natural behavior. Although Dyna-Q+ produced better results than Q-learning since it uses an environment model that runs in simulation, it still presented most of the drawbacks of classical RL methods.

For this reason, in this approach, we consider a high-dimensional state space consisting of 7 variables (sleep, social entertainment, self-entertainment, cognitive interaction, stress, energy, and the dominant motivation) representing how artificial biological processes evolve in the robot and drive the selection of 6 actions (wait, sleep, talk, play, dance, and meditate). We use Deep Q-Networks (DQN) simulation to run the model and then transfer the knowledge to the social robot Mini. Therefore, the system goal is to map situations (states) to actions to maintain an optimal internal state during HRI.

This manuscript introduces DRL in Sect. 2 as the learning method used in this work. Then, Sect. 3 presents our social robot Mini, the biologically inspired model used for producing behaviors, and the actions that Mini can execute. Section 4 shows the results we have obtained while testing our architecture. Finally, Sect. 5 closes this work with the main conclusions and future work.

2   Methods

Deep Q-Networks (DQNs), an algorithm proposed by Mnih et al. [11] in 2015, learns how to map situations to actions from trial and error. DRL considers an agent $\mathcal{A}g$ that executes actions in an environment $\mathcal{E}$ following a specific policy π. In each time step t, the agent is in state $s \in \mathcal{S}$ and it has to select an action $a \in \mathcal{A}$ that produces a reward r which brings it to a new state s'. The agent's goal is to select actions to maximize its future cumulative reward using a reward function $\mathcal{R}$. DQN uses a deep neural network to approximate a solution of the action-value function (also known as the Q function) that can be expressed as

$$Q^*(s,a) = \max_{\pi} \mathbb{E}\left[r_t + \gamma r_{t+1} + \gamma^2 r_{t+2} + ... | s_t = s, a_t = a, \pi\right], \tag{1}$$

by maximizing the expected $\mathbb{E}[\cdot]$ sum of rewards discounted by factor γ at each time step following the behavior policy $\pi = P(a|s)$ after executing action a in state s.

DQN includes experience replay, a novel method that stores the agent's experiences in a dataset of experiences used to speed up and stabilize learning. For learning, the loss function in Eq. 2 has to be optimized

$$\mathcal{L}(\theta) = \mathbb{E}_{s,a,r,s'}\left[\left(r + \gamma \max_{a' \in \mathcal{A}} Q(s', a'; \theta_i^-) - Q(s, a, \theta_i)\right)^2\right], \tag{2}$$

where θ_i are the parameters of the Q-network at iteration i, θ_i^- are parameters of the target network updated with θ_i every C steps with $C = 4$, and γ is the discount factor.

The agent learning depends on the reward function $\mathcal{R}$, whose optimization leads the agent to decide the most appropriate action in each time step. Since in this work the robot's goal is to maintain its biological processes in good condition while sustaining HRI, we propose a reward function that considers a weighted variation of the robot's well-being to recognize the benefits of executing each action in each time step. Therefore, we must provide a background of the learning environment before defining the reward function.

Table 1. Biological processes evolving in the social robot Mini.

Process	Evolution	Ideal value	Range	Description
Sleep	+0.2	0	0 to 100	Represents the robot need to sleep
Social entertainment	−0.3	100	0 to 100	Represents the robot need to play
Self-entertainment	−0.3	100	0 to 100	Represents the robot need of socializing with the user
Cognitive interaction	−0.2	100	0 to 100	Represents the robot need to do entertainment activities alone
Stress	+0.1	0	0 to 100	Represents the evolution of the robot's stress in arousing situations
Energy	−0.2	100	0 to 100	Represents the robot tiredness when executing activities

3   Environment

Mini (see Fig. 1) is a desktop social robot that operates in a broad diversity of HRI applications. It is intended for face-to-face interactions with people who can execute many activities like playing games, visualizing multimedia content, or performing cognitive stimulation therapies. The robot can dynamically drive personalized entertainment, cognitive, and physical stimulation sessions to maintain engagement when working with some sectors of society like older adults. Thanks to its autonomous behavior using the biologically inspired DRL model presented below, Mini can work without human intervention facilitating its deployment in houses and care centers to assist older adults.

3.1   Biologically Inspired Processes

The autonomous behavior selection of the social robot Mini originates in an artificial biologically inspired model that emulates living beings' processes to produce more natural actions. Mini has seven biological processes that evolve with time, representing the robot's needs as defined in Table 1. These biological processes exhibit different evolution dynamics with time (see Fig. 1). Every time step t, they evolve following specific rhythms.

When the current value $cv_i(t)$ of a process in time step t deviates from their ideal value $iv_i(t)$, a deficit $d_i(t)$ appears in the process. Mathematically, deficits can be expressed using Eq. 3.

$$d_i(t) = |iv_i - cv_i(t)|, \tag{3}$$

The robot's internal state deficits urge it to execute actions through motivation. Thus, we define motivations as processes that urge behavior. Drawing on Lorenz's ideas [8] and Cañamero's modeling [3], the motivations' intensity m_i depend on the magnitude of the deficit d_i of specific biological processes modulated by the stimuli we perceive from the environment. In this work, Mini can perceive two different stimuli whose intensity s_i range from 0 to 100, as indicated in Table 2. These stimuli regulate motivations as Table 3 shows.

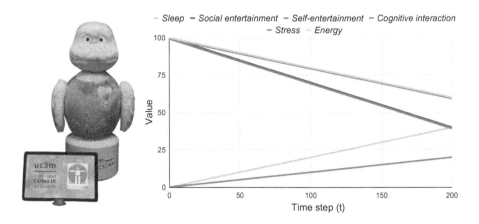

Fig. 1. The social robot Mini and the evolution of its internal biological processes. As we can see, the evolution of social entertainment–self-entertainment and energy–cognitive stimulation evolve following the same dynamics.

Table 2. Stimuli that the social robot Mini can perceive from the environment with influence on its motivations.

Stimulus	Range	Description
User	0 to 100	Person that interacts with Mini performing activities
Light	0 to 100	Light intensity perceived in the room

In this work, we shape the intensity of a motivation as

$$m_i(t) = d_i(t) + \beta_i \times d_i(t) \times s_i(t), \tag{4}$$

where $s_i(t)$ is the intensity with which the robot perceives a stimulus with influence on the motivation m_i and β_i is a weight that modulates how strong the influence is.

Motivations compete among them to become dominant and urge specific behavior. Thus, we define the dominant motivation as the motivation with the highest level of intensity. In this work, the dominant motivation is essential in the robot's state and is used to reinforce actions related to motivations boosted by environmental stimuli.

Mini has to execute actions to reduce its internal deficits and maintain a good internal condition. Table 4 shows the actions that Mini can execute and their effects on the biological processes applied every time step t. It is worth noting that every time an action effect corrects a deficit, the dynamic evolution of the process is not applied.

Table 3. Motivations in the social robot Mini. The weights β_i define the influence of stimuli on some motivation scaling the stimuli intensity and the associated deficit.

Motivation	Biological process	Stimulus	β_i	Description
Sleep	Sleep	Light	–	Motivation to reduce the sleep deficit
Play with user	Soc. entertainment	User	10^{-3}	Motivation to reduce the social entertainment deficit
Play alone	Self-entertainment	Not user	10^{-3}	Motivation used to reduce the self-entertainment deficit
Socialize	Cogn. interaction	User	10^{-3}	Motivation to reduce the cognitive social need
Relax	Stress	None	–	Motivation to reduce the stress levels
Rest	Energy	None	–	Motivation used to reduce the robot's fatigue

3.2 Learning Setup

The learning environment we have designed in this contribution has an input shape of (1×7) and an output shape of (1×6). On the one hand, the input is the robot's state, which consists of the six continuous biological processes that evolve in Mini (see Table 1) plus the discrete dominant motivation. On the other hand, the output is the Q-values associated with the six actions, shown in Table 4, that the robot can execute.

We have used the neural network based on DQN for training and making autonomous decisions, consisting of four layers. The input is a flattened layer with size 1×7 connected to two dense hidden layers with 24 neurons, each connected to a dense output layer with size 1×6. We used the Adam optimizer [17] to reduce the learning rate parameter α exponentially and a Boltzmann policy [6] to control action selection in the output layer. The discount rate γ was set to 0.9 units.

The learning phase consisted of 300 steps per episode and 50 warming steps. Besides, the number of steps we set to finish learning was 100000. Although our model is intended to operate in continuous applications without episodes, during learning, we considered as stopping criteria the agent's "dead", which is produced when one of its internal deficits raised the maximum level of 100 units.

The reward function we use to compute the benefits of executing each action in each state is represented by Eq. 5. This function considers a weighted variation in the robot's deficits in two consecutive time steps.

$$r(t) = \Delta WWb = WWb(t) - WWb(t-1) \tag{5}$$

where the weighted well-being WWb is

$$WWb(t) = \frac{1}{N} \sum_{i=1}^{N} d_i(t) \times \frac{cv_i(t)}{\max(bp)} \tag{6}$$

Table 4. Mini's actions and their effects to regulate its biological processes.

Action	Effects	Description
Wait	Energy +1.2	The robot waits for new upcoming events without executing an action
Sleep	Sleep –0.8 Energy +0.3	Mini simulates it is sleeping by closing its eyes and performing sounds like snores
Play	Energy –0.3 Soc. entert. +1.2	The robot plays with the user different activities like quiz games
Dance	Energy –0.3 Self-entert. +1.2	Mini plays a song and dances
Meditate	Stress –1.2 Energy +0.1	Mini simulates it is meditating by reducing its breath rate and closing its eyes
Talk	Energy –0.1 Cog. inter +1.2	Mini talks with the user by asking about different topics like music to maintain a conversation

where $\max(bp)$ is the maximum value of a biological process bp in time step t and N is the number of biological processes that the robot has to regulate by executing actions.

To consider the effects of stimuli on motivation, if the action reduces the deficit of the biological process related to the dominant motivation, the reward is multiplied by 2. With this mechanism, we allow behaviors related to the dominant motivation that are boosted by stimuli to become active more easily (e.g., reducing the entertainment deficit when the user motivates the robot to play together).

3.3   Experiment and Evaluation

After transferring the knowledge obtained by the DRL model to the social robot Mini, we tested its regulation of biological processes using the learning model. In this scenario, the robot exhibited autonomous behavior using the DRL model for action selection and exploiting the behavior policy learned. The test lasted 1000 s (2000 steps of 0.5 s each), where the user was seated in front of the robot and positively interacted with Mini executing the activities requested. From the robot's point of view, a positive interaction means the user is playing when the robot starts a game and answering the robot's questions.

The evaluation proposed in this contribution follows two different approaches. On the one hand, we use standard metrics like the loss, the mean squared error, and episode reward to appraise the reward function's optimization during simulation learning. On the other hand, we use the robot's well-being to verify whether the robot correctly learns to maintain an optimal internal state in real HRI after transferring the learned knowledge. The well-being metric is needed to guarantee the correct definition of our reward function because the standard metrics only provide information about its correct optimization.

We define the robot's *Well-being* (Wb) as an indicator of the deficits in the robot's artificial internal state. As Eq. 7 shows, the *Wb* value ranges from 0 to 100. High values indicate that Mini can efficiently regulate its internal state, while low values indicate the opposite results. This equation is very similar to the reward function, but the deficits are not weighted since we want to obtain their average value by giving them the same weight.

$$\text{Well-being (Wb)}(t) = \frac{1}{N} \sum_{i=1}^{N} d_i(t) \tag{7}$$

4 Results

Figure 2a shows the loss optimization, Fig. 2b the mean squared error considering the predicted and real output, and Fig. 2c the average episode reward during the learning process before transferring the information to the social robot Mini. As we can see, the loss and mean squared error decay with time, indicating that the

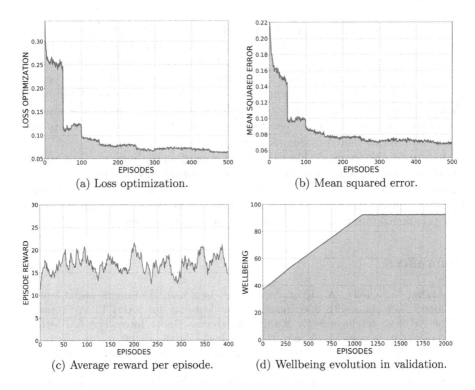

(a) Loss optimization.

(b) Mean squared error.

(c) Average reward per episode.

(d) Wellbeing evolution in validation.

Fig. 2. Metrics obtained during learning and validation of the DRL setting.

DRL algorithm correctly optimizes the reward function. Concerning the average episode reward shows a different dynamic. Since the average episode reward in our approach is stochastic, it is impossible to perceive how it is optimized as the number of episodes increases.

Regarding how Mini maintains an optimal internal state, Fig. 2d shows how Mini regulates its internal state, maintaining high Wb levels once learning has finished. At the beginning of the test, we initialized the robot's biological processes at low random values, leading Mini to be in a weak internal state to analyze if it could overcome this situation with action execution. As we can see, the Wb evolution rapidly increases to very high values. This indicates that action selection is adequate because the Wb value increases step by step, and when it reaches an optimal value of around 90 units, the Wb maintains stability until the end of the testing phase. This fact suggests that Mini exhibits a non-repetitive behavior since, to reduce all its deficits, the action selection has to consider and combine all the actions the robot can execute. Although Fig. 2d seems to evolve rapidly towards stability, the robot's Wb suffers variations that can not be perceived as it shows 2000 time steps. Maintaining an optimal internal state is not ideal since not all the robot's deficits can be reduced simultaneously.

5   Conclusion

In this manuscript, we have presented a DRL environment for the internal regulation of the biologically inspired process of a social robot devoted to HRI. The results show how DRL deals with a high-dimensional state-action space that includes six continuous variables representing the robot's biological processes and the dominant motivation, representing the influence of external stimuli on eliciting certain behaviors. Besides, the robot has to map each possible state to one of the six actions it can execute to maximize the cumulative reward and reduce its internal deficits while affording HRI.

In future work, we would like to continue expanding the number of stimuli and situations the robot considers to make a more complex environment where Mini can exhibit a more diverse behavior. Besides, we would like to explore adaptation to different users using social rules to operate in dynamic environments where user personalization is needed to execute goal-directed actions.

References

1. Akalin, N., Kiselev, A., Kristoffersson, A., Loutfi, A.: Enhancing social human-robot interaction with deep reinforcement learning. In: FAIM/ISCA Workshop on Artificial Intelligence for Multimodal Human Robot Interaction (AI-MHRI), Stockholm, Sweden 14–15 July, 2018, pp. 48–50. MHRI (2018)
2. Akalin, N., Loutfi, A.: Reinforcement learning approaches in social robotics. Sensors **21**(4), 1292 (2021)
3. Cañamero, D.: Designing emotions for activity selection in autonomous agents. Emotions Humans Artifacts **115**, 148 (2003)

4. Chen, C., Liu, Y., Kreiss, S., Alahi, A.: Crowd-robot interaction: Crowd-aware robot navigation with attention-based deep reinforcement learning. In: 2019 International Conference on Robotics and Automation (ICRA), pp. 6015–6022. IEEE (2019)
5. Gao, Y., Sibirtseva, E., Castellano, G., Kragic, D.: Fast adaptation with meta-reinforcement learning for trust modelling in human-robot interaction. In: 2019 IEEE/RSJ International Conference on Intelligent Robots and Systems (IROS), pp. 305–312. IEEE (2019)
6. Kouretas, I., Paliouras, V.: Hardware implementation of a softmax-like function for deep learning. Technologies 8(3), 46 (2020)
7. Liu, L., Dugas, D., Cesari, G., Siegwart, R., Dubé, R.: Robot navigation in crowded environments using deep reinforcement learning. In: 2020 IEEE/RSJ International Conference on Intelligent Robots and Systems (IROS), pp. 5671–5677. IEEE (2020)
8. Lorenz, K.: The foundations of ethology. Springer Science & Business Media (2013). https://doi.org/10.1007/978-3-7091-3671-3
9. Maroto-Gómez, M., Castro-González, Á., Castillo, J.C., Malfaz, M., Salichs, M.A.: A bio-inspired motivational decision making system for social robots based on the perception of the user. Sensors 18(8), 2691 (2018)
10. Maroto-Gómez, M., González, R., Castro-González, Á., Malfaz, M., Salichs, M.Á.: Speeding-up action learning in a social robot with dyna-q+: A bioinspired probabilistic model approach. IEEE Access 9, 98381–98397 (2021)
11. Mnih, V., et al.: Human-level control through deep reinforcement learning. Nature 518(7540), 529–533 (2015)
12. Mousavi, S.S., Schukat, M., Howley, E.: Deep reinforcement learning: an overview. In: Bi, Y., Kapoor, S., Bhatia, R. (eds.) IntelliSys 2016. LNNS, vol. 16, pp. 426–440. Springer, Cham (2018). https://doi.org/10.1007/978-3-319-56991-8_32
13. Qureshi, A.H., Nakamura, Y., Yoshikawa, Y., Ishiguro, H.: Robot gains social intelligence through multimodal deep reinforcement learning. In: 2016 IEEE-RAS 16th International Conference on Humanoid Robots (Humanoids), pp. 745–751. IEEE (2016)
14. Qureshi, A.H., Nakamura, Y., Yoshikawa, Y., Ishiguro, H.: Intrinsically motivated reinforcement learning for human-robot interaction in the real-world. Neural Netw. 107, 23–33 (2018)
15. Salichs, M.A.: Mini: a new social robot for the elderly. Int. J. Soc. Robot. 12(6), 1231–1249 (2020)
16. Samsani, S.S., Muhammad, M.S.: Socially compliant robot navigation in crowded environment by human behavior resemblance using deep reinforcement learning. IEEE Robot. Autom. Lett. 6(3), 5223–5230 (2021)
17. Zhang, Z.: Improved adam optimizer for deep neural networks. In: 2018 IEEE/ACM 26th International Symposium on Quality of Service (IWQoS), pp. 1–2. Ieee (2018)

Share with Me: A Study on a Social Robot Collecting Mental Health Data

Raida Karim[✉][iD], Edgar Lopez[iD], Katelynn Oleson, Tony Li[iD],
Elin A. Björling[iD], and Maya Cakmak[iD]

University of Washington, Seattle, WA 98195, USA
{rk1997,mcakmak}@cs.washington.edu,
{lopeze7,kjoleson,tonywli,bjorling}@uw.edu

Abstract. Social robots have been used to assist with mental well-being in various ways, such as to help children with autism improve on their social skills and executive functioning (e.g., joint attention and bodily awareness). They are also used to help older adults by reducing feelings of isolation and loneliness, as well as supporting mental well-being of teens and children. However, existing work in this sphere has only shown support for mental health through social robots by responding interactively to human activity to help them learn relevant skills. We hypothesize that humans can also get help from social robots in mental well-being by releasing or sharing their mental health data with the social robots. In this paper, we present a human-robot interaction (HRI) study to evaluate this hypothesis. During the five-day study, a total of fifty-five (n=55) participants shared their in-the-moment mood and stress levels with a social robot. Our statistical analysis showed no significant relation between weekdays, and mood/stress levels. We saw a majority of positive results indicating it is worth conducting future work in this direction, and the potential of social robots to largely support mental well-being.

Keywords: Social robot · Mental health · Data sharing

1 Introduction

Apart from genetic or birth related causes, any kind of mental health issues in our daily lives are usually caused by some kind of trouble such as stressful events, grief from accidents or deaths, and trauma from tragic or fearful incidents [18]. Research shows that sharing these troubling experiences helps gain insights from others which helps develop coping skills, and makes one feel less alone in pain which helps to tackle trouble more effectively [3,13]. Therefore,

We thank Patrícia Alves-Oliveira for her guidance on this work. We also thank Yufei Zhang, the study participants, and the anonymous reviewers for sharing valuable feedback. Raida Karim was supported by a Mary Gates Research Scholarship, and a Levinson Emerging Scholars Award at the University of Washington, Seattle. This work was supported in part by the NSF NRI: INT EMAR Project Award #1734100.

F. Cavallo et al. (Eds.): ICSR 2022, LNAI 13817, pp. 218–227, 2022.
https://doi.org/10.1007/978-3-031-24667-8_20

sharing about trouble can potentially help treat or lessen mental health issues. However, people are not always willing to share their personal information with others or publicly, even with their family members, let alone outside community members due to social stigma, personal beliefs or limitations [17]. Therefore, to tackle mental health issues, the main source of support is usually individualized therapy, which is expensive and thus inaccessible to many [7,16]. Digital therapy is a relatively more accessible option compared to in-person therapy because of lower cost and availability in any location [1,19]. However, digital therapy has drawbacks, such as lack of face-to-face interaction, user disengagement, and software incompatibility [9]. So, we hypothesize that sharing mental health with an endearing social robot that overcomes these challenges of therapy options can help support mental health.

2 Related Work

When people share their personally relevant emotions in social media like Facebook, they can experience satisfaction causing positive mental state [3]. People tend to be discreet about sharing their emotional data, as we see Facebook users share more intense and negative emotions in private messages [3]. In prior research, participants reported a positive association between emotional sharing via an online virtual mood wall and reduced negative emotions [13]. Social robots are often perceived as friendly or pet-like companions for their endearing appearances (e.g., outfit, facial expressions) and capabilities that can include haptics, sounds, and movements [15]. Such perceptions or relationships boost user engagement with social robots [4]. Thus, social robots may better foster emotional support with mental health data compared to other technologies (e.g., smartphone apps, websites rendered by touch screen devices) [6]. In a study conducted by Björling et al. [5], teens reported a social robot as a desired tool with which to share stressors for emotional support. Additionally, social robots have been studied in the context of assisting mental healthcare by sharing its emotions with people [12], having behavioral models fulfilling user needs [14], and providing companionship [10]. To the best of our knowledge, the existing literature in this domain indicates that social robots have not yet been used as a means for collecting mental health data from humans, which makes this research direction a novel one in HRI.

3 Methodology

3.1 Sample

We conducted a study where participants interacted with a social robot to share their mood and stress data. The study took place at the Computer Science & Engineering (CSE) department of the University of Washington (Seattle), which is a top CSE school. We had a total of fifty-five (n=55) study participants.

Fig. 1. Participants sharing mental health data with a social robot in the study.

3.2 Experimental Setup

In a five-day study, we deployed the robot in the main entrance atrium of the CSE department easily accessible to students and staff. After informed consent, we invited participants to share their mood and stress levels with a social robot. We used a FLEXI social robot embodiment kit [2] to prepare our social robot, and we used its end-user programming tool to implement programs collecting and storing data autonomously. The software of FLEXI is open-source[1] and its hardware can be customized [2]. We designed the robot with a colorful hat and body frame to make it look endearing (see Fig. 1). Before performing the study in the CSE department, we conducted a trial run[2] with a female participant for ensuring that the planned experimental interaction can help us find out more about the participants' shared mental health data as expected.

3.3 Study Protocols for Data Collection and Data Analysis

The goal of this study was to answer the following questions:

(A) How will participants feel about sharing their mental health data with a social robot?
(B) What mental health information will participants share about their mental health with a social robot?

We plan to investigate these research questions with findings from the study results as discussed later in the paper. A previous study conducted by our lead author [11] showed that rather than using English words like "Good", "Bad", and "Fine" to express different mood and stress levels, using an emoji Likert scale can enhance coherence and accessibility by reducing the need to read

---

[1] FLEXI software open-access link: https://mayacakmak.github.io/emarsoftware/.
[2] A video of the trial run of the mental health data sharing interaction by one participant with a social robot can be found here: https://youtu.be/J6srKDg6OE0.

text and increase dependency on globally understandable graphics and symbols, especially in diverse communities like in the United States. Thus we used an emoji Likert scale with 3 buttons expressing 3 different levels of mood or stress data (see Fig. 3). The brief (about 20 s) interaction had 3 stages: greeting, data sharing, and exit. In the data sharing or second stage, participants were asked to input their *mood* and *stress* data by clicking on the appropriate emoji as answers to these two questions, respectively (see Fig. 3): *"How do you feel today?"* and *"Are you stressed today?"* Their shared data responses were then stored in a secured Firebase database[3]. Apart from showing the questions in its belly screen, there were sounds incorporated in the robot that asked the questions aloud in a female voice in English language. The robot also had head and neck movements in different stages of the interaction. The first three authors of this paper invited passerby on different days verbally to participate in the study. After each passerby completed the interaction, they were interviewed to respond either verbally or by writing in post-its to a prompt as shown in Fig. 2.

We conducted both qualitative and quantitative analysis on the collected study data that include participants' comments responding to the prompt of *"Sharing my mental health data makes me feel...."* (see Fig. 2) as well as the shared mood and stress levels data through the emoji Likert scale counts. A chi-squared test was conducted to analyze the relationship between weekdays and mood/stress levels. We conducted a modified thematic analysis of participant feedback data (prompt responses as shown in Fig. 2) using Miro[4]. A specific theme was assigned based on the nature of prompt response. For instance, comments like *"Sharing my mental health data makes me feel more aware of my stress."* has been assigned to the theme of "self-awareness". And comments like *"I am a bit scared about sharing my data but hope it will go towards a good cause."* has been assigned to the theme of "privacy" as it shows concerns about how participants' data will be used and possible risks to their privacy.

4   Results

Participants' reported moods varied by day of the week. Participants reported mostly a positive mood on Monday, Tuesday, and Thursday. A neutral mood was prevalent on Wednesday. On Friday, both positive and neutral moods were prevalent. A negative mood was the lowest average mood in this community on all weekdays. Participants' stress levels also varied by day of the week. High stress was prevalent on Wednesday, medium stress was prevalent on Monday, Tuesday and Friday. On Thursday, both medium and low stress levels were prevalent. Of course, these observations are true for that specific week, and might not necessarily hold true for other weeks. However, these findings illustrate the usefulness of gathering stress and mood over time in a community setting. We saw the least positive prompt responses on Friday, which may mean this community was exhausted after a long busy week, and thus did not think

---

[3] Firebase: https://firebase.google.com/.
[4] Miro: https://miro.com/.

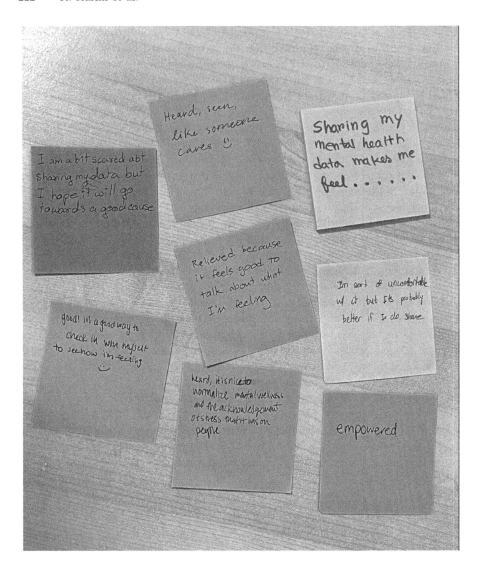

Fig. 2. Written prompt used in the study & responses in post-its.

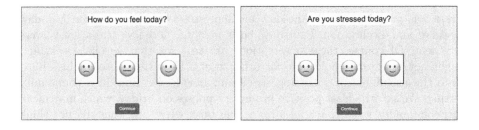

Fig. 3. Emoji likert scale for 3 types of mood & stress levels, respectively.

much or see many positive aspects of this new type of interaction on that day. For mood, the null hypothesis for the chi-squared test was that each person's mood is independent of weekday. The expected number of positive mood people was the highest than other mood types ranging between 5–8 people per weekday. Total 32 people reported positive mood in n=55. The chi-square test results showed no significant association between weekdays and mood levels, $X^2(8, N = 55) = 13.5, p = .0962$. For stress, the null hypothesis was that each person's stress is independent of weekday. The expected number of medium stressed people was the highest than other stress levels ranging between 5–7 people per weekday. Total 28 people reported medium stress in n=55. The chi-square test results showed no significant association between weekdays and stress levels, $X^2(8, N = 55) = 11.1, p = .1964$. A limitation of this analysis is that at least 20% of expected values were less than 5 in stress data table, and at least one expected value was less than 1 in mood data table, which may make these chi-squared test results unreliable [8].

We discuss specific themes below:

Theme 1: Emotions Resulting from Sharing Data

Emotions revealed by users' post-interaction comments ranged between positive (e.g., *"happy"*, *"good, could be myself"*), unchanged (e.g., *"Neutral. No change in how I feel"*, *"didn't feel anything"*), and validated (e.g., *"Accepted"*, *"welcomed, nice to check-in with someone"*, *"Heard, seen, like someone cares :)"*).

Implications: This theme reinforces that sharing mental health data with a social robot can indeed have various effects in people's emotions. These findings can inform future designs of data sharing interaction with social robots targeted to impact the users' mental health for the better.

Theme 2: Positive Interactions

Some people commented about how they felt interacting with a robot specifically while sharing their mental health data. One type of comments expressed the robot's figure positively impacting mental health: *"I feel relaxed by the face"*, *"It made my day to share with the robot"*. Some other people suggested how this interaction could be beneficial to the community. One comment towards this: *"helpful to others"*.

Implications: These findings indicate that the robot's appearance may be an important component in ensuring a positive robot interaction. Also, further research is needed to evaluate how this interaction can be beneficial for people or communities. Depending on in what ways these can be beneficial, the design of such interactions or used social robots could be modified for maximum benefit in specific contexts.

Theme 3: Negative or Confusing Interactions

Some users had somewhat negative responses to the robot interaction after sharing their stress and mood data. One participant expressed doubts in the robot's capability: *"As it's a robot, I know that it will lack human level empathy. The set of responses would be fixed. I knew it won't be capable of doing much like releasing my stress."* Another participant described confusion about the robot's behaviors: *"[I was] confused, not sure what happened or what's happening here, does it have voice and movements"*. Some users made suggestions for improvement: *"weird...as I'm not sure if my mental health can be quantified by data alone"*, *"unusual"*, and one comment on robot design: *"It didn't feel like a robot. Maybe one integrated system might make it feel like a robot. A frame around the belly might help hide the belly ipad, and make it look like an integrated system. But, you can think more about it like arms coming out, or to make it more humanoid; maybe remove distance between face and belly. If the question appears in the face and I answer in the belly, it might be more like an integrated or full system interaction."* These comments indicate some concrete areas for improvement in this interaction and robot design.

Implications: These findings indicate that some participants had a negative experience resulting from unmet expectations or confusion about the robot's abilities. This feedback suggests that further research is needed to better explore both user expectations as well as participants' understanding of the robot's function. In general, mental health is a bit abstract and it can be hard to design convincing short (e.g., 20-seconds) interactions to collect accurate mental health data. Incorporating these feedback and conducting further research might lead to new developments in this regard.

Theme 4: Inward-Looking
This theme is comprised of comments that show users contemplating themselves during the interaction. Some keywords users conveyed: *"reflective"*, *"Transparent"*, *"introspective"*.

Implications: These findings suggest this interaction's ability to compel humans for self-reflection, which can inform future design of such interactions to allow space for reflection.

Theme 5: Impact on Stress Level
This theme reveals how this interaction impacts users' stress levels. Some comments demonstrated alleviation in stress for example: *"Less Stressed"*, *"like some weight has been lifted off of me"*, whereas one comment shows no change in stress level: *"same level of stress"* after the interaction.
Implications: These findings show potential for this type of interaction in alleviating stress. Further research needs to be conducted to solidify this possibility. Diverse communities, targeted interaction experiments, and a larger number of participants can be used to conduct research in different settings.

Theme 6: Self-Awareness
This theme shows user comments with regards to increased awareness in various ways, such as: *"more aware of my stress"*, *"more conscious about my overall health, since mental health is even more important than physical health in my opinion :)"*, *"I feel more self-aware"*.

Implications: These findings are promising in the context of using this type of interactions in different communities as a means of raising awareness of mental health care or fighting associated stigma.

Theme 7: Privacy
This theme indicates users' feelings when sharing their "private" mental health data in this interaction. Some comments didn't express any concerns: *"I typically don't like sharing my data, but I liked this one. I liked that there were options given that I could choose from, so I didn't have to think a lot about my mood, etc.", "I am not concerned at all about sharing my data this way, as it seems low granularity. Not invasive."* Some other comments showed users' concerns: *"I am a bit scared about sharing my data but hope it will go towards a good cause.", "I'm sort of uncomfortable w/it but it's probably better if I do share."*

Implications: These findings demonstrate the need for further work in making users feel comfortable and gaining their trust with their private data shared with a robot. Establishing a good relationship with users may increase effectiveness of such interactions.

5   Discussion and Future Directions

The participant themes found suggest that sharing mental health data with a social robot can support mental healthcare. However, some participants did suggest privacy concerns which are important considerations in this type of implementation. We can mitigate these concerns by incorporating participants' feedback on the robot's design and ensuring participants about the privacy of their shared data in our secured data storage. One observation we made was that this community is part of an academically competitive department, so these results seem to align with this competitive mentality. For instance, from overall community counts, it seems this community most commonly has a good or positive mood and medium stress. Good mood could be a result of the satisfaction and achievement that comes with being part of a prestigious academic department, and being able to pursue the profession they are very passionate about in a competitive place. The medium stress might result from the busy nature of academic or engineering work– deadlines of homework, projects, papers, presentations, demos, etc. that all are constantly working on.

Another potential limitation is data bias. As we collected data through the robot placed in an open space of a community, this might have caused data bias. For instance, if the user is aware that the study coordinators or other community members can observe them when they are entering their data, they might not be truthful (especially if it's negative or sensitive mental health data, they might feel hesitation or shame to share that in public). This could be the reason why we did not get very high counts of negative data (high stress, negative mood, or negative comments about mental health). One way to avoid this bias might be to experiment with data collection in a closed space. For example, placing the robot in a closed room, where only the user can enter to share their data, or placing a cover around the belly of the robot that will not allow the user's interaction (or at least what data they are entering) to be seen. Lastly, the medium of data collection can pose limitations. Instead of using an emoji Likert scale, if we had used a 10-pt slider scale on a 0–9 range, we might have more nuanced data of mood and stress levels indicated by specific values (e.g., 7) as well as provided participants with more options to accurately express their mental health data.

To conclude, our study findings revealed mostly optimistic feelings about this type of human-robot mental health data sharing interaction among participants, as well as different arousal this interaction can have on people such as self-awareness, emotional sharing, etc. as discussed in the "Results" section above. The majority of positive results indicate such interactions with social robots need to be studied further in different settings to evaluate their potential in mental healthcare holistically. Future studies can be conducted with some changed variables in current study settings such as a different location (e.g., hospital, high school, public library, online), population (e.g., teens, seniors, wheelchair users), and robot (e.g., NAO, Moxi). It would also be interesting to gather information about participant demographics (e.g., age, ethnicity, citizenship, gender), and experience or attitude towards robotic technologies. Furthermore, conducting studies in a closed space to give participants a bit more comfort in sharing personal data, and informing them about their data security in our secure storage might produce more positive or interesting results. Another consideration in future studies is to have the robot respond based on participants' shared data as a two-way interaction, since valuable responses tying to their mental health can be impactful [3].

References

1. Aboujaoude, E., et al.: Digital interventions in mental health: current status and future directions. Front. Psychiatry **11**, 111 (2020)
2. Alves-Oliveira, P., et al.: FLEXI: a robust and flexible social robot embodiment kit. In: Designing Interactive Systems Conference (2022)
3. Bazarova, N.N., et al.: Social Sharing of Emotions on Facebook: Channel Differences, Satisfaction, and Replies. In: CSCW (2015)
4. Bishop, L., et al.: Social robots: the inuence of human and robot characteristics on acceptance. Paladyn J. Behav. Robot. **101**, 346–358 (2019)
5. Björling, E.A., Rose, E., Davidson, A., Ren, R., Wong, D.: Can we keep him forever? teens' engagement and desire for emotional connection with a social robot. Int. J. Social Robot. **12**(1), 65–77 (2019). https://doi.org/10.1007/s12369-019-00539-6
6. Boucenna, S., et al.: Interactive technologies for autistic children: A review. Cogn. Comput. **64**, 722–740 (2014)
7. Brown, G.D., et al.: Discussing out-of-pocket expenses during clinical appointments: an observational study of patient-psychiatrist interactions. Psych. Serv. **686**, 610–617 (2017)
8. Cochran, W.G.: Some methods for strengthening the common chisquare tests. Biometrics **104** (1954)

9. Howells, A., Ivtzan, I., Eiroa-Orosa, F.J.: Putting the 'app' in happiness: a randomised controlled trial of a smartphone-based mindfulness intervention to enhance wellbeing. J. Happiness Stud. **17**(1), 163–185 (2014). https://doi.org/10.1007/s10902-014-9589-1

10. Joshi, S., Collins, S., Kamino, W., Gomez, R., Šabanović, S.: Social robots for socio-physical distancing. In: Wagner, A.R., Feil-Seifer, D., Haring, K.S., Rossi, S., Williams, T., He, H., Sam Ge, S. (eds.) ICSR 2020. LNCS (LNAI), vol. 12483, pp. 440–452. Springer, Cham (2020). https://doi.org/10.1007/978-3-030-62056-1_37

11. Karim, R., et al.: Community-Based Data Visualization for Mental Well-Being with a Social Robot. In: Proceedings of the 2022 ACM/IEEE International Conference on Human-Robot Interaction, pp. 839–843 (2022)

12. Ling, H., Björling, E.: Sharing stress with a robot: what would a robot say?. Human-Mach. Commun. **1** (2020)

13. Liu, X., Pan, M., Li, J.: Does Sharing Your Emotion Make You Feel Better? An Empirical Investigation on the Association Between Sharing Emotions on a Virtual Mood Wall and the Relief of Patients' Negative Emotions. Telemed. e-Health **25**(10) (2018)

14. Nocentini, O., et al.: A survey of behavioral models for social robots. Robotics **83**, 54 (2019)

15. Onyeulo, E.B., Gandhi, V.: What Makes a Social Robot Good at Interacting with Humans?. Information **11**(1), 43 (2020)

16. Pella, J.E., et al.: Pediatric anxiety disorders: a cost of illness analysis. J. Abnorm. Child Psychol. **48**(4), 551–559 (2020)

17. Sartorius, N.: Stigma and mental health. The Lancet **370**(9590), 810–811 (2007)

18. Schomerus, G., Matschinger, H., Angermeyer, M.C.: Public beliefs about the causes of mental disorders revisited. Psychiatry Res. **144**(2-3), 233–236 (2006)

19. Taylor, C.B., Fitzsimmons-Craft, E.E., Graham, A.K.: Digital technology can revolutionize mental health services delivery: the COVID-19 crisis as a catalyst for change. Int. J. Eating Disorders **53**(7), 1155–1157 (2020)

Classification of Personal Data Used by Personalised Robot Companions Based on Concern of Exposure

Lewis Riches[✉][iD], Kheng Lee Koay[iD], and Patrick Holthaus[iD]

Adaptive Systems Research Group, University of Hertfordshire, College Lane,
Hatfield AL10 9AB, UK
{l.riches,k.l.koay,p.holthaus}@herts.ac.uk

Abstract. We present a paper looking at the accidental exposure of personal data by personalised companion robots in human-robot interaction. Due to the need for personal data, personalisation brings inherent risk of accidental personal data exposure through multi-modal communication. An online questionnaire was conducted to collect perceptions on the level of concern of personal data being exposed. The personal data examined in this paper has been used to personalise a companion robot along with links to the UK general data protection act. The level of concern for these personal data has been classified into high, medium, and low concern with guidelines provided on how these different classifications should be handled by a robot. Evidence has also been found that age, gender, extroversion, and conscientiousness influence a person's perceptions on personal data exposure concern.

Keywords: Human-robot interaction · Companion robots · Personalisation · Personal data security · General data protection regulation

1 Introduction

Companion robots have been defined as specifically designed robots for personal use in the home [3], this key aspect of bringing robots into the home has led a push towards making them personalised within human-robot interaction (HRI). Personalising companion robots allows the systems to use personal data to adapt their functions/actions to be specific to the user. Examples within literature include, a personalised healthcare assistant robot requiring user health data such as a current medication list to enable medication reminders, a personalised bartender robot [17] requiring personality traits and personal preferences to provide personalised communication and drink recommendations and, a personalised robot tutor [9] requiring an initial skill assessment (educational activities) before being able to apply personalised lessons.

As shown a key requirement of personalisation is personal data, without the personal data of the user, the robot is not able to personalise its actions or functions. Personal data has been defined under UK law by the UK general data

F. Cavallo et al. (Eds.): ICSR 2022, LNAI 13817, pp. 228–237, 2022.
https://doi.org/10.1007/978-3-031-24667-8_21

protection regulation (UK GDPR) as "any information relating to an identified or identifiable natural person". The requirement of personalisation to need personal data is a potentially limiting factor for the adoption and use of personalised features within robots, due to data privacy and security concerns by the user. Lutz et al. [11] identified the potential of a privacy paradox within personalised robots, showing users wanting personalised actions but being unwilling to provide personal data to a robot due to data security concerns. Denning et al. [4] and Krupp et al. [7] demonstrate the potential security vulnerabilities current commercially available companion robots have such as being stolen/hacked or personal information stored being accessed by someone external. Butler et al. [2] identified data privacy concerns related to a robots ability to capture visual data that could contain sensitive information for example bank cards. Syrdal et al. [20] identified privacy concerns with sharing personal data with a robot companion such as concerns of the robot sharing the personal data with a third party and data on the robot being hacked or stolen.

A key theme through robot data privacy concern literature, is the concern of personal data being stolen or obtained by unauthorised people. For personalised robots to overcome these concerns they need to develop a state of trust with the human they interact with, otherwise the robots personalised features/functions will not be used due to the user not trusting the robot with their personal data. Martin et al. [13] found a relationship between trust and data privacy, identifying that even a small data breach has negative effects on trust. With the goal of promoting trust in HRI so humans use personalised behaviours, personalised robots need to demonstrate data privacy features, with Richards [15] identifying data privacy behaviour as a key in enabling trust. Current solutions deployed in human-computer interaction (HCI) to promote trust in personal data storage such as, the encryption of stored personal data or double authentication can be used in HRI but cannot be the sole data protection method. The provided HCI solutions protected the personal information while being stored on the robot, but companion robots within HRI need to decide when personal information can be exposed, for example not saying personal data in-front of strangers in the home such as a plumber when the robot communicates with its user.

An initial step in teaching robots when personal data can be exposed is for these systems to understand the social contexts personal data is allowed to be shared in to prevent accidental exposure of personal data as identified by Marchang and Di Nuovo [12]. They provide a blockchain authentication method as a potential solution to this challenge, the use of a blockchain approach increases the transparency of personal data being stored and worked on within the robot while also providing the security of blockchain. However, blockchain requires the user to define levels of sensitivity/security of personal data in order to operate, this is an issue as with the varying and large quantity of personal data within HRI, this could be a tedious task in identifying the sensitivity of each personal data or be inaccurate when grouping them. A potential solution to this issue is by using a contextual integrity framework as identified by Rueben et al. [18]. Contextual integrity [14] states that a data breach has occurred when the norm of appropriateness or distribution have been broken within a given social context, within HRI this would enable a robot to understand when it can share personal data within a social context and not cause a personal data breach autonomously.

The first step in implementing a contextual integrity framework or something similar, is having robots understand how concerning personal data is if it is exposed. These systems will make the decisions of when personal data can be exposed which requires the robot to judge how concerning the personal data would be if it was exposed in that given context. For example, Rossi et al. [16] investigated a Customers' perceived sensitivity of information shared with a robot bartender. However, before a robot can make decisions based on the social context influences, its first needs to understand generally how concerning that personal data is if exposed in a generalised context. UK law provides some classification of the potential concern of personal data exposure by classifying some personal data into a special category [21] meaning we would consider this as high concern personal data. However, the range of personal data this law covers is limited, for example this law does not cover personal preferences which were used by personalised bar tending robot [17] or educational activities used by a personalised robot tutor [9].

This paper will investigate human perception on how concerning personal data is if it was available to the general public to derive a context independent classification. The personal data analysed within this study has all been used or could be used to personalise companion robots within HRI. Individual differences such as personality type, age and gender all influence how we behave as a person and make us unique, within HCI Li et al. [10] has shown a link between a user's personality traits and their views on data privacy sensitivity. Due to these factors this paper will also be investigating if individual differences such as personality types, age or gender influence a persons' judgement on how concerning personal data is when exposed to the general public. This paper aims to answer the following research questions: research question 1 (**RQ1**) can personal data used by a companion robot for personalised assistance be classified based on the concern of exposure?, and research question 2 (**RQ2**) can individual differences influence a person's views on how concerning personal data is if exposed to the general public?. For that purpose, we present the design and conduction of an online questionnaire in Sect. 2, analyse the obtained results in Sect. 3 and discuss implications of our findings to how our classification could be used within HRI in Sect. 4 before concluding the paper in Sect. 5.

2   Methodology

To investigate the research questions listed previously, we conducted an online questionnaire ethically approved by the Health, Science, Engineering and Technology ECDA committee (SPECS/PGR/UH/04859), with recruitment being done through social media and personal social networks. Participants voluntarily filled in the questionnaire with no compensation given for filling it in. To maintain the aim of a context independent classification of personal data exposure concern, the questionnaire was designed to not include the word robot or any information on the social context.

2.1 Participants Details

The first section of the questionnaire was used to collect information about the participant which was: age, gender, and personality trait. This information was collected to enable analysis for **RQ2** and was collected anonymously by not collecting email addresses or names. To collect personality traits the ten item personality measure (TIPI) [6] was used to measure the big five dimensions (Extraversion, Agreeableness, Conscientiousness, Emotional Stability, Openness to Experiences). Along with being a concise scale, TIPI has been shown to provide a strong validity [1], allowing for an accurate representation of a participants personality types, which will then be used to understand the influence personality types have on personal data sensitivity **RQ2**. A text box was used to allow participants to type their gender identity.

2.2 Personal Data

While this paper could not analyse every piece of personal information, thirteen pieces of personal information were chosen due to their link with UK law, use within literature of robot personalisation or use case to enable personalisation for companion robots within HRI (shown in Table 1). Four pieces of personal information come from the special category of UK GDPR [21] that provide information on the user (Health records used by personalised healthcare robots [5], Political opinions, Racial or Ethnic origin and Sexual orientation). Five pieces of personal information pertain to a user's personal preferences (Drink preferences, Food preferences, Movie preferences, Music preferences and Sports preferences) that have been used to personalise a bartending robot when suggesting drinks or topics of conversation [17], and four pieces of personal information have applications to be used for personalisation and use within smart assistant (Calendar appointments, Educational activities used by a personalised tutor robot [9], Employment history, and Financial records).

2.3 General Views on Personal Data Sensitivity

Once participants answered the initial questions, each participant was presented with the same following question "For each item select how you would feel if the following information about you were available to the general public.", with participants rating the thirteen individual items of personal data shown in Sect. 2.2, using a 5-point Likert scale (1=Not at all concerned, 2=Slightly concerned, 3=Somewhat concerned, 4=Moderately concerned and 5=Extremely concerned).

2.4 Participants

A total of 102 participants were recruited with 51 being male and 51 being female, with no participants identifying as another gender. The lowest age of the sample was 19 and the maximum age within the sample was 83 with an interquartile range between 23 years old and 40 years old.

2.5 Statistical Methods

Research question 1 (**RQ1**) aims to provide the classification of concern of personal data being exposed, to achieve this classification factor analysis will be used. Factor analysis is a reduction technique and reduces a large quantity of variables into factors, this technique will be leveraged to provide evidence of why we classify individual personal data (variables) into concern levels (factors).

Research question 2 (**RQ2**) aims to examine the groups within our sample to see if gender, age and personality type have an influence on the concern level identified in **RQ1**. The Shapiro-Wilk test is used to test for normality over a given data set, for this paper this test showed that the dependent variables were not normally distributed meaning only non-parametric tests could be used. To ascertain if there was a statistical difference between participants within a group, gender and personality types were split into binary groups and age was split by generation [19] (Silent, Boomer, Gen X, Gen Y, Gen Z). For binary groups the Mann-Whitney U test was used and for age the Kruskal-Wallis H test was used to see if there were statistical differences between these groups, to measure correlation Kendall's Tau-b was used.

3 Results

3.1 Classification of Personal Data

To classify the results based on the concern of exposure factor analysis was performed across all 13 pieces of personal information. A Kaiser-Meyer-Olkin Measure of Sampling Adequacy (KMO=.878) and Bartlett's Test of Sphericity ($X_2(78)$=1058.843, p<.001) indicate the results obtained are fit for this analysis. Factor analysis indicated three factors (Table 1): (1) Low concern, (2) Medium concern, and (3) High concern. Figure 1 shows a bar chart breakdown of the frequencies within these three factors. Racial or Ethnic Origin which has a median of Not at all Concerned, which coincides with the medians in the Low Concern group has been classified as medium concern by factor analysis showing the median cannot be solely relied on for classifying personal data exposure concern. All personal preferences we grouped into the Low Concern category, Medium concern contains three of the four personal information located in the special category of UK GDPR (Political opinions, Sexual orientation and Racial or ethnic origin) along with educational activities and employment history, and High concern has Financial records, Health records and Calendar appointments.

Table 1. Results of factorial analysis identifying three components across the thirteen items of personal information, personal information marked with a * is personal information within the special category of UK GDPR

Personal information	Components		
	1	2	3
Music interests	0.905		
Sport preferences	0.879		
Interest in movies	0.841		
Drink preferences	0.839		
Food preferences	0.831		
Political opinions*		0.812	
Sexual orientation*		0.71	
Educational activities		0.661	
Racial or ethnic origin*		0.62	
Employment history		0.595	
Financial records			0.92
Health records*			0.897
Calendar appointments			0.807

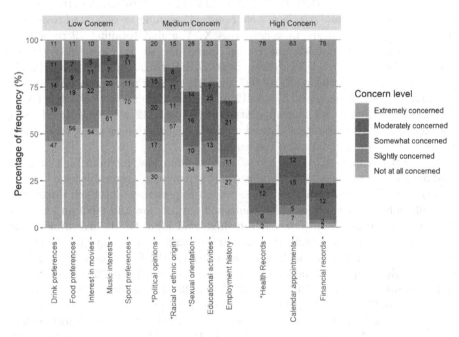

Fig. 1. Participants perceptions on the concern level of each individual item of personal data being available to the general public grouped into components identified in factorial analysis, with X axis being each individual item of personal data, Y axis being the percentage of participants (total participants is 102) and labels on the bar being the frequencies for each bar, personal information marked with a * is personal information within the special category of UK GDPR

3.2   Influencing Factors on Personal Data Sensitivity

Mann-Whitney U tests were conducted across age, gender, and personality types using these as the independent variables and the individual items of personal data as the dependent variable. Statistical significance was only found for age, gender, extroversion, and conscientiousness.

Gender for this paper is considered a binary variable as shown in Sect. 2.4, in our sample 51 participants identified themselves as male and 51 participants identified themselves as female. Results from the Mann-Whitney U tests found gender to be statistically significant only for Sports preferences (U=973, p=.008, r=.264) with males having a lower concern rank compared to females. While only sports preference was found to have statistical significance a clear pattern was identified in the Kendall-Tau B correlation showing that for each individual item of personal data males ranked concern lower than females.

Age was considered to not be binary and initially have 5 groups dictated by generations with the following frequencies N_{Silent}=1, N_{Boomer}=2, N_{GenX}=18, N_{GenY}=43, N_{GenZ}=38. Both the Silent and Boomer generations had frequencies of 1 and 2 so for our analysis these were removed meaning we only used responses from participants who are in generations X, Y and Z totalling 99 responses. Results from the Kruskal-Wallis H test found age to be statistically significant for Health records (X_2=6.686, p=0.035), Political opinions (X_2=9.275, p=0.01), Sexual orientation (X_2=9.097, p=0.011), Drink preferences (X_2=6.937, p=0.031), Music Preferences(X_2=8.412, p=0.015), Educational activities (X_2= 7.543, p=0.023), and Calendar appointments (X_2=11.112, p=0.004). In all cases the Kendall-Tau B correlation showed a positive correlation meaning that as age increases, the concern rank also increases.

The TIPI scale outputs a score of low, medium low, medium high or high ranking for the five personality dimensions (Extroversion, Agreeableness, Conscientiousness, Emotional Stability, Openness to Experiences) [6]. Each dimension was split into 2 groups: Low which contained outputs low and medium low, and High which contained outputs medium high and high. Of the five dimensions only extroversion and conscientiousness were found to have any statistical significance. **Extroversion** had frequencies of 51 for the Low group (G1) and 52 for the High group (G2) and was found to be statistically significant for: Political opinions (U=919, p=0.01, r=0.26, T_B=-0.23), Sexual orientation (U=928, p=0.01, r=0.25, T_B=-0.23), Racial or ethnic origin (U=850, p=<.001, r=0.33, T_B=-0.31), Movie preferences (U=908, p=0, r=0.28, T_B=-0.26), Sport preferences (U=1020.5, p=0.02, r=0.23, T_B=-0.22), and Music preferences(U=922, p=0, r=0.28, T_B=-0.27). A negative correlation was found for all statistically significant results indicating as a participant became more extroverted, their concern ranking decreased. **Conscientiousness** with frequencies of 46 for the Low group (G1) and 56 for the High group (G2), was found to be statistically significant for : Political opinions (U=943, p=0.02, r=0.24, T_B=0.21), Racial or ethnic origin (U=1008.5, p=0.04, r=0.21, T_B=0.19), Drink preferences (U=923, p=0.01, r=0.26, T_B=0.24), and Sport preferences (U=1045.5, p=0.05, r=0.2, T_B=0.19). The Kendall-Tau B correlation for these results was positive, showing as conscientiousness increases, a person's concern ranking also increases.

4   Discussion

The classification outset in Sect. 3.1 provides the first step in being able to train personalised companion robots on how sensitive personal data is (RQ1), enabling such a system to not accidentally expose sensitive personal data while communicating with a user. For example, personal data classified as High concern by default is never exposed and HCI methods such as sending the information via a mobile notification or asking for further verification (e.g. facial or voice recognition) before communicating the personal data, and personal data classified as Low Concern is freely exposed without any restrictions. However, personal data classified as Medium Concern is not as straightforward, this is due to the polarised nature of this information within the classification as shown by the frequencies in Fig. 1. This paper suggests a user input approach for such a classification where a user decides how this personal data should be handled and robots' default to High Concern processes until specified otherwise.

Shown in Sect. 1 to enable personalised behaviours for robots within HRI a user needs to trust the robot with their personal data. Both Richards [15] and Martin et al. [13] shows that trust is promoted by data protection behaviour, meaning if robots exhibit data protection behaviour using our classification as shown above, this will promote user trust of the robot enabling the further sharing of personal data and further personalised behaviour being used. Transparency has been shown to allow users to understand the actions of the robot better [8] and also regain trust quicker if an error does occur transparency. A reason-based approach to personal data communication using our classification, for example, if a robot sends the personal data via a phone notification, will enable transparency for the user as they will know it has been communicated in this way as the personal data is classified as High Concern.

This classification not only provides guidelines for how robots should handle personal data but also for HRI researchers and people actively working in the field of companion robotics/personalised robotics. For example, instead of collecting Health records (High Concern personal data) to assess participants' food allergies, ask only for food preferences (Low Concern personal data). Using less sensitive data within studies to obtain the same result, may make participants feel more comfortable providing such data within the studies, along with potentially improving data collection practices within HRI.

Of particular interest with our classification is the classification received for the personal data derived from the special category data in the UK GDPR [21]. Due to this personal data being derived from law, it could be inferred that this personal data would be classified as High Concern. However, the classification provided shows only one of the four individual items of personal data (Health records) being classified as High Concern with the remaining three being classified as a Medium Concern. A causal factor for this could be due to the person's understanding of what is protected under UK law. For HRI this means robots could provide users with informed consent on local law to make sure they are aware of how their personal data is protected under local law. The classification presented in this paper does not supersede the local law of how personal data should be handled. For example, while only one of the four personal data from the special category data in the UK GDPR was classified as High Concern, all four should be considered high concern and follow the further rules set out by the UK GDPR, then allow users to change this classification manually if they choose to do so.

These results show age, gender, extroversion, and conscientiousness as paramount influencing factors on how participants perceive personal data exposure concerns (**RQ2**). These results are in partial agreement with Li et al. [10] who identified a similar influencing factor within HCI of extroversion, however, this paper found no link between openness and a participant's views on personal data exposure concerns. This paper argues based on the identification of these influencing factors, that not only does the concern classification personal data is in need to be considered but also the age, gender, extroversion, and conscientiousness of the person whose personal data is being communicated needs to be considered. Future work could investigate a combinational effect of both the context and influencing factors may have on personal data exposure concern.

Section 1 identifies the potentiality of using a contextual integrity framework within HRI as a solution to prevent the accidental exposure of personal data by a personalised robot within HRI. Using this classification and the factors that can influence this, robots can start to be trained to understand how sensitive personal data is, working towards the norm of appropriateness/disruption aspects of contextual integrity [14]. This classification also provides motivation for the need of such frameworks within HRI due to different contexts influencing the sensitivity of personal data. Work from Rossi et al. [16] looked at personal data sensitivity within a public bar context and found increased concern rankings for: all personal data that overlapped with this work (Rossi et al. mean (M_R, this papers mean M_L) : political opinions (M_R =4.09, M_L=2.78), sexual orientation (M_R=3.84, M_L=2.92), movie preferences (M_R=2.49, M_L=1.97), drinks preference (M_R=2.34, M_L=2.22), and sports preferences (M_R=2.34, M_L=1.70).

5   Conclusion

This paper has provided a classification of personal data as a solution to concerns of personal data being accidentally exposed within HRI, with a classification of low, medium and high concern. This paper has identified guidelines on how this classification can be used within both robot design and HRI study design. Influencing factors on this classification have been identified as age, extroversion and conscientiousness which need to be factored into a policy derived from these classifications. Care needs to be taken with using any personal data within HRI and all guidance from the local law needs to be considered before this classification is applied.

References

1. Ahmed, A.O., Jenkins, B.: Critical synthesis package: ten-item personality inventory (TIPI). MedEdPORTAL **9**, 9427 (2013)
2. Butler, D.J., Huang, J., Roesner, F., Cakmak, M.: Privacy-utility tradeoff for remotely teleoperated robots, pp. 27–34. ACM (2015)
3. Dautenhahn, K., Woods, S., Kaouri, C., Walters, M., Koay, K., Werry, I.: What is a robot companion - friend, assistant or butler? pp. 1192–1197 (September 2005)
4. Denning, T., Matuszek, C., Koscher, K., Smith, J.R., Kohno, T.: A spotlight on security and privacy risks with future household robots, pp. 105–114. ACM (2009)
5. Fiorini, L., et al.: Enabling personalised medical support for chronic disease management through a hybrid robot-cloud approach. Auton. Robot. **41**, 1263–1276 (2017)
6. Gosling, S.D., Rentfrow, P.J., Swann, W.B.: A very brief measure of the big-five personality domains. Res. Pers. **37**, 504–528 (2003)
7. Krupp, M.M., Rueben, M., Grimm, C.M., Smart, W.D.: A focus group study of privacy concerns about telepresence robots, pp. 1451–1458. IEEE (2017)
8. Kulesza, T., Stumpf, S., Burnett, M., Yang, S., Kwan, I., Wong, W.K.: Too much, too little, or just right? ways explanations impact end users' mental models. In: 2013 IEEE Symposium on VL/HCC, pp. 3–10 (2013)
9. Leyzberg, D., Spaulding, S., Scassellati, B.: Personalizing robot tutors to individuals' learning differences, pp. 423–430. ACM (2014)
10. Li, Y., Huang, Z., Wu, Y.J., Wang, Z.: Exploring how personality affects privacy control behavior on social networking sites. Front. Psychol. **10**, 1771 (2019)
11. Lutz, C., Tamó-Larrieux, A.: The robot privacy paradox. Human-Machine. Communication **1**, 87–111 (2020)
12. Marchang, J., Di Nuovo, A.: Assistive multimodal robotic system: security and privacy issues, challenges, and possible solutions. Appl. Sci. **12**, 2174 (2022)
13. Martin, K.D., Borah, A., Palmatier, R.W.: Data privacy: effects on customer and firm performance. J. Market. **81**, 36–58 (2017)
14. Nissenbaum, H.: Privacy as contextual integrity. Wash. L. Rev. **79**, 119 (2004)
15. Richards, N.M., Hartzog, W.: Taking trust seriously privacy law. SSRN E (2015)
16. Rossi, A., Perugia, G., Rossi, S.: Investigating customers' perceived sensitivity of information shared with a robot bartender. In: Li, H., et al. (eds.) ICSR 2021. LNCS (LNAI), vol. 13086, pp. 119–129. Springer, Cham (2021). https://doi.org/10.1007/978-3-030-90525-5_11
17. Rossi, A., Rossi, S.: Engaged by a bartender robot: Recommendation and personalisation in human-robot interaction, pp. 115–119. ACM (2021)
18. Rueben, M.: Themes and research directions in privacy-sensitive robotics. In: 2018 IEEE Workshop on Advanced Robotics and its Social Impacts (ARSO), pp. 77–84 (2018)
19. Strauss, W., Howe, N.: Generations: The History of America's Future. Quill (1992)
20. Syrdal, D.S., Walters, M., Otero, N., Koay, K.L., Dautenhahn, K.: "he knows when you are sleeping"-privacy and the personal robot companion, pp. 28–33 (2007)
21. United Kingdom Parliment: United kingdom general data protection regulation 2016, no. 679. https://www.legislation.gov.uk/eur/2016/679/contents

Investigating Non Verbal Interaction with Social Robots

Affective Human-Robot Interaction with Multimodal Explanations

Hongbo Zhu[✉], Chuang Yu, and Angelo Cangelosi

The University of Manchester, Manchester, UK
{hongbo.zhu,chuang.yu,angelo.cangelosi}@manchester.ac.uk

Abstract. Facial expressions are one of the most practical and straight-forward ways to communicate emotions. Facial Expression Recognition has been used in lots of fields such as human behaviour understanding and health monitoring. Deep learning models can achieve excellent performance in facial expression recognition tasks. As these deep neural networks have very complex nonlinear structures, when the model makes a prediction, it is not easy for human users to understand what is the basis for the model's prediction. Specifically, we do not know which facial units contribute to the classification more or less. Developing affective computing models with more explainable and transparent feedback for human interactors is essential for a trustworthy human-robot interaction. Compared to "white-box" approaches, "black-box" approaches using deep neural networks, which have advantages in terms of overall accuracy but lack reliability and explainability. In this work, we introduce a multimodal affective human-robot interaction framework, with visual-based and verbal-based explanation, by Layer-Wise Relevance Propagation (LRP) and Local Interpretable Mode-Agnostic Explanation (LIME). The proposed framework has been tested on the KDEF dataset, and in human-robot interaction experiments with the Pepper robot. This experimental evaluation shows the benefits of linking deep learning emotion recognition systems with explainable strategies.

Keywords: Explainable robotics · Facial Expression Recognition (FER) · eXplainable Artificial Intelligence (XAI) · Human-Robot Interaction (HRI)

1 Introduction

Facial expression is a critical non-verbal communication strategy, and human emotions can be expressed through facial expressions, which can be read and interpreted by emotional AI technology [7,27]. Face expression detection is significant for patients with specific diseases or congenital disabilities [13], especially when they cannot express their thoughts through words and actions. In this case, real-time facial emotion detection needs to be performed to take corresponding medical measures for the patient.

Supported by University of Manchester and UKRI Node on Trust (EP/V026682/1).

F. Cavallo et al. (Eds.): ICSR 2022, LNAI 13817, pp. 241–252, 2022.
https://doi.org/10.1007/978-3-031-24667-8_22

The advancement of AI poses challenges for humans to trace model results, especially in the field of deep learning. It is difficult for data scientists and even engineers who write AI algorithms to explain what is happening inside the models and how these AI models come to specific results [1]. XAI is proposed to address this dilemma, which is a set of methods and processes that enable users to understand the output of AI models [2]. AI developers need to have a comprehensive understanding and awareness of the working mechanism, to monitor whether the working process of the model complies with regulations, thereby reducing legal and security risks and gaining the user trust.

In this work, we explored how explainable methods (namely LRP and LIME) could make facial emotion recognition more transparent and trustworthy with visual and verbal explanations. In the visual interpretation extraction part, LRP was utilized to provide a visual explanation on a CNN-based emotion classifier. For the verbal interpretation extraction part, Openface [4] was used to recognise face action units and calculate the related intensity. Then LIME was employed to analyse the contribution of each Action Unit(AU) for model prediction.

The pipeline of our model is shown in Fig. 1. Firstly, the Pepper robot predicts the facial emotion states of the interactor during HRI. Then, Pepper verbalises the predicted emotion as linguistic feedback and shows the heatmap generated from the LRP model as explainable visual feedback. In addition, the robot can give more detailed emotion recognition feedback to increase interaction transparency. This multimodel explanation feedback can help the human interactor understand the robot's internal emotion recognition process, facilitating human-robot trust.

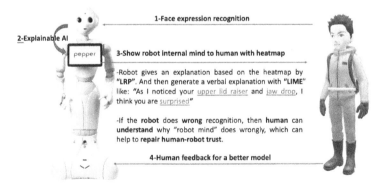

Fig. 1. The proposed multimodel explanation framework

All in all, our paper contributions are as follows:

– We retrained a deep learning model of VGG16 to perform emotion recognition task on KDEF dataset, and LRP was utlized to highlight the crucial pixel-features of the input image and generate heatmap-based explanation.

- We made use of Openface to detact AU and calcualted the corresponding intensity, then random forest was used perform emotion prediction. Finally AU-based explanation was generated by LIME.
- The proposed multimodal explainable method was tested on Pepper robot, the generated heatmap is shown on the screen of chest. Verbal explanation based on AU from LIME is given at the same time. Finally, trust is constructed and the feedback from the interactor can be used to improve the facial expression recognition (FER) model.

2   Related Works and Background

The Deep learning-based model and Facial Action Coding Systems (FACS) based model are two mainstream methods for facial emotion recognition [28]. Compared with traditional ML methods, deep learning-based black-box methods have higher accuracy but usually lack reliability and interpretability due to the complex network structure. Explainable AI is proposed to solve this challenge. Common explainable methods are backpropagation-based Layer-Wise Relevance Propagation (LRP) [3] and perturbation-based Local Interpretable Model-agnostic Explanations (LIME) [17]. The main goal of these methods is to find activation regions in the DL model and highlight the parts of the input image that have a decisive influence on the classifier's decision. While these methods account for the contribution of the input image at the pixel level, they do not give an explanation at the facial action unit level. Facial Action Coding System (FACS) [6] is a standard of most FER models for estimating and recognising AUs. It is based on the activation of facial muscles during facial expressions. These activations are represented by AUs. Action units (AUs) [22] were mostly used as features, feeding classifiers to recognize emotions. AUs are defined as subtle facial muscle movements. According to the physiological distribution of facial muscles and related characteristics, the movements of different facial muscles can be classified into different AUs [23].

Numerous interpretable techniques have been deployed to explain the dynamics process of AI models. We explored backpropagation-based and perturbation-based explainable methods and use them to develop our multimodel explanation architecture for FER in Human-Robot interaction.

2.1   Backpropagation-Based Explanation

Backpropagation is an internal algorithm common across neural network architectures. It is used to calculate the gradient of the loss function with regard to the weights of the connection between the layers of the network, and understand the correlation between the input and output to a network [15]. As for backpropagation-based explainable methods, attributions are calculated by backpropagating once or more times through the network.

Layer-Wise Relevance Propagation is a backpropagation-based interpretable method [14]. It calculates importance scores in a layer-by-layer approximation of backpropagation, which does not interact with the training process of the network and can be easily applied to an already trained DNN model. LRP provides an intuitive human-readable heatmap of input images at the pixel level. It uses the network weights and the neural activation created by the forward-pass to propagate the output back through the network from the predicted output to the input layer [16]. The heatmap is used to visualize the contribution of each pixel to the prediction. The contribution of the intermediate neuron or each pixel is quantified to relevance value R, representing how important the given pixel is to a particular prediction.

2.2 Perturbation-Based Explanation

The perturbation-based XAI method modifies the input of the model to investigate which parts of the input elements are more critical for the model's predictions [8]. Specifically, the disturbance is generated by occluding some pixels or replacing some words in the sentence, then observing the changes in the output. If the input after the disturbance significantly changes the output, it is considered that "the cause behind the disturbance" is very significant. The perturbation-based interpretable methods are generally applicable to the vast majority of deep learning models [18].

Local Interpretable Model-agnostic Explanations is a commonly used post-hoc perturbation-based explainable model [12]. It can generate instance-based explanations for the model predictions. For a given input sample Y, LIME generates perturbed data near Y. The weights of the perturbed data are calculated according to how close they are to the sample Y. LIME then trains an interpretable sparse linear model on the perturbed dataset as a local approximate classifier. In contrast to most backpropagation-based algorithms that need to use the internal information of the classification model to generate explanations, LIME generates explanations without accessing the model's internals. [8].

2.3 Emotion Recognition for HRI

Unlike FER in human-computer interaction, the position of the face relative to the camera is relatively fixed. Robotic emotion recognition is related to environmental factors, making it an extremely challenging task to enable the robot to understand emotions [25]. Emotional robots have many real-life applications, and studies have shown that in treating children with autism, they are more inclined to interact with robots than humans [21]. Therefore, building a robotic system with emotional intelligence will help detect the emotional state of autistic children in real-time, thereby providing more efficient treatment. By dynamically interacting with the external environment, emotional robots can also learn better adaptability and flexibility [26].

3   Methodology

In this paper, explainable emotion recognition was explored in HRI through backpropagation-based model for visual explanation and perturbation-based model for verbal explanation, which will be introduced below.

3.1   Visual-Based Explanation

As for visual-based explanation, we explored explainable facial emotion recognition with LRP. This can explain inputs' relevance for a certain prediction, typically for image processing. Using LRP, the robot can extract the facial heatmap that highlights sufficient parts of the facial pixels most responsible for the emotion prediction task. Face recognition with VGG16 is used in this paper. VGG16 [5] is a simple and widely used convolutional neural network model for image classification tasks. In this work, we reused the pre-trained image classification VGG16 model to fine-tune it for our face emotional recognition task.

The input images of this model are with a fixed size of 224 * 224. The image is passed through a series of convolutional layers, following three fully-connected layers with different depths. As our task has seven emotions, the final fully-connected layer was changed to seven dimensions, as shown in Fig. 2. The whole pre-trained model is further trained on the facial emotional dataset for facial emotion recognition. During this new training, the previous layers of the pre-trained VGG16 are kept fixed.

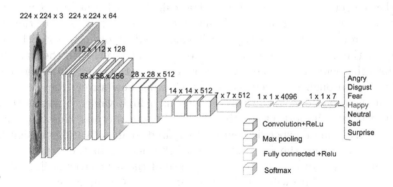

Fig. 2. The architecture of modified VGG16.

Layer-Wise Relevance Propagation (LRP) can explain the relevance of inputs for a certain prediction, typically for image processing. So we can see which part of the input images, or more precisely which pixels, most contribute to a specific prediction. As a model-specific method, LRP generally assumes that the classifier can be decomposed into several layers of computation [24]. In the forward pass process, the image goes through a convolutional neural network for feature extraction from the image. Then, these extracted features are input to a classifier with a fully connected neural network and a softmax layer which gives the final prediction. At this point, we are interested in why the model gets that prediction. LRP goes in reverse order over the layers, we have visited in the forward pass and calculates the relevant scores for each of the neurons in the layer until we arrive at the input again. We can then calculate the relevance for each pixel of the input image. The positive relevant scores indicate how much contributions the pixels make to the model prediction, and the negative values mean these pixels would speak against it, which leads to the heatmap result.

When the LRP model is applied to the trained neural network, it propagates the classification function $f(x)$ backward in the network through pre-defined propagation rules from the output layer to the input layer. Let j and k be neurons at two continuous layers. The propagating relevance scores $R_k^{(l+1)}$ at a given layer $l + 1$ onto neurons of the lower layer l is achieved by applying the following rule [20]:

$$R_j^{(l)} = \sum_k \frac{Z_{jk}}{\sum_{j'} Z_{j'k}} R_k^{(l+1)} \tag{1}$$

The quantity Z_{jk} models how much importance the neuron j has contributed to making the neuron k relevant.

$$Z_{jk} = x_j^{(l)} w_{jk}^{(l,l+1)} \tag{2}$$

The relevance of a neuron is calculated according to Formula 1, which can calculate the relevance R for a neuron j in layer l. So our current layer is l, and the output layer becomes $l + 1$. The calculation for neuron j now works as follows. For each neuron j in the layer l, we calculate the activation based on the neuron j. And the activation is calculated according to Z_{jk}. It simply multiplies the input for the neuron j in our current layer, with the weight that goes into the neuron k in the next layer. This input x comes from passing the pixel values through the previous layers, showing how strong the activation is between these neurons. Intuitively, if there is a high value, it means that the neuron was very important for the output. So we interpret this fraction as a relative activation of a specific neuron, compared to all activations in that layer. Finally, we multiply the relevant score of the neuron in the next layer with this relative value to propagate the relevance of the next layer backwards. The propagation procedure will not stop until it reaches the input layer.

3.2   Verbal-Based Explaination

According to the facial action units (AUs) that make up an expression, FACS[1] divides the face into upper and lower parts and subdivides the facial action units into different AUs to encode facial emotions, shown in Fig. 3. Openface [4] can detect action units and identify the corresponding intensity of each activated AU as an open source software. To explain the relationship between action units and

---

[1] https://imotions.com/blog/facial-action-coding-system/.

emotion, LIME was used to calculate and visualize the contribution of each AU to the predicted emotion in our work. Each AU represents a facial behaviour generated with an anatomically distinct facial muscle group [10]. The combination of AUs can produce most facial expressions, and the goal of facial AU recognition is to detect AU and calculate AU intensity for each input face expression. Here Openface was used in our work to detect and estimate the intensity of AUs from input images, which is shown in Fig. 4.

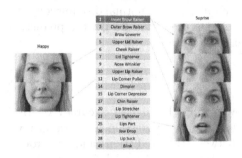

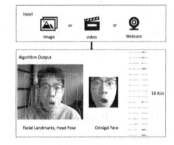

Fig. 3. The illusration of AUs.

Fig. 4. The input and output of Openface.

Local Interpretable Model-agnostic Interpretation (LIME) aims to explain any black-box model by creating a local approximation, which can approximate the original model in the vicinity of an individual instance. It works on almost any input format, such as text, tabular data, images or even graphs.

$$\xi(x) = \operatorname*{argmin}_{g \in G} \mathcal{L}(f, g, \pi_x) + \Omega(g) \tag{3}$$

The idea behind LIME is quite intuitive. For instance, we know the properties of input data point x in a tabular format. In this optimization formula above, the complex model is denoted with f and the simple model or the local model is denoted with g. In this simple model, small g comes from a set of interpretable models which are denoted with a capital G, here capital G is a family of sparse linear models, such as linear regression.

The first loss term L try to find an approximation of the complex model f by the simple model g in the neighbourhood of our data point x. In other terms, we want to get a good approximation in the local neighbourhoods. The third argument π here defines the local neighbourhoods of that data point and is some sort of proximity measure.

The second loss term Ω is used to regularize the complexity of our simple surrogate model for linear regression. For instance, a desirable condition could be to have many zero-weighted input features, so ignoring most of the features and just including a few makes our explanations simpler for the decision tree. It makes sense to have a relatively small depth that stays comprehensible for humans. So overall, this Ω is a complexity measure, and as this optimization problem is a minimization problem, we are trying to minimize Ω. In summary, this loss function says that we look for a simple model g.

To minimize those two-loss terms, it should approximate the complex model in that local area and stay as simple as possible. In the first step, we simply generate some new data points in the neighbourhood of our input data point. More specifically, we randomly generate data points everywhere, but they will be weighted according to the distance to our input data point. As we are just interested in the local area around our input. These data points are generated by perturbations. This can be achieved by sampling from a normal distribution with the mean and standard deviation for each feature. Then we get the prediction for these data points using our complex model f.

$$\mathcal{L}(f, g, \pi_x) = \sum_{z, z' \in \mathcal{Z}} \pi_x(z) \left(f(z) - g(z')\right)^2 \qquad (4)$$

We minimize the first loss term by getting the highest accuracy on that new data set using a simple linear model for linear regression. For instance, we minimize the sum of square distances between the predictions and the ground truth. Then a loss function is used to optimize the linear model. It's basically the sum of squared distances between the label, which comes from the complex model f and the prediction of the simple model g [9]. Additionally, the proximity π is added to weight the loss, according to how close a data point is. Here exponential kernel is used as a distance metric, so we can think of this like a heatmap. The points that are close to our input data points are weighed the most. That is how we ensure that the model is locally faithful. The second loss term Ω is used to make sure that our model stays simple. In LIME, a sparse linear model is used. In practice, this can be achieved by using a regularization technique. This way we ensure to get a simple explanation with only a few relevant variables. In summary, LIME fits a linear interpretable model in that local area, which is a local approximation of a complex model.

4   Model Evaluation and Results

4.1   KDEF Datasets and Pre-processing

The Karolinska Directed Emotional Faces (KDEF) [11] dataset consists of 4900 facial expression photos with 70 individuals (half males and half females, ages from 20 to 30). Each person imitates seven different facial emotions and, each facial expression is recorded from five camera views. In this paper, we only use the front face photos in our experiment as our robot mainly interacts with a human user in a front view. Some examples are as shown in Fig. 5. That means we used one-fifth of the dataset, 980 pictures in total, so each emotion subset contains 140 front view images for each expression. The face images were rescaled to a standard 224 * 224 pixels and three colour channels, to fit the input format of the classification model. And we randomly split the front-face dataset into the trainning part, validation part and testing part with a ratio of 700:140:140.

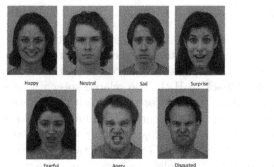

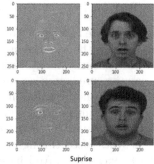

Fig. 5. Sample of the KDEF dataset   **Fig. 6.** Visual based explanation

4.2 Multimodal Explanation

In the affective HRI, the robot will not only recognize the human interactor emotion but also provide the multimodal explainable feedbacks, including visual feedback with explainable heatmap that illustrates emotion recognition contribution extracted from LRP model and verbal feedback with understandable robot speech to explain the face AU activation for emotion recognition.

Based on the pre-trained VGG16 model in the visual explanation part, our face emotion recognition model is further trained on an Nvidia RTX 2080Ti graphic card. We set the batch size to 32 and used Adam as the optimization algorithm, with the learning rate of 0.00001. After 250 epochs of training, the model achieves a classification testing accuracy of 91.4% on the KDEF dataset. The predicted result and model parameters were fed to LRP, and then the pixel wize contribution was calculated and shown on the heatmap for an explanation. For example, the comparison of the two heatmap images in Fig. 6 shows that the robot uses similar feature pixels in two different faces. This means that when VGG16 classifies the face as a 'surprise' emotion, the robot relies more on feature pixes near the eyes, nostrils and lips to make its prediction, which is in line with theories of human emotion perception and cognition [19].

In the verbal explanation part, we use Openface to extract the activation of 16 AUs used for emotion recognition with random forest. Finally, the AUs-based explanation chart was generated by LIME, as shown in Fig. 7. The blue bar indicates positive contribution while the orange bar indicates the negative contribution of surprise prediction. According to the histogram, AU26 (Jaw Drop) and AU05 (Upper Lid Raiser) make the biggest positive contribution to the prediction. Then the blanks of the predefined text template were filled with the AU names that make most significant contribution. Finally, Text-to-Speech (TTS) generates voice explanations for robot speech.

4.3   Test on Pepper Robot

In this work, we have tested our multimodel explanation methods on the Pepper robot. During the experiments, a person interacts with the Pepper robot, who can simultaneously recognise their facial expressions and verbalise the human face emotion prediction as verbal feedback in HRI. The related speech is generated based on the emotion recognition results. For example, if the emotion recognition result is *happy*, the explainable speech sentence will be *As I noticed your Cheek Raiser and Lip Corner Puller, I think you are happy*. The speech voice is synthesized through the Text-To-Speech (TTS) tool of the Naoqi SDK of the Pepper robot. And based on the LRP model, the robot can extract the heatmap images as the pixel-level explanation for the interactor. The original face and the heatmap face are be shown in the Pepper chest screen as interpretable visual feedback. Through verbal and visual feedback, this explainable system has the benefit of supporting trustworthy human-robot interaction.

Explanation Example : As I noticed your upper lid raiser and jaw drop, I think you are surprised

Fig. 7. An example of AUs-based explanation for surprise emotion

5   Conclusion and Future Work

Robotic systems may become more commonplace, but at the same time, more complex. When robots fail to express their intentions, people will feel not only discomfortable but also untrustworthy. It is necessary for people to know how the robot recognize human emotion to assess when such systems can be trusted, even if robots follow a reasonable decision-making process.

In conclusion, this paper integrates two explainable methods in emotion recognition for trustworthy HRI. Using the explainable method LRP, the robot can extract the facial heatmap that highlights significant parts of the facial pixels most responsible for the emotion prediction task. The visualized attention heatmap and verbal feedback, can help the user understand the perceptual mechanism the robot uses to recognise emotions. Thus the explainable method provides essential insights into the natural features of the prediction model.

In this work, we just completed the essential human facial emotion recognition with related explanation, but have not conducted much work on trust validation with our explainable model in human-robot interaction scenes. As for future work, more human-joined tests will be taken for trust evaluation to explore the effectiveness of our multimodel explanation. And we will explore how we can use the feedback for human-in-the-loop robot learning to improve the robot's emotional perception ability in dynamic HRI scenes.

References

1. Adadi, A., Berrada, M.: Peeking inside the black-box: a survey on explainable artificial intelligence (xai). IEEE Access **6**, 52138–52160 (2018)
2. Arrieta, A.B., et al.: Explainable artificial intelligence (xai): concepts, taxonomies, opportunities and challenges toward responsible AI. Inf. Fusion **58**, 82–115 (2020)
3. Bach, S., Binder, A., Montavon, G., Klauschen, F., Müller, K.R., Samek, W.: On pixel-wise explanations for non-linear classifier decisions by layer-wise relevance propagation. PloS One **10**(7), e0130140 (2015)
4. Baltrusaitis, T., Zadeh, A., Lim, Y.C., Morency, L.P.: Openface 2.0: facial behavior analysis toolkit. In: 2018 13th IEEE International Conference on Automatic Face & Gesture Recognition (FG 2018), pp. 59–66. IEEE (2018)
5. Dubey, A.K., Jain, V.: Automatic facial recognition using vgg16 based transfer learning model. J. Inf. Optim. Sci. **41**(7), 1589–1596 (2020)
6. Ekman, P., Friesen, W.V.: Facial action coding system. Environ. Psychol. Nonverbal Behav. (1978)
7. Ekman, P., Friesen, W.V., Ellsworth, P.: Emotion in the human face: Guidelines for research and an integration of findings, vol. 11. Elsevier (2013)
8. Ivanovs, M., Kadikis, R., Ozols, K.: Perturbation-based methods for explaining deep neural networks: a survey. Pattern Recogn. Lett. **150**, 228–234 (2021)
9. Kavila, S.D., Bandaru, R., Gali, T.V.M.B., Shafi, J.: Analysis of cardiovascular disease prediction using model-agnostic explainable artificial intelligence techniques. In: Principles and Methods of Explainable Artificial Intelligence in Healthcare, pp. 27–54. IGI Global (2022)
10. Lien, J.J., Kanade, T., Cohn, J.F., Li, C.C.: Automated facial expression recognition based on facs action units. In: Proceedings Third IEEE International Conference on Automatic Face and Gesture Recognition, pp. 390–395. IEEE (1998)
11. Lundqvist, D., Flykt, A., Öhman, A.: Karolinska directed emotional faces. Cogn. Emot. (1998)
12. Malik, S., Kumar, P., Raman, B.: Towards interpretable facial emotion recognition. In: Proceedings of the Twelfth Indian Conference on Computer Vision, Graphics and Image Processing, pp. 1–9 (2021)
13. Martinez, M., et al.: Emotion detection deficits and decreased empathy in patients with alzheimer's disease and parkinson's disease affect caregiver mood and burden. Front. Aging Neurosci. **10**, 120 (2018)
14. Montavon, G., Binder, A., Lapuschkin, S., Samek, W., Müller, K.R.: Layer-wise relevance propagation: an overview. In: Explainable AI: Interpreting, Explaining and Visualizing Deep Learning, pp. 193–209 (2019)
15. Nie, W., Zhang, Y., Patel, A.: A theoretical explanation for perplexing behaviors of backpropagation-based visualizations. In: International Conference on Machine Learning, pp. 3809–3818. PMLR (2018)
16. Rathod, J., Joshi, C., Khochare, J., Kazi, F.: Interpreting a black-box model used for scada attack detection in gas pipelines control system. In: 2020 IEEE 17th India Council International Conference (INDICON), pp. 1–7. IEEE (2020)
17. Ribeiro, M.T., Singh, S., Guestrin, C.: "why should i trust you?" explaining the predictions of any classifier. In: Proceedings of the 22nd ACM SIGKDD International Conference on Knowledge Discovery and Data Mining, pp. 1135–1144 (2016)

18. Robnik-Šikonja, M., Bohanec, M.: Perturbation-based explanations of prediction models. In: Zhou, J., Chen, F. (eds.) Human and Machine Learning. HIS, pp. 159–175. Springer, Cham (2018). https://doi.org/10.1007/978-3-319-90403-0_9

19. Rosenberg, E.L., Ekman, P.: What the Face Reveals: Basic and Applied Studies of Spontaneous Expression Using the Facial Action Coding System (FACS). Oxford University Press, Oxford (2020)

20. Samek, W., Montavon, G., Vedaldi, A., Hansen, L.K., Müller, K.-R. (eds.): Explainable AI: Interpreting, Explaining and Visualizing Deep Learning. LNCS (LNAI), vol. 11700. Springer, Cham (2019). https://doi.org/10.1007/978-3-030-28954-6

21. Taheri, A., Meghdari, A., Alemi, M., Pouretemad, H.: Human-robot interaction in autism treatment: a case study on three pairs of autistic children as twins, siblings, and classmates. Int. J. Social Rob. **10**(1), 93–113 (2018)

22. Tian, Y.I., Kanade, T., Cohn, J.F.: Recognizing action units for facial expression analysis. IEEE Trans. Pattern Anal. Mach, Intell. **23**(2), 97–115 (2001)

23. Yao, L., Wan, Y., Ni, H., Xu, B.: Action unit classification for facial expression recognition using active learning and svm. Multimedia Tools Appl. **80**(16), 24287–24301 (2021)

24. Yin, P., Huang, L., Lee, S., Qiao, M., Asthana, S., Nakamura, T.: Diagnosis of neural network via backward deduction. In: 2019 IEEE International Conference on Big Data (Big Data), pp. 260–267. IEEE (2019)

25. Yu, C.: Robot Behavior Generation and Human Behavior Understanding in Natural Human-Robot Interaction. Ph.D. thesis, Institut polytechnique de Paris (2021)

26. Yu, C., Tapus, A.: Interactive robot learning for multimodal emotion recognition. In: Salichs, M.A., et al. (eds.) ICSR 2019. LNCS (LNAI), vol. 11876, pp. 633–642. Springer, Cham (2019). https://doi.org/10.1007/978-3-030-35888-4_59

27. Yu, C., Tapus, A.: Multimodal emotion recognition with thermal and rgb-d cameras for human-robot interaction. In: Companion of the 2020 ACM/IEEE International Conference on Human-Robot Interaction, pp. 532–534 (2020)

28. Zhang, H., Yu, C., Tapus, A.: Why do you think this joke told by robot is funny? the humor style matters. In: 2022 31st IEEE International Conference on Robot and Human Interactive Communication (RO-MAN), pp. 572–577. IEEE (2022)

When to Help? A Multimodal Architecture for Recognizing When a User Needs Help from a Social Robot

Jason R. Wilson[(⊠)], Phyo Thuta Aung, and Isabelle Boucher

Franklin & Marshall College, Lancaster, PA 17603, USA
jrw@fandm.edu

Abstract. It is important for socially assistive robots to be able to recognize when a user needs and wants help, and they must be able to do so in a real-time manner so that they can provide timely assistance. We propose an architecture that uses social cues to determine when a robot should provide assistance. Based on a multimodal fusion of eye gaze and language modalities, our architecture is trained and evaluated on data collected in a robot-assisted Lego building task. By focusing on social cues, our architecture has minimal dependencies on the specifics of a given task, enabling it to be applied in many different contexts. Enabling a social robot to recognize a user's needs through social cues can help it to adapt to user behaviors and preferences, which in turn will lead to improved user experiences.

1 Introduction

For socially assistive robots, there is a trade-off between helping too much and too little, helping too early or too late. Helping too little can make the robot seem ineffective or unreliable, leading to a diminished trust in the robot [1]. Helping too much can be annoying, disrupt flow, and harm the user's autonomy [2,3]. How much the robot helps should correspond with how much help the user needs, and the robot must recognize when that help is needed. Simply waiting for when the user explicitly asks for help or makes a mistake may be insufficient and does not enable the agent to provide proactive or unsolicited assistance. The challenge lies in recognizing when the user needs and wants assistance, often through implicit cues [4]. A user may employ a variety of verbal and nonverbal behaviors and other social signals that indicate that assistance may be needed. For example, gaze patterns can be used to recognize when a user becomes disengaged [5,6] or predict user choice in a collaborative task [7]. However, gaze patterns alone are not sufficient (e.g., a user may ask a question without shifting their gaze), and multiple modalities are required to holistically understand when a user needs assistance.

In this paper, we present a real-time architecture that recognizes when a user needs assistance. Our approach automatically analyzes eye gaze and speech of a user and then fuses the outputs from gaze and language models to detect

F. Cavallo et al. (Eds.): ICSR 2022, LNAI 13817, pp. 253–266, 2022.
https://doi.org/10.1007/978-3-031-24667-8_23

whether the user needs help or not. Our main contributions in this paper are the development and validation of models to recognize when a user needs help and an architecture that allows a social robot to interpret social cues to detect when it should help a user. We proceed by first discussing related work in processing social cues and detecting when a user needs help. We then describe the two phases of our work: (1) the development of models to recognize when a user needs help, and (2) the construction of a real-time architecture and its evaluation. Finally, we conclude with a discussion of our approach and its limitations.

2   Related Work

Socially assistive robots have been explored for many tasks from helping in post-stroke rehabilitation [8,9] and managing medications for people with Parkinson's disease [10] to helping students learn language skills [11]. The focus of the robot design may be developing functionality, such as user monitoring or [8,12] retrieving objects [13]. It is often assumed that the robot has a mechanism to determine *when* to help the user and thus the focus is on *how* the robot would assist. However, recognizing the appropriate times for a robot to assist can be critical to protecting the autonomy of the user [10].

Some approaches to determining when to assist employ planning-based approaches that are dependent on the specifics of a task [4,14]. Alternatively, a robot may detect incorrect execution of a task [8,12], but mistakes are better at indicating what they need help with than when they need help. Emotions and eye gaze, on the other hand, provide useful cues for determining when a user would like assistance [4,15]. Social cues are also task-independent, and thus social robots can interpret a user's body posture and eye gaze to determine the level of engagement, regardless of the task at hand [5,6]. Social robots can then interpret these cues to predict the user's intent, detect when users need help, or gauge the user's engagement. Eye gaze data can be used for a sandwich-building robot in determining which ingredient a user is going to select [7], or for a medication-assisting robot in detecting when a user is looking for guidance on medication placement [15]. The user's head position and orientation can help a robot giving directions or an exercise coach robot to detect the user's engagement or affect [6,16]. In addition to non-verbal communication, task-independent language can provide social cues for the robot to interpret. For example, a tour-guide robot detects users' emotions by processing the text of users' speech [17].

3   Phase 1: Model Development

We first describe here the development and evaluation of a set of models to recognize when a user needs help, and in the next section we provide details on how these models are integrated into a real-time architecture. In this first phase, we examine the feasibility of accurately recognizing when a user needs assistance from a social robot. We proceed by first exploring a set of independent models, each examining a distinct approach. Two models look at different eye gaze patterns, one uses language, and a fourth model assesses the user's progress in the task. The intent in developing independent models was twofold: (1) development of each model can focus on identifying relevant features, and (2) robot designs can integrate the appropriate models based on which features are available in the data. We integrate the four independent models using multimodal fusion that provides a more holistic approach to understanding the user.

3.1 Independent Models

Gaze Patterns. We base our eye gaze models on the two models from [15] that were the most effective at predicting when the user needs help: *mutual gaze* and *confirmatory gaze*. The mutual gaze model represents the subject initiating mutual gaze (i.e., eye contact) with the robot by directing their gaze at it. Since it is natural to react to the robot speaking by looking at it, the model excludes these events. However, if the user fixates their gaze on the robot for a longer period, then the model indicates that help is needed. Outputs range from 0 to 1, with 0 meaning the robot is speaking or the subject has not recently looked at the robot, and 1 meaning that the user has gazed at the robot for more than 1 s (threshold determined through empirical testing).

The confirmatory gaze model attempts to recognize when a person is looking back and forth between the task and the robot with the intention of getting feedback on the task. As the person looks back and forth, the duration of the previous gaze direction is relatively short, typically less than 2.5 s (time defined through experimentation). The output of this model is also 0 to 1, proportionate to the duration of the most recent gaze direction. For example, looking at the robot followed by a 0.25 s glance at the task results in a model output of 0.1.

We interpret the output of each model as needing help or not, with values greater than 0.5 meaning the user needs help. The continuous outputs are used to provide more information to our fusion model (see Sect. 3.2).

Language. A person that wants help might say something like "I don't understand." On the other hand, a phrase like "thank you" may indicate the person does not or no longer needs help. In this initial language model we choose to use a simple keyword spotting for terms and phrases that indicate the person either needs help or does not. While this approach clearly will not handle the many subtleties of natural language, it is intended to provide evidence that even a simple language model can help recognize when a person needs help.

Task Progress. To determine if a person needs assistance in a task, a robot may examine the person's progress in the task. Making a mistake indicates a person may need some assistance, whereas actions leading to successful completion of the task indicates help is not needed. Our approach to measuring progress in a task examines whether the length of a plan to complete the task changes [14]. Each time the user takes an action, we use a hierarchical task network

(HTN) planner to generate a list of actions needed to complete the task [18]. If the number of actions remaining decreases, then progress is being made and assistance may not be needed. On the other hand, if the plan length remains the same or increases, the person may need some assistance.

3.2 Multimodal Fusion

Each model on its own is insufficient. The Eye Gaze models cannot capture moments when the user is verbally requesting help, and the Language model cannot recognize unspoken cues. Additionally, recently exhibited behavior also can help interpret the outputs of these components. For example, a confirmatory gaze pattern shortly followed by an "okay" utterance could mean the user is attempting to ask if what the user is looking at is correct. Our approach to combining the outputs of each modality while also taking into account temporal dependencies is to use a decision-level fusion with a sliding window.

The outputs of the language and gaze models represent an inference for a single moment in time. The language model does not incorporate any prior utterances, and the gaze models have only a limited sense of the recent gaze directions. However, previous events should inform how future events are interpreted. To capture these temporal dependencies, we use a sliding window, which concatenates a number (equal to the window size) of the outputs of the specialized models together into a single feature vector as input to the fusion model. We implement the sliding window by concatenating a specified amount of previous feature vectors to the current feature vector, where a feature vector is the set of outputs from the independent models. In our experiments with the model, we vary the window size to assess how much temporal context is necessary.

To determine an optimal integration of our independent models, we experiment with a variety of learning algorithms. Given our limited amount of data, we focus on evaluating learning algorithms that have fewer parameters and thus require less data: support vector machine (SVM), logistic regression, decision tree, naïve Bayes, and random forest (ensemble model). We use a Gaussian model for the naïve Bayes. After empirical testing, we selected a Radial Basis Function (RBF) kernel for the SVM. For the random forest, we use 1600 estimators, a max depth of 20, bootstrap samples, and included a random state.

3.3 Evaluation of Models

Medication Sorting Task. The models are evaluated based on video recordings captured in previous work [3] in which a person is being assisted by a social robot while completing a medication sorting task, which entails organizing pills according to the day of the week and time each pill is to be taken. The assistance provided by the robot includes confirmation of correctness, identification of mistakes, and reminders of constraints.

Data Labeling. Evaluating our models requires data about the user's behavior and labels that indicate when the user needs help. We annotate each video to capture information about the user and the robot. Annotations consist of gaze direction (a qualitative description of where the user was looking), user speech (what the user said), user gestures (whether the user was motioning with their hands), and robot speech (what the robot said). Additionally, task events representing each time the user placed or removed a pill are captured. Lastly, we label segments of the video in which the user appears to need help. We define needing assistance as confused glances, periods of inactivity, verbalization of need, or appearing frustrated. Since judging when a user needs help is a subjective assessment, we use labels from three annotators and resolve differences with a majority vote.

3.4 Experiments and Results

Independent Models. Each of the independent models produced relatively high precision but low recall. Results are in Table 1. Of the independent models, the task model best demonstrates that we can recognize when a user needs help. This result is not surprising since a lack of progress in a task should be a strong indicator of needing help. However, this model is dependent on the particulars of the task and would require accurate recognition of the actions taken. The gaze models are the next best-performing models, and they show that a task-independent approach is feasible. Lastly, the language model is only slightly less precise but has much lower recall and precision. The keyword spotting that the model uses is not expected to handle all the nuances of natural language, and a more sophisticated model is used in phase two.

Fusion Model

Experiment Setup. With the independent models having high precision and low recall, it is likely that integrating these models would lead to increased recall and overall improved performance. To verify this, we conduct a series of experiments using the outputs of the independent models. In each experiment, we vary the size of the sliding window (1–50) and which learning algorithm is used. After applying the sliding window to create the feature vector, the data is shuffled and

Table 1. Each of the independent models has relatively high precision compared to their recall scores.

Model	Precision	Recall	F1
Task	.63	.44	.52
Mutual gaze	.59	.12	.19
Confirmatory gaze	.55	.10	.17
Language	.52	.04	.08

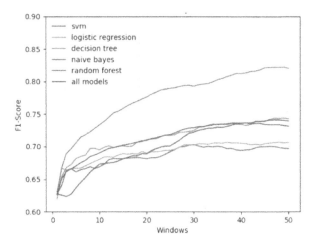

Fig. 1. For each window, the corresponding F1-score is the weighted average of 50 F1-scores to reduce variability from randomization. The all models curve represents the average of all algorithms for each window.

a ten-fold cross-validation is used to train and test the models. To account for random effects from the shuffling, we repeat the shuffling, training, and testing processes for 50 iterations. Overall, we run 12,500 experiments (50 window sizes, 5 algorithms, 50 iterations). We aggregate the results of each of the 50 iterations and calculate F1-scores.

Results. Our best-performing algorithm was the random forest with the window size parameter set to 47. It has a F1-score of .81, far surpassing the best of the independent models. This result validates our hypothesis that integrating the high-precision, low-recall models yields a better-performing model (Fig. 1).

The random forest also shows the most consistent growth in performance as the window size is increased. All of the algorithms generally benefit from larger window sizes, with the greatest increases in performance appearing in the first thirty window sizes. All models have F1-score of .62 or .63 with a window size of one, and performance improves to .70 to .79 at a window size of thirty. After thirty, all models see little to no improvement.

4   Phase 2: Real-Time Architecture

The goal of our architecture is to be able to do real-time recognition of when a user needs assistance by fusing together multiple modalities. The design builds off of the initial prototype of models from the previous section (Sect. 3), though we remove the task model for a task-independent solution. To allow for real-time processing of the data, we introduce architectural components for the automatic processing of audio and video data.

In our initial model development, we rely on manual annotations that labeled the users' speech, gestures, and eye gaze, as well as the robot's speech. Manual

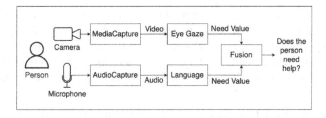

Fig. 2. The architecture has two pipelines for audio and video processing, which are fused together to create the final output.

annotations generally have minimal noise and may not resemble how a robot would need to process live data. We now move towards a more challenging and ecologically valid setup in which the robot needs to automatically detect the user's speech and gaze behavior by processing the audio and video streams in real-time. We also seek to design an approach that is applicable to many tasks in which a social robot is assisting with a physical task. We focus on the social cues that a person exhibits, and thus our architecture does not include a model of the task, in contrast to phase 1.

The architecture, shown in Fig. 2, takes in video and audio inputs of a person through a camera and a microphone, and the data are then fed into the Eye Gaze component and the Language component, respectively. The components independently compute *need values*, which is an estimate of how much assistance the user needs. The need values are then used by the fusion component to determine whether the person needs help or not. To facilitate the processing of real-time data, we have built the system on Microsoft's Platform for Situated Intelligence (\psi) [19].

4.1 Components of Architecture

Eye Gaze. To enable our mutual gaze and confirmatory gaze models to automatically detect when a user needs assistance, we need architectural components to process streaming video data. The Eye Gaze component (see Fig. 3) consists of three subcomponents: OpenFace, Gaze Analyzer, and Gaze Classifier. We use OpenFace to extract eye gaze vectors from images of the incoming video stream [20]. The vectors are translated to qualitative gaze directions by the Gaze Analyzer to describe whether the user is looking at the task, the robot, or elsewhere. Qualitative gaze directions are Up, UpRight, Right, DownRight, Down,

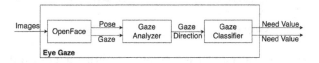

Fig. 3. The Eye Gaze component uses three subcomponents to produce two need values (one for each gaze pattern).

DownLeft, Left, UpLeft, and Center. The GazeClassifier assumes the robot is directly in front of the user and the task is on the table in front of the user. Center is then interpreted as looking at the robot, and down directions are interpreted as looking at the task. The Gaze Classifier subcomponent also contains the gaze models from Sect. 3.1 and outputs two need values, one for each gaze model.

Language. Our initial prototype of the language model (see Sect. 3.1) uses a simple keyword spotting to recognize likely indicators, but this can be too task-specific and not robust enough. Instead, our Language component uses a learned model to classify utterances based on whether the user needs help.

The Language component decomposes into two parts: Speech Recognizer and Text Classifier (see Fig. 4). The Speech Recognizer processes the raw audio input to produce the text of what the user says. The Speech Recognizer is psiDeep-Speech, a \psi component for the Deep Speech[1] (v0.9.3) speech-to-text engine. The text is passed to the Text Classifier, which contains a naïve Bayes model. The model includes two additional features that may indicate a person needs help. We aggregate all question words (i.e., what, who, which, where, when, how, why) into an additional feature. We also have a feature for negations, which includes no, not, none, nothing, isn't, don't, and, can't.

Fusion. Based on our experiments with the fusion model (see Sect. 3.4), the Fusion component uses a random forest algorithm and a window size of 20. While less than the optimal size of 47, we found that 20 is effective while providing better real-time performance. Implementing a sliding window is straightforward with the built-in functionality of \psi, but a challenge is that the Language component produces outputs far less frequently than the Gaze component. Since the output of the Language component may be stale (e.g., the user said something minutes ago that is no longer relevant to their current situation), we apply a linear degradation function to the output of the Language component.

4.2   Data for Training and Evaluation

To evaluate the effectiveness of the architecture, we design an experiment to collect the necessary data. In this data collection, we also lay the foundation for future work with more nuanced labeling of the help that users need.

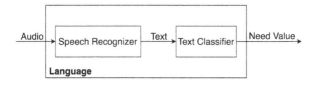

Fig. 4. The Language component has two subcomponents to process the audio input and produce a need value.

---

[1] https://github.com/mozilla/DeepSpeech.

Fig. 5. The Lego pieces, some of which were partially assembled, were on the table directly between the robot and the participant. The black-and-white photo on the participant's right showed the structure they were asked to build. The pouch on the left contained a concealed piece necessary for the structure. Two webcams, on top of a monitor and in front of the robot, were both directed at the participant's face.

Data Collection. Participants (N = 21) interacted with a social robot as they constructed a creature from Legos. The setup (see Fig. 5) involved a physical task performed by the user, as well as a physical agent and printed image, all designed to optimize different gaze directions as well as encourage the participant to speak to the agent. Additionally, there was a hidden piece that was intended to create at least one moment in which all participants would need help.

The interaction began with an orientation phase to familiarize the participant with interacting with the robot. Once the participant completed the orientation phase, the robot instructed the participant to begin building the structure shown in the image on the table. The robot provided encouragement, answered questions, and gave suggestions on how to proceed. All robot behaviors were conducted with a Wizard-Of-Oz setup. After completing the task, participants completed a questionnaire regarding engagement, trust, helpfulness, and assistance.

Labeling. All data were manually labeled using five labels, each describing a different level of need that the user required at a specified time interval. The intent of having multiple levels of need is to allow the robot to alter its assistance in accordance with the amount of need. While the current work does not leverage these distinctions, our architecture design is expected to accommodate this future enhancement.

The level of need of the user was determined by inferring the participant's mental state based on perceptions of the participant's behavior. A person that does not need help may appear engaged, concentrated, and absorbed into a task (i.e., in a flow state [21]). Alternatively, a participant may appear distressed or look around, suggesting that the person may need help. We distinguish between the participant's status in the task and their mental state while completing the task. This is because a person may be making mistakes on the task but is actively working towards a solution. The person's activity is an indicator that they do not need as much help as a person who is making mistakes and is becoming disengaged.

We use labels representing increasing amounts of help needed. For each video, all time after the orientation phase was labeled with one of five need levels (see Fig. 6 for an example). Need levels 1–3 are intended to mirror the first three levels of assistance [22]. The following criteria were used when labeling the data.

- **Flow** represents the participant's steady activity on the task while showing no signs of distress, signifying a steady mental state. This state represents the participant distinctly not needing help.
- **Level 0** is used as a transition from Flow to level 1 when the participant may be pausing and thinking about how to proceed.
- **Level 1** represents a confirmatory stage when a participant appears uncertain. The participant may be checking their work and seeking some form of validation.
- **Level 2** represents when the participant is missing information and may seek it from an external source (e.g., a picture), but not an agent.
- **Level 3** represents when the participant recognizes that they do not have access to the necessary knowledge and seeks input from another agent.

Fig. 6. Every second of the data for each participant was labeled. The annotator had access to the two video streams and the audio that was recorded.

Data Description. The experiment resulted in a total of 146.2 min of labeled video and audio, with 74.3 min of the data being labeled as when the participant needs some level of help. The average length of time it took the participants to complete the task was 7 min with a standard deviation of 4.2 min. Out of the 21 participants, 4 participants completed the task without speaking to the robot at any time throughout the experiment.

As a measurement of the validity of the labels we compare the average level of help in each video to whether the participant indicated whether there was any item other than the missing piece for which they sought the robot's help (item 9 in the questionnaire). To get the average help in each video, we calculated a weighted sum (level · duration) of the labels, using a value of −1 for the Flow label (negative value means help is not needed), and divided by the total seconds. Average help ranged from −0.49 (no help typically needed) to 2.24 (high degree of help regularly needed) ($\mu = 0.32, \sigma = 0.55$). We found that the average help correlated with whether the participant indicated they needed help on more than the missing piece ($r = .47, p = .03$). This shows that the labels correspond with participants self-reports, giving some evidence for the validity of the labels.

4.3 Evaluation of Architecture

The architecture needs to produce a signal that the robot can use as an indicator that it should try to help. Since the final output of the architecture is the result of the Fusion component, it is this component that is the focus of our evaluation. To understand the Fusion component performance, we also examine how well the Gaze and Language components perform. We avoid any comparison with the results of the initial model evaluation since the models in the architecture have modifications, use noisy inputs, and are evaluated with a different data set.

All analysis is based on the components indicating the user needs help or not. We interpret need levels 2 and 3 as needing the robot's help. At level 1, the user appears to need some help but the robot should not interrupt the user. This simplification addresses our primary interest – detecting when the robot should help. See Sect. 5 for how we envision all levels may be incorporated.

Since the language and fusion models require training, we report the results of a ten-fold cross-validation. The gaze models, which are rule-based, do not require training, and thus we report results using all of the recorded data. Table 2 shows that the fusion model generally performs well, suggesting that the architecture has the necessary components to recognize when a user needs help. Greatly contributing to the performance of the fusion model is the language model.

The confirmatory gaze model has relatively high precision, suggesting brief glances at the robot was a good indicator of needing help, but the lower recall of this model suggests that this pattern did not occur often in our data. The

Table 2. Performance of each of the need detection models

Model	Precision	Recall	F1
Mutual gaze	.37	.07	.12
Confirmatory gaze	.65	.04	.08
Language	.61	.76	.68
Multimodal fusion	.77	.81	.79

mutual gaze model performs the least well, possibly indicating that most users do not direct their gaze to the robot too often.

4.4 Demonstration of Architecture

We also demonstrate the ability of the architecture to work in real-time and in a different task. In the video demonstration[2], the robot is assisting a user who is preparing to bake cookies. The provided video shows two instances of a user needing help, causing the robot to give some assistance. The video also shows increasing amount of help provided, which is a feature that will be tied to the level of need in future versions of the architecture. For the purposes of this demonstration, the robot assumes the next step in the recipe is to add vanilla.

5 Discussion

The initial model development explores different approaches that a social robot may use to recognize *when* a person may need help. The gaze and language models are not able to independently capture all the ways a person communicates that they need help. However, the relatively high precision of each model suggests that when the relevant cues are present, the model is able to accurately recognize the user's need for help. Combining these models then allows us to recognize more instances of the user needing help, and the results of the fusion model confirm this. However, these results have two noteworthy drawbacks. First, the task model is a large contributor to the overall performance of the fusion model, possibly making the success of the approach dependent on the specifics of the task. Second, the inputs to all of the models (i.e., gaze direction, speech, user actions) are manual annotations of video recordings. To demonstrate that a social robot can make the same inferences, it must process noisy data from audio/video inputs to produce an accurate recognition of when a person needs assistance.

The results of the model development provide sufficient evidence that it is feasible to recognize when a user needs help from a robot, but a real-time architecture is necessary for a robot to practically make these inferences. We also focus the architecture on interpreting social cues and not relying on the specifics of the task. Collectively, the results show that the architecture has a high rate of accurately recognizing when the user needs assistance. To compensate for the lack of task model in the architecture, the revised language model shows to be a key contributor to the success of our real-time approach.

There are many improvements needed to make the gaze models more effective and applicable to a broader range of setups. Our processing of the user's gaze divided the space into nine qualitative directions and assumes that the user looks at the robot when looking center, the task when looking down, and the picture when down and to the right. While we believe that dividing the gaze space into nine directions is sufficient, we need to be able to adapt how gaze directions map

---

[2] https://youtu.be/eW2uVBgi9r4.

to looking at the robot, task, or goal for any task. Additionally, the models use the duration of the user's gaze as a metric, and altering some of the thresholds in the model would affect the model's performance. Improving the gaze models needs to include a manner by which these duration thresholds can be learned or customized to an individual's behavior. Additionally, we also need to consider other gaze patterns (e.g., goal referencing and gaze aversion), as they may be more informative for some tasks.

In evaluating the real-time architecture, we introduce five levels of needing assistance. While we currently reduce this to a binary classification, the additional categories prepare us for future work that will enable the robot to respond more appropriately to the amount of help the person needs. The different levels of help needed should correspond with different types of assistance. For example, a robot may make a small confirmatory gesture, such as saying "yes" or giving a head nod, in response to recognizing a level 1 help needed. Whereas when recognizing a level 2 help, the robot may interject with where the user may be able to find the necessary information. In order for the robot to have these nuanced responses, we will use our architecture and the data we have already collected to develop refined models to recognize these distinctions.

6   Conclusion

We present the development of models and a real-time multimodal architecture to recognize when a user needs help while working with a socially assistive robot. Accurate recognition relies on a fusion of language and gaze models. The architecture is designed to be task-independent and interprets social cues presented by the user. By recognizing a user's needs through just social cues, we provide a means for assistive robots to give more timely help in a variety of tasks.

Acknowledgment. We thank Ulyana Kurylo, Alex Reneau, Roxy Wilcox, Kevin Hou, and Anzu Hakone for their contributions.

References

1. Langer, A., Feingold-Polak, R., Mueller, O., Kellmeyer, P., Levy-Tzedek, S.: Trust in socially assistive robots: considerations for use in rehabilitation. Neurosci. Biobehav. Rev. **104**, 231–239 (2019)
2. Greczek, J.: Encouraging user autonomy through robot-mediated intervention. In: Proceedings of the Tenth Annual ACM/IEEE International Conference on Human-Robot Interaction Extended Abstracts, pp. 189–190 (2015)
3. Wilson, J.R., Lee, N.Y., Saechao, A., Tickle-Degnen, L., Scheutz, M.: Supporting human autonomy in a robot-assisted medication sorting task. Int. J. Social Rob. **10**(5), 621–641 (2018)
4. Görür, O.C., Rosman, B.S., Hoffman, G., Albayrak, S.: Toward integrating theory of mind into adaptive decision-making of social robots to understand human intention. In: Workshop on Intentions in HRI at ACM/IEEE International Conference on Human-Robot Interaction (HRI 2017) (2017)

5. Sidner, C.L., Lee, C., Kidd, C.D., Lesh, N., Rich, C.: Explorations in engagement for humans and robots. Artif. Intell. **166**(1–2), 140–164 (2005)
6. Bohus, D., Saw, C.W., Horvitz, E.: Directions robot: In-the-wild experiences and lessons learned. In: Proceedings of the 2014 International Conference on Autonomous Agents and Multi-Agent Systems. International Foundation for Autonomous Agents and Multiagent Systems, pp. 637–644 (2014)
7. Huang, C.-M., Andrist, S., Sauppé, A., Mutlu, B.: Using gaze patterns to predict task intent in collaboration. Front. Psychol. **6**, 1049 (2015)
8. Matarić, M.J., Eriksson, J., Feil-Seifer, D.J., Winstein, C.J.: Socially assistive robotics for post-stroke rehabilitation. J. NeuroEng. Rehabil. **4**(1), 1–9 (2007)
9. Polak, R.F., Tzedek, S.L.: Social robot for rehabilitation: Expert clinicians and post-stroke patients' evaluation following a long-term intervention. In: Proceedings of the 2020 ACM/IEEE International Conference on Human-Robot Interaction, pp. 151–160 (2020)
10. Wilson, J.R., Tickle-Degnen, L., Scheutz, M.: Challenges in designing a fully autonomous socially assistive robot for people with parkinson's disease. ACM Trans. Human-Robot Interact. (THRI) **9**(3), 1–31 (2020)
11. Kory-Westlund, J.M., Breazeal, C.: A long-term study of young children's rapport, social emulation, and language learning with a peer-like robot playmate in preschool. Front. Rob. AI **6**, 81 (2019)
12. Fasola, J., Matarić, M.J.: A socially assistive robot exercise coach for the elderly. J. Hum.-Robot Interact. **2**(2), 3–32 (2013)
13. Fischinger, D.: Hobbit, a care robot supporting independent living at home: first prototype and lessons learned. Rob. Auton. Syst. **75**, 60–78 (2016)
14. Wilson, J.R., Wransky, R., Tierno, J.: General approach to automatically generating need-based assistance. In: Proceedings of the Sixth Annual Conference on Advances in Cognitive Systems (2018)
15. Kurylo, U., Wilson, J.R.: Using human eye gaze patterns as indicators of need for assistance from a socially assistive robot. In: Salichs, M.A., et al. (eds.) ICSR 2019. LNCS (LNAI), vol. 11876, pp. 200–210. Springer, Cham (2019). https://doi.org/10.1007/978-3-030-35888-4_19
16. Shao, M., Alves, S.F.D.R., Ismail, O., Zhang, X., Nejat, G., Benhabib, B.: You are doing great! only one rep left: an affect-aware social robot for exercising. In: 2019 IEEE International Conference on Systems, Man and Cybernetics (SMC), pp. 3811–3817. IEEE (2019)
17. Graterol, W., Diaz-Amado, J., Cardinale, Y., Dongo, I., Lopes-Silva, E., Santos-Libarino, C.: Emotion detection for social robots based on NLP transformers and an emotion ontology. Sensors **21**(4), 1322 (2021)
18. Nau, D., Cao, Y., Lotem, A., Munoz-Avila, H.: Shop: simple hierarchical ordered planner. In: Proceedings of the 16th International Joint Conference on Artificial Intelligence, vol. 2, pp. 968–973 (1999)
19. Bohus, D., et al.: Platform for situated intelligence (2021)
20. Baltrušaitis, T., Robinson, P., Morency, L.-P.: Openface: an open source facial behavior analysis toolkit. In: 2016 IEEE Winter Conference on Applications of Computer Vision (WACV), pp. 1–10. IEEE, 2016
21. Csikszentmihalyi, M., Csikzentmihaly, M.: Flow: The Psychology of Optimal Experience, vol. 1990. Harper & Row New York (1990)
22. Rogers, J., Holm, M.: Performance assessment of self-care skills (pass-home) version 3.1. University of Pittsburgh, Pittsburgh (1994)

If You Are Careful, So Am I! How Robot Communicative Motions Can Influence Human Approach in a Joint Task

Linda Lastrico[1,2]([✉]), Nuno Ferreira Duarte[3], Alessandro Carfí[2],
Francesco Rea[1], Fulvio Mastrogiovanni[2], Alessandra Sciutti[4],
and José Santos-Victor[3]

[1] Robotics, Brain and Cognitive Science Department (RBCS),
Italian Institute of Technology, Genoa, Italy
linda.lastrico@iit.it
[2] Department of Informatics, Bioengineering, Robotics, and Systems Engineering
(DIBRIS), University of Genoa, Genoa, Italy
[3] Institute for Systems and Robotics (ISR), Instituto Superior Técnico,
Universidade de Lisboa, Lisbon, Portugal
[4] Cognitive Architecture for Collaborative Technologies Unit (CONTACT),
Italian Institute of Technology, Genoa, Italy

Abstract. As humans, we have a remarkable capacity for reading the characteristics of objects only by observing how another person carries them. Indeed, how we perform our actions naturally embeds information on the item features. Collaborative robots can achieve the same ability by modulating the strategy used to transport objects with their end-effector. A contribution in this sense would promote spontaneous interactions by making an implicit yet effective communication channel available. This work investigates if humans correctly perceive the implicit information shared by a robotic manipulator through its movements during a dyadic collaboration task. Exploiting a generative approach, we designed robot actions to convey virtual properties of the transported objects, particularly to inform the partner if any caution is required to handle the carried item. We found that carefulness is correctly interpreted when observed through the robot movements. In the experiment, we used identical empty plastic cups; nevertheless, participants approached them differently depending on the attitude shown by the robot: humans change how they reach for the object, being more careful whenever the robot does the same. This emerging form of motor contagion is entirely spontaneous and happens even if the task does not require it.

Keywords: Communicative robots' movement · Implicit
communication · Generative adversarial networks · Robots' motion
generation · Objects' manipulation · Human-robot interaction

This paper is supported by the European Commission within the Horizon 2020 research and innovation program, under grant agreement No 870142, project APRIL (multipurpose robotics for mAniPulation of defoRmable materIaLs in manufacturing processes). N. F. Duarte is supported by FCT-IST fellowship grant PD/BD/135116/2017 and LARSyS-FCT project UIDB/50009/2020.

F. Cavallo et al. (Eds.): ICSR 2022, LNAI 13817, pp. 267–279, 2022.
https://doi.org/10.1007/978-3-031-24667-8_24

1 Introduction

Humans routinely engage in joint actions and coordinate their movements with others, e.g. working together, playing a team sport, or merely moving objects. These tasks involve a collaborative process to coordinate attention, communication, and actions to achieve a common goal. During this process, humans observe the behavior of their partners to anticipate their actions and plan their own accordingly. Verbal communication is not the only means to express intentions. Since verbalizing every step of the interaction would be time-consuming and cognitively expensive, humans also exploit their bodies and movements to exchange information. While executing an intended action, we also implicitly communicate to others our goal, its urgency, and the required effort. This ability is referred to as non-verbal communication (i.e., non-verbal cues), and it can be expressed with our body: from turning the head or torso to a simple eye movement.

In ordinary life, humans are very proficient at monitoring different components of other people's kinematics, which they leverage to disclose hidden qualities of a handled item. For instance, studies on human non-verbal cues found that joints kinematics and dynamics of hand manipulation are crucial features to estimate the weight of a manipulated object [1,19,23] or predicting action duration [9].

Given the importance of implicit cues in human-human communication, we believe it should be taken into account also in the robotic field. A robot meant to interact with humans, able to exploit the same communication channels as the partner, would guarantee a natural and less cumbersome experience. Indeed, numerous channels of communication may be employed to convey information between robots and people (such as synthetic speech, light-based, digital display, mixed or augmented reality [7,16,18]). However, a valuable alternative that does not require any training or explicit instruction is mediated by movement, and it should be sought whenever feasible. The impact of legibility and predictability of robot motion in human-robot interaction has been extensively studied by Dragan et. al [4], where especially the trajectory of the movements was modulated to convey information associated to the robot next task or goal. When designing a robot movement, other factors such as the velocity or the curvature can be taken into account, for instance to make the emotional attitude of the action more legible [24]. Human non-verbal cues from eyes, head, and arm movements encode the intention driving the action; when such cues are embedded onto a robot, they similarly allow to read the robot's intention [6]. Regarding object manipulation, object affordances was popularized in robotics and linked to (i) the action associated with the object, (ii) a physical property, or (iii) the type of behavior required to manipulate the object [11,21]. Specifically, works on affordance reasoning examine the object's properties [10,26,28], e.g., how to infer the water level in cups [17], although trying to directly detect such property from the object appearance, making it only possible with transparent cups and glasses.

To overcome the need to understand the properties of objects from their appearance alone, it is relevant to quantify the effect their features have on the kinematics of the action during manipulation. In our previous works, we focused on carefulness associated to human motion and we exploited human kinematics to infer the impact of cup water content on human motion, irrespective of the cup's transparency [5,12]. Indeed, it has been shown that humans alter their behavior, adapting to the properties of the object they transport, such as weight, fragility, or content. Additionally, depending on the type of cup, these behaviors may be more predominant or less, which may indicate that the difficulty of the manipulation impacts the human motion [20]. Knowing from the mentioned studies that humans reveal some object properties through movements, in this work, we investigate if it is possible to modulate the movements adopted by a robot end-effector during the transport of an object to communicate some of its hidden properties. In a previous study [14], we assessed the communicative potential of movements on different humanoid robots, by asking participants to explicitly judge the robotic motion's carefulness after observing it in videos; we also investigated which possible object features may induce a careful manipulation, since carefulness definition is not univocal. This study proposes a dyadic interaction with a new robotic manipulator in a realistic collaborative context. We used Generative Adversarial Networks (GANs) to synthesize and design the robot movements to convey a particular style feature associated with object manipulation: carefulness [8]. By using a generative approach, we can consistently produce novel but meaningful robot actions. Other strategies, such as dynamic motion primitives [22], transformer GANs [15] or variational autoencoders [3] may be applied to synthesize artificial kinematics data; however, our goal is not a comparison with other state of the arts methods: the main novelty is represented by how we apply synthetic data to generate communicative robots' actions. In this study, we first explore (H1) whether the attitude conveyed by the robot's movements is perceived as expected, i.e., if the carefulness (or its absence) is correctly expressed by our controller; in this sense, we hypothesize (H1.1) that participants would properly classify if the observed action was careful or not. We also verify (H2), if a robot transporting objects and expressing the appropriate human-like behavior can invoke motor adaptation in the human response. We assume (H2.1) that, if a contagion emerges, careful actions from the robot would elicit slower movements in the human, and vice versa.

2 Materials and Methods

The objective of our study is to assess whether the generated robot's movements are informative of the properties of the transported object. Moreover, we evaluate if the robot behavior affects how humans perform their tasks.

We will now explain how we synthesized the required velocity profiles and controlled a Kinova Gen3 robot with 7 degrees of freedom to execute them; then, we will describe the experimental setup and design.

2.1 Generation of Robot Movements

To have the robot communicate through its movements the object properties, the robot's end-effector follows the velocity profiles generated by the Generative Adversarial Networks (GANs) model. Our interest is in generating movements to convey whether the transported object requires caution and care to be transported (*careful* movement) or it is safe to move without any particular concern (*not careful* movement). Previous studies assessed this kind of object manipulation and showed a marked difference in the kinematics of the human hand associated with the two classes of motions [5,12]. The velocity profile in the case for *careful* movements are characterized by lower maximum velocity, a prolonged deceleration phase, and longer duration, compared to *not careful* movements. The modulation allows for the distinction of *careful* and *not careful* movements [5,13].

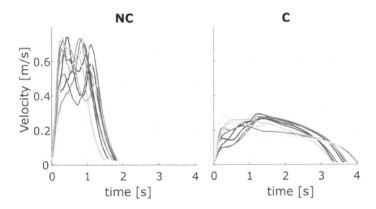

Fig. 1. Velocity profiles generated by the GANs associated to Not Careful (NC) and Careful (C) transportation of objects. These velocity profiles were used to control the robot during the human-robot experiment.

GAN. To define meaningful movements associated with the properties of the carried object, we decided to modulate the velocity profile adopted by the robot end-effector. We used GANs to synthesize novel velocity profiles using an approach already tested [8]. The details on the Time-GAN model [27] and its training are described in [8]. The original data used to feed the GANs consisted of hand velocity profiles recorded with a Motion Capture System during the transport of glasses, either empty or containing water, at two possible weight levels. The trajectories followed by participants during the manipulations were designed to grant a good degree of variability. After training, each generative model can produce novel yet meaningful velocity profiles belonging to the distribution of the human data used during the training. This approach provides new and unlimited synthetic data, always falling into the desired class of motion (careful or not), avoiding a trivial copy of the human velocity profiles. Moreover, learning the velocity norm is useful in generalization terms since the same pattern of motion can be applied to multiple spatial trajectories.

For this specific study, from the trained GANs, we synthesized ten velocity profiles for each of the two classes to be replicated by the Kinova robot. A representation of the generated data is available in Fig. 1.

Robot Controller. The Kinova Gen3 robot is controlled using ROS and the package kortex_ros[1]. Such package provides a velocity controller in Cartesian space, which moves the end-effector 40 Hz in linear (m/s) and angular (rad/s) velocities. Attached to the end-effector is the Robotiq 85 two-finger gripper[2] used to grasp the cups. This work applies two high-level controllers: (i) a velocity PI controller and (ii) a velocity GAN controller. The first controller is responsible for picking the cups from the table, and the second is for transporting and handing over the cups to the participant. The former generates a constant velocity profile throughout the trials, while the latter follows one of the 20 GAN velocity profiles selected (10 careful and 10 not careful) during the experiment. For each GAN motion trajectory, the velocity profile is decomposed into the 3D Cartesian velocity coordinates by setting the current location and final location (handover point) at each time step. The handover location was fixed in advance to avoid any variability that could influence participants during the experiment. The position of the participant's wrist was tracked with the motion capture system, while the position of the gripper is computed by the robot's forward kinematics given the known joint angles and the location of the robot base also tracked with the motion capture system. More details on the sensors are provided in Sect. 2.2. The handover release moment was obtained by applying a threshold: the robot opened the gripper to release the cup whenever the distance between the gripper and the participant's wrist was below a fixed value. This simple design was enough to grant a smooth and reactive handover required for our experiment.

2.2 Setup, Sensors and Experiment Design

Participants were asked to sort the items handled by the Kinova Gen3 robot by positioning them on the appropriate areas marked on the table where they were seated. We designed the experiment for the participants to focus on the robot behavior and not on the characteristics of the items. For this reason, we used identical plastic cups: in the instructions, we explained that we were simulating a cocktail bar scenario, where the robot and the human had to collaborate in sorting the glasses between those full to be served to the clients, and the used and empty ones, to be washed; in such context, the cups were meant to be either

---

[1] Official repository of the Kinova Gen3 ROS package: https://github.com/Kinovaro botics/ros_kortex.

[2] Official website of the gripper: https://robotiq.com/products/2f85-140-adaptive-robot-gripper.

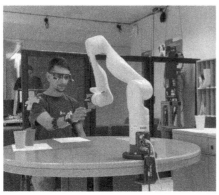 

(a) Setup frontal view   (b) Setup lateral view

Fig. 2. *Setup:* when interacting with the Kinova Gen3 robot, participants seated at a table. Once grasped the cup from the robot gripper, they had to put it down on one of the three areas delimited on the table. The motion capture markers used to analyse the human kinematics are visible on the participants' right wrist.

full of a liquid or empty: however, we explained to the participants that due to the danger of having a robot transporting water, all the cups were empty. This granted that participants could not rely on any visual cue or the actual object features to decide where to place the cup. In every trial, the Kinova robot grasped a cup from the table next to it (see Fig. 2b) and transported it towards the participant, following either a careful (or not) velocity profile generated by the GANs (associated respectively, to the transport of a full or empty glass). The task for the participants was then to grasp the cup from the robot gripper and place it in the appropriate area on the table: on the "To be served" area, on the right, if they thought that the cup was actually meant to be full, or on the "To be washed" area, in case they assumed the cup was indeed empty. A third area, in the middle, was available to place the cups whose virtual content was not clear to the participant to avoid forcing them into making a decision. They were not informed about the modulation of the robot transport movements and, since the cups were all the same, they had to rely on the robot behavior to make their decision[3].

We used Optitrack[4] motion capture system, with an acquisition frequency 120 Hz, to track the position of the participant wrist and shoulder.

Twelve healthy participants, all members of Instituto Superior Técnico, voluntarily took part in the experiment. Each evaluated 20 robot movements, where the sequence of careful and not careful modulation was randomized once and then maintained for every participant. The interactions were organized as five blocks of a sequence of four trials. At the end of each block, the experimenter put the

---

[3] Sample video of the human-robot interaction: https://www.youtube.com/watch?v =HVahS-0tn6g.

[4] Optitrack website: https://optitrack.com/cameras/flex-13/.

cups on the table next to the robot. This resulted in a total of 240 movements evaluated, equally balanced between careful or not robot behavior.

3   Results

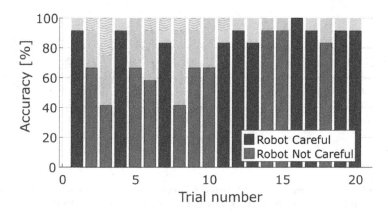

Fig. 3. *Perception of robot's movements:* Percentage of correct interpretation of the robot's transportation movements during the experiment. When the robot performed careful movements, in blue, they were correctly perceived 90% of the times. NC motions required more trials to be consistently classified. The dark bars represent the percentage of correct classification of the movement from the participant, the transparent bars the percentage of wrong attribution; finally, the light gray bars with a wavy pattern, the percentage of "Unknown" answers in each trial. (Color figure online)

One of the aims of this study was to verify whether modulating the robot end-effector velocity to express carefulness can inform participants about the virtual content of the manipulated glasses. Figure 3 shows the participants' accuracy in evaluating, for each trial, if the observed transportation motion was meant to be associated with a delicate object, i.e., careful robot movement, or not. We represented with a dark bar the percentage of correct answers given by the participants, i.e., when they correctly interpreted the robot's attitude. Considering the total number of evaluated trials (240), 189 were correctly classified with no indecision, resulting in an accuracy of 78.75%. The transparent colored bars represent the misclassified movements. For instance, when we generated a robot action modulated to communicate a not careful attitude, while participants associated it with the transport of a full cup. As it can be noticed, misunderstanding a not careful action for a careful one was the most frequent occurrence, especially in the first trials. In detail, 90% of the careful robot movements were perceived as such, whereas 75% of the not careful ones were correctly interpreted. Finally, the grey bars with a wavy pattern represent those trials where participants preferred not to make a choice and placed the cup on the neutral area on the table. Also, these occurrences, which happened in 9 trials out of 240, decrease as the experiment progresses.

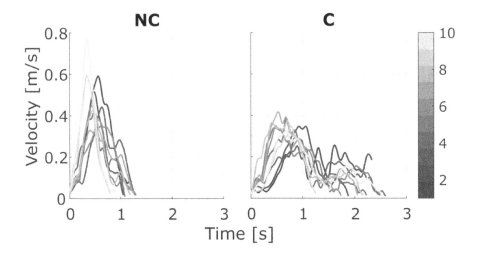

Fig. 4. *Velocity reaching movement:* profiles adopted by one participant when reaching for the cup in the robot gripper. It is noticeable a modulation of both the duration and the maximum velocity depending on the style of the movement adopted by the robot: not careful (NC) or careful (C). The colormap is associated to the trial numbers, in order.

Another aspect we were interested in investigating is if the two attitudes shown by the robot had any effect on how participants performed their tasks. An exploratory inspection of the hand velocity data encouraged us to deepen this intuition: Fig. 4 reports an example of the velocity adopted by one participant when reaching for the cup in the robot gripper. There is a noticeable modulation in the participant's movements that correlates with the attitude shown by the robot. When the robot handled the cup with a careful attitude, also the participant reached for it with slower and prolonged action compared to the not careful situation. To assess this modulation quantitatively in human actions, we considered the duration and median velocity of the movements as relevant features. To perform statistical analyses on the acquired data, we used Jamovi software[5], in particular the GAMLj module[6] for mixed models. Figure 5a shows the mean durations of the participants reaching movements toward the robot gripper. We ran a mixed model assuming the duration of the participants' reaching movements as the dependent variable, the carefulness in the robot movement as a factor, and the subjects as cluster variables. The effect of condition resulted significant ($C - NC$, $estimate = 0.443$, $SE = 0.055$, $t = 8.00$, $p < 0.001$), indicating that when the robot end-effector was following a careful velocity profile, the subsequent human reaching action was longer, with an extended duration estimate of 0.443 s. A second mixed model was used to evaluate the median

---

[5] Jamovi software website: https://www.jamovi.org.
[6] General analyses for linear models Jamovi module: https://gamlj.github.io/.

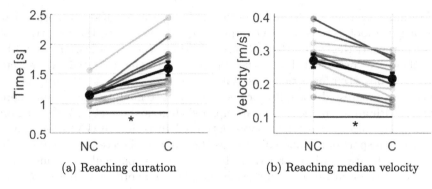

(a) Reaching duration   (b) Reaching median velocity

Fig. 5. *Reaching movement:* in (Fig. 5a) mean duration of the participants reaching movements towards the robot's gripper. When the robot performs a Careful (C) transportation movement, participants are significantly slower in reaching for the cup. Also the median velocity adopted in the reaching movements (Fig. 5b) is modulated by how the robot moved when transporting the cup. The mean values for each participant are represented in a different color. The thick black lines represent the mean over the twelve participants, with the standard error. The star indicates a significant difference with $p < 0.001$.

velocity adopted by the participants when reaching the robot gripper (see Fig. 5b), using this time the median velocity as dependent variable: when the robot was careful, participants significantly diminished their median velocity, with an estimated reduction in speed of 0.055 m/s ($C - NC$, *estimate* = 0.055, $SE = 0.012$, $t = -4.60$, $p < 0.001$). These findings prove that the modulation of the robot movements affected how participants moved to reach and take the cup from the robot. This happened even when there was no reason to adapt to the object properties since we consider a reaching movement and all the cups had exactly the same characteristics. We also verified, for both the duration and the median velocity of the reaching movements, if there was an interaction with the participants' accuracy in evaluating the robot's behavior in every trial. We used the accuracy in their classification as an additional factor in the mixed model, but we found no interaction with how they performed the reaching duration or velocity. The modulation in response to the robot attitude also occurred when participants did not recognize it explicitly.

4   Discussion

In our study, we exploited a generative approach to produce robot movements that could implicitly communicate if a handled object required or not carefulness to be transported. To avoid influencing the choice, all the items transported by the Kinova robot were identical (empty plastic cups). The participants had to decide if they were supposed to be virtually full or empty, without any particular hint or instruction on how to proceed. Firstly, we assessed (H1) whether our controller can express caution in the gestures or its absence. According to the results shown in Fig. 3, our hypothesis (H1.1) was verified: we notice that the *careful* robot actions have been perceived as such since the first trials of the experiment. Regarding the *not careful* actions, there is a learning trend in how they were perceived during the experiment. In the first trials, they were sometimes mistaken for actions associated with transporting a full cup. As the experiment progressed, the difference between the two modulations became more evident, with an accuracy in the participants' choices above 80%. Reflecting on the original dataset of human movements used to train the GANs associated with the transport of full and empty cups [12], we can observe that a *not careful* attitude is the standard in our actions. Indeed, when no particular circumstances are forcing us, for instance when picking and placing an ordinary object, we tend to move in a "neutral" way, and we can shortly describe our approach as not careful. On the contrary, a strong kinematics modulation appears when we are paying attention to not spill the contents of a glass [5,13]. This careful kinematics shaping is what we truly modeled in the communicative robot's movements, and it is rewarding that careful movements were perceived correctly from the beginning.

This study also allows us to evaluate (H2), the effect that the implicit modulation of the robot actions has on the interaction. Even though participants knew from the beginning that the plastic cups were all the same and all empty, there was a modulation in how they approached the robot gripper, confirming our second hypothesis (H2.1). We gave an overview of this phenomenon in Fig. 4 and a quantitative assessment in Fig. 5. If the robot manifested a careful attitude, adopting a lower magnitude in the velocity profile and a longer duration of the movement (see Fig. 1 for reference), also the reaching movement of the humans was significantly slower. Interestingly, this also happened when participants had trouble explicitly recognizing the motion style and classifying the cup: the contagion in how they performed the reaching task was still present. This result emphasizes how important it is to modulate the actions of robots appropriately, with a view towards collaborative interaction. Indeed, we proved a motor contagion from the robot to the human, even if there was no need for the participants to directly associate with the task and adapt their motor strategy. We observed natural coordination emerging from such a simple task, where the pace of the human spontaneously adapted to the robot one, mimicking, even unconsciously, the attitude observed. Human-robot motor contagion on velocity was already observed whenever the robot velocity profile is biologically plausible [2,25]. In our approach, the reasonableness of the velocity profiles was granted using a generative network trained on human examples. The findings in our study extend the existing evidence of motor contagion in Human-Robot Interaction, proving that robotics arms can also leverage it to convey appropriate ways of handling fragile objects.

5 Conclusion

In this study, we showed how a generative approach could be used to generate meaningful and communicative robot actions that a human partner can successfully interpret to infer some properties of the involved objects. This modulation on the robot side also led to a motor contagion in how the human performed its actions and synchronized with the pace of the robot; through motion alone, it was possible to open a channel of communication between the two agents, with measurable effects on the interaction.

Finally, it should be noted that we obtained these results by modulating the movements of a 7 degrees of freedom robotic manipulator, not a humanoid robot. Nevertheless, even though its kinematics was far from the one of a human arm, it was possible to achieve the desired communication intent by simply modulating the end-effector control. This proves the power of the proposed approach and its potential scalability in other contexts and with other robots, also industrial ones, where implicit communication through motion could improve the efficiency and safety of a joint collaborative task.

In future works, we plan to exploit the same controller and have the robot actually manipulate full and empty cups to assess how the movement's modulation affects trust, perceived competency, and efficiency in a dyadic interaction, while facing a challenging task.

References

1. Bingham, G.P.: Kinematic form and scaling: further investigations on the visual perception of lifted weight. J. Exp. Psychol.: Human Percept. Perf. **13**(2), 155–177 (1987)
2. Bisio, A., et al.: Motor contagion during human-human and human-robot interaction. PLOS ONE **9**(8), 1–10 (2014)
3. Desai, A., Freeman, C., Wang, Z., Beaver, I.: Timevae: a variational auto-encoder for multivariate time series generation (2021). arXiv:2111.08095
4. Dragan, A.D., Lee, K.C., Srinivasa, S.S.: Legibility and predictability of robot motion. In: 2013 8th ACM/IEEE International Conference on Human-Robot Interaction (HRI), pp. 301–308 (2013)
5. Duarte, N.F., Chatzilygeroudis, K., Santos-Victor, J., Billard, A.: From human action understanding to robot action execution: how the physical properties of handled objects modulate non-verbal cues. In: 2020 Joint IEEE 10th International Conference on Development and Learning and Epigenetic Robotics (ICDL-EpiRob), pp. 1–6. IEEE, Valparaiso (2020)
6. Duarte, N.F., Rakovic, M., Tasevski, J., Coco, M.I., Billard, A., Santos-Victor, J.: Action anticipation: reading the intentions of humans and robots. IEEE Rob. Autom. Lett. **3**(4), 4132–4139 (2018)
7. Fulton, M., Edge, C., Sattar, J.: Robot communication via motion: a study on modalities for robot-to-human communication in the field. ACM Trans. Hum.-Rob. Interact. **11**(2), 1–40 (2022)

8. Garello, L., Lastrico, L., Rea, F., Mastrogiovanni, F., Noceti, N., Sciutti, A.: Property-aware robot object manipulation: a generative approach. In: 2021 IEEE International Conference on Development and Learning (ICDL), pp. 1–7. IEEE, Beijing (2021)

9. Hamilton, A.F.C., Joyce, D.W., Flanagan, J.R., Frith, C.D., Wolpert, D.M.: Kinematic cues in perceptual weight judgement and their origins in box lifting. Psychol. Res. **71**(1), 13–21 (2007)

10. Hassanin, M., Khan, S., Tahtali, M.: Visual affordance and function understanding: a survey. ACM Comput. Surv. **54**(3), 1–35 (2021)

11. Jamone, L., et al.: Affordances in psychology, neuroscience, and robotics: a survey. IEEE Trans. Cogn. Dev. Syst. **10**(1), 4–25 (2018)

12. Lastrico, L., et al.: Careful with that! observation of human movements to estimate objects properties. In: Saveriano, M., Renaudo, E., Rodríguez-Sánchez, A., Piater, J. (eds.) HFR 2020. SPAR, vol. 18, pp. 127–141. Springer, Cham (2021). https://doi.org/10.1007/978-3-030-71356-0_10

13. Lastrico, L., Carfi, A., Rea, F., Sciutti, A., Mastrogiovanni, F.: From movement kinematics to object properties: online recognition of human carefulness. In: Social Robotics, pp. 61–72 (2021)

14. Lastrico, L., et al.: Robots with different embodiments can express and influence carefulness in object manipulation. In: 2022 IEEE International Conference on Development and Learning (ICDL), London, UK (2022)

15. Li, X., Metsis, V., Wang, H., Ngu, A.H.H.: TTS-GAN: a transformer-based time-series generative adversarial network. In: Artificial Intelligence in Medicine, pp. 133–143. Springer, Cham (2022). https://doi.org/10.1007/978-3-031-09342-5_13

16. Macciò; S., Carfi, A., Mastrogiovanni, F.: Mixed reality as communication medium for human-robot collaboration. In: 2022 International Conference on Robotics and Automation (ICRA), pp. 2796–2802 (2022)

17. Mottaghi, R., Schenck, C., Fox, D., Farhadi, A.: See the glass half full: reasoning about liquid containers, their volume and content. In: 2017 IEEE International Conference on Computer Vision (ICCV), pp. 1889–1898. IEEE, Venice (2017)

18. Rosen, E., et al.: Communicating and controlling robot arm motion intent through mixed-reality head-mounted displays. Int. J. Rob. Res. **38**(12–13), 1513–1526 (2019)

19. Rosen, J., Perry, J.C., Manning, N., Burns, S., Hannaford, B.: the human arm kinematics and dynamics during daily activities - toward a 7 DOF upper limb powered exoskeleton. In: 12th International Conference on Advanced Robotics, p. 8 (2005)

20. Rosenbaum, D.A., Chapman, K.M., Weigelt, M., Weiss, D.J., van der Wel, R.: Cognition, action, and object manipulation. Psychol. Bull. **138**(5), 924–946 (2012)

21. Saponaro, G., Jamone, L., Bernardino, A., Salvi, G.: Interactive robot learning of gestures, language and affordances. In: GLU 2017 International Workshop on Grounding Language Understanding, pp. 83–87. ISCA (2017)

22. Schaal, S.: Dynamic movement primitives -a framework for motor control in humans and humanoid robotics, pp. 261–280. Springer, Tokyo (2006). https://doi.org/10.1007/4-431-31381-8_23

23. Sciutti, A., Patanè, L., Sandini, G.: Development of visual perception of others' actions: children's judgment of lifted weight. PLoS ONE **14**(11), 1–15 (2019)

24. Vannucci, F., Di Cesare, G., Rea, F., Sandini, G., Sciutti, A.: A robot with style: can robotic attitudes influence human actions? In: 2018 IEEE-RAS 18th International Conference on Humanoid Robots (Humanoids), pp. 1–6 (2018)

25. Vasalya, A., Ganesh, G., Kheddar, A.: More than just co-workers: presence of humanoid robot co-worker influences human performance. PLOS ONE **13**(11), 1–19 (2018)
26. Yamani, Y., Ariga, A., Yamada, Y.: Object affordances potentiate responses but do not guide attentional prioritization. Front. Integrat. Neurosci. **9**, 74 (2016)
27. Yoon, J., Jarrett, D., van der Schaar, M.: Time-series generative adversarial networks. In: Wallach, H., Larochelle, H., Beygelzimer, A., Alché-Buc, F.D., Fox, E., Garnett, R. (eds.) Advances in Neural Information Processing Systems, vol. 32. Curran Associates, Inc. (2019)
28. Yu, L.F., Duncan, N., Yeung, S.K.: Fill and transfer: a simple physics-based approach for containability reasoning. In: 2015 IEEE International Conference on Computer Vision (ICCV), pp. 711–719. IEEE, Santiago (2015)

Exploring Non-verbal Strategies
for Initiating an HRI

Francesco Vigni[1(✉)] and Silvia Rossi[1,2]

[1] Interdepartmental Center for Advances in Robotic Surgery - ICAROS,
University of Naples Federico II, Naples, Italy
{francesco.vigni,silvia.rossi}@unina.it
[2] Department of Electrical Engineering and Information Technologies - DIETI,
University of Naples Federico II, Naples, Italy

Abstract. The growing deployment of robots in social contexts implies
the need to model their behaviour as social agents. In this context, the
way a robot approaches a user and eventually engages in an interaction
is a crucial aspect to take into account for the acceptance of these tools.
In this work, we explore how the approaching policy and gaze behaviours
can influence the perceived intention to interact before the interaction
starts. The conducted user study highlights the importance of the robot's
gaze behaviour when approaching a human with respect to its approaching behaviour. In particular, if the robot moves in the surroundings of
a human, even not straightforward in their direction, but locks the gaze
at them, the intention to interact is recognised clearer and faster with
respect to the direct approaching of the user but with an adverse gaze.

Keywords: Approach policy · Social behaviour · Gaze · Proxemics

1 Introduction

A typical first encounter with a robot and the subsequent interaction provide
important insights to the user on the robot's capabilities. When the latter
presents humanoid characteristics, the interaction can elicit social expectations
[6,30]. However, if during the interaction the robot fails to comply with social
norms, dissatisfaction can arise [27]. To tackle these issues, research is pushing
toward the definition of *natural* Human-Robot Interaction (nHRI) [26], which
can enable robots to display and perceive all the modalities used by humans in
face-to-face interactions.

The spontaneity of Human-Human Interactions (HHIs) is inherently unconstrained and strongly depends on the nonverbal cues employed by the participants in the interaction. These cues can vary with the participant, the context,
and also their willingness in taking part in the interaction. However, it becomes

This work has been supported by the European Union's Horizon 2020 research and
innovation programme under the Marie Skłodowska-Curie grant agreement No 955778.

F. Cavallo et al. (Eds.): ICSR 2022, LNAI 13817, pp. 280–289, 2022.
https://doi.org/10.1007/978-3-031-24667-8_25

very hard to keep spontaneity in the nonverbal channel of the encounter if one of the participants is a social robot. The question "How does a social HRI begin, and what factors trigger it?" becomes increasingly important and embeds how the nonverbal behaviours of a robot are perceived by a user.

In this work, we start from the assumption that two participants (a human and a robot) about to start a social HRI continuously exchange social signals in a bidirectional manner that could lead to initiating the interaction. In this sense, the behaviour of both (potential) participants of an HRI can lead to initiating or avoiding the interaction at will. If one of the (potential) participants in an HRI is constrained, the behaviour of the partner is considered responsible for initiating or avoiding, the interaction. This claim is inspired by the work presented in [13], in which authors model an HRI in a multimodal fashion and consider the bidirectional component of the communication channels. Similar policies happen among humans. For instance, if we would like to prevent an interaction to start while walking in a public space, we can use an aversive gaze or deviate our path to avoid a specific person. When translating this behaviour to HRI, we can exploit the anthropomorphism of a robot to design behaviours that can purposefully convey the intention to start or avoid an interaction.

To investigate these concepts, we conducted a user study where the approach policy and gaze of a humanoid robot (Pepper) approaching a standing user were manipulated to convey various degrees of intention to initiate the interaction. Our results show that, given a robot approaching a user, the robot's gaze conveys the social intention quicker and clearer than its motion toward the user.

2   Background and Related Work

With the increasing deployment of robots in social contexts, it is relevant to understand how the interactions evolve. Among the well-known metrics used in HRI, engagement evaluation is crucial as it allows estimating the process or state (according to the chosen definition) of the interaction [16].

Engagement in HRI is a widely studied topic that has its roots in human sciences and exploits recent technologies for building effective and robust tools. In a key work in the field, authors define engagement in HRI as "the process by which individuals involved in an interaction start, maintain, and end their perceived connection to one another" [23]. In a similar fashion, we model the interaction in three separate phases namely: approaching, interacting and terminating. In the first phase, the user might infer the intention to initiate an interaction of the robot but no HRI is ongoing. In the second phase the HRI is occurring, and in the last phase, the social cues of the participants convey that the interaction is terminating.

Metrics like engagement [16] and visual focus of attention (VFoA) [3] can be used to track how the interaction unfolds. For example, the authors in [5] present a dataset (EU-HRI dataset) containing a rich set of data streams obtained from a 56 days experiment performed in the wild, in which a (static) humanoid robot Pepper was used to interact with users and record data from its sensors. In that work, a distance threshold from the fixed standing robot defines the logic for considering the user as part of the HRI. Hence, engagement evaluation is deployed as a metric "during" the interaction while does not provide information on a social interaction that is about to start. Indeed, among humans, social intelligence can be used to understand a partner that seeks an interaction or that would like to terminate it [25]. Social robots should be able to employ, or at least mimic, similar social intelligence. When an interaction with an anthropomorphic robot is about to start, Kendon's model [11] can be used to define the social robot skills [2] and greetings behaviours [9, 28].

Gaze [1, 24], proxemics [14] and body movements [21] are among the nonverbal features that can be interpreted as social signals and can be used to convey the robot's intentions. The interpersonal space, relative body pose and mutual gaze [18] can be used to capture a snapshot of the evolution of an HRI. The way these variables develop over time can give us more insights into the dynamics of the interaction. Yet, an orchestrated employment of these in a multimodal fashion is expected to improve natural HRIs [4, 10].

The approaching phase in a social HRI provides a first impression that can be used to deduct social intentions. Research highlights that proxemics and the robot's body motions in this phase are pivotal for the users' perception of the robot's intention [10, 14, 20]. The way a robot approaches a human can be interpreted by the latter in different ways [19]. A fast movement towards the human might elicit fear and discomfort [12]. On the other hand, if the robot approaches the human too slowly, the latter might not understand its intention to interact. Moreover, if the robot embeds anthropomorphic features, the motion of each body part can also affect the interaction. In particular, gaze can be manipulated to convey positive or negative robot's mental states and intentions during an interaction [1]. Yet, a robot that stares a human during a social interaction is not positively perceived [29]. In [22], authors developed a model that predicts the walking behaviour of a person in the proximity of the robot, plans a path towards them and finally conveys the intention to start a conversation in a nonverbal fashion. In contrast to the design choices of [22], this work constrains the movement of the humans and focuses on how various nonverbal features of the robot can influence the perceived intention to interact only during the approaching phase. The main idea is that, despite the perception strategies that are currently in use in anthropomorphic robots, users might infer the robot's social intentions by its body expressions from afar.

3   Methods

A 2×2 experimental design was implemented, to investigate the effects of gaze and approach policy of a robot navigating toward a user in a hall. The controlled variables modulate the nonverbal behaviour of the robot and can be interpreted by the users as social signals [4]. For the robot's gaze, two conditions are chosen by employing a *social* or an *adverse* gaze during the approach phase. In this sense, a *social* gaze consists in the robot employing a face-directed gaze [1] during the approach phase, while an *adverse* gaze consists in the robot gazing the location that is specular to the human's face with respect to the robot's path. Hence, the robot is gazing an empty location in the hall. We assume this last condition to be perceived as asocial as Normoyle et al. [15] link similar behaviours to low trust.

The approach policy is controlled by the position of the standing user in space (front vs side approach). The user can either stand in front of the robot or with a lateral offset from the trajectory at the end of the approaching phase (30° clockwise, see Fig. 1). Given the symmetry of the scenario, only one lateral condition is implemented. In both conditions, the user is instructed to face the robot. These two configurations are expected to well mimic a spontaneous encounter with a robot in a public space while still fitting with the social space range defined in [17]. Table 1 shows an overview of the experimental conditions. The conditions are named according to their controlled variables where SF refers to social front, AF to adverse front, SS to social side and AS to adverse side.

An initial pilot study is performed to validate the designed conditions and to improve the survey. The outcome of it allowed us to rephrase some unclear entries in the survey and optimize the experimental protocol. Then a user study is conducted with a within-subject design in which each participant is exposed to the four experimental conditions. We recruited 26 participants in total, which would allow us to detect an effect size of $d = 0.25$ with .80 power at an alpha level of .05 (calculated using the G*Power software [7]).

Table 1. Overview of the experimental conditions.

	Social	Adverse
Front	Condition 1 (SF)	Condition 2 (AF)
Side	Condition 3 (SS)	Condition 4 (AS)

Most of the participants (93%) have already interacted with a robot prior to this experiment and are in average 28.3 years old ($SD = 8.74$). The experiment was carried out in a hall with controlled illumination and no outside distraction. Only the robot, the participant and the experimenter were present in the hall throughout the duration of the experiment (ca. 20 min). The robot performs a frontal straight segment of 4 m (*approaching phase* 0–14 s), stops at 1.7 m from the user, gazes at them and says a short greeting sentence (*interacting phase* 14–24 s) and finally goes back to the starting position (*terminating phase* 24–51 s). It is important to notice that despite the position of the participant (frontally or with the lateral offset), once the robot has finished the approaching phase, it regulates its face towards them before playing the greeting sentence. Figs. 1a, 1b, 1c, 1d shows snapshots of the experimental conditions SF, AF, SS and AS, respectively. The initial distance of 4 m as well as the distance during the interacting phase of 1.7 m are selected according to [8]. We are aware that proxemics can differ among participants, however, this work focuses on the role

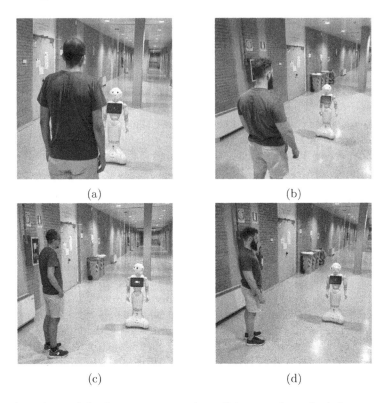

(a)   (b)

(c)   (d)

Fig. 1. Snapshots of the four experimental conditions at the end of the approaching phase.

of gaze and proximity as drivers for initiating a social HRI and the selected values are reasonable for the goal. Each participant is instructed to stand still throughout the experiment, observe the robot's behaviour and ask themself the question:

– (1) "Would the robot like to start an interaction with me?".

Participants are instructed to say "yes" as soon as they can answer the question (1) positively. At this point, the experimenter halts a stopwatch that keeps track of the time passed between the initial motion of the robot and the time when the participant responded to question (1) with "yes". If the robot can reach the interacting phase location and the participant still has not answered positively to (1), we consider the stopwatch to halt at the end of the interacting phase ($t = 24$ s). With this logic, the stopwatch values are taken into account only if belong to the approaching phase and are saturated if answered during the interacting phase or later. Bearing this in mind, the multimodal interaction that unfolds during the interacting phase and its effects on the question (1) are out of the scope of this work. The interpersonal space together with the gaze directed to the participant and a short spoken sentence, allow us to consider that participants surely perceive the intention to interact with the robot during the interacting phase. The controlled variables (gaze and approach policy) differ across the conditions only during the approaching phase. The conditions are administered to the user in a pseudo-randomized fashion to mitigate order effects. After being exposed to each condition the participants answered a brief post-interaction survey comprising of the following 5-point Likert scale entries. In italic are shown the corresponding keywords used in Fig. 3.

1. The robot's behaviour is *social*.
2. The robot would like to *interact* with me.
3. I would feel *comfortable* of encountering this robot in a social context.
4. I like the *quality* of the robot.
5. I quickly understood when the robot wanted to *start* the interaction.
6. I quickly understood when the robot wanted to *finish* the interaction.

The response could range between 1 (I fully disagree) to 5 (I fully agree). Finally, after experiencing the four conditions the experimenter tells the participant the goal of the research in detail.

4 Result

The responses to question (1) are collected in terms of seconds (time between the start of the robot motion and the keyword pronounced by the participants).

A paired t-test with 95% confidence intervals is performed on the mean of these for each condition. Figure 2 shows the mean time to answer the question (1) and the standard deviation at each condition is shown in terms of error bar length.

In this measure, we found a significant difference between SF ($M = 16.59$, $SD = 6.45$) and AF ($M = 21.06$, $SD = 3.75$), with $t(25) = -2.56$, $p < .05$ and between SF and AS ($M = 22.26$, $SD = 2.06$), $t(25) = -3.76$, $p < .001$. This shows that participants were able to answer significantly faster to question (1) when the robot employed a social gaze compared to the robot that used an asocial gaze despite its base motion trajectory. Significant difference is found between AF and SS ($M = 12.58, SD = 4.80$) with $t(25) = 7.84$, $p < .001$ and between SS and AS with $t(25) = 8.27$, $p < .001$. Participants took significantly longer to answer question (1) when the robot employed an adverse gaze despite its base motion trajectory. Finally, significant difference is found between SF and SS with $t(25) = 2.20$, $p < .05$. This latter result shows that question (1) was answered significantly faster when the robot employed a social gaze and the user was not in front of the trajectory of the robot.

We could deduct that the base motion trajectory is less relevant than the gaze direction for eliciting the intention to start a social HRI. It is interesting to notice that in Fig. 2 only the condition SS obtained a mean time within the approaching phase window. Figure 3 shows the mean responses of the survey grouped by conditions with the respective significant differences.

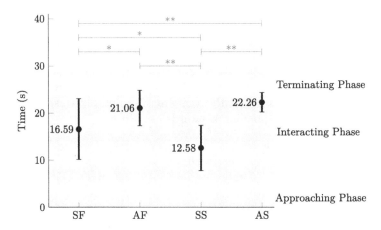

Fig. 2. Responses' means of question (1) per condition. Significant differences between conditions have been indicated with * for $p < .05$ and with ** for $p < .001$.

Regarding the questions presented in Sect. 3, a Wilcoxon signed-rank test is performed on the mean responses per each condition. In particular significant differences are found in the *social* question between SF and AS $(T = 55, p < .05)$, between AF and AS $(T = 48, p < .05)$ and between SS and AS $(T = 18, p < .05)$. Regarding the *interact* question significant differences are found between SF and AF $(T = 22, p < .05)$ and between SF and AS $(T = 20, p < .05)$. The experiments were designed so that the robot 1) approaches the user in four different ways and 2) terminates the interaction using the same behaviour across all conditions. Surprisingly, no significant difference was found in the *start* question, but a significant difference was found in the *finish* question between SS and AS $(T = 41, p < .05)$. We suspect that this result is given by the short time allocated to the interaction and the difference in the yaw of the robot head between SS and AS. However, further investigation will help us understand this trend.

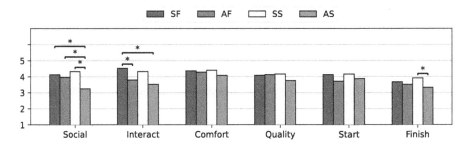

Fig. 3. Average responses of the survey. Significant differences between conditions have been indicated with * for $p < .05$.

5   Discussion

Interpersonal distance and gaze are some preceptors of the interaction but cannot always reflect the intention of initiating an interaction. In the scenarios that we build, despite the motion constraint given to the user, we could simulate unstructured spontaneous encounters with a robot. While the robot is approaching a user, its arm gestures and body pose can influence the way the user perceives it [6]. The interactions developed for this study aim to simulate a spontaneous' one that can happen in the wild. Clearly, an unstructured scene is far more complex and the environment can influence the interaction in a positive or negative fashion. For instance, if two users are in a hall without illumination, it would be very hard to establish an interaction. Hence, the social cognition is preceded by the perception of the surroundings.

Figure 2 suggest that the robot's head acts as a stronger social cue with respect to the user's relative body position while approaching a social HRI. Furthermore, in SS the robot gives the impression to actively looking for the user while in FS since the user is already on the robot's trajectory, the intentionality of it is not clearly perceived.

Some participants described the behaviour of the robot during SS as secure and more natural, while other participants suggested that the relative torso pose would have also benefited the study. Additionally, few participants described the behaviour of the robot during SF as aggressive and unnatural. Despite the slight changes among the conditions, our results show that even when the robot is far from the human, its gazing behaviour is read as a social signal and can convey the intention to initiate an interaction.

6   Conclusion

In this work, we investigate the role of nonverbal robot behaviour before a social HRI takes place. We model the time evolution of an HRI with a three-phase representation and conduct a user study to investigate the effects of gaze and approach policy when the interaction has not started yet. Participants are instructed to pronounce the keyword "yes" as soon as they can answer positively to the question "Would the robot like to start an interaction with me?". At this point, a stopwatch records how long it took each participant to pronounce the keyword in each condition. Each participant also fills in a post-interaction survey after experiencing each condition. Results show that participants significantly preferred conditions in which the robot employs a social gaze while approaching them. However, it might be that when the user is directly on the path of the robot the intentionality of the social gaze is perceived as a consequence of the robot's motion.

Future research will investigate the effects of different robot designs and more complex robot paths have on the perceived robot's intentions in similar scenarios. Moreover, we plan to target different age groups of participants to investigate whether their perception of the robot's intention differs.

References

1. Admoni, H., Scassellati, B.: Social eye gaze in human-robot interaction: a review. J. Hum.-Rob. Interact. **6**(1), 25–63 (2017)
2. Avelino, J., Garcia-Marques, L., Ventura, R., Bernardino, A.: Break the ice: a survey on socially aware engagement for human-robot first encounters. Int. J. Social Rob. **13**(8), 1851–1877 (2021)
3. Ba, S.O., Odobez, J.M.: Recognizing visual focus of attention from head pose in natural meetings. IEEE Trans. Syst. Man Cybern. Part B (Cybern.) **39**(1), 16–33 (2008)
4. Belpaeme, T., et al.: Multimodal child-robot interaction: building social bonds. J. Hum.-Robot Interact. **1**(2) (2012)
5. Ben-Youssef, A., Clavel, C., Essid, S., Bilac, M., Chamoux, M., Lim, A.: Ue-hri: a new dataset for the study of user engagement in spontaneous human-robot interactions. In: Proceedings of the 19th ACM International Conference on Multimodal Interaction, pp. 464–472 (2017)
6. Breazeal, C., Dautenhahn, K., Kanda, T.: Social robotics. In: Springer Handbook of Robotics, pp. 1935–1972 (2016)
7. Faul, F., Erdfelder, E., Lang, A.G., Buchner, A.: G* power 3: a flexible statistical power analysis program for the social, behavioral, and biomedical sciences. Behav. Res. Methods **39**(2), 175–191 (2007)
8. Hall, E.T.: The Hidden Dimension, vol. 609. Anchor (1966)
9. Heenan, B., Greenberg, S., Aghel-Manesh, S., Sharlin, E.: Designing social greetings in human robot interaction. In: Proceedings of the 2014 Conference on Designing Interactive Systems, pp. 855–864 (2014)
10. Hong, A., et al.: A multimodal emotional human-robot interaction architecture for social robots engaged in bidirectional communication. IEEE Trans. Cybern. **51**(12), 5954–5968 (2021)
11. Kendon, A.: Conducting Interaction: Patterns of Behavior in Focused Encounters, vol. 7. CUP Archive (1990)
12. MacArthur, K.R., Stowers, K., Hancock, P.A.: Human-robot interaction: proximity and speed-slowly back away from the robot! In: Advances in Human Factors in Robots and Unmanned Systems, pp. 365–374. Springer, Heidelberg (2017). https://doi.org/10.1007/978-3-319-41959-6_30
13. Maniscalco, U., Storniolo, P., Messina, A.: Bidirectional multi-modal signs of checking human-robot engagement and interaction. Int. J. Social Rob., 1–15 (2022)
14. Neggers, M.M., Cuijpers, R.H., Ruijten, P.A., Ijsselsteijn, W.A.: Determining shape and size of personal space of a human when passed by a robot. Int. J. Social Rob. **14**(2), 561–572 (2022)
15. Normoyle, A., Badler, J.B., Fan, T., Badler, N.I., Cassol, V.J., Musse, S.R.: Evaluating perceived trust from procedurally animated gaze. In: Proceedings of Motion on Games, pp. 141–148 (2013)
16. Oertel, C., et al.: Engagement in human-agent interaction: an overview. Front. Rob. AI **7**, 92 (2020)
17. Patompak, P., Jeong, S., Nilkhamhang, I., Chong, N.Y.: Learning proxemics for personalized human-robot social interaction. Int. J. Social Rob. **12**(1), 267–280 (2020)
18. Pereira, A., Oertel, C., Fermoselle, L., Mendelson, J., Gustafson, J.: Effects of different interaction contexts when evaluating gaze models in hri. In: Proceedings of the 2020 ACM/IEEE International Conference on Human-Robot Interaction, pp. 131–139 (2020)

19. Rossi, S., Ercolano, G., Raggioli, L., Savino, E., Ruocco, M.: The disappearing robot: an analysis of disengagement and distraction during non-interactive tasks. In: 2018 27th IEEE International Symposium on Robot and Human Interactive Communication (RO-MAN), pp. 522–527 (2018)
20. Rossi, S., Staffa, M., Bove, L., Capasso, R., Ercolano, G.: User's personality and activity influence on hri comfortable distances. In: Social Robotics, pp. 167–177. Springer, Cham (2017). https://doi.org/10.1007/978-3-319-70022-9_17
21. Sanghvi, J., Castellano, G., Leite, I., Pereira, A., McOwan, P.W., Paiva, A.: Automatic analysis of affective postures and body motion to detect engagement with a game companion. In: Proceedings of the 6th International Conference on Human-Robot Interaction, pp. 305–312 (2011)
22. Satake, S., Kanda, T., Glas, D.F., Imai, M., Ishiguro, H., Hagita, N.: How to approach humans? strategies for social robots to initiate interaction. In: Proceedings of the 4th ACM/IEEE International Conference on Human Robot Interaction, pp. 109–116 (2009)
23. Sidner, C.L., Lee, C., Kidd, C.D., Lesh, N., Rich, C.: Explorations in engagement for humans and robots. Artif. Intell. **166**(1), 140–164 (2005)
24. Staffa, M., Gregorio, M.D., Giordano, M., Rossi, S.: Can you follow that guy? In: 22th European Symposium on Artificial Neural Networks, ESANN 2014, Bruges, Belgium, 23–25 April 2014 (2014)
25. Sternberg, R.J., Smith, C.: Social intelligence and decoding skills in nonverbal communication. Social Cogn. **3**(2), 168 (1985)
26. Strazdas, D., Hintz, J., Felßberg, A.M., Al-Hamadi, A.: Robots and wizards: an investigation into natural human-robot interaction. IEEE Access **8**, 207635–207642 (2020)
27. Syrdal, D.S., Dautenhahn, K., Walters, M.L., Koay, K.L.: Sharing spaces with robots in a home scenario-anthropomorphic attributions and their effect on proxemic expectations and evaluations in a live hri trial. In: AAAI Fall Symposium: AI in Eldercare: New Solutions to Old Problems, pp. 116–123 (2008)
28. Vigni, F., Knoop, E., Prattichizzo, D., Malvezzi, M.: The role of closed-loop hand control in handshaking interactions. IEEE Rob. Autom. Lett. **4**(2), 878–885 (2019)
29. Zhang, Y., Beskow, J., Kjellström, H.: Look but don't stare: mutual gaze interaction in social robots. In: International Conference on Social Robotics, pp. 556–566. Springer, Heidelberg (2017). https://doi.org/10.1007/978-3-319-70022-9_55
30. Złotowski, J., Proudfoot, D., Yogeeswaran, K., Bartneck, C.: Anthropomorphism: opportunities and challenges in human-robot interaction. Int. J. Social Rob. **7**(3), 347–360 (2015)

On the Emotional Transparency
of a Non-humanoid Social Robot

Francesco Vigni[1]([✉])[iD], Alessandra Rossi[2][iD], Linda Miccio[2], and Silvia Rossi[2][iD]

[1] Interdepartmental Center for Advances in Robotic Surgery - ICAROS,
University of Naples Federico II, Naples, Italy
francesco.vigni@unina.it
[2] Department of Electrical Engineering and Information Technologies - DIETI,
University of Naples Federico II, Naples, Italy
{alessandra.rossi,silvia.rossi}@unina.it

Abstract. Non-anthropomorphic robots have issues in conveying internal state during a Human-Robot Interaction (HRI). A possible approach is to let robots communicate their states or intentions through emotions. However, the robot's emotional responses are not always clearly identified by people, and it is also difficult to identify which and how many cues are most relevant in affecting people's ability of recognition of robots' emotions during the ongoing interaction. We involved 102 participants in an online questionnaire-based study where they rated the robot's behaviours, designed in terms of colours, movements and sounds, according to the perceived emotions in order to identify the cues to be used for making robots more legible. The results suggest that emotional transparency can benefit from multimodal interaction. Our results underline that single modes can be capable of conveying effectively the desired emotion, and little benefit is obtained by the use of additional modes that may be not necessarily noticed by the users.

Keywords: Affective robotics · Human-robot interaction · Emotional transparency

1 Introduction

People are able to communicate and interpret multimodal communication signals, including natural language, gesture, pose, and body language. In addition to those, they might engage other humans with a bidirectional and mutual understanding [25] that allows them to understand and predict others' intentions and behaviours.

Current literature has identified a number of social cues that could influence people's perception of a robot as social entity, and, as a consequence, their behaviours and trust towards a robot during an interaction [21]. However, it is

This work has been supported by the European Union's Horizon 2020 research and innovation programme under the Marie Skłodowska-Curie grant agreement No 955778, and Italian PON R&I 2014–2020 - REACT-EU (CUP E65F21002920003).

F. Cavallo et al. (Eds.): ICSR 2022, LNAI 13817, pp. 290–299, 2022.
https://doi.org/10.1007/978-3-031-24667-8_26

not clear if the cues composing the multimodal interaction affect equally the quality of the interaction, or if one or some of them are shadowed by the others [24]. In this work, we investigate how emotions are attributed to the behaviour of a non-humanoid social robot whose main purpose is to help the learning experience of students in schools. The robot used in this work is the ClassMate developed in collaboration with Protom Group S.p.a.[1]. It is designed as a social robot for classroom environments and allows the development of social expressions in terms of body motion, facial expression, tactile interaction and sounds [5]. Thanks to its design, it can be deployed on top of a standard desk without the need of securing the structure to it.

We design a set of affective behaviours on the robot and vary the multimodal dimension of these to investigate whether users can match the desired emotions to them. To span the most important emotions perceived by humans, we developed six affective behaviours where each aims to represent the desired emotion. As target emotions, we used the distinctive universal emotions defined by Ekman [8]: anger, fear, disgust, sadness, joy and surprise. We consider facial expression, body motion, and sound as a component for achieving multimodal interaction.

2   Background and Related Work

The social behaviours of a robot designed to constantly be exposed to users must be carefully designed in order to improve its acceptance.

2.1   Robots in Education

Vernier et al. [27] present a science lesson mediated by a life-size humanoid robot. Parts of the lesson were given through the Wizard of Oz (WoZ) and the authors show that the interaction with the robot teacher achieved its educational objectives. Kanda et al. [11] design interactive behaviours for long-term interaction in an elementary school and report how the design principles promote such interaction. Their field study lasted two months and the authors have found that once the novelty effect vanishes two-thirds of students become bored and reject social robots over time. Once the interaction is prolonged in time, relationships are likely build. In this sense, the children-teacher relationship evolves and when a robot is deployed as a teacher, children treat it as a social actor [9].

Davison et al. [7] present the results of a four-month study in which the interactions between children and a social robot were totally motivated by the firsts. In their work, the robot is not actively looking for the interaction but is behaving socially if triggered. The authors investigated also the extent to which the children could self-regulate the learning process if exposed to a prolonged interaction with the robot. However, if the robot takes initiative in a team during a learning task, perceived engagement does not necessarily improve [10].

---

[1] https://www.protom.com.

A typical learning scenario aims to maximize the quality and quantity of content that students are receiving. Introducing a robot in this type of context surely creates a novelty effect at first, but for long-term interactions, the robot should be capable to adapt its behaviour to the interacting user [1]. However, in this field, the problem of maintaining the interest of the students is yet to be solved. Low interest in a classroom can come from individual physical status, lack of interest in the content or the way the content is exposed by the robot teacher. Such use-case, despite its great benefits [20], should also be treated carefully in terms of ethics [26]. However, on a robot-perception level, engagement can be measured on the students and the robot could employ behaviours to recover it. For instance, Leite et al. [12] presents a strategy by which the robot could classify disengagement automatically with the aim to adjust its behaviour to re-acquire the attention of the children. More recently, Nasir et al. [17] showed that in educational HRI engagement does not necessarily correlate with learning performances. In their work, authors show that in order to maximize learning a robot should seek a productive engagement that allows gaps in which the student is not engaged. Suggesting that a little bit of distraction can actually improve learning.

Clearly, in order to successfully adopt robots in social contexts, the emotional response of the users has also to be taken into account.

2.2 Emotional Robotics

The future of social robotics is strictly related to the capability of these to elicit emotions on humans [4]. Beck et al. [2] evaluated children's ability to interpret a robot's emotional body language, demonstrating, for instance, the impact of head position on the perception of various body postures. The goal of these studies is to improve educational objective performance with the aid of robotics. However, a common issue when conducting user studies in HRI is the gap between users' expectations of the robot and its real capabilities. The expectations are driven by socio-cultural factors like movies, books and other types of arts. Frequently robots are represented as embodied Artificial Intelligent (AI) agents that can process information and interact smoothly with surrounding users. When focusing on learning context, it is important to realize the effect of robotics on younger generations. Ligthart et al. [13] investigate the role of expectations in child-robot interaction and found that the effectiveness of the social assistance of the robot is negatively influenced by misaligned expectations.

Despite Beck et al. [2] suggests that the lack of an anthropomorphic face in a social robot does not impede emulating emotions, Löffler et al. [14] highlights the importance of empowering social robots with artificial emotions that are effective given by a combination of three low-cost output channels (colour, motion and sound). For instance, when focusing on the latter, Rossi et al. [23] presented show that children aged 3–8 years perceive the robot's behaviours and the related selected emotional semantic free sounds in terms of different degrees of arousal, valence and dominance: while valence and dominance are clearly perceived by the children, arousal is poorly distinguished. Designing behaviours for non-humanoid robots with the goal of intentionally eliciting emotions is not a trivial task.

In this work, we present the results of an online user study in which the robot ClassMate is showing five different artificial emotions via using its face, body movements and sounds to users that are asked to associate an emotion with each behaviour.

3   The ClassMate Robot

The ClassMate Robot is an open chain robot with 6 degrees of freedom (DoF) implemented as revolute joints. The robot could be divided into (fixed) base, body and head. The base allows a rotation of the body along the vertical axis, the body contains 4 parallel-axes joints. Finally, the head is controlled by a revolute joint whose axis is orthogonal to its parent's. Figure 1 shows one of the first prototypes of the robot and highlights (1) Infrared (IR) Sensors, (2) Touch Sensors, (3) Camera with a built-in microphone, (4) LCD Display, (5) Left and right RGB LEDs + Frontal camera flash, (6) Sound Sensors and (7) Motors. The robot is designed to engage students, teachers and school personnel in social interactions while providing different functionalities, such as small talks, and

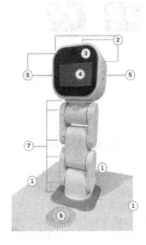

Fig. 1. Robot's prototype

learning applications [5]. The ClassMate's framework has been developed following four main principles that allow an easy personalization, update, and extension of the available skills/applications: 1) the robot needs to be interacting and have personalised behaviours, 2) the robot needs to be able to have natural and social interactions, 3) new applications can be easily added by non-programmers, and 4) the applications/services provided need to be perceived as part of the robot and not external tools.

To this purpose, affective modalities can be used by social robots to convey their internal states and intentions [3], and improve the success of the social interaction. The social component of the interaction is manipulated on the ClassMate robot's facial gestures, body motions and sounds, as suggested by [14]. In particular, we endowed the robot with the capability of expressing Ekman's basic emotions (joy, sadness, disgust, fear, surprise and anger) [8]. The next sections describe how the robot's face, body and sounds are controlled and combined in order to simulate the desired emotions.

3.1   Facial Expressions

The screen located on the head of the robot shows two simple eyes on a black background. The shape and colour of the robot's eye animations have been designed considering relevant studies [6,18]. Figure 2 shows examples of the facial expressions designed in this work with the relatively intended emotion.

Fig. 2. Examples of facial expression with relative intended emotion.

3.2 Body Expressions

The body movements of a robot are also used to convey emotions [22]. However, the kinematics of this robot allow limited motion of the joints, so the range of emotional expressions that can be designed is also limited. To convey emotions, we can rotate the last joint (head), control the body to represent "closeness" or "openness" to the interaction [16], and rotate the whole body using the base joint. As discussed in [15], the emotions that a robot's body can express, surely depend on its design and anthropomorphism. In this work, only three separate body expressions are implemented. Bearing in mind that across all the body motions the robot always starts at the initial configuration (Fig. 3a).

Figure 3b, 3c, 3d show the final configuration of the body at the end of the expression of each motion.

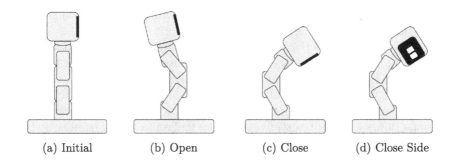

Fig. 3. Examples of ClassMate's body motions for emotional expression.

3.3   The Sound

Several non-verbal sounds are used to mimic the natural backchannelling cues that are often used by humans to express a specific emotion. In HRI, backchannelling cues are important as they can be used to maintain a person engaged with a robot or to attract attention [23].

4   User Study

The purpose of this study was to evaluate which is the minimum type of modalities needed by the ClassMate robot for expressing internal states and responses to effectively communicate with people. This is not a trivial task since developed emotions are not always perceived as intended both in humanoid and non-humanoid robots [22]. A misinterpretation of the emotions may have negative effects on the legibility of the robot's intentions and, as a consequence, on the overall success of the interaction. In this context, we classified several multimodal affective (para-verbal and non-verbal) behaviours according to people's perceived emotions. In particular, we hypothesised that multimodal interactions for such non-humanoid social robot improve the legibility of its simulated emotions. Therefore, we combined three modalities to identify which are the social cues that make transparent a robot's emotional state for people.

4.1   Methodology

We conducted an online questionnaire-based study that was organised as a between-subject experimental design to evaluate the perceived expressions of the robot's animations. Participants watched several animations in which the ClassMate robot simulated emotions using: 1) **C1** only one modality, i.e. facial expressions; 2) **C2** facial expressions and body motions; and 3) **C3** facial expressions, body motions and sounds.

Overall, we developed six robot affective behaviours that mimic distinctive universal emotions (anger, fear, disgust, sadness, joy and surprise). In condition **C1**, the robot's eyes displayed on the screen were white eyes with a fixed shape[2]. In condition **C2**, the robot's eyes assumed the colour as described in Sect. 3.1[3]. In condition **C3**, we used the same facial animations of **C2**, and we added paraverbal sounds that are often used by people to convey the respective emotion[4]. In our design, condition **C3** is the baseline, and we expect that people would clearly associate these animations to the respective emotional expression.

The presented animations also included two variations of the fear and anger emotions using a different movement directions. The combinations of the body

---

[2] The animations used in **C1** condition can be viewed on https://tinyurl.com/2a9bhjzj.

[3] The animations used in **C2** condition can be viewed on https://tinyurl.com/yc72srkp.

[4] The animations used in **C3** condition can be viewed on https://tinyurl.com/ycynm64d.

expressions and emotions was inspired by the results presented in Löffler et al. [14]. Each animation lasted about 3 s, and were displayed in random order to the participants.

During the different stages of the questionnaire study, we asked participants to complete several questionnaires. A pre-experimental questionnaire collected participants' demographics data (age, gender), and their previous experience with robots, including what kind of previous interactions and type of robots they interacted with.

After each video, participants were asked to associate to the robot's behaviours one of Ekman's six basic affective states (joy, sadness, disgust, fear, anger and surprise), and rate their own confidence in the choice on a 5-point Likert Scale [1 = "Not at all" to 5 = "Very much"].

At the end of their interaction, we assessed their overall perception of robot by asking them whether they would like to interact with a physical robot on a scale from 1 ["Not at all"] to 7 ["Very much"].

4.2   Participants

An a priori sample size calculation using G*Power considering ANOVA as analysis ($\alpha = .05$, power $= .95$, number of groups $= 3$, number of measurements $= 5$), and moderate effects ($f(V) = 0.25$), resulted in a sample size of 96 participants.

We recruited 102 participants (54 male, 48 female, no non-binary), aged between 18 and 66 years old (avg. 36.45, stdv. 13.99). The majority of participants (79.4%) did not have any experience with robots, 7.8% of participants were programmers, researchers, while the remaining participants had mainly saw robots on TV, social media, or demos. Participants' experience with robots included Furhat, Pepper and Roomba robot.

Each participant was assigned to one condition, and they were overall distributed among the three experimental conditions as follows: 1) 33 people in the only-face (**C1**) condition, 2) 32 participants in the pose-face (**C2**) condition, and 3) 37 participants in the pose-face-sound condition (**C3**) condition.

5   Result

Our results allowed us to classify a set of modalities for expressing robot emotions (see Fig. 4). Note that Fig. 4a and 4b share a common y-label.

The heatmap in Fig. 4a shows that participants were able to correctly recognise sadness and surprise emotions with the robot's pose showed. They were more undecided in associating the robot's poses to the disgust, joy and fear emotions, even though we can observe that they were confused with emotions having similar polarity. These results also show that anger was the only emotions completely misinterpreted in the condition **C1**.

In conditions **C2**, participants correctly associated the robot's animations with the disgust, joy, anger, surprise and sadness emotions (see Fig. 4b). Observing this heatmap, we can also notice that both animations representing fear were

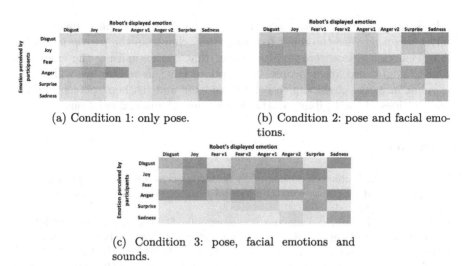

(a) Condition 1: only pose.

(b) Condition 2: pose and facial emotions.

(c) Condition 3: pose, facial emotions and sounds.

Fig. 4. A heatmap for the affective expressions associated with the robot's behaviours by the participants. Colors ranging from low scores in red to high scores in green. (Color figure online)

not as clear as the others. Interestingly, previous studies [19, 22] also highlighted the difficulty for participants to recognise it as expressed by most robots.

As expected, the sounds used in condition **C3** allowed participants to almost uniquely associate an emotion to the robot's animation showed (see Fig. 4c).

Finally, at the end of the study, participants were asked to express their desire to use in person the robot. The majority of participants (76%) stated that they would like to interact with a physical ClassMate, the 9% of participants were unsure if they would like to interact the ClassMate, and the remaining expressed a negative response.

6   Conclusion

The emotional transparency of a non-anthropomorphic robot deployed in schools is important for long-term interactions. In this regard, we developed six different social expressions that aim to represent emotions and manipulate the multi-modality degree in an online questionnaire-based user study. We observed that participants were able to differentiate most of the emotions using either one or two modalities, i.e. robot's pose or robot's pose and facial expression. Interestingly, we also found that participants were not able to differentiate clearly fear from other negative emotions. Löffler et al. [14] show that multimodal interaction improves emotional transparency, however, our results suggest that for robot emotions designed with single modes and correctly identified, little improvement is obtained by the use of additional modes. Moreover, in line with [23], this work shows that para-verbal cue is extremely important for improving human's emotional understanding of social robots.

In future studies, we want to conduct a similar study with participants physically interacting with the robot to observe any change in the perception of the robot's emotion. Moreover, we also expect that contextualising the emotional response might also affect people's perception. For this reason, we will deploy the robot in a real classroom to collect students and teachers' perception and considerations of the legibility of the robot's behaviours and emotions.

References

1. Ahmad, M.I., Mubin, O., Orlando, J.: Adaptive social robot for sustaining social engagement during long-term children-robot interaction. Int. J. Hum.-Comput. Interact. **33**(12), 943–962 (2017)
2. Beck, A., Cañamero, L., Damiano, L., Sommavilla, G., Tesser, F., Cosi, P.: Children interpretation of emotional body language displayed by a robot. In: Mutlu, B., Bartneck, C., Ham, J., Evers, V., Kanda, T. (eds.) ICSR 2011. LNCS (LNAI), vol. 7072, pp. 62–70. Springer, Heidelberg (2011). https://doi.org/10.1007/978-3-642-25504-5_7
3. Broekens, J., Chetouani, M.: Towards transparent robot learning through tdrl-based emotional expressions. IEEE Trans. Affect. Comput. **12**(2), 352–362 (2019)
4. Chuah, S.H.W., Yu, J.: The future of service: the power of emotion in human-robot interaction. J. Retail. Cons. Serv. **61**, 102551 (2021)
5. Cucciniello, I., L'Arco, G., Rossi, A., Autorino, C., Santoro, G., Rossi, S.: Classmate robot: a robot to support teaching and learning activities in schools. In: 2022 31st IEEE International Symposium on Robot and Human Interactive Communication (RO-MAN). IEEE (2022)
6. Da Pos, O., Green-Armytage, P.: Facial expressions, colours and basic emotions. Colour Des. Creat. **1**(1), 2 (2007)
7. Davison, D.P., Wijnen, F.M., Charisi, V., van der Meij, J., Evers, V., Reidsma, D.: Working with a social robot in school: a long-term real-world unsupervised deployment. In: 2020 15th ACM/IEEE International Conference on Human-Robot Interaction (HRI), pp. 63–72. IEEE (2020)
8. Ekman, P.: An argument for basic emotions. Cogn. Emot. **6**(3–4), 169–200 (1992)
9. Ekström, S., Pareto, L.: The dual role of humanoid robots in education: as didactic tools and social actors. In: Education and Information Technologies, pp. 1–36 (2022)
10. Ivaldi, S., Anzalone, S.M., Rousseau, W., Sigaud, O., Chetouani, M.: Robot initiative in a team learning task increases the rhythm of interaction but not the perceived engagement. Front. Neurorob. **8**, 5 (2014)
11. Kanda, T., Sato, R., Saiwaki, N., Ishiguro, H.: A two-month field trial in an elementary school for long-term human-robot interaction. IEEE Trans. Rob. **23**(5), 962–971 (2007)
12. Leite, I., et al.: Autonomous disengagement classification and repair in multiparty child-robot interaction. In: 2016 25th IEEE International Symposium on Robot and Human Interactive Communication (RO-MAN), pp. 525–532. IEEE (2016)
13. Ligthart, M., Henkemans, O.B., Hindriks, K., Neerincx, M.A.: Expectation management in child-robot interaction. In: 2017 26th IEEE International Symposium on Robot and Human Interactive Communication (RO-MAN), pp. 916–921. IEEE (2017)

14. Löffler, D., Schmidt, N., Tscharn, R.: Multimodal expression of artificial emotion in social robots using color, motion and sound. In: 2018 13th ACM/IEEE International Conference on Human-Robot Interaction (HRI), pp. 334–343. IEEE (2018)
15. Marmpena, M., Lim, A., Dahl, T.S., Hemion, N.: Generating robotic emotional body language with variational autoencoders. In: 2019 8th International Conference on Affective Computing and Intelligent Interaction (ACII), pp. 545–551. IEEE (2019)
16. McColl, D., Zhang, Z., Nejat, G.: Human body pose interpretation and classification for social human-robot interaction. Int. J. Social Rob. 3(3), 313–332 (2011)
17. Nasir, J., Bruno, B., Chetouani, M., Dillenbourg, P.: What if social robots look for productive engagement? Int. J. Social Rob. 14(1), 55–71 (2022)
18. Plutchik, R.: The nature of emotions: human emotions have deep evolutionary roots, a fact that may explain their complexity and provide tools for clinical practice. Am. Sci. 89(4), 344–350 (2001)
19. Reyes, M.E., Meza, I.V., Pineda, L.A.: Robotics facial expression of anger in collaborative human-robot interaction. Int. J. Adv. Rob. Syst. 16(1) (2019)
20. Rosanda, V., Istenic Starcic, A.: The robot in the classroom: a review of a robot role. In: Popescu, E., Hao, T., Hsu, T.-C., Xie, H., Temperini, M., Chen, W. (eds.) SETE 2019. LNCS, vol. 11984, pp. 347–357. Springer, Cham (2020). https://doi.org/10.1007/978-3-030-38778-5_38
21. Rossi, A., et al.: Investigating the effects of social interactive behaviours of a robot on people's trust during a navigation task. In: Althoefer, K., Konstantinova, J., Zhang, K. (eds.) TAROS 2019. LNCS (LNAI), vol. 11649, pp. 349–361. Springer, Cham (2019). https://doi.org/10.1007/978-3-030-23807-0_29
22. Rossi, A., Scheunemann, M.M., L'Arco, G., Rossi, S.: Evaluation of a humanoid robot's emotional gestures for transparent interaction. In: Li, H., et al. (eds.) ICSR 2021. LNCS (LNAI), vol. 13086, pp. 397–407. Springer, Cham (2021). https://doi.org/10.1007/978-3-030-90525-5_34
23. Rossi, S., Dell'Aquila, E., Bucci, B.: Evaluating the emotional valence of affective sounds for child-robot interaction. In: Salichs, M.A., et al. (eds.) ICSR 2019. LNCS (LNAI), vol. 11876, pp. 505–514. Springer, Cham (2019). https://doi.org/10.1007/978-3-030-35888-4_47
24. Rossi, S., Ruocco, M.: Better alone than in bad company: effects of incoherent non-verbal emotional cues for a humanoid robot. Interact. Stud. 20(3), 487–508 (2019)
25. Sciutti, A., Mara, M., Tagliasco, V., Sandini, G.: Humanizing human-robot interaction: on the importance of mutual understanding. IEEE Technol. Soc. Maga. 37(1), 22–29 (2018)
26. Sharkey, A.J.C.: Should we welcome robot teachers? Ethics Inf. Technol. 18(4), 283–297 (2016). https://doi.org/10.1007/s10676-016-9387-z
27. Verner, I.M., Polishuk, A., Krayner, N.: Science class with robothespian: using a robot teacher to make science fun and engage students. IEEE Rob. Autom. Maga. 23(2), 74–80 (2016)

Transparent Interactive Reinforcement Learning Using Emotional Behaviours

Georgios Angelopoulos[1]([✉])(iD), Alessandra Rossi[1,2](iD), Gianluca L'Arco[2], and Silvia Rossi[1,2](iD)

[1] Interdepartmental Center for Advances in Robotic Surgery - ICAROS, University of Naples Federico II, Naples, Italy
{georgios.angelopoulos,alessandra.rossi,silvia.rossi}@unina.it
[2] Department of Electrical Engineering and Information Technologies - DIETI, University of Naples Federico II, Naples, Italy

Abstract. This work presents a model for improving transparency during robot learning tasks in Human-Robot Interaction scenarios. Our model puts the human in the learning loop by using two categories of robot's emotional/behavioural reactions, one associated with the learning process of the robot and another elicited as a response to the feedback provided by the user. Preliminary results from a between-subjects study show that people empathized more with a robot expressing its emotions in both the above categories. We noticed a slight increase in the transparency of the robot while it expressed emotions during the learning process and as a response to the user. These findings highlight the importance of emotional behaviours for improving the transparency in the learning systems, which are fundamental for social learning scenarios in future humanoid robotic applications.

Keywords: Interactive reinforcement learning · Human-robot interaction · Emotional behaviour · Transparency

1 Introduction

The ability of people who lack programming skills (children, older adults, and other non-expert users) to easily teach robots new tasks is becoming critical in domains that involve closer user interactions. As a result, robots need to develop task-related skills with humans as tutors, in similar ways children do, as this will improve the robot's performance and acceptance.

One way for roboticists to provide a robot with learning capabilities is by applying an Interactive Reinforcement Learning (IntRL) algorithm where the human can provide corrections or preferable constraints to enhance the robot's learning [16,17]. Furthermore, robots are built with anthropomorphic features

This work has been supported by the European Union's Horizon 2020 research and innovation programme under the Marie Skłodowska-Curie grant agreement No 955778, and CHIST-ERA IV COHERENT project "COllaborative HiErarchical Robotic ExplaNaTions", and Italian PON R&I 2014-2020 - REACT-EU (CUP E65F21002920003).

F. Cavallo et al. (Eds.): ICSR 2022, LNAI 13817, pp. 300–311, 2022.
https://doi.org/10.1007/978-3-031-24667-8_27

to allow them to engage people in an interactive learning style that is socially accepted. If a robot's learning behaviour is familiar to people, they will find it more natural to teach it [3].

In this respect, the careful management of robots' behaviour during learning is paramount; when done correctly, people's natural tendencies to anthropomorphize can facilitate and enhance their interaction with robots. However, to better understand how to design the robots' behaviours appropriately, we should understand how human teachers teach their pupils, and how this knowledge can be used to teach robots. In a natural Human-Human environment, a classroom is an emotional place where students frequently express their emotions. For example, students can be excited during studying, hope for success, feel pride in their accomplishments, be surprised at discovering a new solution, or experience anxiety about failing examinations [13]. Another fundamental attribute in educational milieus seems to be teacher's empathy [12]. Arghode et al. [1] showed the significant role of empathy in facilitating the academic development of teachers and students. Baron-Cohen [2] defined empathy as the drive to identify another person's emotions and thoughts. Consequently, just as most adults and children elicit a response to nurture, care, and tutor, robots should elicit a similar response. Indeed, Broekens and Chetouani [4] affirm that the lack of robot transparency has a direct impact on learning. In addition, they highlight the vital link between emotion and expression of the internal state, suggesting that the expression of emotion is a valuable and universal tool, independent of language and species, to transmit one's internal state.

The present work designs, tests, and compares emotional expression mechanisms as a solution for a transparent learning system. In particular, the study explores emotional responses during a robot's learning task based on the progress of the learning and on the certainty of the subsequent actions. We also explore the feedback/reward of humans, and how these behaviours affect their responses. By increasing robots' behaviour transparency, we can design more effective and social robots that are perceived as more acceptable and trustworthy in human-centred environments [14].

2   Related Work

Despite the increasing deployment of humanoid robots in our everyday life, developing transparent interactive learning methods in HRI has just very recently received attention. In particular, robots rarely use emotions to express transparency while learning new tasks from a human teacher.

In a recent study, Hindemith et al. [7] investigated the influence of the feedback type on the user experience of interacting with the different interfaces and the performance of the learning systems. Specifically, they investigated using either absolute scale (e.g., 5-point Likert-scales) or preference-based user feedback (e.g., the participant was shown two movements of the robot and could select which one was better) for an interface to teach a robot a new skill of the game cup-and-ball. While there is no significant difference in the subjective user experience between the conditions, they discovered a significant difference in the learning performance.

Lin et al. [9] proposed an IntRL method to allow a virtual agent to learn from human feedback, such as facial feedback via an ordinary camera and gestural feedback via a leap motion sensor. Their experiments showed that human social signals can effectively improve the learning efficiency of virtual agents. Furthermore, facial feedback recognition error had a larger effect on the agent performance in the beginning training process than in the later training stage.

Suay et al. [16] explored an interactive reinforcement learning approach that enables humans to advise a robot via multiple modalities, such as speech and gestures. Their experimental evaluations in a simulated grid world scenario showed that their method is more robust and converges significantly faster than standard Q-learning algorithms.

Most approaches in the literature generally investigated different feedback types that people use to the virtual learning agent, and they are not focused on how the robot should behave during learning tasks, resulting in a black-box learning system for the users. Therefore, there is still a need for natural and efficient behaviours implemented into humanoid robots during the learning process. Matarese et al. [11] proposed a model to improve the robot's transparency during reinforcement learning tasks by designing non-verbal emotional/behavioural cues into a humanoid robot. Their model considered human feedback as the reward of the RL algorithm, and the robot presented emotional/behavioural responses based on the learning progress. Their results highlighted that people preferred to interact with an expressive robot over a mechanical one. Nevertheless, their model resulted in a misinterpretation when the robot was expressing doubt or uncertainty, and, as a consequence, it negatively affected the robot's transparency. Moreover, the robot's facial expressions were interpreted as a reaction to the user feedback while they were also linked to the learning (certainty/uncertainty) process. Starting from this work, here we present a different model that takes into account also reactions to users' feedback independently of the status of the learning progress and different emotional behaviours. The user perception of every single individual behaviour was previously validated in [15].

3   Methods

During the learning, one of the main challenges is to make the whole process transparent to users, experts or not. This study presents a method where emotions can be used as an effective and transparent solution for communicating the state of the learning process to users. The robot can express emotions that intrinsically represent the current state.

The proposed emotional model relies on the use of four emotions: fear, hope, sadness, and joy. Here, fear and hope are associated with the learning process of the robot, and, therefore, they are elicited during the execution of the robot's actions (e.g., the pointing actions in our application). In this paper, we refer to them as *pointing emotions*. Sadness and joy are, instead, elicited as a response to the feedback provided by the user. In the paper, they are called *feedback emotions*. It is essential to underline that, unlike the approach of Broekens and Chetouani [4], we do not use the pointing emotions as a manifestation of anticipation of a negative or positive adjustment but as the degree of uncertainty in the execution of a specific action a, in a specific state s. Therefore, the pointing emotions represent the robot's degree of certainty about the task execution.

These emotions are expressed based on the CMS model (Color, Motion, Sound) [10]. Following the results of our previous work [15], the robot expresses its emotions through movement and sound, the colour of the LEDs, and also uses its tablet on its chest to make them more recognizable.

3.1 Elicitation of Pointing Emotions

Pointing emotions, E_p, can vary based on intensity. In detail, they fluctuate in a range from maximum fear to maximum hope:

$$E_p = [fear_{high}, fear, fear_{low}, hope_{low}, hope, hope_{high}] \tag{1}$$

where $fear_{high}$ determines the maximum negative uncertainty, and $hope_{high}$ determines the maximum positive uncertainty. The stimulation of pointing emotions considers the temporal difference error TD (the assessment of how much better or worse a situation just became) and the variation of the temporal difference error Δ_{TD}.

The value of the temporal difference error (initially set at $-\infty$) determines the value of the emotion. When the temporal difference error TD decreases, the valence increases. This behaviour defines the uncertainty of the pointing emotions while executing a specific action a in a state s. The negative uncertainty of an action is mapped as fear, while positive uncertainty as hope. When the TD of a state s converges to 0, the knowledge for the specific state is maximum; in this case, the emotion expressed is $hope_{high}$, and over time, the agent's emotions converge to this emotion.

The intensity of emotions is determined by the variation of the temporal difference error Δ_{TD} (initially set at $-\infty$ as the temporal difference error TD). A significant variation in the temporal difference error Δ_{TD} determines a greater intensity in fear and lower intensity in hope. In contrast, a slight variation in the temporal difference error Δ_{TD} determines a lower intensity in fear and a greater intensity in hope. These emotions were selected based on the work of Tiedens and Linton [18].

In details, let s be a generic non-terminal state, a the action that the agent has chosen to perform; if the absolute value of the relative difference between the new $Q'(s,a)$ and the old $Q(s,a)$, D_q, is less than or equal to 0.1 (so the difference between the two values is at most 10%) to avoid steep changes, then the pointing emotion has a positive value; otherwise negative.

$$valence = \begin{cases} \text{positive, if } D_q = \left| \frac{Q'(s,a) - Q(s,a)}{Q(s,a)} \right| \leq 0.1 \\ \text{negative, otherwise} \end{cases} \tag{2}$$

Once the valence has been established, the absolute value of the relative difference between the new TD' and the old TD, called the Δ_{TD} value, is calculated to determine the specific emotion.

Table 1. Selection of pointing emotions.

Δ_{TD}	Emotions	
	Positive valence	Negative valence
< 0.25	$hope_{high}$	$fear_{low}$
$\geq 0.25 \wedge < 0.50$	$hope$	$fear$
≥ 0.50	$hope_{low}$	$fear_{high}$

$$\Delta_{TD} = \left| \frac{TD'(s,a) - TD(s,a)}{|TD(s,a)|} \right| \tag{3}$$

Having determined the value and the absolute value of the relative difference between the new and the old TD, Δ_{TD} value, it is possible to identify the corresponding emotion from Table 1.

3.2   Elicitation of Feedback Emotions

Feedback emotions, E_f, just like pointing emotions, can vary based on their intensity; they fluctuate in an interval that goes from maximum sadness to maximum joy:

$$E_f = [sadness_{high}, sadness, sadness_{low}, joy_{low}, joy, joy_{high}] \tag{4}$$

Unlike pointing emotions, feedback emotions do not express information; in fact, they are used only as a direct response to the feedback provided by the user. Furthermore, they are also subject to convergence to an emotion; however, the latter depends on the user's evaluation method. The elicitation of these emotions is based on the feedback provided by the user and on its variation. The feedback value of the user determines the value of the emotion. Negative feedback corresponds to a negative valence, zero feedback corresponds to indifference, while positive feedback corresponds to a positive valence. Once the valence has been established, the specific emotion is determined based on the absolute value of the relative difference between the new R' and old feedback R provided by the user, called Δ_R. In the absence of emotion, the variation of the feedback is indifferent.

$$\Delta_R = \left| \frac{R' - R}{|R|} \right| \tag{5}$$

Having determined the absolute value of Δ_R, it is possible to identify the corresponding emotion from Table 2. Finally, Table 3 presents the adopted CMS model.

Table 2. Selection of feedback emotions

Δ_R	Emotions	
	Positive valence	Negative valence
< 0.25	joy_{low}	$sadness_{low}$
$\geq 0.25 \wedge < 0.50$	joy	$sadness$
≥ 0.50	joy_{high}	$sadness_{high}$

Table 3. Expression of emotions.

Emotions	Led	Movement	Sound
Fear low		Indecisive aiming	Not applicable
Fear		Indecisive aiming and gaze distortion	Not applicable
Fear high		Indecisive pointing	Not applicable
Hope low		Fast and decisive aiming	Not applicable
Hope		Strong and fast aiming	Not applicable
Hope high		Strong and very fast aiming	Not applicable
Sadness low		Slightly hunched forward posture	Discouraged
Sadness		Posture hunched forward	Discouraged
Sadness high		Very hunched forward posture	Discouraged
Joy low		Slightly open posture	Joyful
Joy		Open posture	Joyful
Joy high		Very open posture	Joyful

3.3 The Teaching Scenario

In the proposed study, we use a simple interactive scenario based on the board game Mastermind, invented by Mordecai Meirowitz [5] in which a player, called a decoder, must guess a secret code composed by the opposing player, called the encoder. In our scenario, the robot takes the role of the decoder, and the user is the encoder. The secret code consists of a multi-set of two elements, where each element is a ball of three possible colours. The user's task is limited to choosing the secret code and teaching the robot by evaluating each attempt of the robot to guess the code using feedback $r : r \in [-3, 3] \subset \mathbb{N}$ from a user interface.

The robot's task is to guess the secret code by learning from the ratings provided by the user. Its actions are limited to the choice, and consequent the pointing, of a coloured ball. Based on that, we engineered two behavioural conditions for the robot. Specifically, the conditions are:

- **Condition 1 (C1):** The robot provides emotional behaviour based on the user reward only (feedback emotions).
- **Condition 2 (C2):** The robot's behaviour is composed of emotional responses based on the users' rewards (feedback emotion) and emotional behaviour based on the uncertainty of the action (pointing emotion).

We expect that when the emotional expressions of the pointing actions are present in the learning process (C2) will make the robot's behaviours more transparent to the human (**Hypothesis 1**).

In addition, previous studies showed that humans' empathy increases when the robot expresses emotions related to its internal state [8]. Therefore, we expect people to empathize more with the robot in C2 and consequently receive more favourable reward values than in C1 (**Hypothesis 2**).

3.4   Learning Architecture

Considering the interactive scenario described previously, we arrange the coloured balls on the table and enumerate them from 0 to 2; it is possible to formalize the robot's action a as the pointing of the a-th ball. Therefore, the available actions are three (one for each coloured ball available). The state is made up of the set of balls pointed to by the robot, up to that moment, which cannot be greater than the number of balls of the secret code (i.e., 2), and each possible state is a combination of balls with possible repetitions.

The update phase requires a generic sequence of states seq (e.g. $seq = (s_0 = \{\varnothing\}, s_1 = \{1\}, s_2 = \{1,2\})$) and a feedback r provided by the user for the sequence of states seq. The Q value of state s is propagated by updating the Q value of all states that can reach s. This set of states is called coverage $C(s)$ (e.g., the coverage of state $\{x,y\}$ is $C(\{x,y\}) = \{\varnothing, \{x\}, \{y\}, \{x,y\}\}$. For every coverage state s_c the $Q(s_c, a)$ values: $s_c \cup \{a\} \in C(s)$ are updated using the classic update equation of the Q-Learning algorithm, with the only particularity that the feedback r is always equal to 0, since the feedback is "assignable" only to the terminal states:

$$Q(s_c, a) = Q(s_c, a) + \alpha \cdot \overbrace{(\gamma \cdot maxQ\left(s_c \cup \{a\}, a'\right) - Q(s_c, a))}^{\text{Temporal Difference error}} \qquad (6)$$

The Q value of the reached terminal state s_2 is updated using the following expression:

$$Q(s_2, a') = Q(s_2, a') + \alpha \cdot \overbrace{(r - Q(s_2, a'))}^{\text{Temporal Difference error}} \qquad (7)$$

It is important to note that $\forall a : a \in [0, 2] \Rightarrow \gamma \cdot maxQ\left(s_c \cup \{a\}, a'\right) = 0$ since there are no states subsequent to the terminal one. This approach allows the agent to correctly guess the code in a few attempts. Discovering the sequence quickly is essential to avoid participants facing repetitive and potentially dull tests.

4   User Study

A user study was conducted to assess whether the robot's learning process was more transparent to the human teachers when the robot expressed emotions as a reaction to the user feedback or taking into account also the certainty in its action. We designed a between-participant study in a designated environment at the University of Naples Federico II.

4.1 Procedure

Upon arrival, participants were asked to read and sign an informed consent form about the experiment's aims and procedure. Then, the robot and the experimental environment were introduced. Each participant was randomly assigned to one of the conditions. Furthermore, they were told to select a secret code represented by a multi-set of two elements (where each element is a ball of three possible colours) and that they had to evaluate each attempt of the robot to guess the code by providing feedback. Participants were left free to choose their two elements and what feedback to give to the robot. The feedback was provided using the graphical interface by selecting values between -3 and 3. The experimental trial lasted approximately 10–15 min.

4.2 Measurement

At the beginning of the study and before the interaction with the robot, participants were asked to complete a questionnaire containing demographic questions (i.e., age, gender, education), their previous experience with robots, and their perception of robots. We also wanted to evaluate the possible negative bias of participants toward robots, so we asked them to answer the following question on a 5-point Likert Scale: "To what extent do you fear that machines will become out of control?".

To understand and measure the individual differences in empathy, we adopted IRI (Interpersonal Reactivity Index) [6], a well-established and validated questionnaire in the social psychology literature, applying it before the experiment. In particular, the participants rated the "Empathic Concern" (EC) subscale, which assesses the feelings of sympathy and concern for unfortunate others, using seven questions on a 5-point Likert Scale.

At the end of the experiment, a questionnaire was administered to the participants *to measure the transparency of the learning process*. We collected their responses on whether they believed that the robot learned through them ("Do you think the robot learned from your feedback?"), and their expectations ("What was your expectation of the robot after your feedback?"). Finally, we used a 5-point Likert Scale to evaluate to what extent the robot met participants' expectations ("How well does the robot meet your expectations?"). The aforementioned questions evaluate transparency by considering the robot's legibility and predictability attributes.

5   Preliminary Results

We recruited 28 participants (equally distributed in the two conditions) between the University's community, 19 males and 9 females. Their age ranges from 18 to 60 (Mean = 28, Std. Deviation = 9), and they were not familiar with the setup of the study. The majority of the participants (75%) already had previous experience with robots, while 25% of the participants stated that they had never interacted with robots before. Furthermore, we observed that they had no negative bias towards robots (Max. Value = 3, Mean = 1.5, Std. Deviation = 0.6). For this reason, we did not exclude any participants who successfully participated in the study. Nevertheless, while the limited number of participants in our study makes it difficult to draw definite conclusions, our results, however, indicate some interesting preliminary directions to further investigate.

A Cronbach's α test assessed the internal reliability of the Empathic Concern subscale of the IRI questionnaire, where we found an acceptable value of $\alpha_{EC} = 0.72$. Afterwards, we investigated the mean scores of the EC per each condition, revealing similar mean scores. In particular, in C1, the mean score of Empathic concern was 3.2 ± 0.4, while in C2, we found a mean score of 3.1 ± 0.4.

5.1 System's Transparency

In order to investigate the legibility of the learning system, we analysed participants' responses about their belief that the robot learned from their evaluation. Figure 1 shows that 75% of the respondents in C2 believed that their evaluation helped the learning process of the robot, while there has been a slight decrease of 25% in the number of participants answering positively in C1. In addition, we can also observe a 21% difference between the participants' uncertainty; in C1, half of them stated that they were unsure or replied negatively. However, an Independent Samples T-test did not observe a statistically significant difference, $t(22.414) = -1.375$, $p = 0.18$.

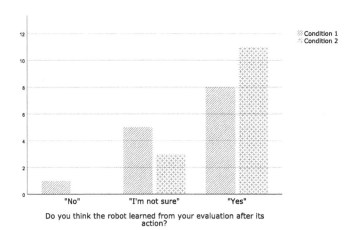

Fig. 1. Humans' confidence about robot's learning per each condition.

Then, we analysed participants' expectations after providing feedback to the robot. Figure 2a shows a slight difference in the participants' answers between the two conditions. Specifically, 64% of the participants in C1 and 78% in C2 believed that it understood what to do in its next move, thanks to their feedback. Nevertheless, we did not observe a statistically significant difference between the two conditions, t(25.194) = −0.460, p = 0.65

In a secondary exploratory analysis, we examined the participants' responses to the question, "How well the robot met your expectations?". Participants in C1 replied with a mean score of 3.3 and a standard deviation of 0.9, while in C2, we had a mean score of 3.9 with a standard deviation of 0.8. Furthermore, as depicted in Fig. 2b the robot in C1 did not fully meet the participants' expectations. In addition, the Independent Samples T-test comparing the two conditions was not statistically significant, t(25.181) = −1.858, p = 0.07.

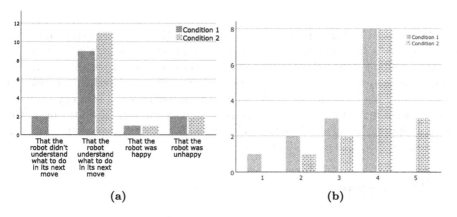

(a)   (b)

Fig. 2. Participants' expectations. (a) What was your expectation of the robot after your feedback? (b) How well does the robot meet your expectations?

5.2 Participants' Feedback

In terms of the participants' rewards, our study showed that human tutors had a positive bias toward the robot. Our results showed that they opted to reward rather than punish the robot. We can also observe that the robot in C2 received a more favourable reward than in C1 since we have a higher mean value in C2 (Mean = 0.93) than in C1 (Mean = 0.09). Moreover, Fig. 3 shows that participants empathized more with the robot in C2 and gave a more favourable reward than in C1. An Independent Samples T-test observed a tendency (p<0.1) between the two conditions, t(22.907) = −1.847, p = 0.07. Therefore, Hypothesis 2 was confirmed. We also noticed that even though we told participants that their feedback could vary between −3 to 3, the participants tended to avoid extreme positive or negative rewards in both conditions. However, participants told the experimenter that they wanted to reward the robot with the most positive feedback (+3) when it learned the sequence. Unfortunately, we did not include a final reward at the end of the learning process. In future works, we would also like to refine our model to consider rewards after learning the sequence.

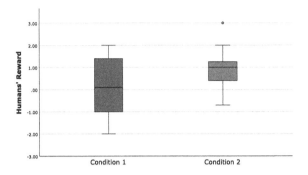

Fig. 3. Humans' reward per each condition.

Observing the participants' behaviours, we noticed that a participant (who was assigned to C2) started with a series of high positive rewards in the first five trials (Mean = 2.4) and then continued with a series of smaller rewards (Mean = − 0.8). The participant said, "between humans, positive reinforcement works, but not with robots". We assume that this change in participants' strategy is due to the transparency of the learning system. This phenomenon (the alter in participants' approach) occurred in the 14% and 43% of participants in C1 and C2, respectively, ($t(23.400) = -1.700$, p = 0.1).

6   Conclusions

The work presented in this paper aimed at integrating emotional behaviours into the robot's social learning to improve the transparency of the learning process for human tutors. We compared a robot showing only emotional/behavioural responses based on the user feedback (C1) and a robot expressing emotional/ behavioural responses based on the user feedback and emotional expressions based on the certainty of the action (C2). From the experimental results, we observed the transparent effects of the designed human-robot learning system in C2. Furthermore, C2 received more favourable rewards confirming our hypothesis. These findings imply that emotional expressiveness is essential for social robots to interact with people transparently while learning. However, we aim at recruiting a larger and more variate group of participants to confirm the applicability of the phenomenon on a larger scale.

We conclude that our preliminary study offers a starting point for a broader experiment on emotional behaviours during learning with human tutors to achieve transparency and overcome the limitation of previous works. In the future, we will also consider different types of human rewards beyond a user interface that may impact the interaction and the learning process.

References

1. Arghode, V., Yalvac, B., Liew, J.: Teacher empathy and science education: a collective case study. Eurasia J. Math. Sci. Technol. Educ. **9**(2), 89–99 (2013)
2. Baron-Cohen, S.: The essential difference: the male and female brain. In: Phi Kappa Phi Forum, vol. 85, pp. 23–26 (2005)
3. Breazeal, C.: Designing sociable machines. In: Socially Intelligent Agents, pp. 149–156. Springer, Heidelberg (2002). https://doi.org/10.1007/0-306-47373-9_18
4. Broekens, J., Chetouani, M.: Towards transparent robot learning through tdrl-based emotional expressions. IEEE Trans. Affect. Comput. **12**(2), 352–362 (2019)
5. Chvátal, V.: Mastermind. Combinatorica **3**(3), 325–329 (1983)
6. Davis, M.H.: Measuring individual differences in empathy: evidence for a multidimensional approach. J. Pers. Soc. Psychol. **44**(1), 113 (1983)
7. Hindemith, L., Bruns, O., Noller, A.M., Hemion, N., Schneider, S., Vollmer, A.L.: Interactive robot task learning: Human teaching proficiency with different feedback approaches. IEEE Trans. Cogn. Dev. Syst. (2022)
8. Kwak, S.S., Kim, Y., Kim, E., Shin, C., Cho, K.: What makes people empathize with an emotional robot?: the impact of agency and physical embodiment on human empathy for a robot. In: 2013 IEEE RO-MAN, pp. 180–185. IEEE (2013)
9. Lin, J., Zhang, Q., Gomez, R., Nakamura, K., He, B., Li, G.: Human social feedback for efficient interactive reinforcement agent learning. In: 2020 29th IEEE International Conference on Robot and Human Interactive Communication (RO-MAN), pp. 706–712. IEEE (2020)
10. Löffler, D., Schmidt, N., Tscharn, R.: Multimodal expression of artificial emotion in social robots using color, motion and sound. In: 2018 13th ACM/IEEE International Conference on Human-Robot Interaction (HRI), pp. 334–343. IEEE (2018)
11. Matarese, M., Sciutti, A., Rea, F., Rossi, S.: Toward robots' behavioral transparency of temporal difference reinforcement learning with a human teacher. IEEE Trans. Hum.-Mach. Syst. **51**(6), 578–589 (2021)
12. McAllister, G., Irvine, J.J.: The role of empathy in teaching culturally diverse students: a qualitative study of teachers' beliefs. J. Teach. Educ. **53**(5), 433–443 (2002)
13. Pekrun, R.: Emotions and learning. Educ. Pract. Ser. **24**(1), 1–31 (2014)
14. Rossi, A., Dautenhahn, K., Lee Koay, K., Walters, M.L.: How social robots influence people's trust in critical situations. In: RO-MAN 2020, pp. 1020–1025 (2020)
15. Rossi, A., Scheunemann, M.M., L'Arco, G., Rossi, S.: Evaluation of a humanoid robot's emotional gestures for transparent interaction. In: Li, H., et al. (eds.) ICSR 2021. LNCS (LNAI), vol. 13086, pp. 397–407. Springer, Cham (2021). https://doi.org/10.1007/978-3-030-90525-5_34
16. Suay, H.B., Chernova, S.: Effect of human guidance and state space size on interactive reinforcement learning. In: 2011 Ro-Man, pp. 1–6. IEEE (2011)
17. Thomaz, A.L., Hoffman, G., Breazeal, C.: Real-time interactive reinforcement learning for robots. In: AAAI 2005 Workshop on Human Comprehensible Machine Learning, pp. 9–13 (2005)
18. Tiedens, L.Z., Linton, S.: Judgment under emotional certainty and uncertainty: the effects of specific emotions on information processing. J. Pers. Social Psychol. **81**(6), 973 (2001)

What Do I Look Like? A Conditional GAN Based Robot Facial Self-Awareness Approach

Shangguan Zhegong[1], Chuang Yu[2(✉)], Wenjie Huang[2], Zexuan Sun[1], and Adriana Tapus[1]

[1] Autonomous Systems and Robotics Lab/U2IS, ENSTA Paris, Institut Polytechnique de Paris, 828 boulevard des Maréchaux, Palaiseau 91120, France
{zhegong.shangguan,zexuan.sun,adriana.tapus}@ensta-paris.fr
[2] Cognitive Robotics Laboratory, University of Manchester, Oxford Rd, Manchester, UK
{chuang.yu,wenjie.huang}@manchester.ac.uk

Abstract. In uncertain social scenarios, the self-awareness of facial expressions helps a person to understand, predict, and control his/her states better. Self-awareness gives animals the ability to distinguish self from others and to self-recognize themselves. For cognitive robots, the ability to be aware of their actions and the effects of actions on self and the environment is crucial for reliable and trustworthy intelligent robots. In particular, we are interested in robot facial expression awareness by using action joint data to achieve self-face perception and recognition, passing a deep learning model. Our methodology proposes the first attempt toward robot facial expression self-awareness. We discuss the crucial role of self-awareness in social robots and propose a CGAN (Conditional Generative Adversarial Network) model to generate robot facial expression images from motors' angle parameters. By using the CGAN method, the robot learns its facial self-awareness from a series of facial images. In addition, we introduce our robots facial self-awareness dataset. Our methodology can make the robot find the difference between self and others from its current generated image. The results show good performance and demonstrate the ability to achieve real-time robot facial self-awareness.

Keywords: Self-aware robot · Human-robot interaction · Generative adversarial network

1 Introduction

Self-awareness refers to "the capacity of becoming the object of one's attention" [1,7] and helps one to recognize the divergence between self and standards [23].

This work was supported by ENSTA Paris, Institut Polytechnique de Paris, France and the CSC PhD Scholarship.

Furthermore, self-awareness occurs to a person when one reflects on the knowledge of the perception and the process of the stimuli like seeing colorful objects or tasting food [19]. There is no doubt that human beings have the cognition of themselves and their facial expressions, speech, or other context experiences, even without seeing, smelling, touching, or hearing them. After around 2 years old, most kids can recognize themselves in a mirror [22]. For an adult, "What do I look like?", "Is my facial expression suitable in this situation?" are usually echoing or recalled in his/her minds [21]. We use the self-facial-awareness ability to appraise and manage our social behaviors. An accurate interpretation and representation of one's facial expression show crucial roles in social communications and interactions to control our emotional expression. In previous research [8], two types of self-awareness are given: private and public self-awareness. Private self-awareness means one's self-attention on internal aspects. Public self-awareness refers to one's self-attention on external, observable aspects [10]. The facial expression self-awareness, discussed in this paper, is part of public self-awareness, which means an imagery of one's face.

In order to develop autonomous robots capable of assisting humans in complex environments or solving complicated tasks, the development of cognitive abilities is considered to play an important role in accessing artificial intelligence [4]. Nowadays, physical machines have multiple sensors and powerful perceptual capabilities. With the development of computer vision methods, robots have acquired abilities to perceive and model the objective world in real-time with high precision [29,30]. However, for a social robot, perceiving only the information from the environment is not sufficient [27]. Social robots are expected to play a social role in our daily life [28,31]. They should have capabilities to understand humans, other robots, and themselves in social terms [3]. We are mainly interested in answering the following question: *How can robots understand themselves in social terms?*. Our approach to addressing this question is to make robots able to have facial self-awareness. In particular, we focus on making robots know about their facial appearance. We believe that a robot embodied by self-awareness in a control loop can perform better from a social point.

In the foreseeable future, the picture of artificial intelligence research is to make the machine think like humans [15]. By using deep learning (DL) methods, the knowledge is captured from data. The DL model will learn the distribution of data and generate new data by new stimuli from environments, which are sampled from the same data distribution. Our main idea is to use a DL model to make robots learn the knowledge about their own face. After learning, robots can memorize their own face and know how do they look like or what expressions they have expressed. Also if the robot have planed a sequence of motions, the robots can know what they will look like in the future and what will their expressions effect in the future to modify their current motions. Our approach to solving this problem is to use a GAN (Generative Adversarial Network) learning model.

In this paper, we propose a CGAN (Conditional Generative Adversarial Network) approach to achieve the robot facial self-awareness by generating robots facial images from servo motors angles. More specifically, we build a facial expression images dataset of Zeno robot [33]. This dataset is utilized as the knowledge to train a CGAN model. In this dataset, images of a Zeno robot face are recorded. These images show rich different facial expressions. The images are labeled with 6 motors' angle parameters. These parameters are corresponding to the motors, which drive the Zeno robot's facial expression at the same time. In this context, by using our CGAN model, we can generate Zeno robots' facial images from facial joints angles without monitor devices. By using the generated face images, the robot can recognize its current face among several face images. By PCA anlysis, the distinction of self's and the other's face images is visualised and clustered. We believe that this model is able to help robots better understand themselves in social terms and can be employed in various social scenarios.

The rest of the paper is structured as follows: Sect. 2 introduces the related works about self-awareness and GAN methods. Section 3 describes the methodology of problem definition, mapping solution, and evaluation methods; Sect. 4 shows the dataset building and the experiments. The experimental results are summarized in Sect. 5. The discussion is presented in Sect. 6. And finally, Sect. 7 concludes the paper.

2 Related Works

Many researchers have developed several robot facial expressions. For a long time, by using the Facial Action Coding System (FACS), researchers successfully designed and completed the emotion display robot [25]. Ishiguro et al. analyze and generate laughter motions in an android robot [14]. In [11], Goury et al. used a numerical method to model a flexible manipulator robot. Our goal is to generate humanoid robots face 2D images with robots joint state vector. Previous researches have proved the value of GAN in image generation [6]. Since CGAN was proposed in [17], controllable image generation techniques are gaining popularity. Researchers have used CGAN to make text2video generation [9] or image colourisation [2].

Robot self-awareness gives robots abilities to build self-model of robot bodies in a computational way without extra monitors. The traditional way to model robots morphology depends on special physical simulators [26]. Most of these methods are used in model rigid-body robots' joints action and self-collision avoidance. For robots with flexible material and facial expression (see Fig. 1), the self-modeling is still a difficult problem [11]. It is hard for some robots (e.g., Geminoid, see Fig. 1) to model facial skin variation linearly. However, robots could learn by themselves. Recently, progress in fully data-driven methods has enabled machines to learn their kinematics with interaction data. In [5], Chen et al. used a robot joint state vector to generate an entire robot arm 3D model with collected visual 3D data. This model can be aware of its shape and the distance to target efficiently.

Robot Geminoid HI   Robot Sophia   Robot Zeno   Robot ibuki   Eva Robot

Fig. 1. Humanoid Robots with facial expressions

Furthermore, in [24], the effects of perceptions of robotic self-recognition on service robots are investigated. The author suggests that the impact of self-recognition of service robots influences service quality. Researchers in [20] argue that the robot conceptually reasons on the context with self-awareness. And they make the robot pass the mirror test by inner speech. Authors in [16] used a theoretical model in a robot's brain for perception and action, with machine learning methods. Their robot achieves relation learning of its motions and its body. In [13], authors used machine learning methods to make robots pass the mirror test. Typically developed human beings have the self-awareness capability to imagine their appearance without actual visual information about their bodies by using the Mirror Self-Recognition (MSR) process. Theories suggested that self-knowledge is needed for MSR [18]. Our approach is more intuitive than the above methods, and the distinctions between self and others are presented in a clustered and visual way.

In our work, we use a CGAN model to generate robots facial images to equip humanoid robots with facial self-awareness.

3 Methodology

3.1 Problem Definition

Our experiment platform is a Zeno robot that has been depicted in Fig. 2. In our research, we are focusing on facial expressions. The Zeno's face structure and motors (PMW Driver) distribution are shown in Fig. 2. Six facial joints are driven by six motors. We aim at generating facial images from robot joints state space. The framework is shown in Fig. 1. It is a generation task in which the model should be able to map the motors' joints state to the facial self-awareness images. Similar to Zeno, most humanoid robots are built on a set of motor actions. These actions change the facial morphology directly. For a general humanoid robot, at one moment, the facial motor actions state X is defined in (1):

$$X = \{x_1, x_2, ..., x_i\} \tag{1}$$

Fig. 2. Zeno Robot. It is made for HRI research with 32 distinct facial expressions. There are 5 motors behind the face and 2 motors in the neck. To some extent, this platform can contribute to research about the treatment of autism spectrum disorder.

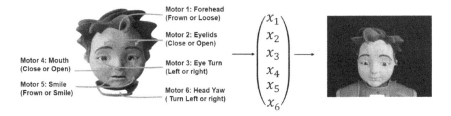

Fig. 3. Facial Self-Awareness Framework. We use 6 motors to map self facial images. These servo motors are driven by commands from the robot's computing center. Every command is a parameter that ranges from 0 to 10 ($0°$ to $180°$) in 0.03 s.

In (1), x_i is the i motor's joint state at time t. Therefore, there is a robot facial expression self-awareness A corresponding to X. In our research, we try to build a map from motor action space to facial self-awareness space as in (2):

$$X \longrightarrow A \tag{2}$$

The motors' angles $M = \{m_1, ..., m_i\}$ represent the states of actions X, therefore, $M \longrightarrow X$. We use a self facial RGB image $Y_{self} = Y_{self}^{w \times h \times 3}$ to present the facial self-awareness A, therefore, $Y \longrightarrow A$. Hence, the problem is defined as in (3).

$$M \longrightarrow Y_{self}^{w \times h \times 3} \tag{3}$$

When the robot recognize itself in a mirror or perceive others' face in social situations, we use the detected face image Y_{other} to compare with the robot self-facial-expression Y_{self}. The distance $D_{self-aware}$ between two face is the difference between self and the detected object (4).

$$D_{self-aware} = Y_{self} - Y_{perception} \tag{4}$$

3.2   Mapping Solution

As discussed in Sect. 3.1, CGAN is used to make this mapping. In a basic GAN, the goal is to train a generator G, which is able to generate high-quality images, and a discriminator D, which is able to classify images whether they are from the original distribution. In (5), it shows the training process of GAN.

$$\min_{G} \max_{D} V(D, G) = \mathbb{E}_{Y \sim p_{\text{data}}(Y)}[\log D(Y)] \\ + \mathbb{E}_{z \sim p_z(z)}[1 - \log D(G(z))] \tag{5}$$

Moreover, with CGAN, we can generate images with corresponding labels. Therefore, in our paper, the training process of GAN is shown in (6). Therefore, Y represents the facial images, M represents the motors' angles, z is the Gaussian noise.

$$\min_{G} \max_{D} V(D, G) = \mathbb{E}_{Y \sim p_{\text{data}}(Y)}[\log D(Y \mid M)] \\ + \mathbb{E}_{z \sim p_z(z)}[1 - \log D(G(z \mid M))] \tag{6}$$

The generator G is composed of Deconvolutional Networks [32]. For one layer Deconvolutional Network, an image y, is composed of K_0 color channels. Each channel c is a linear sum of K_1 latent feature map z_k convolved with filters $f_{k,c}$ (7).

$$\sum_{k=1}^{K_1} z_k \oplus f_{k,c} = y_c \tag{7}$$

The discriminator D is composed with Convolutional Networks. For one layer Convolutional Network, an image y is extracted to a latent feature map z_k with filters $f_{k,c}$ (8).

$$\sum_{k=1}^{K_1} y_c \oplus f_{c,k} = z_k \tag{8}$$

In the generator G, we use multiple ReLU (see (9)) as layers activation function and one Tanh (see 10) as output activation function. In the discriminator, LeakyReLUs (see 11) are used as layers activation function one Sigmoid (see 12) is output activation function.

$$Relu(z) = max(0, z) \tag{9}$$

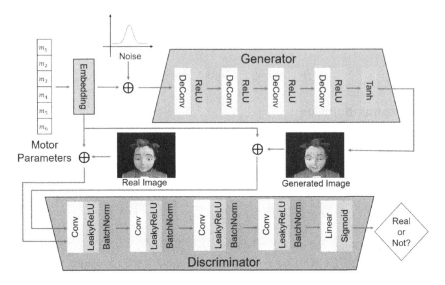

Fig. 4. The pipeline of facial self-awareness CGAN model. The commands of motors' parameters are directly calculated in the robot computing center. Therefore, when a robot shows its facial expression, there is an image of its self-face generated at the same time. This is how we check if the robot is aware of its own face.

$$Tanh(z) = \frac{e^z - e^{-z}}{e^z + e^{-z}} = \frac{1 - e^{-2z}}{1 + e^{-2z}} \tag{10}$$

$$LeakyReLu(z) = max(0, z) + \alpha * min(0, z) \tag{11}$$

$$\sigma(z) = \frac{1}{1 + e^{-z}} \tag{12}$$

In the whole model, the training loss is evaluated by two Binary Cross Entropy (BCE) function (see 13).

$$Loss = -(y\log(p) + (1 - y)\log(1 - p)) \tag{13}$$

Above all, the facial self-awareness framework is shown in Fig. 3. Our CGAN approach structure is shown in Fig. 4.

3.3   Evaluation

Evaluation of Generation. The Frechet Inception Distance (FID) is used to evaluate the quality of generated images and to find the best generation model. FID can capture the similarity of generated images to real ones [12]. It is commonly used in GAN methods. Equation (14) shows the calculation of FID scores. d^2 is FID, which will be high when images are quite far from original distribution. The μ_1 and μ_2 refer to the mean features of the original and generated images. C_1 and C_2 are the covariance matrix of original and generated feature vectors. Tr is the trace of the matrix.

$$d^2 = ||\mu_1 - \mu_2||^2 + Tr(C_1 + C_2 - 2 * \sqrt{C_1 * C_2}) \tag{14}$$

Evaluation of Generation of Self/Other of Distinction. Part of the Mirror Test is used to evaluate the robot self-facial-awareness abilities. We give the robot kinds of images (i.e., its face currently, its face currently with a mark, others' similar face) to recognize whether the images are its current self-face. Specifically, we subtract the generated image from the image, and then use PCA to reduce the dimension and plot the distance out.

4   Database Building and Experiment Process

4.1   Database Building

To build our model, we developed an experimental environment to collect facial data labeled by motors' angles. We installed a camera in front of the robot and recorded the images of robot facial expression. To avoid environmental variations, the light in the room was constant. The robot stood in front of a black curtain. A script capable of changing the different facial expressions of the robot by changing the 6 motors' angle parameters inside the robot's head was developed. We recorded the 6 motors angle parameters and the robot face image of different facial expressions. The dataset is composed of more than 200,000 images, and each image matches 6 motors' parameters inside the robot's head. For each image, the resolution is $640 \times 480 \times 3$. In this way, we get a mapping from the robot's joints states data to the facial expression images. This dataset is available upon request. Other details and discussion about self-awareness can be found in our previous work [33].

4.2   Experiment Process

For our experiment, we resized the images to $320 \times 240 \times 3$. Then, we normalized the tensor images with mean ($[0.5, 0.5, 0.5]$) and standard deviation ($[0.5, 0.5, 0.5]$). The batch size is 64. The Adam optimizer was used with an initial learning rate of 2×10^{-4}. As shown in Fig. 4, in the generator G, the label matrix $M_{6 \times 1}$ is embedded to be $M'_{6 \times 48}$. The $noise_{1 \times 256}$ is sampled from a Gaussian Distribution and transferred to be $noise'_{1 \times 48}$. $M'_{6 \times 48}$, and the $noise'_{1 \times 48}$ are concatenated and converted by several transposed CNN to generate image $Y^{320 \times 240 \times 3}$. For the discriminator D, embedded label $M'_{6 \times 48}$ is concatenated to real or fake images $Y^{320 \times 240 \times 3}$ and converted by several CNN layers to make the classification. The model was trained for 200 epochs. The training loss changes of G and D are shown in Fig. 5. We saved the modal every 4 epochs. Each model generated 5000 images after every 4 epochs to calculate the FID score between original data and generated data. The FID performance of the model in training processing is shown in Fig. 6. The Neural Network experiment platform is Pytorch.

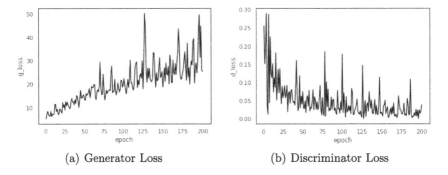

(a) Generator Loss   (b) Discriminator Loss

Fig. 5. Training loss

5   Results

After model training and selection, we chose the model in the 192 epoch to be the final model. We generated a set of images from the angles parameters and we compared them with ground truth images (real facial images in the same motor angles, see Fig. 8). We also tested the time cost of generating one image (see Fig. 7). The average time cost of generation is of 0.023 s, which is lower than 0.03 s. The execution time of robot motors is set to be 0.03 s. However, in real scenarios, the execution time is much longer than the set parameter. Therefore, we can achieve real-time facial images awareness. By using this model, we evaluate the self/other distinction abilities.

We give the robot several face images as we have discussed in Sect. 3.3 to calculate the distinction between self and others. After calculation, we use PCA to reduce the dimension of the result and visualize it. The distinction cluster is

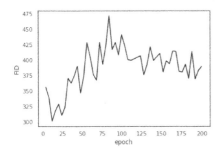

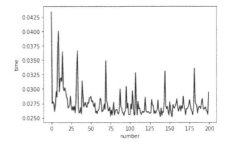

Fig. 6. FID score   **Fig. 7.** Time cost of once generation

shown in Fig. 9. As is shown in Fig. 9, the self-images captured by the camera, no matter with or without a mark, are clustered together in the center, and the self-images recorded by the camera in the past are clustered and far away from the center.

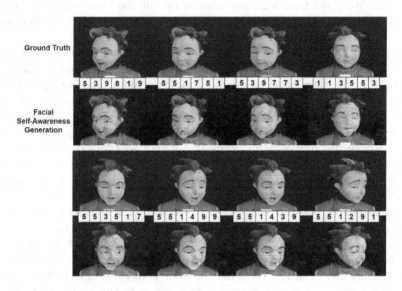

Fig. 8. The generation performance of CGAN Model. The 6 numbers refer to the 6 motors parameters (0° to 180°).

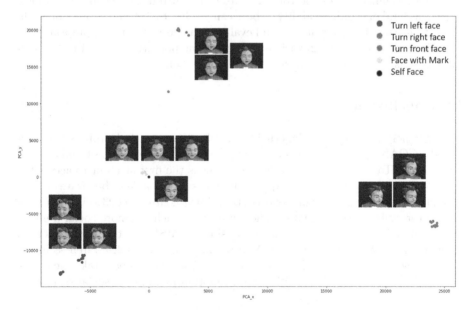

Fig. 9. The self/others distinction visualization

6   Discussions

Self-awareness has attracted much attention and has been discussed for several years. It is defined as being aware of oneself, including one's traits, feelings, and behaviors. We posit that self-awareness as one of the basic cognitive abilities in human beings will always be an interesting construct that will allow social robots to achieve cognitive abilities.

Obviously, the key to this ambition is to understand the relationship between knowledge, perception, and the action of a robot. In our opinion, for a self-aware robot, the perception is not only about including the perception of the environment but also about the perception of itself. The actions of the motor also can capture knowledge and influence decision-making. Our experiment and the work in [5] suggest that a robot with more prior knowledge about itself is able to reduce the information capture in different scenarios in which the robot needs information about the self. Deep learning provides a way to memorize and learn prior knowledge in a more general way. One big shortage of deep learning is that the model is too big to run in real-time.

In our research, the data generation is sufficiently fast to react to environmental stimuli. In [19], authors support that the inner speech and the imagery are two ways to exchange information with self and to make reflected appraisals, taking others' perceptive, and audience. Our approach achieves part of self-imagery by generating facial images. By using the prior knowledge-based DL model, the robots have the potential to recognize themselves in the mirror and pass the MSR. Our facial self-awareness model based on visual knowledge can provide real-time visualization of the robot's state of its current 2D facial morphology. With this kind of cognitive ability, robots can predict their facial expression without actually moving their motors and evaluate the impact of the appropriateness of their facial expressions in various contexts. The potential of multi-modal self-awareness is therefore an important question to address.

7   Conclusion

In our paper, we discussed the crucial role of self-awareness in robots and proposed a CGAN approach to generate facial images from the robot's facial motors' parameters. To the best of our knowledge, this is the first attempt to access the facial self-awareness robot. This approach makes robots able to be aware of their own facial expressions. The model execution time ($Mean = 0.023\,s$) is lower than the motor reaction time ($0.03\,s$). Therefore, it can achieve more social abilities in real-time. Future work will focus on passing the MSR and the development of multi-modal self-awareness robots. Also the application of self-awareness in the context-awareness tasks in HRI is considered: Making the robots take the future action effects into consideration in current motion planning in social situations.

References

1. Birlo, M., Tapus, A.: The crucial role of robot self-awareness in hri. In: 2011 6th ACM/IEEE International Conference on Human-Robot Interaction (HRI), pp. 115–116. IEEE (2011)
2. Blanch, M.G., Mrak, M., Smeaton, A.F., O'Connor, N.E.: End-to-end conditional gan-based architectures for image colourisation. In: 2019 IEEE 21st International Workshop on Multimedia Signal Processing (MMSP), pp. 1–6. IEEE (2019)
3. Breazeal, C.: Designing Sociable Robots. MIT press, Cambridge (2004)
4. Cangelosi, A., Asada, M.: Cognitive robotics (2022)
5. Chen, B., Kwiatkowski, R., Vondrick, C., Lipson, H.: Full-body visual self-modeling of robot morphologies. arXiv preprint arXiv:2111.06389 (2021)
6. Creswell, A., White, T., Dumoulin, V., Arulkumaran, K., Sengupta, B., Bharath, A.A.: Generative adversarial networks: an overview. IEEE Signal Process. Maga. **35**(1), 53–65 (2018)
7. Duval, S., Wicklund, R.A.: A theory of objective self awareness (1972)
8. Fenigstein, A., Scheier, M.F., Buss, A.H.: Public and private self-consciousness: assessment and theory. J. Consult. Clin. Psychol. **43**, 522–527 (1975)
9. Ganguli, S., Garzon, P., Glaser, N.: Geogan: A conditional gan with reconstruction and style loss to generate standard layer of maps from satellite images. arXiv preprint arXiv:1902.05611 (2019)
10. George, L., Stopa, L.: Private and public self-awareness in social anxiety. J. Behav. Therapy Exp. Psychiat. **39**(1), 57–72 (2008)
11. Goury, O., Carrez, B., Duriez, C.: Real-time simulation for control of soft robots with self-collisions using model order reduction for contact forces. IEEE Rob. Autom. Lett. **6**(2), 3752–3759 (2021)
12. Heusel, M., Ramsauer, H., Unterthiner, T., Nessler, B., Hochreiter, S.: Gans trained by a two time-scale update rule converge to a local nash equilibrium. Adv. Neural Inf. Process. Syst. **30**, 1–12 (2017)
13. Hoffmann, M., Wang, S., Outrata, V., Alzueta, E., Lanillos, P.: Robot in the mirror: toward an embodied computational model of mirror self-recognition. KI-Künstliche Intelligenz **35**(1), 37–51 (2021)
14. Ishi, C.T., Minato, T., Ishiguro, H.: Analysis and generation of laughter motions, and evaluation in an android robot. APSIPA Trans. Signal Inf. Process. **8**, 1–10 (2019)
15. Lake, B.M., Ullman, T.D., Tenenbaum, J.B., Gershman, S.J.: Building machines that learn and think like people. Behav. Brain Sci. **40**, 1–72 (2017)
16. Lanillos, P., Cheng, G., et al.: Robot self/other distinction: active inference meets neural networks learning in a mirror. arXiv preprint arXiv:2004.05473 (2020)
17. Mirza, M., Osindero, S.: Conditional generative adversarial nets. arXiv preprint arXiv:1411.1784 (2014)
18. Mitchell, R.W.: Mental models of mirror-self-recognition: two theories. New Ideas Psychol. **11**(3), 295–325 (1993)
19. Morin, A.: Self-awareness part 1: definition, measures, effects, functions, and antecedents. Social Pers. Psychol. Compass **5**(10), 807–823 (2011)
20. Pipitone, A., Chella, A.: Robot passes the mirror test by inner speech. Rob. Auton. Syst. **144**, 103838 (2021)
21. Qu, F., Yan, W.J., Chen, Y.H., Li, K., Zhang, H., Fu, X.: "You should have seen the look on your face": self-awareness of facial expressions. Front. Psychol. **8**, 832 (2017)

22. Rochat, P.: Five levels of self-awareness as they unfold early in life. Conscious. Cogn. **12**(4), 717–731 (2003)
23. Silvia, P.J., Duval, T.S.: Self-awareness, self-motives, and self-motivation. In: Motivational Analyses of Social Behavior: Building on Jack Brehm's Contributions to Psychology, pp. 57–75 (2004)
24. Söderlund, M.: When service robots look at themselves in the mirror: an examination of the effects of perceptions of robotic self-recognition. J. Retail. Cons. Serv. **64**, 102820 (2022)
25. Sosnowski, S., Bittermann, A., Kuhnlenz, K., Buss, M.: Design and evaluation of emotion-display eddie. In: 2006 IEEE/RSJ International Conference on Intelligent Robots and Systems, pp. 3113–3118. IEEE (2006)
26. Todorov, E., Erez, T., Tassa, Y.: Mujoco: a physics engine for model-based control. In: 2012 IEEE/RSJ International Conference on Intelligent Robots and Systems, pp. 5026–5033. IEEE (2012)
27. Yu, C.: Robot Behavior Generation and Human Behavior Understanding in Natural Human-Robot Interaction. Ph.D. thesis, Institut Polytechnique de Paris (2021)
28. Yu, C., Changzeng, F., Chen, R., Tapus, A.: First attempt of gender-free speech style transfer for genderless robot. In: 2022 ACM/IEEE International Conference on Human-Robot Interaction, pp. 1110–1113 (2022)
29. Yu, C., Tapus, A.: Interactive robot learning for multimodal emotion recognition. In: Salichs, M.A., et al. (eds.) ICSR 2019. LNCS (LNAI), vol. 11876, pp. 633–642. Springer, Cham (2019). https://doi.org/10.1007/978-3-030-35888-4_59
30. Yu, C., Tapus, A.: Multimodal emotion recognition with thermal and rgb-d cameras for human-robot interaction. In: Companion of the 2020 ACM/IEEE International Conference on Human-Robot Interaction, pp. 532–534 (2020)
31. Yu, C., Tapus, A.: Srg 3: speech-driven robot gesture generation with gan. In: 2020 16th International Conference on Control, Automation, Robotics and Vision (ICARCV), pp. 759–766. IEEE (2020)
32. Zeiler, M.D., Krishnan, D., Taylor, G.W., Fergus, R.: Deconvolutional networks. In: 2010 IEEE Computer Society Conference on Computer Vision and Pattern Recognition, pp. 2528–2535. IEEE (2010)
33. Zhegong, S., Yu, C., Tapus, A.: What do i look like? dataset for social robot facial expression self-awareness. In: Workshop on Robot Curiosity in Human Robot Interaction (RCHRI). University of Waterloo (2022)

Modeling and Evaluation of Human Motor Learning by Finger Manipulandum

Amr Okasha[1]([✉]), Sabahat Şengezer[2], Ozancan Özdemir[1], Ceylan Yozgatlıgil[1], Ali E. Turgut[1], and Kutluk B. Arıkan[2]

[1] Middle East Technical University, Ankara, Turkey
okasha.amr@metu.edu.tr
[2] TED University, Ankara, Turkey

Abstract. A finger manipulandum was developed to assess human motor learning in a virtual mirror game. The task is the leader-follower modality in the mirror paradigm. The follower in the virtual dynamic system is controlled by the force generated by the interaction between human and manipulandum due to pinching. One participant played the game for five consecutive days. The player's kinematic tracking error was found to fit the free energy model leading to motor learning. In addition, the acquired data were processed with a machine learning algorithm to predict the retention data. Both the free energy model and predictors were found to provide promising results for more detailed motor learning models of healthy subjects and stroke patients.

Keywords: Finger manipulandum · Mirror paradigm · Free energy · Machine learning

1 Introduction

Stroke is one of the leading causes of the loss of motor functions in patients [1]. Stroke patients often require intensive sessions of rehabilitation to partially or completely regain their lost motor abilities [2]. Robot-aided rehabilitation utilizes the advantage of using robotics to provide rehabilitation for patients [3–6]. Moreover, it has been shown to be beneficial in upper-limp rehabilitation [7]; however, more work needs to be done make robot-aided rehabilitation more accessible. Virtual reality (VR) systems, on the other hand, provide further possibilities, as demonstrated in [8], where Sveistrup assessed several settings. According to the assessment, the combination of VR and haptic interfaces offered greater outcomes in terms of patient engagement by giving more diversity. These haptic interfaces are frequently used as an assistive device to help motor learning/relearning of daily activities (ADLs) [9]. The recovery goal of rehabilitation for stroke patients is to regain the motor function they were performing before the stroke. Motor relearning is assumed to govern the motor recovery if the type of loss to be addressed by rehabilitation is known, the type of motor learning to be targeted is known, and the patient has an undamaged learning ability [10]. Motor relearning is thought to take the same elements as motor learning in healthy people. Therefore, understanding

© The Author(s), under exclusive license to Springer Nature Switzerland AG 2022
F. Cavallo et al. (Eds.): ICSR 2022, LNAI 13817, pp. 325–334, 2022.
https://doi.org/10.1007/978-3-031-24667-8_29

and modeling motor learning in healthy individuals will help to understand the process of motor relearning that aids the patient to reach motor recovery [11].

Various models for studying motor learning exist in the literature. A recently developed model of motor learning is based on the free energy principle. The Free Energy Principle (FEP) is a mathematical theory that attempts to explain brain structure and function by drawing on developments in statistics, physics, theoretical biology, and the machine learning [12]. In general, the FEP states that all biological agents strive to maintain their equilibrium in the face of negative external influences and to actively control internal equilibrium under changing environmental conditions [13]. The FEP, therefore, proposes to conceptualize human learning as a process of entropy minimization through "active inference," while the brain encodes a Bayesian network whose neural dynamics are governed by a generative model that predicts sensory data [14]. In addition, model-based and model-free approaches to learning motor control schedules are also discussed in [15]. Ueyama applied system identification techniques to model motor learning and recovery revealing adaptation and generalization functions by linear state space models [16]. Similarly, Casadio et al. proposed a linear model to predict the performance of impaired subjects during robot-assisted exercise, and they claim that using computational models is promising to predict the outcomes of robotic rehabilitation [17]. In [18, 19], a feedforward type of artificial neural network is used to model the use-dependent recovery of locomotor force and learning is simulated by a biologically plausible reinforcement learning algorithm. They show that the model makes predictions that are consistent with clinical and brain imaging data. In [20], the effects of control systems on motor relearning in a robotic hand exoskeleton are simulated. Reinforcement learning is used to model voluntary torque generation by the subject during the rehabilitation process. It is shown that the kinematic control system that does not interact with the patient results in slacking. Finally, the mirror paradigm is used as the control task in this work. ADLs can also include activities in conjunction with others [21]. Thus, a commonly used approach in the literature to promote imitation and social coordination is the mirror game, in which players attempt to imitate each other's movements in one of two modalities: Leader-Follower (LF) or Joint Improvisation [22]. Indeed, several works have shown that through haptic interactions, better overall motor performance can be achieved for both the leader and the follower [23, 24].

Accordingly, a new experimental setup is proposed in this paper, consisting of a pinching manipulandum and a VR-based mirror game in LF mode as a motor control task. The virtual leader makes a compound movement consisting of three sine waves. The follower avatar is controlled by the unidirectional force generated by the interaction between human and manipulandum due to pinching. To move the avatar in the opposite direction, the user must learn to use the gravity prevailing in the virtual reality system. The data collected during the compound learning task is expected to provide models for motor learning. The manipulandum is used by a healthy individual for five consecutive days in this proof-of-concept study, and the data collected is analyzed to model and assess the motor learning of the participant.

2   Materials and Methods

In this section, the physical setup containing a mirror game that is driven by a finger manipulandum is presented. In this human-robot interaction setup, the user learns to gauge the force that is applied using the manipulandum to achieve an acceptable tracking performance.

2.1   Virtual Mirror Game and Pinching Manipulandum

Virtual Mirror Game. A leader-follower type mirror game is implemented in Simulink® Desktop Real-Time 2021b where the player controls the vertical motion of a box in free fall. The game environment is designed using V-Realm Editor and is shown in Fig. 1. Given a predefined leader motion [23, 25], the user attempts to track the leader by applying a unidirectional force that is used to move the box upwards; the downwards motion is achieved by using simulated gravity (~0.5 g). The unidirectional nature of the force created a demanding experience in which the participants had to somewhat oppose the gravitational force during descending action in order to maintain synchronized motion with the leader. The tracking performance is calculated in real-time using a position error-based score metric and displayed to the user on the screen [26]. The score is calculated as,

$$T_f^{-1} \int_0^{T_f} e_{max} - |y_F(t) - y_L(t)| \, dt \tag{1}$$

In Eq. 1, t is the elapsed time, e_{max} is the maximum tolerable error, y_F and y_L are the follower's and leader's positions, respectively, T_f is the round duration.

Fig. 1. Hand pinching the manipulandum (Left). The tracking mirror game. (Right)

Pinching Manipulandum. End-effector-based rehabilitation tools are widely used in robot-assisted rehabilitation applications. Planar manipulanda [27, 28] are used in various studies to assess motor learning behavior in healthy individuals and patients. They are commonly driven by interaction-type controllers and are used to provide haptic interaction between the users and a virtual environment [24]. A pinching manipulandum refers to an apparatus designed to facilitate pinching action applied with the index and thumb fingers [29, 30]. In this paper, a pinching manipulandum is developed to perform haptic interaction between the users and the mirror game. To achieve pinching action, two ergonomic finger pads were constrained by horizontal sliders. These sliders were controlled using a centered, double slider-crank mechanism that is actuated by a single motor (Maxon EC-max 60W). A force sensor (Honeywell FSG15N1A) was placed against the finger pad such that the force is directed through lever action from the fingertips. The measured force was used to drive an admittance controller which rendered a virtual spring-damper system at the fingertips, creating a human-robot interaction scheme, Fig. 2. The generated pinching force is transmitted through a data acquisition board (National Instruments PCI-6229 M Series) at 2 kHz to a real-time control system to control the manipulandum motor and run the aforementioned mirror game.

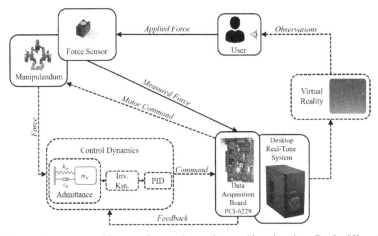

Fig. 2. Shows the system architecture for sensing, using, and logging data. Dashed lines indicate systems implemented in software.

2.2 Models for Motor Learning

As stated in [31], the FEP involves the Bayesian brain hypothesis, which states that brain function explores how well the nervous system can operate under uncertain conditions in a way that approximates the ideal recommended by Bayesian statistics: the idea that the brain is an inference machine [32]. In this work, an exponential model is used to describe the complex nature of motor learning [14]. The model is given as,

$$y = ae^{bx} \tag{2}$$

where, the coefficients a and b can be interpreted as the initial magnitude of variability and the decay rate, respectively, where x is the round number and y is a performance error metric.

In addition, two machine learning approaches are utilized to predict the performance of the participant. The first approach trains a Long Short-Term Memory (LSTM) [33, 34] network using the training dataset to predict the last day's performance. The second approach uses a tree-based machine learning models to evaluate which rounds were the most prominent for the motor learning of the participant.

2.3 Experimental Design

In this proof-of-concept study, one participant (female, age 31) played the mirror tracking game using the manipulandum. Over five consecutive days, the participant played a total of 104 rounds. A round is defined as the 30- or 60-s-long tracking task that is described in Sect. 2.1. At the beginning, the baseline skill level is assessed by playing two 60-s rounds (BL), afterwards and over 5 consecutive days, the participant played 20 30-s rounds per day for a total 100 rounds (T). On the fifth day, the skill level was assessed again by two 60-s rounds (R) identical to the baseline. The experimental protocol is shown in Fig. 3. Importantly, BL and R rounds had identical leader motion patterns, whereas the TR rounds had reversed leader motion pattern [14, 26].

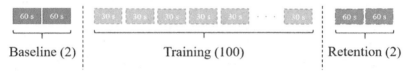

Fig. 3. Presents the experimental protocol used to collect the data. The training data is collected as batches of 20 rounds over 5 consecutive days.

The RMSE provides a measure of the error between the leader and follower's position. As a result, this metric can be thought of as a measure of synchrony between the leader and the follower. It is defined as, [35]

$$RMSE = \frac{1}{L}\sqrt{\sum_{k=1}^{n} \frac{1}{n}\left(x_{L,k} - x_{F,k}\right)^2} \tag{3}$$

where L is the position range, n is the number of time intervals, and the x's refer to the positions of the leader and follower at the kth sample step. It is expected to see this metric decrease as the participants play more rounds of the game; this can be correlated with the motor learning performance. Indeed, this metric is used to fit the free energy function.

3 Results and Discussion

3.1 Free Energy Model

The free energy model is fitted to the data collected over 5 days. The position data of the leader and the pursuer for 100 training rounds were used to determine the RMSE for each round separately. The resulting scatter plot is shown in Fig. 4. Each data point refers to the RMSE of a single round. Then the free energy model (Eq. 2) is fitted to the scatter plot. The exponential fitting coefficients $a = 0.234$ and $b = -0.00914$ are determined with 95% confidence and are consistent with the expectations of the model in [14]. According to the FEP, the data fit shows the specific rate and variance of the subject's motor learning during the training period. To evaluate the error densities, Bayesian Regression modeling is used [36–38]. The entire distribution of Fig. 4 is defined as the density of the error of the participant. While the black line (y) represents the density of the original error, the other thin lines represent the posterior predictive distribution (y_{rep}), which represents the predicted error based on the Bayesian model. The density distribution figure demonstrates that the posterior projected data is more comparable to the true data. The validation of the Bayesian model also supports the free energy model for motor learning.

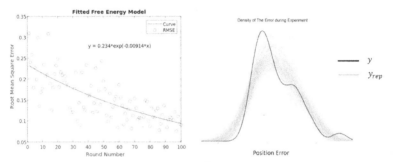

Fig. 4. (Left) The free energy fitted model $y = ae^{bx}$ for the obtained RMSE values. (Right) The probability of the position error density of the Bayesian model for multiple predictors (day and rounds).

3.2 Use of Long Short-Term Memories (LSTM) and Tree-Based Predictive Models

Using the training data from the training session, an LSTM type of artificial neural network [34] is trained to predict the subject's position response (i.e., the location of the follower avatar) on the fifth day. Each day's 20th training session is utilized in the network to narrow down the data, Fig. 5 (left). In this study, the past 4 lags were given to the LSTM architecture as a time-delay embedding to capture the auto-correlation [39]. In the architecture of LSTM, 1 recurrent layer and 2 features in the hidden state are used. The nonlinearity is supplied by the tanh function. The LSTM layer ends with one linear layer which applies the linear transformation to incoming data. For training the network, an Adam optimizer with a learning rate of 0.01 is used, and the loss function is set as the mean square error. 2000 epochs are needed to train the LSTM. Figure 5 (right) shows the performance of the predictor. In addition to the visual representation, the forecasting performance of the LSTM is evaluated by calculating the RMSE score on the test data. The RMSE of the model for the test data is 0.053 which indicates that the model has a considerable prediction capability.

Furthermore, a tree-based machine learning algorithm for predicting the user's R1 and R2 responses is developed with the aim of understanding which training round is effective in the prediction of R1 and R2; this is achieved through the variable importance property of tree algorithms. All processes are conducted using Jupyter Notebook and related Python libraries including Pandas, Sklearn, Xgboost, and Shap.

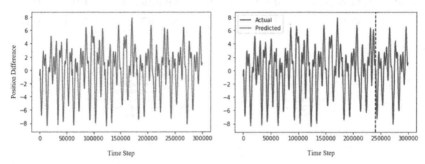

Fig. 5. (Left) Shows serially-combined position error data for each T20 in the five consecutive days. (Right) Shows the prediction of the LSTM.

Before starting the modeling, the dataset is divided randomly into two parts; train (80%) and test (20%). After that, the train data is again randomly divided into the train (80%) and validation sets (20%). The parameters of applied models are tuned using the random search approach. Two tree-based algorithms, which are Random Forest and Xgboost, are applied and compared concerning R^2 and $RMSE$. The prediction performance of both models for validation and test sets is given in Table 1. It is seen that the Xgboost model outperforms Random Forest in the prediction of the position of the user in the R1 and R2. Next, which round of the game is the most effective in the prediction of the position of the user can be explored using a beeswarm plot of the model created by SHAP. SHAP is a game-theoretical Shapley value-based method to explain the machine learning model. It is seen in Fig. 6 that the most effective training round on R1 is the 6th round, followed by the 14th and 7th rounds. Therefore, it can be said that when the performance of the user in the 6th round increases, then the performance of the user in the R1 round also increases. On the other hand, it can be said that when the score of the user in the 14th round increases, the score of the user in R1 decreases. It is seen in Fig. 6 that the most effective training round on R2 is the 14th round, followed by the 9th and 7th rounds. It can be said that when the position score of the user in the 14th round increases, then the position score of the user in R2 decreases. A similar interpretation can be also made for round 9. However, the R2 score decreases when the 7th round score decreases.

Table 1. The performance of Random Forest and Xgboost in the prediction of R1 and R2

		R^2	RMSE		R^2	RMSE
Random Forest	Validation (R1)	0.276	2.316	Validation (R2)	0.313	2.229
	Test (R1)	0.278	2.311	Test (R2)	0.314	2.233
XgBoost	Validation (R1)	0.998	0.120	Validation (R2)	0.998	0.120
	Test(R1)	0.998	0.126	Test (R2)	0.998	0.116

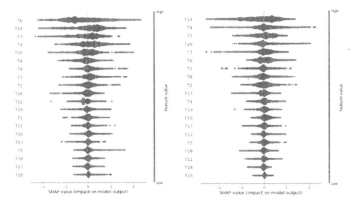

Fig. 6. Shows the SHAP plots for R1 (left) and R2 (right).

4 Conclusion

In this paper, we briefly described the pinching manipulandum system, which was developed to measure motor learning in healthy people at first. Continuous implicit learning in the leader-follower modality is combined with learning to generate unidirectional force and use the gravitational field to locomote the follower. Such a challenge must be tailored to the skill level of the participants. The primary goal of our study is to develop subject-specific motor learning models. The initial phase of model construction is led by basic exponential functions derived from the free energy principle and predictors derived from machine learning methods. These models will then be combined with more structured learning models to replicate more complex motor control policies. They will also serve as previous knowledge for subject-specific reinforcement learning models. It is critical to evaluate the most efficient rounds or sessions for motor learning to develop optimal rehabilitation programs. It is important to increase the number of participants in order to demonstrate that data from the proposed experimental platform is used to construct subject-specific and distinguishable models. Manipulandum will be used as an end effector kind of rehabilitation robot for stroke patients, as well as in conjunction with an exoskeleton type of robotic system to serve as an interaction environment for the VR mirror therapy protocol. Finally, it is proposed to construct patient-specific optimal robotic hand rehabilitation systems with control systems that impose personalized entropic sources in order to maximize motor relearning.

References

1. Raffin, E., Hummel, F.: Restoring motor functions after stroke: multiple approaches and opportunities. Neuroscientist **24**(4), 400–416 (2017)
2. Hatem, S., et al.: Rehabilitation of motor function after stroke: a multiple systematic review focused on techniques to stimulate upper extremity recovery. Front. Hum. Neurosci. **10** (2016)
3. Krebs, H., Hogan, N., Aisen, M., Volpe, B.: Robot-aided neurorehabilitation. IEEE Trans. Rehabil. Eng. **6**(1), 75–87 (1998)
4. Colombo, R., et al.: Design strategies to improve patient motivation during robot-aided rehabilitation. J. NeuroEng. Rehab. **4**(1) (2007)
5. Volpe, B., Krebs, H., Hogan, N., Edelstein, L., Diels, C., Aisen, M.: A novel approach to stroke rehabilitation. Neurology **54**(10), 1938–1944 (2000)
6. Oña, E., Garcia-Haro, J., Jardón, A., Balaguer, C.: Robotics in health care: perspectives of robot-aided interventions in clinical practice for rehabilitation of upper limbs. Appl. Sci. **9**(13), 2586 (2019)
7. Babaiasl, M., Mahdioun, S., Jaryani, P., Yazdani, M.: A review of technological and clinical aspects of robot-aided rehabilitation of upper-extremity after stroke. Disab. Rehab. Assist. Technol. 1–18 (2015)
8. Sveistrup, H.: J. NeuroEng. Rehab. **1**(1), 10 (2004)
9. Colombo, R., Sanguineti, V.: Assistive controllers and modalities for robot-aided neurorehabilitation. Rehab. Robot. 63–74 (2018)
10. Krakauer, J.: The applicability of motor learning to neurorehabilitation. Oxford Textbook of Neurorehabilitation, pp. 55–64 (2015). https://doi.org/10.1093/med/9780199673711.003.0007
11. Krakauer, J., Hadjiosif, A., Xu, J., Wong, A., Haith, A.: Motor Learning. Comprehensive Physiology, pp. 613–663 (2019). https://doi.org/10.1002/cphy.c170043
12. Friston, K.: The free-energy principle: a rough guide to the brain? Trends Cogn. Sci. **13**(7), 293–301 (2009)
13. Demekas, D., Parr, T., Friston, K.J.: An investigation of the free energy principle for emotion recognition. Front. Comput. Neurosci. **14** (2020)
14. Brookes, J., et al.: Exploring disturbance as a force for good in motor learning (2019)
15. Haith, A., Krakauer, J.: Model-based and model-free mechanisms of human motor learning. Advances in Experimental Medicine and Biology, pp. 1–21 (2013). https://doi.org/10.1007/978-1-4614-5465-6_1
16. Ueyama, Y.: System identification of neural mechanisms from trial-by-trial motor behaviour: modelling of learning, impairment and recovery. Adv. Robot. **31**(3), 107–117 (2016). https://doi.org/10.1080/01691864.2016.1266966
17. Casadio, M., Sanguineti, V.: Learning, retention, and slacking: a model of the dynamics of recovery in robot therapy. IEEE Trans. Neural Syst. Rehab. Eng. **20**(3), 286–296 (2012). https://doi.org/10.1109/tnsre.2012.2190827
18. Reinkensmeyer, D., et al.: Computational neurorehabilitation: modeling plasticity and learning to predict recovery. J. NeuroEng. Rehab. **13**(1) (2016). https://doi.org/10.1186/s12984-016-0148-3
19. Reinkensmeyer, D., Guigon, E., Maier, M.: A computational model of use-dependent motor recovery following a stroke: Optimizing corticospinal activations via reinforcement learning can explain residual capacity and other strength recovery dynamics. Neural Networks **29–30**, 60–69 (2012). https://doi.org/10.1016/j.neunet.2012.02.002
20. Yağmur, O.: Model-based Evaluation of the Control Strategies of a Hand Rehabilitation Robot Based on Motor Learning Principles. Middle East Technical University, MSc (2022)

21. Konvalinka, I., Vuust, P., Roepstorff, A., Frith, C.: Follow you, follow me: continuous mutual prediction and adaptation in joint tapping. Quar. J. Exper. Psychol. **63**(11), 2220–2230 (2010)
22. Noy, L., Dekel, E., Alon, U.: The mirror game as a paradigm for studying the dynamics of two people improvising motion together. Proc. Natl. Acad. Sci. **108**(52), 20947–20952 (2011)
23. Takagi, A., Ganesh, G., Yoshioka, T., Kawato, M., Burdet, E.: Physically interacting individuals estimate the partner's goal to enhance their movements. Nature Hum. Behav. **1**(3) (2017)
24. Ganesh, G., Takagi, A., Osu, R., Yoshioka, T., Kawato, M., Burdet, E.: Two is better than one: physical interactions improve motor performance in humans. Sci. Rep. **4**(1) (2014)
25. Künzell, S., Sießmeir, D., Ewolds, H.: Validation of the continuous tracking paradigm for studying implicit motor learning. Exper. Psychol. **63**(6), 318–325 (2016). https://doi.org/10.1027/1618-3169/a000343
26. Özen, Ö., Buetler, K., Marchal-Crespo, L.: Promoting motor variability during robotic assistance enhances motor learning of dynamic tasks. Front. Neurosci. **14** (2021). https://doi.org/10.3389/fnins.2020.600059
27. Howard, I., Ingram, J., Wolpert, D.: A modular planar robotic manipulandum with end-point torque control. J. Neurosci. Methods **181**(2), 199–211 (2009)
28. Millman, P., Colgate, J.: Design of a four degree-of-freedom force-reflecting manipulandum with a specified force/torque workspace. In: Proceedings. 1991 IEEE International Conference on Robotics and Automation (1991)
29. Metzger, J., Lambercy, O., Chapuis, D., Gassert, R.: Design and characterization of the ReHapticKnob, a robot for assessment and therapy of hand function. In: 2011 IEEE/RSJ International Conference on Intelligent Robots and Systems (2011). https://doi.org/10.1109/iros.2011.6094882
30. Metzger, J., Lambercy, O., Gassert, R.: High-fidelity rendering of virtual objects with the ReHapticKnob - novel avenues in robot assisted rehabilitation of hand function. In: 2012 IEEE Haptics Symposium (HAPTICS) (2012). https://doi.org/10.1109/haptic.2012.6183769
31. Karl, F.: A free energy principle for biological systems. Entropy **14**(11), 2100–2121 (2012)
32. Clark, A.: Whatever next? predictive brains, situated agents, and the future of cognitive science. Behav. Brain Sci. **36**(3), 181–204 (2013)
33. Hochreiter, S., Schmidhuber, J.: Long short-term memory. Neural Comput. **9**(8), 1735–1780 (1997). https://doi.org/10.1162/neco.1997.9.8.1735
34. Sherstinsky, A.: Fundamentals of Recurrent Neural Network (RNN) and Long Short-Term Memory (LSTM) network. Phys. D Nonlinear Phenomena **404**, 132306 (2020). https://doi.org/10.1016/j.physd.2019.132306
35. Zhai, C., Alderisio, F., Słowiński, P., Tsaneva-Atanasova, K., di Bernardo, M.: Design of a virtual player for joint improvisation with humans in the mirror game. PLoS ONE **11**(4), e0154361 (2016)
36. Friston, K.J., Stephan, K.E.: Free-energy and the brain. Synthese **159**(3), 417–458 (2007). https://doi.org/10.1007/s11229-007-9237-y
37. Annis, J., Miller, B.J., Palmeri, T.J.: Bayesian inference with Stan: a tutorial on adding custom distributions. Behav. Res. Methods **49**(3), 863–886 (2016). https://doi.org/10.3758/s13428-016-0746-9
38. Muth, C., Oravecz, Z., Gabry, J.: User-friendly bayesian regression modeling: a tutorial with RSTANARM and Shinystan. Quant. Meth. Psychol. **14**(2), 99–119 (2018). https://doi.org/10.20982/tqmp.14.2.p099
39. Pan, S., Duraisamy, K.: On the structure of time-delay embedding in linear models of nonlinear dynamical systems (2019)

Motor Interference of Incongruent Hand Motions in HRI Depends on Movement Velocity

Mertcan Kaya and Kolja Kühnlenz[✉]

Robotics Research Lab, Department of Electrical Engineering and Computer Science,
Coburg University of Applied Sciences and Arts, 96450 Coburg, Germany
{mertcan.kaya,kolja.kuehnlenz}@hs-coburg.de
http://www.hs-coburg.de/

Abstract. This paper presents results from a study on the dependency of motor interference (in terms of deviation of human hand movement from task direction) on movement velocity during simultaneous robot arm movement. Test participants and a robot arm perform synchronous vertical and horizontal movements in all combinations, while robot velocity is varied in three levels. Significant results show, that motor interference decreases in case of fast movement velocity and increases for slow and medium velocities. These findings can contribute to refined motor interference modeling in order to predict the extent of motor interference during more general movements with varying velocity profiles and this way reduce movement uncertainty and increase safety.

Keywords: Human-robot interaction · Motor interference

1 Introduction

Motor interference is an effect, first observed in human-human motion coordination, resulting in variabilities of Cartesian hand position trajectories of humans depending on those of their interaction partner in case of incongruent motion directions and vice versa [11]. This effect is commonly measured in terms of standard deviations of hand position progressions, which increase for incongruent motions. This is explained by perception of the interaction partners as animate subjects and the tendency to imitate those. This is assumed to be caused by the mirror neuron system as any observation of an action of a human counterpart elicits activation of corresponding areas of the premotor cortex [2,3], e.g. an increase in the motor-evoked potentials of hand muscles during observation of hand movements can be found [6]. So, any perceived action influences outgoing actions in terms of supporting similar action and distracting from different action [1]. Motor interference was e.g. investigated using biological motions realized as dot motions [10].

Especially in close and fast interaction and motion coordination, uncertainty and predictability of human motion and trajectory tracking behavior of humans as well as of robots are important aspects, which influence overall performance

F. Cavallo et al. (Eds.): ICSR 2022, LNAI 13817, pp. 335–343, 2022.
https://doi.org/10.1007/978-3-031-24667-8_30

of a cooperative task. The effect of motor interference, however - the standard deviation of which can well be in the order of centimeters [12] -, may have a variable and significant impact on the interaction quality in close human-robot interaction depending on the specific and situational robot embodiment and motion optimization. Moreover, additional uncertainty may be considered a safety risk.

More recent studies included biologically grounded motion profiles based on the biologically motivated minimum-jerk (MJ) optimization principle [7]. The social relevance of MJ trajectories is also indicated by [5], showing a reduced sensitivity to MJ biological motion in test subjects with autism spectrum disorders. In order to render robotic motion more human-like, MJ optimization is applied in various works, e.g. [8,12]. It is observed, that interaction with robots with humanoid appearance in terms of motion coordination results in motor interference in terms of higher variability of the motions of the human if MJ optimization is applied [14] or if pre-recorded human controlled natural motion profiles are used [4,14], similarly to the effects observed in human-human motion coordination. This is explained by the perceived social presence of the robot. In contrast, studies with pure industrial robots with a table-mount embodiment and MJ optimization do not observe motor interference, even in spite of the biological motion pattern [11].

Other related works consider human perception of robot motions with different degrees of anthropomorphism involving fMRI-based activity measurement of brain areas, where it was found, that the level of anthropomorphism is reflected by the intensity of mirror neuron activity [13], which is in line with findings of other state-of-the-art works. Another work in this context investigates the prediction quality of a human collaborator showing a shorter prediction time for anthropomorphic robot motions without an increase of prediction errors. Especially, an increased mental effort was not observed, yet, only in terms of an observer's not an interactor's point of view [15]. It is concluded, that anthropomorphism generally would contribute to higher acceptance than safety, however, safety was not explicitly evaluated in terms of perceived or physical safety. Further, it was not considered, that the beneficial findings might be at the cost of increased motor interference, which was not investigated, but which might very well impact safety, e.g. in terms of potentially increased collision probabilities due to increased movement uncertainty.

Further, in previous works, it was shown, that incongruent movements contributed to higher subjective ratings of performance and effort during movement coordination compared to congruent movements, which was measured using NASA-TLX for task load and which is connected to the effect of motor interference, where humans continually have to work against [9]. This effect suggests, that incongruent task movement components should be avoided, at least in terms of parallel execution, in order to reduce continuous task load for an interacting human and decrease stress. In many cases, execution of incongruent movements is not avoidable due to task requirements, and in this context, it would be of high interest, whether velocity could be a parameter to be tuned in order to potentially reduce the effect of motor intefrerence.

With respect to more refined modeling of the motor interference effect, this paper investigates the impact of different movement velocities on motor interference during congruent and incongruent movements. A shoulder-mounted robot arm and minimum-jerk trajectory profiles are chosen in order to appear more human-like and elicit motor interference more effectively. Sequences of vertical and horizontal human and robot arm movements are varied and realized in a Latin square manner in order to reduce complexity, while a within-subjects design is used with respect to the presentation of three velocity levels, which are fully counterbalanced for each motion sequence. Hand movements are tracked using an optical tracking system and standard deviations of hand movements orthogonally to the (vertical or horizontal) respective task directions are evaluated as a measure for motor interference in order to be comparable to related works, e.g. [12].

The remainder of the paper is structured as follows: In Sect. 2, the experimental study design is described; Sect. 3 presents experimental results on motor interference, which are then discussed in Sect. 4; conclusions are given in Sect. 5.

2   Experimental Study Design

2.1   Hypotheses

Considering an extreme case, where hand velocity is nearly zero, it is expected, that motor interference decreases for for small velocities. For high velocities, it is expected, that human arm inertia and higher muscle tension also could result in reduced motor interference. So, it is hypothesized, that:

- H1: Motor interference depends on movement velocity.
- H2: Motor interference decreases for small and high arm velocities.

These hypotheses are investigated in an experimental study using a commercial cooperative robot arm (UR3) in a within-subjects design with repeated measures factor 'velocity'. The study design and measures are described in the following.

2.2   Study Design and Measures

A strongly controlled scenario is chosen, in order to minimize artefacts. Human participant and robot are positioned in front of each other. The robot performs arm movements with the arm fully stretched in either vertical or horizontal direction with three different velocity levels starting from an initial position, where its arm directly points towards the participant. Participants then perform synchronous arm movements in either the same direction (vertical/horizontal) or the orthogonal direction (vertical/horizontal) with respect to robot movement. Using an optical marker-based tracking system (OptiTrack Trio), human hand movements are recorded and deviations from the intended arm movement are evaluated in terms of standard deviations in the direction orthogonal to the intended task-related direction.

Because a full counterbalance design including the three velocity levels and all four combinations of vertical and horizontal human and robot arm movements is impractical, a compromise is chosen varying the possible movement combinations A, B, C, and D (see below) for the participants in a Latin square manner, while presenting all permutations of the velocity levels (approx. 4 min duration) in each movement combination. So, the balanced Latin square results in four sequence variants, which are presented to different test persons (between-subjects factor). For each velocity level, three periods of the vertical, respectively, horizontal movement are presented as a trade-off between data acquisition and exhaustion of the test participants, in order to limit the overall trial duration for each test person to about 15 min. Motor interference is computed evaluating the trajectory data over all the movement periods corresponding to the respective velocity level in the corresponding congruent, respectively, incongruent conditions. Cycle times (one period) are 6 s, 4 s, and 2 s for low, medium, and high velocities. Low and high velocity levels are chosen in such a way, that the participants just managed to keep up with the synchronous motion (prior study).

- A - human: vertical, robot: vertical (congruent)
- B - human: horizontal, robot: vertical (incongruent)
- C - human: vertical, robot: horizontal (incongruent)
- D - human: horizontal, robot: horizontal (congruent)

The experimental set-up consists of a UR3 robot arm (Universal Robots) shoulder-mounted on a test stand as shown in Fig. 1. The human participant is placed in front of the robot with about a meter of distance between their finger tips or end-points, if the arms of both are fully stretched horizontally in the directions of each other. An optical marker is placed at the top of the participants right hand wrist and tracked 120 Hz by a Trio tracking system (OptiTrack).

The study was approved by the Coburg University ethics committee and informed consent of the participants is obtained (Table 1).

3   Results

Results are deduced from data sets of 16 test participants (9 male and 7 female, age between 20 and 60 years). Shapiro-Wilk test is non-significant, so a repeated-measures ANOVA is applied with repeated-measures factor 'velocity'. Mauchly's test indicated, that the assumption of sphericity is violated ($p < 0.05$), so a Greenhouse-Geisser correction is applied.

Focusing on the main effects, the ANOVA results of the within-subjects effects show significant differences of standard deviations of human hand trajectories orthogonal to movement direction (motor interference) for incongruent human and robot movements with a medium effect.

Fig. 1. Experimental setup (UR3, shoulder mounted).

Table 1. Sequence and durations of tasks of experimental trial of one test person.

Task	Duration	Comments
Briefing		Introduction to procedure and tests
Pre-questionnaire	∼5 min	Demographical data, dispositional parameters
Set-up		Place test person
Adjustment	1 min	Let person adjust to setting
Trajectory 1	4 min	Trajectory type 1
Trajectory 2	4 min	Trajectory type 2
Trajectory 3	4 min	Trajectory type 3
Trajectory 4	4 min	Trajectory type 4
De-briefing		

Post hoc comparisons show significant differences of motor interference effects between low and high as well as medium and high velocities with strong effects. Between low and medium velocities, no significant effect is found (Tables 2 and 4).

Table 2. Within Subjects Effects of motor interference (standard deviations orthogonal to task direction) of incongruent movements

	Sphericity correction	Sum of squares	df	Mean square	F	p	η_p^2
Velocity	Greenhouse-Geisser	6.725e-5	1.383	4.864e−5	7.572	0.007	0.335
Residual	Greenhouse-Geisser	1.332e-4	20.742	6.423e−6			

Table 3. Descriptives (motor interference in terms of means of standard deviations [m] orthogonal to task direction) for incongruent movements

Velocity	Mean	SD	N
Low	0.019	0.005	16
Medium	0.019	0.006	16
High	0.016	0.004	16

Table 4. Post Hoc Comparisons of motor interference (standard deviations orthogonal to task direction) for incongruent movements

		Mean difference [m]	SE	t	Cohen's d	p_{holm}
High	Low	−0.002	8.808e−4	−2.678	−0.669	0.034
	Medium	−0.003	8.384e−4	−3.148	−0.787	0.020
Low	Medium	−2.809e−4	4.320e−4	−0.650	−0.163	0.525

For comparisons, also standard deviations for congruent movements are evaluated, in order to illustrate, that the standard deviations for incongruent movements are substantially higher, which is due to the effect of motor interference. The ANOVA results of the within-subjects effects for congruent movements show significant differences of standard deviations of human hand trajectories orthogonal to movement direction with a small effect. Post hoc comparisons, however, do not show significant differences. Looking at the data more deeply, a strong skewness towards lower standard deviations can be noted in contrast to the incongruent data set. A non-parametric Friedman test then revealed significant differences between low and high velocities (Fig. 2).

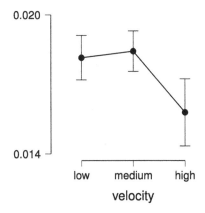

Fig. 2. Motor interference (standard deviations [m] orthogonal to task direction) of incongruent human and robot movements for different velocity levels and standard errors.

Interactions with gender, previous experience with robots or sports activity are not observed (Table 5).

Table 5. Within Subjects Effects of motor interference (standard deviations orthogonal to task direction) for congruent movements

	Sphericity correction	Sum of squares	df	Mean square	F	p	η_p^2
Velocity	Greenhouse-Geisser	2.417e−5	1.276	1.893e−5	4.994	0.030	0.250
Residual	Greenhouse-Geisser	7.259e−5	97.146	3.792e−6			

4 Discussion

It can be noted, that standard deviations of hand position progressions orthogonally to movement direction decrease for high velocities compared to medium velocities in case of incongruent human and robot hand movements. This indicates a decrease of the motor interference effect supporting H1 (Tables 6 and 7).

With respect to low velocity, no significant differences are found compared to medium velocity. So, a change of motor interference is only detected with respect to high velocity and H2 is only partially supported in terms of the mentioned decrease of motor interference for high velocities. Based on a power analysis accounting for the descriptives in Table 3, a necessary sample size in the order of 10^5 for obtaining significant results with respect to differences between low and medium velocity is estimated. Even then differences are small, indicating low relevance to practical implications for this part of the initial assumption.

Table 6. Descriptives (motor interference in terms of means of standard deviations [m] orthogonal to task direction) for congruent movements

Velocity	Mean [m]	SD	N
Low	0.013	0.004	16
Medium	0.013	0.004	16
High	0.012	0.005	16

Table 7. Post Hoc Comparisons of motor interference (standard deviations orthogonal to task direction) for congruent movements

		Mean difference [m]	SE	t	Cohen's d	p_{holm}
High	Low	−0.002	7.102e−4	−2.435	−0.609	0.084
	Medium	−0.001	5.412e−4	−1.874	−0.469	0.096
Low	Medium	7.150e−4	3.320e−4	2.154	0.538	0.096

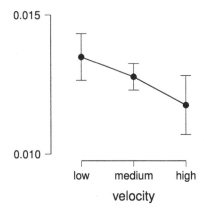

Fig. 3. Motor interference (standard deviations [m] orthogonal to task direction) of congruent human and robot movements for different velocity levels and standard errors.

Summarizing, the overall results show, that the interference effect of robot movement on human movement is most prominent for medium to low velocities. In terms of practical implications, it is concluded, that this velocity range poses a higher risk of deviations of human hand movements from task direction, if robot movements are incongruent and, thus, may impact task performance or even safety in terms of collision probabilities.

The strongly controlled scenario is limited in terms of the chosen velocity combinations as human velocity is always identical to robot velocity. This was chosen as a first step because synchronization was more easily and effectively realizable for the test persons. An interesting aspect and next step for further research is, how different robot and human velocities interact and if the findings of this paper still hold in those cases, which would require additional signals for the participants in order to be able keep up with their trajectory task, while the robot executes different cycle times (Fig. 3).

5   Conclusions

In this paper, motor interference as a result of robot arm movement impacting human arm movement is investigated in terms of velocity dependency as a potential component for motor interference modeling. It is found, that a significant dependency of motor interference on velocity exists. For higher arm velocities, the motor interference effect is smaller than for low and medium velocities. It is concluded, that human task movements may perform better in terms of task accomplishment in case of higher arm velocities, if performed in the vicinity of a moving robot. Moreover, movement uncertainty is reduced, which may be beneficial in terms of safety.

Future work will target different combinations of human and robot velocities and consideration of real-world interaction scenarios, in order to check, if the findings can be generalized contributing to a refined model of motor interference for more general human-robot interaction.

Acknowledgment. This work has been supported in part by the German Research Foundation (DFG), grant no. KU 2486/8-1.

References

1. Brass, M., Bekkering, H., Prinz, W.: Movement observation affects movement execution in a simple response task. Acta Psychologica **106**(1–2), 3–22 (2001)
2. Buccino, G., et al.: Action observation activates premotor and parietal areas in a somatotopic manner: an fMRI study. Eur. J. Neurosci. **13**, 400–404 (2001)
3. Buccino, G., Binkofski, F., Riggio, L.: The mirror neuron system and action recognition. Brain Lang. **89**(2), 370–376 (2004)
4. Chaminade, T., Franklin, D., Oztop, E., Cheng, G.: Motor interference between humans and humanoid robots: effect of biological and artificial motion. In: Proceedings of the IEEE International Conference on Development and Learning (2005)
5. Cook, J., Saygin, A.P., Swain, R., Blakemore, S.J.: Reduced sensitivity to minimum-jerk biological motion in autism spectrum conditions. Neuropsychologia **47**(14), 3275–3278 (2009)
6. Fadiga, L., Fogassi, L., Pavesi, G., Rizzolatti, G.: Motor facilitation during action observation: a magnetic stimulation study. J. Neurophysiol. **73**(6), 2608–2611 (1995)
7. Flash, T., Hogan, N.: The coordination of arm movements: an experimentally confirmed mathematical model. J. Neurosci. Soc. Neurosci. **5**(7), 1688–1703 (1985)
8. Huber, M., Rickert, M., Knoll, A., Brandt, T., Glasauer, S.: Human-robot interaction in handing-over tasks. In: Proceedings of the IEEE International Symposium on Robot and Human Interactive Communication (RO-MAN) (2008)
9. Kühnlenz, K., Kühnlenz, B.: Motor interference of incongruent motions increases workload in close hri. Adv. Rob. **34**(6), 400–406 (2020). https://doi.org/10.1080/01691864.2020.1717614
10. Kilner, J., Hamilton, A., Blakemore, S.: Interference effect of observed human movement on action is due to velocity profile of biological motion. Social Neurosci. **2**(3), 158–166 (2007)
11. Kilner, J., Paulignan, Y., Blakemore, S.: An interference effect of observed biological movement on action. Curr. Biol. **13**(6), 522–525 (2003)
12. Kupferberg, A., Glasauer, S., Huber, M., Rickert, M., Knoll, A., Brandt, T.: Biological movement increases acceptance of humanoid robots as human partners in motor interaction. AI Soc. **26**(4), 339–345 (2011)
13. Kuz, S., Schlick, C.: Anthropomorphic motion control for safe and efficient human-robot cooperation in assembly system. In: Proceedings of the Triennial Congress of the International Ergonomics Association (IEA) (2015)
14. Oztop, E., Franklin, D., Chaminade, T., Cheng, G.: Human-humanoid interaction: is a humanoid robot perceived as a human? Int. J. Hum. Rob. **2**, 537–559 (2005)
15. Petruck, H., Kuz, S., Mertens, A., Schlick, C.: Increasing safety in human-robot collaboration by using anthropomorphic speed profiles of robot movements (2016)

Foster Attention and Engagement Strategies in Social Robots

Attributing Intentionality to Artificial Agents: Exposure Versus Interactive Scenarios

Lorenzo Parenti[1,2], Serena Marchesi[1], Marwen Belkaid[1,3], and Agnieszka Wykowska[1(✉)]

[1] Social Cognition in Human-Robot Interaction, Italian Institute of Technology, Genova, Italy
agnieszka.wykowska@iit.it
[2] Department of Psychology, University of Turin, Turin, Italy
[3] ETIS Lab, CY Cergy Paris Université, ENSEA, Paris CNRS UMR8051, France

Abstract. Recent studies suggest that people can interact with robots as social agents. However, it is still unclear what mental processes people rely on when interacting with robots. One core process in social cognition is the adoption of intentional stance, a strategy that humans use to interpret the behavior of others with reference to mental states. In this work, we sought to examine how the adoption of intentional stance may be modulated by the type of behaviors exhibited by a virtual robot and the context in which people are exposed to it. We developed an interactive virtual task and used the InStance Test to measure the attribution of intentionality to the robot. Our results show that participants attributed more intentionality to the virtual robot after interacting with it, independently of the type of behavior. Leveraging data from a previous study, we also show this increase is stronger than in a non-interactive, purely observational scenario. This study thus improves our understanding of how different contexts can affect the attribution of intentional stance and anthropomorphism in Human-Robot Interaction.

Keywords: Intentional stance · Human-likeness · Human-Robot Interaction

1 Introduction

One of the key process of human social cognition that entails perceiving other agents as social entities is the attribution of intentionality to their behaviors [1]. This process is thoroughly explained by Daniel Dennett [2, 3], who defines the concept of "stances" (or strategies) that humans adopt to explain and predict others' behaviors. Dennett presents two stances that we can adopt: (i) the intentional stance, that is adopted when we interpret the agents' behavior with reference to mental states; and (ii) the design stance, which is adopted when we interpret the behavior of observed agents with reference to how they were designed to behave. When it comes to human agents, adopting the intentional stance is a default strategy enabling an efficient way to navigate the social environment (for a review see [4]). It remains to be answered, however, if and how humans adopt the intentional stance towards artificial agents.

To operationalize and empirically address the philosophical concept of intentional stance, Marchesi and colleagues [5] developed the InStance Test (IST). For example,

F. Cavallo et al. (Eds.): ICSR 2022, LNAI 13817, pp. 347–356, 2022.
https://doi.org/10.1007/978-3-031-24667-8_31

using IST, it was shown that individuals' tendency to adopt the intentional stance toward robots is characterized by differences in their neural activity at rest [6]. In addition, studies found that the adoption of the intentional stance can be modulated by numerous factors: (i) related to the robot, such as appearance and repetitive behavior[7]; (ii) related to the human, like prior exposure to robots[8]; and related to the task, like collaborative framing [9] Moreover, multiple exposures to robots over time could result in negative subjective perceptions of robotic agents [10] and can decrease the likelihood to attribute mental states to them [7, 11].

In this paper, we sought to investigate whether the quality of the robot's movements would influence the adoption of the intentional stance toward it. Indeed, motion plays a crucial role in social cognition in humans [12]. For example, it has been shown that the movements of simple shapes can evoke attributions of intentions [13]. In HRI, the type of movements performed by robots were found to affect the adoption of the intentional stance [14]. The human-likeness of the machine's movements and the extent to which it resembles biological motion could potentially provide the basis for mentalistic explanations [15, 16]. However, in a previous study using robotic virtual agents [17], we showed that IST scores increased after observing the robot with mechanistic behaviors but not to the robot with human-like behaviors. In other words, machine-like behaviors of the robotic virtual agent had a positive effect on participants' adoption of intentional stance. Overall, how the human-likeness of robots' motion may affect the adoption of intentional stance toward them remains unclear.

Another important factor, which may influence intentionality attribution, is the context of the interaction. Following the second-person neuroscience framework presented by Schilbach and colleagues [18], we focused on the domain of second-person robotics proposed by Dominey [19]. This framework suggests that the mental processes engaged during an interaction differ from those engaged by the observation of another agent. Thus, since our previous study mentioned above [15] was merely observational, results may be different in case participants fully interacted with the robot. For example, previous studies found that interactive scenarios are also beneficial for general attitudes toward the robot (e.g. likeability and perceived intelligence) [20, 21]. By integrating the behaviors to which participants were exposed in the previous study in an interactive task, we seek to investigate whether intentionality attribution depends on the type of encounter, i.e. observational or interactive.

1.1 Aim of the Study

This study aimed to examine behavioral and contextual factors that may affect the adoption of intentional stance toward robots. Specifically, we investigated the effects of quality of the robot behavior (human-like vs robot-like motion) and of the nature of the task (interactive vs observational). Based on the literature described above, we hypothesized that the adoption of the intentional stance (i) would be modulated by the human-likeness of the robot behavior, even though, based on the literature, it remains difficult to clearly predict the direction of such modulation; (ii) would positively correlate with perceived intelligence and likability; and (iii) would be stronger in an interactive scenario compared to a mere exposure to the same agent exhibiting the same behaviors. To test these hypotheses, we designed an experiment involving an interactive task occurring in a virtual environment, and used IST and the Godspeed questionnaire (GSQ). The virtual environment incorporated a 3D avatar modeled after the humanoid robot iCub, which allowed us to overcome the mechanical constraints of the embodied robot, manipulate the human-likeness of the agent's motion and compare behaviors that follow the properties of biological motion with jerky, mechanistic movements that are more typical of robots.

2 Methods and Materials

2.1 Participants

Forty-one participants (M/F: 16/25; age: 26.7 ± 7) took part in the study. All participants had normal or corrected-to-normal vision and were not informed about the purpose of the experiment. All participants gave their informed written consent. The experiment was conducted under the ethical standards (Declaration of Helsinki, 1964) and approved by the local Ethical Committee (Comitato Etico Regione Liguria). The data of one participant (male, age 24) have been excluded because they did not complete the experiment. Therefore, data of forty participants were included in the final analysis.

2.2 Apparatus

Participants were seated facing two 22" LCD monitors. The first screen displayed the virtual environment for the decision task running on a computer with an AMD Ryzen Threadripper 2950X 16-core 3.5 GHz CPU, 128 GB of RAM and a NVIDIA GeForce GTX 1060 3 GB video card. The 3D-animated virtual environment including avatars with the appearance of the iCub robot [22] was developed using Unreal Engine (Epic Games: www.unrealengine.com). An ad-hoc Python program (version 3.9.5) handled stimulus presentation and data collection. Participants responded on a QWERTY keyboard. The second monitor was used to display the InStance Test and Godspeed Questionnaire (GSQ), which were administered through SoSci (https://www.soscisurvey.de).

2.3 Procedure

After providing consent, participants were instructed about the structure of the experiment. Participants completed the first part of the IST (IST Pre). After that, they performed an interactive task with a virtual agent presented on a screen (see Sect. 2.4). At the end of the task, participants were asked to complete the second part of IST (IST Post) and 2 GSQ subscales. Participants were randomly assigned to one of the two experimental groups. In one group, the behavior of the iCub avatar in the interactive task was characterized by biological motion resulting in human-like movements (human-like iCub). In the other group, the iCub avatar was exhibiting the same types of behaviors but moving mechanically, in a typical robotic fashion (robot-like iCub). In summary, the task included one between-subjects manipulation related to the human-likeness of the avatar behavior (human-like vs robot-like movements). Task and subjective measures are described in details in the next sections. Participants did not have a specified time limit to complete the experiment and could take break between the task and IST. Average time required to complete the experiment and read instructions was around 1 h and 30 min.

2.4 Task

The interactive task was loosely inspired by the Shell Game [23]. In our version, the game required the presence of a game partner (here the robot) and a player (here the participant) to guess the position of a ball hidden under one of the cups. The game and the instructions were not explicitly framing the task as collaborative or competitive. In the virtual environment displayed on the monitor, the robot was facing the participant on the other side of a table on which two identical red cups and one ball were placed. As in typical cups and ball games, the cups were shuffled to hide the ball position then the player had to guess under which of the two cups the ball was hidden.

Each trial began with iCub looking at the participants and then at the movement of the cups on the table game. After the cups stopped moving, participants were asked to press 'a' to choose the cup on their left and 'd' to choose the cup on their right. After this decision step, cups were lifted to show the ball position and thus the outcome of the trial (i.e., hit or miss). In order to create an interactive scenario, iCub then provided social feedback in the form a non-verbal behavior. Feedback from iCub were always congruent with participant performance, meaning positive feedback after a hit and negative feedback after a miss. Positive feedbacks were iCub clapping hands or nodding, in both feedback types, iCub was also showing a happy face expression. Negative feedback were iCub punching the table and shaking its head and iCub was showing a sad expression during both negative behaviors (see Fig. 1). Behavioral data were collected (e.g. response times and accuracy) but their analysis is out of the scope of this paper.

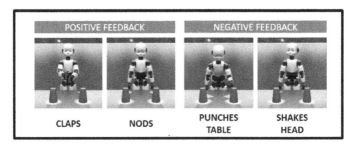

Fig. 1. Feedback from iCub presented to the participants at the end of the trial. Positive feedback were always including a happy face expression and negative feedback were always presented with a sad face expression.

2.5 Subjective Measures

To measure whether interacting with the virtual robot modulated participants' tendency to adopt intentional stance toward the robot, the IST [5] was administered before and after exposure to the robot (pre- and post-). In order to avoid participants to rate twice the same items, we split the IST in two halves, based on a prior work [24]. IST pre- and post- consisted of 17 items each. Each IST item consists of a scenario made of three different pictures of iCub involved in an action alone or with a human partner (see Fig. 2). Two sentences describing the situation are presented below the scenario. One description is written with mentalistic words and the other with mechanistic terms. Participants were asked to indicate whether the mentalistic or mechanistic description was fitting the scenario better by moving a slider placed on a line between the two sentences. IST scoring was calculated by assigning 0 to the extreme of the slider line on the mechanistic side (adopting the mechanistic stance) and 100 to the extreme side of the line on the mentalistic side (adopting the intentional stance). IST pre- and post- averaged scores were calculated for each participant. IST delta scores were calculated for each participant subtracting IST pre- score from IST post- score, to have a unique measure for modulation of IST related to the interaction.

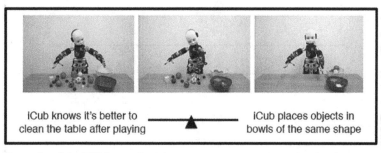

Fig. 2. Example of the IST items. Each item presents a scenario made of 3 pictures. Two sentences are presented below the scenario: one giving a mentalistic explanation and one a more mechanistic description.

In addition, we used the Godspeed questionnaire (GSQ) to assess participants' attitude toward the robot. In GSQ, Bartneck and colleagues identified five subscales (anthropomorphism, animacy, likeability, perceived intelligence, and perceived safety) which are useful to investigate people's perception of robots [25]. To limit the duration of the experiment, we selected the two most relevant GSQ subscales: likeability and perceived intelligence. Both subscales are composed by 5 items on 5-points scale with opposite poles (e.g. dislike-like, incompetent-competent). These two subscales were shown to be associated with the quality of the interaction scenario [21].

3   Results

First, we examined if the two groups were different based on demographic information. The t-test showed no differences between the two groups based on age ($t(38) = 0.63$, $p = 0.533$, Cohen's d $= 0.199$, $M_{human-like} = 27 \pm 7.7$; $M_{robot-like} = 25.7 \pm 6.2$). The Chi-Squared analysis showed a significant difference based on sex ($X^2 = 3.956$, $p = 0.047$, M/F$_{human-like} = 4/16$; M/F$_{robot-like} = 10/10$). Given that sex was unbalanced, we performed an independent samples t-test to test whether this could affect IST and GSQ measures. No effect of sex was found (all p-values > 0.063).

3.1 InStance Test

We submitted IST scores averaged individually to a two-way ANOVA with groups as a between-subject factor and IST pre/post as a within-subject factor. The results showed a within-subjects effect of IST score ($F(1,38) = 68.535$, $p < 0.001$, $\eta^2 = 0.461$) and no effect of the group ($p = 0.38$) or interaction ($p = 0.11$) (see Fig. 3).

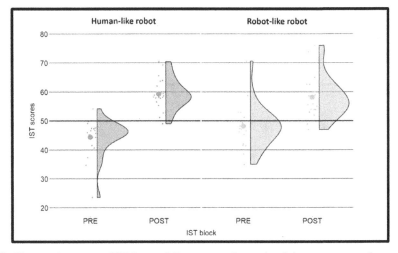

Fig. 3. The graph presents IST Pre and Post scores for each of the two groups (human-like or robot-like behavior of iCub). Bigger dots represent the mean score, smaller dots are single participant IST score and on the side the distribution of the sample. The score of 50 represents a neutral response between "completely mechanistic explanation" (0) and "completely intentional explanation" (100).

To check whether IST PRE and POST scores were significantly different from 50 we performed two separate one-sample t-test. Results showed that IST PRE scores are significantly lower than 50 ($t(39) = -3.284$, $p = 0.002$, Cohen's $D = 6.368$) and IST POST scores are significantly higher than 50 ($t(39) = 8.643$, $p < 0.001$, Cohen's $D = 9.212$), meaning that participants had a bias towards one or the other stance, rather than being ambivalent.

3.2 Godspeed Questionnaire

We first looked for between-subjects difference using an independent t-test and found no difference between the human-like and the robot-like group, neither on the Likability subscale ($p = 0.955$) nor on the Perceived Intelligence subscale ($p = 0.999$). Mean score of the Likability subscale was 3.79 ± 0.624 for the human-like agent and 3.78 ± 0.476

for the robot-like agent. Mean score of the Perceived Intelligence subscale was 4.11 ± 0.685 for the human-like agent and 4.11 ± 0.61 for the robot-like agent. Then, we performed a correlation analysis to examine possible association between IST and GSQ scores. The analysis did not show any significant correlation (all p-values > 0.123).

3.3 Differences with Previous Exposure Study

To examine differences in intentional attribution based on different type of interaction with the virtual agents, we proceeded to compare IST scores with those reported in our previous study [15], in which participants watched the same behaviors exhibited by the virtual robots here but without any interactive context (i.e. non-interactive task). The non-interactive task consisted in watching short video clips of the robot behaviors and rating them in terms of how human-like the movements were. Previous study sample counted 97 participants (M/F: 49/48; age: 26 ± 6.5). Forty-nine participants watched and rated the virtual human-like robot (M/F: 24/25; age: 25.7 ± 6.5) and 48 did the same with the robot-like robot (M/F: 25/23; age: 26.2 ± 6.6). We submitted Delta IST scores to an ANCOVA with type of interaction as a between-subject factor and IST PRE scores as a covariate in the model. The Deltas IST calculation helps to investigate the magnitude of the changes in the IST scores. Results showed a significant effect of the type of interaction on Delta IST ($F(1,134) = 28.12$, $p < 0.001$, eta sq = 0.163) where the interactive scenario increased IST scores significantly more than the exposure (M exposure = 2.609 vs M interaction = 12.478) (see Fig. 4). No other main effect or interaction was found to be significant.

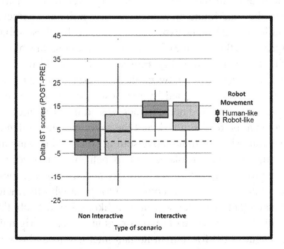

Fig. 4. The graph shows the delta of IST scores (IST Post – IST Pre scores) comparing the exposure with the interactive task, divided by the type of behavior the avatar was showing (human-like vs robot-like). Each boxplot shows a thicker black line as median value, colored part representing interquartile range and vertical lines as upper and lower whiskers. The dashed line represents the delta value of 0, meaning no difference between pre and post-IST score. Delta above "0" represent an increase in IST scores from Pre to Post.

4 Discussion

The aim of this study was to investigate whether adoption of the intentional stance toward robots their perception as likeable or intelligent is influenced by the human-likeness of their movements (human-like vs robot-like motion) and by the context of the task (interactive vs observational). To this aim, we asked participants to interact with a virtual robot and administered IST and GSQ to measure intentionality attribution, likeability, and perceived intelligence. Because mechanical constraints make it difficult to implement biological motion on real, embodied robots, we designed this study in a virtual environment as a first step. This allowed us to implement jerky, robot-like movements and compare them to more human-like movements.

Consistently with previous IST studies [5, 17], participants showed a general bias toward a mechanistic explanation of robot actions in the IST Pre phase. As stated in our first hypothesis, we were expecting the human-likeness of the robot's behavior during the task to modulate attribution of intentionality after the interaction. Contrary to our hypothesis, we found an increase in IST scores independently of the type of behavior; meaning that after interacting with robot in our setting, participants tended to adopt the intentional stance more, independent of the type of movement it was exhibiting. One possible explanation for this is that the robot with which participants interacted was virtual rather than physically embodied. As such, the behavior might not have modulated the IST as much as in physical presence settings [10].

Our second hypothesis was also not confirmed. Indeed, unlike previous studies [26], we found no correlation between intentionality attribution and the levels of likeability and perceived intelligence in the GSQ; which were overall high with relatively low variability. Other studies had found an increase in likeability and perceived intelligence in interactive scenarios [20, 21]. One explanation could be that these subjective measures were generally high due to the positive effect of the interaction, thus blurring the possible relation with attribution of intentionality. Future studies should investigate the factors that might influence the correlation between these measures in HRI.

Our last hypothesis was confirmed by the observed difference in the increase of IST scores between interactive and non-interactive settings. The interactive setting was characterized by a dynamic decision task and the robot was giving feedback to partici-pants after the decision. The non-interactive setting consisted in watching short videos of the robot and rating the human-likeness of its behaviors. Indeed, participants who merely observed the robot's behavior without any social context (non-interactive set-ting) attributed less intentionality to it compared to those who interacted with it. This result was also independent of the level of human-likeness of the robot's behavior. This finding is in line with the perspective of second-person approach originally presented by Schilbach and colleagues [18] for human-human interactions and extended to human-robot interactions by Dominey [19]. Indeed, it suggests that even in virtual environments, the possibility to interact with the virtual agent can affect the strategy we use to predict and interpret their behaviors.

Interestingly, our previous results with merely observational exposure to the same behaviors that we used in this study showed that IST scores only increased in case of robot-like motion. This suggested that intentionality attribution was dependent on prior expectations about the agent [17]. In other words, given that humans expect robots to move in a jerky, mechanistic fashion, violating such expectation might hinder the adoption of the intentional stance toward them. The results of the present study indicate that such an effect could be attenuated in interactive scenarios. While further studies are needed to confirm these results, we believe this is an important finding, as it suggests that the quality of the robot's motion might matter less than the interactive nature of the task. The attribution of mental states to robots can increase the acceptance and positive attitudes towards them [26]. Therefore, the ability to create scenarios (i.e. interactive) that favor the adoption of the intentional stance may be key to successful human-robot interaction and more broadly to human-agent interaction. Moreover, we believe that implementing communicative gestures on the robotic agent (i.e. feedback in this study) could make the experimental scenario more interactive and engaging for participants and so future users.

References

1. Frith, C.D., Frith, U.: Mechanisms of social cognition. Ann. Rev. Psychol. **63**(1), 287–313 (2012). https://doi.org/10.1146/annurev-psych-120710-100449
2. Dennett, D.C.: The journal of philosophy, Inc., intentional systems: J. Philos. **68**(4), 87–106 (1971). https://doi.org/10.2307/2025382
3. Dennett, D.C.: Intentional systems in cognitive ethology: the panglossian paradigm defended. Behav. Brain Sci. **6**(3), 343–355 (1983). https://doi.org/10.1017/S0140525X00016393
4. Perez-Osorio, J., Wykowska, A.: Adopting the intentional stance toward natural and artificial agents. Philos. Psychol. **33**(3), 369–395 (2020). https://doi.org/10.1080/09515089.2019.168 8778
5. Marchesi, S., Ghiglino, D., Ciardo, F., Perez-Osorio, J., Baykara, E., Wykowska, A.: Do we adopt the intentional stance toward humanoid robots? Front. Psychol. **10**, 450 (2019). https://doi.org/10.3389/fpsyg.2019.00450
6. Bossi, F., Willemse, C., Cavazza, J., Marchesi, S., Murino, V., Wykowska, A.: The human brain reveals resting state activity patterns that are predictive of biases in attitudes toward robots. Sci. Robot. **5**(46), eabb6652 (2020). https://doi.org/10.1126/scirobotics.abb6652
7. Abubshait, A., Wykowska, A.: Repetitive robot behavior impacts perception of intentionality and gaze-related attentional orienting. Front. Robot. AI **7**, 565825 (2020). https://doi.org/10.3389/frobt.2020.565825
8. Perez-Osorio, J., Marchesi, S., Ghiglino, D., Ince, M., Wykowska, A.: More than you expect: priors influence on the adoption of intentional stance toward humanoid robots. In: Salichs, M.A., et al. (eds.) ICSR 2019. LNCS (LNAI), vol. 11876, pp. 119–129. Springer, Cham (2019). https://doi.org/10.1007/978-3-030-35888-4_12
9. Abubshait, A., Perez-Osorio, J., Tommaso, D.D., Wykowska, A.: Collaboratively framed interactions increase the adoption of intentional stance towards robots. In: 2021 30th IEEE International Conference on Robot & Human Interactive Communication (RO-MAN), Vancouver, BC, Canada, pp. 886–891 (2021). https://doi.org/10.1109/RO-MAN50785.2021.951 5515
10. Bergmann, K., Eyssel, F., Kopp, S.: A second chance to make a first impression? how appearance and nonverbal behavior affect perceived warmth and competence of virtual agents over time. In: Nakano, Y., Neff, M., Paiva, A., Walker, M. (eds.) IVA 2012. LNCS (LNAI), vol. 7502, pp. 126–138. Springer, Heidelberg (2012). https://doi.org/10.1007/978-3-642-33197-8_13

11. Epley, N., Waytz, A., Cacioppo, J.T.: On seeing human: a three-factor theory of anthropomorphism. Psychol. Rev. **114**(4), 864–886 (2007). https://doi.org/10.1037/0033-295X.114.4.864

12. Williams, E.H., Cristino, F., Cross, E.S.: Human body motion captures visual attention and elicits pupillary dilation. Cognition **193**, 104029 (2019). https://doi.org/10.1016/j.cognition.2019.104029

13. Heider, F., Simmel, M.: An experimental study of apparent behavior. Am. J. Psychol. **57**(2), 243 (1944). https://doi.org/10.2307/1416950

14. Bossema, M., Saunders, R., Allouch, S.B.: Robot body movements and the intentional stance, presented at the first international workshop on designerly HRI knowledge. In: IEEE International Conference on Robot and Human Interactive Communication (ROMAN) (2020)

15. Perez-Osorio, J., Wykowska, A.: Adopting the intentional stance towards humanoid robots. In: Laumond, J.-P., Danblon, E., Pieters, C. (eds.) Wording Robotics. STAR, vol. 130, pp. 119–136. Springer, Cham (2019). https://doi.org/10.1007/978-3-030-17974-8_10

16. Ciardo, F., De Tommaso, D., Wykowska, A.: Human-like behavioral variability blurs the distinction between a human and a machine in a nonverbal turing test. Sci. Robot. **7**(68), eabo1241 (2022). https://doi.org/10.1126/scirobotics.abo1241

17. Parenti, L., Marchesi, S., Belkaid, M., Wykowska, A.: Exposure to robotic virtual agent affects adoption of intentional stance. In: Proceedings of the 9th International Conference on Human-Agent Interaction, Virtual Event Japan, pp. 348–353 (2021). https://doi.org/10.1145/3472307.3484667

18. Schilbach, L., et al.: Toward a second-person neuroscience. Behav. Brain Sci. **36**(4), 393–414 (2013). https://doi.org/10.1017/S0140525X12000660

19. Dominey, P.F.: Reciprocity between second-person neuroscience and cognitive robotics. Behav. Brain Sci. **36**(4), 418–419 (2013). https://doi.org/10.1017/S0140525X12001884

20. Weiss, A., Bartneck, C.: Meta analysis of the usage of the godspeed questionnaire series. In: 2015 24th IEEE International Symposium on Robot and Human Interactive Communication (RO-MAN), Kobe, Japan, pp. 381–388 (2015). https://doi.org/10.1109/ROMAN.2015.7333568

21. Bruna, M.T., Cuijpers, R.H., Ham, J.R.C., Torta, E.: The benefits of using high-level goal information for robot navigation. Technische Universiteit Eindhoven (2011)

22. Metta, G., Sandini, G., Vernon, D., Natale, L., Nori, F.: The iCub humanoid robot: an open platform for research in embodied cognition. In: Proceedings of the 8th Workshop on Performance Metrics for Intelligent Systems - PerMIS '08, Gaithersburg, Maryland, p. 50 (2008). https://doi.org/10.1145/1774674.1774683

23. Editors of Encyclopaedia Britannica, Encyclopedia Britannica (2014). https://www.britannica.com/art/cups-and-balls-trick

24. Spatola, N., Marchesi, S., Wykowska, A.: the intentional stance test-2: how to measure the tendency to adopt intentional stance towards robots. Front. Robot. AI **8**, 666586 (2021). https://doi.org/10.3389/frobt.2021.666586

25. Bartneck, C., Kulić, D., Croft, E., Zoghbi, S.: Measurement instruments for the anthropomorphism, animacy, likeability, perceived intelligence, and perceived safety of robots. Int. J. Soc. Robot. **1**(1), 71–81 (2009). https://doi.org/10.1007/s12369-008-0001-3

26. Marchesi, S., De Tommaso, D., Perez-Osorio, J., Wykowska, A.: Belief in sharing the same phe-nomenological experience increases the likelihood of adopting the intentional stance toward a humanoid robot. Technol. Mind Behav. **3**(3), 11 (2022). https://doi.org/10.1037/tmb0000072

Does Embodiment and Interaction Affect the Adoption of the Intentional Stance Towards a Humanoid Robot?

Ziggy O'Reilly[1,2] , Uma Prashant Navare[1,3] , Serena Marchesi[1] ,
and Agnieszka Wykowska[1(✉)]

[1] Social Cognition in Human-Robot Interaction, Istituto Italiano di Tecnologia, Genova, Italy
agnieszka.wykowska@iit.it
[2] Department of Psychology, University of Turin, Turin, Italy
[3] Department of Computer Science, University of Manchester, Manchester, UK

Abstract. Humanoid robots are a useful research tool to understand which factors trigger the adoption of the Intentional Stance (i.e., the attribution of mental states). The InStance Test (IST), assesses this with the isolated robot subscale and the social robot subscale - where higher scores reflect a greater tendency to adopt the Intentional Stance. Previous work found that when a human interacts with an embodied robot exhibiting human-like behaviour, their IST scores increase. However, it is not yet known whether this effect is robust to changes in embodiment or interaction. Subsequently, we administered both subscales before and after participants witnessed a humanoid robot exhibiting human-like behaviour. There was a significant increase in both scales after participants (1) interacted with the embodied robot, (2) watched a video of the robot interacting with a human and (3) watched a video of the robot without interaction. Secondly, to check there were no differences across the human-like experiments, we compared the differences of the magnitude of the IST score increase. We found no significant differences across the experiments. Additionally, we conducted follow-up control analyses' with the robot exhibiting machine-like behaviour, to ensure the increases were not due to exposure effects. We found no significant difference in the IST after participants (1) interacted with the embodied robot or (2) watched a video of the robot interacting with a human. These results show that the increased IST scores after witnessing iCub behaving in a human-like way, is not due to mere exposure and is robust to changes in embodiment and interaction.

Keywords: Intentional Stance · Human-robot interaction · Physical embodiment

1 Introduction

The second-person neuroscience framework of Schilbach et al. [1] argues that to better understand the mechanisms of social cognition, one needs to observe these in reciprocal interactions, rather than through passive observation. Indeed, evidence suggests that physical presence and embodiment is crucial for the development of various cognitive

F. Cavallo et al. (Eds.): ICSR 2022, LNAI 13817, pp. 357–366, 2022.
https://doi.org/10.1007/978-3-031-24667-8_32

mechanisms, higher order social-cognition and learning [2]. As such, a humanoid robot could be a useful research tool to investigate social cognition as they are physically embodied, able to exhibit social gestures, and can be programmed for experimental control [3, 4]. Specifically, they can be used to investigate questions around the degree to which physical embodiment and interaction effects the attribution of mental states.

According to Daniel Dennett's framework, attributing mental states to entities to explain behaviour, reflects the adoption of the Intentional Stance [5, 6]. Dennett argued that it is the most efficient strategy to navigate and understand social interactions with humans. However, he claims that it is not the only stance individuals adopt to explain and predict the behaviour of entities. For example, adopting the Design Stance could be more efficient to explain the behaviour of a robot by referring to knowledge about its functional design (i.e., 'the robot grabbed a glass because it was *programmed* to'), rather than to describe the robot's behaviours based on mental states (i.e., 'the robot grabbed a glass because it *wanted* to').

One way to assess the tendency to adopt the Intentional or the Design Stance towards a humanoid robot is by administering the InStance Test (IST) [7]. The IST consists of multiple questions each with a sequence of images of a child-like humanoid robot called iCub [8] (see Fig. 1). Participants choose between two descriptions that best describes the sequence of images. One description contains mentalistic vocabulary, whereas the other contains mechanistic vocabulary. The IST can be further split into two subscales; the social robot subscale, which depicts images of iCub next to a human(s), and the isolated robot subscale, which depicts iCub alone.

O'Reilly et al. [9], administered both subscales before and after participants watched a short film displaying a human interacting with a humanoid robot arm using human-like gestures. They found that the film affected scores on the social robot subscale and the isolated robot subscale differently. The isolated robot subscale increased for individuals with low autistic traits (reflecting an increase in the adoption of the Intentional Stance), whereas the social robot subscale decreased. This suggests that the subscales of the IST may in fact capture different cognitive processes [7], and that passive observation of an interaction could be sufficient to increase scores on the isolated robot subscale only. However, as there was no direct comparison to a film without an interaction, nor with a physically embodied interaction, it is unclear whether the differences in the subscales was driven by the interaction between the human and the robot nor whether this pattern of results would be replicated in an embodied interaction.

Marchesi et al. [10] also administered the IST to individuals in the context of a humanoid robot. They administered it to two separate groups of participants before and after they watched a film together with a physically embodied iCub. Depending on the group, iCub either behaved in a machine-like or a human-like way. They found a significant increase in the scores of the IST after participants interacted with the iCub displaying human-like behaviour, but not after the machine-like behaviour. Marchesi et al. [10] interpreted the results from a non-representationalist perspective of social cognition; that the moment-to-moment embodied interaction between the two subjects in the human-like condition could have contributed to enhanced social understanding (i.e., enactive intersubjectivity [11]). However, there was no direct comparison to passive observation of iCub, so the degree to which the embodied interaction affected the adoption of the Intentional Stance remains unknown. Furthermore, it is difficult to directly compare these results to O'Reilly et al. [9] due to differences in measurement and stimuli.

Thus, to understand whether different degrees of embodiment and interaction affects the adoption of the Intentional Stance, the current study aimed to use standardised behaviours (iCub's pre-existing behaviours) and measures (the subscales of the IST). Specifically, we first re-analyzed the human-like data from Marchesi et al. [10] according to the subscales. Secondly, we used video recordings of iCub's human-like behaviour from Marchesi et al.'s. [10] study and only manipulated interaction (i.e., the presence of a human in the video). Thirdly, we compared the magnitude change in the IST scores per subscale, across the human-like experiments. Finally, to ensure the findings from the human-like experiments were not due to mere exposure to the items in the IST, we re-analyzed the machine-like data from Marchest et al. [10] and conducted an online experiment where participants watched a video of iCub interacting with a human in a machine-like way.

We expected that a physically embodied interaction with a robot behaving in a human-like way would enhance the scores on the IST, compared to passive observation of a video of a robot behaving in a human-like way with and without interaction [1, 11]. Furthermore, we expected that watching a video of iCub interacting in a human-like way with an interaction, will affect the subscales differently [9]. Finally, we did not expect any changes in the IST scores after participants were exposed to iCub behaving in a machine-like way [10].

2   Common Methods and Procedures

2.1   InStance Test (IST)

The IST contains sequences of images (i.e., 'scenarios') of the humanoid robot iCub interacting with objects and/or a human(s). These scenarios establish whether participants are more biased towards explaining iCub's behaviour in reference to mental states (i.e., Intentional Stance), or in reference to its mechanical functions (i.e., Design Stance) [7]. Underneath the scenarios are two possible explanations of the robot's behaviour. One explanation always explains iCub's behaviour functionally (i.e., 'iCub *tracked* the girls hand movements'), while the other always describes its behaviour using mental state terms (i.e., 'iCub is *interested* in these objects'). Each sentence is located on opposite poles of a bipolar continuous scale. Participants move a slider toward the sentence they think best describes the scenario. The scale is a continuum ranging from 0 to 100, where a mean of 0 corresponds to a bias for the mechanistic explanation and 100 to the mentalistic explanation. Their InStance Scores (ISS) are calculated by converting the scale into a 0–100 scale for each item and averaging across the items. The average corresponds to the participants' bias. The complete IST contains 34 items, and is associated with high internal consistency ($a = 0.83$, [7]). This study used the shortened version developed by Spatola et al. [7] which contains 12 items, containing two subscales: the isolated robot subscale and the social robot subscale (see Fig. 1).

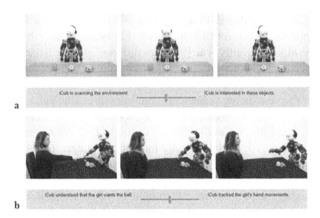

Fig. 1. Items from the InStance Test representative of (a) the isolated robot subscale and (b) the social robot subscale.

2.2 Stimuli

For the human-like behaviour, iCub communicated the appearance of emotions through emotive sound, facial expression and social communicative gesture. The robot's reactions were contingent with the events in an animal documentary. For example, it expressed enjoyment by audibly giggling, raising its arm to its face, and smiling. For the machine-like behaviour, iCub made mechanical sounds, and movement (see Fig. 2 and Marchesi et al., [10] for further details of the behaviours).

Fig. 2. Frames from the human-like video with interaction (left), machine-like video with interaction (middle) and human-like video without interaction (right). See full video in [https://osf.io/xnm5c/]. Marchesi et al. [10].

2.3 Procedure

All studies were approved by the local Ethical Committee (Comitato Etico Regione Liguria) and were conducted in accordance with the Code of Ethics of the World Medical Association (Declaration of Helsinki). Each participant provided informed consent, answered demographic questions, were naive to the purpose of the experiment and received monetary compensation. Each experiment consisted of three main parts; part one (IST pre), part 2 (exposure to iCub: either on a screen or physically embodied), and part 3 (IST post). Before the experiment each participant completed a practise item from the IST. The presentation order of the scenarios from the IST were counterbalanced and presented in a pseudo-randomized order.

2.4 Analysis

Based on an a priori hypothesis, a 2×2 repeated measures ANOVA was conducted to investigate whether the subscale affected the IST before and after participants engaged with iCub (i.e., through physically embodied interaction or by watching a video). Subscale (social robot vs. isolated) and time (before and after) were the within subjects' factors. Post-hoc pairwise comparisons were run, and Bonferroni correction was applied where necessary. All the data were normally distributed (all ps > .05). All analyses were performed using JASP statistical package version 0.14.1.0 (JASP Team).

3 Experiment One: Physically Embodied Interaction

3.1 Aim

We aimed to investigate how human-like behaviour affects the social robot and isolated robot subscale in a physically embodied interaction by re-analysing the data from Marchesi et al. [10]. We hypothesised that both the isolated robot and the social robot subscale would increase after participants engaged in the human-like condition.

3.2 Participants and Procedure

For the details of the experimental procedure, see Marchesi et al. [10]. Here we only report the re-analysis of the data obtained in [10] which considers the two subscales of IST. The re-analysis of the human-like data was performed on 40 data sets collected in [10] ($M_{age} = 29.12$, $SD_{age} = 8.87$, R = 18–60, 23 females).

3.3 Results

A repeated measures ANOVA showed a significant main effect of the time in which participants completed the IST ($F(1,39) = 5.819$, $p = .021$, $\eta_p^2 = .130$), confirming the results of Marchesi et al. [10]. There was also a significant main effect of subscale ($F(1, 39) = 50.943$, $p < .001$, $\eta_p^2 = .566$). There was no interaction between the time participants took the IST and the subscale ($F(1,39) = .016$, $p = .899$, $\eta_p^2 = 0.00$). Post-hoc pairwise comparisons were conducted to investigate the effect of time and subscale. The average ISS significantly increased after participants engaged in the human-like embodied experiment, $t(39) = -2.41$, $p = .021$, d $= -.381$ (Pre $M = 48.1$, $SD = 34.366$; Post $M = 57.742$, $SD = 31.759$). There was a significant difference in the ISS scores for the social robot subscale compared to the isolated robot subscale, $t(39) = 7.137$, $p < .001$, d $= 1.129$, with the means for the social robot subscale being higher than the isolated robot subscale (Isolated $M = 42.879$, $SD = 32.014$; Social $M = 62.962$, $SD = 31.762$).

4 Experiment Two: Video of Human-Robot Interaction

4.1 Aim

We aimed to investigate how human-like behaviour affects the social robot and isolated robot subscale when participants watched a video of the robot interacting with a human. Based on findings from O'Reilly et al. [9], we hypothesised that after participants watched the video, the social subscale scores will decrease whereas the isolated subscale scores will increase.

4.2 Procedure and Participants

For this study, a new group of 50 participants were recruited through Prolific and received a monetary compensation of £7.11 per hour. Seven participants were excluded because they selected only the extreme ends of a scale, which, in an online experiment might be an indicator of inattentiveness [12]. The final sample was $N = 43$ participants (M_{age} = 28.07, SD_{age} = 9.025, R = 19–59, 22 females, 20 males, 1 non-binary). Before the main experiment begun, participants checked video playback and audio by watching a short animation which was unrelated to the task. The study took approximately 11 min to complete.

4.3 Results

The repeated measures ANOVA showed a significant main effect of time ($F(1,42)$ = 7.673, p = .008, η_p^2 = .154). There was also a significant main effect of subscale ($F(1, 42)$ = 44.850, $p < .001$, η_p^2 = .516). There was no interaction between the time the participants took the IST and the subscale ($F(1,42)$ = .065, p = .801, η_p^2 = 0.002; left). Post-hoc pairwise comparisons were conducted to investigate the effect of time and subscale. The average ISS significantly increased after participants watched the video of the human-robot interaction, $t(42)$ = -2.770, p = .008, d = .422 (Pre M = 46.295, SD = 38.558; Post M = 55.593, SD = 35.034). There was a significant difference in the ISS scores for the social robot subscale compared to the isolated robot subscale, $t(42)$ = 6.697, $p < .001$, d = 1.021, with the means for the social robot subscale being higher than the isolated robot subscale (Isolated M = 41.434, SD = 35.853; Social M = 60.453, SD = 35.924).

5 Experiment Three: Video of Robot Without Interaction

5.1 Aim

We aimed to investigate how human-like behaviour affects the social robot and isolated robot subscale when participants watch a video of the robot without an interaction partner. We did not form any a priori hypotheses.

5.2   Procedure and Participants

The experimental procedure was identical to Experiment Two. 50 participants were recruited through Prolific and received a monetary compensation of £7.11 per hour. We excluded individuals who participated in Experiment Two. One participant was excluded due to incomplete data. The final sample was $N = 49$ participants ($M_{age} = 29.69$, $SD_{age} = 10.098$, $R = 19$–57, 22 females, 26 males, 1 non-binary).

5.3   Results

The repeated measures ANOVA showed a significant main effect of time ($F(1,48) = 8.120$, $p = .006$, $\eta_p^2 = .146$). There was also a significant main effect of subscale ($F(1, 48) = 24.650$, $p < .05$, $\eta_p^2 = .339$). There was no interaction effect between the time the participants took the IST and the subscales ($F(1,48) = .714$, $p = .402$, $\eta_p^2 = 0.015$; left). Post-hoc pairwise comparisons were conducted to investigate the effect of time and subscale. The average ISS significantly increased after participants watched the video, $t(48) = -2.865$, $p = .006$, d $= -.409$ (Pre $M = 45.680$, $SD = 38.165$; Post $M = 54.078$, $SD = 36.634$). There was a significant difference in the ISS scores for the social robot subscale compared to the isolated robot subscale, $t(48) = 4.965$, $p < .001$, d $= .709$, with the means for the social robot subscale being higher than the isolated robot subscale (Isolated $M = 43.320$, $SD = 36.747$, Social $M = 56.439$, $SD = 37.381$).

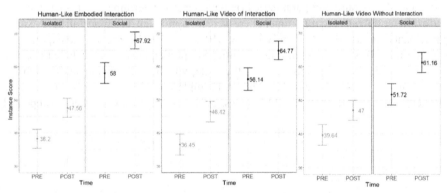

Fig. 3. The average ISS for the isolated and social robot subscale before and after participating in Experiment One (left), Experiment Two (middle) and Experiment Three (right).

6   Comparison Between Human-Like Experiments

To check that there was no effect of experiment type (i.e., physical embodiment and interaction) nor subscale (i.e., isolated and social) on the magnitude of change in the ISS before and after engaging with the human-like iCub, we compared the results between the experiments. We calculated a Δ-ISS separately for the isolated robot and the social robot subscale as the absolute difference between the ISS after and before, for each participant. A Shapiro-Wilk test was performed which showed that the distribution of the ISS departed significantly from normality for both subscales in Experiment One (Isolated $W = .863, p < .001$; Social $W = .833, p < .001$), Experiment Two (Isolated $W = 0.943, p = .034$; Social $W = .918, p = .005$) and Experiment Three (Isolated $W = .883, p < .001$; Social $W = .923, p = .003$). Subsequently, we ran a non-parametric Kruskal-Wallis test with the Δ-ISS delta score as our dependent variable, and experiment and subscale as fixed factors. There was no significant main effect of study type, $\chi^2(2) = .857, p = .651$, nor of subscale, $\chi^2(1) = 1.227, p = .268$.

7 Control Conditions: Machine-Like Behaviour

To confirm that the increase in the ISS was not due to mere exposure to the IST, we ran two control experiments with iCub exhibiting machine-like behaviour; (1) where participants interacted with a physically embodied iCub and (2) where participants watched a video of iCub interacting with a human (see Fig. 2). We hypothesised that there would be no difference in ISS after each experimental manipulation. For the first experiment we re-analysed the machine-like data collected in Marchesi et al. [10]. The sample was $N = 40$ participants ($M_{age} = 34.27$, $SD_{age} = 12.29$, R = 18–54, 30 females). A Shapiro-Wilk test showed that the distribution of the ISS departed significantly from normality for the isolated robot subscale scores before exposure to iCub ($W = .942, p = .039$) and for the social robot subscale scores after exposure to iCub ($W = .929, p = .015$). Subsequently, we ran a non-parametric Friedman's test to determine whether participants had a differential rank order for time. There were no significant differences in the ISS after participants interacted with iCub ($\chi^2(1) = .010, p = .920$). For the second experiment, we recruited 50 participants through Prolific. Six participants were excluded because they only selected the extreme ends of the scale, which, in an online study might be an indicator of inattentiveness [12]. The final sample was $N = 44$ participants ($M_{age} = 29$, $SD_{age} = 9.589$, R = 19–55, 22 females, 20 males, 1 intersex, 1 other). A repeated

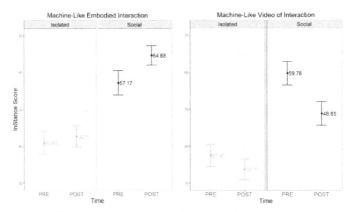

Fig. 4. The average ISS for the isolated and social robot subscale before and after participants interacted with the machine-like physically embodied iCub (left) and watched a video of an interaction with the machine-like iCub (right).

measures ANOVA also showed no significant differences in the ISS after participants watched iCub ($F(1,43) = 3.589, p = .065, \eta_p^2 = .031$). The results from the two control experiments (Fig. 4) confirm that the increase in the ISS in the human-like experiments (Fig. 3) was not due to exposure to the IST, but due to the experimental manipulation.

8 Discussion

We investigated whether the degree of embodiment and interaction affects the tendency to adopt the Intentional Stance towards iCub which is behaving in a human-like way, across two subscales of the IST. Participants either interacted with a physically embodied iCub (Experiment One), watched a video of an interaction between iCub and a human (Experiment Two), or watched iCub without an interaction (Experiment Three). Additionally, we compared the differences in the magnitude of the ISS increase across the human-like experiments. Finally, to ensure the increases in the ISS after exposure to the experimental manipulation was not due to mere exposure to the IST, we included two controls in which participants either (1) interacted with a physically embodied iCub behaving in a machine-like way or (2) watched a video of a human interacting with iCub behaving in a machine-like way.

Our hypothesis for Experiment One was supported: participants ISS increased on both subscales after they interacted with iCub. However, our hypothesis for Experiment Two was not supported. We hypothesised that a video of a human-robot interaction would affect the subscales differently [9]. Instead, both subscales increased after participants watched the video. It is possible that we found a different pattern of results compared to O'Reilly et al. [9] due to the different humanoid robots used in this study. O'Reilly et al. [9] used a humanoid arm which was 3D printed from the open-source designs by InMoov, rather than iCub. For Experiment Three, we did not have any a priori hypothesis. We found that ISS on both subscales increased after participants watched the video of iCub without an interaction partner. Furthermore, our hypothesis that physical embodiment and interaction would enhance the adoption of the Intentional Stance towards a humanoid robot compared to passive observation [10], was not supported. Instead we found no difference in the magnitude difference before and after participants completed the IST, per subscale, across the studies. For the follow-up controls with the machine-like behaviour, we hypothesised that there would be no significant difference in the ISS after participants (1) interacted with the embodied robot or (2) watched a video of the robot interacting with a human. This was supported.

This pattern of results within and across the human-like experiments, suggests that the increase in the adoption of the Intentional Stance was not due to mere exposure to the IST, but rather due to the human-like behaviour of iCub. Furthermore, the increase in ISS after witnessing iCub behaving in a human-like way, across different levels of embodiment and interaction, suggests that the enhanced tendency to adopt the Intentional Stance is robust to changes in embodiment and interaction. This implies that enactive intersubjectivity [11] is not a necessary condition to increase the adoption of the Intentional Stance. Instead, the increase in the adoption of the Intentional Stance in Experiment Two and Three, could be explained by a representationalist perspective. This perspective argues that social cognition arises from a process of simulating internal models of behaviour based on passive observation [11]. Indeed, it is possible that neither the representationalist nor the non-representationalist perspective is the only route towards adoption of the Intentional Stance. Perhaps, individuals flexibly employ either model dependent on the context (i.e., embodied interaction or passive observation). The debate around the appropriate accounts of social cognition, and their interaction deserves further research and humanoid robots could be a useful tool to explore these complexities.

Acknowledgements. This work has received support from the European Research Council under the European Union's Horizon 2020 research and innovation programme, ERC Starting grant ERC-2016-StG-715058, awarded to Agnieszka Wykowska. The content of this paper is the sole responsibility of the authors. The European Commission or its services cannot be held responsible for any use that may be made of the information it contains.

References

1. Schilbach, L., et al.: Toward a second-person neuroscience 1. Behav. Brain Sci. **36**(4), 393–414 (2013)
2. Roseberry Lytle, S., Garcia-Sierra, A., Kuhl, P.K.: Infant language learning in the presence of peers. Proc. Natl. Acad. Sci. **115**, 9859–9866 (2018)
3. Wiese, E., Metta, G., Wykowska, A.: Robots as intentional agents: using neuroscientific methods to make robots appear more social. Front. Psychol. **8**, 1663 (2017)
4. Wykowska, A.: Robots as mirrors of the human mind. Curr. Dir. Psychol. Sci. **30**(1), 34–40 (2021)
5. Dennett, D.C.: Intentional systems. J. Philos. **68**(4), 87–106 (1971)
6. Dennett, D.C., Haugeland, J.: Intentionality. Oxford University Press, In The Oxford companion to the mind (1987)
7. Spatola, N., Marchesi, S., Wykowska, A.: The Instance Task: how to measure the mentalistic bias in human-robot interaction (2021). https://doi.org/10.31234/osf.io/b3wtq
8. Metta, G., Sandini, G., Vernon, D., Natale, L., Nori, F.: The iCub humanoid robot: an open platform for research in embodied cognition. In: Proceedings of the 8th Workshop on Performance Metrics for Intelligent Systems, pp. 50–56 (2008)
9. O'Reilly, Z., Ghiglino, D., Spatola, N., Wykowska, A.: Modulating the intentional stance: humanoid robots, narrative and autistic traits. In: Li, H., et al. (eds.) ICSR 2021. LNCS (LNAI), vol. 13086, pp. 697–706. Springer, Cham (2021). https://doi.org/10.1007/978-3-030-90525-5_61
10. Marchesi, S., De Tommaso, D., Perez-Osorio, J., Wykowska, A.: Belief in sharing the same phenomenological experience increases the likelihood of adopting the intentional stance toward a humanoid robot (2022)
11. Fuchs, T., De Jaegher, H.: Enactive intersubjectivity: participatory sense-making and mutual incorporation. Phenomenol. Cogn. Sci. **8**(4), 465–486 (2009)
12. Hamilton, D.L.: Personality attributes associated with extreme response style. Psychol. Bull. **69**(3), 192 (1968)

A Case for the Design of Attention and Gesture Systems for Social Robots

Romain Maure, Erik A. Wengle[(✉)], Utku Norman, Daniel Carnieto Tozadore, and Barbara Bruno

Swiss Federal Institute of Technology in Lausanne (EPFL), Lausanne, Switzerland
{erik.wengle,barbara.bruno}@epfl.ch

Abstract. The success of social robots, even (or, especially) in use cases as simple as "manning" a booth to promote a product in a shopping mall, depends on their ability of interacting with humans in a timely, effective and enjoyable way. In this paper we present an attention system and a gesture system for use by an autonomous social robot in applications related to product promotion. Our attention system employs a modular approach and attention functions, to allow for rich run-time behaviours to arise from simple rules, while the proposed gesture system allows for tuning the gestures to convey different emotions and robot personalities. The two systems were tested in an experiment involving 790 participants, aiming to explore the attractive power of different robot behaviours.

Keywords: Social robotics · Attention system · Gesture system

1 Introduction

Imagine to enter a shopping mall. On the side, a young woman is standing next to a booth, to promote a new product among customers. Her job description is simple: 1) identify potentially interested customers and attract them towards the booth, 2) describe them the key features of the product, typically on the basis of a script learned by heart, 3) conclude the (short) interaction by giving them a sample, leaflet, or gadget, as a reminder of the product. Such a job is repetitive, tiring (often requiring people to stand still for long shifts), usually poorly paid, possibly demoralising (since most customers ignore the vendors, or treat them as nuisances) and even enforcing gender biases and stereotypes, as it typically employs young, good-looking women to attract more customers. These characteristics, which make the job unappealing for people, also make it a perfect task for social robots: repetitive, short, interactions are their *forte*, they have a natural talent for standing still and do not possess feelings that rude customers can hurt. Moreover, robots, still a rare sight in everyday life, arguably exert a strong attraction on humans, with the added benefit of not enforcing stereotypes. As an example, a recent study revealed that people who saw an advertisement

R. Maure and E.A. Wengle—Contributed equally to this work.

F. Cavallo et al. (Eds.): ICSR 2022, LNAI 13817, pp. 367–377, 2022.
https://doi.org/10.1007/978-3-031-24667-8_33

of a robot hotel service had a significantly higher purchase intention than those who watched a traditional hotel service advertisement [11].

Designing a social robot for product promotion poses a number of not-yet-fully-solved challenges, among which: 1) the robot needs to be able to identify potentially interested customers among the passers-by, 2) the robot needs to know *how* to successfully attract them to the booth and show them the product.

The first challenge requires the robot to be equipped with an *attention system* [4], allowing it to detect passers-by, identify the interested ones among them and hold their attention throughout the interaction. Early attention systems relied on psychophysical models of human attention, supported by neurobiological evidence [7]. Attempts at achieving human-like processing efficiency include VOCUS, which combines a bottom-up approach for the detection of elements of (possible) interest with a top-down extension for the identification of regions of (more) interest [3].

The second challenge requires the robot to be equipped with a *gesture* system [8], allowing it to perform gestures prior to and during the interaction, to attract a passer-by's attention and guide it towards the product on display. While it is established that the robots' non-verbal behaviour is correlated with their likeability [6], literature findings are not conclusive concerning what is the best behaviour for attracting attention. As an example, [9] suggests that multimodal behaviours draw more attention, but [10] reveals that they generate slower response times than unimodal behaviours.

In this article, we tackle the two above-listed challenges, with the overarching goal of contributing to the design and development of social robots for product promotion. We propose a fast, easily customisable *attention system* for social robots, allowing to display a natural, complex behaviour arising from the combination of simple features and a *gesture system* which allows for conveying different emotional and personality cues. Building on an experiment involving 790 passers-by, we investigate the success rate of different unimodal and multimodal behaviours in attracting the attention of passers-by.

2   System Architecture

2.1   Attention System

A key requirement for our attention system is to allow for the easy customisation of *what* is interesting and *how* to react to the detection of an element of interest. To this aim, our attention system relies on *events* and associated *attention functions*, which the system manipulates at run-time.

At the lowest level, the system relies on a portfolio of detectors of elements of interest (e.g., faces and objects), which work on the camera stream and provide in output, frame by frame, a 2D bounding box within the image space for each detected element. The goal of the attention system is to identify at all times, within the image space, the most interesting element to look at.

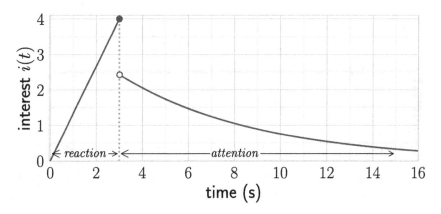

Fig. 1. The attention function, defined as $i(t)$ with $t_r = 3$, $I = 4$, $a = 6$ and $b = 0$.

At the core of the attention system there are the *events*. Each category of element of interest can be associated with one or more events, of three types: *detection* events are triggered when an element of that category first appears in the robot's field of view; *change* events are triggered when an element, already present in the robot's field of view, changes in one or more of its perceived properties; *departure* events are triggered when an element, previously present in the robot's field of view, disappears from the scene. As an example, in our experimental evaluation we consider human faces as elements of interest and define four events associated with face detection: 1) the *detection event* is raised when a new face appears in the robot's field of view; 2) the *movement event* is a change event raised when a tracked face moves within the robot's field of view; 3) the *head tilt event* is another change event, raised when a tracked face changes its orientation (e.g., to turn towards, or away from the robot); 4) the *departure event* is raised when a tracked face disappears from the robot's field of view.

Each event is supposed to raise the attention of the robot quickly, and lowering it slowly over time if no new event is triggered. An event is therefore associated with an *attention function*, which computes an interest score $i(t) \in \mathbb{R}_{\geq 0}$ for each time instant $t \in \mathbb{R}_{\geq 0}$ given as an input.

The function, shown in the graph of Fig. 1, is defined by four parameters:

- The reaction time t_r defines how quickly $i(t)$ should increase after activation and corresponds to the time for which $i(t)$ reaches its peak.
- The interest value I is the value of $i(t)$ at the peak. In our implementation, this parameter is set at run-time for tilt events, proportional with the angle between the person's gaze and the robot's orientation.
- The attention factor a defines how slowly $i(t)$ should decay after the peak.
- The base value b allows for chaining events (i.e., their attention functions) and shall be elaborated on in the following.

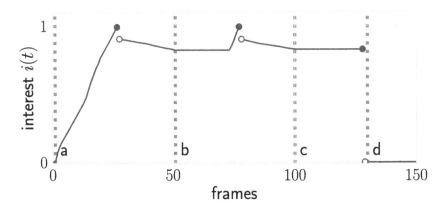

Fig. 2. Evolution of the interest score, for a person in following events: event (a) entering the robot's field of view, (b) turning to look at the robot, (c) looking away and (d) leaving. The score is computed by chaining the attention functions associated with the triggered events.

The function is then computed as follows:

$$i(t) = \begin{cases} \max\{b, I\frac{t}{t_r}\} & \text{if } t \le t_r \\ e^{-t/a} \max\{b, I\} & \text{if } t > t_r \end{cases} \tag{1}$$

At run time, whenever an element of interest is detected, the corresponding detection event is triggered, and the associated attention function is activated and linked with the element's bounding box. The interest value $i(t)$ of the attention function thus represents the interest that the element within the bounding box has for the robot, at any given time. Later events related to the same element (e.g., if a detected face changes orientation) cause the previous and new attention functions to be merged as follows. Let us assume that at time t^* an element of interest generated by a previous detection event has an interest value $i_d(t^*) = i^*$, where $i_d(t)$ denotes the attention function associated with the detection event. If, at time t^*, the element experiences a change, the associated attention function is re-set as:

$$i(t) = i_c(t - t^*) \text{ such that } b_c = i_d(t^*) = i^* \tag{2}$$

where $i_c(t)$ denotes the new attention function associated with the change event and b_c is its base value. Note that $i_c(0) = b_c$.

As an example, the graph of Fig. 2 illustrates the evolution of the interest score associated with a face that (a) enters the robot's field of view, (b) turns to look at the robot, (c) looks away and (d) leaves.

The tracking of the elements of interests is done via the Euclidean distance metric, that first associates each bounding box detected at frame n with the closest bounding box detected at frame $n - 1$ of the same type and then, by evaluating the difference between the previous and current element within the box, triggers the appropriate event, if any. To allow the aggregation of the interest score of multiple, possibly overlapping, bounding boxes, the robot's field of view is partitioned into a grid of equally sized cells. The interest score of each cell corresponds to the sum of the interest scores of all the bounding boxes it intersects with. Finally, at each frame, the output of the attention system is the coordinates of the cell with the highest interest value. If no bounding box is present, the interest score of all cells defaults to 0, and no cell is returned.

2.2 Gesture System

The gesture system endows the robot with the ability to perform *deictic*, or pointing, gestures [1], aiming to attract others' attention to a specific entity in the environment. In our use case, deictic gestures can be used to attract the passers-by's attention on the robot, as a form of attractive behaviour, as well as on the product on display, once a person has approached the booth.

The system is designed as a hierarchy of ROS2 services. At the lower level, a `goto` service relies on the robot's inverse kinematic model to allow the robot's end effectors reach any reachable pose within the workspace from their current pose. The service provides two types of motion trajectories, the *linear* trajectory and the *minimum jerk* trajectory, and allows for tuning the motion speed in terms of a percentage of the actuators' maximum velocity.

The `point_to` service relies on the `goto` service to endow the robot with the ability to point towards an entity or direction of interest. Given a point of interest $P = (x_P, y_P, z_P)$ in the Cartesian space whose origin O is located at the robot's torso, the direction of interest is defined by the vector $\overrightarrow{OP}$ and the final position P^* of the robot's end effector can be located anywhere along the $\overline{OP}$ segment. A parameter allows to specify the end effector's position along the segment, as a percentage of the farthest reachable point along the segment, defined as the intersection point between $\overrightarrow{OP}$ and the robot's workspace boundary.

The service provides several types of pointing gestures. The *basic pointing* gesture aims to mimic human's pointing gestures: the robot simply moves its end effector from its current position to P^*, oriented along the direction of interest. The *two-steps pointing* gesture is a combination of two successive movements. The robot first moves the end effector from its current position to a home position near the shoulder, then moves it along $\overrightarrow{OP}$ from this home position to P^*, keeping its orientation always aligned with $\overrightarrow{OP}$. Intuitively, this gesture type aims to attract viewers' attention on the direction of interest and make it easier for them to follow it. Lastly, the *self-pointing* gesture aims to attract viewers' attention on the robot itself. This gesture can be seen as a reversal of the *two-steps pointing* gesture, where the robot first points towards the human whose attention it intends to attract and then follows the direction of interest backwards, bringing the end effector close to itself.

The gesture system also allows to simultaneously move the robot's head during a pointing gesture, to increase the impact of the attractive behaviour. Finally, for the purposes of the experimental evaluation described in Sect. 3, a simple *waving* gesture has also been developed, to allow for a comparison between its attraction power and the one of other types of gestures and behaviours.

Fig. 3. Experiment setup.

3 Experimental Evaluation

3.1 Experiment Design

The primary goal of the experimental evaluation is to assess the effectiveness of various types of robot behaviours in attracting the attention of passing-by people. The experiment also allows for an evaluation of the attention system's performance in identifying and responding to events of interest, in a highly dynamic context and for events not necessarily defined a-priori.

We placed the robot at the entrance of the EPFL's library (Fig. 3), sideways with respect to the path followed by student to enter/exit the study area. This choice ensures a large variability in the type of situations presented to the attention system (people moving alone or in groups, walking in a hurry or leisurely strolling, etc.). Moreover, it guarantees that attracted passers-by visibly alter their behaviour w.r.t. not-attracted passers-by (e.g., by turning their head to the side, or by changing their path to come closer to the robot). We deem this setting to be a reasonable example of a product promotion use case, typically taking place in a crowded environment, in which people move with a purpose and where the booth is placed sideways to not block the customers' path.

The experiment is a natural experiment study [5], with random-like assignment of participants to the five conditions determined by the behaviour used by the robot to attract passers-by. The robot ran each condition for thirty consecutive minutes, changed manually by the experimenters. In the *control* condition, the robot only moves its head, as determined by the attention system. This behaviour is identical across all conditions. In the *waving* condition, the robot waves every time a new passer-by currently ignoring it (henceforth referred to as "target person") is detected by the attention system, while in the *self-pointing* condition the robot, upon detecting a new "target person", performs a self-pointing gesture. In the *speaking* condition, the robot's attractive behaviour is to utter the sentence "Hey, would you come over here?" while, lastly, in the *multimodal* condition the robot's reaction to a new "target person" envisions the concurrent uttering of a sentence and execution of a self-pointing gesture. Our hypothesis is that the order in which conditions are listed above corresponds to the attraction effectiveness of the corresponding robot behaviours, i.e., it increases from the control to the multimodal.

The interaction unfolded as follows. The robot's attention system continuously scans the environment at three frames per second. Once a person is detected, the attention system orients the robot's head toward the point of maximum interest (if needed), checks if the person has already been detected or not and whether they are already moving and/or looking towards it (on the basis of their head orientation). A not-currently-tracked participant whose head is not oriented towards the robot is a "target person". Upon identifying a new "target person", the robot computes and stores a metric related to the distance between the human and itself and performs the attractive behaviour associated with the currently active condition. After executing the behaviour, the robot recomputes the distance to the person: if it is significantly smaller than the one computed before the attractive behaviour (concretely, if the ratio of the area of the current bounding box over the initial area of the bounding box at the detection event has increased beyond 125%), the robot invites the person to take a chocolate from a nearby box, by pointing to it, and utters a goodbye sentence. If the distance has not reduced, the robot murmurs "I blame myself", lowers the arm used to attract the "target person" (in the conditions which imply arm movement) and resumes scanning its surroundings.

3.2 Evaluation Metrics

The simplest metric to measure the effectiveness of the different robot behaviours in attracting passers-by is to consider how many among them came close enough to the robot and picked up a chocolate from the chocolate box. Let us denote with P the number of all passers-by, and with P_{Choc} the number of people who came close enough and picked a chocolate. The *strong attraction rate* A_{strong} is thus computed as:

$$A_{strong} = \frac{P_{Choc}}{P} \tag{3}$$

Conversely, the *weak attraction rate* measures the number of times the robot elicited any type of response from a participant, even if they did not move closer. Let us denote with P_{Int} the number of passers-by who displayed at any time an interest in the robot, e.g., by coming closer, or verbally, or by hand-waving to it. The *weak attraction rate* A_{weak} is thus computed as:

$$A_{weak} = \frac{P_{Int}}{P} \tag{4}$$

Finally, we introduce the notion of *persuasiveness* of the robot to solely focus on those people that, while initially uninterested in the robot, changed their behaviour as a response to the robot's action. Let us denote with P_{Att} the number of passers-by not interested in the robot upon entering its field of view (i.e., not walking toward the robot and not looking at the robot) that the robot identified as "target people" and thus tried to attract, and with P_{React} those among them who responded in any way to the robot's action. The robot's *persuasiveness Per* is thus computed as:

$$Per = \frac{P_{React}}{P_{Att}} \qquad (5)$$

3.3 Participants

The participants of the study are EPFL students and personnel, passing by the EPFL library on the day the experiment took place. No personal information was collected before, during nor after the experiment. The age of participants can be estimated to lie in the $[16, 65]$ range, with most participants likely below 30. Concerning gender, our participants' pool is likely skewed towards men, since women represent approx. 30% of all EPFL students [2]. The experiment took place on a Tuesday morning and lasted approximately 2.5 h (30 min per condition). A total of 790 people passed by the robot during the study. The average interaction time of the users which showed interest in the robot (P_{Int}) was 22.93 s (with a standard deviation of 15.12 s). A Kruskal-Wallis H test indicated no statistically significant differences between attractive behaviours for the duration of interaction of the users that showed interest ($H = 2.81, p = .59$).

4   Results

4.1   Attractive Behaviours Evaluation

Table 1 shows the attraction rates obtained for the various attractive behaviours.

Table 1. Attraction rates and robot liveliness.

Condition	P	P_{Choc}	A_{strong}	P_{Int}	A_{weak}	P_{Att}	P_{React}	Per
Control	104 (66)	9	8.65% (13.64%)	8	7.69% (12.12%)	0	0	0.00%
Waving	172 (86)	18	10.47% (20.93%)	26	15.11% (30.23%)	14	5	35.71%
Self-pointing	177 (84)	28	15.82% (33.33%)	25	14.12% (29.76%)	19	3	15.78%
Speaking	145 (63)	37	**25.52% (58.73%)**	22	15.17% (34.92%)	17	3	17.64%
Multimodal	192 (99)	45	23.44% (45.45%)	35	**18.23% (35.35%)**	7	4	**57.14%**

As expected, the table shows that the addition of attractive behaviours has a non-negligible impact on the number of passers-by being attracted towards the robot. In terms of the strong attraction rate A_{strong}, the best performance is achieved by the *speaking* condition (25.52%), closely followed by the *multimodal* condition (23.44%). Conversely, in terms of the weak attraction rate A_{weak}, the best performance is achieved by the *multimodal* condition (18.23%), while all other attractive behaviours display similar rates. Lastly, although the small number of people involved and the imbalance between the conditions do not allow to draw significant conclusions, the persuasiveness analysis suggests that the *multimodal* attractive behaviour (57.14%) is remarkably more persuasive than all others, with a 60% improvement over the performance of the second-best behaviour (*waving* with 35.71%).

4.2 Attention System Evaluation in the Wild

The face detection rates in the various experimental conditions are reported in Table 2: in total, 277 out of 398 (69.60%) people walking towards the robot were detected and therefore considered by the attention system.

Table 2. Number of passers-by per condition and face detection rates.

Condition	Total	Facing away	Facing towards	Detected	Detection rate
Control	104	38	66	37	56.06 %
Waving	172	86	86	61	70.93 %
Self-pointing	177	93	84	55	65.48 %
Speaking	145	82	63	40	63.49 %
Multimodal	192	93	99	84	84.85 %
TOTAL	790	392	398	277	69.60 %

We think that these detection rates are reasonably high, considering that (1) the experiment was performed over multiple hours, with different natural lighting conditions (2) the experiment took place in December 2021, when COVID-19 countermeasures still enforced the use of masks indoor. Indeed, most mis-detection were caused by the concurrent use of surgical masks, glasses, scarfs and/or hats, which left only a very small portion of the face actually visible. Lastly, on average, half of the people entering the robot's field of view were not facing the robot and thus impossible to detect. We hypothesise that, exactly as the robot had difficulties seeing people facing away from it, those people might have had difficulties in seeing the robot. To account for this possibility, in Table 1 we report, in parenthesis, the total number of participants whose moving direction was to walk towards the robot and the corresponding A_{strong} and A_{weak} rates. The considerations reported in Sect. 4.1 still apply.

The experiment generated a large amount of events (both foreseen and not foreseen at design time), where 4 scenarios are worth reporting.

In the first situation, the two people moved their gaze from the robot to each other throughout the interaction, which caused the robot to similarly shift its attention from the first person to the second, in a natural manner. Conversely, in the second situation the two people in the robot's field of view never looked away from it. This caused the robot to continuously move its gaze from one to the other, in a rather unnatural fashion. In the third situation four people entered the scene and moved towards the box of chocolate, completely oblivious to the robot. Upon noticing it, they thanked it for the chocolate and left. Throughout this interaction, the robot's gaze stayed stably on one single person, only moving towards a different person as the first one moved to take a piece of chocolate and looked away from the robot. This behaviour is deemed correct and natural. Lastly, in the fourth situation, two people entered the robot's field of view, with one way more interested in the robot than the other. In an attempt at catching the robot's attention, the first person caused the face of the second person to be repeatedly obstructed, and thus, by repeatedly appearing as a new face, be counted as more interesting for the attention system. This behaviour is deemed not correct, as the robot behaved differently from the person's expectation.

The good performance of the system even in unforeseen and "stressful" conditions (e.g., with four people surrounding the robot, or with a number of passers-by in the background) give us hope that the proposed approach could strike a good balance between speed, simplicity of setup and complexity and richness of the run-time behaviour.

5   Conclusions

In this paper we investigate the requirements posed on an autonomous social robot by the use case of manning a booth for product promotion in a shopping mall, a job which, while pervasive in our societies, has a number of drawbacks making it unattractive for humans. Such a robot requires a fast and simple-to-tune attention system, allowing it to identify potentially interested customers among the passers-by. To this end, we propose an attention system which allows for obtaining rich run-time behaviours as a combination of simple events, with associated attention functions. At the same time, this application requires the robot to be capable of gestures-based non-verbal interaction. To this end, we propose a gesture system allowing for the parameterisation of the robot's movements. In an experiment involving 790 participants, we compared the performance of five different uni-modal and multimodal behaviours in attracting the attention of passing-by people, showing that a multimodal behaviour combining an utterance with a self-pointing gesture not only elicits more responses from passers-by, but seems more persuasive (i.e., better able of attracting the interest of previously uninterested people) than all other behaviours.

Acknowledgments. This project was supported by the European Union's Horizon 2020 Research and Innovation Programme under grant agreement No 765955 (ANIMATAS) and as a part of NCCR Robotics, a National Centre of Competence in Research, funded by the Swiss National Science Foundation (grant number 51NF40_185543).

References

1. Ekman, P., Friesen, W.V.: The repertoire of nonverbal behavior: categories, origins, usage, and coding. Semiotica **1**(1), 49–98 (1969)
2. Equal opportunity office: gender monitoring EPFL 2019–2020. Technical Report, EPFL (2020). https://www.epfl.ch/about/equality/wp-content/uploads/2020/10/GenderMonitoring_EPFL_2020_en.pdf
3. Frintrop, S.: Computational visual attention. In: Salah, A., Gevers, T. (eds.) Computer Analysis of Human Behavior, pp. 69–101. Springer, London (2011). https://doi.org/10.1007/978-0-85729-994-9_4
4. Lanillos, P., Ferreira, J.F., Dias, J.: Designing an artificial attention system for social robots. In: 2015 IEEE/RSJ International Conference on Intelligent Robots and Systems (IROS), pp. 4171–4178. IEEE (2015). https://doi.org/10.1109/IROS.2015.7353967
5. Leatherdale, S.T.: Natural experiment methodology for research: a review of how different methods can support real-world research. Int. J. Soc. Res. Method. **22**(1), 19–35 (2019). https://doi.org/10.1080/13645579.2018.1488449
6. Lewandowski, B., et al.: Socially compliant human-robot interaction for autonomous scanning tasks in supermarket environments. In: 2020 29th IEEE International Conference on Robot and Human Interactive Communication (RO-MAN), pp. 363–370. IEEE (2020). https://doi.org/10.1109/RO-MAN47096.2020.9223568
7. Norman, D.A.: Toward a theory of memory and attention. Psychol. Rev. **75**(6), 522–536 (1968). https://doi.org/10.1037/h0026699
8. Van de Perre, G., De Beir, A., Cao, H.L., Esteban, P.G., Lefeber, D., Vanderborght, B.: Reaching and pointing gestures calculated by a generic gesture system for social robots. Robot. Autonom. Syst. **83**, 32–43 (2016). https://doi.org/10.1016/j.robot.2016.06.006
9. Saad, E., Neerincx, M.A., Hindriks, K.V.: Welcoming robot behaviors for drawing attention. In: 2019 14th ACM/IEEE International Conference on Human-Robot Interaction (HRI). pp. 636–637. IEEE (2019). https://doi.org/10.1109/HRI.2019.8673283
10. Torta, E., van Heumen, J., Piunti, F., Romeo, L., Cuijpers, R.: Evaluation of unimodal and multimodal communication cues for attracting attention in human-robot interaction. Int. J. Soc. Robot. **7**(1), 89–96 (2014). https://doi.org/10.1007/s12369-014-0271-x
11. Zhong, L., Sun, S., Law, R., Zhang, X.: Impact of robot hotel service on consumers' purchase intention: a control experiment. Asia Pacific J. Tourism Res. **25**(7), 780–798 (2020). https://doi.org/10.1080/10941665.2020.1726421

Introducing Psychology Strategies to Increase Engagement on Social Robots

Fernando Alonso-Martin$^{(\boxtimes)}$ (iD), Sara Carrasco-Martínez,
Juan José Gamboa-Montero, Enrique Fernández-Rodicio,
and Miguel Ángel Salichs

University Carlos III of Madrid, Getafe, Spain
`famartin@ing.uc3m.es`

Abstract. One of the challenges facing the field of social robotics research is to achieve useful robots that users trust and regularly employ in their daily lives. That is, robots with a high degree of engagement with their users. To date, few social bots have achieved massive sales success coupled with a satisfactory and continuous user experience over time by the users who interact with them. This may be partly due to the lack of maturity of certain technologies involved in developing these social robots, but undoubtedly a key factor —and one that is being taken into account very little— is the psychological factor when designing and developing these technological devices. There are several psychological techniques that, when correctly applied and combined, can significantly increase the engagement in the interaction between humans and robots. In this paper, we will unravel what these techniques are and how we can apply them in this field of research.

Keywords: Engagement · Social robots · Human-robot interaction

1 Introduction

Scientists studying addictions in the early 20th century believed that people exhibiting addictive behaviors lacked morality and willpower. This concept was erroneous and was gradually corrected. In the second half of the 20th century, some scientific research began to appear linking addictions to brain behavior. Thanks to these groundbreaking discoveries, addictions are classified as a disorder that affects the brain and modifies its behavior. In the 21st century, a large part of the planet lives and coexists in digital environments. Surrounded by the so-called new technologies, immersed in them. There are people, the new generations, who are unable to imagine a non-digital world. Since they were born, their lives have developed in constant digital interaction. They are the so-called digital natives. Human behavior in this digital environment is closely related to the theory of behaviorism studied by psychologist B.F. Skinner. Behaviorism is a

Acknowledgments to Spanish Ministry of Science, Innovation, and Universities.

F. Cavallo et al. (Eds.): ICSR 2022, LNAI 13817, pp. 378–387, 2022.
https://doi.org/10.1007/978-3-031-24667-8_34

branch of psychology based on the observation and analysis of behavior. Behaviorism emerged as a counterpoint to psychoanalysis, and it aimed to provide a scientific, demonstrable, and measurable basis for psychology.

Watson and Pavlov began to conduct experiments with various animals, laying the foundation for behaviorism and conditioning [22]. A few years later, B. F. Skinner added a great discovery to this branch of psychology: operant conditioning [19]. Skinner wanted to discover how to get certain animals to reproduce a specific behavior based on rewards. To do so, he invented the Operant Conditioning Chamber, better known as "Skinner's Box". He experimented mainly with pigeons.

Skinner's boxes contained some mechanism - for example, a lever - that the pigeons had to manipulate. This behavior is not in the pigeon's nature, so it had to learn it. When the pigeon presses the lever, it receives a reward, usually food. Receiving the food is a positive stimulus that favors the conditioning that is intended to be achieved in the experiment. At first, the animal guesses by chance and later learns. This is called learning by reinforcement, and for it to work, it must have a more or less immediate and satisfactory reinforcement. That is, the reward must be something pleasant. The Skinner Box also has a device that records the responses of the pigeons as a function of time and the sequential order in which they have been given. In addition, it signals which responses have been reinforced, depending on whether the rewards have been fixed or variable. This data is essential, and with it comes another of Skinner's great discoveries.

After testing different rewards and intervals, Skinner and his team found —almost by chance— a type of reward that made the animals press the lever more times and for more extended periods. When the reward frequency was variable, with no particular pattern, it turned out that the animals pressed the lever impulsively and compulsively. This is how was discover the variable reward system, where the unknown and randomness of not knowing when the reward would be received made the repetitive behavior of the animals complicated to extinguish. In other words: they became tremendously addicted to constantly pressing the lever.

An American neuroendocrinology scientist, Robert Sapolsky, studied dopamine to discover how this molecule was related to human behavior [16]. He discovered that dopamine is not a substance that rewards us when we do something, but rather it is the substance that directly drives us to do something. In other words, the substance gives us the push (in that moment of uncertainty) that we need to act when we perceive a given stimulus. The action of dopamine is so decisive that there are studies with laboratory rats in which when their dopamine receptors are inhibited, the rats do not perform any action and end up dying from not eating.

As we have seen, dopamine is the substance that gives us the push we need, just in that previous moment of uncertainty in which we feel desire, and it is the one that moves us to act when we see the signal. This is how it works in a simplified way: we receive a signal, we feel desire, the brain gives us a shot of dopamine so that we take action, we take action and when we consume the action, we feel pleasure [4].

This signal and dopamine hook is exploited in the digital and technological world, where the variable reward system is flourishing, especially in free-to-play video games [23]. In these, the game is free to play, but the creators fill it with variable reward items such as boxes and chests, which require the user to make a micropayment to open or obtain them.

We find it in video games and almost all bars and restaurants, such as the famous "slot machines". These machines are designed to make us lose money (and we know it), but the randomness of the game and the instinct of "I am sure I will get the next one" make that we cannot stop playing and it becomes a real vice [20].

Variable reward systems can be combined with another set of techniques, especially from studies in social psychology and game theory, which will be discussed later in this paper. One of this paper's key and main contributions is to propose using these potential techniques to increase engagement in the field of social robotics. These techniques have been used in isolation, in some cases with some combination, in other fields such as games, video games, social networks, etc. However, their use in robotics has not begun. Therefore, in this paper, we introduce their use and suggest how to integrate them into the dynamics of human-robot interaction.

2   Strategies to Enhance Engagement

In this section, we will analyse the twelve relevant strategies related to hooking science and psychology that we can apply directly in the field of social robotics. We will try to explain them concisely and give some examples of practical application in our area.

2.1   Variable and Unpredictability Rewards

Humans, like the pigeons in Skinner's box, or Sapolsky's mice, crave predictability and struggle to find patterns, even when they do not exist. Variability is the brain's cognitive nemesis, and our minds make deducing cause and effect a priority over other functions such as self-control and restraint. Variable rewards seem to keep the brain busy, removing its defenses and providing an opportunity to plant the seeds of new habits. It is, therefore, perhaps the most powerful technique to increase engagement.

Strangely, we perceive this trance state as fun. It is because our brains are programmed to endlessly search for the next reward and novelty, never being satisfied. Recent neuroscience has revealed that our dopamine system does not reward our efforts but keeps us searching by inducing that semi-stressful response we call desire [10]. Though it sometimes pains us, it is this mental wiring that keeps us alive as a species. We are the most relentlessly curious species on the planet, and we have found more meaning in our environment than any other animal. Nevertheless, this same impulse to search endlessly, never satisfied, creates the habitual behavior of many new technologies.

Variable rewards respond to three basic human needs [6]:

- Need for *social rewards*. We seek them out to feel part of the group. The need to belong is vital for humans and some animal species. The feeling of belonging brings us security and exclusion generates anxiety and stress. Evolutionarily we have developed this need because it guaranteed our survival. Thousands of years ago being expelled from the group was a guarantee of dying soon. We are social and gregarious beings. We need to feel accepted, valued and important. Pages and social networks where members can rate and "like" each other are based on this need to feel accepted, valued and important.
- Need for *information rewards* or *rewards that reduce uncertainty*. Our brain is programmed with the need to obtain physical objects and information. Uncertainty produces anxiety, eliminating it makes us feel good. Showing part of the content and letting the person look for the rest, generates engagement: leaving news and photographs half seen at the end of the screen, suggestive clothes that show a little but not everything, giving you an appetizer to taste an exquisite dish. When we leave a glimpse of something, the impulse is to discover what is hidden from us, the desire to get it, increases.
- Need for *rewards for the ego*. We have an instinct to complete tasks and solve mysteries. We have grown up with riddles, jigsaw puzzles, puzzles, games of assembling and disassembling pieces and structures, convertible dolls... In video games: leveling up, getting new skills, etc.

Suggestions for use in social robotics: In the games included in the robot, a ranking of users with better scores (social reward) and personal (ego reward) could be added. During the interaction with the robot, it can offer the user information related to and relevant to that user (information reward). The robot can gamify the experience as a reward by offering them "prizes" in a variable and simple way when they complete specific tasks, explore certain functionalities, or reach a particular interaction time.

2.2 The Beginner's Luck

One of the most potent effects of hooking in casinos is to have a good run right from the start [11]. The same thing happens on many dating sites, when the user makes a profile, they are quickly presented with seductive profiles to arouse interest and then supposedly irresistible offers of payment. On the contrary, if you start losing or without understanding its dynamics at the beginning of a new activity or game, you will likely stop doing it in the future. That is to say, the engagement is much lower.

Suggestions for use in social robotics: In the repertoire of games that the robot consists of, it is possible to incorporate dynamics that facilitate engagement so that in the first interactions, the user starts winning, although with a certain level of difficulty. If the level of difficulty were excessive, the user would not be motivated to continue playing. Concerning interaction in general, the same concept is applicable, the robot can "premiate" in the first interactions with the user to encourage engagement. E.g. the robot detects a new user, it can try to "engage" him with some compliment, joke, or call for attention.

2.3   Supernormal Stimuli

They are something studied in biology and psychology [14,21]. It is a specific type of stimuli that exaggerates the qualities of others, causing the organism that perceives it to emit a much stronger response than to those normal stimuli. Junk food, foods that generate a great appetite because of their appearance and taste, are terrible for our organism at a nutritional level. Flavors are intensified to make food very palatable and challenging to resist. Feminine images where attributes and curves are clearly exaggerated. Breast and lip implants are a supernormal stimulus. Clichés to the extreme, exaggerating features, for example of romantic cut, looking for an emotional response. Filters in photos showing perfect faces. These are some of the supernormal stimuli of our modern world. They exaggerate the features that are naturally attractive to us, and as a result, our instincts go wild, leading us to excessive consumption habits and abusive habits of social networks, pornography, junk food, and many others.

Suggestions for use in social robotics: Robots can be designed in the shape of a domestic pet (generally preferred) but exaggerate some preferences that we humans have in general. For example, design it to look like or inspire the shape of a cat, but perhaps with more enormous eyes and an even more cuddly appearance. We can also coat the robot with a fabric that is incredibly comfortable to the human touch.

2.4   Illusion of Control

It is a cognitive bias based on the need to control our decisions or environment inherent to human beings [2,5]. Many superstitions stem from this. Some people believe that if they do not pick the lottery numbers themselves, they will not win. In a panic room (gradual increase in sound), installing a button to ask for the sound to stop made patients endure more volume. The button was a fake. Similarly, some traffic lights and elevators have fake buttons. Giving false control generates engagement. In personal relationships and recruiting and sales techniques, "I will just be 1 min" (you give them false control of their time) is used a lot. Surveys that tell you it takes 2 min and it is not valid. A sign on the highway that says that such and such a place (a shopping mall, a hypermarket) is 5 min away and it is not true. Or the famous phrase "you are free, you choose", but they offer you limited options that prevent you from choosing what you want (you are free to choose from what I decide you can choose). Alternatively, simply by telling you that you are free to choose, you lower your resistance and you are already more hooked.

Suggestions for use in social robotics: Devices can be added to the robot, such as buttons, which in theory allow the user to control the interaction, although these buttons may not do anything.

2.5   Accumulation of Temptations

Take advantage of "the accumulation of temptations" or also called "Premack's Principle" [3]: try to induce the behavior you want to generate in combination with a pleasurable activity that the user already likes to do. For example, associate watching a movie at the cinema with eating popcorn. This is an association to an already established habit: habits are compelling, once they are well acquired, they will remain in our minds for the rest of our lives. That is why the product that manages to relate to a deep habit will get the same hook. Other examples: breakfast cereals. Of the most recent ones, many people already relate waking up with looking at Instagram and Twitter.

Suggestions for use in social robotics: We have to study what kind of hobbies and tastes the users have. If our user loves listening to the radio, let us try to make the social robot offer him to listen to his favorite program. Another example would be, if the user likes to watch Sunday mass, let us try that the robot when the time comes automatically offers him this possibility to watch Sunday mass on his tablet or project, at the same time that the robot can complement the interaction by making gestures or saying some timely comment.

2.6   High Frequency of Actions: High Degree of Multimodal Interactivity

A habit becomes firm the more times it is repeated. Some products can be used several times a day [15]. That is the goal. Create incentives for them to open the app several times. Notifications with sound, flashing LEDs, etc., make them look at their mobile to find out what has arrived. It could even generate a need that does not exist: do not miss the latest news, always stay informed. Many people open their social networks every hour throughout the day.

Suggestions for use in social robotics: We should try to make the user take an active and interactive role, for that we will request "calls to action" frequently. We are trying to turn these calls to action into multimodal signals: voice, light, screens, etc.

2.7   Losses Masquerading as Gains

It happens that, especially when employing variable rewards (as described above), increases the possibility of delivering rewards that do not compensate for the net losses suffered during a full game of chance (especially if money is at stake). As a result, an inflated estimate of the long-term reward may be conveyed [1]. There are problems with the statistics of large numbers and not understanding the mathematical mean of negative expectation in that "behavior" or "game" [9,17].

Suggestions for use in social robotics: We can try to generate the feeling that the time spent interacting with the robot is always useful time spent. To do this, we will frequently remind him of the number of actions or skills he has been able to learn, how much fun he has had during the interaction or the social contact he has been able to have with his friends and family thanks to the interaction with the social robot.

2.8   Chaining Actions

Also known as "Diderot Principle" [13] or "the Abstruse trap". A new one appears below when you have just read a news item from an online newspaper. *YouTube, Spotify*, and *Tik Tok* quickly automatically offer you more content. The key is for systems always to offer something to follow the user's current action, which is chosen with high probability and without much cognitive effort on the user's part. In this way, actions are concatenated in a way that together can build a habit of using the system, in this case, the social robot.

Suggestions for use in social robotics: The robot will take a proactive attitude in the interaction, especially with less proactive users. Once any activity with the robot is finished, automatically and by default - based on the user's activity history and preferences - it could suggest a new activity, which, unless canceled by the user (related to the illusion of control), would start automatically.

2.9   Reduced Friction: High Usability

All technologies evolve and solve more and more problems with less and less effort on the user's part. In other words, they are easier to use, with less friction: reduced loading times, delays, unforeseen errors [12]. In addition, interoperability between different technologies, creating ecosystems, is greater. There is no doubt that any technology that can be used intuitively, without a high learning curve, that is comfortable with our tastes, and that does not generate excessive physical or mental fatigue has the potential to produce greater engagement.

Suggestions for use in social robotics: We will try to keep the loading times between the different robot activities as short as possible, so that the responses of the robot in each communicative turn in the interaction are as fluid and fast as possible. In addition, all robot behavior should be as intuitive as possible and be done in the most natural way for the human it is interacting with. We will try to avoid the use of instruction manuals and long configuration phases.

2.10   The Paradox of Choice

In 2004, the American psychologist Barry Schwartz argued that offering many options to a customer or user creates anxiety, generating "choice paralysis" [18]. And not only does it create paralysis when it comes to buying or using technology, but also, due to the wide range of products available, we are increasingly dissatisfied with the products we buy. Customers like to be free to find exactly what they are looking for, but this is often impossible to achieve, as there is always a new and better product just around the corner. A list of specifications will convince them that another product is better than what they initially wanted to buy, making them fear making a wrong decision. It is such a stressful process that is often giving up and not buying anything is the most attractive option.

On the modern world, the Paradox of Choice is even more relevant as there is a vast catalog of products accessible at any time. Users are continually switching between stores and comparing products, reflected in bounce rates and abandoned carts. The good news is that there are ways to make decision-making easier. The challenge is to keep them interested and get them to act. We must keep in mind that people generally have a relatively short attention span. The product or technology may have many advantages that you would like your potential user to know about, but you must keep in mind that showing much information can make the reading very tedious and cause the user to abandon it. Anything that amuse the user from our objective can be considered a distraction.

Suggestions for use in social robotics: In social robotics applications, we should keep this effect in mind. When the user is presented with several options to choose from, a reduced set of options should always be presented, as intuitive as possible and adjusted to the user's level of experience interacting with the robot. In the case of displaying on-screen menus, we should limit the set of possible options to no more than 4 or 5 options, including, if possible, some clue (*nudges*) as to which is the option usually chosen by default by most users or which is more convenient for the interaction at that moment.

2.11 Feeling Useful

Logotherapy is psychotherapy that proposes that the will to meaning is the primary motivation of the human being [8]. Logotherapy was founded and developed by the Viennese psychiatrist Viktor Frankl (1905–1997). He talks about values and the meaning of life. Frankl understands the difference of motivation concerning therapy as an expression of his attitude towards life and separates it from his primary disorder, from his neurosis.

We use logetherapy as a piece to maximize engagement because the feeling of being useful, with a certain purpose, such as taking care of another pet, robot, or virtual agent, helps the user to have that feeling of fulfilling a certain purpose [7].

Suggestions for use in social robotics: We can try to design social robots that mimic the behavior of domestic pets that the user must take care of, feed or protect. In this way, the user could experience this feeling of being useful.

2.12 Exchange Costs: Collectibility and Customization

The goal is to get users to invest in the form of time or money in the app, service, or in our case, the social robots. In the form of storing images, already having an extensive list of contacts, virtual objects collected, specific customizations adapted to our tastes, or even having earned a reputation. Human beings are loss averse, so you get hooked and do not lose the content, points, or whatever you have already earned.

Suggestions for use in social robotics: In order to prolong and maximize user interaction with social bots over time, we have to try to implement strategies that increase the so-called "costs of change". This can be done in many ways, for example, if: the interaction is more adapted and personalized to the user as he spends more time interacting; he has a large number of multimedia files stored in the robot; he has the history of conversations held with other users through the robot and can consult it at any time; he has personalized reminders that warn him when he has to take specific medication; he has medals for overcoming particular challenges.

3   Conclusions

This work presents twelve techniques or tools extracted from other research fields, such as social psychology and game theory, for their application in social robotics. The objective is to try to enhance the use of a useful tool for users, such as social robots that act as companions of people. Especially, elderly people, with some degree of illness or who feel lonely.

The study of techniques to increase engagement in human-robot interaction has led us to select twelve techniques with the potential to be used successfully in social robotics, as well as propose some suggestions for use in this field.

Using these tools in social robotics can be the first step to getting users to regularly use social robots, as an aid tool, in their daily lives. In future work, we will present some of these techniques in practical and real scenarios, measuring quantitatively and qualitatively the degree of engagement between the users and the social robot.

Acknowledgements. The research leading to these results has received funding from the projects: Robots Sociales para Estimulación Física, Cognitiva y Afectiva de Mayores (ROSES), RTI2018-096338-B-I00, funded by the Ministerio de Ciencia, Innovación y Universidades; Robots sociales para mitigar la soledad y el aislamiento en mayores (SOROLI), PID2021-123941OA-I00, funded by Agencia Estatal de Investigación (AEI), Spanish Ministerio de Ciencia e Innovación; the project PLEC2021-007819, funded by MCIN/AEI/10.13039/501100011033 and by the European Union NextGenerationEU/PRTR, and RoboCity2030-DIH-CM, Madrid Robotics Digital Innovation Hub, S2018/NMT-4331, funded by "Programas de Actividades I+D en la Comunidad de Madrid" and cofunded by the European Social Funds (FSE) of the EU.

References

1. Auer, M., Hopfgartner, N., Griffiths, M.D.: The effect of loss-limit reminders on gambling behavior: a real-world study of Norwegian gamblers. J. Behav. Addictions **7**(4), 1056–1067 (2018). https://doi.org/10.1556/2006.7.2018.106

2. Burger, J.M., Schnerring, D.A.: The effects of desire for control and extrinsic rewards on the illusion of control and gambling. Motiv. Emot. **6**(4), 329–335 (1982). https://doi.org/10.1007/BF00998189
3. Clear, J.: Atomic Habits (2018)
4. Di Chiara, G., Bassareo, V.: Reward system and addiction: what dopamine does and doesn't do (2007). https://doi.org/10.1016/j.coph.2007.02.001
5. Dixon, M.R.: Manipulating the illusion of control: variations in gambling as a function of perceived control over chance outcomes. Psychol. Record **50**(4), 705–719 (2000). https://doi.org/10.1007/BF03395379
6. Eyal, N.: Hooked: how to build habit-forming products (2014)
7. Ghadampour, E., Fazlollah Mirderikvand, K.B.: The effectiveness of logotherapy training on academic engagement in student. Adv. Cogn. Sci. **19**(2), 52–62 (2017)
8. Frankl, V.E.: The will to meaning: foundations and applications of logotherapy. Angewandte Chemie Int. Edition **6**(11), 151 (2014)
9. Graydon, C., Dixon, M.J., Stange, M., Fugelsang, J.A.: Gambling despite financial loss-the role of losses disguised as wins in multi-line slots. Addiction **114**(1), 119–124 (2019). https://doi.org/10.1111/add.14406
10. Ibrahimov, S.: Dopamine, and its effect on the human brain. **9**, 402–405 (2021). https://doi.org/10.36074/grail-of-science.22.10.2021.72
11. Lane, M.: Model. Irrational Gambling Behav. Math. Enthusiast worth the risk? **12**(1–3), 31–37 (2015)
12. Lemieux, C., McDonald, D.: Frictionless : why the future of everything will be fast, fluid & made just for you (2020)
13. Lorenzen, J.A.: Diderot effect. In: The Blackwell Encyclopedia of Sociology. Wiley, New York, September 2008. https://doi.org/10.1002/9781405165518.wbeosd046
14. Morris, P.H., White, J., Morrison, E.R., Fisher, K.: High heels as supernormal stimuli: How wearing high heels affects judgements of female attractiveness. Evol. Hum. Behav. **34**(3), 176–181 (2013). https://doi.org/10.1016/j.evolhumbehav.2012.11.006
15. Nasti, L., Michienzi, A., Guidi, B.: Discovering the impact of notifications on social network addiction. In: Bowles, J., Broccia, G., Nanni, M. (eds.) DataMod 2020. LNCS, vol. 12611, pp. 72–86. Springer, Cham (2021). https://doi.org/10.1007/978-3-030-70650-0_5
16. Sapolksy, R.: Behave: the biology of humans at our best and worst, vol. 134 (2017). https://doi.org/10.1016/j.anbehav.2017.09.025
17. Scarfe, M.L., Stange, M., Dixon, M.J.: Measuring Gamblers' behaviour to show that negative sounds can reveal the true nature of losses disguised as wins in multiline slot machines. J. Gambl. Stud. **37**(2), 403–425 (2020). https://doi.org/10.1007/s10899-020-09976-9
18. Schwartz, B.: The Paradox of Choice - Why More is Less (2004)
19. Skinner, B.: Science and human behavior (1965)
20. Volkow, N.D., Wang, G.J., Fowler, J.S., Tomasi, D., Telang, F.: Addiction: Beyond dopamine reward circuitry (2011). https://doi.org/10.1073/pnas.1010654108
21. Ward, A.F.: Supernormal: how the internet is changing our memories and our minds. Psychol. Inquiry **24**(4), 341–348 (2013). https://doi.org/10.1080/1047840X.2013.850148
22. Watson, J., Pavlov, I., Skinner, B., Bandura, A.: Conductisme (1947)
23. Zack, M., St. George, R., Clark, L.: Dopaminergic signaling of uncertainty and the aetiology of gambling addiction (2020). https://doi.org/10.1016/j.pnpbp.2019.109853

Hey, Robot! An Investigation of Getting Robot's Attention Through Touch

Hagen Lehmann[1,2] (iD), Adam Rojik[2], Kassandra Friebe[3,4],
and Matej Hoffmann[2(✉)] (iD)

[1] Universitá di Bergamo, Dipartimento di Scienze Umane e Sociali, Bergamo, Italy
hagen.lehmann@unibg.it
[2] Department of Cybernetics, Faculty of Electrical Engineering Czech Technical University in Prague, Prague, Czech Republic
matej.hoffmann@fel.cvut.cz
[3] Faculty of Mathematics, Physics and Informatics, Comenius University, Bratislava, Slovakia
[4] Department of Cognitive Science, Central European University, Vienna, Austria

Abstract. Touch is a key part of interaction and communication between humans, but has still been little explored in human-robot interaction. In this work, participants were asked to approach and touch a humanoid robot on the hand (Nao – 26 participants; Pepper – 28 participants) to get its attention. We designed reaction behaviors for the robot that consisted in four different combinations of arm movements with the touched hand moving forward or back and the other hand moving forward or staying in place, with simultaneous leaning back, followed by looking at the participant. We studied which reaction of the robot people found the most appropriate and what was the reason for their choice. For both robots, the preferred reaction of the robot hand being touched was moving back. For the other hand, no movement at all was rated most natural for the Pepper, while it was movement forward for the Nao. A correlation between the anxiety subscale of the participants' personality traits and the passive to active/aggressive nature of the robot reactions was found. Most participants noticed the leaning back and rated it positively. Looking at the participant was commented on positively by some participants in unstructured comments. We also analyzed where and how participants spontaneously touched the robot on the hand. In summary, the touch reaction behaviors designed here are good candidates to be deployed more generally in social robots, possibly including incidental touch in crowded environments. The robot size constitutes one important factor shaping how the robot reaction is perceived.

Keywords: Tactile human-robot interaction · reaction to touch · Touch type analysis

This work was supported by the Czech Science Foundation (GA ČR), project no. 20-24186X. H.L. was supported by the International Mobility of Researchers in CTU, Nr. CZ.02.2.690.00.016_0270008465.

F. Cavallo et al. (Eds.): ICSR 2022, LNAI 13817, pp. 388–401, 2022.
https://doi.org/10.1007/978-3-031-24667-8_35

1 Introduction

People constantly use a variety of nonverbal cues while interacting. These include gaze and eye movement, gesture, mimicry and imitation, touch, posture and movement, interaction rhythm and timing [4, Chapter 6]. For successful human-robot interaction (HRI), machines should be able to understand as well as produce these cues. According to [5], "humans are born as *tactile creatures*. Physical touch is one of the most basic forms of human communication." Even a single gentle touch can have important effects as demonstrated by the so-called "Midas touch" effect [10], for example. At the same time, physical contact is a very intimate type of interaction that is to be used with caution. Heslin [15] studied the pleasantness vs. intrusiveness of touch between sexes in relation to a stranger, a friend, and a close friend in the United States. The body areas where touch was rated as pleasant or unpleasant strongly depend on the combination of these factors. In HRI, touch has still been relatively unexplored to date.

The bottleneck of wider use of touch in HRI has largely been technological—robust and affordable tactile sensors were lacking. Recently, the number of available technologies is growing (see e.g., the 2019 special issue of Proceedings of the IEEE [11]). The focus has largely been on tactile sensing for manipulation, as equipping only robot hands/fingers with tactile sensors requires relatively small patches of electronic skin. Whole-body artificial skins for robots have been an exception, with only a few successful technologies deployed on complete robots and over extended time periods (e.g., [17] on the iCub humanoid or the multimodal skin of Mittendorfer, Cheng, and colleagues [18]). Large patches of sensitive skin are also important for the safety of robot manipulators, as demonstrated by Airskin, for example (see [26]). Silvera-Tawil et al. [25] provide a review of artificial skin and tactile sensing for socially interactive robots. For example, tactile sensors on the therapeutic seal robot PARO are an important sensory modality supporting its interactions [22]. The Nao and Pepper social humanoids use capacitive touch sensors on the head and arms to detect human contact.

There are several ways in which touch enters HRI (see [2,24] for surveys). The first division comes from who initiates the contact. More studies investigated the case where the robot initiated contact [3,7,8,27–29]. Humans touching robots has been less explored [1,19,20]. Cramer et al. [9] had participants rate videos of both interaction types and found that communicative touch could be considered a more appropriate behavior for proactive agents rather than reactive agents. Affective touch, as manifested by the PARO robot [22], constitutes a different context compared to communicative touch. Finally, while most studies focus on deliberate touch, incidental contacts like in a crowded environment and reactions to them [12] are also relevant for HRI.

In this work, participants were instructed to get the attention of a humanoid robot (Nao or Pepper) looking to the side by touching its hand. The hand was chosen as touch on this body part is the most acceptable across different contexts (gender, stranger/friend) [15]. The robot reactions were preprogrammed and consisted in four different combinations of arm movements with the touched hand moving forward or back and the other hand moving forward or staying in place, accompanied by leaning back and followed by looking at the participant. The goal was to design behaviors that would be perceived as natural by participants. We were loosely inspired by prank videos like the "Touching Hands on Escalator Prank", https://youtu.be/BTl5HC9VfAE. We studied: (i) which reaction of the robot participants found the most appropriate and what was the reason for their choice; (ii) where and how participants touched the robot on the hand. With the focus on designing and assessing robot reactions to touch, this study provides a new contribution to the field, complementing the work of Shiomi et al. [23] who investigated pre-touch reactions.

2   Related Work

Here we review previous studies specifically relevant to our scenario, structured as follows: robots touching humans, humans touching robots, and robot reactions to touch.

2.1   Robots Touching Humans

Guidelines for robots how to touch humans are provided in [27]. Chen et al. [7,8] studied responses to robot-initiated touch in a nursing context and found that instrumental touch—cleaning the person's skin—was perceived more favorably than affective touch (providing comfort). Zheng et al. [29] used the female android Erica to touch participants' hand or finger, varying the touch type (contact or pat) and the duration and intensity of the contact. They studied the effect on participants' arousal and whether the robot succeeded to communicate a specific emotion through the touch.

Other studies used videos, with participants rating sequences in which humans were touched by a robot. Arnold and Scheutz [3] using the PR2 robot found that touch improves people's evaluation of a robot's social performance. In [28], participants rated the pleasantness of touch when a person on the video was touched on the hand by a human hand, Nao robot hand, mannequin arm, or plastic tube. Stroking touches with a velocity of ca. 3 cm/s were rated as most pleasant. Robot touch was not rated as significantly more pleasant than either touches applied with the mannequin hand or tube.

2.2   Humans Touching Robots

The studies in which humans touch robots are of two main types. The first group is constituted by studies in which participants are asked to touch a robot in a specific fashion. In [1], people were asked to touch a Nao robot, expressing one of eight emotions: anger, disgust, fear, happiness, sadness, gratitude, sympathy, or love. In [6], specific instructions about affective touch communication gestures (hitting, poking, squeezing, stroking, and tickling) at two force intensities (gentle and energetic) and sensor locations were provided to participants.

In a second group of studies, humans touched robots spontaneously. Robins et al. [19,20] studied interaction of autistic children with the robot KASPAR and identified grasping, stroking and poking. The intensity of touch varied between tight or firm and very light or 'gentle'. In [12], contacts were not deliberate but incidental, as a Pepper robot was moving trough a crowd. Impact, push, and clamp were the touch types identified and 70% of them were with the arms and hands of the robot.

2.3   How Should the Robot Respond?

In many studies on social touch in HRI, experiments end their evaluation with the moment of touch and the reaction to touch and its appropriateness is not assessed (e.g., [1,6]). Shiomi et al. [23] studied pre-touch reactions. As participants were approaching the face of a female android with their hand, the robot displayed a reaction—turning the head toward the person—either at 45 or 20 cm before contact (pre-touch) or only after contact. The pre-touch reaction at 20 cm was rated most positively. For the KASPAR robot, several responses were designed: for example, touching the robot hand caused the robot to raise its hand; touching the shoulder caused the robot to move the arm to the side [19]. The robot responded to 'aggressive' tactile interaction by displaying its 'sad' expression, face covered by hands, evasive body movements, or by saying "ouch - this hurts" [20]. Garcia et al. [12] experimented with a Pepper robot in a crowd. The impacts (contact, push, clamp) were not detected by tactile sensors but through joint torques. The reactions consisted in local or whole-body compliant behaviors in the direction of the impact.

Different than in the works described above, we designed the following responses to touch on the robot's hand: (1) look at the touched hand; (2) lean back; (3) move the arms in 4 different ways. Rather than asking the participants about their perception of the robot (e.g., [3]) or pleasantness or appropriateness of the situation involving touch in general (e.g., [7,9,28,29]), we specifically asked them to rate the robot reactions.

3   Methods

3.1   Participants

There were 26 participants (13 female; mean age 29.8 years; ranging from 21 to 68) interacting with the Nao robot and 28 participants (12 female; mean age 28.5, ranging from 20 to 53) interacting with the Pepper robot. On a 5-point Likert scale concerning their experience with robots and ranging from 1 = no experience to 5 = very experienced, the "Nao group" reported an average experience with robots of 2.3; the "Pepper group" 2.1. Participants were recruited from Facebook local area groups, experimenters' social circles such as family and friends, and from the administrative personnel of the Department.

3.2   Nao and Pepper Humanoid Robots

Both robots were manufactured by Aldebaran, now Softbank Robotics. They use the same middleware (NAOqi) and programming environment. The robot movements used in this work were designed in Choregraphe.

Nao Robot. We used Nao version Evolution V5 (H25 V50). Our robot exemplar was uniquely equipped with artificial sensitive skin (black parts on Fig. 1), making the robot slightly taller (59 cm compared to 57.4 cm) than the original. The skin is a capacitive tactile system commonly used on the iCub robot [17] and custom-designed for the Nao robot.

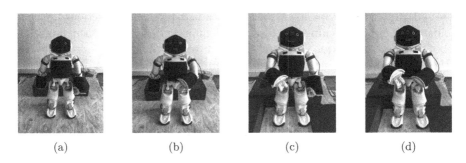

(a)   (b)   (c)   (d)

Fig. 1. Nao – arm movements for startle reaction. (a) Touched hand back, other hand still. (b) Touched hand back, other hand forward. (c) Touched hand forward, other hand still. (d) Touched hand forward, other hand forward. Other components of the behavior (gaze, lean back) not shown here.

Pepper Robot. Humanoid robot Pepper (version 1.8a) was used (Fig. 2). It is 120 cm tall and has touch sensors on its arms.

3.3   Touch Detection

Touch on the robot arm is detected differently for the two robots. On the Pepper, the touch sensors on the outer part of its hand were used. On the Nao, the capacitive pressure-sensitive skin surrounding the whole hand and wrist and comprising 240 sensors was used (Fig. 1). To detect and then respond to touch in real time, the asynchronous calls available in NAOqi API 2.4.3 were used.[1]

In the Pepper robot, touch sensors' output was true or false and could be directly registered to trigger a response. In our Nao, sensitive skin outputs were sensed by the YARP middleware. Contact detection was then performed by a module running in a separate thread, comparing the signals with a threshold value—if crossed, a contact event was triggered.

---

[1] NAOqi API 2.4.3 was standard in the Pepper robot. In the Nao robot used (NAOqi API version 2.1.4) the newer NAOqi API version had to be used in addition to allow for these calls to be used.

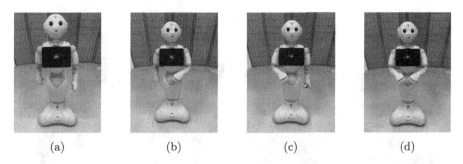

(a)   (b)   (c)   (d)

Fig. 2. Pepper – arm movements for startle reaction. (a) Touched hand back, other hand still. (b) Touched hand back, other hand forward. (c) Touched hand forward, other hand still. (d) Touched hand forward, other hand forward. Other components of the behavior (gaze, lean back) not shown here.

3.4 Reactions to Touch

A key contribution of this work is the design of robot reactions to unexpected touch. We took inspiration from how humans react in such situations (e.g., https://youtu.be/BTl5HC9VfAE) and we tested several behaviors on ourselves. An illustration of the behaviors we developed is available in the accompanying video https://youtu.be/TI_oy6uO0Kw.

Arm Movements. Since it was the robot hand that was unexpectedly touched, some reaction with the contacted limb seems natural. An instinctive reaction appears to be to retract the arm/hand that was unexpectedly contacted (Fig. 3, A). This may be accompanied by moving the contralateral arm forward (B), constituting a defensive reaction. However, people may not find a robot defensive reaction the most appropriate and could perceive it as detached. We thus added also the other two possible combinations of arm movements with the touched hand moving forward and the other hand remaining still (C) or moving forward as well (D). Those movements were created in Choregraphe and then exported into Python code. We experimented with additional behaviors like raising the touched hand or both hands to shoulder height, but these movements appeared too aggressive and were omitted.

Lean Back. Movements of the whole body are more natural than isolated arm movements. After experimentation, we accompanied the arm movements with simultaneous leaning back of the torso, taking advantage of the implementation in [16].

Gaze. Furthermore, when confronted with an unexpected sensory percept such as a touch, it is natural to seek the cause of the stimulation. One possibility would be to look at the touched hand. After initial experimentation, we decided to design this component of the reaction differently. Rather than adding to the immediate startle reaction (move arms, lean back), we decided to add a slower

Fig. 3. Startle reactions – arm movements schematics. (Top) Nao, (Bottom) Pepper. (A) Touched hand back, other hand still. (B) Touched hand back, other hand forward. (C) Touched hand forward, other hand still. (D) Touched hand forward, other hand forward. See Figs. 1, 2 for complete robot photos.

head movement that directs the gaze on the participant, looking approximately into his eyes. This seems a more natural reaction in case the unexpected touch was not threatening. In the Pepper robot, this was accompanied by blinking.

3.5   Experimental Procedure

Before each experiment, the participants filled in an informed consent form. With the goal of assessing the personality dimensions of our participants we asked them at the beginning of the experiment to complete the Ten Item Personality Inventory (TIPI) questionnaire, a brief measure of the "Big-Five" personality dimensions [13].[2] The participants were then instructed to approach the robot (Nao or Pepper) and touch the robot's right hand. The robot was initially looking to the other side and did not know about the participant. After the robot detected the touch, it displayed one of the four reactions (Sect. 3.4). The scenario was repeated four times, with the order of startle reactions randomized for individual participants. After this, the participants filled in a custom questionnaire choosing which reaction they liked best, followed by questions whether they noticed and liked the leaning back. Finally, participants had the opportunity to add any comments regarding their general impression from the experiment.

4   Results

4.1   Which Reaction Was the Most Appropriate?

The main result consists in the assessment of the four reaction types by the participants. A summary is in Table 1 below. For the Nao robot, the preferred

---

[2] Prof. Marek Franěk kindly provided the Czech version [21].

reaction type was B—the touched hand moving back and the other hand moving forward. For the Pepper, the preferred reaction was the touched hand moving back and the other hand remaining still. Taking both robots together, the reactions involving the touched hand moving backward (A, B) were preferred over those where the touched hand moved forward (C, D). We performed a χ^2 test comparing the number of A and B together versus C and D with the expected probability distribution 0.5 for each. The result did not yield statistical significance ($\chi^2 = 2.3$, $df = 1$, $p = 0.13$).

Table 1. Most appropriate reaction reported by participants. For example, the top left number means that 6 participants interacting with the Nao liked the reaction "A" best.

Robot\Reaction	A	B	C	D
Nao	6	10	6	4
Pepper	11	6	5	6
both robots	**16**	**16**	**11**	**10**

Further, we evaluated the free text answers from the questionnaires where the participants commented on their choices. Most participants advocated their choice that the chosen reaction was the most natural, appropriate, or logical to them. Some mentioned that this is what "they would do" in such a context. Some participants reported that the most natural reaction depends on the context. If unexpectedly touched by a stranger (our case), a more defensive reaction (A,B) is expected. If the robot was touched by a friend and not taken by surprise, reaction involving movement toward the participant (C or D) would be natural. There were also some qualitative differences between the words the two participant groups used, which could be attributed to the different robot size. For the Nao robot, some participants that opted for C or D reported that they found the reactions A or B too fearful—the robot appears frightened and unfriendly and does not want to interact with them. Reactions C and D were found more interactive and friendly by some. For the Pepper group, the word "aggressive" or its synonyms was more present in the dictionary, mostly in relation to assessing reactions C or D that involved forward movements toward the participant.

Most participants reported in the questionnaire that they noticed the leaning back component of the behavior (21/26 for the Nao; 26/28 for the Pepper) and most evaluated it positively (18/26 for Nao; 22/28 for Pepper).

4.2   Interaction with Personality Traits and Experience with Robots

Correlation of Anxiety Scores with Preferred Reaction Type. The robot reactions (Fig. 3 for an overview of the arm movements) can be approximately ordered from the most passive (A – touched hand moves back), over less passive (B – touched hand moves back, other hand moves forward) to more active or perhaps even "aggressive"—the touched hand moves forward (C) and both hands move forward (D). We hypothesised that the assessment of the reactions by the participants could correlate with their anxiety score as reported by the TIPI subscale 'Anxious, easily upset.' We hypothesized that participants with higher anxiety scores may prefer more passive robot reactions. Spearman's rank correlations were computed to assess this relationship. A negative correlation between participants' anxiety and the "aggressiveness" of the robot reaction, i.e. people with higher anxiety scores avoiding aggressive and preferring more passive robot reactions was found for the Pepper robot ($r(26) = -0.25$, p-value $= .202$, not significant). Interestingly, for the Nao robot, a significant positive correlation ($r(24) = 0.49$, $p = .011$) was found. One can speculate that the robot size makes the difference here. For the Nao robot that is small and perceived as not threatening, participants with higher anxiety scores may not be concerned about their safety, but instead may fear that the robot will not interact with them and hence they may prefer more active robot reactions.

Correlation of Experience with Preferred Reaction Type. A Spearman's rank correlation did not reveal any significant correlation of participants' experience with robots and their preferred reaction, $r(52) = -0.09$, p-value $= .518$.

4.3   Touch Location and Type

How touch is delivered—location, duration, intensity, type—importantly modifies this act of communication and allows to express different emotions, for example (see [1,14] for application to HRI). In this work, the participants were only instructed to get the robot's attention by touching its right hand. After contact was detected, the robot response was triggered so the touch duration could not be studied. Intensity was not available from the sensors on the Pepper; the skin our Nao is retrofitted with could detect pressure values, but in our experiments, it was binarized. Therefore, we used the video recordings of the experiments to study: (i) which hand participants used to contact the robot hand; (ii) which part of their hand they used for contact; (iii) which part of the robot hand did they contact; (iv) what was the type of touch (e.g., brief contact, grasp). Due to a technical problem (full memory card), some videos with the Nao robot were not saved. Thus, in this section, 15 Nao participants and all 28 Pepper participants' interactions are analyzed. Examples of the different combinations are in Fig. 4a.

Participants' Hand and Location. As the participants were instructed to approach the robot that was facing them and touch the robot's right hand in a habitual resting posture next to the robot's body, it was natural for them to use their left hand to touch the robot. Most people indeed used their left hand (80% with Nao; 85.7% with Pepper). The rest used the right hand; one participant used both hands to contact the Nao robot.

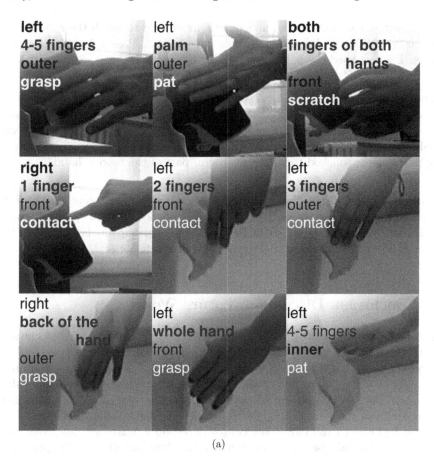

(a)

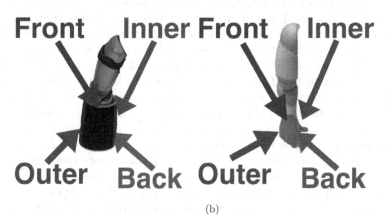

(b)

Fig. 4. a) Touch location and type – examples. We distinguished which hand the participants used for contact (left/right/both), what part of their hand (1, 2, 3, 4–5 fingers, palm, whole hand, or back of the hand), what part of the robot hand was contacted (front/back/inner/outer), and the type of contact (contact/grasp/pat/scratch). b) Touch location on robot hand (Left) Nao (Right) Pepper.

Regarding the part of the participants' hand used to touch the robot, more than 60% of the participants used their fingers (1, 2, 3, or 4–5) to contact the robot. The rest used the palm or the whole hand.

Location on Robot's Hand. Given the nature of the Nao's hand in our case—basically a cylinder—we limited the classification to whether the participants touched the front, back, inner, or outer part of the robot hand. The same was applied to the Pepper. See Fig. 4a. As would be expected, the vast majority of the participants touched the outer or frontal part of the robots' hands.

Contact Type. Finally, we classified the type of contact—how participants touched the robot. The majority of the participants used a brief, "atomic", touch or contact (62.5% for Nao; 75% for Pepper). Some participants have grasped the robot hand (12.5% Nao; 14.3% Pepper). Pat or scratch was also used occasionally.

5   Conclusion, Discussion, Future Work

In this study, we presented participants with a new type of HRI scenario involving touch, in which they were asked to approach a robot (Nao or Pepper) looking elsewhere and get its attention by touching its hand. The main contribution of this work is the focus on the design and participants' assessment of the robot reactions. The key component of the robot response were four different combinations of arm movements. For both robots, most participants preferred when the touched robot hand moved backwards in response to contact. Such reactions seem most natural also in interaction between humans. On the Pepper robot (120 cm tall), participants preferred that the other hand of the robot remained still (reaction A). For the Nao (60 cm tall), the reaction with the contralateral hand moving simultaneously forward was preferred (reaction B)[3]. However, the participants' assessments were not clear-cut and the effect of preferring A or B (touched hand moved back) over C or D (touched hand moved front) was only marginally significant. This may have to do with to what extent participants anthropomorphized the robot. When asked to comment on the scenario and their choice of the preferred reaction, some said "this is what I would do". This perspective was probably not shared by all participants though—in other words, the most natural reaction one expects from a robot may be different.

The experiments were conducted on two humanoid robots that differed in several aspects. We speculate that a key factor possibly explaining some of the differences in participants' ratings was the robot size. The Pepper, which is twice as tall as the Nao, may be perceived as potentially more threatening and movements toward a person may not be perceived well—this may explain the preferrence for reaction A in the Pepper. Furthermore, participants with higher scores on the anxiety subscale of the TIPI questionnaire preferred the more

---

[3] This reaction was identified as one that is taught in courses of self-defense.

passive robot reactions (A,B) (effect not significant). Interestingly, a significant correlation in the opposite direction—more "anxious, easily upset" participants preferring reactions C or D—was found for the Nao robot. We speculate that people did not fear the Nao robot; instead more anxious participants were more eager to see a friendly, engaging response of the robot with one or both arms moving forward.

The robot reactions we designed additionally consisted in leaning back after the unexpected touch, followed by looking at the participant (and blinking in case of Pepper). These were identical in all conditions. In a questionnaire, we asked the participants whether they noticed the leaning back and whether they liked it—the majority of participants responded positively to both questions. Looking at the participant after the contact was not specifically rated; few participants appreciated it in unstructured comments on the experiment. Looking at the touched body part instead of at the face of the participant constitutes an alternative that could be tested in the future.

We also studied where on the hand and how people contacted the robot. Similarly for both robots, participants typically used the fingers of their left hand to touch the outer or frontal part of the robot hand. Most participants used a brief touch/contact; only few participants used other touch types like pat, grasp, or scratch.

In summary, this study provides a new contribution to the design of robot responses to touch. In other works on social touch in HRI, experiments end their evaluation with the moment of touch and the reaction to touch and its appropriateness is not assessed (e.g., [1,6]). Participants are asked about their perception of the robot (e.g., [3]) or pleasantness or appropriateness of the situation involving touch in general (e.g., [7,9,28,29]). Instead, we specifically asked them to rate the robot reactions. Furthermore, unlike in studies in which participants are asked to touch a robot in a specific fashion [1,6], we studied the natural way in which participants touch a robot to get its attention.

The implications of this work are the following. First, it seems that high-level behavioral patterns such as "I move a hand that was unexpectedly touched back" can be carried over from human-human to human-robot interaction. However, the size of the robot seems to be an important factor, shaping how participants rate the robot reactions. Furthermore, there may be interaction with the personality traits of the interlocutor and hence, if possible, the reactions may be personalized. Second, the analysis of touch location and type revelaed a preference for brief contact with the outer or inner part of the robot hand, which should be taken into account in robot design—placement and type of contact sensors. Finally, our scenario involved deliberate contact. It remains to be tested whether the reactions we designed would be also be positively rated in incidental contact scenarios like when a robot is traversing a crowded place [12].

References

1. Alenljung, B., Andreasson, R., Lowe, R., Billing, E., Lindblom, J.: Conveying emotions by touch to the Nao robot: a user experience perspective. Multimodal Technol. Interact. **2**(4), 82 (2018)

2. Argall, B., Billard, A.: A survey of tactile humanrobot interactions. Robot. Autonom. Syst. **58**(10), 1159–1176 (2010). https://doi.org/10.1016/j.robot.2010.07.002

3. Arnold, T., Scheutz, M.: Observing robot touch in context: how does touch and attitude affect perceptions of a robot's social qualities? In: Proceedings of the 2018 ACM/IEEE International Conference on Human-Robot Interaction, HRI 2018, pp. 352–360. Association for Computing Machinery, New York (2018). https://doi.org/10.1145/3171221.3171263

4. Bartneck, C., Belpaeme, T., Eyssel, F., Kanda, T., Keijsers, M., Šabanović, S.: Human-robot interaction: an introduction. Cambridge Univ. Press (2020). https://doi.org/10.1017/9781108676649

5. Breazeal, C., Dautenhahn, K., Kanda, T.: Social Robotics. In: Siciliano, B., Khatib, O. (eds.) Springer Handbook of Robotics, pp. 1935–1972. Springer, Cham (2016). https://doi.org/10.1007/978-3-319-32552-1_72

6. Burns, R.B., Lee, H., Seifi, H., Faulkner, R., Kuchenbecker, K.J.: Endowing a Nao robot with practical social-touch perception. Front. Robot. AI 86 (2022)

7. Chen, T.L., King, C.H., Thomaz, A.L., Kemp, C.C.: Touched by a robot: an investigation of subjective responses to robot-initiated touch. In: 2011 6th ACM/IEEE International Conference on Human-Robot Interaction (HRI), pp. 457–464. IEEE (2011)

8. Chen, T.L., King, C.H.A., Thomaz, A.L., Kemp, C.C.: An investigation of responses to robot-initiated touch in a nursing context. Int. J. Soc. Robot. **6**(1), 141–161 (2014)

9. Cramer, H., Kemper, N., Amin, A., Wielinga, B., Evers, V.: 'Give me a hug': the effects of touch and autonomy on people's responses to embodied social agents. Comput. Animation Virtual Worlds **20**(2-3), 437–445 (2009). https://doi.org/10.1002/cav.317, https://onlinelibrary.wiley.com/doi/abs/10.1002/cav.317

10. Crusco, A.H., Wetzel, C.G.: The Midas touch: the effects of interpersonal touch on restaurant tipping. Pers. Soc. Psychol. Bull. **10**(4), 512–517 (1984). https://doi.org/10.1177/0146167284104003

11. Dahiya, R., Akinwande, D., Chang, J.S.: Flexible electronic skin: From humanoids to humans [scanning the issue]. Proc. IEEE **107**(10), 2011–2015 (2019)

12. Garcia, F., Mazel, A., Cruz Maya, A.: Safe human-robot interaction through crowd contact video analysis. In: Salichs, M.A., et al. (eds.) ICSR 2019. LNCS (LNAI), vol. 11876, pp. 588–598. Springer, Cham (2019). https://doi.org/10.1007/978-3-030-35888-4_55

13. Gosling, S.D., Rentfrow, P.J., Swann, W.B., Jr.: A very brief measure of the big-five personality domains. J. Res. Pers. **37**(6), 504–528 (2003)

14. Hertenstein, M.J., Holmes, R., McCullough, M., Keltner, D.: The communication of emotion via touch. Emotion **9**(4), 566 (2009)

15. Heslin, R., Nguyen, T.D., Nguyen, M.L.: Meaning of touch: the case of touch from a stranger or same sex person. J. Nonverbal Behav. **7**, 147–157 (1983)

16. Lehmann, H., Rojik, A., Hoffmann, M.: Should a small robot have a small personal space? investigating personal spatial zones and proxemic behavior in human-robot interaction. In: CognitIve RobotiCs for intEraction (CIRCE) Workshop at IEEE International Conference On Robot and Human Interactive Communication (RO-MAN) (2020)

17. Maiolino, P., Maggiali, M., Cannata, G., Metta, G., Natale, L.: A flexible and robust large scale capacitive tactile system for robots. IEEE Sens. J. **13**(10), 3910–3917 (2013)

18. Mittendorfer, P., Cheng, G.: Humanoid multimodal tactile-sensing modules. IEEE Trans. Robot. **27**(3), 401–410 (2011)
19. Robins, B., Dautenhahn, K.: Developing play scenarios for tactile interaction with a humanoid robot: a case study exploration with children with autism. In: Ge, S.S., Li, H., Cabibihan, J.-J., Tan, Y.K. (eds.) ICSR 2010. LNCS (LNAI), vol. 6414, pp. 243–252. Springer, Heidelberg (2010). https://doi.org/10.1007/978-3-642-17248-9_25
20. Robins, B., Dautenhahn, K., Dickerson, P.: Embodiment and cognitive learning – can a humanoid robot help children with autism to learn about tactile social behaviour? In: Ge, S.S., Khatib, O., Cabibihan, J.-J., Simmons, R., Williams, M.-A. (eds.) ICSR 2012. LNCS (LNAI), vol. 7621, pp. 66–75. Springer, Heidelberg (2012). https://doi.org/10.1007/978-3-642-34103-8_7
21. Šefara, D., Franěk, M., Zubr, V.: Socio-psychological factors that influence car preference in undergraduate students: the case of the Czech republic. Technol. Econ. Dev. of Econ. **21**(4), 643–659 (2015)
22. Shibata, T.: Therapeutic seal robot as biofeedback medical device: qualitative and quantitative evaluations of robot therapy in dementia care. Proc. IEEE **100**(8), 2527–2538 (2012)
23. Shiomi, M., Shatani, K., Minato, T., Ishiguro, H.: How should a robot react before people's touch? Modeling a pre-touch reaction distance for a robot's face. IEEE Robot. Autom. Lett. **3**(4), 3773–3780 (2018)
24. Shiomi, M., Sumioka, H., Ishiguro, H.: Survey of social touch interaction between humans and robots. J. Robot. Mech. **32**(1), 128–135 (2020). https://doi.org/10.20965/jrm.2020.p0128
25. Silvera-Tawil, D., Rye, D., Velonaki, M.: Artificial skin and tactile sensing for socially interactive robots: a review. Robot. Autonom. Syst. **63**, 230–243 (2015). https://doi.org/10.1016/j.robot.2014.09.008, http://www.sciencedirect.com/science/article/pii/S0921889014001833, Advances in Tactile Sensing and Touch-based Human Robot Interaction
26. Svarny, P., et al.: Effect of active and passive protective soft skins on collision forces in human-robot collaboration. Robot. Comput.-Integr. Manuf. **78**, 102363 (2022). https://doi.org/10.1016/j.rcim.2022.102363, https://www.sciencedirect.com/science/article/pii/S0736584522000515
27. Van Erp, J.B., Toet, A.: How to touch humans: Guidelines for social agents and robots that can touch. In: 2013 Humaine Association Conference on Affective Computing and Intelligent Interaction, pp. 780–785. IEEE (2013)
28. Willemse, C.J.A.M., Huisman, G., Jung, M.M., van Erp, J.B.F., Heylen, D.K.J.: Observing touch from video: the influence of social cues on pleasantness perceptions. In: Bello, F., Kajimoto, H., Visell, Y. (eds.) EuroHaptics 2016. LNCS, vol. 9775, pp. 196–205. Springer, Cham (2016). https://doi.org/10.1007/978-3-319-42324-1_20
29. Zheng, X., Shiomi, M., Minato, T., Ishiguro, H.: What kinds of robot's touch will match expressed emotions? IEEE Robot. Autom. Lett. **5**(1), 127–134 (2020)

Gaze Cueing and the Role of Presence in Human-Robot Interaction

Kassandra Friebe[1,2]([✉]) [ID], Sabína Samporová[2], Kristína Malinovská[2] [ID],
and Matej Hoffmann[3] [ID]

[1] Department of Cognitive Science, Central European University, Vienna, Austria
kassandra.friebe@web.de
[2] Faculty of Mathematics, Physics and Informatics, Comenius University,
Mlynská Dolina, 84248 Bratislava, Slovakia
[3] Faculty of Electrical Engineering, Czech Technical University in Prague,
Technická 1902/2, 166 27 Praha 6 - Dejvice, Prague, Czechia

Abstract. Gaze cueing is a fundamental part of social interactions, and broadly studied using Posner task based gaze cueing paradigms. While studies using human stimuli consistently yield a gaze cueing effect, results from studies using robotic stimuli are inconsistent. Typically, these studies use virtual agents or pictures of robots. As previous research has pointed to the significance of physical presence in human-robot interaction, it is of fundamental importance to understand its yet unexplored role in interactions with gaze cues. This paper investigates whether the physical presence of the iCub humanoid robot affects the strength of the gaze cueing effect in human-robot interaction. We exposed 42 participants to a gaze cueing task. We asked participants to react as quickly and accurately as possible to the appearance of a target stimulus that was either congruently or incongruently cued by the gaze of a copresent iCub robot or a virtual version of the same robot. Analysis of the reaction time measurements showed that participants were consistently affected by their robot interaction partner's gaze, independently on the way the robot was presented. Additional analyses of participants' ratings of the robot's anthropomorphism, animacy and likeability further add to the impression that presence does not play a significant role in simple gaze based interactions. Together our findings open up interesting discussions about the possibility to generalize results from studies using virtual agents to real life interactions with copresent robots.

Keywords: Human-robot interaction · Gaze cueing · Presence

1 Introduction

Human social interactions are based on a complex exchange of a variety of signals, including facial expressions, gaze, gestures, and posture. Gaze plays a special part as it serves to perceive objects or other humans and at the same time it communicates to others where one focuses the attention [22]. For instance, our

© The Author(s), under exclusive license to Springer Nature Switzerland AG 2022
F. Cavallo et al. (Eds.): ICSR 2022, LNAI 13817, pp. 402–414, 2022.
https://doi.org/10.1007/978-3-031-24667-8_36

gaze helps us indicate social interest [24], understand other people's mental and emotional state [3], and see what they are attending to [10]. This process of using someone else's eye movement as information of what they are attending to and shifting one's own attention accordingly is called gaze cueing and is discussed as a prerequisite for joint attention [8], the case in which both persons visually attend the same object.

Social gaze has been mostly studied in human and non-human primates, and with the emergence of social robots has become introduced into robotic systems [6,14] and has become a growing branch of research ever since. A great amount of research on gaze cueing in human-robot interaction (HRI) uses virtual agents or pictures of robots instead of physically copresent robots. From other work on human-robot interaction, we know however, that the physical presence of a robot fundamentally shapes the way we perceive and interact with it [2,16,26]. What we do not know, however, is how the physical presence of an agent and gaze cueing relate. This paper thus explores whether the physical presence of an agent affects the strength of the gaze cueing effect in human-robot interaction.

2   Related Work

The common paradigm used to study gaze cueing is a variation of the Posner paradigm [21], in which participants are asked to localize a target stimulus while that stimulus is consistently and inconsistently cued by a facial stimulus. In several studies using schematic and human faces as stimuli, a gaze cueing effect (GCE) has been observed, evidenced by faster reaction times in responding to congruent (gazed-at) target stimuli compared to incongruent (non-gazed-at) target stimuli [7,9].

In contrast to these common findings, studies using robotic stimuli show mixed results. While Admoni and colleagues [1] find a gaze cueing effect with images of human, schematic, and no GCE for the robot faces in one study, Wiese and colleagues [27] report a more pronounced GCE for robotic face stimuli compared to human face stimuli in a study with individuals with autism spectrum disorder (ASD). Notably, most studies on gaze cueing in HRI used only static images of gazing robots. For instance, in a study investigating the effect of human-likeness of a robot on the strength of the gaze cueing effect, Martini et al. used morphed images of human and robot faces as stimuli [17]. To date, however, it is still unclear to what extent these results can be generalized to copresent robots in real human-robot interaction.

Physical presence appears to be an important factor shaping our perception of and interaction with robots [16]. For example, in an early study conducted by Lee et al. [15], in which participants were either introduced to a physical Aibo robot dog, or its virtual equivalent, a positive effect of embodiment on ratings of the interaction with the robot and the robot's social presence was found. These results indicate the importance of physical embodiment in HRI, even if it is not necessary to complete the interaction successfully.

Wiese and colleagues employed a gaze cueing paradigm using a copresent humanoid robot [28]. Participants were instructed to indicate the appearance of a light stimulus on their left or right side, which was cued by a Meka robot's gaze shift. Even though the researchers informed the participants that the robot's gaze is uninformative of the appearance of the light stimulus, participants seemed to follow the robot's gaze, as a congruency effect could still be found. Using a similar setup, Kompatsiari et al. [13] were able to replicate these results with an iCub robot when the robot established mutual gaze with the observer before turning to the target stimuli, as in the previously reported experiment [28], but not when no mutual gaze was established.

Further controlled investigations will be needed, in which participants are faced with scenarios and robots that are constant except for the way they are presented, to better grasp the role of presence on gaze cueing effects in HRI. To our knowledge, there is only one systematic study conducted to date that explores the relation of embodiment, presence and facial cueing. Mollahosseini et al. [19] investigated the effect of robot embodiment and presence on interaction tasks that involved typical measures of communication, and found that these factors affect recognition of facial expressions, and especially eye gaze. While further analysis of the data revealed a significant effect of embodiment, unlike other studies examining social interaction in HRI, no main effect of presence was found. This could be due to the nature of the task, which involved only still representations of the gaze rather than actual movements, or to the fact that it generally did not rely on social attributions that could relate to the presence of the robot, but on purely geometric cues.

3   Methods and Material

We chose a mixed experimental design with two independent variables: (1) type of robot presence (between-subject) with two levels: a physical robot and a virtual version of the same robot as depicted in Fig. 1 (2) gaze cue congruency (within-subject) with two levels: congruent, and incongruent as depicted in Fig. 2. Participants were randomly assigned to one type of robot and observed it gazeing at one of two light stimuli situated on either side of the table. The robot shifted its gaze in 80 trials, 40 congruent trials in which the robot looked at the lamp that was to change color and 40 incongruent trials in which the robot looked at the opposite lamp (see Fig. 2). In half of the conditions the robot looked at the left side and in the other half at the right side. All conditions were pseudo-randomly shuffled. Most of the features detailed in this section are also illustrated in this video https://youtu.be/n_rU9XNE-bI.

3.1   Participants

A total of 42 participants were recruited via posters in the university building, Facebook advertisement, and email. Three participants were excluded due to technical problems with the setup.

Fig. 1. Copresent (left) and virtual iCub (right) used in the experiment.

The final sample consisted of 42 participants (16 females; mean age = 29.98). All participants provided written informed consent in line with the ethical approval of the study granted by the Committee for Research Ethics at the Czech Technical University in Prague. When asked about their experience with robots on a scale from 1 (very poor) to 5 (very good), the mean score was 2.33 (SD = 1.2) and only one participant answered 5. Data was stored and analysed anonymously. Testing time was about fifteen minutes.

3.2 Measures

Similar to previous studies on gaze cueing [7,28], the influence of gaze cueing on participants' gaze following behavior was determined by measures of mean correct reaction time. A response was considered incorrect if it was made with the wrong key press, and considered correct if the correct key was pressed. Responses that were given in a response time that was more than 2.5 standard deviations away from the individual mean response time of a participant were excluded from further analyses. To further check for possible effects of a robot's physical presence on gaze following behavior, average correct response times (RTs) were calculated for each participant and each experimental condition.

3.3 Experimental Set-Up and Procedure

The present experiment was designed to examine both self-reported and behavioral effects of a robot's presence and gaze cues in a human-robot interaction task. During the experiment, participants were instructed to indicate the appearance of a target stimulus that was either congruent or incongruent with the position being gazed at by an iCub robot that was either physically present in the same room with the participants (copresence condition) or presented via a monitor (virtual agent condition) by pressing a corresponding key on a keyboard. After completion of the task, participants were asked to indicate the way they perceived the robot by completing the Czech translation of the three subscales "Anthropomorphism", "Animacy" and "Likeability" of the Godspeed series [4][1]. The experiment was conducted in April 2022 in the laboratories of the Department of Cybernetics of the Czech Technical University in Prague.

At the beginning of the experiment, participants received written and oral instructions and gave informed consent. They were informed that the task was to respond as fast as possible to the color change of one of two light stimuli. Responses had to be given by pressing the appropriate key on a keyboard. Participants were also informed that iCub might move randomly during the time of the experiment. Reaction times were measured as a dependent variable. After receiving the instructions participants had the opportunity to ask questions about the task.

Each trial began with iCub making eye contact by looking straight ahead in the direction of the observer. After 250 ms, iCub shifted his gaze either toward the lamp that was on his left side or toward the lamp that was on his right side. Subsequently, after 200 ms, one of the two lamps changed color, either on the corresponding side of the gaze cue or on the non-corresponding side of the gaze cue. When the target stimulus was presented, participants responded as quickly and as accurately as possible to the position of the target stimulus by pressing the "x" or "m" key on a standard keyboard. The target stimulus remained unchanged until a response was made or a time-out criterion (5000 ms) was reached. Then the light was turned off again and iCub looked straight ahead again to signal readiness to begin the next trial. Figure 2 shows an exemplary trial sequence.

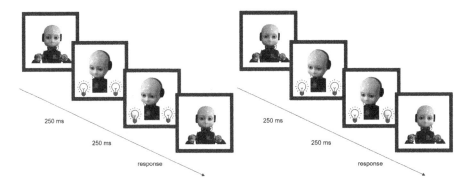

Fig. 2. Example trial sequence with (left) congruent condition and (right) incongruent condition for the physically presence condition. Target stimuli are represented as schematic depiction (light bulb vs. self-made light stimuli in the actual experiment).

---

[1] https://www.bartneck.de/2008/03/11/the-godspeed-questionnaire-series/.

3.4   Hardware and Software

The iCub [18] is a small humanoid robot that resembles a 4-year old child. It is one meter tall and has 53 Degrees of Freedom (DoF). Most relevant to gaze, it has 3 DoF in the neck and 3 coupled DoF for the two eyes (tilt, version, and vergence) in an anthropomorphic arrangement. For the virtual iCub we used the freely available simulator [25]. The iCub gaze controller [23] is used to command where the robot should look. Our custom made C++ program that controls the movement of the robot using the YARP middleware and records the reaction times in the experiment is publicly available[2]. For our experiment we designed custom lamps which consisted of mate covered red led lamps controlled via Arduino Nano.

3.5   Analysis

Statistical analyses were conducted using R (version 4.1.2). The average correct RTs for congruent and incongruent trials were compared for each robot presence condition individually to check for consistency with previous studies regarding the strength of the gaze cueing effect. To test for the effect of cue-target congruence, for the virtual robot condition a t-test was calculated comparing the mean reactions times of congruent trials and incongruent trials. For the copresent robot condition a Wilcoxon test was calculated instead, to account for non-normally distributed data. A gaze cueing effect is evidenced by significant differences in reaction times of congruent and incongruent trials.

Moreover, a mixed model analysis of variance (ANOVA) with a between-subject factor of robot presence (2: copresence vs. virtual presence), and within-subject factors of cue-target congruency (2: congruent vs. incongruent) was calculated. This analysis was used to assess the individual effect of cue-target congruency and the effect of presence specificity of gaze cueing. Robot presence specific gaze-cueing effects would be evidenced by a significant interaction between presence condition and cue-target congruency (over and above a main effect of congruency). By contrast, presence nonspecific gaze cueing would manifest in terms of a main effect of cue-target congruency (not accompanied by a presence × congruency interaction), with equal facilitation for all robot presence conditions of interest.

4   Results

4.1   The Effect of Presence and Gaze

Mean reaction times were subjected to a two-way analysis of variance with two levels of robot presence (copresent robot, virtual agent) and two levels of cue-target congruence (congruent, incongruent) to test the effect of robot physical

---

[2] github.com/Sabka/icub-hri-cuing.

presence and gaze cueing behavior on participants' reaction times in a localization task (see Table 1). It is important to note that the data was not normally
distributed in each group. An ANOVA was conducted either way, as F-Tests have
been reported to be relatively robust to violations of normality when homogene-
ity of variance is given [5].

Table 1. Gaze Congruence x robot presence analysis of variance

Source	Df	F	$\mu2$	p
Robot Presence	1	0.64	0.02	0.43
Gaze Congruence	1	18.71	0.32	.001***
Presence x Gaze	1	2.22	0.05	0.14
Error	40			

*Note. *** p<.001, ** p<.01, * p<.05*

The main effect of gaze congruency yielded an F-ratio of $F(1, 40) = 18.71$,
$p < .001$, indicating that mean reaction times differed significantly between
congruent and incongruent trials, with faster reaction times on congruent cue-
target trials (M = 288 ms, SD = 37.2 ms) than on incongruent cue-target trials
(M = 298 ms, SD = 43.2 ms).

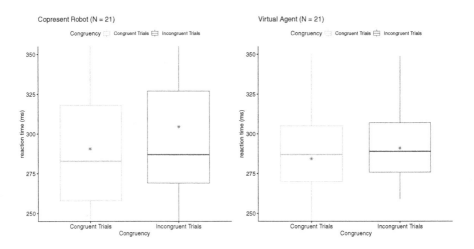

Fig. 3. Mean reaction times by robot presence group. Values are reported in millisec-
onds. Group means are illustrated as red stars. (Color figure online)

To illustrate the size of the GCE by robot presence group, individual analyses were performed for both robot conditions as displayed in Fig. 3. For the
comparison of mean reaction times in congruent and incongruent trials in the

copresent robot group a Wilcoxon signed-rank test was calculated to account for non-normally distributed data as indicated by a significant Shapiro-Wilk test (W = .9, p = .009). On average, participants in the copresent robot condition responded faster on congruent trials (M = 291 ms) than on incongruent trials (M = 305 ms). Results of the Wilcoxon signed-rank test showed that this difference was statistically significant (p = .001), with a large effect size, r = 0.7. An additional t-test conducted on the mean reaction times of participants in the virtual agent group revealed a significant difference between congruent and incongruent trials (t (20) = -2, p = .03) with shorter reaction times for congruent (M = 284 ms) than incongruent trials (M = 291 ms). The effect size was at a moderate level, r = 0.5.

While participants in the virtual agent group (M = 287 ms) on average reacted faster than participants in the copresent group (M = 298 ms), the main effect of robot presence on participants' mean reaction times was non-significant $F(1, 40) = 0.64$, p > .05. Yet, it is worth noting that the variances of the reaction times of the two robot conditions were significantly different, p =.012. Moreover, no significant interaction effect of gaze congruency and presence could be found, $F(1, 40) = 2.22$, p > .05.

4.2 Analysis of Godspeed Indices

To further test how robot presence influences the way participants perceive the robot, responses of the participants to the Godspeed subscales Anthropomorphism, Animacy and Likeability were taken into account. A standard t-test was used to examine the influence of robot presence on animacy ratings. Significant results in a Shapiro-Wilk test with mean ratings of anthropomorphism and likability as outcome variables indicated non-normally distributed data, so an unpaired two-samples Wilcoxon test was computed to test the influence of robot presence on perceived anthropomorphism and likability. Mean ratings for all three Godspeed subscales by robot presence condition can be found in Fig. 4.

Anthropomorphism. For ratings of the robot's perceived anthropomorphism, participants in the virtual agent condition assessed the robot's anthropomorphism slightly higher (M = 12.29, SD = 2.83) than people in the copresent robot condition (M = 12.05, SD = 4.03). Results of the independent samples Wilcoxon test, however, were not significant; W = 208.5, p = .77, r = −0.05. A linear model including sex as an additional predictor was tested due to the significant correlation of anthropomorphism ratings and sex. The model revealed no significant difference between presence groups, whereas ratings between sexes significantly differed (p < .05), with females (M = 13.56, SD = 3.44) rating the robot as more anthropomorphic on average than males (M = 11.31, SD = 3.21).

Animacy. On average, participants in the copresent robot condition rated the robot's perceived animacy higher (M = 15.19, SD= 4.50) than participants in the virtual agent group (M = 13.95, SD = 3.67). This difference was not significant; t(38.43) = 0.98, p = .33.

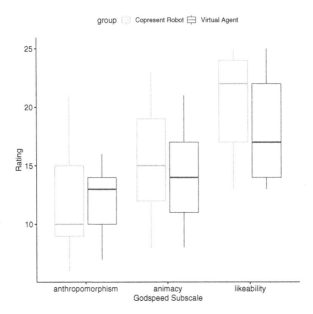

Fig. 4. Ratings of the Godspeed Indices by Group. Scores are summed for each individual subscale. The Anthropomorphism and Likeability scale consist of 5 sub-questions on a 5-point Likert scale with a maximum score of 25 points, and the Animacy scale consists of 6 sub-questions on a 5-point Likert scale with a maximum score of 30 points.

Likeability. Participants in the copresent robot condition assessed the robot's likeability slightly higher (M = 20.19, SD = 4.25) than people in the copresent robot condition (M = 18.10, SD = 3.94). Results of the independent samples Wilcoxon test indicate that this difference was not significant; W = 289, p = .09, r = 0.26. A linear model including sex as an additional predictor was tested due to the significant correlation of likeability ratings and sex. The model revealed no significant difference between presence groups, whereas ratings between sexes significantly differed (p < .01). On average, females (M = 21.23, SD = 3.41) rated the robot as more likeable than males (M = 17.84, SD = 4.13).

5   Discussion

Our results are consistent with previous research on gaze following with copresent robots [28]: Participants consistently exhibited gaze-following behavior, as evidenced by slower reaction times on trials in which the robot cued the wrong target compared to trials in which the cued location and target location matched. Hence, our results replicate the well-known finding that participants locate a target that is congruent with the cued direction more quickly than a target that is incongruent with the cued direction [7,9]. In particular, our results are in line with findings by Wiese [28] and by Kompatsiari [13] showing that a gaze cueing effect can be found when the target stimulus is predicted by the gaze of an embodied robot. This finding is particularly valuable given the ongoing replication crisis in psychological research, which has highlighted the problem of replicating the results of many scientific studies [20] and allows for the generalization of the gaze cueing effect across different robotic platforms. Crucially, with an effect of 14 ms, the gaze cueing effect in our study is smaller than the 25 ms found by [28] but in line with findings of other studies using more controlled settings [29,30]. Differences in the extent of the effect might be explained by the design of the robot—possibly, the Meka robot used in [28] offers more social cues or other affordances than the iCub robot used in the present study or other robotic platforms. Further studies will be needed to better understand the relationship of robot design and gaze following behavior. Moreover, our results show that even the virtual version of our robot consistently triggered a gaze cueing effect as indicated by slower reaction times in incongruent compared to congruent trials, showing that gaze following in HRI is not limited to physically present versions of embodied robots.

Importantly, however, the same stimuli did not elicit varying degrees of gaze-cueing when comparing the different ways the robot was presented to the participants, as evidenced by a non-significant interaction of robot presence and cue-target congruency. Across conditions participants consistently followed the gaze, independently of whether they were confronted with a copresent iCub or a virtual iCub. As the novelty of this study lies in comparing the way the different ways of presenting the robot influence simple social attention mechanisms, as evidenced by the gaze cueing effect, there exists hardly any literature indicating similar or contradictory results. However, these results add to findings of Mollahosseini [19] who were comparing the effect of embodiment and presence of four different types of agents on similar outcome variables. Results showed that embodiment but not physical presence was the factor that accounts for the significant difference in the participants' response, as indicated by no significant difference in results when presenting the participants with a copresent robot compared to a telepresent robot. However, the outcomes differed significantly for the comparisons of virtual agents and both forms of embodied robots. In contrast, our study found no significant difference in gaze following behavior between the presence conditions, as participants' reaction times were not significantly different when interacting with a virtual agent compared to a copresent robot.

There are multiple possible reasons why physical presence might not additionally influence the gaze cueing effect. One could be that our results are based on the fact that robots in both conditions moved in a similar, human-like manner. Previous research has shown that (natural) movement is linked to mind attributions—famously for example in the Heider and Simmel illusion [11], in which participants attribute mental states to three moving geometrical figures (two triangles that seem to "hunt" a circle). Studies examining how mental state attributions alter gaze following behavior in trials with photographs of robots have shown that this manipulation led to the occurrence of a gaze cueing effect that was not otherwise present [30]. Differences between our results and those of studies using only photos of agents or robots [1] or non-moving agents, as in the research of Mollahosseini [19], might be due to the association of motion and mind attributions leading to typical social interaction phenomena, such as gaze cueing.

Moreover, in contrast to previous findings [16], the copresent robot did not generate more positive ratings than the virtual agent, as indicated by participants' ratings of the robot's anthropomorphism, animacy, and likability. Similar results were reported in a study [12], in which the ratings of four types of agents that differed in terms of their embodiment and physical presence were compared after a simple conversational interaction. Notably, neither the interaction reported by [12] nor the interaction reported in our study involved physical touch or a particular focus on spatial relations. The differences between the results of this and other studies could be explained by the advantages of the physical presence of a robot in more complex interaction scenarios.

6   Conclusion

Social gaze is a fundamental part of human interactions and becomes more relevant in the scope of social human-robot interaction. Gaze cueing, the event in which we observe our interaction partner's gaze and shift our own attention accordingly, is broadly studied using images or virtual versions of robots. As previous research has pointed to the broad range of effects physical presence has in human-robot interaction, the question arises whether it affects the strength of the gaze cueing effect and hence, whether results from studies using images or virtual agents can be generalized to copresent robots. We designed a study to investigate the relationship of physical presence and social gaze by adapting a gaze cueing paradigm with two types of agents (1) a copresent robot and (2) a virtual version of the same robot. The results of our study indicate that gaze cueing is a stable effect in basal human-robot interaction across different robot presence conditions. Thereby, we add to the understanding of possibilities to generalize results from studies using virtual agents and pictorial stimuli to real life human-robot interaction.

Acknowledgements. This research was supported by the by the Czech Science Foundation (GAČR), project 20-24186X. The authors from Comenius University were additionally supported by the Slovak Research and Development Agency, project APVV-21-0105 and by Slovak Society for Cognitive Science. We would like to dearly thank Jakub Rozlivek and Lukáš Rustler for their help in programming the iCub and Adam Rojík for organizing the recruitment of participants.

References

1. Admoni, H., Bank, C., Tan, J., Toneva, M., Scassellati, B.: Robot gaze does not reflexively cue human attention. In: Proceedings of the Annual Meeting of the Cognitive Science Society, vol. 33 (2011)

2. Bainbridge, W.A., Hart, J., Kim, E.S., Scassellati, B.: The effect of presence on human-robot interaction. In: RO-MAN 2008-The 17th IEEE International Symposium on Robot and Human Interactive Communication, pp. 701–706. IEEE (2008)
3. Baron-Cohen, S., Wheelwright, S., Jolliffe, T.: Is there a "language of the eyes"? evidence from normal adults, and adults with autism or asperger syndrome. Vis. Cogn. 4(3), 311–331 (1997)
4. Bartneck, C., Kulić, D., Croft, E., Zoghbi, S.: Measurement instruments for the anthropomorphism, animacy, likeability, perceived intelligence, and perceived safety of robots. Int. J. Soc. Robot. 1(1), 71–81 (2009)
5. Blanca Mena, M.J., Alarcón Postigo, R., Arnau Gras, J., Bono Cabré, R., Bendayan, R., et al.: Non-normal data: Is anova still a valid option? Psicothema (2017)
6. Breazeal, C., Scassellati, B.: How to build robots that make friends and influence people. In: Proceedings 1999 IEEE/RSJ International Conference on Intelligent Robots and Systems. Human and Environment Friendly Robots with High Intelligence and Emotional Quotients, vol. 2, pp. 858–863. IEEE (1999)
7. Driver, J., IV., Davis, G., Ricciardelli, P., Kidd, P., Maxwell, E., Baron-Cohen, S.: Gaze perception triggers reflexive visuospatial orienting. Vis. Cogn. 6(5), 509–540 (1999)
8. Emery, N.J., Lorincz, E.N., Perrett, D.I., Oram, M.W., Baker, C.I.: Gaze following and joint attention in rhesus monkeys (macaca mulatta). J. Comp. Psychol. 111(3), 286 (1997)
9. Friesen, C.K., Kingstone, A.: The eyes have it! reflexive orienting is triggered by nonpredictive gaze. Psychon. Bull. Rev. 5(3), 490–495 (1998)
10. Frischen, A., Bayliss, A.P., Tipper, S.P.: Gaze cueing of attention: visual attention, social cognition, and individual differences. Psychol. Bull. 133(4), 694 (2007)
11. Heider, F., Simmel, M.: An experimental study of apparent behavior. Am. J. Psychol. 57(2), 243–259 (1944)
12. Kiesler, S., Powers, A., Fussell, S.R., Torrey, C.: Anthropomorphic interactions with a robot and robot-like agent. Soc. Cogn. 26(2), 169–181 (2008)
13. Kompatsiari, K., Ciardo, F., Tikhanoff, V., Metta, G., Wykowska, A.: On the role of eye contact in gaze cueing. Sci. Rep. 8(1), 1–10 (2018)
14. Kozima, H., Ito, A.: Towards language acquisition by an attention-sharing robot. In: New Methods in Language Processing and Computational Natural Language Learning (1998)
15. Lee, K.M., Jung, Y., Kim, J., Kim, S.R.: Are physically embodied social agents better than disembodied social agents?: The effects of physical embodiment, tactile interaction, and people's loneliness in human-robot interaction. Int. J. Human-Comput. Stud. 64(10), 962–973 (2006)
16. Li, J.: The benefit of being physically present: a survey of experimental works comparing copresent robots, telepresent robots and virtual agents. Int. J. Hum.-Comput. Stud. 77, 23–37 (2015)
17. Martini, M.C., Buzzell, G.A., Wiese, E.: Agent appearance modulates mind attribution and social attention in human-robot interaction. In: ICSR 2015. LNCS (LNAI), vol. 9388, pp. 431–439. Springer, Cham (2015). https://doi.org/10.1007/978-3-319-25554-5_43
18. Metta, G., et al.: The icub humanoid robot: an open-systems platform for research in cognitive development. Neural Netw. 23(8–9), 1125–1134 (2010)
19. Mollahosseini, A., Abdollahi, H., Sweeny, T.D., Cole, R., Mahoor, M.H.: Role of embodiment and presence in human perception of robots' facial cues. Int. J. Hum.-Comput. Stud. 116, 25–39 (2018)

20. Open Science Collaboration: estimating the reproducibility of psychological science. Science **349**(6251), aac4716 (2015)
21. Posner, M.I.: Orienting of attention. Quart. J. Exp. Psychol. **32**(1), 3–25 (1980)
22. Risko, E.F., Richardson, D.C., Kingstone, A.: Breaking the fourth wall of cognitive science: real-world social attention and the dual function of gaze. Curr. Dir. Psychol. Sci. **25**(1), 70–74 (2016)
23. Roncone, A., Pattacini, U., Metta, G., Natale, L.: A Cartesian 6-DoF gaze controller for humanoid robots. In: Robotics: Science and Systems, vol. 2016 (2016)
24. Stass, J.W., Willis, F.N.: Eye contact, pupil dilation, and personal preference. Psychon. Sci. **7**(10), 375–376 (1967). https://doi.org/10.3758/BF03331131
25. Tikhanoff, V., Cangelosi, A., Fitzpatrick, P., Metta, G., Natale, L., Nori, F.: An open-source simulator for cognitive robotics research: the prototype of the icub humanoid robot simulator. In: Proceedings of the 8th Workshop on Performance Metrics for Intelligent Systems, pp. 57–61 (2008)
26. Wainer, J., Feil-Seifer, D.J., Shell, D.A., Mataric, M.J.: The role of physical embodiment in human-robot interaction. In: ROMAN 2006-The 15th IEEE International Symposium on Robot and Human Interactive Communication, pp. 117–122. IEEE (2006)
27. Wiese, E., Müller, H.J., Wykowska, A.: Using a gaze-cueing paradigm to examine social cognitive mechanisms of individuals with autism observing robot and human faces. In: Beetz, M., Johnston, B., Williams, M.-A. (eds.) ICSR 2014. LNCS (LNAI), vol. 8755, pp. 370–379. Springer, Cham (2014). https://doi.org/10.1007/978-3-319-11973-1_38
28. Wiese, E., Weis, P.P., Lofaro, D.M.: Embodied social robots trigger gaze following in real-time hri. 2018 15th International Conference on Ubiquitous Robots (UR), pp. 477–482 (2018). https://doi.org/10.1109/URAI.2018.8441825
29. Wiese, E., Wykowska, A., Zwickel, J., Müller, H.J.: I see what you mean: How attentional selection is shaped by ascribing intentions to others. PLoS ONE **7**, 1–7 (2012). https://doi.org/10.1371/journal.pone.0045391
30. Wykowska, A., Wiese, E., Prosser, A., Müller, H.J.: Beliefs about the minds of others influence how we process sensory information. PLoS ONE **9**(4), e94339 (2014)

Special Session 1: Social Robotics Driven by Intelligent Perception and Endogenous Emotion-Motivation Core

An Efficient Medicine Identification and Delivery System Based on Mobile Manipulation Robot

Meiyuan Zou, Qingchuan Xu, Jianfeng Bian, Dingfeng Chen,
Wenzheng Chi[✉], and Lining Sun

Robotics and Microsystems Center, School of Mechanical and Electric Engineering,
Soochow University, Suzhou 215021, China
{myzou,qcxu,jfbian,dfchen1105,wzchi,lnsun}@suda.edu.cn

Abstract. In recent years, with the emergence of COVID-19, the shortage of medical resources has become increasingly obvious. However, current environments such as hospital wards still require a large number of medical staff to deliver medicines. In this paper, we propose a mobile robot that can complete medicine grabbing and delivery in a hospital ward scenario. First, a lightweight neural network is built to improve the detection efficiency of Faster R-CNN algorithm for boxed medicine. Then, the pose of the robotic arm grasping the pill box is determined by point cloud matching to control the mechanical grasping of the pill box. Finally, a discomfort function representing the collision risk between the robot and the pedestrian is incorporated into the Risk-RRT algorithm to improve the navigation performance of the algorithm. By building a real experimental platform, the experiments verify the performance of our proposed medicine delivery robot system.

Keywords: Target detection · Network model lightweight · Mobile robot navigation

1 Introduction

Object detection is a basic research direction of machine vision, which aims to enable robots to recognize objects in images and mark the location of objects. It is widely used in different fields including industrial robotic arms, service robots, self-driving cars, autonomous sweepers, *etc.* In general, object detection methods can be divided into two categories. Detection methods based on sliding windows such as YOLO [1] is to divide the image into many regular windows, and then classify each window after judgement. The algorithm based on

Supported by National Key R&D Program of China grant #2020YFB1313601, National Science Foundation of China grant #61903267 and China Postdoctoral Science Foundation grant #2020M681691 awarded to Wenzheng Chi.
M. Zou and Q. Xu—contribute equally to this paper.

sliding window has high timeliness, but the accuracy is relatively low. Detection methods based on candidate regions, such as R-CNN and its derivatives [2] have gained popularity for their capability of high detection accuracy. Through the segmentation method, some candidate regions are first extracted. Then, the candidate regions are identified and regressed to find the regions containing the target objects. Segmentation-based object detection algorithms usually first extract some candidate regions. Next, the recognition and regression processing is performed within the candidate regions to find the regions containing objects, and finally these regions are merged.

Grishick *et al.* [3] designed a new R-CNN network structure and successfully used convolutional neural networks in the field of target detection. Compared with the traditional target detection algorithm, the performance of R-CNN algorithm has been significantly improved. Ren *et al.* [2,4] proposed the Faster R-CNN algorithm, which solves the problem that Fast R-CNN generates candidate proposal frames slowly to improve the accuracy of the algorithm. In this paper, we combine the inverted residual structure [5] and depthwise separable convolution to build a lightweight neural network and integrate it into the Faster R-CNN algorithm. In this way, the amount of parameters generated by the model operation is reduced, and the timeliness of model detection is improved.

In the field of robot motion planning, many advanced algorithms have been proposed. Lavalle *et al.* [6] proposed the Rapid Exploration Random Tree (RRT) algorithm, which laid the foundation for sampling-based motion planning algorithms. Karaman *et al.* [7] proposed the RRT* algorithm with asymptotic optimality. On the basis of RRT node expansion, random geometric graph and pruning optimization theory are added to ensure that the nodes of the random tree can converge to the current optimal value. Fulgenzi *et al.* [8] proposed a Risk-RRT algorithm, which introduced the RRT algorithm into a dynamic environment by estimating moving obstacles with a Gaussian process.

Aiming at the problem that the sampling point of the Risk-RRT algorithm will fall inside the pedestrian during the path planning process, resulting in the failure of navigation. In this paper, we propose a discomfort function representing collision risk, and integrate it into the Risk-RRT algorithm to improve the navigation success rate of the algorithm.

The rest of this paper is organized as follows. In Sect. 2, we will explain our methods in detail. In Sect. 3, we conduct a series of experimental studies and discuss the results. We finally draw conclusions in Sect. 4.

2   Methods

2.1   Identification of Boxed Medicine

In this paper, a lightweight neural network model is built by combining the ideas of depthwise separable convolution and inverse residual structure.

Compared with ordinary convolution, depthwise separable convolution not only reduces the amount of calculation during operation, but also generates less parameters during the calculation process. The comparison between the

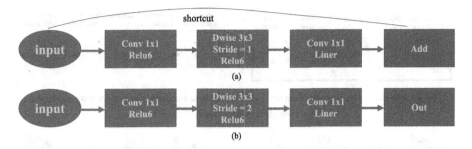

Fig. 1. Linear bottleneck structure with two step sizes. (a) shows a linear bottleneck structure with stride one. (b) shows a linear bottleneck structure with stride two.

depthwise separable convolution and the standard convolution in the convolution operation is listed as follows:

$$\frac{P_1}{P_2} = \frac{D_f^2 D_k^2 Y + D_f^2 Y X}{D_f^2 D_k^2 X Y} = \frac{1}{N} + \frac{1}{D_k^2}. \tag{1}$$

Herein, (P_1) and (P_2) represent the calculation amount of depthwise separable convolution and standard convolution respectively. (D_f) represents the side length of the feature map, (X) represents the number of channels output by the feature map, (D_k) represents the side length of the depthwise convolution kernel, and (Y) represents the number of input channels. It can be seen from the above formula that in the calculation process of the depthwise separable convolution, the amount of parameters and the amount of calculation generated by the ordinary convolution is less.

In addition, the reverse residual structure can not only deepen the number of layers extracted by the network when extracting feature information, but also improve the extraction ability.

The linear bottleneck structure is used to replace the nonlinear bottleneck to reduce the loss of low-dimensional feature information [9]. The network structure of the linear bottleneck structure is shown in Fig. 1. First, we increase the feature vector dimension by point-by-point convolution (1×1 ordinary convolution). Then, feature extraction is performed on each channel of the upscaled vector through 3×3 convolution. Finally, we reduce the dimension of the feature vector by point-by-point convolution. It should be noted that when the stride of the pointwise convolution is one, the input and output can be connected directly. When the stride of pointwise convolution is two, pointwise convolution, activation function and depthwise convolution can only be simply concatenated together.

As shown in Fig. 2, the lightweight neural network model independently built in this study consists of 13 Linear Bottlenecks. In the network model, the activation function of the inverted residual structure is ReLU6. The final activation function is changed to a linear activation function, which can reduce the loss of information on low-dimensional features. The final output channel of the model is 1280.

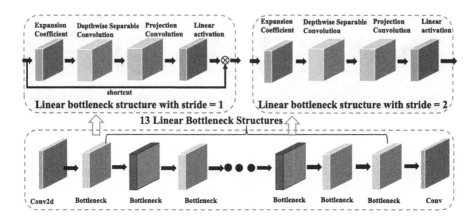

Fig. 2. The model network framework proposed in this paper.

Parameter pre-training [10] is a machine learning method that usually refers to the transfer of knowledge from source domain to target domain.

2.2 Motion Control of the Robotic Arm

The traditional grasping method of the robotic arm is to detect obstacles visually and grasp the target object according to the artificially calibrated path [11]. However, once the environment changes, it is necessary to manually set the halfway point of the movement. Therefore, it has become a research focus to allow the robotic arm to independently plan the obstacle avoidance route and realize the grasping function according to the detected environmental information in the working environment. In this paper, we adopt an improved RRT-Connect [12] algorithm with a heuristic strategy based on the Rapidly-exploring Random Trees [13] algorithm. Two trees created in the space and using each other as inspiration, exploring their directions until the paths of exploration intersect. Compared with Rapidly-exploring Random Trees algorithm, the search speed and search efficiency of our algorithm have been significantly improved. In order to determine the grasping pose of the robotic arm, we also performed point cloud registration. First, we used the depth camera to capture point cloud images of the pillbox at six different angles, as shown in Fig. 3. After point cloud filtering and point cloud fusion, clear medicine box point cloud data is obtained. Finally, the ICP registration algorithm [14] is used to obtain the transformation matrix of the point cloud pose, so as to determine the grasping pose of the robotic arm.

2.3 Research on Autonomous Navigation Technology

Inspired by research results in the field of psychology [15,16] , in this paper, we adopt a pedestrian discomfort function with utilizes distance [17], pedestrian density, height, size and speed to calculate the discomfort value and then integrate the discomfort function into the moving obstacle model in the Risk-RRT

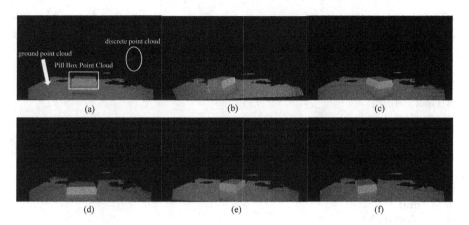

Fig. 3. Point cloud data obtained by using the depth camera. (a)(b)(c)(d)(e)(f) are the point cloud data obtained from different angles.

simulation package to create a pedestrian model. The discomfort function is defined as:

$$f(x,y) = \begin{cases} exp(-\frac{x^2+y^2}{2\sigma^2}) & x < 0 \\ exp(-\frac{w_v^2 x^2+y^2}{2\sigma^2}) & x \geq 0 \end{cases}. \tag{2}$$

$$\sigma = \frac{PS_l * h * s}{\rho_i * h_{avr} * s_{avr}}. \tag{3}$$

$$\omega_v = \frac{PS_u}{PS_u + v * t}. \tag{4}$$

The variables in the discomfort function include: (1) Pedestrian position (x, y, z); (2) Pedestrian moving direction, that is, the rotation angle θ around the $z - axis$; (3) Pedestrian moving speed; (4) Pedestrian height; (5) The size of the pedestrian s using the length of the shoulder to represent the size of the pedestrian; (6) The density of the pedestrian ρ_i [18,19] . The modified Risk-RRT pseudocode is shown in Algorithm 1. The algorithm introduces the RRT algorithm into the dynamic environment, and estimates the trajectory of pedestrian based on the Gaussian process, thereby predicts the position of pedestrian in a short time. If the environment changes, the algorithm is capable of updating the path in real time based on robot coordinates and pedestrian positions to determine the best path.

3   Experimental Studies and Results

3.1   Feature Extraction Network Performance Experiment

This paper uses Labeling, a visual image calibration tool, to annotate 585 medicine box images. The file format generated by this tool is the same as the

Algorithm 1: Modified Risk-RRT

Input: *Goal*; *Map*
Output: *Trajectory*
1 *Trajectory* = empty
2 *Tree* = empty
3 *Goal* = read()
4 *t* = clock()
5 **while** *Goal not reached* **do**
6   **if** *Trajectory is empty* **then**
7 | Brake
8   **else**
9 | move along *Trajectory* for one step
10   **end**
11   observe(X)
12   delete unreachable *trajectories*(T, X)
13   observe(*Map, pedestrian*)
14   *t* = clock()
15   predict at time $t, ..., t + N * \Delta t$
16   **if** *environment different* **then**
17 | update *trajectories*($T, Map, pedestrian$)
18   **end**
19   **while** *clock()* ¡ $t + \Delta t$ **do**
20 | Grow()
21   **end**
22   *Trajectory* = Choose best *trajectory* in T
23   *t* = clock()
24   **return** *Trajectory*
25 **end**

data set format, so when training the model, the labeled images can be mixed with the PASCAL VOC2012 data set to improve the training effect of the model.

We mix the prepared dataset and PASCAL VOC2012 dataset with a total of 16,710 images, then divide them into training set and validation set according to the ratio of 1:1. We train the Faster R-CNN neural network model with VGG16 and our model as the feature extraction network respectively. The equipment used for training is a server with NVIDIA GeForce 3080 graphics card with 10G memory. The training epoch is set to 25, the optimizer SGD learning rate is set to 0.005, the momentum is set to 0.9, and the weight decay is set to 0.0005. We use the trained model to detect 4000 pictures, and count their detection timeliness and the detection accuracy of the medicine box. Using our model as the feature extraction network has 84.2% detection accuracy for pill boxes, and it only takes 22.1 ms to recognize a picture. The model with VGG16 as the feature extraction network has a detection accuracy of 18.5% for the medicine box, but it takes 46.3 ms to detect a picture.

Finally, as shown in Table 1, it can be seen that the detection timeliness of the YOLO algorithm is slightly better than the model we proposed in this paper,

Table 1. Accuracy and Timeliness of Various Neural Network Detection boxed medicine

Method	Transfer learning	mAP	Test time
VGG16	✗	18.5%	46.3 ms
Our model	✓	84.2%	21.9 ms
YOLO V3	✓	57.4%	13.8 ms

Table 2. Navigation results of two algorithms

	Number of intrusions	Number of navigation failures	Navigation time
Risk-RRT	15/20	4/20	22 s
Ours	3/20	0/20	23 s

which is 13.8 ms. However, the detection of the YOLO algorithm accuracy is only 57.4%, which is much lower than our model.

The experimental results show that the ICP algorithm can obtain an effective transformation matrix after 15 iterations, and each registration takes about 1.5 s, which meets the research requirements of the project.

3.2 Autonomous Navigation Simulation Experiments

The experimental scene is designed as a small space to simulate the hospital corridor scene. In the experiments the robot needs to pass through six randomly moving pedestrians in a small space to reach the destination. We set the space within 1.2 m of the pedestrian as the private space of pedestrian, and count the number of times the robot intrudes into the private space of pedestrian. After that we observe the obstacle avoidance trajectory after the robot detects pedestrians during the movement process, The experimental process is shown in Fig. 4. Our improved algorithm can effectively predict the trajectory of pedestrians when the mobile robot is running, and the obstacle avoidance route re-planned according to the prediction results is obviously far away from pedestrians. This type of navigation route not only makes pedestrians feel psychologically comfortable, but also greatly reduces the risk of collision between mobile robots and pedestrians.

We compared the RRT algorithm with our improved algorithm, and carried out comparative experiments. The experimental results are shown in Table 2. Our improved Risk-RRT algorithm greatly reduced the number of intrusions into the private space of pedestrians and the number of times of getting stuck, and the success rate of pedestrian obstacle avoidance had been significantly improved.

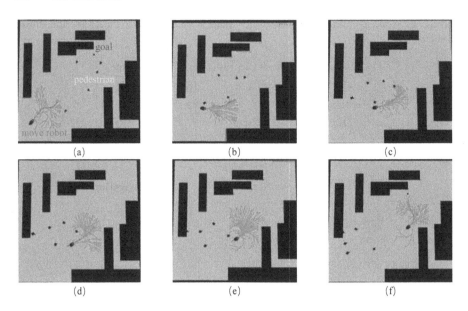

Fig. 4. Experimental results of our improved algorithm. (a) is the experimental environment of the robot. (b) is the start of the experiment and the robot is running. (c)(d)(e) represent the obstacle avoidance process of robot. (e) is the robot reaching the target point.

3.3   Real-World Experiments

We simulated the hospital ward environment and built a real experimental scene to carry out the robot grasping and obstacle avoidance experiments, respectively. The experimental procedure is shown in Fig. 5. It can be seen that the robot moved to the medicine according to the set path to complete the medicine grasping. The experimental result proves that the drug delivery robot proposed in this work can complete boxed medicine grabbing, transportation and pedestrian obstacle avoidance in a complex human-robot environment.

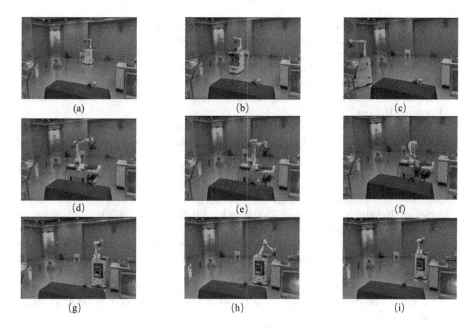

Fig. 5. The experimental process of navigation and scraping. (a)(b)(c)(d) are the navigation process of the robot. (e)(f) are the process of the robot grabbing the pill box. (g)(h)(i) are the process of the robot delivering the pill box.

4   Conclusion

In this paper, we design a hospital ward medicine delivery robot. By independently building a lightweight neural network, the efficiency of detecting pill boxes is improved, and the performance of the Faster R-CNN algorithm is improved. By incorporating the pedestrian discomfort function representing the risk into the Risk-RRT algorithm, the navigation of robots success rate is improved. Through real experiments, it is verified that the medicine delivery robot proposed in this paper can better complete drug grasping, transportation and autonomous navigation.

References

1. Redmon, J., Divvala, S., Girshick, R., Farhadi, A.: You Only Look Once: Unified, Real-Time Object Detection. In: 2016 IEEE Conference on Computer Vision and Pattern Recognition (CVPR), pp. 779–788(2016)
2. Dong, P., Wang, W.: Better region proposals for pedestrian detection with R-CNN. In: 2016 Visual Communications and Image Processing (VCIP), pp. 1–4(2016)
3. Gkioxari, G., Girshick, R., Malik, J.: Contextual Action Recognition with R CNN. In: 2015 IEEE International Conference on Computer Vision (ICCV), pp. 1080–1088(2015)

4. Ren, S., He, K., Girshick, R., Sun, J.: Faster R-CNN: towards real-time object detection with region proposal networks. IEEE Trans. **39**(6), 1137–1149 (2017)
5. Sandler, M., Howard, A., Zhu, M., Zhmoginov, A., Chen, L.: MobileNetV2: Inverted Residuals and Linear Bottleneck. In: 2018 IEEE/CVF Conference on Computer Vision and Pattern Recognition, pp. 4510–4520(2018)
6. Lavalle, S.M.: Rapidly-Exploring Random Trees: A New Tool for Path Planning. Research Report
7. Karaman, S., Frazzoli, E.: Sampling-based algorithms for optimal motion planning with deterministic μ-calculus specifications. In: 2012 American Control Conference (ACC), pp. 735–742(2012)
8. Fulgenzi, C., Spalanzani, A., Laugier, C., Tay, C.: Risk based motion planning and navigation in uncertain dynamic environment. Hal Inria (2010)
9. Sandler, M., Howard, A., Zhu, M., Zhmoginov, A., Chen, L.: MobileNetV2: Inverted Residuals and Linear Bottlenecks. In: 2018 IEEE/CVF Conference on Computer Vision and Pattern Recognition, pp. 4510–4520(2018)
10. Örnek, A., Çelik, M., Ceylan, M.: Mask Detection From Face Images Using Deep Learning and Transfer Learning. In: 15th Turkish National Software Engineering Symposium (UYMS), pp. 1–4(2021)
11. Liu, X., Li, X., Su, H., Zhao, Y., Ge, S. S.: The opening workspace control strategy of a novel manipulator-driven emission source microscopy system. ISA Transactions. (2022)
12. Abidin, Z., Muis, M., Djuriatno, W.: Omni-Wheeled Robot with Rapidly-exploring Random Tree (RRT) Algorithm for Path Planning. In: 2019 International Conference on Advanced Mechatronics, Intelligent Manufacture and Industrial Automation (ICAMIMIA), pp. 288–292(2019)
13. Zhang, D., Xu, Y., Yao, X.: An Improved Path Planning Algorithm for Unmanned Aerial Vehicle Based on RRT-Connect. In: 37th Chinese Control Conference (CCC), pp. 4854–4858(2018)
14. Guan, W., Li, W., Ren, Y.: Point cloud registration based on improved ICP algorithm. In: 2018 Chinese Control And Decision Conference (CCDC), pp. 1461–1465(2018)
15. Huang, K., Li, J., Fu, L.: Human-oriented navigation for service providing in home environment. In: Proceedings of SICE Annual Conference 2010, pp. 1892–1897(2010)
16. Lam, C., Chou, C., Chiang, K., Fu, L.: Human-centered robot navigation-towards a harmoniously human-robot coexisting environment. IEEE Trans. **27**(1), 99–112 (2011)
17. Chi, W., Kono, H., Tamura, Y., Yamashita, A., Meng, Q. H.: A human-friendly robot navigation algorithm using the risk-RRT approach. In: 2016 IEEE International Conference on Real-time Computing and Robotics (RCAR), pp. 227–232 (2016)
18. Eric, S., Knowles: The proximity of others: A critique of crowding research and integration with the Social Sciences. Population Environ. **2**(1) 3–17 (1979)
19. Hayduk, L. A.: Personal space: Where we now stand. Psychol. Bull. **94**(2), 293–335 (1983)

A Generative Adversarial Network Based Motion Planning Framework for Mobile Robots in Dynamic Human-Robot Integration Environments

Yuqi Kong, Yao Wang, Yang Hong, Rongguang Ye, Wenzheng Chi[✉],
and Lining Sun

Robotics and Microsystems Center, School of Mechanical and Electric Engineering,
Soochow University, Suzhou 215021, China
{yqkong,ywang,yhong,rgye,wzchi,lnsun}@suda.edu.cn

Abstract. In the human-robot integration environment, efficient and
safe navigation is of great significance for mobile service robots. At
present, human-robot integration environment is highly uncertain and
dynamic, which brings new challenges to motion planning. In order to
solve this problem, this paper proposes a dynamic obstacle avoidance
strategy based on imitation learning in a Generative Adversarial Network (GAN) framework. When the robot detects a pedestrian around it,
it generates an active obstacle avoidance point that maintains an appropriate distance from the pedestrian according to the pedestrian pose and
the global path planned by the A* algorithm as a sub-goal to guide the
robot for motion planning. In the experiment, the performance of the
algorithm is evaluated by the number of entering the pedestrian person space, the time cost and the trajectory length. Compared with the
Dynamic Window Approach (DWA) and Proactive Social Motion Model
(PSMM) algorithms, the experimental results show that our proposed
algorithm has better performance than the other two algorithms in the
human-robot integration environment.

Keywords: Human-robot integration environment · Dynamic obstacle
avoidance · Generative adversarial networks

1 Introduction

In recent years, with the rapid development of mobile robots, mobile service
robots have been widely used in human-robot integration environments. This
requires the robot to avoid not only regular obstacles but also walking pedestrians during navigation. Therefore, how to plan a feasible and smooth trajectory in
the human-robot integration environment has received extensive attention from
related researchers.

In the past decades, many related researchers have proposed various path
planning algorithms, in the field of robot motion planning, which can be roughly

© The Author(s), under exclusive license to Springer Nature Switzerland AG 2022
F. Cavallo et al. (Eds.): ICSR 2022, LNAI 13817, pp. 427–439, 2022.
https://doi.org/10.1007/978-3-031-24667-8_38

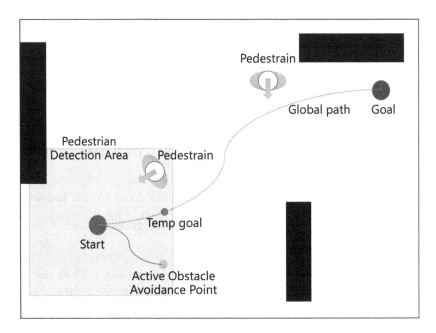

Fig. 1. Illustration of the proposed navigation method. When a pedestrian is detected near the robot, an active obstacle avoidance point is generated by a GAN framework according to the pedestrian pose and the goal position to guide the robot to perform motion planning.

divided into four categories. The artificial potential field algorithm [1] based on minimizing the potential energy function can effectively plan a safe path in the map. However, it is easy to fall into a local minimum value during the planning process, causing the robot to get stuck. The grid-based A* algorithm [2] can efficiently find the shortest path in the map. The sampling-based RRT algorithm [3,4] can quickly plan a feasible path in the map. Some algorithms can plan in a dynamic environment, but it only treats pedestrians as obstacles without taking into account the pedestrian feelings, such as widely adopted Dynamic Window Approach (DWA) [5]. There are also algorithms that focus on the next moment of action according to some specific interaction rules, such as Reciprocal Velocity Obstacles (RVO) [6] and Optimal Reciprocal Collision Avoidance (ORCA) [7]. These navigation algorithms avoid obstacles by reacting passively after encountering pedestrians, and have achieved good results in environments with few pedestrians. However, in crowded environments, the movement trajectory of the robot will be unnatural ,and the robot may be too close to pedestrians, or even collide due to the lack of long-term considerations which the robot should try to navigate to a place with low pedestrian density while meeting the navigation task.

To address these issues, we draw inspiration from human obstacle avoidance strategies. In crowded environments, people usually choose obstacle avoidance strategies based on different factors, such as pedestrian density, pedestrian movement speed, pedestrian movement direction. For example, when encountering a group of people walking straight towards a person quickly, the person will generally move to a nearby relatively empty area to avoid obstacles based on long-term considerations, which is defined as the active obstacle avoidance point in this article, and then re-plan a suitable feasible path. Although the process of moving to the active obstacle avoidance point for obstacle avoidance will deviate from the original path, it can help people to avoid obstacles effectively and generate a continuous, natural and safe trajectory. Inspired by this idea, this paper proposes an active obstacle avoidance method based on imitation learning, as shown in Fig. 1. When there is a pedestrian near the robot, the robot will generate an active obstacle avoidance point based on the pedestrian pose and the global path planned by the A* algorithm, and then the robot will plan a path to the active obstacle avoidance point. When the robot reaches the active obstacle avoidance point, it will repeat the above operations until the robot reaches the goal. In the above process, the position of the active obstacle avoidance point generated by the robot should be affected by factors such as pedestrian pose and goal. Therefore, the crucial problem is how to generate active obstacle avoidance points that conform to the human conventions.

1.1 Related Work

With the development of society and technology, people put forward increasing requirements, in the process of navigation, the robot should not only navigate to the goal without collision but also try not to interfere with the normal movement of pedestrians, so as to make pedestrians feel comfortable. Therefore, how to make pedestrians feel comfortable during robot navigation is also a major research hotspot in this field.

Hall *et al.* [8] proposed the concept of spatial agency for human interaction, which revealed that humans choose different social interaction distances based on social relationships and intentions. Without special circumstances, people should not easily enter other people personal space. Pacchierotti *et al.* [9,10] suggested that in order to ensure the psychological comfort of pedestrians, robots should not get too close to pedestrians even if there is no risk of collision with pedestrians.

Dragan *et al.* [11] found that the more natural the trajectory of the robot, that is, the more similar it is to pedestrians, the higher the comfort level of pedestrian. Therefore, many researchers focus on making robots plan a trajectory similar to that of pedestrians, which can be mainly classified into inference-based methods and learning-based methods.

The inference-based methods rely on manually constructed mathematical models, such as constant speed model [12], discrete choice model [13], social force model and its variants [14,15], and Proactive Social Motion Model [16]. However, pedestrians usually show high randomness in motion planning, so inference-based methods is not very similar to the motion of pedestrians.

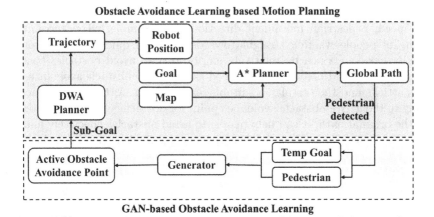

Fig. 2. The system architecture of the proposed obstacle avoidance learning based motion planning method.

In recent years, with the development of deep learning technologies, many researchers have used deep learning methods to study such problems, which have achieved good results, such as the social Long Short-Term Memory (LSTM) method [17]. In addition, many researchers have also used deep reinforcement learning to solve such problems. The robot accumulates experience through continuous trial and error in the virtual environment, and finally plans a trajectory similar to that of pedestrians. Recent work in [18] has demonstrated the superior navigation ability of this method, but the effectiveness of this method relies on pre-set subtle reward functions.

Path planning can be regarded as a generation problem, and an appropriate motion path is generated according to external information. Generative Adversarial Networks (GAN) have recently become popular in the field of deep learning due to their powerful generative capabilities. Gupta *et al.* [19] used GAN to predict future actions of pedestrians by observing pedestrian historical trajectories, and achieved good results. Zhang *et al.* [20] used GAN to predict the promising regions of RRT sampling to guide the growth of RRT and perform path planning tasks. However, this method can only perform path planning in a static environment. Given such powerful generative capabilities of GANs, we adopt the GAN framework to learn human obstacle avoidance strategies in dynamic environments.

1.2   The Proposed System and Approach

This paper proposes a new motion planning method for mobile robots by designing a dynamic obstacle avoidance strategy based on imitation learning in the GAN framework. With the proposed method, mobile robots can better cooperate with humans in a human-robot integration environment and successfully complete their navigation tasks. The system architecture is shown in the Fig. 2.

First, a fixed-size rectangular area is determined with the robot as the center to detect whether there are pedestrians in the surrounding of the robot. If there are pedestrians, the pedestrian pose in the rectangular area is recorded, and the A* algorithm is used to plan a path from the robot current position to the goal. The point where the path intersects the rectangle is defined as the temp goal. During the learning process, the input information includes the position of the temp goal, the pedestrian pose in the rectangular area, and the artificially marked active obstacle avoidance point. Whenever there is a pedestrian in the rectangular area, the GAN is triggered to generate an active obstacle avoidance point, which is used as a sub-goal of the robot for planning, to achieve the effect of active obstacle avoidance.

The contributions of our work are summarized as follows:

- A novel dynamic obstacle avoidance strategy to improve the robot navigation ability in a human-robot integrated environment;
- A GAN-based active obstacle avoidance learning framework;
- Case studies to demonstrate the effectiveness and efficiency of the proposed GAN-based active obstacle avoidance learning framework.

The rest of the paper is organized as follows: In Section, we formulate our research question. In Sect. 2, we explain the details of the proposed robot motion planning algorithm. In Sect. 3, we conduct a series of experimental studies, discuss the results, and finally draw conclusions in Sect. 4.

2   Algorithms

This paper proposes an active obstacle avoidance method based on GAN framework learning, which takes pedestrian pose around the robot, the position of the temp goal, and the position of manually-labeled active obstacle avoidance points as input in a human-robot integration environment in the learning process. In the testing phase, the temp goal and the pedestrian pose in the rectangular area centered on the robot in the human-robot integration environment are taken as input, and the model can then output an active obstacle avoidance point. Since the positions of the active obstacle avoidance points in the training set are in line with the human obstacle avoidance conventions, guiding the robot to perform path planning through the active obstacle avoidance points output by the model will conform to the human obstacle avoidance conventions through thorough learning.

2.1   GAN-Based Obstacle Avoidance Learning

In this part, we will introduce the learning model of GAN. The basic framework of GAN consists of a generator G and a discriminator D. The generator accepts external noise z and outputs an active obstacle avoidance point coordinate. The discriminator accepts the obstacle avoidance point y from the training set and $G(z)$ from the generator, respectively, and outputs the probability that the point is from the training set. The generator and the discriminator are in a confrontation game. The generator generates the coordinates of the obstacle avoidance point similar to the training data set, in an attempt to deceive the discriminator. The discriminator is constantly evolving, trying to accurately distinguish the source of the coordinates of the input obstacle avoidance point, and the objective function can be defined as

$$\mathcal{L}_{GAN}(G, D) = \mathbb{E}_y[logD(y)] + \mathbb{E}_z[log(1 - D(G(z)))]. \tag{1}$$

The symbol $\mathbb{E}$ represents a mathematical expectation. The generator is trained by minimizing the objective function, while the discriminator is trained by maximizing the objective function. Then the objective function of a GAN model is represented as

$$\theta^* = arg \min_G \max_D \mathcal{L}_{GAN}(G, D). \tag{2}$$

The symbol θ^* represents the network optimal parameters of the generator and discriminator satisfying the maximum minimum game. In order to control the generation process, the generator and discriminator can be given a condition. Let c be the given condition and let them perform generation and discrimination tasks according to c. In this way, the objective function can be expressed as

$$\mathcal{L}_{GAN}(G, D) = \mathbb{E}_{c,y}[logD(y|c)] + \mathbb{E}_c[log(1 - D(G(c)|c)]. \tag{3}$$

In order to make the generated obstacle avoidance points as close as possible to the obstacle avoidance points in the training set, we add $L1$ loss, so the final objective function is defined as:

$$\theta^* = arg \min_G \max_D [\mathcal{L}_{GAN}(G, D) + \lambda \mathcal{L}_{L1}(G)] \tag{4}$$

where λ is the weight coefficient, which is set to 1 empirically.

Before the training phase, we firstly construct the dataset. Taking the robot as the center, the pedestrian pose and temp goal position relative to the robot are randomly generated by the program in a square area with a side length of 6 m. It is assumed that there will be at most five pedestrians in this area, so the pedestrian pose and temp goal position relative to the robot are represented by 15-dimensional and 2-dimensional vectors, respectively. The size of dataset is 3000.

Figure 3 shows the structure of the generator and discriminators. The input to the generator is 4-dimensional noise z, 2-dimensional temp goal g_t, and 15-dimensional pedestrian pose p. The output is a 2-dimensional active obstacle avoidance point p_a. The number of all hidden layer neurons in the fully connected structure of the generator is 128, and a dropout layer with a dropout rate of 0.5 is added between the hidden layer neurons of each layer. The dropout layer can deactivate each hidden layer neurons with a probability of 50% in the training phase, so it can effectively alleviate the phenomenon of over-fitting and improve

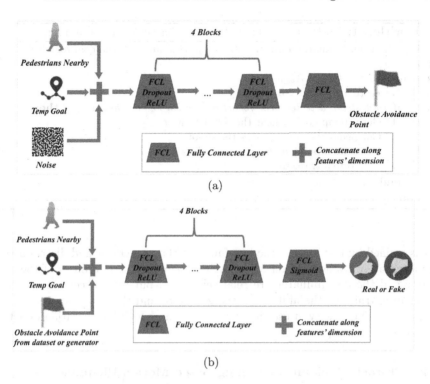

Fig. 3. Illustration of the proposed GAN model. (a) The architecture of the generator. (b) The architecture of the discriminator

the generalization ability of the generator [21]. A rectified linear unit (ReLU) activation layer is added after each hidden layer of neurons, which can also help avoid the over-fitting problem [22]. The mathematical expression of the ReLU activation function is $f(x) = max(0, x)$, where x is the input value.

The input to the discriminator is 2-dimensional temp goal g_t, 15-dimensional pedestrian pose p, and 2-dimensional active obstacle avoidance point p_a from training set or generator. The output is a 1-dimensional probability value representing the probability that the input active obstacle avoidance point a is from the training set. Similar to the network structure of the generator, the number of hidden layer neurons in all fully connected layers in the discriminator network structure is 128. A dropout layer with a dropout rate of 0.5 is added between neurons in each hidden layer. A ReLU activation function is added after each hidden layer of neurons. Different from the generator structure, because the output of the discriminator is the probability that the active obstacle avoidance point comes from the training set, it needs to be between 0 and 1, so a layer of sigmoid activation function is added after the output neuron of the discriminator. The mathematical expression of the sigmoid activation function is $f(x) = \frac{1}{1+e^{-x}}$, where x is the input value. The training process is as follows: According to the Eq. (4), the generator is trained by minimizing the loss function, and discrimina-

---

Algorithm 1: Obstacle Avoidance Learning based Motion Planning

---

Input: Scenario Information: the start x_{init}, the map M, the goal region $\mathcal{X}_{goal}$;

1 $p_a \leftarrow x_{init}$
2 **while** *robot not reach $\mathcal{X}_{goal}$* **do**
3   Generate a trajectory σ to $\mathcal{X}_{goal}$;
4   **if** *(pedestrian detected near robot) && (robot has reached the p_a)* **then**
5   Get a temp goal g_t near the robot from σ;
6   Get pedestrian pose p near the robot;
7   Generate a point p_a from G according M, g_t and p;
8   Generate a trajectory σ_{active} to p_a;
9   **end**
10 **end**

---

tor is trained by maximizing the loss function. The generator and discriminator are alternately trained an iter ation. At the beginning, the abilities of the generator and the discriminator are relatively weak, but after a certain epoch of adversarial training, the abilities of the generator and the discriminator will be enhanced. Finally, we will use the trained generator for the generation of active obstacle avoidance points.

2.2 Obstacle Avoidance Learning Based Motion Planning

After the learning process, we incorporate the learned policy into the motion planning of the mobile robot, as shown in the Algorithm 1. First, the traditional path planning method is used to plan the path σ from the start x_{init} to the goal region $\mathcal{X}_{goal}$. If a pedestrian is detected around the robot during navigation, the pedestrian pose p around the robot, the position of the temp goal g_t and the randomly sampled noise distribution z are input into the trained generator G to generate an active obstacle avoidance point p_a, and then the traditional path planning method is adopted to plan a path σ_{active} from the current position of the robot to the active obstacle avoidance point p_a. After the robot reaches the active obstacle avoidance point p_a, the above operations are repeated until the robot reaches the goal region $\mathcal{X}_{goal}$. This method can successfully plan a feasible and smooth path in the human-robot integration environment, and meet the comfort requirements of pedestrians for mobile robots.

3 Experimental Studies and Results

To verify the effectiveness of our proposed GAN-based active obstacle avoidance learning method for path planning in a human-robot integration environment, we conducted the experimental studies on a laptop equipped with an Intel Pentium G4600 CPU and adopted the 8 G RAM. We evaluate the adaptive performance of the method under different scene conditions, and then conduct motion planning

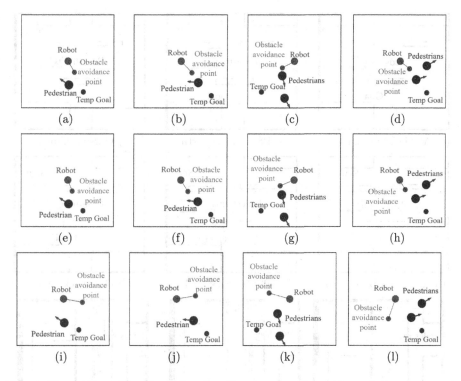

Fig. 4. The GAN model trained the effect of active obstacle avoidance points generated by different epochs. (a) (b) (c) and (d) show the effect of training for 10 epochs, (e) (f) (g) and (h) show the effect of training for 50 epochs, and (h) (i) (j) and (k) show the effect of training for 200 epochs.

experiments using the proposed obstacle avoidance strategy and compare it with some other state-of-the-art navigation methods.

3.1 GAN-Based Obstacle Avoidance Learning in Different Situation

In this part, we evaluate the generated active obstacle avoidance points. As shown in Fig. 4, the red circle represents the location of the robot, which is always in the center of the rectangular box, the blue circle represents the temp goal, the purple circle represents pedestrians, and the arrows represent the direction of pedestrian movement, and the green circle represents the generated active obstacle avoidance point. The direct connection between the active obstacle avoidance point and the position of the robot can approximately represent the trajectory of the robot planning to the active obstacle avoidance point. Usually, the robot should not collide with pedestrians, and the distance between the robot and pedestrians should not be too small during the movement process, so as to protect the pedestrian person space and guarantee the psychological comfort of pedestrians. With the above conditions met, the robot should move roughly

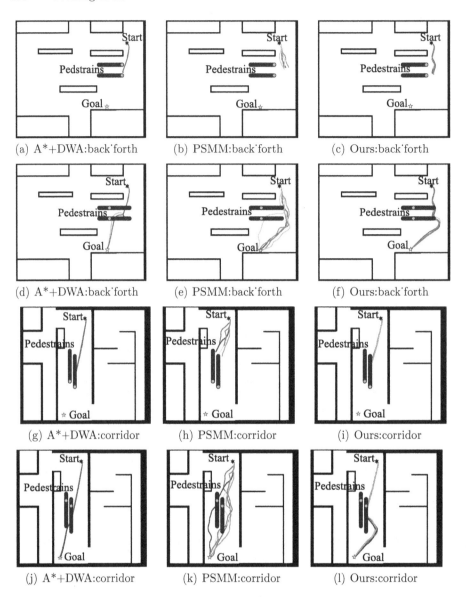

Fig. 5. Comparison of trajectories generated by the A*+DWA, PSMM, and Ours method in two scenarios. (a) (b) (c) (g) (h) and (i) show the intermediate state while (d) (e) (f) (j) (k) and (l) demonstrate the final trajectories.

towards the temp goal. It can be seen from Fig. 4 that as the training epoch of the GAN model increases, the generated active obstacle avoidance point positions are more conform to the human conventions. When the model is trained to 200 epoch, it can well complete the task of dynamic environment obstacle avoidance.

Table 1. Statistics of navigation experiment results.

Methods	back_forth			room		
	Offenses	Time(s)	Length(m)	Offenses	Time(s)	Length(m)
A*+DWA	5/5	42.80 ± 3.40	14.00 ± 0.50	5/5	43.30 ± 0.10	18.55 ± 0.05
PSMM	3/5	45.60 ± 3.10	15.04 ± 0.56	1/5	59.76 ± 5.64	19.76 ± 0.36
Ours	1/5	34.62 ± 1.82	15.44 ± 0.36	0/5	40.38 ± 1.78	20.42 ± 0.22

3.2 Obstacle Avoidance Learning Based Motion Planning in Different Scenario

In this part, we combine the proposed dynamic obstacle avoidance strategy with the A* algorithm and the DWA algorithm, and use the A* algorithm as the global path planner and the DWA algorithm as the local path planner to conduct simulation experiments. With the original A*+DWA algorithm and PSMM algorithm as a reference, repeated experiments are carried out in two different scenarios, and the comparison results are shown in the Fig. 5. The red pentagram represents the starting point of the robot, the yellow pentagram represents the goal, the dark blue circle represents the trajectory of the pedestrian, and the light blue circle represents the current position of the pedestrian. Because the DWA algorithm only treats the pedestrian as a dynamic obstacle, the distance between the robot and the pedestrian will be relatively close during the navigation process, which will lead to navigation failure. The PSMM algorithm is based on the social force model, it calculates the social force of each pedestrian and obstacle on the robot at every moment, which will make the trajectory of the robot unnatural. The algorithm proposed by us will comprehensively consider the density and moving direction of pedestrians, and generate an active obstacle avoidance point that conform to the human conventions to guide the robot to generate a anthropomorphic trajectory. We can find that the dynamic obstacle avoidance strategy proposed in this paper is more effective in avoiding pedestrians in advance than the other two methods, and the generated paths look more natural and smooth.

In order to intuitively compare the performance of different algorithms, we set three experimental indicators as shown in Table 1. "**Offenses**" refers to the number of times that the robot enters the pedestrian person space or hits an pedestrian during the navigation process, i.e., the distance between the robot and the pedestrian is less than 1.2 m. "**Time**" refers to the running time of the robot to complete the navigation task, and "**Length**" refers to the length of the robot trajectory. Three methods are carried out for the navigation task in the above two scenarios, and we record the above three metrics in Table 1. We can see that, compared with the other two navigation methods, the method proposed in this paper has less interference to pedestrians. Furthermore, the average navigation time of this method is also smaller than the other two methods. In addition, we also recorded the time spent on each generation of active obstacle avoidance points in the simulation environment. We found that in the above two scenarios, the average time spent on generating active obstacle avoidance points is 9.48 ms, which can fully meet the real-time requirements. In summary, this method can not only ensure the comfort of pedestrians, but also improve the navigation efficiency.

4 Conclusions

In this paper, a novel dynamic obstacle avoidance strategy is proposed to improve the navigation ability of robots in a human-robot integration environment. A GAN-based active obstacle avoidance learning framework is proposed. According to the information around the robot, the framework can effectively generate an active obstacle avoidance point to guide the robot to effectively avoid pedestrians in a human-robot integration environment, thereby improving the navigation efficiency. The experimental results show that this method can effectively avoid pedestrians in advance and has good navigation efficiency in a human-robot integration environment.

Acknowledgements. This work was made possible through funding from the National Key R&D Program of China grant #2020YFB1313601, National Science Foundation of China grant #61903267 and China Postdoctoral Science Foundation grant #2020M681691 awarded to Wenzheng Chi.

References

1. Khatib, O.: Real-time obstacle avoidance for manipulators and mobile robots. In: 1985 IEEE International Conference on Robotics and Automation, pp. 500–505 (1985)
2. Hart, P.E., Nilsson, N.J., Raphael, B.: A formal basis for the heuristic determination of minimum cost paths. IEEE Trans. Syst. Sci. Cybern. **4**(2), 100–107 (1968)
3. LaValle, S.M.: Rapidly-exploring random trees: a new tool for path planning. Tech. Rep (TR98-11), Computer Science Dept, Iowa State University (1998)
4. Liu, X., Li, X., Su, H., Zhao, Y., Ge, S.S.: The opening workspace control strategy of a novel manipulator-driven emission source microscopy system. ISA Transactions (2022)
5. Fox, D., Burgard, W., Thrun, S.: The dynamic window approach to collision avoidance. IEEE Robot. Autom. **4**(1), 23–33 (1997)
6. Van den Berg, J., Lin, M., Manocha, D.: Reciprocal velocity obstacles for real-time multi-agent navigation. In: 2008 IEEE International Conference on Robotics and Automation, pp. 1928–1935 (2008)
7. Cheng, H., Zhu, Q., Liu, Z., Xu, T., Lin, L.: Decentralized navigation of multiple agents based on ORCA and model predictive control. In: 2017 IEEE/RSJ International Conference on Intelligent Robots and Systems (IROS), pp. 3446–3451 (2017)
8. Hall, E.T.: Proxemics. Curr. Anthropol. **9**(2–3), 83–108 (1968)
9. Pacchierotti, E., Christensen, H.I., Jensfelt, P.: Human-robot embodied interaction in hallway settings: a pilot user study. In: 2005 IEEE International Workshop on Robot and Human Interactive Communication, pp. 164–171 (2005)

10. Pacchierotti, E., Christensen, H.I., Jensfelt, P.: Evaluation of passing distance for social robots. In: 2006 IEEE International Symposium on Robot and Human Interactive Communication, pp. 315–320 (2006)
11. Dragan, A.D., Bauman, S., Forlizzi, J., Srinivasa, S.S.: Effects of robot motion on human-robot collaboration. In: 2015 10th ACM/IEEE International Conference on Human-Robot Interaction (HRI), pp. 51–58 (2015)
12. Pellegrini, S., Ess, A., Schindler, K., Van Gool, L.: You'll never walk alone: Modeling social behavior for multi-target tracking. In: 2009 IEEE 12th International Conference on Computer Vision, pp. 261–2680 (2009)
13. Antonini, G., Bierlaire, M., Weber, M.: Discrete choice models of pedestrian walking behavior. Transport. Res. Part B: Methodol. **40**(8), 667–687 (2006)
14. Helbing, D., Molnar, P.: Social force model for pedestrian dynamics. Phys. Rev. E **51**(5), 4282–4286 (1995)
15. Ellis, D., Sommerlade, E., Reid, I.: Modelling pedestrian trajectory patterns with gaussian processes. In: 2009 IEEE 12th International Conference on Computer Vision Workshops, ICCV Workshops, pp. 1229–1234 (2009)
16. Truong, X.-T., Ngo, T.D.: Toward socially aware robot navigation in dynamic and crowded environments: a proactive social motion model. IEEE Trans. Autom. Sci. Eng. **14**(4), 1743–1760 (2017)
17. Alahi, A., Goel, K., Ramanathan, V., Robicquet, A., Fei-Fei, L., Savarese, S.: Social lstm: Human trajectory prediction in crowded spaces. In: 2016 IEEE Conference on Computer Vision and Pattern Recognition (CVPR), pp. 961–971 (2016)
18. Nishimura, M., Yonetani, R.: L2B: Learning to balance the safety-efficiency trade-off in interactive crowd-aware robot navigation. In: 2020 IEEE/RSJ International Conference on Intelligent Robots and Systems (IROS), pp. 11004–11010 (2020)
19. Gupta, A., Johnson, J., Fei-Fei, L., Savarese, S., Alahi, A.: Social gan: Socially acceptable trajectories with generative adversarial networks. In: 2018 IEEE/CVF Conference on Computer Vision and Pattern Recognition, pp. 2255–2264 (2018)
20. Zhang, T., Wang, J., Meng, M.Q.-H.: Generative adversarial network based heuristics for sampling-based path planning. IEEE/CAA J. Automatica Sinica. **9**(1), 64–74 (2021)
21. Srivastava, N., Hinton, G., Krizhevsky, A., Sutskever, I., Salakhutdinov, R.: Dropout: a simple way to prevent neural networks from overfitting. J. Mach. Learn. Res. **15**(1), 1929–1958 (2014)
22. Nair, V., Hinton, G.E.: Rectified linear units improve restricted boltzmann machines. In: Proceedings of the 27th International Conference on Machine Learning (ICML-10), pp. 807–814 (2010)

Research on 3D Face Reconstruction Based on Weakly Supervised Learning

Zewei Su[1](✉), Lanfang Dong[1], Xuejie Ji[1], Guoming Li[2], and Xierong Zhu[2]

[1] University of Science and Technology of China, Hefei 230026, China
{zwsu,jijay2020}@mail.ustc.edu.cn, lfdong@ustc.edu.cn
[2] AI Lab, China Merchants Bank, Shenzhen 518040, China
{lkm,zxr8192}@cmbchina.com

Abstract. Social robots may reshape the entire society in the future, and human-computer interaction is its key technology. The advent of virtual human enables the robot to show the realistic appearance of human face. A high-precision face model helps the robot to obtain a favorable impression of the interacting object and better realize the human-computer interaction. Because 3D face data is not enough, many existing face reconstruction algorithms first use traditional methods to construct 3D labels for 2D images as training data, but these synthetic data generally lack real facial features, which affects the reconstruction quality of the algorithm. Based on these questions, we first propose a weakly supervised model based on the multi-level loss to directly learn 3D features from a large number of images without 3D labels. In addition, to avoid the influence of wearing and face pose on the reconstruction, this paper uses the most advanced face segmentation network to preprocess the images and remove the invisible areas generated by face occlusion or rotation. The experimental results show that our model has achieved a certain improvement in reconstruction quality and reconstruction accuracy.

Keywords: 3D face reconstruction · Weakly supervised learning · 3D morphable model · Face segmentation · Multi-level loss

1 Introduction

The virtual human is a key medium for human-computer interaction, and a highly accurate face model can effectively improve the favorability of the interaction object. Early 3D face reconstruction used scanning methods to reproduce the 3D structure of the face [11,20]. Although a high-precision face can be reconstructed, the expensive equipment and complex operation make it impossible to widely use. In 1972, Parke et al. first proposed a method of parametric modeling [12]. This method could generate various face with some control parameters,

Supported by the National Key Research and Development Program of China under Grant No.2020YFB1313602.

which greatly simplifies the face reconstruction. Since then, various automatic face modeling techniques have emerged [22]. We classify these works into two categories: traditional methods and deep learning methods.

Traditional face reconstruction mainly uses 3D Morphable Mode(hereinafter referred to as 3DMM) [1]. 3DMM is a face model based on statistics, and its main idea is to regard the face space as a linear space and any face can be linearly synthesized by different faces in the database. 3DMM implements parametric modeling of the face, but its main problem is that the computational price is too big and the reconstruction efficiency is low.

Recently, with the great achievements of deep learning in CV, people have started to apply deep learning to the face reconstruction [4,18]. They used neural network to calculate 3DMM parameters, and then decoded the parameters to reconstruct a 3D face. The reconstruction quality and speed have been greatly improved compared with the traditional methods. But because 3D face data is hard to obtain, deep learning methods for face reconstruction have been facing bottlenecks.

There are two common ways to solve the shortage of training data, one is to use synthetic data. Richardson et al. [14] randomly sampled the 3DMM face model, modified the model parameters to generate a new 3D model and then rendered it to a 2D image. By this method, they generated sufficient 3D faces and 2D images as training pairs for training. But the synthetic images generally lack real facial features, which affects the reconstruction quality of the algorithm. Another method is to use weakly supervised learning. Tewari et al. [17] used differentiable rendering to render the reconstructed model into 2D space, and only establish model loss between the rendered image and the input, thereby getting rid of the dependence on the 3D label. Based on this, Genova et al. [5] added high-level face feature constraints to the model loss through a pre-trained recognition network. However, these weakly supervised learning methods also have disadvantages. Since the model is directly trained on unconstrained wild images, there may be problems such as face occlusion and large pose faces in these images, which will affect the effect of face reconstruction.

Based on above problems, we first proposes a weakly supervised learning model based on multi-level loss, which would learn multiple weakly supervised information from 2D face images to supervise the network. In order to measure the loss of the network in 2D space, we render the reconstructed 3D model into 2D space by the differentiable renderer SoftRas [9], and establish the loss between the rendered image and the input. In this way, our approach does not need any 3D labels. In addition, to avoid the effects of occlusion and large pose faces on the face reconstruction, we use the latest face segmentation model [7] to remove occlusions. The results indicate that our approach achieves a certain improvement in reconstruction quality and reconstruction accuracy.

2   Models and Related Technology

Figure 1 shows the overall framework of our face reconstruction algorithm. Given a 2D face I as input, we first use FAN [2] to label 68 landmarks as one of the weakly supervised signals for computing the model loss. At the same time, we use the segmentation model to calculate the mask of face, so that the network is trained to focus only on the real face region. After that, the input is fed into the encoder to regress the feature vectors of each key coefficient, including 3DMM and rendering parameters. Then two decoders decode the 3DMM parameters to reconstruct the shape and albedo of the 3D face. Due to the lack of 3D labels, we adopt the differentiable renderer to render the 3D model into 2D space to get a rendered image I_r. At last, We would set a multi-level loss between I and I_r to constrain the network parameters to converge as shown in Fig. 1.

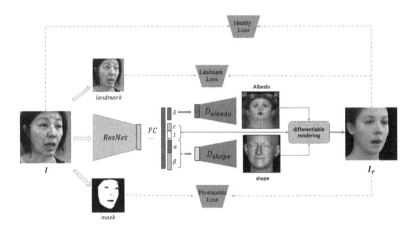

Fig. 1. Network architecture

2.1   Model Parameters

In order to achieve weakly supervised face reconstruction, the Encoder needs to calculate the corresponding 3DMM parameters and rendering parameters. The 3DMM parameters are used to reconstruct the 3D face, which includes shape and albedo. The rendering parameters include camera parameters and lighting parameters, which are used to adjust the 3D face position, size and light during rendering to generate realistic rendered images.

3DMM Face Model. Traditional 3DMM unifies the 3D face represented by two vectors:

$$S = (x_1, y_1, z_1, x_2, y_2, z_2, \cdots, x_n, y_n, z_n)^T \in R^{3n} \tag{1}$$

$$T = (r_1, g_1, b_1, r_2, g_2, b_2, \cdots, r_n, g_n, b_n)^T \in R^{3n} \tag{2}$$

where S represents 3D face shape vector, and T represents 3D face texture vector. 3DMM treats the face space as a linear space, any 3D face can be represented by a linear combination of other faces model. After dimensionality reduction and decorrelation by PCA, any new faces can be represented as:

$$S_{new} = \bar{S} + A_{id}\alpha + A_{exp}\beta \tag{3}$$

$$T_{new} = \bar{T} + A_{tex}\delta \tag{4}$$

where $\bar{S}$ and $\bar{T}$ represent the average shape and texture vectors of face. And A_{id}, A_{exp}, and A_{tex} represent the face shape, expression, and texture PCA principal components.

In our method, the 3D face shape and expression data is sourced from the FLAME [8], and the texture data is sourced from the BFM [13]. In order to reduce the model computation and speed up the model training, we select the first 100, 50, and 50 principal components in face shape, expression, and texture space. Adding face pose parameters which control of neck, chin and eye rotation, the encoder needs to calculate a total of 215 dimensions of face parameters.

Camera Model. It should be noted that our method cannot reconstruct a 3D model that is consistent with the real face size, it usually requires some additional information (such as the true distance between some landmarks). The existing face reconstruction methods are generally only used to reconstruct the basic shapes similar to the face in the image while ignoring the face size, then they use the camera model to control the rotation, translation and scaling of the 3D face so that the reconstructed face is strictly aligned with the input image in terms of face pose and size. However, this also does not represent the true size of the face, but only corresponds to the picture size in rendering. For the camera model, assuming that V_{3d} is a vertex in base 3D Model, the process of projecting it to a 2D plane vertex v can be calculated as:

$$v = f * P * R * V_{3d} + t \tag{5}$$

where f is the scaling factor. R is the rotation matrix, and t is the translation vector. P is the camera matrix, and since we use the weak perspective projection model, P is the matrix $[[1, 0, 0], [0, 1, 0]]$. Therefore, the camera parameters of our model are composed of $[f, R, t]$.

Illumination Model. The illumination model is used to calculate the real light intensity of face. Since the model is trained on unconstrained field images, there are complex shadows and lighting variations among them. Therefore, we will use spherical harmonic function [16] to estimate the lighting information of the image and reduce the effect of lighting on the face texture. For a point p in 3D face, the true texture is the albedo (skin texture after removing light and shadows) at p multiplied by a linear combination of spherical harmonic basis functions:

$$I(p) = t \cdot \sum_{j=1}^{9} \gamma_j h_j(n) \tag{6}$$

where t represents the albedo at vertex p, $\mathrm{n} = (n_x, n_y, n_z)$ represents the normal direction, and h_j represents the nine spherical harmonic basis functions. And γ_j represents the coefficients of the spherical harmonic basis functions.

In summary, in order to achieve the 3D face reconstruction from a single image, the encoder needs to accurately predict each key parameter of the face. These parameter include the 3DMM shape parameter $\alpha \in R^{100}$, expression parameter $\beta \in R^{50}$, texture parameter $\delta \in R^{50}$, pose parameter $\theta \in R^{15}$ and the camera parameter $\mathrm{c} = [f, R, t] \in R^7$, and lighting parameter $\gamma \in R^{27}$.

2.2   Face Segmentation Model

Semantic segmentation of faces is one of the important data pre-processing processes. In our method, a weakly supervised face reconstruction model is proposed by training from a large number of unlabeled field images. These images often have complex backgrounds and face occlusions(e.g., glasses, hat, etc.). These regions should obviously not be involved in the computation of losses in the network. So we will use the latest face segmentation model Focus [7] to calculate the face mask for each image so that the network focuses only on the real face region. Its face segmentation effect is shown in Fig. 2.

Fig. 2. Face segmentation in focus [7]

The Focus model contains of two parts: reconstruction network as N_{rec} and segmentation network as N_{seg}. To use the segmentation model, we reproduced the main work of Focus using the VGGFace2 dataset. More specifically, we adopted an EM-type training strategy in two networks to create a synergistic effect, which the N_{seg} prevents the reconstruction network from fitting to the occlusion, enhancing the N_{rec}. Then the improved reconstruction network, in turn, enables the N_{seg} to better predict the occlusion. In this way, we could continuously improve the accuracy of the semantic segmentation model. Finally, we saved the best model from the training process for calculating face masks for our data.

2.3   Differentiable Renderer - SoftRas

In order to establish the model loss between the 3D model and the 2D image, it is necessary to project the reconstructed 3D face into 2D space. In this paper, We use a differentiable renderer called SoftRas [9] to achieve projection process.

The SoftRas treats the rendering process as an aggregation function. Unlike traditional renderers that only select the color of the nearest triangle in a discrete sampling operation, SoftRas assumes that all mesh triangles contribute probabilistically to each rendered pixel, and it fuses all probabilistic contributions of each triangle to the pixel to get the final result. As a truly differentiable rendering framework, SoftRas is capable of generating effective gradients from pixels to 3D model vertices, textures, normal vectors, and other attributes. Therefore, SoftRas can be applied as a general framework in a deep neural network model to provide a pixel-level supervised signal for 3D reconstruction tasks based on a single unlabeled 3D image.

2.4   Model Loss

Due to the lack of 3D labels, we could only calculate model losses in the 2D space. But thanks to the excellent work of SoftRas, we succeeded in projecting the reconstructed model onto the 2D plane to obtain a 2D rendered image and it could obtain effective gradients from 2D to 3D. In this way, we could construct the model loss between the input and the rendered image in 2D, and pass the loss penalty to the 3D model via the gradient saved by SoftRas.

For 2D model loss, some networks [17] focus only on the low-dimensional pixel differences between images, leading to models that tend to fall into a local optimum. To avoid this problem, we considered different-level features of the 2D image as supervised signals to guide the training of the model. More specifically, the multi-level loss includes pixel-level photometric loss, landmarks loss and face identity loss. The entire network aims to minimize the following loss functions.

$$L = \lambda_{\text{pho}} \, L_{\text{pho}} + \lambda_{lmk} L_{lmk} + \lambda_{id} L_{id} + \lambda_{\text{reg}} \, L_{reg} \tag{7}$$

For the photometric loss, we will calculate the difference between the rendered image and the input in pixels, which is used to constrain the rendered image to be as similar as possible to the input in terms of color. Considering the background and face occlusion, we use face mask to focus only the pixel in the non-occluded facial region.

$$L_{\text{pho}} = \|Mask_I \odot (I - I_r)\|_2 \tag{8}$$

In addition, we will calculate the difference between two images in terms of landmark positions. By constraining the landmark locations, we can effectively guide the network to reconstruct real facial shape, expression and pose. The loss is calculated as:

$$L_{lmk} = \sum_{i=1}^{68} \|v_i - \widehat{v_l}\|_2 \tag{9}$$

In this paper, we use the face recognition network [3] trained in VGGFace2 to calculate the high level feature loss of faces. We feed the input and rendered image into the recognition network to extract their identity vectors. Then we calculate the cosine distance between two vectors as the identity loss of the model. By constraining the identity similarity between images, we can ensure that I and I_r are from the same face. The identity loss is calculated as follows.

$$L_{id} = 1 - \frac{f(I)f(I_r)}{\|f(I)\|_2 \cdot \|f(I_r)\|_2} \tag{10}$$

Finally, this is the regularization loss of the model, which is used to constrain the 3DMM face parameters to obey a normal distribution. We use this loss to prevent extreme cases such as reconstructing a non-human face.

$$L_{re.g.} = w_{id}\|\alpha\|^2 + w_{exp}\|\beta\|^2 + w_{tex}\|\delta\|^2 \tag{11}$$

3   Experiments and Results

3.1   Dataset

In this paper, we train our model on two publicly available datasets: VGGFace2 [3] and CelebA [10]. The VGGface2 contains pictures of move than $8k$ identities, with an average of over 300 pictures per people, and the CelebA offers over $200k$ pictures of $10k$ identities. After excluding some extreme data, we selected 20 to 50 images for each identity. In total, our model is trained on over $500k$ face images. We divided these data into training sets and test sets in the ratio of $8 : 2$.

During the pre-processing of the dataset, we first done data enhancement, including random image flipping, rotation, and changing illumination. When changing the illumination, we randomly multiply the RGB channels of the image by $0.7 \sim 1.3$ and operate independently between channels. With light enhancement, we can effectively improve the robustness of the algorithm to illumination. After this, we used the pre-trained FAN and Focus models to calculate the landmarks positions and masks of the faces, and save them for calculating the loss of the models when training.

3.2   Implementation Details

Our algorithm is implemented in PyTorch. The encoder uses the Resent-50 network model, and the last fully connected layer is modified to 249 dimensions to fit the output of the model. The decoders are from the FLAME [8]. We use Adam as optimizer. The learning rate is set to $1e-4$ and the input images are scaled to 224^2. The weights of each loss function (λ_{pho}, λ_{lmk}, λ_{id}, and λ_{reg} are set to 2.0, 1.0, 0.2, and $1e-4$.

3.3   Results

Qualitative Evaluation. In the qualitative evaluation of the model, we use some face images from real scenes to verify the effect of 3D face reconstruction. To enhance the robustness of the model, we add a face detection function, so that if no face is detected in the input image, the result will not be displayed. In the inference of the model, given a single face image, our model would reconstructs a 3D face, which includes shape and albedo. Some reconstruction results are shown in Fig. 3.

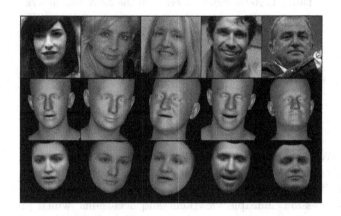

Fig. 3. 3D face shape and texture reconstruction

The first row of Fig. 3 is the input image, and the second and third rows correspond to the shape and albedo of the reconstructed face. The results show that the 3D model reconstructed by our method can fit the facial contour and expression of face in images well. And the model can also truly reflect the texture information of the face for images with different skin tones and different lighting. In addition, to avoid occlusion and large pose face problems, we use a segmentation model to calculate the visible area of the face. Therefore, even if the face is obscured or there is a large pose of the face (for example, only half of the face is exposed), our model can still reconstruct the basic shape of human face very well, just as shown in Fig. 4.

Fig. 4. Reconstruction effect with occlusion and different pose

Quantitative Evaluation. We compare our model with publicly available methods, which include 3DMM-CNN [18], RingNet [15] and 3DDFA-V2 [6]. In order to quantitatively compare the differences between ours and these models, we use the NoW [15] benchmark to evaluate the reconstruction error of ours and follow the same procedure to calculate the error of other models. The result is shown in Table 1. Note that our model achieves better performance on 3D reconstruction without any 3D labels in training.

Table 1. Reconstruction error on the NoW benchmark

Method	Median(mm)	Mean(mm)	Std(mm)
3DMM-CNN [18]	1.84	2.33	2.05
RingNet [15]	1.21	1.54	1.31
3DDFA-V2 [6]	1.23	1.57	1.39
ours	**1.18**	**1.46**	**1.25**

The NoW benchmark consists of 2054 pictures from 100 people, divided into a validation set (20 people) and a test set (80 people), each with a reference 3D facial scan. These face images cover different indoor and outdoor environments, multiple expression, multiple viewpoint and occlusions, which provide a good measure of the robustness of the algorithm. Considering that our model is in different local coordinate system from the ground truth, we first need to rigidly align the reconstructed model with the scan data. In this paper, we select a set of corresponding landmarks between the prediction and the scan to achieve the alignment process, and make the predicted and scanned meshes strictly aligned by translating, rotating and scaling the predicted meshes. After alignment, we count the Euclidean distance of the corresponding 3D vertices as the reconstruction error of the model as shown in Table 1. The results show that our method shows superiority over other face reconstruction algorithms on the NoW benchmark.

4   Conclusion

Although a lot of research has been done on 2D faces [19, 21], 3D faces contain more deep features than 2D faces and can be widely used in many fields such as face recognition and expression recognition. In this paper, we propose a weakly supervised 3D face reconstruction model based on multi-level loss, which could directly learn 3D features from field images without 3D labels. By designing a multi-level loss function, the rendered image is constrained from different dimensions to prevent the model from falling into a local optimum. Meanwhile, to avoid the effect of occlusion and large pose faces, we use the latest segmentation network to calculate the real face region. The experimental results show that the reconstruction quality and reconstruction accuracy of this algorithm are significantly improved compared with other algorithms, and our method is more robust to the presence of occlusion and large pose faces in 2D images.

References

1. Blanz, V., Vetter, T.: A morphable model for the synthesis of 3d faces. In: Proceedings of the 26th Annual Conference on Computer Graphics and Interactive Techniques, pp. 187–194 (1999)
2. Bulat, A., Tzimiropoulos, G.: How far are we from solving the 2d & 3d face alignment problem?(and a dataset of 230,000 3d facial landmarks). In: Proceedings of the IEEE International Conference on Computer Vision, pp. 1021–1030 (2017)
3. Cao, Q., Shen, L., Xie, W., Parkhi, O.M., Zisserman, A.: Vggface2: A dataset for recognising faces across pose and age. In: 2018 13th IEEE International Conference on Automatic Face & Gesture Recognition (FG 2018), pp. 67–74. IEEE (2018)
4. Chang, F.J., Tran, A.T., Hassner, T., Masi, I., Nevatia, R., Medioni, G.: Expnet: Landmark-free, deep, 3d facial expressions. In: 2018 13th IEEE International Conference on Automatic Face & Gesture Recognition (FG 2018), pp. 122–129. IEEE (2018)
5. Genova, K., Cole, F., Maschinot, A., Sarna, A., Vlasic, D., Freeman, W.T.: Unsupervised training for 3d morphable model regression. In: Proceedings of the IEEE Conference on Computer Vision and Pattern Recognition, pp. 8377–8386 (2018)
6. Guo, J., Zhu, X., Yang, Y., Yang, F., Lei, Z., Li, S.Z.: Towards fast, accurate and stable 3D dense face alignment. In: Vedaldi, A., Bischof, H., Brox, T., Frahm, J.-M. (eds.) ECCV 2020. LNCS, vol. 12364, pp. 152–168. Springer, Cham (2020). https://doi.org/10.1007/978-3-030-58529-7_10
7. Li, C., Morel-Forster, A., Vetter, T., Egger, B., Kortylewski, A.: To fit or not to fit: Model-based face reconstruction and occlusion segmentation from weak supervision. arXiv preprint arXiv:2106.09614 (2021)
8. Li, T., Bolkart, T., Black, M.J., Li, H., Romero, J.: Learning a model of facial shape and expression from 4d scans. ACM Trans. Graph. 36(6), 194–1 (2017)
9. Liu, S., Li, T., Chen, W., Li, H.: Soft rasterizer: A differentiable renderer for image-based 3d reasoning. In: Proceedings of the IEEE/CVF International Conference on Computer Vision, pp. 7708–7717 (2019)
10. Liu, Z., Luo, P., Wang, X., Tang, X.: Deep learning face attributes in the wild. In: Proceedings of the IEEE International Conference on Computer Vision, pp. 3730–3738 (2015)
11. Moss, J., Linney, A., Grindrod, S., Mosse, C.: A laser scanning system for the measurement of facial surface morphology. Opt. Lasers Eng. 10(3–4), 179–190 (1989)
12. Parke, F.I.: Computer generated animation of faces. In: Proceedings of the ACM Annual Conference-Vol. 1, pp. 451–457 (1972)
13. Paysan, P., Knothe, R., Amberg, B., Romdhani, S., Vetter, T.: A 3d face model for pose and illumination invariant face recognition. In: 2009 sixth IEEE International Conference on Advanced Video and Signal Based Surveillance, pp. 296–301. Ieee (2009)
14. Richardson, E., Sela, M., Kimmel, R.: 3d face reconstruction by learning from synthetic data. In: 2016 Fourth International Conference on 3D Vision (3DV), pp. 460–469. IEEE (2016)

15. Sanyal, S., Bolkart, T., Feng, H., Black, M.J.: Learning to regress 3d face shape and expression from an image without 3d supervision. In: Proceedings of the IEEE/CVF Conference on Computer Vision and Pattern Recognition, pp. 7763–7772 (2019)
16. Seeley, R.T.: Spherical harmonics. The American Mathematical Monthly 73(4P2), pp. 115–121 (1966)
17. Tewari, A., Zollhofer, M., Kim, H., Garrido, P., Bernard, F., Perez, P., Theobalt, C.: Mofa: Model-based deep convolutional face autoencoder for unsupervised monocular reconstruction. In: Proceedings of the IEEE International Conference on Computer Vision Workshops, pp. 1274–1283 (2017)
18. Tuan Tran, A., Hassner, T., Masi, I., Medioni, G.: Regressing robust and discriminative 3d morphable models with a very deep neural network. In: Proceedings of the IEEE Conference on Computer Vision and Pattern Recognition, pp. 5163–5172 (2017)
19. Wang, D., Ma, G., Liu, X.: An intelligent recognition framework of access control system with anti-spoofing function. AIMS Math. 7(6), 10495–10512 (2022)
20. Woodham, R.J.: Photometric method for determining surface orientation from multiple images. Opt. Eng. 19(1), 139–144 (1980)
21. Xu, Y., Su, H., Ma, G., Liu, X.: A novel dual-modal emotion recognition algorithm with fusing hybrid features of audio signal and speech context. Complex Int. Syst. 1–13 (2022). https://doi.org/10.1007/s40747-022-00841-3
22. Zollhöfer, M., et al: State of the art on monocular 3d face reconstruction, tracking, and applications. In: Computer Graphics Forum. vol. 37, pp. 523–550. Wiley Online Library (2018)

Robot Differential Behavioral Expression in Different Scenarios

Zhonghao Zhang[1], Wanyue Jiang[1(✉)], Rui Zhang[1], Yuhan Zheng[1], and Shuzhi Sam Ge[1,2]

[1] Institute for Future, School of Automation, Qingdao University, Qingdao, China
jwy@qdu.edu.cn
[2] Department of Electrical and Computer Engineering, National University of Singapore, Singapore, Singapore

Abstract. During human-robot interaction, a robot is commonly considered dull since it follows very limited programmed orders repeatedly. Although faced with different people in different scenarios, a robot behaves the same. In this paper, we aim to construct a robot emotion system with respect to the personality of the robot and the reaction of the interactor. The robot's behaviors, including its facial expression, voice, and motion, are all parameterized and interrelated with the robot's emotions. In this way, the robot will perform much richer behavioral expressions in different situations. Two typical experiments are conducted, where the robot acts as a guard at a school gate and a study partner in a house, respectively. According to the questionnaire, most of the participants agree that the robot behaves differently in the two scenes.

Keywords: Social robot · Different scenarios · Emotion expression · Human-robot interaction

1 Introduction

Over the past few years, artificial intelligence [1] has been advancing by leaps and bounds. To address the lack of relevant skilled workers [2] caused by demographic changes, research of social robots [3–5] continue to emerge. One of the main capabilities of social robots is to establish natural interactions with humans. Considering the domain intersection of humans and robots, how to obtain and utilize the relationships between the two to make social robots successful in human-robot interaction (HRI) [6,7] is becoming more and more important. In recent years, based on a growing interest in HRI, robots are not only in industry but also in other fields such as schools [8,9] , homes[10] , hospitals [11] and rehabilitation centers [12]. However, these works have only taken into account a

---

This work was supported by the National Key Research and Development Project under Grant 2020YFB1313604.

F. Cavallo et al. (Eds.): ICSR 2022, LNAI 13817, pp. 451–462, 2022.
https://doi.org/10.1007/978-3-031-24667-8_40

single scenario so that the behavioral expression of robots in different scenarios appears repetitive and monotonous.

Emotional signals have been shown as important factors in human-robot relationships. With the improvement of robot imitation ability, their expression is increasingly favorable for HRI [13–15]. Whether and how expressive whole-body movements of real humanoid robots influence cooperative decision-making has been investigated in [16]. In [17], facial emotion expression during human-robot interaction has been discussed. It has been verified in [18] that humanoid robot head position has a certain influence on imitating human emotions. The paper [19] discussed emotional expression and its application in social robots. However, neither of them investigated the differences in robot behavioral expression in multiple aspects, including motion, voice, and facial expression.

The paper designs an emotion block diagram for robot emotion-based behavioral expression. In the diagram, based on social rules, we consider robot personality, internal impacts, and external impacts as the factors that affect robot emotions. Then according to the emotion value, the robot can choose the appropriate emotion quantization level and show the corresponding performance in movement, voice, and facial expression. The main contributions of the paper are proposed as follows.

1) Different robot characters in different scenarios are designed to achieve the robot's differential behavioral expression. In the family scene, the robot behaves as a lively partner. And the robot behaves like a serious guard in the school scene.
2) Three factors are presented to parameterize the robot's emotional value. Robot personality is determined by the pre-set according to the task. According to user needs, external impacts are brought up to change robot emotions. Internal impacts are proposed to make robot emotions stable in the corresponding character.
3) Emotion expression is manifested in three aspects: movement, voice, and facial expression. Robots can better display emotions and make themselves more anthropomorphic to interact with people by emotion quantization level.

2   Method

Figure 1 is the block diagram that is used to describe the process of emotion control and expression of the robot. We make the robot behave as a serious guard in school and a lively partner in the family to accord with the usual social norms. The robot's emotions can be more flexible by adapting self-feedback to regulate its emotion within a range. User evaluation and user behavior are used to appropriately change the robot's emotions to cater to people's needs.

The diagram contains seven modules of emotion model, personality related to environment scenes, body self-feedback, external impact, emotion level, processing unit, and execution unit. It can be seen that the value of robot personality p is firstly determined by the task environment. The robot's emotions are influenced by the internal parameter self-feedback which is used to regulate itself like

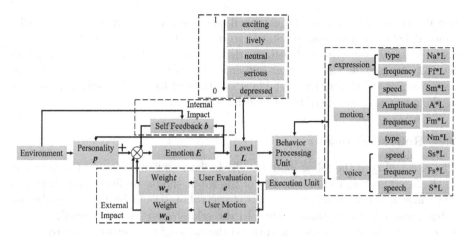

Fig. 1. Emotion block diagram

Table 1. Processing unit parameters

Parameter	Description	Parameter	Description
N_a	The number of expression types	F_f	Expression switching frequency
S_m	Movement speed	A	Action amplitude
F_m	Action switching frequency	N_m	The number of action types
S_s	Speaking speed	F_s	Speaking frequency
S	Language complexity		

the self consolation process, and the external parameter which is used to imitate some social behaviors such as user evaluation and user behavior. Then through the adder, we can obtain the value of the emotion model E. We divide emotions into exciting, lively, neural, serious, and depressed so that emotion level L can select one of five emotions according to E. The behavior processing unit utilizes the parameters saved in advance as depicted in Table 1 to compute and pass the quantized value to the execution unit. According to the current emotion, the execution unit receives and implements the corresponding orders.

2.1 Social Emotion Model

Based on the impacts of personality, user evaluation, user motion, and self-feedback, the social emotion model E of the robot is proposed as follows:

$$
E = \begin{cases} p + w_a a + w_e e + b, & 0 < E < 1 \\ 0, & E \leq 0 \\ 1, & E \geq 1 \end{cases} \tag{1}
$$

where $E \in [0, 1]$ denotes the emotional value and is positively correlated with the liveliness of the robot, p denotes the initial personality variable in the specific environment, a is the user behavior variable which is related to distance d between man and robot, w_a is the weight parameter of the behavior variable a, e is the user evaluation variable which is related to the satisfaction level of the user as the external influence of robot emotion, w_e is the weight parameter of the evaluation variable e, b is the self-feedback regulation variable as the internal influence of robot emotion.

2.2 Robot Personality

The personality of the robot should be dissimilar in different scenes. For instance, in the family scene, the personality of the robot should be lively and chatty, so the value of the personality variable of the robot should be high to make the robot have a high emotional value. In the school scene, the personality of the robot should be serious and taciturn, so the value of the personality variable of the robot should be low to make the robot have a low emotional value. As a consequence, p as the personality variable of the robot is proposed to make the robot play different roles and meet people's needs as follows:

$$p = \begin{cases} 0.7, & \text{family scene} \\ 0.3, & \text{school scene} \\ E_p \end{cases} \qquad (2)$$

where $p \in [0,1]$, $p = 0.7$ denotes a lively character in the family scene, and $p = 0.3$ denotes a serious character in the school scene. E_p is the recorded last score value of E. It can be seen that personality is the main factor for the emotion of robots so that robots can better show the differentiation of different personality expressions in different scenes.

2.3 User Behaviour

Taking into account general social rules, during a conversation, the emotion should change due to the distance between two people. When the distance between the two is close, it often indicates that the relationship between the two is closer, that is, a more lively emotion should be displayed. Then we present the functional relation between the variable a and the distance d between the robot and person to describe the social relationship. The user behavior variable a is defined as follows:

$$a = 5 - 5d \qquad (3)$$

where $a \in [0,1]$, and we choose $d \in [0.8, 1.2]$ denotes the commonly social distance. The reason why d is in the range of 0.8m to 1.2m is that we let robots maintain a safe and normal social distance from humans so that better HRI can be achieved safely.

Figure 2 shows that the robot's emotion elevates when the social distance is getting closer, on the contrary, the robot gets gradually serious if the distance is getting further. We choose d = 1m as the median social distance. Since a is a

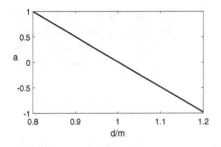
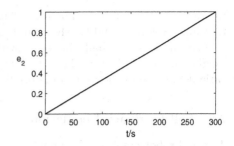

Fig. 2. Behaviour variable   **Fig. 3.** Evaluation variable

secondary factor, we need to consider that its change can not seriously affect the robot's emotions without ignoring its role. We propose the weight parameter of the behavior variable $w_a = 0.1$ to constrain the behavior variable of user a to be in the range of $[-0.1, 0.1]$.

2.4 User Evaluation

For user evaluation, we consider that different users have different evaluation methods. Some people like to express themselves directly, some like to suggest indirectly. Under comprehensive consideration, we divide e into direct evaluation e_1 and indirect evaluation e_2 two parts. The user evaluation e is presented as follows:

$$e = e_1 + e_2 \tag{4}$$

where $e \in [-1, 2]$. According to the verbal evaluation of users, the judgment should be made accordingly by the robot to make appropriate adjustments promptly. Then by dividing user reviews into five kinds, the user direct evaluation variable e_1 is defined as:

$$e_1 = \begin{cases} 1, & \text{very satisfied} \\ 0.5, & \text{satisfied} \\ 0, & \text{generally satisfied} \\ -0.5, & \text{dissatisfied} \\ -1, & \text{very dissatisfied} \end{cases} \tag{5}$$

where $e_1 \in \{-1, -0.5, 0, 0.5, 1\}$, because of its immediacy, its value is discrete and variable. The degree of satisfaction including very satisfied, satisfied, generally satisfied, dissatisfied, and very dissatisfied five kinds is judged by the robot itself according to the user's speech. As for indirect user evaluation, we choose the relationship of the user indirect evaluation variable e_2 and interaction time t to describe. The equation is defined as follows:

$$e_2 = \begin{cases} \frac{t}{300}, & 0 \le t \le 300 \\ 1, & t \ge 300 \end{cases} \tag{6}$$

where $e_2 \in [0,1]$, and we choose $t = 300s$ as the HRI time threshold. The relationship between e_2 and t is shown in Fig. 3. It can be seen that the indirect user evaluation value gradually increases with the interaction time. We present the weight parameter of the evaluation variable $w_e = 0.1$ to constrain user evaluation variable e to be in the range of $[-0.1, 0.2]$.

2.5   Self Feedback Regulation

To avoid robot emotions dominated by user behavior and losing themselves, we consider a self-regulating mechanism to compensate for this deficiency. Different emotions need to be maintained in different scenarios, which also requires that the self-regulation mechanism has different roles in different scenarios. For example, in the family scene, the robot needs to maintain a lively personality, which requires the self-regulation mechanism to quickly resist depression and slowly suppress excitement. In the school scene, the robot needs to maintain a serious personality, which requires the self-regulation mechanism to slowly resist depression and quickly suppress excitement. Then the variable of self-feedback regulation b is divided into two cases according to the environment. In the family scene, due to various environmental impacts, the emotion of the robot is always changing. To keep the personality of the robot stable, the self-regulatory mechanism need to be used to make the robot maintain the corresponding character in different scenes. The variable of self-feedback regulation b is defined as follows:

$$b = \begin{cases} -7.5E^2 + 12E - 4.8, & 0.8 < E \le 1 \\ 0, & 0.7 \le E \le 0.8, family\ scene \\ -\frac{10}{7}E^2 + 0.7, & 0 \le E < 0.7 \end{cases} \quad (7)$$

where $b \in [-0.3, 0.7]$.

The figure of self-feedback regulation b is illustrated in Fig. 4, it can be seen that in the family scene when the emotion parameter is lower than 0.6, the self-feedback regulation b increases its value quickly to make the robot lively. And within an acceptable range, the self-feedback regulation b doesn't work. When the emotion parameter is higher than 0.8, the self-feedback regulation b decreases its value slowly to make the robot not get too excited. The overall idea is that the robot can keep lively in the family scene when emotions fluctuate. In the school scene, taking into account environmental needs the self-feedback regulation b should keep robots serious to create a formal atmosphere. The equation is defined as follows:

$$b = \begin{cases} \frac{10}{7}E^2 - \frac{20}{7}E + \frac{51}{70}, & 0.3 < E \le 1 \\ 0, & 0.2 \le E \le 0.3, school\ scene \\ 7.5E^2 - 3E + 0.3, & 0 \le E < 0.2 \end{cases} \quad (8)$$

where $b \in [-0.7, 0.3]$.

In Fig. 5, it can be seen that in the school scene when the emotion parameter is lower than 0.2, the self-feedback regulation b increases its value slowly to

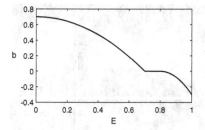

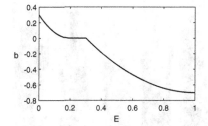

Fig. 4. Self-feedback regulation in the family scene

Fig. 5. Self-feedback regulation in the school scene

make the robot not get too serious. And within an acceptable range, the self-feedback regulation b doesn't work. When the emotion parameter is higher than 0.4, the self-feedback regulation b decreases its value quickly to make the robot a little serious. The overall idea is that the robot can keep serious in the school scene when emotions fluctuate. Comparing two pictures Fig. 4 and 5, we can obtain that robot emotion can maintain the desired level under the impact of self-feedback regulation. In the family scene, the robot is more active in facial expressions, voice, and movement, such as higher movement speed, richer facial expressions, and fuller language. On the contrary, in the school scene, the robot is more solemn in facial expressions, voice, and movement, such as normal movement speed, simple facial expressions, and refined language.

2.6   Processing and Execution

Table 2. Emotion level

Emotion	$0-0.2$	$0.2-0.4$	$0.4-0.6$	$0.6-0.8$	$0.8-1$
Level	Depressed	Serious	Neutral	Lively	Exciting

According to the value of the emotion variable E and Table 2, the robot can choose the appropriate behavior level L. The behavior processing unit chooses the parameters saved in advance to quantify based on the corresponding emotion level. The execution unit controls the various actuators of the robot to perform corresponding actions according to the received parameters.

3   Results and Discussion

In the family scene, the robot's emotional expression examples are shown in Fig. 6 and 7. In the school scene, the robot's emotional expression examples are shown in Fig. 8 and 9. Comparing Fig. 6 and Fig. 8, when the robot is idle, the

Fig. 6. Movement in the family scene

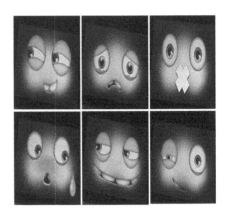

Fig. 7. Facial expressions in the family scene

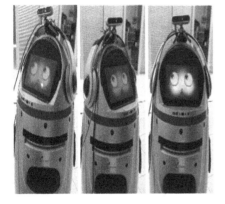

Fig. 8. Movement in the school scene

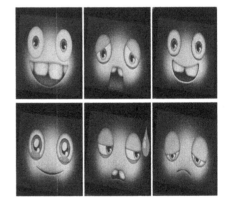

Fig. 9. Facial expressions in the school scene

robot turns the body with a lively personality in the family scene and turns the head with a serious personality in the school scene. According to Figs. 7 and 9, in contrast with expressions in the school scene, the expressions of the robot are more lively and vivid in the family scene. It can be obtained that the robot performs differently in different scenarios.

Relevance Interpretation for Robotic Expression is listed in Table 3. It can be seen that the emotion parameter values in the family scene are higher than those in the school scene, which means that the robot in the school scene is more serious. The emotion value change and interaction distance are shown in Fig. 10(a) in the family scene and Fig. 10(b) in the school scene. It can be seen that self-feedback b, user evaluation e and user motion a can influence the emotional value. The emotion level L is illustrated as the orange lines. In the family scene, as Fig. 10(a) shows, the robot gets an initial lively personality based on

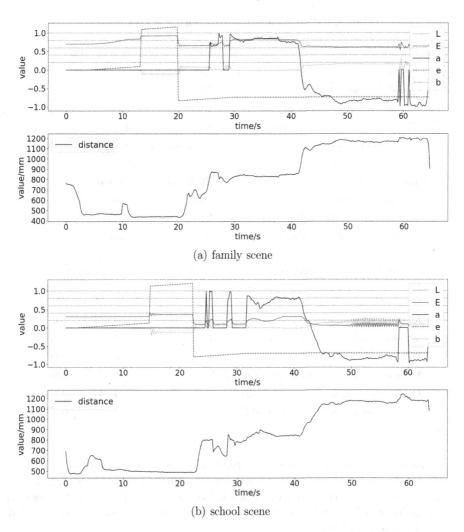

(a) family scene

(b) school scene

Fig. 10. Emotion Value Changes with parameters changes

the current environment. Then for user evaluation e, when we talk to the robot, its emotional value gradually increased. When we make a subjective assessment, good evaluations accordingly improve robot emotions and bad evaluations lower the emotion value. For user motion a, when the interaction distance is close to $0.8m$, the robot gets high emotion to behave excitedly to respond to people's interests. When the interaction distance is close to $1.2m$, the robot thinks people are a little uninterested or unsatisfactory in it and becomes peaceful. With self-feedback b, the robot can avoid seriousness when robot emotion drop to keep itself behaving lively so that robot emotions can be maintained around the lively level. In the school scene, as Fig. 10(b) shows, the robot gets an initial serious

Table 3. Relevance interpretation for robotic expression

Robotic expression	Family scene	School scene
Speed of wing/head(0-100)	80	40
Speed of wheel(0-400)	320	160
Action switching frequency	High	Low
The number of action types(10)	8	4
Action amplitude	Big-amplitude	Small-amplitude
Speed of speech(0-15)	12	6
Language complexity	Talkative	Concise
Speaking frequency	High	Low
The number of expression types(1-40)	32	16
Expression switching frequency	High	Low

Table 4. Descriptive statistics for each item of the questionnaire

Question	N	Mean	SD
Identity information and scene matching degree(0–100)	50	84.2	10.21
The pleasure of talking to a robot(0–100)	50	81.4	9.16
Whether the emotional expression is reasonable(0–5)	50	4.28	0.66
Does the robot have a personality(0–5)	50	3.98	0.90
Do robot emotions infect you(0–5)	50	3.68	0.85
Diversity of robot behaviors and identities(0–5)	50	4	0.77

personality based on the current environment. The user evaluation e and user motion a could influence robot emotion as described in the family scene. And with self-feedback b, the robot could avoid liveliness when robot emotion boosts to keep itself behaving seriously so that robot emotion could be maintained around the serious level.

To verify the actual performance of robot emotion models, we adopted a questionnaire to ask 50 people to evaluate the robots performance by watching our demo in two scenarios. As shown in Table 4, six questions were chosen to discuss rationality, diversity, and acceptability of people's perceptions of robot personalities. The first question was used to test whether the robot's personality matches the current environment. The second question was used to test whether people are willing to interact with the robot. The third question was used to check whether the robot's behavioral expression meets expectations. The fourth question was used to test the satisfaction of people with robot personality differences in different scenarios. The fifth question was used to check how people feel about robot emotions. The sixth question was used to test whether robots have diverse personalities. The results demonstrate that most people are more accepting of the emotional expression of robots.

4 Conclusion

In the paper, the robot emotion diagram was presented to describe the process of robot emotion changes and expression in different scenarios. We chose family and school two scenes. By considering the influence of personality, internal impacts, and external impact three factors, robot emotions could change accordingly to show different roles. Then the motion, the voice, and the facial expression were used to make the robot demonstrate anthropomorphic behavioral expression. Based on emotion, the performances of the robot were shown in the results. Questionnaires were used to demonstrate user satisfaction.

References

1. Osawa, H., Miyamoto, D., Hase, S., et al.: Visions of artificial intelligence and robots in science fiction: a computational analysis. Int. J. Soc. Robot. 1–11 (2022)
2. Bieling, G., Stock, R.M., Dorozalla, F.: Coping with demographic change in job markets: how age diversity management contributes to organisational performance. German J. Hum. Resou. Manag. **29**(1), 5–30 (2015)
3. Allan, D.D., Vonasch, A.J., Bartneck, C.: "I have to praise you like i should?" the effects of implicit self-theories and robot-delivered praise on evaluations of a social robot. Int. J. Soc. Robot. **14**, 1013–1024 (2022)
4. Law, T., Malle, B.F., Scheutz, M.: A touching connection: how observing robotic touch can affect human trust in a robot. Int. J. Soc. Robot. **13**(8), 2003–2019 (2021). https://doi.org/10.1007/s12369-020-00729-7
5. Nocentini, O., Fiorini, L., Acerbi, G., Sorrentino, A., Mancioppi, G., Cavallo, F.: A survey of behavioral models for social robots. Robotics **8**(3), 54 (2019)
6. Fong, T., Thorpe, C., Baur, C.: Collaboration, dialogue, human-robot interaction. In: 10th International Symposium on Robotics Research. Tracts in Advanced Robotics, vol. 6, pp. 255–266. Springer (2003). https://doi.org/10.1007/3-540-36460-9_17
7. Stock-Homburg, R.: Survey of emotions in human-robot interactions: perspectives from robotic psychology on 20 years of research. Int. J. Soc. Robot. **14**, 389–411 (2021)
8. Conti, D., Trubia, G., Buono, S., Di Nuovo, S., Di Nuovo, A.: Evaluation of a robot-assisted therapy for children with autism and intellectual disability. In: Proceedings of the Annual Conference towards Autonomous Robotic Systems, Bristol, UK, pp. 405–415 (2018)
9. Alhaddad, A.Y., Cabibihan, J.J., Bonarini, A.: Real-time social robot's responses to undesired interactions between children and their surroundings. Int. J. Soc. Robot. (2022)
10. Cavallo, F., et al.: Improving domiciliary robotic services by integrating the astro robot in an ami infrastructure. In: Röhrbein, F., Veiga, G., Natale, C. (eds.) Gearing Up and Accelerating Cross-fertilization between Academic and Industrial Robotics Research in Europe: STAR, vol. 94, pp. 267–282. Springer, Cham (2014). https://doi.org/10.1007/978-3-319-03838-4_13
11. Johnson, M.J., Mohan, M., Mendonca, R.: Therapist-patient interactions in task-oriented stroke therapy can guide robot-patient interactions. Int. J. Soc. Robot. (2022)

12. Loi, S.M., et al.: A pilot study exploring staff acceptability of a socially assistive robot in a residential care facility that accommodates people under 65 years old. Int. Psychogeriatr. **30**(7), 1075–1080 (2018)

13. Haslam, N.: Dehumanization: an integrative review. Pers. Soc. Psychol. Rev. **10**(3), 252–264 (2006)

14. Parkinson, B.: Emotions are social. Br. J. Psychol. **87**(4), 663–683 (1996)

15. Andreasson, R., Alenljung, B., Billing, E., et al.: Affective touch in human-robot interaction: conveying emotion to the nao robot. Int. J. Soc. Robot. **10**, 473–491 (2018)

16. Takahashi, Y., Kayukawa, Y., Terada, K., et al.: Emotional expressions of real humanoid robots and their influence on human decision-making in a finite iterated prisoner's dilemma game. Int. J. Soc. Robot. **13**, 1777–1786 (2021)

17. Rawal, N., Stock-Homburg, R.M.: Facial emotion expressions in human-robot interaction: a survey. Int. J. Soc. Robot. (2022)

18. Johnson, D.O., Cuijpers, R.H.: Investigating the effect of a humanoid robot's head position on imitating human emotions. Int. J. Soc. Robot. **11**, 65–74 (2019)

19. Ahn, H.S., Lee, D.-W.: Emotional expression and its applications. Int. J. Soc. Robot. **5**(4), 419–421 (2013). https://doi.org/10.1007/s12369-013-0216-9

Building an Affective Model for Social Robots with Customizable Personality

Ziyan Zhang, Wenjing Yang, and Wei Wang$^{(\boxtimes)}$

Robotics Institute, Beihang University, Beijing 100191, China
wangweilab@buaa.edu.cn

Abstract. As robot technology advances, there is a progressively growing demand to empower robots with human-like emotions. Designing appropriate personality features for social robots can enhance user contact with them as well as help them complete their works more effectively. In this paper, an affective model for social robots with adjustable personality is proposed. This model describes the changing process between emotional states using emotion, mood, and personality. Our model can convincingly mimic the emotional fluctuations of individuals with various personalities by using the results of experiments on real humans. First, we proposed a bowl-shaped affective model with eight fundamental feelings in three dimensions of emotional space, and then we provide a way for modeling personality. Second, we use the emotional arousal methods to contrast and examine how various personality groups responded to the same emotional stimulus. Based on this, we build two models that can fully capture introverted and extroverted personality traits, and then we use the validation data set to assess the validity and reliability of the parameters in our model. The results show that the model can effectively simulate the emotional change process of different personality groups after being subjected to varied emotional stimuli.

Keywords: Social robots · Affective model · Personality · Human-robot interaction

1 Introduction and Related Works

People now have higher expectations for robots as a result of the development of robot technology, which expands application scenarios for robots and makes it possible for robots entering people's daily lives from factories in recent years. For instance, people are more likely to consider robots as partners for projecting emotions than just to regard them as machines for completing tasks [1, 24], and robots that can replicate empathy sensitively will be much more well-liked by their users [2]. Building "natural" human-robot interaction (HRI) solutions with implicit communication channels and a certain level of emotional intelligence are therefore becoming increasingly crucial [3]. An affective model can make social robots better meeting user's needs. Additionally, affective models can be sensitive to empathy and satisfy the special demands of users. Therefore,

---

Z. Zhang and W. Yang—These authors contributed equally to this work.

F. Cavallo et al. (Eds.): ICSR 2022, LNAI 13817, pp. 463–474, 2022.
https://doi.org/10.1007/978-3-031-24667-8_41

an affective model which can be customized and shows some kind of "personality" can address the aforementioned problems.

Robot personality has not yet been adequately defined by academics. However, a person's personality is characterized by their distinctive thought, emotion, and behavior patterns as well as the psychological mechanisms behind it [4, 25]. In terms of the user's emotional demands, users have psychological expectations for the robot's personality traits [5]. The robot's personality has a substantial impact on the user's behavior, experience, and appraisal in HRI [6–8], and in the long-term interaction process, the robot's personality plays a role [9]. In terms of product functional needs, robots in different jobs need to have diverse personalities to fit their jobs. For example, companion robots must be kind and compassionate, and security robots may be expected to possess courage, among other traits [1, 10].

The development of accurate computational emotion models for robots has drew significant attention from researchers. There are two categories of robot emotion model programs: one is devoted to a more reasonable expression of emotions "externally", while the other is devoted to an endogenous human-like emotion regulation "internally" of the robot [11]. We focus more on the latter. A small number of researchers have concentrated on the function of personality in emotion regulation in robots. In particular, Naoki Masuyama et al. [12] proposed an emotion model containing personality traits, memories, and five fundamental emotions with the P-A-D emotion space theory and the Big Five personality theory. They demonstrated how the emotions of robots with three different personality parameters changed. By modifying the personality suppression of expression parameters, Xue Hu et al. [13] built an emotion model for robots with various personalities and measured the emotion regulation process of Gross using the Hidden Markov Model (HMM). Meng-Ju Han et al. [14] developed an "emotion-mood-personality" three-level emotion model and showed three robots with various personalities by altering the parameters of the five-factor personality model. Itoh C et al. [15] proposed an emotion-generating model with emotion transmission to evaluate a robot's personality and internal condition. However, the majority of studies have treated personality parameters as set variables rather than parameters to be adjusted, and this will result in our inability to test whether the robot's personality achieves the desired effect, furthermore, we are also unable to accurately generate robotic personalities that meet the needs of users through models.

Our study proposes and validates a reliable robot personality creation approach, extending the work of Qi X et al. [16], and proposes a modeling method for a three-dimensional emotion space based on Plutchik's wheel of emotions (PWE), with "emotion-mood-personality" as the emotional interaction mechanism.

This paper has the following contributions:

(1) Propose a new approach to model a 3D emotional space, including theoretical and calculational mechanisms;
(2) Suggest a method for creating various personality robots based on the affective model, simulates the various personalities that robots may need in a variety of scenarios, and confirms the validity of the personality model.

2 The Framework of Customizable Personality Affective Model (CPAM)

2.1 Overview of Previous Work PWE Inspired Affective Model

In our previous work [16], we have proposed a PWE [17] inspired affective model which can simulate the motivation of stimuli on emotions, emotion natural decay, and the effect of mood on emotional responses and emotional decay. The model contains 8 basic bipolar emotions together with the interactions with moods, and uses exponential decay processes to describe the natural changes of emotions and moods. The process of the affective changes is corresponding to different update equations in four conditions, which are based on comparing the combined effect and the single factor effect of the previous emotion, previous mood, and current stimulus. Any detailed discussion can be found in [16].

Personality is an important factor in understanding robot emotions during human-robot interaction [5, 17, 18]. Specifically, we believe that it is necessary to represent personality figuratively in the robot emotion model. The above model only lies in the differences between a few threshold parameters and the variable of personality bias, thus will make the differences in emotional change under different personalities incomplete and intuitive, and will influence us to shape the affect of a robot from the perspective of personality. And even further, there is still a lack of a clear parameterized method to explain the mechanisms involved in controlling the differences in affective change. To address the above problems of PWE, we propose an improved model named Customizable Personality Affective Model (CPAM).

2.2 Parametric Approaches to Personality

On the basis of the previous work, the interaction mechanism among emotion, mood, stimulus and personality is improved, shown in Fig. 1. It includes three instantaneous effects on emotion, and two cumulative effects produced by emotion and mood.

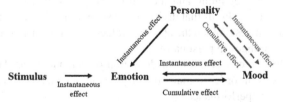

Fig. 1. The interaction mechanism among variables. (The blue dotted line belongs to our previous model, the red solid line belongs to the improved model, others belong to both two models) (Color figure online)

The improvement mainly focuses on the parametric definition of the two cumulative effects. In terms of mood update, as it lasts more longer and does not relate to specific events, we regard it as a cumulative effect of emotion, and model it as a state variable that changes slowly.

$$m(t) = m(t-1) + \Delta m \tag{1}$$

where t is the time that the event happened and i represents the corresponding emotion and Δm is the amount of change in every update period of mood dt.

And to map stimulus emotions into mood states, we simply adopt the mean emotion mapping function [19], as well as consider the two sources of effect including stimulus and natural attenuation of emotion.

$$\Delta m = \begin{cases} \frac{1}{n} \sum\limits_{i=1}^{w} \alpha_i k_{ei} a_{it}, & t \in [t_{i0}, t_{i0} + d_{it}] \\ \dfrac{\sum\limits_{i=1}^{8} \alpha_i \int_{t_s}^{t_s+dt} (e_i(t) - e_i(t_s)) dt}{dt}, & otherwise \end{cases} \tag{2}$$

where n is the number of dt while the stimulus still works, w is the total number of active emotions, α_i is the emotional polarity variable that divides emotions into positive ($\alpha_i = 1$) and negative ($\alpha_i = -1$) according to whether they are user-friendly or not, a_{it} is the intensity of the stimulus event, t_{i0} is the natural decay start time, k_{ei} is the influence factors of emotions to mood, d_{it} is the duration of stimulus that effects on emotion i, $e_i(t)$ is the intensity of emotion i at moment t, and t_s is the start time of each dt while the mood is naturally decaying.

Moreover, the previous research has documented that maintaining a unipolar emotional experience for a long time will affect personality shaping [20]. Accordingly a variable $m_{ac}(t)$ is defined to record the cumulative effect of mood that not in neutral state as in Eq. (3).

$$m_{ac}(t) = \begin{cases} \left| \int_{t_{ac}}^{t'_{ac}} m(t) dt \right|, & if \ R_3 \\ 0, & otherwise \end{cases} \tag{3}$$

$$R_3 : \forall m(t), t \in [t_{ac}, t'_{ac}], m(t) \in [-1, h_n] \cup [h_p, 1], m(t-1) \in (h_n, h_p) \tag{4}$$

where t_{ac}, t'_{ac} are the beginning and the end of the period that satisfy R_3, h_n and h_p represent 2 different thresholds that divide mood state into 3 intervals (positive, neutral, and negative mood states). When the absolute value of $m_{ac}(t)$ reaches a certain standard m_{ac}, it will cause changes in personality.

Following this we can give a clear definition of personality as the union of eight countable locus sets, in order to make the changes in personality caused by the mood has obvious concrete performance:

$$P = \bigcup_{i=8} P_i, \forall P_i \in \{P\}, P_i = \{p_{i0}, p_{i1}, \dots, p_{in_i}\}, n_i \in N \tag{5}$$

For any personality $P_x \in \{P\}$, each of its 8 subsets P_{ix} covers some loci of control $\{p_{ik}\}$ that consist of various degrees of stimuli and the corresponding emotional intensity it aroused.

$$p_{ik} = (e_{ik}(t_{i0}), a_{ik}), a_{ik} \in \{a_{it}\}, k \in n_i \tag{6}$$

These loci of control can concretely reflect the differences between various personalities. On the one hand, the loci of control shape a 3D model shown in next subsection, through which we can more intuitively observe differences in emotional traits exhibited by different personalities. On the other hand, they directly affect the computational parameters, which in turn play a decisive role in the model. Consequently, the changes in personality can be parameterized as changes in these loci of control.

In order to show the personality changes in a more intuitive parameterized way, we simply select 33 loci as observation objects, whose emotional intensity is equal to the emotional threshold. These loci are the most representative ones, thus we can observe the most obvious personality traits and changes by focusing on them. And the update equations for them can be written as follows.

$$h = \begin{cases} \frac{(m(t)-h')}{\beta * \beta'}, & if \ |m_{ac}(t)| > m_{ac} \\ 0, & otherwise \end{cases} \tag{7}$$

$$\beta' = \begin{cases} 1, & if \ h_{ij} = h_{im} \\ \frac{h_{im}}{h_{ij}}, & otherwise \end{cases}, \quad h' = \begin{cases} h_{n,}, & m(t) \leq h_n \\ h_p, & m(t) \geq h_p \end{cases} \tag{8}$$

where β and β' are the update factors of personality, and $\{h_{ij}\}$ contains all the emotional thresholds. For any selected locus of control (h_{ij}, a_{ik}), after an update process of personality, the new value will become $(h_{ij} + \Delta h, a_{ik})$.

In like manner, any remaining locus of control p_{ik} will also changes the emotional intensity aroused by the same stimulation. The change will follow a linear fit between two adjacent threshold loci of control.

2.3 3D Model Structure

On the basis of the affective model with detailed definition of personality, a 3D model that contains the emotion curves and balls can be proposed as shown in Fig. 2a. It can describe the spatial form of personality locus of control, and show the process of emotion change.

Compared with the previous 2D model [16], the 3D one can not only cover all the visualizations that the original model can display, but also having a huge advantage on showing the personality traits obviously, as well as visualizing the relationship between stimuli and emotions clearly.

Taking Fig. 2b as an example, for the same kind of personality we give a stimulus having the same intensity on both joy and trust. But even though the Joy-Ball and the Trust-Ball having the same spatial height, the horizontal projection distance of the Joy-Ball to its initial position is much longer than another. It's on this basis that we can conclude this personality having a more explicit characteristic on joy than on trust. Besides, focus on the two bowl-shaped affective model mentioned above, we can also analyze the traits of different personalities by comparing the spatial position of corresponding threshold loci, for instance, the personality in Fig. 2a can achieve more intense trust.

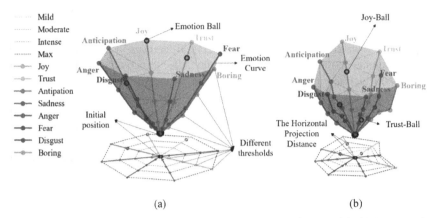

Fig. 2. The proposed 3D affective model. (a) The components of the model; (b) An example of the model.

3   Building Introverted/Extroverted Robot Affective Models

3.1   Questionnaire of Personality Parameters

To evaluate the effectiveness of the proposed affective model, we use text to simulate and quantify the stimuli first, then compare the emotional arousal of real people and the model under the same conditions. So, the first step is to run a preliminary experiment to determine the model parameters, which can help building the robot affective models for comparison. And in view of the measure of introversion/extroversion being more popular in the current academic research on robot personality [6], we adopt these two personalities as the classification of our sample affective model.

The whole preliminary experiment is conducted through a series of online questionnaires, which can be divided into personality test and stimulus simulation test. The questionnaire material for the personality test is Eysenck Personality Inventory (E Scale) [21]. And the text type materials for stimulus simulation test are selected from the Affective Norms for English Words (ANEW) [18], which contains 718 sentences of 5–23 words, and labeled with emotional valence and emotional arousal. It's worth mentioning that this data set was evaluated and validated by 148 psychology students from University of Warsaw and 2,091 students from different faculties, in the case of a male-to-female ratio maintaining at 1,030:1,209. Therefore, it fully meets the requirements of authority for the experiments. On this basis, we screen out some representative texts with different levels of emotional arousal from ANEW, then we translate the text and slightly adjust them according to Chinese context to fit our testee in China.

Our testee for the preliminary experiment are 67 people from all over China, who ranges in age from 16 to 80 (M = 27.01, SD = 6.38). We divide them into 4 groups by age, spaced 10 years apart. And the sample size ratio of these seven groups is 6:45:11:5, sorted from the youngest to the eldest. Besides, there is an equal proportion of men and women in the population, and in the 20 to 29-year-old group, whose sample size is the largest, the ratio of men and women is 22:23.

In the process of the experiment, we publish the questionnaire through the Internet, with controlling the age distribution of the testee. After that each testee will start with the personality test, then read 36 stimulus-texts in turn and rate their emotional intensity of 8 emotions, with the experimental guidance and the self-emotional rehabilitation having completed.

In the first place, we test the reliability and validity of the questionnaire, the result is shown in Table 1.

Table 1. The reliability and validity of the questionnaire.

Item	Reliability		Validity [23]		
Index	Standardized Cronbach's Alpha [22]	CITC for each problem	KMO(p)	Cumulative variance interpretation rate after rotation	Communalities
Value	0.968(>0.7)	<0.49(97%+) <0.40(78%+)	0.659(0.000 < 0.05)	75.452%(>50%)	>0.40(100%)

As seen from the table, the Standardized Cronbach's Alpha shows the results of this questionnaire have excellent consistency and stability, the CITC value shows that each stimulus has a high independence, and the KMO value with p, together with the cumulative variance interpretation rate after rotation and the communalities tell us that the results of the questionnaire are suitable for extracting information. In conclusion, our questionnaire has excellent reliability and validity.

3.2 Calculation of Personality Parameters

Based on the results of questionnaire, we calculate the initial parameters of the loci of control for introverted and extroverted affective model, the detailed process of which is listed as followed:

1. Divide the testee into two groups according to the score of introversion and extroversion, and calculate the mean of each data in each group.
2. Use K-means clustering to estimate a few sets of data that can represent the personality traits of the crowd, with using the mean data in last step as the original cluster center, and the clustering number being two. In this step, both personality and emotional arousal traits are considered, and the final clustering center should be retained.
3. Compare the cluster members in step2 with members of the similar group in step1, and use the mean values of the disputed members and clustering centers to be the final representative data.
4. Correspond the data in step3 to the loci of control according to the emotional arousal value ANEW given.

In the actual process, the ratio of the size of two clusters is 16:19, and there is only one disputed member. The final introverted and extroverted affective model are shown in Fig. 3.

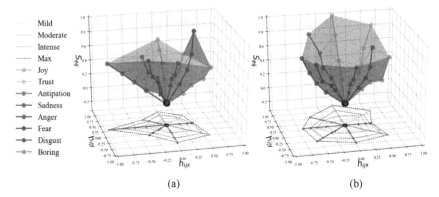

Fig. 3. The introverted/extroverted robot affective models.(a) introverted; (b) extroverted

4 Validation and Evaluation

4.1 Model Test

Based on the introverted and extroverted robot affective models we have built, we can carry out a new round of human-computer interaction experiment, to verify the accuracy of emotion model compared with real human emotion under the same stimulus. In this round of formal experiment, we adopt some online questionnaires with a similar structure to the preliminary experiment. But the difference is that we select texts from ANEW with a new emotional arousal, and we conduct 8 groups of experiments with 25 testee each, categorized according to the category of emotion. The configuration of each group is as follows.

4.2 Results

We use all the texts whose emotional arousal can act as the intensity of input stimulus in the questionnaire mentioned above to prove that our model has a good fit. We feed the stimulus into two emotion models and record the estimated values of the model as e_{es} first. Then by comparing e_{es} with the average observed values in the experiment e_{os}, it can infer that the smaller the absolute value of the difference between the two b, the better the fitting degree of the affective model. The partial results are listed in Table 3.

In the other six emotions, the maximum b are 0.081, 0.124, 0.103, 0.941, 0.065, 0.088, thus it can be seen that our model closely mimicked real people in the emotional expression both introverted and extroverted.

Additionally, we feed the same predefined stimulus to the introverted and extroverted model, while controlling other irrelevant parameters at the same level, to test the difference representation ability of the affective model.

Table 2. The configuration of each experiment group.

Group	Emotion	M_{age}	SD_{age}	Standardized Cronbach's Alpha	KMO(p)
A	Joy	26.28	5.70	0.975	0.723(0.000)
B	Sadness	26.20	5.13	0.801	0.698(0.000)
C	Anticipation	29.08	7.97	0.984	0.602(0.000)
D	Anger	27.76	6.40	0.988	0.649(0.000)
E	Fear	31.00	11.03	0.977	0.601(0.000)
F	Surprise	27.04	7.79	0.959	0.617(0.000)
G	Disgust	29.44	6.82	0.966	0.622(0.000)
H	Trust	27.48	6.62	0.973	0.674(0.000)

Table 3. Comparison of estimated values of affective model with observed values of experiments.

Stimulus intensity		Introverted			Extroverted		
		e_{es}	e_{os}	b	e_{es}	e_{os}	b
Joy	$a_{11} = 2.87$	0.102	0.127	0.025	0.196	0.117	0.079
	$a_{12} = 4.08$	0.231	0.304	0.073	0.311	0.249	0.062
	$a_{13} = 4.25$	0.267	0.279	0.012	0.312	0.339	0.027
	$a_{14} = 4.35$	0.274	0.240	0.034	0.349	0.433	0.084
	$a_{15} = 5.02$	0.398	0.307	0.091	0.447	0.430	0.017
	$a_{16} = 5.75$	0.447	0.508	0.061	0.549	0.571	0.022
	$a_{17} = 6.17$	0.526	0.569	0.043	0.607	0.574	0.033
	$a_{18} = 6.79$	0.607	0.659	0.052	0.729	0.740	0.011
Sadness	$a_{41} = 3.55$	0.279	0.335	0.056	0.191	0.112	0.079
	$a_{42} = 4.10$	0.318	0.399	0.081	0.303	0.334	0.031
	$a_{43} = 4.37$	0.362	0.454	0.092	0.311	0.366	0.055
	$a_{44} = 4.48$	0.373	0.339	0.034	0.351	0.399	0.048
	$a_{45} = 6.07$	0.546	0.621	0.075	0.436	0.360	0.076
	$a_{46} = 6.43$	0.599	0.665	0.066	0.505	0.530	0.025
	$a_{47} = 7.38$	0.670	0.64	0.030	0.551	0.634	0.083
	$a_{48} = 7.46$	0.681	0.728	0.047	0.599	0.647	0.048

It can be seen in Fig. 4. That under the same stimulation, the more explicit emotion include joy, anticipation and trust, will be higher arousal in the extroverted model. Meanwhile, the introverted model shows greater ability to maintain the high level of emotions longer.

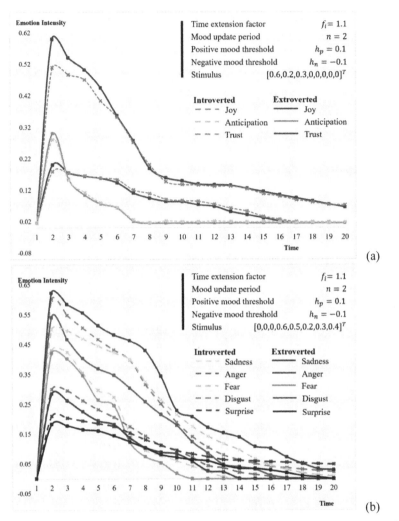

Fig. 4. Comparison of emotion changes under different personality. (a) Positive emotions; (b) Negative emotions.

5   Conclusion and Future Work

In this paper, we have proposed a method for modeling the affective model and personality creation of a 3D social robot based on Plutchik's Wheel of Emotions, built sample models with introverted and extroverted personalities, and modeled different personalities to broaden the application of the affective model. The findings have been analyzed from questionnaires ratings that were given by 270 individuals of various ages, genders, and personality qualities.

Based on the results of the experiments, the affective model has been preliminarily shown to accurately mimic human multiple personalities, and its affective mechanisms of customized personalities are consistent with humans with the same type of personality.

To further support and confirm our findings, future work such as examining differences in attitudes of people towards robots with and without appropriate personalities in multiple positions can be done. On the other hand, studies based on endogenous emotions in robots concentrate on the behavior of emotional processes acting in people [12], so we will expand our experimental scenarios and consider combining robotic personality mechanisms with behavioral decision-making mechanisms to apply the model to various real-life contexts.

Acknowledgements. This work was supported by the fund provided by National Key Research and Development Program of China (Grant No. 2020YFB1313600). We would also like to thank Yutong Hu for his assistance that promoted our research.

References

1. Darling, K.: The New Breed: What Our History with Animals Reveals About Our Future with Robots. Henry Holt and Company, New York (2021)
2. Marcos-Pablos, S., García-Peñalvo, F.J.: Emotional intelligence in robotics: a scoping review. In: de Paz Santana, J.F., de la Iglesia, D.H., López Rivero, A.J. (eds.) DiTTEt 2021. AISC, vol. 1410, pp. 66–75. Springer, Cham (2022). https://doi.org/10.1007/978-3-030-87687-6_7
3. Picard, R.: Affective computing. Massachustes Institute of Techonology, Cambridge (1997)
4. Funder, D.C.: The Personality Puzzle. WW Norton & Co., New York (1997)
5. Kiesler, S., Goetz, J.: Mental models of robotic assistants. In: CHI 2002 Extended Abstracts on Human Factors in Computing Systems, pp. 576–577 (2002)
6. Robert, L.: Personality in the human robot interaction literature: a review and brief critique. In: Robert, L.P. (ed.) Personality in the Human Robot Interaction Literature: A Review and Brief Critique, Proceedings of the 24th Americas Conference on Information Systems, pp. 16–18, August 2018
7. Robert, L.P., Jr., et al.: A review of personality in human–robot interactions. Found. Trends® Inf. Syst. **4**(2), 107–212 (2020)
8. Whittaker, S., Rogers, Y., Petrovskaya, E., Zhuang, H.: Designing personas for expressive robots: personality in the new breed of moving, speaking, and colorful social home robots. ACM Trans. Hum. Robot Interact. (THRI) **10**(1), 1–25 (2021)
9. Leite, I., Martinho, C., Paiva, A.: Social robots for long-term interaction: a survey. Int. J. Soc. Robot. **5**(2), 291–308 (2013)
10. Hendriks, B., Meerbeek, B., Boess, S., Pauws, S., Sonneveld, M.: Robot vacuum cleaner personality and behavior. Int. J. Soc. Robot. **3**(2), 187–195 (2011)
11. Damiano, L., Dumouchel, P., Lehmann, H.: Towards human–robot affective co-evolution overcoming oppositions in constructing emotions and empathy. Int. J. Soc. Robot. **7**(1), 7–18 (2015)
12. Masuyama, N., Loo, C.K., Seera, M.: Personality affected robotic emotional model with associative memory for human-robot interaction. Neurocomputing **272**, 213–225 (2018)
13. Hu, X., Xie, L., Liu, X., Wang, Z.: Emotion expression of robot with personality. Mathe. Probl. Eng. **2013**, 10 (2013)
14. Han, M.J., Lin, C.H., Song, K.T.: Robotic emotional expression generation based on mood transition and personality model. IEEE Trans. Cybern. **43**(4), 1290–1303 (2012)

15. Itoh, C., Kato, S., Itoh, H.: Mood-transition-based emotion generation model for the robot's personality. In: 2009 IEEE International Conference on Systems, Man and Cybernetics, pp. 2878–2883. IEEE (2009)
16. Qi, X., Wang, W., Guo, L., Li, M., Zhang, X., Wei, R.: Building a Plutchik's wheel inspired affective model for social robots. J. Bionic Eng. **16**(2), 209–221 (2019)
17. Gockley, R., MatariC, M.J.: Encouraging physical therapy compliance with a hands-off mobile robot. In: Proceedings of the 1st ACM SIGCHI/SIGART Conference on Human-Robot interaction, pp. 150–155 (2006)
18. Koay, K.L., Syrdal, D.S., Walters, M.L., Dautenhahn, K.: Living with robots: Investigating the habituation effect in participants' preferences during a longitudinal human-robot interaction study. In: RO-MAN 2007- The 16th IEEE International Symposium on Robot and Human Interactive Communication, pp. 564–569. IEEE (2007)
19. Katsimerou, C., Heynderickx, I., Redi, J.A.: Predicting mood from punctual emotion annotations on videos. IEEE Trans. Affect. Comput. **6**(2), 179–192 (2015)
20. Diener, E., Smith, H., Fujita, F.: The personality structure of affect. J. Pers. Soc. Psychol. **69**(1), 130 (1995)
21. Eysenck, H.J., Strelau, J., et al.: The biosocial approach to personality. In: Explorations in Temperament: International Perspectives on Theory and Measurement, p. 87 (1991)
22. Tavakol, M., Dennick, R.: Making sense of Cronbach's Alpha. Int. J. Med. Educ. **2**, 53 (2011)
23. Brown, T.A.: Confirmatory Factor Analysis for Applied Research. Guilford Publications, New York (2015)
24. Liu, X., Jiang, W., Su, H., Qi, W., Ge, S.S.: A control strategy of robot eyehead coordinated gaze behavior achieved for minimized neural transmission noise. IEEE/ASME Trans. Mechatron. (2022)
25. Xu, Y., Su, H., Ma, G. et al.: A novel dual-modal emotion recognition algorithm with fusing hybrid features of audio signal and speech context. Complex Intell. Syst. (2022). https://doi.org/10.1007/s40747-022-00841-3

A Multimodal Perception and Cognition Framework and Its Application for Social Robots

Lanfang Dong[1], PuZhao Hu[1], Xiao Xiao[1(✉)], YingChao Tang[1], Meng Mao[2], and Guoming Li[2]

[1] University of Science and Technology of China, Hefei 230031, China
lfdong@ustc.edu.cn, 1213622420@qq.com
[2] AI Lab, China Merchants Bank, Shenzhen 518040, China
{melvinmaonn,lkm}@cmbchina.com

Abstract. With the development of artificial intelligence and computer technology, more and more intelligent robots come into people's view. And we can see the application of social robots in various scenarios, but these robots are insufficient in terms of anthropomorphism and personalization. In this paper, an interaction framework based on multimodal perception and cognition is proposed. This framework allows for more individualized engagement behaviors while also enhancing the cognitive system of social robots by gathering information on users' words, expressions, and posture. The application of the interactive framework was demonstrated in the hospital scenario.

Keywords: Social robots · Multimodal perception · Interaction framework · Interaction behaviors · Cognitive system

1 Introduction

The ability to have harmonious and natural social interaction is one of the important signs that intelligent robots and human society have entered the era of human-machine integration. At present, social robots have been applied in some scenarios, such as navigation machines that can help assist driving [3], robots used to monitor social distancing during the epidemic [11], assistance robots to help direct traffic [5], and robots for cylindrical bore diameter measurement [7]. Even though there has been some advancement in the theory and technology of robot social interaction in short-term and specific scenarios, there are still issues with the personification and personalization of robot social behavior as well as the lack of a multi-modal perception and cognitive system. The language, expressions, gestures, eye movements and other information of social objects contain rich social clues. Multimodal information collection and recognition is an important prerequisite for realizing human-computer interaction. Robots obtain this

Supported by the National Key Research and Development Program of China under Grant No.2020YFB1313602.

F. Cavallo et al. (Eds.): ICSR 2022, LNAI 13817, pp. 475–484, 2022.
https://doi.org/10.1007/978-3-031-24667-8_42

information of social objects to understand various social objects. Intent to complete the interactive function. A social robot based on multimodal information interaction can form a variety of modules with different functions. We designed a social robot framework for multimodal information interaction, has implemented face detection, age and gender prediction, emotion recognition, intention prediction, gesture recognition and other functions. This framework can complete interactive tasks based on these multimodal information. The general framework diagram of our social robot is as shown in Fig. 1.

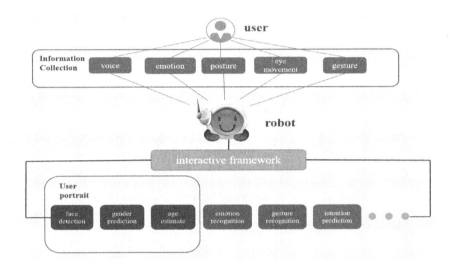

Fig. 1. A multimodal natural perception and interaction module

We collect the acoustics, visual and lingustic information of users from the robot side, and transmit it to the server side through the internet. The server side transfers the collected information to different functional modules to complete the corresponding recognition works. According to the recognition result, the robot is driven to complete the corresponding recognition work. So far, we have implemented face detection, age and gender prediction, emotion recognition, intention prediction, gesture recognition, and we can continue to expand other functions in the future.

2   Module Introduction

We constructed a multi-modal perception and cognition interactive framework to extract features from the collected information and transmit the features to each module for detection and recognition. At the same time, modules communicate with each other to transfer information. Our framework mainly includes four modules: user portrait, emotion recognition, intention prediction and gesture recognition.

2.1   User Portrait

The user portrait module includes face detection, gender and age recognition, and identity confirmation,and involves many sub-tasks. How to realize a lightweight and concise user portrait system while ensuring the final accuracy is an urgent problem to be solved. We design an identity comparison system based on face information, which will identify the user's age and gender immediately after detecting the user's face information.

Identity Comparison System Based on Face Information. Face detection is the basis for age and gender prediction and emotion recognition. At present, face detection technology is relatively mature, such as fast and lightweight SSH [8] algorithm, anti-fraud detection algorithm [15]. We use PyramidBox [13] for face detection, which can assist face detection through the context information of the face. The information of head, shoulder and body can assist face detection and improve the accuracy of face detection. Face detection needs to establish a corresponding face database, and we use the face-encodings method of the python face detection library face-recognition to encode the face. We compare the face encoding detected by the module with those in the database one by one. The matching distance lower than 0.4 is considered to be the same person. Users who do not match the results in the database need to register their identity. The overall process is as shown in Fig. 2.

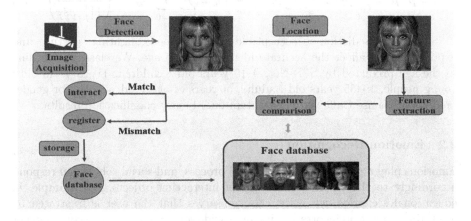

Fig. 2. The process of identity matching system

We first collect the images of social objects through the camera, and then perform face detection on the images to obtain the faces. We locate the features of the obtained face, then extract the features, obtain the feature codes, and compare the feature codes with the face database one by one. If the match is successful, the human-computer interaction can be continued. If the match fails, the user is required to register the identity, and the information is registered to the face database for updating.

Age and Gender Prediction. We use convolutional neural network CNN for age prediction, we adopt SSR-Net [18], which transforms age prediction from a classification problem to a regression problem. Unlike DEX [10], it divides the prediction is performed in stages, which greatly saves the overhead of inference. DEX divides the age [0, V] into s intervals, and the age span of each interval is V/s, as shown in Eq. (1).

$$\tilde{y} = \boldsymbol{p} \cdot \boldsymbol{\mu} = \sum_{i=0}^{s-1} p_i \cdot \mu_i = \sum_{i=0}^{s-1} p_i \cdot i \left(\frac{V}{s} \right) \tag{1}$$

If the model predicts that the probability of being located in each interval is p, the representative value of each interval multiplied by its probability is accumulated to be the final prediction result. SSR-Net is divided into k stages for prediction, for example, the prediction age interval [0, 90], the first stage prediction the probability of interval [0, 30], [30, 60], [60, 90]. In the second stage, each interval continues to be predicted in three stages, and each stage uses the same weight. However, dividing the interval in this way lacks flexibility. SSR-Net also adds a dynamic range to each interval, allowing each interval to move and scale according to the input image. The final calculation formula is as shown in Eq. (2).

$$\tilde{y} = \boldsymbol{p} \cdot \boldsymbol{\mu} = \sum_{i=0}^{s-1} p_i \cdot \mu_i = \sum_{i=0}^{s-1} p_i \cdot i \left(\frac{V}{s} \right) \tilde{y} = \sum_{k=1}^{K} \sum_{i=0}^{s_k-1} p_i^{(k)} \cdot \bar{i} \left(\frac{V}{\prod_{j=1}^{k} \bar{s}_j} \right) \tag{2}$$

Since age prediction is susceptible to interference, lighting, posture and expressions will affect the accurate identification of age. We classify according to the age predicted by SSR-Net, 0–10 years old : children, 11–18 years old : young people, 19–55 years old : adults, 56 years of age : old people. For gender prediction, we use CaffeNet [6] to obtain final binary classification results.

2.2   Emotion Recognition

Emotions play a pivotal role in the social process, and social robots can respond accordingly to the emotional changes of interacting objects. For example, in educational scenarios, when the robot observes that the user is frustrated by answering a question incorrectly, it can provide some appropriate encouragement to increase the user's interest in participating. If the emotional expression of the interacting object is integrated into the interaction process, it is more conducive to customize the personalized interaction behavior. Emotion recognition is the intelligent recognition of human emotions, which is a multi-modal recognition that can be comprehensively recognized based on multiple levels, including facial, speech, and physiological emotion recognition. Analyze and identify human emotions through facial expressions, eye movements, and muscle movements of social objects. It is also possible to obtain semantics through the speed and intonation of people speaking, or through text analysis through NLP after speech is converted into text. The combination of the two can analyze and identify human emotions. In addition, human emotions can also be identified by analyzing the gestures and actions of human behavior, and physiological signals such as breathing, heart rate, and body temperature. The technologies used in emotion recognition are image emotion recognition and speech emotion recognition. Image emotion recognition is the analysis of facial expressions using computers. Speech emotion recognition is to extract the structural characteristics and distribution rules of the time structure, amplitude structure, fundamental frequency structure and formant structure of the tone signal, compare and analyze and fuzzy judgment, to find the most similar features of a certain basic expression. In addition, there are also methods for face recognition by combining text features and speech features [16].

The emotion recognition task suffers from lower accuracy in real-life scenarios due to its large intra-class differences and small inter-class differences. Our emotion recognition module is mainly based on image emotion recognition. We applied the VGG16 [12] as the base model and add an attention mechanism to help the model to ignore unimportant information such as hair and background when performing emotion recognition. Pay attention to eye movement, mouth shape and other information to obtain better recognition results. We hope that the robot can recognize 7 different emotions of anger, disgust, fear, happiness, neutrality, sadness and surprise, change the output of the last layer of VGG16 to 7-dimensional, and replace the previous convolutional layers with self- attention module.

2.3   Intention Prediction

Intention prediction is the key to voice interaction. Robots can only interact correctly if they predict the intention of each sentence of the user. Since Google proposed the pre-trained language representation model BERT [4] in 2018, natural language processing tasks have undergone fundamental changes, and the two-stage method of pre-training and fine-tuning has become the mainstream. The BERT network architecture is mainly based on the encoder of the deep bidirectional Transformer [14]. In the pre-training stage, it uses an unsupervised way to generate deep bidirectional language representations and automatically mine semantic knowledge; in the fine-tuning stage, the model is fine-tuned for specific downstream tasks. The two-stage process of BERT makes it easy to adapt to the task of intent recognition. We directly use BERTbase to process the input text. The number of BERTbase parameters is small, which can reduce the inference consumption of the model. We continue to use BERTbase pre-training to Extract intent-related features. At the same time, the MLM task in the BERT pre-training task has the greatest significance for intent recognition. The masking language model MLM selects random words for replacement, forcing the model to learn contextual information to predict the replaced word. We choose MLM as the pre-training target for better semantic understanding and lay the foundation for reasoning for intent classification. In order to further analyze the semantics of the input text, and to make the text intent recognition feature output consistent with other task features in dimension, we add a LSTM with two layers with 64 hidden nodes on the basis of the BERTbase output. Its output serves as the final text intent recognition feature.

2.4 Gesture Recognition

Gesture interaction is also an important interaction method. Due to the flexibility of the hand and the variety of gestures, different semantics can be set for different gestures, and interactive instructions can be given to the robot directly through gestures. In practical applications, we hope that the gesture recognition method is as fast and lightweight as possible to facilitate the deployment of applications on low-power computing devices. Therefore, we use a lightweight gesture recognition model that combines three features extracted from the skeleton sequence as the input of the model. We use Mediapipe [1] to obtain skeleton sequences of gestures, and then recognize skeleton sequences based on DD-Net [17]. We extract features from the skeleton sequence from space and time. In space, we use the joint point set distance JCD as the first feature, which calculates the Euclidean distance between each pair of joint point coordinates. The distance forms a symmetrical joint point pair distance matrix, which is calculated following Eq. (3).

$$
JCD^k = \begin{bmatrix} \left\| \overrightarrow{J_2^k J_1^k} \right\| & & \\ \vdots & \ddots & \\ \vdots & \cdots \ddots & \\ \left\| \overrightarrow{J_N^k J_1^k} \right\| & \cdots\cdots & \left\| \overrightarrow{J_N^k J_{N-1}^k} \right\| \end{bmatrix} \tag{3}
$$

where $\left\| J_i^k J_j^k \right\|$ $(i \neq j)$ resents the distance between joint points i and j.

The joint point set distance only obtains the distance relationship between the skeleton nodes. We also need to obtain the direction information between the skeleton nodes. We use the joint point direction cone JDC as the feature in the direction. It selects a node as the starting point, and then calculate each node and the direction between it one by one, the calculation method is shown in Eq. (4).

$$
JDC^k = \left(\overrightarrow{J_1^k J_2^k}, \overrightarrow{J_1^k J_3^k}, \cdots, \overrightarrow{J_1^k J_N^k} \right) \tag{4}
$$

where $\overrightarrow{J_i^k J_j^k} = \left(x_j^k - x_i^k, y_j^k - y_i^k, z_j^k - z_i^k \right)$.

Furthermore, temporally, we utilize a 1*3 convolution kernel to extract the motion features of the skeleton sequence. Obtaining these three features, we add them point by point, and then get the recognition result after multiple convolutional layers, pooling layers and fully connected layers.

3 Frame Display

In order to facilitate the demonstration of the multimodal interaction framework, we have made a concise interactive interface through which we can conduct real-time human-computer interaction. The interface is shown in Fig. 3.

Fig. 3. An interface to a multimodal perception and recognition framework

There are five areas in the figure, of which area A is the text intent prediction module, area B is the age, gender and emotion recognition module, area C is the interaction mode selection module, area D is the image display area, and area E is the interactive dialog box.

The Input button in area A can input text data, and the Scenes button can select different scenarios according to the application site of the robot. Based on the Chinese corpus, we have trained 8 consultation intentions to be processed by the consultation robot in the hospital scene, which are human-computer interaction, entry Dialysis room, printing of test sheets, temperature measurement, dialysis appointment, registration of strangers, daily chat and general instructions. Figure 4 shows our text intention prediction results:

Fig. 4. Results of text intention prediction

From Fig. 4, we can see that the intent recognition module can accurately analyze the intent contained in each sentence, thus laying the foundation for subsequent human-computer interaction functions. In the following modules, we will demonstrate the application in the hospital scene. The Model button can directly predict the intent of the text information entered in the Input. In area C, we can select an image through the Select button, and then perform age and gender prediction and emotion recognition on the image through the Age, Gender, and Emotion buttons in area B. We selected some images from the IMDB-WIKI face database [9] for testing. Figure 5 shows our test results.

Fig. 5. Results of age gender prediction and emotion recognition

From Fig. 5, we can see that the age, gender and expression of the characters in each image have been successfully predicted, and we can accurately predict whether it is male, female, old or young, whether happy or depressed. In addition, we can also conduct real-time voice interaction with the robot through the Chat button in the C area. We use Python's Pyaudio [2] toolkit to collect and process the voice. The robot will make the next interactive behavior according to the intention of each sentence we say. In addition to direct voice interaction, we can also call the camera through the Visit button in the C area to obtain the current user image, so that the corresponding interaction can be performed according to the user's identity attributes. We can also use the gesture recognition module through the Gesture button in the C area. Figure 6 shows the result of gesture recognition.

Fig. 6. The result of gesture recognition

The robot can recognize the information represented by our different gestures, and we can also set different gestures to guide the robot to complete the corresponding functions. For example, the ok gesture can express the meaning of confirmation, and when selecting the menu bar, different numbers can also be used to represent different options.

4 Conclusion

We designed a multimodal perception and cognition social robot framework that can collect information such as images, voices, gestures and other information of social users, so as to complete the interactive work according to these information, and we established a face information based on face information. The comparison system, which fuses the age and gender prediction networks, significantly reduces the amount of inference overhead needed to run the software. In the emotion recognition module, we use the attention mechanism to decrease the distances among expressions in intra-classes and increase the distances among those in inter-classes, and improve the accuracy of the model in actual operation. In the gesture recognition module, we use a lightweight model to improve the running speed of the software. In addition, we can give meanings to various specific gestures, directly instructing the robot to complete the corresponding tasks or completing the selection of various functions of the interactive interface through gestures. We can also expand more functions on the basis of this framework, so that robots can be competent for more powerful work, and robots in different scenarios can complete their social duties.

References

1. https://github.com/google/mediapipe
2. https://pypi.org/project/PyAudio
3. Chen, C., Liu, Y., Kreiss, S., Alahi, A.: Crowd-robot interaction: Crowd-aware robot navigation with attention-based deep reinforcement learning. In: 2019 International Conference on Robotics and Automation (ICRA), pp. 6015–6022 (2019). https://doi.org/10.1109/ICRA.2019.8794134
4. Devlin, J., Chang, M.W., Lee, K., Toutanova, K.: Bert: Pre-training of deep bidirectional transformers for language understanding. arXiv preprint arXiv:1810.04805 (2018)
5. Ghaffar, F.: Controlling traffic with humanoid social robot. arXiv preprint arXiv:2204.04240 (2022)
6. Krizhevsky, A., Sutskever, I., Hinton, G.E.: Imagenet classification with deep convolutional neural networks. In: Advances in Neural Information Processing Systems, vol. 25 (2012)
7. Liu, X., Li, X., Su, H., Zhao, Y., Ge, S.S.: The opening workspace control strategy of a novel manipulator-driven emission source microscopy system. ISA Trans. (2022)
8. Najibi, M., Samangouei, P., Chellappa, R., Davis, L.S.: Ssh: Single stage headless face detector, pp. 4875–4884 (2017)

9. Rothe, R., Timofte, R., Gool, L.V.: Deep expectation of real and apparent age from a single image without facial landmarks. Int. J. Comput. Vision **126**(2–4), 144–157 (2018)

10. Rothe, R., Timofte, R., Van Gool, L.: Dex: Deep expectation of apparent age from a single image. In: Proceedings of the IEEE international conference on computer vision workshops, pp. 10–15 (2015)

11. Saaybi, S., Majid, A.Y., Prasad, R.V., Koubaa, A., Verhoeven, C.: Covy: An ai-powered robot for detection of breaches in social distancing. arXiv preprint arXiv:2207.06847 (2022)

12. Simonyan, K., Zisserman, A.: Very deep convolutional networks for large-scale image recognition. arXiv preprint arXiv:1409.1556 (2014)

13. Tang, X., Du, D.K., He, Z., Liu, J.: Pyramidbox: A context-assisted single shot face detector. In: Proceedings of the European Conference on Computer Vision (ECCV), pp. 797–813 (2018)

14. Vaswani, A., et al.: Attention is all you need. In: Advances in Neural Information Processing Systems, vol. 30 (2017)

15. Wang, D., Ma, G., Liu, X.: An intelligent recognition framework of access control system with anti-spoofing function. AIMS Math. **7**(6), 10495–10512 (2022)

16. Xu, Y., Su, H., Ma, G., Liu, X.: A novel dual-modal emotion recognition algorithm with fusing hybrid features of audio signal and speech context. Complex & Intelligent Systems, pp. 1–13 (2022). https://doi.org/10.1007/s40747-022-00841-3

17. Yang, F., Wu, Y., Sakti, S., Nakamura, S.: Make skeleton-based action recognition model smaller, faster and better. In: Proceedings of the ACM multimedia asia, pp. 1–6 (2019)

18. Yang, T.Y., Huang, Y.H., Lin, Y.Y., Hsiu, P.C., Chuang, Y.Y.: Ssr-net: A compact soft stagewise regression network for age estimation. In: IJCAI. vol. 5, p. 7 (2018)

Indoor Mobile Robot Socially Concomitant Navigation System

Rui Zhang[1], Wanyue Jiang[1], Zhonghao Zhang[1], Yuhan Zheng[1], and Shuzhi Sam Ge[1,2(✉)]

[1] Institute for Future, School of Automation, Qingdao University, Qingdao, China
[2] Department of Electrical and Computer Engineering,
National University of Singapore, Singapore, Singapore
samge@nus.edu.sg

Abstract. With the progress of science and technology and the development of economy, more and more robots have entered the family and become good helpers and partners in people's daily life. As a good partner of human beings, the robot is endowed with humanized emotion and decision-making core, and has harmonious and natural social interaction ability. Among them, the socially concomitant navigation function is a very important social function. For indoor mobile robot to navigate socially with its human companions, a Single-Object Tracking deepsort(SOT deepsort)algorithm is proposed, and a fast, stable and simple socially concomitant navigation system is proposed. In order to make the robot more socialized, questionnaires are designed to investigate the comfortable distance of the robot in the process of following its companion. Endow the robot appropriate behavior when traveling with human companions, so that the robot can play the role of accompanying the pedestrian and complete the task of following the companion. Finally, the proposed system is tested on Fabo mobile robot. The experimental results show that the following accuracy of this method is high and meets the real-time requirements.

Keywords: Social robot · Socially concomitant navigation · SOT deepsort

1 Introduction

With the development of society and the progress of technology, robots are more and more involved in human life. As a fundamental task of service robots, the automatic follow-up function can be applied to many occasions. For example, in the supermarket, the automatic follow-up cart can help users load the purchased goods and free their hands. In the airport or construction site, the automatic follow-up freight car can help users carry luggage or building materials, reducing

This work was supported by the National Key Research and Development Project under Grant 2020YFB1313604.

the work difficulty of handling personnel. In the hotel, the automatic follow-up robot can place luggage for guests and improve the happiness of guests. In this case, tracking moving targets becomes crucial and widely concerned [1–5].

In the past, researchers have developed methods to track targets using various sensors. The non-visual tracking technology mainly realizes the perception of the target azimuth through ultrasonic, UWB, lidar and other sensors. Ferrer et al. [6] established a social force model (SFM) by scanning human body data and three-dimensional environment map with lidar, so that robots can follow targets side by side in crowded environment. Cifuentes et al. [7] synchronized the parameter estimation of each gait cycle for target recognition. Chung [8] et al. collated the two-dimensional laser point cloud to obtain the leg model of the pedestrian, and analyzed the movement of the pedestrian's legs to obtain the position of the target pedestrian, so as to achieve the goal of following the target pedestrian.

In visual tracking, Azrad et al. [9] used Kalman filter to estimate the relative position and attitude of the target and UAV, so that the UAV can stably follow and hover over the target. Farahi et al. [10] proposed a probabilistic Kalman filter (PKF) algorithm, which tracks objects with abnormal behavior according to the constructed probability map and solved the partial occlusion problem. Wang et al. [11] introduced the mixed Gaussian model background method on the basis of continuous adaptive mean shift to weaken the role of background tone and improve the tracking accuracy and stability. Xia et al. [12] used depth and color information to identify the target pedestrian, and then used particle filter to follow the target. Henriques et al. [13] proposed the CSK tracking algorithm, which uses the cyclic matrix to realize the dense sampling of the target image and improves the efficiency. Later, continuing this idea, Henriques et al. [14] further successfully improved the kernel correlation filter (KCF) algorithm and discriminant correlation filter (DCF) algorithm. Vasil et al. [15] used offline trained depth convolution neural network to detect targets, and the robot platform used 2D LRF to track targets. Vasil et al. [16] used multi-sensor data flow, and the control algorithm can locate and track the target object according to its shape. In addition, the robot can recognize human gesture commands. Liu [17] proposed a human tracking method based on monocular vision, which is composed of Kalman filter tracker and recognition module.

In order to realize the fast and stable following of pedestrian targets and simplify the robot system, this paper combines the differential wheel motion model, image recognition, wireless communication and other technologies, and designs a simple and feasible visual based mobile robot socially concomitant navigation system. According to the structure and motion characteristics of the robot, expression, voice and action modules are added to the robot. Based on the deepsort algorithm [18], this paper proposes a Single Object Tracking deepsort algorithm (SOT deepsort), YoloV5 and the improved deepsort algorithm are used for target recognition and tracking, the depth camera is used to measure the distance and angle. Then, the Fabo robot is quickly and real-time controlled through the LAN. The system realizes a fast, stable and simple socially concomitant navigation.

2   System Overview

The system mainly includes two sub modules: the visual detection and tracking module and the mobile robot following control module, as shown in Fig. 1. The visual detection and tracking module is composed of a Realsense depth camera and a bracket, which are used to obtain the image sequence required by the visual detection and tracking system. The following control module of the mobile robot is Fabo Android mobile platform, which is driven by two differential wheels. The external computer is the core of the system. The detection and tracking algorithm program runs on the Windows operating system of the external computer.

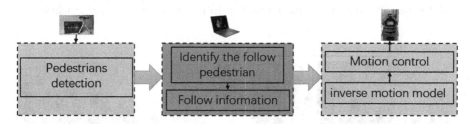

Fig. 1. Structure of the mobile robot pedestrian following system

3   Mobile Robot Socially Concomitant Navigation System

3.1   Pedestrian Target Detection

YoloV5 is used to recognize the human in the image. The SOT deepsort algorithm matches pedestrians in different frames to determine the target pedestrian, and calls the position function in the Realsense camera to calculate the direction and position information between the target pedestrian and the robot. The SOT deepsort algorithm is shown in the Fig. 2.

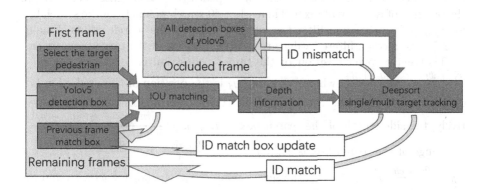

Fig. 2. SOT deepsort algorithm block diagram

In the first frame, select the target pedestrian box and the yolov5 detection box for IOU matching, and the obtained matching box is transmitted to the matching box variable of the previous frame, and then the matching box and depth information are transmitted to the deepsort tracker for single-target tracking. At this time, the ID of the target pedestrian is fed back. In the second frame, the matching box of the previous frame and the yolov5 detection box for IOU matching, and the results are transmitted to the matching box variable of the previous frame, and then the matching box and the depth information are transmitted to the deepsort tracker, Cycle the process all the time. When the target pedestrian is blocked, the ID does not match at this time. All the detection frames of yolov5 are transmitted to the deepsort tracker for multi-target tracking. Until the ID of the target pedestrian appears, the ID matching box updates the previous frame matching box to perform single-target tracking.

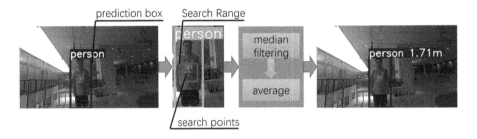

Fig. 3. Pedestrian distance solution block diagram

Since we focus on the pedestrain tracking task, the robot only needs to know the position information of the target, not the pose information of the target. Using the detected result in SOT deepsort, the relative position between the robot and the human is calculated by the image coordinates of the center point of the rectangular box representing the target. As shown in Fig. 3, in order to reduce the amount of calculation, the search box for distance information collection between the robot and the target pedestrian is calculated according to the position of the central pixel. Then select 40 search points from the search box for ranging, and median filter the effective value of the search points. Finally, average the median filtered values to get the distance of the target pedestrian.

The central pixel position of the target pedestrian is $M = (x_0, y_0), x_0 = \frac{x_r + x_l}{2}, y_0 = \frac{y_u + y_d}{2}$, where, x_l, x_r, y_u, y_d is the position of the prediction box denote the left, the right, the top, and the bottom coordinates, respectively, the side length of the search box is $a_{search} = \frac{min\{|x_r - x_l|, |y_u - y_d|\}}{2}$, the range of the search box is $x_{search} \in \left[x_0 - \frac{a_{search}}{2}, x_0 + \frac{a_{search}}{2}\right], y_{search} \in \left[y_0 - \frac{a_{search}}{2}, y_0 + \frac{a_{search}}{2}\right]$, the search point $P_{search} = (x_0 + \delta, y_0 + \delta)$, and the deviation range is $\delta \in \left[-\frac{a_{search}}{2}, \frac{a_{search}}{2}\right]$.

When one arm of a person is raised, the central pixel position will deviate from the human body, leading to the incorrect positioning of the search point. As a result, a large relative distance is wrongly generated as shown in Fig. 4a. In this paper, In order to solve this problem, the median filter is modified to the following method. The predicted distance of the pedestrian in the next frame is calculated based on the distance $d_p(t)$ and speed $v_p(t)$ of the pedestrian detected in the previous frame. Predicted distance:

$$d_p(t + \Delta t) = d_p(t) + v_p(t)\Delta t - v_r(t)\Delta t \tag{1}$$

where, $v_r(t)$ is the speed of the robot in the previous frame. Values outside the error range are removed from the data sequence. The average value of the values within the error range is taken as the final distance. Error range is $[d_p(t + \Delta t) - \varepsilon, d_p(t + \Delta t) + \varepsilon]$. The result of this method is shown in Fig. 4b.

(a) Solving distance by median filter method (b) Solving distance by predicting distance method

Fig. 4. Comparison of two distance calculation methods

After testing, the depth field of view of the depth camera is about 60 °C. The image size is 640 × 480. Denote the front direction of the robot as 0°, left range as negative, and right range as positive, the angle coordinate is illustrated in Fig. 5. Correlating the camera FOV to the image coordinates, the relative angle θ_p between the robot and the target pedestrian can be calculted. x_{image} is the picture coordinate. According to Eq. 2, the angle information of the target pedestrian can be obtained, as shown in Fig. 6. The relative angle:

$$\theta_p = 0.09375 \times x_{image} - 30 \tag{2}$$

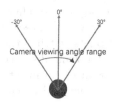  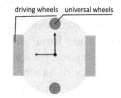

Fig. 5. Angle coordinates   **Fig. 6.** Detected pedestrian angle   **Fig. 7.** Two wheel differential model

3.2 Mobile Robot Visual Follow Control

The mobile robot has two driving wheels and two universal wheels, as shown in Fig. 7. Movements of the robot can be realized by changing the speed of the two driving wheels. The pedestrian following task is achieved by controlling the speed of the driving wheels. The speed of the left and right wheels (v_l and v_r) are calculated based on the inverse motion model:

$$\begin{bmatrix} v_r \\ v_l \end{bmatrix} = \begin{bmatrix} v_c + \dfrac{d_{wb}}{2}w \\ v_c - \dfrac{d_{wb}}{2}w \end{bmatrix} = \begin{bmatrix} 1 & \dfrac{d_{wb}}{2} \\ 1 & -\dfrac{d_{wb}}{2} \end{bmatrix} \begin{bmatrix} v_c \\ w \end{bmatrix} \tag{3}$$

where v_c is the linear velocity, w is the angular velocity, and d_{wb} is the distance between the two driving wheels.

In Eq. (3), the linear velocity and angular velocity of the robot are consistent with those of the pedestrian. The relative angle θ_p^i and distance d_p^i of the ith pedestrian in the robot's field of view. $v_c(t)$ is the linear velocity of the robot at time t. Linear velocity and angular velocity of the robot at the current time:

$$v_c = \frac{d_p^i(t + \Delta t) - d_p^i(t) + v_c(t)\Delta t}{\Delta t} \tag{4}$$

$$w = \frac{\theta_p^i(t + \Delta t) - \theta_p^i(t)}{\Delta t} \tag{5}$$

4 Robot Social Behavior

4.1 Investigation on Comfort Degree of Human Robot Distance

Table 1. Survey results of robot following distance comfort questionnaire

Question	Quantized value	Proportion
Follow distance	120 ~ 140 cm	82%
Interaction distance	100 ~ 120 cm	78%

When the robot moves to the target pedestrian, the whole process may cause discomfort to the pedestrian. The cause of discomfort may be too close, too fast, too slow, etc., which hinders people's normal travel. In this study, we recruited 50 participants from university, aged between 19 and 29. Participants watched the demonstration on site. Questionnaires were conducted on the following distance and safety distance. For the following distance, we divide 0.8 m ~ 1.6 m into four grades. For safety distance, 0.6 m ~ 1.4 m is divided into four grades. The results are shown in Table 1.

82% of the respondents think that the comfortable distance of the robot following the pedestrian is 1.2 m ~ 1.4 m. 78% of the respondents believe that the interaction distance between the robot and the pedestrian is 1.0 m ∼ 1.2 m. The following distance is greater than the interaction distance, which can not only avoid collision, but also avoid the emotional discomfort that humans may feel when observing the robot approaching its safe distance.

4.2 Expression, Voice and Action Modules

In this research, we consider adding expression, voice and action modules in the robot's following process, which can better reflect the robot's sociability. We design that when the robot's following distance is greater than the set following distance, the robot will show sweaty and tired expressions. When the following distance is within the set range, the robot will show happy expressions. When the following distance is less than the set range, the robot will show nervous expressions. When the robot walks up to a pedestrian, it will greet people and wave its wings. The following distance is far greater than the following distance, and the robot will voice to remind pedestrians to wait for it. If the following distance is less than the safe distance, the robot will voice to remind pedestrians to walk quickly or avoid it. Due to the limitation of the robot platform, we can only do some simple wing waving operations. The range of set follow distance in this paper is 1.2 m ∼ 1.4 m.

5   Experiment

5.1   Experiment Environment

The hardware system includes the mobile robot, the external computer, the depth camera, etc. The specific experimental environment parameters are shown in Table 2. Detailed parameters of Intel Realsense depth camera D415 (Fig. 8a) are shown in Table 3. In this paper, Fabo is selected as the mobile experimental platform of robot navigation system, as shown in Fig. 8b.

Table 2. Hardware experiment environment related parameters

Devices	Parameter
Mobile robot	Fabo
Depth camera	Intel Realsense depth camera D415
Robot control host	Android
External computer	Equipped with NVIDIA geforce GTX 1050 Graphic Processing Unit, Windows 10 system

Table 3. Depth camera related parameters

Feature	D415
Use Environment	Indoor/Outdoor
Image Sensor Technology	Rolling Shutter
Depth FOV (H × V)	65° × 40°
Ideal Range	0.3 m to 10 m
Connectors	USB 3.0 Type-C

5.2 Pedestrian Following Experiment

In order to illustrate the effectiveness and accuracy of the SOT deepsort algorithm proposed in this paper. Figure 9 shows the occlusion following experiment. When the target pedestrian is occluded, the algorithm switches to multi-target tracking. The target pedestrian reappears and switches to single-target tracking. The last six figures are following effects.

Figure 10 shows the emotional expression of the robot. First, the robot walks to the target pedestrian and greets him, including the expression of speech, wings waving and voice(Left 2, 3). In the process of following, the robot shows happiness. If the distance is large, the robot shows sweat and fatigue(Left 1). If the distance is short, the robot shows nervous mood(Right 1).

Since the maximum linear speed of Fabo mobile robot is only 0.4 m/s, the pedestrian target moves slowly in the experiment.

Figure 11 shows a complete experimental process in which the mobile robot follows the target pedestrian in a straight line. First, the target pedestrian stands still and waits for the mobile robot move near, then the pedestrian moves slowly. The mobile robot keeps a safe distance behind the pedestrian to follow the target. When the distance between the mobile robot and the target increases, the robot accelerates to follow. When the distance between the mobile robot and the tracked target is reduced, the robot will slow down to follow.

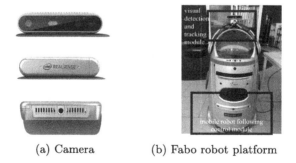

(a) Camera   (b) Fabo robot platform

Fig. 8. Hardware environment

Fig. 9. Pedestrian occlusion following experiment based on SOT deepsort

Fig. 10. Emotion expression of robot at different following distances

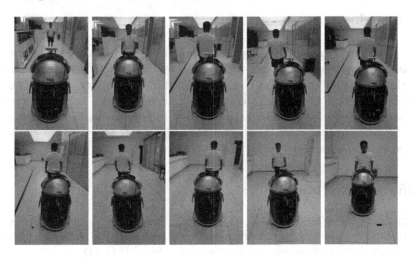

Fig. 11. Pedestrian following experiment of mobile robot

Figure 12 plots the real-time relative distance and real-time frame rate between the robot and the human during the pedestrian following process. The average frame rate is 13.18, with good real-time performance. Due to the limitation of the robot speed, the pedestrian needs to keep moving at a low speed, so the relative distance between the robot and the pedestrian fluctuates. According to the analysis of the experimental data, the distance between the robot and the target pedestrian fluctuates around 1370 mm. As can be seen from Fig. 11. Before the pedestrian starts moving, the system detection and tracking module detects the target pedestrian, and the robot quickly moves to the vicinity of the pedestrian target. The robot speed increases as their relative distance becomes larger, and decreases in the opposite case. Thus ensures pedestrian safety. When the pedestrian target stands still, the robot slows down and stops at 1000 mm.

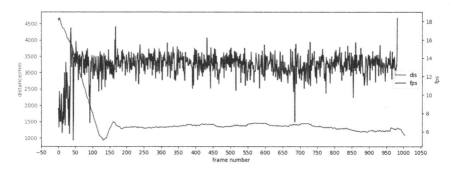

Fig. 12. The results of mobile robot pedestrian following experiments

6   Conclusion

This paper gives the robot emotion, and designs a simple and feasible system to realize the target pedestrian following of the mobile robot. The system transmitted the pedestrian distance and angle provided by the pedestrian detection and tracking module to the following control module in real time. The robot was kept at the desired distance and angle to completed the following task. Experiments on fabo mobile robot have shown that the vision tracking algorithm can follow the pedestrian accurately, stably and in real time.

References

1. Gritti, A.P.F., Tarabini, O.S., Guzzi, J.T.: Kinect-based people detection and tracking from smallfootprint ground robots. In: IEEE/RSJ International Conference on Intelligent Robots and Systems, pp. 4096–4103 (2014)
2. Wang, J.E.F., Xiao, X.Q.S.: Mobile robot integrated navigation method based on QR code vision positioning. Chinese J. Sci. Instrum. **39**(8), 230–238 (2018)

3. Su, D.F., Miro, J.V.S.: An ultrasonic/RF GP-based sensor model robotic solution for indoors/outdoors person tracking. In: 13th International Conference on Control Automation Robotics & Vision (ICARCV)2014, pp. 1662–1667 (2014)

4. Vincze, M.F., Schlemmer. M.S., Gemeiner, P.T.: Vision for robotics: A tool for model-based object tracking. IEEE Robot. Autom. Mag. **12**(4), 53–64 (2005)

5. Li, P.F., Zhang, J.Y.S., Han, G.Ch.T.: Local search tracking algorithm for LiDAR mobile robot. Electron. Measure. Technol. **41**(11), 6–9 (2018)

6. Ferrer, G.F., Zulueta, A.G.S., Cotarelo, F.H.T.: Robot social-aware navigation framework to accompany people walking side-by-side. Auto. Robots **41**(4), 775–793 (2017)

7. Cifuentes, C.A.F., Frizera, A.S., Carelli, R.T.: Human-robot interaction based on wearable IMU sensor and laser range finder. Robot. Auto. Syst. **62**(10), 1425–1439 (2014)

8. Chung, W.F., Kim, H.S., Yoo, Y.T.: The detection and following of human legs through inductive approaches for a mobile robot with a single laser range finder. IEEE Trans. Indust. Electron. **59**(8), 3156–3166 (2012)

9. Azrad, S.F., Kendoul, F.S., Nonami, K.T.: Visual servoing of quadrotor micro-air vehicle using color-based tracking algorithm. J. Syst. Design Dyn. **4**(2), 255–268 (2010)

10. Farahi, F.F., Yazdi, H.S.S.: Probabilistic Kalman filter for moving object tracking. Signal Processing: Image Commun. https://doi.org/10.1016/j.image.2019.115751 (2020)

11. Wang, X.D.F., Wang, Y.W.S., Wang, H.T.: Continuously adaptive mean-shift tracking algorithm with suppressed background histogram model. J. Electron. Inform. Technol. **41**(6), 1480–1487 (2019)

12. Xia, K.F.F., Li, P.F.S., Chen, X.P.T.: People tracking of mobile robot using improved particle filter. J. Front. Comput. Sci. Technol. **11**(11), 1849–1859 (2017)

13. Henriques, J.F., Caseiro, R., Martins, P., Batista, J.: Exploiting the circulant structure of tracking-by-detection with kernels. In: Fitzgibbon, A., Lazebnik, S., Perona, P., Sato, Y., Schmid, C. (eds.) ECCV 2012. LNCS, vol. 7575, pp. 702–715. Springer, Heidelberg (2012). https://doi.org/10.1007/978-3-642-33765-9_50

14. Henriques, J.F.F., Caseiro, R.S., Martins, P.T.: High-speed tracking with kernelized correlation filters. IEEE Trans. Pattern Anal. Mach. Intell. **37**(3), 583–596 (2015)

15. Vasil, L.P., F.Sevil, A.A.S., Andon, V.T.T.: Development of Mobile Robot Target Recognition and Following Behaviour Using Deep Convolutional Neural Network and 2D Range Data. IFAC-PapersOnLine **51**(30), 210–215 (2018)

16. Vasil, L.P.F., Nikola, G.S.S., Andon, V.T.T.: Detection and Following of Moving Target by an Indoor Mobile Robot using Multi-sensor Information. IFAC-PapersOnLine **39**(8), 357–362 (2021)

17. Liu, J.H.F., Chen, X.Y.S., Wang, C.Q.T.: A person-following method based on monocular camera for quadruped robots. Biomimetic Intell. Robot. **2**(3), 2667–3797 (2022)

18. Wojke, N.F., Bewley, A.S., Paulus, D.T.: Simple online and realtime tracking with a deep association metric. In: 2017 IEEE International Conference on Image Processing (ICIP), pp. 3645–3649 (2017)

NRTIRL Based NN-RRT* Path Planner in Human-Robot Interaction Environment

Yao Wang, Yuqi Kong, Zhiyu Ding, Wenzheng Chi$^{(\boxtimes)}$, and Lining Sun

Robotics and Microsystems Center, School of Mechanical and Electric Engineering,
Soochow University, Suzhou 215021, China
{ywang,yqkong,zyding,wzchi,lnsun}@suda.edu.cn

Abstract. In human-robot interaction environment, it is of great significance for mobile robots to have the awareness of social rules, to realize the socialization and anthropomorphism of robot navigation behavior, and enhance the scene adaptation ability of socialized navigation. Learning from Demonstration (LfD) can obtain an optimized robot trajectory by learning the expert path. Inspired by the LfD method, we propose a new navigation method to learn navigation behaviors form demonstration paths of experts by Neural Network Rapidly-exploring Random Trees (NN-RRT*) planner in the human-robot interaction environment. First, we propose a new NN-RRT* planner to generate paths. Next, the features of demonstration paths and planned paths are extracted for Inverse Reinforcement Learning (IRL) process. The cost function of the path planner is updated. Finally, a new NN-RRT* that can adapt to the complex human-robot interaction environment is obtained. The experimental results show that comparing with the state-of-the-art methods, the path generated by the new navigation method has a higher degree of anthropomorphism and is suitable for navigation in a complex human-robot interaction environment.

Keywords: Robot navigation · NN-RRT* · IRL

1 Introduction

Nowadays, mobile robots are increasingly common in our daily life. In the social environment, how to reasonably coexist with humans has become an urgent problem for mobile robots. The navigation behaviors without social consciousness bring many troubles to pedestrians. The robot lacking social awareness interrupts human behaviors frequently. Most of the traditional navigation planning methods regard pedestrians as dynamic obstacles, and use the path planning algorithm of dynamic obstacle avoidance to complete autonomous navigation. The planned paths lack social awareness and do not take into account the psychological comfort of users during the interaction process. Therefore, it is of great significance to design a social adaptive navigation method for mobile robot navigation.

In order to solve the existing problems of autonomous navigation of mobile robots, many scholars have introduced Proxemics [1] into navigation, taking the

F. Cavallo et al. (Eds.): ICSR 2022, LNAI 13817, pp. 496–508, 2022.
https://doi.org/10.1007/978-3-031-24667-8_44

distance from pedestrians as an important consideration in path planning. Pérez-Higueras [2] proposed a method for learning a cost function from demonstration paths (RTIRL), which combines inverse reinforcement learning and Rapidly-exploring Random Trees to learn the weights of the cost function for the planning of robot navigation. It makes the robot have social awareness, and its planned path is similar to the demonstration path generated by human, i.e., it is more anthropomorphic.

When the cost function of the path planner is updated, a linear model is adopted. However, in the actual environment, we usually consider the interaction between these features comprehensively, and the impact of these features on the cost may be nonlinear. Therefore, the results obtained by using a linear model may be inaccurate. In this paper, a nonlinear navigation social rule model method is proposed, which systematically analyzes the complex influence of various pedestrian feature attributes on their movement patterns, replacing the relatively simple linear model method.

1.1 Related Work

In the past few years, more and more scholars have focused their attention on the comfort of pedestrians during human-robot interaction. Chi et al. [3] proposed a pedestrian comfort function model and a Comfort and Collision Risk (CCR) map. By combing the CCR graph and Risk-based Rapidly exploring Random Tree (Risk-RRT), a human-friendly robot navigation algorithm was proposed. Ratsamee et al. [4] proposed a modified social force model based on estimated human motion and facial pose, enabling robots to perform human-like navigation by avoiding face-to-face confrontation. Truong [5] proposed an effective proactive social motion model (PSMM), which comprehensively considered the information of human-robot interaction, and then made the designed navigation framework to make the robot more anthropomorphic when planning the path. Hoang et al. [6] proposed a social timed elastic band (STEB)-based navigation framework based on motion dynamics constraints and social rules, which can safely avoid pedestrians during navigation.

In addition, many scholars have conducted in-depth research on how to dynamically avoid pedestrians during navigation. Chen [7] proposed a navigation framework that can identify pedestrian movement patterns and generate local optimal trajectories to protect pedestrian safety. Chen et al. [8] proposed a multiagent collision avoidance algorithm based on deep reforcement learning. Li [9] proposed the Guided Dynamic Window Approach (GDWA) navigation algorithm to guide the robot to move towards the feasible region of the local target.

In recent years, much progress has been made in solving navigation problems in human-robot integration scenarios based on LfD [10]. LfD can introduce more features in the path planning process, and the diversity of features enables the excellent performance of the robot to be generalized to multiple scenarios [11]. Kollmitz et al. [12] proposed to allow the volunteer to physically interact with the robot under navigation through IRL, thereby enabling the robot to adapt to the volunteer's personal preferences. Ratliff [13] extended the Maximum Margin Planning (MMP) framework to learn nonlinear cost functions, and experiments show that the new framework can perform nonlinear optimization more efficiently. Brys *et al.* [14] compares the respective advantages and limitations of RL and LfD, and proposes a reward shaping-based approach with higher robustness. As one of the LfD methods, IRL [15] directly applies the cost function learned from the demonstration path to the specific path planning algorithm, which is more robust to environmental changes. Imani [16] proposed Bayesian Inverse Reinforcement Learning (BIRL) based on Q-Learning, which effectively estimated the parameters of the cost function. Konar [17] proposed a risk-based interaction feature based on the IRL framework. Pérez-Higueras *et al.* [2, 18–20] proposed a set of features that can represent the pedestrian state and combined these features with RRT* [21] planner. Through Inverse Reinforcement Learning process, a feature model that can adapt to the complex human-robot interaction environment is obtained. Ding [22] proposed the Penalty based Rapidly-exploring Random Trees Inverse Reinforcement Learning (PRTIRL) algorithm framework and derived a socially adaptive feature model for mobile robots to navigate in a human-robot interaction environment.

1.2   The Proposed System and Approach

This paper proposes a new algorithm framework, an NN-RRT* based Inverse Reinforcement Learning (NRTIRL), and applies it to autonomous robot navigation tasks. In this paper, we propose a cost function based on neural network and combine the cost function with IRL to make the robot navigation more anthropomorphic. The datasets for this experiment are different demonstration paths which volunteers generate on the Rviz simulation platform through control robot with the handle. Through the NRTIRL framework we realize the back-propagation of the neural network, and the neural network is optimized. Our work contributions are summarized as follows:

- A cost function based on neural network;
- An NN-RRT* planner for complex human-robot interaction environments;
- An NRTIRL based social adaptive path planning framework for mobile robots.

The rest of the paper is organized as follows: Section 2 introduces the design of NN-RRT* and the construction of NRTIRL. The dataset collection and experimental results are reported in Sect. 3. We further discuss the results and the proposed system, and draw some conclusions at the end of this paper in Sect. 4.

2   Methods

2.1   NN-RRT* Planner

RRT* [23] planner can quickly find the initial path, and then continue to optimize with the increase of sampling nodes until the target point is found. The optimization process is the reconnection of the new node.

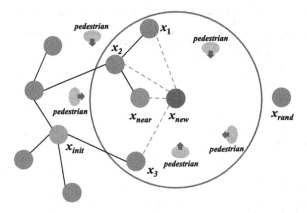

Fig. 1. The reconnection process of the new node.

As shown in Fig. 1, the planner first samples from the map and obtains the node x_{rand}. After the nearest node $x_{nearest}$ to the x_{rand} is found on the tree, a new node x_{new} can be generated by the $x_{nearest}$ and the x_{rand}. If x_{new} is free from the collision detection, a group of candidate nodes will be obtained within a certain range. Among them, the new node x_{new} can select a node which can make the cost of it smallest as the parent node x_{parent}. And then, the new node x_{new} also can be selected by other nodes within the certain range as the parent node.

The node cost in RRT* only considers the distance between the nodes on the tree. Based on RRT*, five features are selected to represent the state of the node in the human-robot interaction environment. Considering the complexity of the social model and the interaction between the five features, we replace the original linear function with a neural network which can approximately represent any function. And then, we propose the new NN-RRT* path planner. The pseudo code of NN-RRT* is shown in Algorithm 1. In line 10 of the Algorithm 1, the cost of C_{min} is added by the cost of $x_{nearest}$ and the incremental cost (IncCost) of the nearest node to the new node. The cost of $x_{nearest}$ is the output value of the neural network when we take the features of the node as input. The IncCost of the nearest node to the new node is calculated by $C_{\Omega}(nearest)$ and $C_{\Omega}(new)$.

$$\text{IncCost}_{\Omega}(nearest, new) = \frac{C_{\Omega}(nearest) + C_{\Omega}(new)}{2}$$
$$* \, distance(nearest, new)$$
(1)

To represent the state of the node on the NN-RRT* tree in the human-robot interaction environment, we adopt a feature vector F. The architecture of the neural network is shown in Fig. 2.

- f_1 represents the Euclidean distance from the point to the target point.
- f_2 represents the normalized Euclidean distance from the point to the nearest obstacle.

Algorithm 1: NN-RRT*

Input: Start, Goal, Map and Neural Network Ω
Output: The NN-RRT* $Tree = (V, E)$
1   $V \leftarrow \{x_{init}\}$; $E \leftarrow \emptyset$;
2   **for** $i = 1,...,n$ **do**
3     $x_{rand} \leftarrow$ Sample;
4     $x_{nearest} \leftarrow$ Nearest$(Tree = (V, E), x_{rand})$;
5     $x_{new} \leftarrow$ Steer$(x_{nearest}, x_{rand})$;
6   **if** $ObstcalFree(x_{new})$ **then**
7       $X_{near} \leftarrow$ Near$(Tree = (V, E), x_{new}, r)$;
8       $V \leftarrow V \cup \{x_{new}\}$;
9       $x_{min} \leftarrow x_{nearest}$;
10      $c_{min} \leftarrow C_\Omega(x_{nearest}) + \text{IncCost}_\Omega(x_{nearest}, x_{new})$;
11   **if** $CollisionFree(x_{new}, x_{near})$ **then**
12   **for** $x_{near} \in X_{near}$ **do**
13   **if** $C_\Omega(x_{near}) + \text{IncCost}_\Omega(x_{near}, x_{new}) < c_{min}$ **then**
14            $x_{min} \leftarrow x_{near}$;
15            $c_{min} \leftarrow C_\Omega(x_{near}) + \text{IncCost}_\Omega(x_{near}, x_{new})$;
16   **end**
17   **end**
18        $E \leftarrow E \cup \{(x_{min}, x_{new})\}$;
19   **for** $x_{near} \in X_{near}$ **do**
20   **if** $C_\Omega(x_{new}) + \text{IncCost}_\Omega(x_{new}, x_{near}) < C_\Omega(x_{near})$ **then**
21            $x_{parent} \leftarrow$ SetParent(x_{near});
22            $E \leftarrow (E \setminus \{(x_{parent}, x_{near})\}) \cup \{(x_{new}, x_{near})\}$;
23   **end**
24   **end**
25   **end**
26   **end**
27 **end**
28 **return** $Tree = (V, E)$

- f_{3-5} represent the cost related to the pedestrian. The cost function is defined by the Gaussian function, which is divided into three directions: front, back, and right of the pedestrian, respectively.

These features form a set of feature vectors, and the feature vector F(x) is used as input of the NN, and the output is used as the cost of the NN-RRT* planner at the current node.

$$C_{NN-RRT^*}(x) = f(\sum_{i=1}^{n} w_i x_i - b) \tag{2}$$

When the cost is smaller, it means that the current state is more ideal, and based on this, the parent node with the smallest cost is selected for this node from the candidate parent nodes.

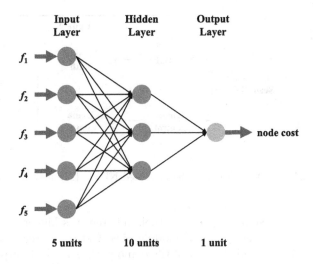

Fig. 2. The proposed neural network architecture.

Next, according to the reward function, the cost function in the path planning process is designed. There are mainly two cost functions in the motion planning algorithm based on random sampling. $C_1(x)$ is the cost function of sampling points on the random tree growth process, and $C_2(\sigma)$ is the cost function of the trajectory on the random tree:

$$C_1(x) = \hat{C}_1(x) + C_{NN-RRT*}(x) \tag{3}$$

$$C_2(\sigma) = \hat{C}_1(\sigma) + \sum_{j=1}^{M} C_{NN-RRT*}(x) \tag{4}$$

Among them, σ represents the trajectory on the random tree, $\hat{C}_1(x)$ and $\hat{C}_2(\sigma)$ represent the original cost function in the motion planning algorithm based on random sampling, and M represents the number of nodes on the trajectory.

We train our neural network through IRL, so that the network can better discriminate the ideal state of the robot and make planned paths and demonstration paths more similar.

2.2   NRTIRL Framework

Based on the above NN-RRT* planner, we propose the NRTIRL framework, as shown in Fig. 3. When constructing a demonstration path, we take information of map, pedestrian, start point and target point as prior information, and volunteers are asked to generate demonstration paths by controlling the robot with a remote control handle.

The planned paths are generated by NN-RRT* planner. We extract the feature vectors of demo and plan paths, and then input them into the neural network

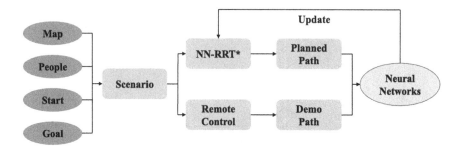

Fig. 3. Description of the proposed NRTIRL framework.

to obtain their corresponding cost. If their difference is higher than allowable error, we input them into the IRL module. The feature vector of the planned path is used as input, and the cost of the demo path is used as output of neural network. When the feature difference between demo and plan paths is lower than the allowable error we set, the training stops. At this time, the features of demo and plan paths tend to be consistent, and the trajectories of them are more similar. After the whole training process is over, we can get a new NN-RRT* planner that adapts to the dynamic and complex human-robot interaction environment. The description of the proposed NRTIRL framework is shown in Fig. 3.

In this work, LfD method is proposed to introduce more features in the path planning process to make path planner have social awareness. We propose NRTIRL framework to optimize NN-RRT* planner. The pseudo code of the NRTIRL is shown in Algorithm 2. During the training process, the social adaptive feature model derived from PRTIRL is used for pre-training. In the IRL module, the demonstration paths are used as input, and the output is neural network. For different human-robot interaction scenarios, the path generated by the NN-RRT* planner can be represented by two sets of features, the global features F_L and local feature F_{NH}. On this basis, the non-homotopic path is penalized, and finally a set of feature vectors that can represent the planned path is obtained. With the features of demo and plan paths, the difference of them can be calculated. We optimize the neural network until the difference of demo and plan paths is lower than our allowable error. When the parameters of the neural network converge, the new NN-RRT* planner can generate more anthropomorphic paths.

3   Experiments

In this work, we carry out simulations based on the Robot Operating System (ROS) with Ubuntu 16.04 on a laptop equipped with Intel i7-11800H CPU @2.3 GHz and 16 GB of RAM. The robot is equipped with a 360-degree lidar to collect the information, such as obstacles and surrounding pedestrians.

Algorithm 2: NRTIRL

Input: Demo paths $D = \{\zeta_{D1}, ..., \zeta_{DS}\}$ from S scenarios
Output: Neural Network $\Omega = [w_1, ..., w_m, b_1, ..., b_n]$

1 $\Omega \leftarrow$ Pre-training(W_{PRTIRL})
2 **while** Ω *not converge* **do**
3   **for** $s \in S$ **do**
4   **for** *repetitions* **do**
5              $\zeta_{pi} \leftarrow$ NN-RRT*(s,w,b)
6              $F_L \leftarrow$ LocalFeature(ζ_{pi})
7              $F_{NH} \leftarrow$ GlobalFeature(ζ_{pi}, ζ_{DS})
8              $f(\zeta_{pi}) \leftarrow$ Penalty($f(\zeta_{pi}), F_L, F_{NH}$)
9   **end**
10         $\bar{f}^s_{NN-RRT^*} \leftarrow \left(\sum_{i=1}^{repetitions} f(\zeta_{pi})/repetitions \right)$
11   **end**
12     $\bar{f}_{NN-RRT^*} \leftarrow \left(\sum_{i=1}^{S} \bar{f}^i_{NN-RRT^*} \right)/S$
13   error $\leftarrow \Omega\left(\bar{f}_{NN-RRT^*}\right) - \Omega\left(\bar{f}_D\right)$
14     $\Omega \leftarrow$ Update(*error*)
15 **end**
16 **return** Ω

3.1 Dataset Collection

Data collection process can be roughly divided into three steps. Firstly, we draw a static map and publish it to RVIZ simulation platform for visualization. Secondly, we set the start point and target point, and then visualize the robot in the map. Finally, the volunteers are asked to remotely control the robot through the handle to generate the demonstration path. In the RVIZ simulation platform, we configure a lidar for the robot to obtain information about the surrounding environment. While the volunteers control the robot to walk out of the demonstration path, the rosbag tool is used to record the environmental information of the robot at each time stamp, such as the start point, target point, obstacles, and surrounding pedestrians. The packaged dataset is used for the IRL module. We finally designed 25 human-robot interaction scenarios. The data set is divided into two parts: training set and validation set. Among the 25 scenarios, 15 scenarios are used as training set and 10 scenarios are used as validation set.

3.2 Experimental Metrics

We set a group of metrics to evaluate the path planners from three aspects: dissimilarity, feature difference and homotopic rate.

1) The dissimilarity between planned paths and demonstration paths: The dissimilarity is numerically approximately equal to the area of the enclosed area composed of two paths (demonstration path and planned path) with the same start point and target point calculated according to the Riemann

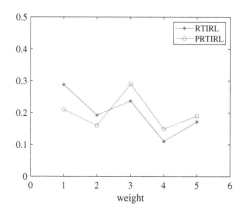

Fig. 4. Weights of RTIRL and PRTIRL.

integral. The smaller the dissimilarity between the paths, the closer the planned path is to the demonstration path.

2) The difference of features between planned paths and demonstration paths: The difference is numerically equal to the absolute value of the difference of the corresponding features of the planned path and the demonstration path. The smaller the difference between the two paths, the closer the planned path is to the demonstration path.

3) The homotopic rate of the planned path with respect to the demonstration path: For two paths with the same start point and target point, if one trajectory can be smoothly deformed into the other without colliding with obstacles, then call these two paths are homotopic [24]. The higher the homotopic rate, the smaller the difference between the two paths, and the closer the planned path is to the demonstration path.

3.3   Comparative Results

In this section we compare the navigation effects of NRTIRL, RTIRL and PRTIRL. Firstly, we train RTIRL and PRTIRL to obtain the corresponding linear weights, as shown in the Fig. 4. Secondly, we train NRTIRL to get trained neural networks weights. Finally, with the above three evaluation indicators, the comparative experiments have been carried out with the three methods based on the same validation set.

In order to make the experimental results more reliable, we conducted experiments on the training set and the validation set, as shown in Fig. 5 and Fig. 6.

On the training set, the homotopic rate of RTIRL is 73.3%, the rate of PRTIRL is 80% and the rate of NRTIRL is 86.7%. On the validation set, the homotopic rates of RTIRL and PRTIRL are both 70% and the homotopic rate of NRTIRL is 90%. The experimental result indicates that paths planned by NRTIRL are more anthropomorphic.

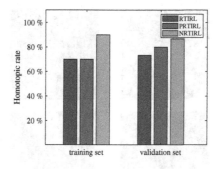

Fig. 5. The homotopic rate of RTIRL, PRTIRL and NRTIRL.

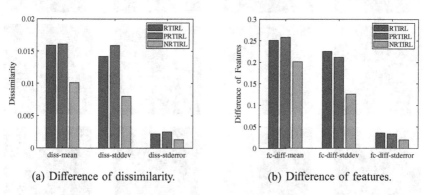

(a) Difference of dissimilarity.

(b) Difference of features.

Fig. 6. Difference of dissimilarity and features among RTIRL, PRTIRL and NRTIRL.

As shown in Fig. 7(a) and Fig. 7(b), in terms of mean dissimilarity and mean feature difference, NRTIRL is the lowest among the three, which indicates that the paths generated by the NN-RRT* planner are more similar to demonstration paths. In the aspect of standard deviation of both dissimilarity and feature difference, the value of NRTIRL is less than others, which indicates that the paths generated by NN-RRT* are more similar to each other. In the filed of standard error, the value of NRTIRL is also the lowest among the three, which reflects that the sample can represent the scenarios we set better.

In response to the above non-homotopic phenomenons, we selecte four scenarios with large differences for comparative analysis: The paths in the first line of Fig. 7 are generated by RTIRL. The paths in the second line of Fig. 7 are generated by PRTIRL. The paths in the third line of Fig. 7 are generated by NRTIRL. The paths in the fourth line of Fig. 7 are the demonstration paths generated by volunteers.

As shown in Fig. 7(a)–(d), the path planner of RTIRL are more biased toward the target attraction factor. As shown in Fig. 7(e)–(h), the path planner of PRTIRL are more biased toward the socially adaptive factor. As shown in Fig. 7(i)–(l), the path planner of NRTIRL which takes both target attraction

506   Y. Wang et al.

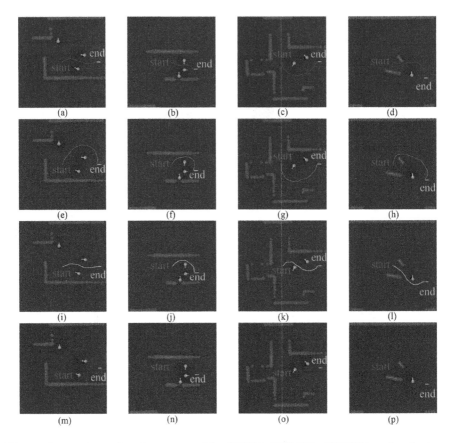

Fig. 7. Comparison of paths generated by RTIRL, PRTIRL, NRTIRL and volunteers in four scenarios.

factor and socially adaptive factor into consideration. The paths generated by NRTIRL are more similar to the demonatraion paths.

In Scenario 1, the path generated by PRTIRL is longer than demonstration path. The path planner of PRTIRL considers the factor of socially adaption than other factors in navigation. In Scenario 2, the length of path generated by RTIRL is shorter than that of demonstration path. However, the path planner of RTIRL invades the social space of pedestrians. In Scenario 3, the path generated by NRTIRL is more similar to the demonstration path, comparing with the paths generated by RTIRL and PRTIRL. In Scenario 4, the path generated by NRTIRL is shorter than the paths generated by RTIRL and PRTIRL, and the planner of NRTIRL consider the social space of pedestrians.

In summary, the navigation effect of NRTIRL is better than that of RTIRL and PRTIRL in the human-robot interaction environment.

4   Conclusion

In this paper, we have proposed an NN-RRT* path planner for the robot to generate the path in the human-robot interaction environment. An NRTIRL based learning framework has been proposed for NN-RRT* path planner to learn from the demonstration paths. After the learning process, the path planner that can adapt to the complex human-robot interaction environment has been obtained. Verified in different scenarios, the new path planner can generate the socially adaptive path, and the path generated has been confirmed more similar to the demonstration path. The experimental studies have also revealed that the path planner obtained from NRTIRL framework can guide the robot to generate the anthropomorphic path in the human-robot interaction environment.

References

1. Hall, E.T.: Proxemics. Curr. Anthropol. **9**, 83–108 (1968)
2. Pérez-Higueras, N., Caballero, F., Merino, L.: Teaching robot navigation behaviors to optimal RRT planners. Int. J. Soc. Robot. **10**, 235–249 (2018)
3. Chi, W., Kono, H., Tamura, Y., Yamashita, A., Meng, Q.H.: A human-friendly robot navigation algorithm using the risk-RRT approach. In: 2016 IEEE International Conference on Real-time Computing and Robotics (RCAR), pp. 227–232 (2016)
4. Ratsamee, P., Mae, Y., Ohara, K., Takubo, T., Arai, T.: Modified social force model with face pose for human collision avoidance. In: 2012 7th ACM/IEEE International Conference on Human-Robot Interaction (HRI), pp. 215–216 (2012)
5. Truong, X.T., Ngo, T.D.: Toward socially aware robot navigation in dynamic and crowded environments: a proactive social motion model. IEEE Trans. Autom. Sci. Eng. **14**, 1–18 (2017)
6. Hoang, V.B., Nguyen, V.H., Nguyen, L.A., Quang, T.D., Truong, X.T.: Social constraints-based socially aware navigation framework for mobile service robots. In: 2020 7th NAFOSTED Conference on Information and Computer Science (NICS), pp. 84–89 (2020)
7. Chen, Y., Lou, Y.: A unified multiple-motion-mode framework for socially compliant navigation in dense crowds. IEEE Trans. Autom. Sci. Eng., 1–13 (2021)
8. Chen, Y.F., Liu, M., Everett, M., How, J.P.: Decentralized non-communicating multiagent collision avoidance with deep reinforcement learning. In: 2017 IEEE International Conference on Robotics and Automation (ICRA), pp. 285–292 (2017)
9. Li, G., Wu, Y., Wei, W.: Guided dynamic window approach to collision avoidance in troublesome scenarios. In: 2008 7th World Congress on Intelligent Control and Automation, pp. 5759–5763 (2008)
10. Argall, B.D., Chernova, S., Veloso, M., Browning, B.: A survey of robot learning from demonstration. Rob. Auton. Syst. **57**(5), 469–483 (2009)
11. Silver, D., Bagnell, J.A., Stentz, A.: Learning from demonstration for autonomous navigation in complex unstructured terrain. Int. J. Rob. Res. **29**, 1569–1592 (2010)
12. Kollmitz, M., Koller, T., Boedecker, J., Burgard, W.: Learning human-aware robot navigation from physical interaction via inverse reinforcement learning. In: 2020 IEEE/RSJ International Conference on Intelligent Robots and Systems (IROS), pp. 11025–11031 (2020)

13. Ratliff, N.D., Silver, D., Bagnell, J.A.: Learning to search: Functional gradient techniques for imitation learning. Auton. Rob. **27**, 25–53 (2009)

14. Brys, T., Harutyunyan, A., Suay, H.B., Chernova, S., Taylor, M.E., Nowé, A.: Reinforcement learning from demonstration through shaping. In: Proceedings of the 24th International Conference on Artificial Intelligence, pp. 3352–3358 (2015)

15. Ng, A.Y., Russell, S.J.: Algorithms for inverse reinforcement learning. In: Proceedings of the Seventeenth International Conference on Machine Learning, pp. 663–670 (2000)

16. Imani, M., Braga-Neto, U.: Control of gene regulatory networks using Bayesian inverse reinforcement learning. IEEE/ACM Trans. Comput. Biol. Bioinf. **16**, 1250–1261 (2018)

17. Konar, A., Baghi, B.H., Dudek, G.: Learning goal conditioned socially compliant navigation from demonstration using risk-based features. IEEE Rob. Autom. Lett. **6**, 651–658 (2021)

18. Pérez-Higueras, N., Ramón-Vigo, R., Caballero, F., Merino, L.: Robot local navigation with learned social cost functions. In: 2014 11th International Conference on Informatics in Control, Automation and Robotics (ICINCO), pp,618–625 (2014)

19. Pérez-Higueras, N., Caballero, F., Merino, L.: Learning robot navigation behaviors by demonstration using a RRT* planner. In: International Conference on Social Robotics, pp. 1–10 (2016)

20. Ramon-Vigo, R., Perez-Higueras, N., Caballero, F., Merino, L.: Analyzing the relevance of features for a social navigation task. In: Robot 2015: Second Iberian Robotics Conference, pp. 235–246 (2016)

21. Liu, X., Li, X., Su, H., Zhao, Y., Ge, S.S.: The opening workspace control strategy of a novel manipulator-driven emission source microscopy system. ISA Trans. (2022)

22. Ding, Z., Chi, W., Wang, J., Chen, G., Sun, L.: PRTIRL based socially adaptive path planning for mobile robots. Int. J. Soc. Rob. (2022)

23. Karaman, S., Frazzoli, E.: Sampling-based algorithms for optimal motion planning. Int. J. Rob. Res. **30**, 846–894 (2011)

24. Bhattacharya, S., Kumar, V., Likhachev, M.: Search-based path planning with homotopy class constraints. In: Symposium on Combinatorial Search, pp. 1230–1237 (2010)

Special Session 2: Adaptive Behavioral Models of Robotic Systems Based on Brain-Inspired AI Cognitive Architectures

Can I Feel You? Recognizing Human's Emotions During Human-Robot Interaction

Laura Fiorini[1,2](✉), Federica G. C. Loizzo[2], Grazia D'Onofrio[3],
Alessandra Sorrentino[1], Filomena Ciccone[3], Sergio Russo[4], Francesco Giuliani[4],
Daniele Sancarlo[5], and Filippo Cavallo[1,2]

[1] Department of Industrial Engineering, University of Florence, 50139 Florence, Italy
laura.fiorini@unifi.it
[2] BioRobotics Institute, Scuola Superiore Sant'Anna, 56025 Pontedera, PI, Italy
federica.loizzo@santannapisa.it
[3] Clinical Psychology Service, Health Department, IRCCSFondazione Casa Sollievo della
Sofferenza, 71013, San Giovanni Rotondo, Foggia, Italy
{g.donofrio, f.ciccone}@operapadrepio.it
[4] Innovation and Research Unit, IRCCSFondazione Casa Sollievo della Sofferenza, 71013,
San Giovanni Rotondo, Foggia, Italy
{s.russo, f.giuliani}@operapadrepio.it
[5] Geriatrics Unit, Department of Medical Sciences, IRCCSFondazione Casa Sollievo della
Sofferenza, 71013, San Giovanni Rotondo, Foggia, Italy
d.sancarlo@operapadrepio.it

Abstract. Assistive social robots are becoming increasingly important in our daily life. In this context, humans expect to be able to interact with them using the same mental rules applied to human-human communication, including the use of non-verbal channels. Therefore, over the last years, research efforts have been devoted to develop behavioral models for robots that can perceive the user state and properly plan a reaction. In this context, this paper presents a study where 30 healthy subjects were requested to interact with the Pepper robot that elicited three emotions (i.e. positive, negative, and neutral) using a set of 60 images, retrieved from a standardized database. The paper aimed to assess the robot's performance in the recognition of emotion and to analyze the role of the robot's behavior (coherent and incoherent) using three supervised machine learning, namely Support Vector Machine, Random Forest, and K-Nearest Neighbor. The results underline a good recognition rate (accuracy higher than 0.85 with the best classifiers), suggesting that the use of multimodal communication channels improves the recognition of the user's emotional state.

Keywords: Social robotics · Emotion recognition · Human-robot interaction

1 Introduction

The field of assistive social robotics has significantly matured in the last thirty years, moving from addressing robots that assist people with physical disabilities to connect multi-robots systems that provide complex services through physical and cognitive cooperation

F. Cavallo et al. (Eds.): ICSR 2022, LNAI 13817, pp. 511–521, 2022.
https://doi.org/10.1007/978-3-031-24667-8_45

in different environments. In this regard, the design of robots was based on the implementation of capabilities for human-robot interaction in unstructured and unprotected environments, which included psychological and social aspects for intimate interaction and consequently to anthropomorphic characteristics [1]. In this context, Human-Robot Interaction (HRI) is becoming increasingly important. When interacting with a robot, especially a humanoid robot, we expect to use the same mental structure and social rules that guide us in human-human communication, expecting empathetic interaction since social robots may be perceived as social actors [2]. In this sense, the design of a reliable and affordable social robot is composed of two essential parts. Firstly, it is devoted to design and implement the robot's congruent emotional behavior; this behavior could be implemented by using verbal and non-verbal cues, such as voice tone, body posture, gesture, and gaze. Secondly, it is inherent to the user's emotional response to these behaviors [3] to fine-tune the robot's reaction feedback and close the loop (Fig. 1). Over the last years, several research groups have focused their efforts on the development of sensing and perceptual robots' abilities to detect emotion, action, and other social cues, based on artificial intelligent techniques (e.g. machine learning, deep learning, and reinforcement learning) [4]. As for the verbal cues, research is devoted to design and to develop a Speech-To-Text module and advanced tools to analyse the content of sentences as well as the tones and prosody of users' voices [5]. The robot's ability to perceive and recognize non-verbal cues such as facial expressions, body gestures, poses and gaze plays a key role in the development of a robotic agent capable of performing meaningful interactions [6]. Namely, non-verbal cues represent spontaneous expressions of the user's thoughts and emotions.

In this context, the aim of this paper is two-fold. First, since related literature studies employed non-standard elicitation modality, it aims to assess the accuracy of the proposed emotion recognition system using a standard emotion dataset, namely the International Affective Picture System (IAPS). Second, this work aims to investigate the role of robot non-verbal coherent and incoherent behaviors in the robot perception of user's emotions and, consequently, of their recognition.

2   Emotion and Assistive Social Robotics

2.1   USEr's Emotion Detection in Social Assistive Robotics

The capability of inferring and interpreting emotions plays a key role in establishing intuitive and engaging human-robot interactions [7]. On one side, a robot endowed with emotion recognition skills could adapt its behavior based on the detected user emotion. On the other side, a robot expressing recognizable emotions positively influences the evaluation of the robot's capabilities [8]. Regarding the first point, the models proposed for describing emotions rely on two main categories [7]: categorical, which treat emotions as discrete entities (e.g. Ekman model [9]), and dimensional models, which describe emotions in a continuous form (e.g. Russell's theory [10]). Besides the chosen model, the emotional state of the user is commonly assessed by detecting specific behaviors from the sensory equipment mounted on the robot. As described in our previous review [11], the visual modality is the most adopted one, since it permits the detection of non-verbal behaviors which are representative of the emotional state of the user, i.e. facial expressions, body posture, movements, and gestures. Other studies have used wearable sensors to capture changes in physiological parameters (e.g. galvanic skin responses, heart rate, breathing rate). Several classification methods have been proposed to learn the mapping between the detected behavior and the annotated emotion, mostly adopting machine- and deep-learning approaches. A complete overview is also reported in [7].

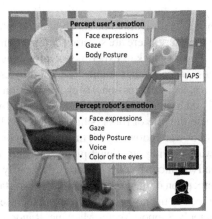

Fig. 1. Participant is interacting with Pepper robot.

2.2 Express Emotions in Assistive Social Robotics

To foster the quality of the interaction, one common trend is to endow a social robot with the capability of expressing the appropriate emotional response. Several efforts have been made to design and evaluate the appropriateness of robotic emotional expressions, especially using humanoid robots. Salem et al. [8] evaluated the effects of endowing a robot with the capability of producing speech-accompanying gestures, and the results suggested that the non-verbal behaviors positively impacted the perception of the ASIMO robot. Costa et al. [12] investigated the meaning attributed by the participants to the facial expressions and gestures of the ZECA robot. The results suggested that the participants correctly identified the expressions of happiness, neutrality, sadness, and surprise. Similarly, the study conducted by Aly et al. [13] reported that the multimodality of the robot's behavior increased the clearness of the emotional content of the interaction, especially due to the presence of facial expressions. When a robot has a static facial expression (e.g. Pepper and NAO robots), the emotion is conveyed by non-verbal signals obtained by body movement and LED illumination. Marmpena et al. [14] used the pre-defined set of animations of the Pepper robot to evaluate the perception of valence and arousal dimensions of the emotional body language expressed by the robot. Exploiting the possibility of endowing robots with multimodal emotional responses, several studies investigated the appropriateness of robot behavior. Tsiourti et al. [15] showed that the contextual incongruence of Pepper's reactions confused the observers and negatively impacted the perception of the robot in terms of likelihood and perceived intelligence. Rossi et al.

[16] evaluated the perception of coherent and incoherent behaviors of the Pepper robot in a movie recommendation task. Their results suggested that the incoherent behaviors of the robot in this context increased user engagement producing a sort of humorous effect.

2.3 Study Design

In this direction, we aimed at investigating the capability of a robot of recognizing emotions during the HRI. In literature, there are several attempts to measure emotions using robots [7, 11], however, there is a lack of experimental protocols that use standard emotion elicitation modalities. Indeed, other studies rely on movies, as well as on robots' actions (e.g., body gestures, facial expressions) to evoke emotions in humans. Therefore, in this paper, we will rely on a standard image dataset (namely IAPS). Additionally, this paper aims also to evaluate the role of robot behavior in a standard emotion elicitation protocol. In detail, the robot was endowed with the capability of exhibiting three different behaviors while it was showing emotional pictures: (i) no reaction, (ii) congruous emotional expression, and (iii) incongruent behavior. To properly investigate the effect of robot animacy on the perception of the user emotions, current state-of-the-art automatic tools are included for detecting the non-verbal cues from the user behavior. Then, three supervised classifiers, namely Support Vector Machine, Random Forest, and K-Nearest Neighbor, were used to classify the perceived emotions.

3 System and Experiment

3.1 System Components

The instrumentation used in this setting is composed of i) Pepper robot, ii) RoboMate interface to program its behavior; iii) a custom interface that contains pictures from IAPS, and iv) an external camera placed on Pepper to record the participant's emotion during the interaction. Pepper is a humanoid robot (SoftBank Robotics, SoftBank Group) widely used for experimentation in the social robotics field. It is 120 cm tall and weighs 28 kg. RoboMate interface was used to animate Pepper, when necessary, selecting among the behavior classified as "positive social stimulus" or "negative social stimulus". Particularly, the selected stimulus was modeled using three modalities: body gesture (upper limb and head), gaze, and sound (Fig. 1, blue arrow). The IAPS is a database of images devoted to elicit standardized emotions. It was developed by the Center for Emotion and Attention (CSEA) at the University of Florida. This database is commonly used in psychological studies of emotion and attention. The emotion linked with each image is labeled, thus, enabling researchers to properly select the stimulus [17]. Particularly, for this study, 60 images were selected from the psychologists' team of the hospital "Casa Sollievo della Sofferenza". According to the IAPS valence dimension, of the selected images, 21 were rated as positive, 19 as negative, and 20 as neutral. A customized web-based interface was developed to standardize the emotional stimulation.

3.2 Experimental Protocol

A psychologist welcomed the participant, briefly explaining the experimental setup. The participant was asked to sit down in front of the Pepper robot. Pepper was placed 0.5–0.6 m far from the user (i.e. personal distances according to [18]) with the arms along the body in a neutral position. Pepper showed the selected 60 IAPS images on its tablet through the customized web application (Fig. 1). Each image was shown for 7s. The participant was randomly assigned to one of the following elicitation modalities: i) *Static behavior (STA)* where Pepper face was looking at the participant with its arms in a neutral position. ii) *Coherent behavior (COH)*: By using the RoboMate application, the psychologist assigned to Pepper a coherent behavior synchronized to the shown IAPS images (i.e. positive, negative or neutral). For example, Pepper gestures were chosen to look friendly, looking in the user's direction and giving verbal comments as positive reinforcement. Iii) *Incoherent behavior (INC)*: similar to COH behavior, the psychologist assigned an incoherent behavior to Pepper robot concerning the IAPS images shown on the tablet. For example, this behavior was characterized by funny/sad expressions and movements, which were discordant with the shown images. After seeing each image, the participants were requested to rate the perceived emotion in terms of valence, arousal and dominance using the 9-point Self-Assessment Manikin (SAM) scale [19]. The psychologist was present for all the test duration and using RoboMate coupled the behavior to the images. She/he was ready to intervene in case of necessity. All the tests took place at the research hospital "Casa Sollievo della Sofferenza".

3.3 Participants

Participants were recruited among employees and staff of the research hospital "Casa Sollievo della Sofferenza" located in Apulia (Foggia). Participants were excluded if they had a hearing or visual impairment. Before entering the study, the participant signed the informed consent form. A total of thirty participants were enrolled for this study, 10 for each elicitation modality (i.e. STA, COH, INC). Particularly, as for the STA cohort, 4 males and 6 females were recruited and the average age was 37 ± 8 years old. The COH group has an average age of 45 ± 13 years old, and it was composed of 5 males and 5 females. The INC group was composed of 1 male and 9 females and has an average age of 44 ± 12 years old. The approval of the study was obtained from the local Ethics Committee on human experimentation (Prot. N. 3038/01DG).

4 Data Analysis

Two data analyses were computed: on SAM values and data extracted from the video. The average valence values acquired with the SAM questionnaire were computed to verify if the emotions were successfully elicited. We acquired valence, arousal, and dominance values, but we use only valence values in this paper. The data analysis computed on the video was described in the following sub-sections.

4.1 Pre-processing

The data captured by the camera were processed and analyzed offline. As a first step, the videos were pre-processed using Avidemux software, to keep in the analysis only the frames that contained the face of the user who was performing the test. This preliminary step was performed because sometimes the camera was filming external people who were not performing the test, and this could lead to later errors. Then, the pre-processed videos were synchronized with the timestamp corresponding to the appearance of each IAPS image and were segmented; in this way, short videos, that corresponded to the user's reaction to each image proposed, were obtained, for a total of 60 videos per user.

4.2 Features Extraction and Normalization

The Openface software was used to extract from each video 150 features related to gaze and body postures (Fig. 1, yellow arrow), as well as to the quality (i.e. confidence) of the extracted features. In detail:

- From feature 1 to feature 3: eye gaze direction vector in world coordinates (x, y, z) for eye 0;
- From feature 4 to feature 6: eye gaze direction vector in world coordinates (x, y, z) for eye 1;
- From feature 7 to feature 8: eye gaze direction in radians in world coordinates (x, y) averaged for both eyes;
- From feature 9 to feature 56: location of 2D eye region landmarks in pixels;
- From feature 57 to feature 150: location of 2D face region landmarks in pixels.

Once these features were extracted, a data filtering phase was performed. When the face was not well detected from the video (e.g. the face was too close to the camera, it was cut in half, or the person was wearing glasses), the confidence values associated with the features extracted by OpenFace software were very low. To guarantee the reliability of the extracted features, frames with average confidence < 0.90 were discarded from the analysis. The resulting data were labeled, based on the IAPS-labeled emotions (i.e., positive, negative, neutral). After labeling the data (i.e. positive, negative, neutral), a normalization step was performed. In detail, the parameters related to the positions of the 2D landmarks in pixels were normalized user by user through a Min-Max normalization, whose formula is:

$$x_{new} = \frac{(x - x_{\min})}{(x_{max} - x_{\min})}, \tag{1}$$

where x is a set of the observed values of the current landmark, $x_{\min}$ and $x_{\max}$ are the minimum and the maximum observed values of the current landmark. The features related to the gaze direction were already normalized by OpenFace, thus, they were excluded from the normalization step.

4.3 Feature Selection and Emotion Classification

To remove redundancy from the detected features, we applied a feature selection step to the normalized data. To obtain features that are relevant for all the users, we merged the normalized features of all the users in a unique dataset. From this initial dataset, only those features with a correlation coefficient < 0.85 were selected so to exclude from the analysis the ones with high correlation (which may represent redundant information). After the feature selection, the data of the merged dataset were split again into sub-datasets (one for each user), and the emotion classification was performed using the selected features. In literature, several supervised classification methods, deep learning, and reinforcement learning approaches are used for the recognition of emotions [7, 11]. In this paper three commonly used supervised classifiers were employed, namely: Support Vector Machine (SVM) with the third-order polynomial kernel, Random Forrest (RF), and K-Nearest Neighbor (KNN). In the latter case, we set $K = 1$, meaning that the object was simply assigned to the class of that single nearest neighbor, and the Euclidean distance was set as the distance metric. The use of well-known benchmark classification algorithms makes the results directly comparable with other literary works. The data were classified user by the user using a 10-fold cross-validation technique. Classification performance was evaluated in terms of accuracy, precision, recall, and F-measure. Results were organized in confusion matrices and the final performance for each emotion was computed as the average metrics of each sub-dataset. All the analyses were performed using Matlab2020a.

Table 1. Distribution of the average valence values and of the standard deviation computed for the three IAPS groups (positive, negative and neutral) for each elicitation.

	Average			Standard deviation		
	Positive	Negative	Neutral	Positive	Negative	Neutral
STA	7.69	3.58	6.42	0.64	1.09	0.95
COH	7.86	3.63	6.75	0.49	1.28	0.80
INC	7.72	4.77	6.90	0.50	1.09	0.74

Table 2. Distribution of the three IAPS groups (positive, negative and neutral) for each elicitation (static, coherent and incoherent).

	Positive	Negative	Neutral
STA	35.16%	31.67%	32.35%
COH	34.29%	32.15%	33.55%
INC	40.65%	28.77%	30.58%

Table 3. Performances of the KNN and RF classifiers for each group.

	Accuracy		Precision		F-measure		Recall	
	KNN	RF	KNN	RF	KNN	RF	KNN	RF
STA	0.85	0.64	0.85	0.64	0.85	0.64	0.85	0.64
COH	0.96	0.66	0.96	0.65	0.96	0.65	0.96	0.66
INC	0.98	0.80	0.98	0.84	0.98	0.84	0.98	0.83

5   Results

The SAM average values were summarized in Table 1. Generally, the participants were successfully elicited, it is worth noticing that with the INC behavior, the negative emotions were perceived as less negative. As for the emotion recognition process, at the end of the feature extraction process, the dataset was split to create a database for each person, obtaining 30 datasets of different sizes. In particular, the number of instances for each elicitation modality was: 170602 for the static, 151930 for the coherent, and 63147 for the incoherent group. The number of features composing each dataset corresponded to the number of features selected after the correlation analysis process. The features selection process returned six features, namely: i) The x,y, and z coordinates of the eye gaze direction vector for eye 0 (3 features); ii) The z coordinate of the eye gaze direction vector for eye 1 (1 feature); iii) The x and y coordinates of the location of the landmark 8 of the eye 0 (2 features). The generated 30 datasets were used as input to the three classifiers discussed in the previous section, leading to a classification of the data into three emotional groups. The evaluation metrics reported in the following were computed as mean values among the participants belonging to the same stimulation cohort (i.e. static, coherent, and incoherent). The datasets were quite balanced across the three categories as depicted in Table 2. The best classification performances are obtained with the KNN classifier, obtaining values of accuracy up to 0.85 for the STA behavior and higher than 0.95 for the other two behaviors. The SVM classifiers obtained the worst performances (accuracy up to 0.55, 0.58, and 0.82 for STA, COH, and INC, respectively), so it was discarded from further analysis. The complete results for KNN and RF are reported in Table 3. In particular, the accuracy, F-measure, precision, and recall values are shown for each group. KNN reached the best performance also in terms of F-measures with respect to the RF classifier. To better investigate the classification performances of the best classifiers (i.e. KNN and RF) in detecting each emotion (i.e. positive, negative, and neutral), the confusion matrices were computed for the three groups (i.e. STA, COH, INC), as shown in Fig. 2. It emerged that both classifiers were less prone to errors in predicting the positive emotion, both when the robot was set in the STA and INC elicitation modalities. As for the COH behavior, the three emotions show a comparable recognition rate (around 95%) for the KNN classifiers; as for the RF classifier, the positive and neutral emotions reached a similar and higher recognition rate than the negative emotion.

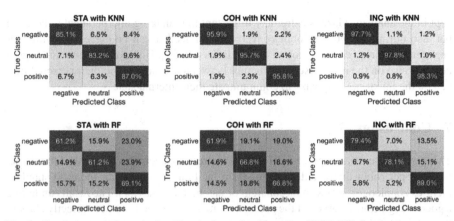

Fig. 2. Confusion matrices obtained by the best classifiers (i.e. KNN, RF) for the three groups (i.e. STA, COH, INC).

6 Discussion

The purpose of this paper is two-fold. First, it aims to assess the performances of an emotion recognition system during the HRI when a standard emotion elicitation modality is used (i.e. IAPS dataset). Secondly, it aims to evaluate how the non-verbal cues influence the emotions' perceptions, and, consequently, their detection from the robotic agent. Each participant was asked to interact 60 times with Pepper, therefore we collected and analyzed a dataset composed of more than 380'000 labeled frames. Observing Table 1, it emerges that participants felt fewer negative emotions when elicited with INC behavior. These findings are aligned with the previous qualitative works that have pointed out how incoherent behavior can generate hilarious reactions in humans [16], or it can generate discomfort - in the case of negative images and positive robot behavior - and impact the robot's perception [9]. The emotion recognition results confirm a good accuracy in emotion recognition related to the standard elicitation channel for the KNN classifiers despite the other two. In this case, the emotions were recognized with an average accuracy higher than 0.85 over the three elicitation conditions. Additionally, as for the secondary aim, this paper aims to investigate how the accuracy of the recognition system can change if the robot uses also non-verbal cues to stimulate the participants. According to the results, the classifiers reached a better performance in the COH and INC cases with respect to the STA case (an increase of +10% in KNN). These results suggest that the use of multiple non-verbal channels is better understandable than using a single channel even from a robot perception point of view. This finding is aligned with the state of the art since the users declared to be more engaged when more than one communicative channel is used. In other words, the users seem to be "strongly" stimulated in COH and INC cases and those stimulations cause a better recognition of the emotional status. Observing Table 3 it emerges that INC values are slightly better than the ones obtained within the COH condition. Based on these findings, future studies should investigate more where the user focuses his/her attention when the observed reactions are in contrast. It is also worth underlining that after the feature selection process, only the features related to gaze were kept in the analysis. Gaze is extremely important in managing interpersonal interaction but also during the human-robot conversation, indeed it can be correlated with user engagement during conversation or mutual tasks [20, 21]. However, the amount of gaze depends also on the interpersonal dynamics between the partner and their personalities, and on the intent of using gaze to communicate their internal state.

7 Conclusion

This paper presents an experimental setting where 30 participants were asked to interact with Pepper robot that acted as an emotion facilitator by showing them 60 standard pictures coupled (or not) with its coherent or incoherent behaviors. The results underline a good recognition accuracy of the perception modules. Indeed, we can correctly classify the valence of the emotion (i.e. positive, neutral, and negative) with an accuracy up to 0.98 in the best case. These results suggest that, in the future, features related to emotions, gaze, and facial expression could be used at two levels. On one side, they can be used by the robot agents to tailor appropriate reactions. On the other side, they can be monitored over time and provided to careers or clinicians to monitor the pathology status because of their clinical valence. Indeed, emotions (or absence of emotions) can be also influenced by a person's clinical status. For instance, children affected by autism spectrum disorders have social gaze deficits or they can have problems showing emotions. Social apathy is common in neurocognitive disorders (e.g. Alzheimer's disease, vascular dementia, stroke, traumatic brain injuries) and people affected by Parkinson's disease can also have a deficit in facial expressions. This work presents some limitations due to the sample size and the use of offline state-of-the-art supervised classification methods. Future studies will be carried out to increase the sample size and to apply other AI methods (e.g. deep learning, reinforcement learning) in real time.

References

1. Cavallo, F., et al.: Design impact of acceptability and dependability in assisted living robotic applications. Int. J. Interact. Des. Manuf. (IJIDeM) **12**(4), 1167–1178 (2018). https://doi.org/10.1007/s12008-018-0467-7
2. Horstmann, A.C., Krämer, N.C.: Great expectations? Relation of previous experiences with social robots in real life or in the media and expectancies based on qualitative and quantitative assessment. Front. Psychol. **10**, 939 (2019). https://doi.org/10.3389/fpsyg.2019.00939
3. Guo, F., Li, M., Qu, Q., Duffy, V.G.: The Effect of a humanoid robot's emotional behaviors on users' emotional responses: evidence from pupillometry and electroencephalography measures. Int. J. Hum. Comput. Interact. **35**, 1947–1959 (2019). https://doi.org/10.1080/10447318.2019.1587938
4. Nocentini, O., Fiorini, L., Acerbi, G., et al.: A survey of behavioral models for social robots. Robotics **8**, 54 (2019). https://doi.org/10.3390/robotics8030054
5. McGinn, C., Torre, I.: Can you tell the robot by the voice? An exploratory study on the role of voice in the perception of robots. In: 2019 14th ACM/IEEE International Conference on Human-Robot Interaction (HRI) (2019)
6. Rossi, S., Ferland, F., Tapus, A.: User profiling and behavioral adaptation for HRI: a survey. Pattern Recogn. Lett. **99**, 3–12 (2017). https://doi.org/10.1016/j.patrec.2017.06.002

7. Spezialetti, M., Placidi, G., Rossi, S.: Emotion recognition for human-robot interaction: recent advances and future perspectives. Front. Robot. AI 7, 532279 (2020). https://doi.org/10.3389/frobt.2020.532279
8. Salem, M., Rohlfing, K., Kopp, S., Joublin, F.: A friendly gesture: Investigating the effect of multimodal robot behavior in human-robot interaction. In: 2011 RO-MAN (2011)
9. Ekman, P.: Basic emotions. In: Handbook of Cognition and Emotion, pp. 45–60 (2005)
10. Russell, J.A.: A circumplex model of affect. J. Pers. Soc. Psychol. 39, 1161–1178 (1980). https://doi.org/10.1037/h0077714
11. Cavallo, F., Semeraro, F., Fiorini, L., Magyar, G., Sinčák, P., Dario, P.: Emotion modelling for social robotics applications: a review. J. Bionic Eng. 15(2), 185–203 (2018). https://doi.org/10.1007/s42235-018-0015-y
12. Costa, S., Soares, F., Santos, C.: Facial expressions and gestures to convey emotions with a humanoid robot. In: Herrmann, G., Pearson, M.J., Lenz, A., Bremner, P., Spiers, A., Leonards, U. (eds.) ICSR 2013. LNCS (LNAI), vol. 8239, pp. 542–551. Springer, Cham (2013). https://doi.org/10.1007/978-3-319-02675-6_54
13. Aly, A., Tapus, A.: Multimodal adapted robot behavior synthesis within a narrative human-robot interaction. In: 2015 IEEE/RSJ International Conference on Intelligent Robots and Systems (IROS) (2015)
14. Marmpena, M., Lim, A., Dahl, T.S.: How does the robot feel? Perception of valence and arousal in emotional body language. Paladyn 9, 168–182 (2018). https://doi.org/10.1515/pjbr-2018-0012
15. Tsiourti, C., Weiss, A., Wac, K., Vincze, M.: Multimodal integration of emotional signals from voice, body, and context: effects of (in)congruence on emotion recognition and attitudes towards robots. Int. J. Soc. Robot. 11(4), 555–573 (2019). https://doi.org/10.1007/s12369-019-00524-z
16. Rossi, S., Cimmino, T., Matarese, M., Raiano, M.: Coherent and incoherent robot emotional behavior for humorous and engaging recommendations. In: 2019 28th IEEE International Conference on Robot and Human Interactive Communication (RO-MAN) (2019)
17. Lang, P.J., Bradley, M.M., Cuthbert, B.N.: International affective picture system (IAPS): technical manual and affective ratings. In: Bertron, A., Bertron, A., Petry, M., et al. (eds.) NIMH Center for the Study of Emotion and Attention 1997. Psychology (1997)
18. Hall, E.T.: The hidden dimension. Leonardo 6, 94 (1973). https://doi.org/10.2307/1572461
19. Bradley, M.M., Lang, P.J.: Measuring emotion: the self-assessment manikin and the semantic differential. J. Behav. Ther. Exp. Psychiatry 25, 49–59 (1994). https://doi.org/10.1016/0005-7916(94)90063-9
20. Admoni, H., Scassellati, B.: Social eye gaze in human-robot interaction: a review. J. Hum. Robot. Interact. 6, 25 (2017). https://doi.org/10.5898/jhri.6.1.admoni
21. Kompatsiari, K., Bossi, F., Wykowska, A.: Eye contact during joint attention with a humanoid robot modulates oscillatory brain activity. Soc. Cogn. Affect. Neurosci. 16, 383–392 (2021). https://doi.org/10.1093/scan/nsab001

A Reinforcement Learning Framework to Foster Affective Empathy in Social Robots

Alessandra Sorrentino[1(✉)], Gustavo Assunção[2,3(✉)], Filippo Cavallo[1,4], Laura Fiorini[1], and Paulo Menezes[2,3]

[1] Department of Industrial Engineering, University of Florence, Florence, Italy
alessandra.sorrentino@unifi.it
[2] Department of Electrical and Computer Engineering, University of Coimbra, Coimbra, Portugal
gustavo.assuncao@isr.uc.pt
[3] Institute of Systems and Robotics, University of Coimbra, Coimbra, Portugal
[4] BioRobotics Institute, Scuola Superiore Sant'Anna, Pisa, Italy

Abstract. This work aims to endow a social robot with the ability to mimic affective empathy, which represents the skill of inferring the other's emotional state and mirroring the detected emotion. In this direction, we first designed a set of 52 facial expressions that may be representative of the primary emotions. Leveraging on the idea that the robot should learn the matching between emotion and its expressions directly from the final users, we modeled a deep reinforcement learning algorithm, and we recruited 105 users to train it, by rating the coherence of the robot's facial expressions on a web interface. A total of 22251 facial configurations were generated by the algorithm and rewarded by the pool of participants. The results proved that the algorithm exploited every facial configuration, converging towards a subset of 6 facial expressions at the end of the teaching process. Thus, we tested the trained empathetic model on a real robot (i.e. CloudIA robot) in a conversation scenario. The results collected through the interview and the questionnaires' analysis highlighted a general tendency of preferring the empathetic behavior of the robot, more than the not empathetic one. Namely, the robot endowed with empathetic behavior was perceived as more human-like and aware of the context of the interaction.

Keywords: Empathetic framework · Reinforcement learning

1 Introduction

As robots and humans are increasingly sharing the same space and activities, there is a need to make the robots able to understand more about users and to adapt their behaviors to human characteristics and preferences [18]. To foster this understanding and enhance the interaction, one choice is to endow the

F. Cavallo et al. (Eds.): ICSR 2022, LNAI 13817, pp. 522–533, 2022.
https://doi.org/10.1007/978-3-031-24667-8_46

robotic platform with empathetic behavior. Among the several definitions of empathy [9], most of the psychological studies share the idea that there exist different levels of empathy, namely: affective and cognitive. Affective empathy is usually defined as "an observer's reacting emotionally because he perceives that another is experiencing or is about to experience an emotion" [21], while cognitive empathy refers to "the ability to put one-self in the other's place and imagining how he or she feels" [8]. While the former mostly relies on mirroring the perceived emotions focusing on our emotional reactions to people [2], the latter implies a more complex cognitive process, which is usually referred to as perspective-taking. To mimic this process on social agents, computational empathy emerged as a novel field. It aims to equip artificial agents with the capability of showing empathetic behavior during interaction with human users [23]. Previous studies in the human-robot interaction (HRI) research field highlight that empathy fosters the creation of social bonds between people and robots [16] because empathetic agents are perceived as more likable, caring, and trustworthy [12]. When dealing with the empathy concept, many works in HRI focus on the anthropomorphic appearance that the robot should incorporate to obtain a higher level of acceptance from the human user [16,22]. The objective of this study is to improve the robot's social capabilities and create an expressive and empathetic social agent (affect-aware), focusing on the exhibited behavior more than its appearance. We focused on designing a robot capable of interpreting users' emotions during the interaction, and acting accordingly, by mimicking the perceived emotion (i.e. affective empathy [2]). While previous works adopt a Reinforcement Learning approach for evaluating hand-coded behaviors of the robot (e.g., set of utterances [1,11], vocal features [15], facial expressions [4,17]), in this work we designed a Deep Reinforcement Learning (DRL) algorithm to let the robot self-learn the association between emotions and its current expression. Thus, the robot self-associates its available facial expressions to the most representative emotions, based on the reward received by the human teacher. Then, we tested the trained model on a real interaction scenario, asking 20 young users to engage in a conversation with the CloudIA robot, which was endowed with the empathetic module.

The paper is organized as follows: the empathetic framework proposed in this work and its training procedure are reported in Sect. 2. Section 3 details the integration of the empathetic model on the real robotic platform and the experimental results. A complete overview of the achieved results is discussed in Sect. 4.

2   Empathetic Framework

Following the formulation of standard reinforcement learning, the action space of the proposed empathetic module is composed by the set of the facial expressions of the robot (i.e. eye-mouth configurations). The facial expressions of the robot are obtained as the combination of 13 mouth representations and 4 eye configurations. It results in 52 facial expressions, reported in Fig. 1, which are representative of the seven primary emotions [6], namely: happiness, sadness, fear, surprise, disgust, anger, and neutral emotion. The state space is composed of two states: non-empathetic and empathetic. As the names suggest, in the first state the generated facial expression does not match the user's emotions, while in the latter state it does. To foster the robot towards the "empathetic" state, the reward mechanism is designed such that the robot receives a low reward (i.e., $r_t = 2$) when it is moving from the "not empathetic" towards the "empathetic" state, no reward when it remains in the "not empathetic" state, and an high reward (i.e. $r_t = 10$) when it stays in the "empathetic" state. In this work, a deep Q network (DQN) is adopted to compute the state-action value function (Q_π). Namely, the network takes as input the robot's state and the current user's emotions. As shown in Fig. 2, the input is fed into two consecutive dense layers and progressed into two output dense layers, respectively for the eyes and mouth configuration. In terms of training, the DQN followed the standard ϵ-greedy Q-learning procedure. The DQN framework has been implemented by using Keras API with a TensorFlow back-end.

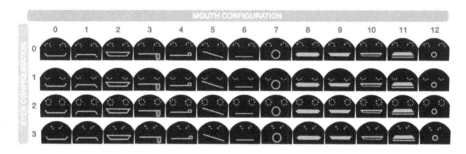

Fig. 1. List of facial expressions obtained by combining eyes and mouth configurations. We will refer to each expression as [index eyes, index mouth] format.

2.1 Training Procedure

We decided to speed up the trial-and-error stages required to learn the optimal policy, by replicating the facial expressions of the robot on a web page, which is easily accessible by different users at the same time. The web page was directly connected with the machine running the algorithm through a WebSocket connection. The web page showed the facial expression returned by the DQN to represent the emotion (reported on the top of the page), which was randomly selected by the algorithm itself. Each user could rate the facial expression as coherent or incoherent by clicking the corresponding button. This feedback was used as part of the reward of the DRL. After reaching 250 trials (i.e., number of steps of each training episode), the algorithm selected another emotion. The experimental procedure could last a maximum of 10 min, but the same user could access the web page several times or disconnect before the timeout. A copy of the trained model was locally stored on the server at the end of each day. For

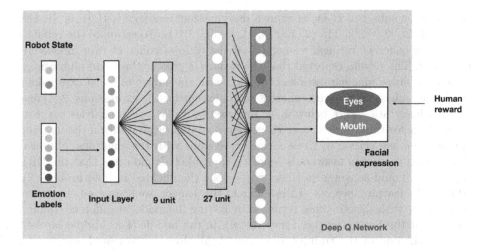

Fig. 2. Architecture of the proposed DQN

this "online" experimental procedure, the participants were recruited by sharing the link to the web page on different social platforms. By accessing the link, the participants found the description of the aim of the experimentation and a brief tutorial. Before being directed to the teaching page, each user needed to fill out a socio-demographic form. Both the user's general data and the user's answers were stored on the server as log files. While the log file with the general data was useful to keep track of the background of the participants, the log file with the user's answers was useful to analyze the associations taught by the participants. In detail, the latter file was parsed to compute the occurrence of coherent and incoherent evaluations for each facial expression. These values and their ratios were used to check the most rated facial expressions and their association with the emotion. Additionally, we evaluated the performance of the DRL algorithm over time, by testing the trained model at different stages of the learning process.

2.2 Training Results

A total of 105 subjects (46 women and 59 men, avg age = 32.01 years old, std age = 10.06) were recruited for the training procedure. Most of the participants were Italians (58.25%) and Portuguese (26.21%). The remaining participants came from other countries in Europe (6.80%), Asia (5.83%), South America (1.94%), and North Africa (0.97%). On average, each participant completed 155.6 trials (std = 92.95). A total of 22251 facial configurations were generated by the algorithm and rewarded by the participants.

By parsing the log file, we noticed that the algorithm exploited every facial configuration, suggesting that the algorithm explored the whole environment during the training phase. By examining the user feedback, it emerged that 42.51% of the facial expressions were rated as coherent with the proposed emotions. By normalizing the number of coherent evaluations by the total number of ratings, a subset of 11 facial expressions emerged, namely: [1, 1], [1, 6], [1, 11], [2, 1], [2, 2], [2, 6], [2, 11], [2, 12], [3, 1], [3, 6], [3, 11]. To estimate the reliability of the coherent ratings, we computed the ratio of coherent over incoherent feedback. The results reported that the ratio was greater than 1 in nine configurations. These nine expressions coincided with the subset of facial expressions with the highest normalized coherent score, except for the expressions [2, 1] and [2, 2] whose ratios were below 1, as reported in Table 1. The analysis suggests that the algorithm iterated over these eleven configurations during the learning phase. The association of these facial expressions with the emotions, obtained by parsing the user's answers is reported in Table 1. It indicates that the DRL approach should converge to these expressions (highlighted in bold in Table 2), during the learning process. To investigate this aspect, we compared the coherent ratings with the outcomes returned by testing the model at different training phases: at the beginning (i.e. First Model), in the middle (i.e., Middle Model), and at the end of the training (i.e., the Final Model). We tested each model by running a total of 7876 trials (i.e., the sum of coherent evaluations of the 11 facial expressions), balanced according to the number of coherent representations associated with each emotion. The results of the three testing phases are reported in Table 2. Among the three models, the associations made by the Final Model mostly reflect the data extracted by the log file (reported in Table 2).

Table 1. Normalized coherent ratings associated with the most exploited expressions. The maximum values of each column and row are highlighted in bold. The colored cells remark on the association learned by the algorithm (Final model).

Expression	Sadness	Fear	Anger	Disgust	Surprise	Happiness	Neutral	Ratio
[1, 1]	**16.4**	0.0	0.1	0.2	0.0	0.0	0.0	2.68
[1, 6]	14.0	0.2	0.0	0.3	0.0	0.6	0.7	3.06
[1, 11]	**16.4**	0.1	0.3	0.2	0.0	0.0	0.2	1.61
[2, 1]	0.8	**5.7**	0.1	1.0	0.0	0.0	0.0	0.70
[2, 2]	0.0	0.1	0.0	0.0	3.3	16.7	0.0	0.75
[2, 6]	0.1	5.9	0.1	1.7	3.8	0.5	28.1	1.13
[2, 11]	0.3	**12.8**	0.0	5.8	**14.9**	0.1	4.6	1.48
[2, 12]	0.0	3.8	0.0	0.0	13.4	0.0	0.0	2.43
[3, 1]	0.2	0.1	**21.9**	12.1	0.0	0.0	0.0	2.90
[3, 6]	0.1	0.2	**10.3**	1.6	0.0	0.0	1.8	1.85
[3, 11]	0.1	0.1	**11.8**	4.5	0.0	0.1	4.1	1.41
[3, 12]	0.0	0.3	0.1	0.0	1.4	0.0	0.1	0.27

3   Integration on a Real Robot

The empathetic module was integrated on a ROS-based robot, named CloudIA. As shown in Fig. 3, the robot is equipped with an RGB-D camera (ASTRA Orbbec, USA), which integrates four microphones, two speakers, and a tablet

Table 2. Facial Expressions associated by the model at different training stages: at the beginning (First Model), in the Middle (Middle Model), and at the end (Final Model).

Emotion	First model	Middle model	Final model
Neutral	[1, 12]	[3, 6]	[2, 6]
Disgust	[2, 7]	[3, 1]	[3, 12]
Surprise	[1, 12]	[2, 12]	[2, 12]
Happiness	[2, 9]	[0, 6]	[2, 2]
Sadness	[2, 9]	[1, 1]	[1, 6]
Anger	[1, 12]	[3, 1]	[3, 1]
Fear	[1, 12]	[0, 12]	[2, 12]

(Samsung, Korea), on which the facial expressions could be shown. The integration of the empathetic module is shown in Block A of Fig. 3. Namely, a pre-trained Convolutional Neural Network[1] is used to assess the current emotion of the user from the image flow of the camera. The detected emotion is passed as input to the trained DRL model, which associates the learned facial configuration (i.e. eyes and mouth indices). The facial configuration is sent back to the robotic platform and displayed on the tablet of the robot. Additionally, the detected emotion is forwarded to the dialog manager (Block B). The dialog manager is a customized Finite State Machine that selects the robot's utterance based on verbal content detected by the user (if any) and the user emotional state. To understand the user's verbal messages, the audio recorded by the microphones is processed by an automatic speech recognition model (i.e. Vosk2). The speaking capabilities of the robot are based on the ROS wrapper of the svox-pico Text-to-Speech.

3.1 Experimental Setting

We evaluated the role of empathy in a conversation scenario. The conversation was guided by the robot, and it was composed of three main stages, namely:

1. SMALL CHAT: the robot welcomed the participant, introduced itself, and asked general questions to get the participant used to the interaction (e.g., "what is your name?", "how are you today?").
2. ELICITING: the robot suggested watching some videos with the participant. The aim was to elicit the primary emotions in the participants, as described in [19]. Each video was created by combining images and sounds from the International Affective Picture System (IAPS) [10] database and the International Affective Digitized Sounds (IADS) [3], respectively. First, we selected the images belonging to the seven emotions from IAPS, following the guidelines reported in [13]. Then, we selected the sound of the IADS that better

---

[1] https://github.com/SanjayMarreddi/Emotion-Investigator.

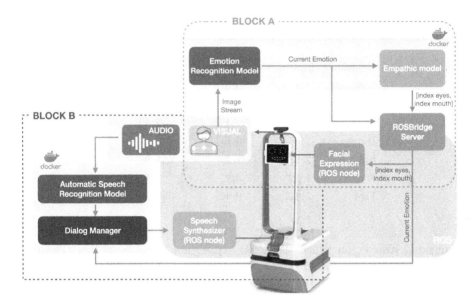

Fig. 3. Software architecture of the empathetic robot.

suited each image. At the end of each video, the robot expresses a comment, using the utterance coded in the robot's behaviour.

3. AKINATOR GAME: the robot asked the participant to think about a character and let the robot guess it, like in [17]. At the end of this stage, the robot thanked the participant.

To properly evaluate the effect of the empathetic behavior on the conversation, each participant was asked to participate in the experimental session twice. In each experimental session, the robot exhibited a certain behavior, i.e., an empathetic (EMP) or a neutral (NOT-EMP) behavior. In the EMP behavior, the DRL model was active, and the robot continuously adapted its facial expression based on the detected user's emotion (shown in Fig. 3). Additionally, in the ELICITING stage, the robot would comment on each video based on the detected emotion. If the detected emotion coincided with the emotion elicited by the video, then the robot would say something like "it seems like the video made you feel ⟨emotion⟩" and "I (don't) like it.", according to the emotional valence. Otherwise, the robot would simply express its own emotion, which coincided with the emotion elicited by the video (e.g. "This video made me feel ⟨emotion⟩. I (don't) like it"). In the NOT-EMP behavior, the DRL was not active, thus, the robot's facial expression was set to the neutral configuration. In the ELICITING phase, the robot would comment on the videos by randomly picking a sentence between: "Wow, impressive" (vague), "Nice, I liked it" (positive comment), and "I did not like it" (negative comment).

The second session was organized five days after the first one, and the behavior of the robot was randomly assigned among the participants. To avoid any bias, the experimenter advised the participants that the experiment was about testing a conversation module of the robot, without mentioning the robot's affective component.

At the beginning of the first experimental session, each participant was asked to compile a socio-demographic questionnaire to collect information about their gender, age, level of education, and previous experience with robots. At the end of each session, the participants were asked to fill out an extended version of the Godspeed questionnaire (GQ) [14]. The Godspeed questionnaire is commonly used in the robotic field to evaluate the perception of five key aspects of the robot behavior, namely: anthropomorphism (ANT), animacy (ANI), likeability (LIK), perceived intelligence (PEI) and perceived safety (PES). The extended version adopted in this work includes three additional dimensions, namely: emotion (EMO), social intelligence (SOI), and extroversion (EXT). The extended version is then composed of 33 items, which could be rated on a 5-point Likert Scale. At the end of the second session, the experimenter conducted a brief interview to investigate if the participant noticed a difference in the behaviors of the robot, and, if detected, asked the participant to describe the difference and express a preference among the two behaviors, if any. The study was approved by the joint Ethical Committee of Scuola Superiore Sant'Anna and Scuola Normale Superiore (Delibera 17/2022).

3.2   Testing Results

A total of 20 participants (8 females and 12 males; avg age = 28.1 years old, std = 2.15) were recruited for this study. Each experimental session lasted for c.a. 15 min. Despite they were all employed at the BioRobotics Institute, six of them had no or few experiences with robots (30%), while the remaining ones had some experience as participants in other experiments and/or researchers in the robotics field. The nationality of the participants was mostly Italian, except for two participants. The answers to the Godspeed questionnaires (GQs) were analyzed to compute the evaluation of the ANT, ANI, LIK, PEI, PES, EMO, SOI, and EXT domains associated with the two behaviors. Since each domain is characterized by a different number of items, the normalized score of each domain was computed to properly compare the results. The internal consistency of the collected answers was verified by computing Cronbach's alpha for each questionnaire. The Cronbach's alpha was ≥ 0.85 for all the GQ ratings, confirming the reliability of the answers.

Several statistical tools were applied for corroborating the analysis. Descriptive statistics was adopted to represent the trends in the GQ ratings. Additionally, the Wilcox-on Signed Rank Test for dependent samples was applied to detect any significant differences in the perception of the empathetic behavior and the neutral behavior. The analysis of the GQ's answers returned that the empathetic behavior received higher scores concerning the neutral one. As shown in Fig. 4, the median of each domain is higher in the EMP behavior more than in the NOT-EMP behavior. Interestingly, the evaluation of the EMP domains is characterized by a more homogeneous distribution. The Wilcoxon Signed Rank

Test for dependent samples highlighted a significant difference in the evaluation of the EMO domain (p = 0.003) of the two behaviors. All the participants stated that they perceived a difference between the behaviors exhibited by the robot. Most of the participants noticed the difference in the comments pronounced in the ELICITING stage (75%) and mentioned that in the EMP case the robot was adapting its facial expressions (70%). Five out of 20 participants noticed some differences in the AKINATOR GAME performances, in terms of the number of answers, and duration of the game. Except for two participants who did not express any preference and five participants that preferred the not empathetic behavior ("today, the robot seems more reactive", statement of user 5), the EMP behavior was the most appreciated one. In the EMP behavior, the robot seemed more expressive and aware of the occurring interaction ("I liked the robot more this time because it had human-like reactions to the videos and it was less creepy" statement user 8; "the expressions were congruent with the interaction", statement user 4; "its expressions also influenced mine, it was very engaging", statement user 2). On the other side, the NOT-EMP behavior was described as "apathetic" (statement user 1), "cold and rigid" (statement user 7). Interestingly, even if they were not aware of the behaviors exhibited by the robot, four users explicitly declared that the robot seemed "more empathetic" referring to the robot with EMP behavior, while one user described the robot expressing the NOT-EMP behavior as "less sensitive and less empathetic".

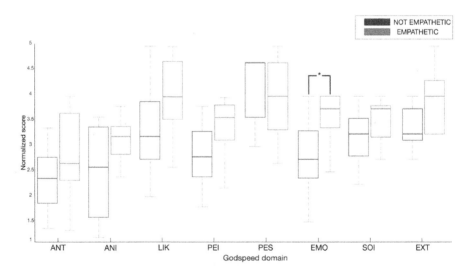

Fig. 4. Box plot of the ratings associated with the Godspeed domains of the two robot's behaviors.

4 Discussion

We proposed our strategy for improving the social behavior of the robotic platform by creating an empathetic framework. On one side, we developed a framework, based on a deep learning strategy, that allows the robot to learn the most appropriate facial representations for each primary emotional state (i.e., Sadness, Neutral, Happiness, Anger, Fear, Surprise, and Disgust). Instead of manually associating the possible facial expressions to the corresponding emotion, our work relies on a DRL algorithm, which allows the robot to incrementally shape its knowledge about emotional response, learning the association between facial expressions and emotions from 105 human teachers. The results of the training process show that the algorithm converged toward a subset of facial configurations. The learned facial expressions are obtained by combining three out of four possible eye representations (i.e., 1, 2, 3) and five out of thirteen mouth configurations (i.e., 1, 2, 6, 11, 12). This result underlines that the emotion representation is both influenced by the eyes and the mouth representation as well by their combinations. Thus, by combining the same eyes with different mouth representations (and vice-versa), the robot could display a different emotion.

We integrated the developed framework on a real robotic platform, and we tested it in a real interaction scenario. It gave us the opportunity of evaluating the consistency of facial expression mimicry with real users. To derive the user's emotions, we included a trained model for emotion recognition on the robotic platform. To avoid the Wizard-of-Oz strategy, we included a dialog manager, responsible of handle the robot interaction capabilities. We evaluated the learned empathetic behavior of the robot in a closed perception-decision-action loop. The results collected through the interview and the questionnaires' analysis highlighted a general tendency of preferring the empathetic behavior of the robot. This result confirms the outcomes of previous studies in the field with different robotic platforms [7,17]. Despite most of the robot's capabilities getting a higher score in the EMP behavior, the only statistically significant difference emerged in the evaluation of the emotion domain (i.e., EMO). This domain refers to the evaluation of expressive and empathetic agents [14]. Thus, this result suggested that the participant recognized the emotional capability of the empathetic behavior of the robot since they associated with that behavior higher values of compassion, emotional stability, active response, and empathetic skills (i.e., four items of the EMO domain). Furthermore, the results of this work highlighted the importance of endowing a robotic platform with an appropriate facial expression, which adapted itself to the context. Without explicitly stating that the robot was mirroring their emotions, some of them mentioned the concept of "empathy" and the consistency between the facial expressions and the context. The mirroring capability changed the perception of the elements composing the robotic platform in a positive way, namely it "seemed that the face is part of the robot's body, not just a tablet hanging in front of you" (statement user 4). Despite the relation between facial expression mimicking and increased engagement being not a new knowledge, the novelty of this work relies on the fact that it occurred with a not human-like robot, in which the participants found human-like aspects during the interaction. The obtained results encourage the idea that empathy mainly depends on the emotional skills of the robot, more than its appearance. Also, they suggest that this affective capability of expressing empathy could also be exploited in clinical context, where the robot could represent a support tool for teaching or stimulate emotional responses [5].

One of the main limitations of this work is that the recruited participants belonged to the same age and working environment, which could represent a bias in the evaluation. As in [20], it may be the case that people with previous experience with robots tend to evaluate the robot's social capability. To draw more robust conclusions, a larger and heterogeneous sample of participants should be included. Additionally, a deep investigation into the role of user traits in the training procedure and the perception of the robot's empathetic behavior should be included. In future work, we will also compare the learning performance of the current model with the learning performances of a supervised algorithm (trained with the same data) to check the pro and cons of adopting a reinforcement solution instead of a classical approach based on machine learning techniques.

References

1. Bagheri, E., Roesler, O., Cao, H.L., Vanderborght, B.: A reinforcement learning based cognitive empathy framework for social robots. Int. J. Soc. Robot. **13**(5), 1079–1093 (2021)
2. Baron-Cohen, S.: The Essential Difference. Penguin UK (2004)
3. Bradley, M., Lang, P.: The international affective digitized sounds: affective ratings of sounds and instruction manual (technical report no. b-3). University of Florida. NIMH Center for the Study of Emotion and Attention, Gainesville, FL (2007)
4. Churamani, N., Barros, P., Strahl, E., Wermter, S.: Learning empathy-driven emotion expressions using affective modulations. In: 2018 International Joint Conference on Neural Networks (IJCNN), pp. 1–8. IEEE (2018)
5. Cifuentes, C.A., Pinto, M.J., Céspedes, N., Múnera, M.: Social robots in therapy and care. Current Rob. Rep. **1**(3), 59–74 (2020)
6. Ekman, P.: An argument for basic emotions. Cogn. Emot. **6**(3–4), 169–200 (1992)
7. Hegel, F., Spexard, T., Wrede, B., Horstmann, G., Vogt, T.: Playing a different imitation game: Interaction with an empathic android robot. In: 2006 6th IEEE-RAS International Conference on Humanoid Robots, pp. 56–61. IEEE (2006)
8. Hoffman, M.L.: Empathy and moral development. Ann. Rep. Educ. Psychol. Japan **35**, 157–162 (1996)
9. Lamm, C., Tomova, L.: The neural bases of empathy in humans. In: Neuronal Correlates of Empathy, pp. 25–36. Elsevier (2018)
10. Lang, P.J., Bradley, M.M., Cuthbert, B.N., et al.: International affective picture system (IAPS): Affective ratings of pictures and instruction manual. Center for the Study of Emotion & Attention Gainesville, FL, NIMH (2005)
11. Leite, I., Castellano, G., Pereira, A., Martinho, C., Paiva, A.: Empathic robots for long-term interaction. Int. J. Soc. Robot. **6**(3), 329–341 (2014)
12. Leite, I., Pereira, A., Mascarenhas, S., Martinho, C., Prada, R., Paiva, A.: The influence of empathy in human-robot relations. Int. J. Hum. Comput. Stud. **71**(3), 250–260 (2013)

13. Mikels, J.A., Fredrickson, B.L., Larkin, G.R., Lindberg, C.M., Maglio, S.J., Reuter-Lorenz, P.A.: Emotional category data on images from the international affective picture system. Behav. Res. Methods **37**(4), 626–630 (2005)

14. Mileounis, A., Cuijpers, R.H., Barakova, E.I.: Creating robots with personality: the effect of personality on social intelligence. In: Ferrández Vicente, J.M., Álvarez-Sánchez, J.R., de la Paz López, F., Toledo-Moreo, F.J., Adeli, H. (eds.) IWINAC 2015. LNCS, vol. 9107, pp. 119–132. Springer, Cham (2015). https://doi.org/10.1007/978-3-319-18914-7_13

15. Niculescu, A., van Dijk, B., Nijholt, A., Li, H., See, S.L.: Making social robots more attractive: the effects of voice pitch, humor and empathy. Int. J. Soc. Robot. **5**(2), 171–191 (2013)

16. Paiva, A., Leite, I., Boukricha, H., Wachsmuth, I.: Empathy in virtual agents and robots: a survey. ACM Trans. Interactive Intell. Syst. (TiiS) **7**(3), 1–40 (2017)

17. Riek, L.D., Paul, P.C., Robinson, P.: When my robot smiles at me: enabling human-robot rapport via real-time head gesture mimicry. J. Multimodal User Interfaces **3**(1), 99–108 (2010)

18. Rossi, S., Ferland, F., Tapus, A.: User profiling and behavioral adaptation for HRI: a survey. Pattern Recogn. Lett. **99**, 3–12 (2017)

19. Siedlecka, E., Denson, T.F.: Experimental methods for inducing basic emotions: a qualitative review. Emot. Rev. **11**(1), 87–97 (2019)

20. Sorrentino, A., Khalid, O., Coviello, L., Cavallo, F., Fiorini, L.: Modeling human-like robot personalities as a key to foster socially aware navigation. In: 2021 30th IEEE International Conference on Robot & Human Interactive Communication (RO-MAN), pp. 95–101. IEEE (2021)

21. Stotland, E.: Exploratory investigations of empathy. In: Advances in Experimental Social Psychology, vol. 4, pp. 271–314. Elsevier (1969)

22. Tapus, A., Mataric, M.J., Scassellati, B.: Socially assistive robotics [grand challenges of robotics]. IEEE Rob. Autom. Mag. **14**(1), 35–42 (2007)

23. Yalçın, Ö.N.: Evaluating empathy in artificial agents. arXiv preprint arXiv:1908.05341 (2019)

Robotics Technology for Pain Treatment and Management: A Review

Angela Higgins[1(✉)], Alison Llewellyn[2], Emma Dures[2], and Praminda Caleb-Solly[1]

[1] School of Computer Science, University of Nottingham, NG8 1BB Nottingham, UK
angela.higgins@nottingham.ac.uk
[2] Faculty of Health and Applied Sciences, UWE, BS16 1QY Bristol, UK

Abstract. The use of robots for pain management is a new and active research field. The aim of this scoping review is to identify current research, which groups or conditions are being targeted for treatment, which devices are being used, and how effective they have been. Using the PRISMA protocol for scoping reviews, papers were identified using university libraries, Google scholar and additional databases relating to healthcare or engineering including AMED, NICE Evidence, and OTSeeker. Included were articles involved user trials of a robot or device to manage or alleviate pain, with a quantitative measure of pain or pain anxiety. 17 articles were analysed, of which 12 reported statistically significant improvement of pain measures. The scope and trial design of these articles varied widely. Most devices used were socially assistive robots, with others using robots for physical therapy. Most robots were used for treatment of procedural pain. Others addressed chronic pain, particularly in people with dementia. A variety of established pain measurement techniques were used to quantify difference in perceived pain or pain anxiety. There may be benefits to using some robotic technologies to manage pain for both acute and chronic pain conditions, within certain populations. However, this research field is still new, and more studies are required to demonstrate efficacy. Future studies should look to use methodologies from clinical trials to improve the quality of their results.

Keywords: Pain · Pain management · Robotics · Socially assistive robots

1 Introduction

During our lifetimes we will all experience pain, whether acute and short-term or chronic and long-term. Both acute and chronic pain can be life restricting, due to temporary anxiety around pain or ongoing debilitation. Chronic pain persists or recurs for more than 3 months [45], and it can be a disease in itself or a symptom of another condition. Acute pain has a duration of less than 3 months, reduces over time, and usually occurs as the result of a singular incidence of trauma, such as an accident or medical procedure [39].

F. Cavallo et al. (Eds.): ICSR 2022, LNAI 13817, pp. 534–545, 2022.
https://doi.org/10.1007/978-3-031-24667-8_47

Due to increasing awareness of potential disadvantages of pharmacological treatments, many researchers are seeking to find non-pharmacological and non-surgical interventions that may help alleviate pain. This scoping review aims to evaluate contemporary research into the use of robotics technologies for pain alleviation or management, including both acute and chronic pain.

Currently, simple electronic devices are sometimes used in medical settings to help those living with pain. These include transcutaneous electrical nerve stimulation (TENS) machines and vibrotactile devices [44]. Additionally, the use of virtual reality (VR) for distraction and relaxation has shown potential for pain alleviation [14]. Other research has combined haptic and VR technology to create multimodal pain alleviation, with some positive outcomes [27]. Whilst these are technologies often linked to robotics, no robots were used in these prior studies therefore they are beyond the scope of this review.

Chronic pain treatment is complex and multifaceted, and the application of technology to aid in self-management at home may benefit pain patients by assisting with daily routines, providing soothing sensations or mimicking physical therapy (PT) [23]. Additionally, those experiencing acute pain in a medical setting, such as a painful procedure, may benefit from technological methods that lessen pain and lead to better outcomes [19]. Generally interventions use one of three existing theoretical approaches to pain management: pain distraction, pain gating or cutaneous stimulation, and affective touch, described below.

Distraction as pain management works by shifting the individual's attention from the painful sensations and onto another stimulus. This includes methods such as visualisation exercises or engaging in an enjoyable hobby. It can also be beneficial during shorter painful medical procedures, however the type of distraction should be adjusted according to patient and procedure [22].

The gate control theory of pain, whilst contested, has been used in the development of pain management techniques currently in use. The theory states that pain signals travelling along the nervous system to the brain can be interrupted at the spinal cord by the generation of other signals [12]. An example of this used in medical settings is TENS machines to reduce pain associated with childbirth, although their efficacy is disputed [6].

Similar to pain gating, in that it involves physical stimulation of the body, cutaneous stimulation involves using tactile stimuli often on or near the pain site [15,18]. However, whilst pain gating seeks to reroute the electrical signals travelling to the brain, cutaneous stimulation seeks to lessen pain sensations by overriding them with pleasant stimuli.

Robotics technologies have already been imagined, researched and deployed in a variety of healthcare scenarios, and it is hoped that robotics will become integrated into a patient's healthcare journey [28]. Even more recently researchers have become interested in the potential for robots to be used in pain alleviation or management. As with other technologies, it may be that robots can be used as alternative or complementary interventions for pain management.

Frequently, pain management research uses a socially assistive robot (SAR), that provides assistance through social interaction including dialogue, sounds and gestures, rather than providing physical assistance [17]. This utilises human-robot interaction (HRI) to distract or relax a patient undergoing a procedure or therapeutic regimen. Research into SARs and HRI has already shown potential uses in healthcare, particularly the care of people in later life, providing assistance, therapy or comfort and improving quality of life [1]. However, sometimes this involves a robot that has no social features designed to interact with the body as part of physical therapy. This scoping review looked for current research into robotic treatments of pain in order to identify trends such as groups and conditions targeted for treatment, devices used and their effectiveness. From this possible recommendations were made for future research.

2   Methods

2.1   Search Methods

The aims of this review were to identify and analyse research which indicates how robots could possibly be used to alleviate or manage pain. This scoping review sought to answer the following research questions:

(i) What research currently exists into the use of robots or robotic devices for pain alleviation and/or management?

(ii) Which groups or conditions are being considered for the potential use of robots for pain alleviation and/or management, and in what form?

(iii) Which robots or robotic devices have shown efficacy for the alleviation and/or management of pain?

(iv) Based on the findings from current research what recommendations can be made for future research?

2.2   The PRISMA Protocol and Search Strategy

Methods from the PRISMA protocol for scoping reviews were used as the search strategy [42]. This involved searching the library database at the University of the West of England, Google Scholar and additional databases relating to healthcare or engineering. Additional records were sourced through Altmetric and cited references in publications. Searches were performed between October 2019 to March 2022 inclusive. The initial search was broad, and all possibly relevant articles were included based on screening of titles, abstracts and references. The inclusion criteria were literature written in English and published between 2000 to spring 2022. However due to the active nature of the research topic no results were found prior to 2010. Search terms are shown in Table 1, where each word from the first column was combined with each word in the second.

2.3   Selection Criteria

Full length articles were included if they contained user trials using a robot or a robotic device, and used a quantitative measurement of pain or perceived pain, including those that used anxiety questionnaires with specific reference to pain. The PRISMA flow diagram is shown in Fig. 1. A robotic device was defined as an interactive device which has an embodied presence. This excluded articles discussing pain treatment methods such as vibration or TENS machines, or those using virtual reality for pain treatment. Duplicate results were also removed, as well as studies which used the same experiments for more than one publication. Results are shown in Table 2.

Table 1. Search terms

First term	Second term
robot	pain
robotics	pain relief
socially assistive robot	pain management
Paro	pain therapy
NAO	pain distraction
assistive robot	analgesia
assistive technology	analgesic

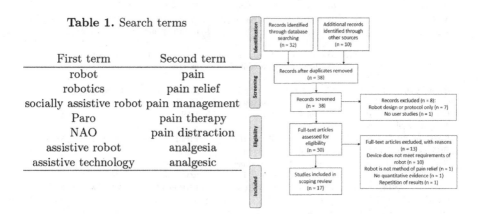

Fig. 1. PRISMA flow diagram

3   Results

3.1   Demographics and Study Design

The search elicited 17 articles, within which participant groups, trial design, type of measurements and study duration varied widely. Articles originated from 8 countries and study locations included clinical settings, such as a hospital or doctor's office (n = 14), long-term care facilities (n = 3) and a university laboratory (n = 1). All articles were published after October 2012, with an increasing amount occurring in subsequent years until the end of the search period.

Participants in user trials were usually members of a specific patient population, for example paediatric patients, from premature infants up to 18 years, plus one study that classified children as up to 19 years (n = 11, total 462 participants). These children were in treatment for long-term medical conditions such as cancer or undergoing an isolated medical procedure, often as part as a long-term treatment program. The largest study involving children examined 86 patients undergoing IV insertion, and the smallest examined 10 premature infants (born at less than 36 weeks of gestation) undergoing a blood test.

Other notable participant groups were: people with dementia (n = 3, total 79 participants); and people receiving post-stroke rehabilitation (n = 2, total 73 participants). Finally, one group contained healthy adults who were subject to experimentally induced pain (n = 1, total 83 participants).

Most participant groups were randomly split into intervention and control groups for comparison, with one article using sample stratification for gender.

Table 2. Results

Authors, Year, Country	Robot	Participants	Pain Condition	Measurements	Technique	Sig. Results
Alemi et al. 2016, Iran [2]	NAO	11 children (7–12yrs)	Cancer	MASC scale	Talk therapy	Yes
Ali et al, 2021, Canada [3]	NAO	86 children (6–11yrs)	IV insertion procedure	FPS-R and OSBD-R	Distraction	Yes
Ariji et al. 2015, Japan[4]	Oral therapy robot	37 adults (19–83yrs)	Myofascial pain	VAS and max mouth opening	PT	Yes
Beraldo et al. 2019, Italy [7]	Pepper and Sanbot	28 children (3-19yrs)	Various medical procedures	Self-designed questionnaire	Distraction	Yes
Beran et al. 2013, Canada[8]	NAO	57 children (4–9yrs)	Vaccination procedure	FPS-R and BAADS	Distraction	Yes
Borboni et al. 2017, Italy [9]	PT robot	25 adults (45-80yrs)	Post-stroke rehab	VAS	PT	Yes
Farrier et al. 2019, Canada [16]	NAO	46 children (2–15yrs)	IV insertion procedure	FPS-R + CFS	Distraction	Yes
Geva et al. 2020, Israel [20]	Paro	83 adults (M = 25.1yrs)	Experimentally induced	VAS and salivary oxytocin	Affective touch	Yes
Holsti et al. 2019, Canada [25]	Calmer	49 premature infants	Blood test	BIIP and heart rate	Affective touch	No
Jibb et al. 2018, Canada [26]	NAO	40 children (4–9yrs)	IV insertion	FPS-R and BAADS	Distraction	No
Kim et al. 2019, Korea [29]	PT robot	38 adults	Post-stroke rehab	VAS and range of motion	PT	Yes
Lane et al. 2016,USA [30]	Paro	23 adults (58–97yrs)	Dementia related	Carer assesed	Affective touch	No
Manaloor et al. 2019, Canada[32]	NAO	86 children (6-11yrs)	IV insertion procedure	FPS-R and OSBD-R	Distraction	Yes
Okita 2013, USA[34]	Paro	18 children (6–16yrs)	Various medical procedures	FPR-S and anxiety questionnaire	Affective Touch	Yes
Pu et al. 2020, Australia [36]	Paro	11 adults (65–94yrs)	Dementia related	COREQ compliant questionnaire	Affective Touch	Yes
Trost et al. 2020, USA [43]	MAKI	31 children (4–14yrs)	IV insertion procedure	FPS-R and CFS	Distraction	No
Williams et al. 2019, Canada [46]	Calmer	10 premature infants	Blood test	Heart rate	Affective touch	Yes

The remainder compared each patient's results and relative improvement over time. Most studies were non blinded, however 3 used blinded analysts to review and encode data after the studies. All articles used at least one standardised qualitative measurement of pain, or questionnaires adherent to the COREQ checklist for qualitative research [41].

3.2 Types of Robots

The majority of articles used commercially available SARs, particularly the small humanoid robot NAO (n = 6) and the baby seal robot Paro (n = 4). Others SARs used included the Maki and the humanoid robots Pepper and Sanbot. The most common experimental robot-participant combination was NAO for pain management in children (n = 6) and Paro for people with dementia (n = 2). These robots and their frequency of use are shown in Fig. 2.

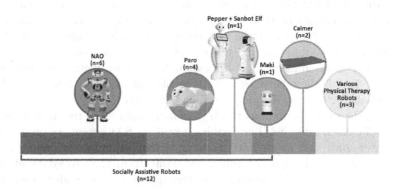

Fig. 2. Robots used in studies

3.3 Pain Conditions

A number of articles observed the treatment of procedural pain (n = 8), including intravenous insertion (n = 4), needles (n = 2) and other one-off medical procedures (n = 3). These medical procedures are brief but common; most people will undergo them at least once during a lifetime.

Other studies were used to treat chronic pain associated with dementia (n = 2) or acute pain associated with ageing in people with dementia (n = 1). Others aimed to mimic physical therapy for specific long-term conditions (n = 3).

In some articles procedural and experimental pain management only lasted for the duration of a singular medical treatment (n = 10), whereas other pain management interventions consisted of a regular therapeutic program (n = 6), for example once a week over a number of months. One trial with people with dementia had no specific protocol for robot use, employing Paro as and when medical staff thought it appropriate.

Several robots were used to recreate physical therapy (n = 3) to help alleviate pain in a specific condition, through therapeutic methods employing massage or joint manipulation. These robots are usually designed to mimic procedures performed a therapy professional, with the aim to provide more frequent therapy and assist recovery.

The Calmer robot, used in two studies, simulates parental warmth, breathing and heartbeat. This was used with premature babies to mimic skin-to-skin contact which is used to soothe infants during medical procedures. The device has the appearance of a small bed which the baby is placed upon with to create calming sensations.

3.4   Pain Management and Techniques

The majority of articles (n = 13) reported a statistically significant improvement in perceived pain or pain anxiety post intervention (p < 0.05). Although in those studies without significant positive effect no difference was found between current standard interventions or those using robots. All articles reviewed gave details of the techniques they employed to manage user pain. These techniques are underpinned by existing theoretical work into pain management and techniques already in use, including medical professionals and therapeutic animals. In the articles reviewed, these theories and protocols were implemented through the use of robots for the specific purpose of investigation.

One of the most common methods to manage pain using robots was distraction (n = 7), often using NAO performing a routine. SARs were pre-programmed or operator-controlled to provide interactions that included performing for the child, to put attention on the robot and away from the procedure at hand. One study used NAO to implement talk therapy to increase understanding and decrease distress and associated pain. The robot interacted with children allowing them to speak about their pain and anxiety.

Other articles applied cutaneous stimulation, using comforting tactile stimuli (n = 6). Paro, as a soft and tactile robot, was often used to deliver therapeutic touch as a substitution for pet therapy, particularly for people with dementia. A notable exception using cutaneous stimulation was the use of the Calmer robotic device to mimic affective touch of a parent.

3.5   Pain Measurement

Pain itself can be difficult to measure, as one person's perceptions and tolerance can be different from the next [13]. Frequent measurements of pain included the self-reported Wong-Baker FACES pain rating scale or Faces Pain Scale - Revised (FSP-R) [24]. Alternative self-report measurements included the visual analogue scale (VAS) for pain [31]. Others used self-reported measurements relating to pain anxiety or behaviours such as the Multidimensional Anxiety Scale for Children (MASC) [33] or their own interviews or questionnaires.

Researchers also used observation and behavioural assessment including Behavioral Approach-Avoidance Distress Scale (BAADS), Children's Fear Scale, Observational Scale of Behavioral Distress - Revised (OSBD-R), Pain Assessment in Advanced Dementia (PAINAD) or observation by trained carers. These measures could be complementary to self-reporting or useful when self-reporting was not appropriate.

Self-report and observational measurements, however, have limitations and can be prone to bias. To complement these measurements some studies therefore used physiological measurements including heart rate and salivary oxytocin, a hormone linked to reduced pain sensitivity and anxiety [37]. In the case of preterm infants, who evidently are unable to self-report, only one physiological measurement, in the form of heart rate, was used. Additionally, for robots treating a particular physical condition, such as post-stroke rehabilitation, improvements in qualities such as range of motion could also be measured. The nature of the scales is summarised in Table 3.

4 Discussion

Research into potential pain interventions using robots is ongoing, and interest in the area is increasing as robots are implemented for new healthcare applications. Early research indicates some positive results for the use of robots for pain treatment, with 13 out of 17 studies reporting statistically significant improvement in quantitative measurements of pain or pain anxiety. However, more studies are needed to prove efficacy.

All included articles based their interventions on existing theories of pain management, including pain distraction, cutaneous stimulation and physical therapy. Further research should investigate which methods of pain management are beneficial for different user groups and conditions. Some methods may be more appropriate in different situations, particularly when it comes to procedural (distraction) as opposed to long term (therapeutic) pain.

Several articles investigated treatment of chronic pain, particularly with people with dementia. Here complementary pain management could prove particularly beneficial, and affective touch may have additional benefits for this population [21]. Other articles concerned the use of distraction for young people undergoing acutely painful medical procedures, like those currently used by medical professionals. Additionally, some robots were used to mimic physical therapies for conditions that require long-term treatment with a human therapist.

A benefit of using social robots and human-robot interaction for pain management is that human-human interaction techniques can be replicated. For example, NAO often performed a routine designed to engage a child and distract them from a medical procedure. The baby seal robot Paro was often used as a replacement for pet therapy which is used in dementia care. Compared to humans or animals, robots are able to provide a more consistent and controlled intervention.

Commercially available socially assistive robots were used in the majority of studies and often demonstrated some efficacy at reducing pain or anxiety in those using them. However, these toy-like robots may also indicate a level of infantilisation, particularly when children and people with dementia are the primary study groups. The use of commercial robots could also be considered technocentric, with existing technology reflectively applied to pain management. It may be beneficial for researchers to consider co-design of robots or interventions alongside stakeholders, particularly when therapeutic treatment may need to be flexible and customisable [47]. Additionally, little mention was made regarding the acceptability or suitability of the robots for pain management from end users, which may improve both uptake and outcomes [35].

Table 3. Pain measurements

Abbrev.	Self-Report	Observation	Physiology
BAADS		x	
BIIP		x	
CFS	x		
FPS-R	x		
Heart Rate			x
MASC	x		
PAINAD		x	
Salivary Oxytocin			x
VAS	x		

Trialing non-pharmacological treatments for pain can be difficult, but future research should consider established protocols, for example, the Stage Model of Behavioural Therapies [38] which has also been adapted specifically to new chronic pain therapies [11]. This guide uses three stages before an intervention can be considered effective, and all articles in this review would be considered at stage 1a (Therapy Design/Manual Writing) or 1b (Pilot and Feasibility Testing).

Furthermore, most articles failed to report detailed demographic information. Participants were often allocated to control or intervention groups randomly, with only one using stratified sampling based on gender. Whilst this is not always necessary, existing research has shown the acceptance of robots varies dependant on factors including age, gender and cultural background [5,10] as well as the task the robot is to perform [40].

Pain is a subjective, personal and lived experience; therefore, it is difficult to quantify the pain a person is feeling. Most studies used well-known methods for self-reporting combined with behavioural observations. Some combined these scales with biometric measurements, providing bodily responses to pain, which may be more reliable as self-report can be tracked alongside physiological outcomes. Finally, there may be some benefit to measuring more long-term quality of life indicators associated with pain for those living with chronic conditions.

The limitations of this review and the included articles are primarily due to emerging nature of the research topic. Whilst positive outcomes have been demonstrated studies are often small and require more rigorous measurements to quantify their results. Future research should look to expand upon initial positive results and investigate why these methods are successful, whilst looking to investigate other patient groups and methods of intervention design.

5   Conclusion

Initial research shows potential for using robots to manage or alleviate pain, however more research is needed to show efficacy. Interventions using robots often use existing theoretical framework for the treatment of pain. Commercially available social robots were used most frequently, for the treatment of children or people with dementia. Further research should look at the appropriateness of different treatment types for different user groups and seek to design interventions based on the needs of these groups. Existing research has demonstrated the need for robots to be appropriate for a user group and task to be effective, so this should also be considered. Further trials should look to models of non-pharmacological clinical trials to ensure the effectiveness of using robots for pain management. Expanded research with more user groups and different intervention approaches should be conducted with more formalised methodology to better explore the potential for robots to be used for pain alleviation or management.

References

1. Abdi, J., Al-Hindawi, A., Ng, T., Vizcaychipi, M.P.: Scoping review on the use of socially assistive robot technology in elderly care. BMJ Open **8**(2) (2018)
2. Alemi, M., Ghanbarzadeh, A., Meghdari, A., Moghadam, L.J.: Clinical application of a Humanoid robot in pediatric cancer interventions. Int. J. Soc. Robot. **8**(5), 743–759 (2016)
3. Ali, S., et al.: A randomized trial of robot-based distraction to reduce children's distress and pain during intravenous insertion in the emergency department. Can. J. Emerg. Med. **23**(1), 85–93 (2021)
4. Ariji, Y., et al.: Potential clinical application of masseter and temporal muscle massage treatment using an oral rehabilitation robot in temporomandibular disorder patients with myofascial pain. CRANIO® **33**(4), 256–262 (2015)
5. Bartneck, C., Nomura, T., Kanda, T., Suzuki, T., Kato, K.: A cross-cultural study on attitudes towards robots. In: Proceedings of the HCI International 2005, Las Vegas. Lawrence Erlbaum Associates (2005)
6. Bedwell, C., Dowswell, T., Neilson, J.P., Lavender, T.: The use of transcutaneous electrical nerve stimulation (TENS) for pain relief in labour: a review of the evidence. Midwifery **27**(5), 141–148 (2011)
7. Beraldo, G., Menegatti, E., De Tommasi, V., Mancin, R., Benini, F.: A preliminary investigation of using humanoid social robots as non-pharmacological techniques with children. In: Proceedings of IEEE Workshop on Advanced Robotics and its Social Impacts, ARSO 2019-Octob, pp. 393–400 (2019)
8. Beran, T.N., Ramirez-Serrano, A., Vanderkooi, O.G., Kuhn, S.: Reducing children's pain and distress towards flu vaccinations: a novel and effective application of humanoid robotics. Vaccine **31**(25), 2772–2777 (2013)
9. Borboni, A., et al.: Robot-assisted rehabilitation of hand paralysis after stroke reduces wrist edema and pain: a prospective clinical trial. J. Manipul. Physiol. Ther. **40**(1), 21–30 (2017)
10. Broadbent, E., Stafford, R., MacDonald, B.: Acceptance of healthcare robots for the older population: review and future directions. Int. J. Soc. Robot. **1**(4), 319–330 (2009)
11. Bruckenthal, P.: Integrating nonpharmacologic and alternative strategies into a comprehensive management approach for older adults with pain. Pain Manag. Nurs. **11**(2), S23–S31 (2010)
12. Cervero, F.: Understanding Pain: Exploring the Perception of Pain. MIT Press, Cambridge, Massachusetts (2012)

13. Chapman, C.R., Casey, K., Dubner, R., Foley, K., Gracely, R., Reading, A.: Pain measurement: an overview. Pain **22**(1), 1–31 (1985)
14. Eijlers, R., et al.: Systematic review and meta-analysis of virtual reality in pediatrics: effects on pain and anxiety. Anesth. Analg. **129**(5), 1344–1353 (2019)
15. Ellingsen, D.M., Leknes, S., Løseth, G., Wessberg, J., Olausson, H.: The Neurobiology Shaping Affective Touch: Expectation, Motivation, and Meaning in the Multisensory Context (2016)
16. Farrier, C.E., Pearson, J.D.R., Beran, T.N.: Reducing childrens fear and pain during medical procedures: a nonrandomized trial with a humanoid robot. Can. J. Nurs. Res. 084456211986274 (2019)
17. Feil-Seifer, D., Matarić, M.J.: Defining socially assistive robotics. In: Proceedings of the 2005 IEEE 9th International Conference on Rehabilitation Robotics 2005, pp. 465–468 (2005)
18. Gallace, A., Spence, C.: The science of interpersonal touch: an overview. Neurosci. Biobehav. Rev. **34**(2), 246–259 (2010)
19. Gates, M., et al.: Digital technology distraction for acute pain in children: a meta-analysis. Pediatrics **145**(2) (2020)
20. Geva, N., Uzefovsky, F., Levy-Tzedek, S.: Touching the social robot PARO reduces pain perception and salivary oxytocin levels. Sci. Rep. **10**(1) (2020)
21. Hansen, N.V., Jørgensen, T., Ørtenblad, L.: Massage and touch for dementia. Cochrane Datab. Syst. Rev. (4) (2006)
22. Hawthorn, J., Redmond, K.: Pain: causes and management. J. Psychiatric Mental Health Nurs.**6**(5), 205–211 (1999)
23. Heapy, A.A., Higgins, D.M., Cervone, D., Wandner, L., Fenton, B.T., Kerns, R.D.: A systematic review of technology-assisted self-management interventions for chronic pain: Looking across treatment modalities. Clin. J. Pain **31**(6), 470–492 (2015)
24. Hicks, C.L., von Baeyer, C.L., Spafford, P.A., van Korlaar, I., Goodenough, B.: The faces pain scale-revised: toward a common metric in pediatric pain measurement. Pain **93**(2), 173–183 (2001)
25. Holsti, L., MacLean, K., Oberlander, T., Synnes, A., Brant, R.: Calmer: a robot for managing acute pain effectively in preterm infants in the neonatal intensive care unit. Pain Rep. **4**(2) (2019)
26. Jibb, L.A., et al.: Using the MEDiPORT humanoid robot to reduce procedural pain and distress in children with cancer: a pilot randomized controlled trial. Pediatric Blood Canc. **65**(9) (2018)
27. Karafotias, G., Korres, G., Teranishi, A., Park, W., Eid, M.: Mid-air tactile stimulation for pain distraction. IEEE Trans. Haptics **11**(2), 185–191 (2018)
28. Khan, A., Anwar, Y.: Robots in healthcare: a survey. In: Arai, K., Kapoor, S. (eds.) CVC 2019. AISC, vol. 944, pp. 280–292. Springer, Cham (2020). https://doi.org/10.1007/978-3-030-17798-0_24
29. Kim, M.S., Kim, S.H., Noh, S.E., Bang, H.J., Lee, K.M.: Robotic-assisted shoulder rehabilitation therapy effectively improved poststroke hemiplegic shoulder pain: a randomized controlled trial. Arch. Phys. Med. Rehabil. **100**(6), 1015–1022 (2019)
30. Lane, G.W., et al.: Effectiveness of a social robot, Paro, in a VA long-term care setting. Psychol. Serv. **13**(3), 292–299 (2016)
31. Langley, G., Sheppeard, H.: The visual analogue scale: its use in pain measurement. Rheumatol. Int. **5**(4), 145–148 (1985)
32. Manaloor, R., et al.: Humanoid robot-based distraction to reduce pain and distress during venipuncture in the pediatric emergency department: a randomized controlled trial. Paediatr. Child Health **24**(Supplement_2), e43–e43 (2019)

33. March, J.S., Parker, J.D., Sullivan, K., Stallings, P., Conners, C.K.: The multidimensional anxiety scale for children (masc): factor structure, reliability, and validity. J. Am. Acad. Child Adolesc. Psychiatry **36**(4), 554–565 (1997)

34. Okita, S.Y.: Self-other's perspective taking: the use of therapeutic robot companions as social agents for reducing pain and anxiety in pediatric patients. Cyberpsychol. Behav. Soc. Network. **16**(6), 436–441 (2013)

35. Pino, M., Boulay, M., Jouen, F., Rigaud, A.S.: Are we ready for robots that care for us? attitudes and opinions of older adults toward socially assistive robots. Front. Aging Neurosci. **7**, 141 (2015)

36. Pu, L., Moyle, W., Jones, C.: How people with dementia perceive a therapeutic robot called PARO in relation to their pain and mood: a qualitative study. J. Clin. Nurs. **29**(3–4), 437–446 (2020)

37. Rash, J.A., Aguirre-Camacho, A., Campbell, T.S.: Oxytocin and pain: a systematic review and synthesis of findings. Clin. J. Pain **30**(5), 453–462 (2014)

38. Rounsaville, B.J., Carroll, K.M., Onken, L.S.: A stage model of behavioral therapies research: getting started and moving on from stage i. Clin. Psychol. Sci. Pract. **8**(2), 133–142 (2001)

39. Sinatra, R.S.: Acute Pain Management. Cambridge University Press (2009)

40. Smarr, C.A., et al.: Domestic robots for older adults: attitudes, preferences, and potential. Int. J. Soc. Robot. **6**(2), 229–247 (2014)

41. Tong, A., Sainsbury, P., Craig, J.: Consolidated criteria for reporting qualitative research (coreq): a 32-item checklist for interviews and focus groups. Int. J. Qual. Health Care **19**(6), 349–357 (2007)

42. Tricco, A.C., et al.: PRISMA extension for scoping reviews (PRISMA-ScR): checklist and explanation. Ann. Inter. Med. **169**(7), 467–473 (2018)

43. Trost, M.J., Chrysilla, G., Gold, J.I., Matarić, M.: Socially-Assistive robots using empathy to reduce pain and distress during peripheral IV placement in children. Pain Res. Manag. (2020)

44. Vance, C.G., Dailey, D.L., Rakel, B.A., Sluka, K.A.: Using TENS for pain control: the state of the evidence. Pain Manag. **4**(3), 197–209 (2014)

45. WHO: Icd-11 for mortality and morbidity statistics (2018) (2018)

46. Williams, N., MacLean, K., Guan, L., Collet, J.P., Holsti, L.: Pilot testing a robot for reducing pain in hospitalized preterm infants. OTJR Occup. Participat. Health **39**(2), 108–115 (2019)

47. Winkle, K., Caleb-Solly, P., Turton, A., Bremner, P.: Mutual shaping in the design of socially assistive robots: a case study on social robots for therapy. Int. J. Soc. Robot. **12**(4), 1–20 (2019)

Implications of Robot Backchannelling in Cognitive Therapy

Antonio Andriella[1]($\boxtimes$), Carme Torras[2], and Guillem Alenyà[2]

[1] Pal Robotics, Carrer de Pujades, 77, 08005 Barcelona, Spain
aandriella@pal-robotics.com
[2] Institut de Robòtica i Informàtica Industrial CSIC-UPC,
C/Llorens i Artigas 4-6, 08028 Barcelona, Spain
{torras,galenya}@iri.upc.edu

Abstract. The social ability of humans to provide active feedback during conversations is known as backchannelling. Recent work has recognised the importance of endowing robots with such social behaviour to make interactions more natural. Nonetheless, very little is known about how backchannelling should be designed in order to be detected and whether it can have an impact on users' behaviour and performance in cooperative tasks. In this article, we aim at evaluating the legibility of robot's backchannelling behaviour on Persons with Dementia (PwDs) and its effect on their performance when playing cognitive training exercises. Aiming to do so, a TIAGo robot was endowed with backchannelling behaviour generated by combining verbal and non-verbal cues. To evaluate our system, two user studies were carried out, in which the social signal was provided first by a human therapist and later on by a robot. Results indicate that patients were capable of identifying such kind of feedback. Nonetheless, our findings pointed out a significant difference in terms of performance between the two studies. They reveal how patients in the study with the robot overused the feedback to obtain the correct answer, putting in place a cheating mechanism that has led them to significantly worsen their performance. We conclude our work by discussing the implications of our findings when deploying robots in sensitive roles and possible solutions to address such unexpected behaviours.

Keywords: Backchannelling cues · Socially intelligent behaviour · Socially assistive robotics · Cognitive training therapy

This project has received funding from the European Union's Horizon 2020 research and innovation programme under the Marie Skłodowska-Curie grant agreement No 801342 (Tecniospring INDUSTRY). This project has also been supported by the European Union's Horizon 2020 under ERC Advanced Grant CLOTHILDE (no. 741930); by MCIN/AEI/10.13039/501100011033 by the "European Union NextGenerationEU/PRTR" under the project ROB-IN (PLEC2021-007859); by the Research Council of Norway under the project SECUROPS (INT-NO/0875); and by the "European Union NextGenerationEU/PRTR" through CSIC's Thematic Platforms (PTI+ Neuro-Aging).

F. Cavallo et al. (Eds.): ICSR 2022, LNAI 13817, pp. 546–557, 2022.
https://doi.org/10.1007/978-3-031-24667-8_48

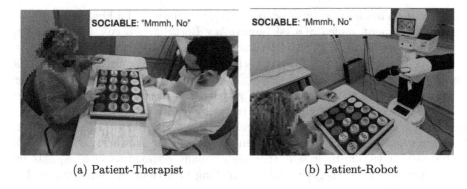

(a) Patient-Therapist   (b) Patient-Robot

Fig. 1. Examples of backchannelling behaviour during the interactions between a patient and the therapist (a), and between a patient and the robot (b).

1 Introduction

Nowadays, robots are increasingly employed in contexts in which they are requested to interact socially with humans. The social robotics field has grown consistently in the last decades, having expanded to domains such as education [8], healthcare [23] and entertainment [1]. In such contexts, robots are expected to have high communication skills almost equivalent to those of humans [7].

Communication in human-human interactions is complex and multi-modal. Our everyday communication is a constant mix of verbal and non-verbal message sending and receiving. Backchannelling in linguistics refers to the cues provided by the listener to the speaker during a conversation without the intent to take a turn, but only to provide feedback. In general, backchannel can be classified by content in: non-lexical ("Hu hu"), phrasal ("Yeah") and substantive ("Come on") [17]. Mimicking such behaviour on robots would make interaction with humans more fluid and natural, which, in turn, would contribute to increasing humans' overall engagement [16].

Despite its importance, very few works in social robotics have explored how to implement such behaviour on robots [2,10,13,15,20,22] and its impact on humans' acceptance and performance in assistive tasks [12,16]. Ding *et al.* [10] describes how an agent can be endowed to elicit conversations with older adults for delivering cognitive training. Similarly, Hussain *et al.* [14] presented a method that learnt to produce non-verbal backchannels, and demonstrated how such feedback had an impact on participants' engagement. Inden *et al.* [16] modelled five different strategies for feedback behaviour in a conversational agent and evaluated their effectiveness in a user study, showing that when the robot took into account the interlocutor's utterance and pauses, participants rated that strategy as more adequate than the others. Likewise, Park *et al.* [22] developed a backchannelling prediction algorithm that detected speaker cues in children's speech and produced backchannelling responses. The results showed that children preferred the robot endowed with such behaviour.

In our preliminary work presented in [2], we modulated a kind of backchannelling behaviour, called SOCial ImmediAcy BackchanneL cuE (SOCIABLE), which was proved to be effective for its immediacy and responsiveness. The system was validated with healthy participants playing a cognitive game. In this work, we go a step further, deploying it in a social robot designed to deliver cognitive training therapy to Persons with Dementia (PwDs) [6]. Indeed, from a set of observational studies conducted with healthcare professionals of Ace Alzheimer Center Barcelona (Fundació ACE), we noticed that patients when playing cognitive training exercises tended to look for the therapist's feedback after each move. On their side, therapists usually respond to such requests by providing positive or negative backchannelling behaviour by combining verbal and non-verbal cues.

Therefore, in this work we are interested in addressing the following research question: *To what extent, if any, would PwDs recognise the robot's backchannelling behaviour, and what would be the impact on their overall performance?*

With the purpose of answering our research question, we evaluated the **legibility** of SOCIABLE and its impact on patients' **performance** during a cognitive training task. Specifically, we designed two user studies in which the therapist was firstly a human, namely, the human-therapist study, and later on a robot, namely, the robot-therapist study (See Fig. 1).

To the best of the authors' knowledge, this is the first work that has evaluated backchannelling social cues with PwDs. With this effort, we aim to shed some light on the implications of using such social signals with vulnerable populations in sensitive contexts in which humans might be inclined to take shortcuts.

2   The Personalised RACT System

The Robot-Assisted Cognitive Training (RACT) system has been presented in detail in [6]. We developed aCtive leARning agEnt aSsiStive bEhaviouR (CARESSER), a personalised framework capable of being customisable by therapists and of adapting to patients' individual needs. In the following, we describe the robot's assistive behaviour. Focusing on the verbal and non-verbal social cues that have been implemented on the robot to provide the robot with backchannelling behaviour.

2.1   Socially Assistive Behaviour

The robot could provide assistance in a multi-modal fashion by combining verbal and non-verbal social cues before any patient's movement. The seven incremental levels of assistance are the following: i) turn-taking, ii) reminding, ii) encouragement, vi) suggesting line, v) suggesting subset, vi) suggesting solution, and finally, vii) offering token. These levels were learnt by the robot using Learning From Demonstrations (LfD) through Inverse Reinforcement Learning (IRL) by combining the therapist's demonstrations and expertise [6]. Besides that, the robot is also endowed with an empathic self-comparative personality in order to be more engaging. For instance, it never compares the performance of the current patient to the other, and it celebrates them when they move the correct token and reassures them when they commit mistakes [3]. These supportive behaviours were provided before and after the patient's move, while SOCIABLE, the backchannelling behaviour object of this study, is provided as soon as the patient makes a move.

2.2   SOCIABLE

SOCIABLE [2] is a kind of backchannelling behaviour that is defined as a combination of verbal and non-verbal cues resulting in an instantaneous response to the user's move. Specifically, SOCIABLE is based on phrasal, non-lexical and substantive backchannelling [17]. When the patient picks the incorrect token, the robot firstly makes a confused/surprised/sad face reproducing a sound like "Mmmh", "Huhu", "Naaa" (non-lexical). Then, if the patient carries on picking wrong tokes, the robot might say "Nope", "Incorrect" (phrasal), "Are you sure?" or "Really want to move this?" (substantive). On the contrary, when the patient picks the correct token, the robot would make a happy/excited face and reproduce sounds like "Yep" (non-lexical), "Ok", "Good", "Wow" (phrasal), "Well done", "Carry on" (substantive). In both cases, the facial expressions and the verbal utterances are reinforced by the robot nodding its head. Here[1], we show a snapshot of a session in which the robot endowed with backchannelling behaviour delivers cognitive training therapy to a patient.

3   Experimental Design

The study was set up as a within-subject design, in which the same patient played the cognitive training therapy session first with the human therapist and later on with the robot therapist. It is worthwhile mentioning that the order of the sessions was fixed due to our experimental design [6]. However, we believe there was no learning effect as between the two studies there was almost a month (M = 26 days).

Each session consisted of two batteries of three trials. In one battery, the therapist (human or robotic) provided backchannelling behaviour and in the next one, the therapist did not offer any social feedback. To avoid any learning effect, the order in which the batteries were delivered was randomised.

In both studies, we manipulated SOCIABLE (independent variable). To demonstrate the presence or the absence of an effect, we analysed the data using regression analysis.

3.1   Experimental Setting

The experiment was carried out in a room where patients were used to receiving their cognitive training therapy at one of the healthcare centres of Fundació ACE

---

[1] https://youtu.be/a2Ktz6ADlwo.

The therapist, either a human or a robot, was sit in front of the patient and the board was placed on the table. Cameras were installed to record audiovisual data and monitor the interactions during the session. Only the therapist (human or robotic), the experimenter and the patient were present in the room. Figure 1 shows the experimental setup for both studies.

3.2 Cognitive Exercises

The cognitive exercises delivered by the therapist (human or robotic) were designed by the professional staff according to the well-known Syndrom-Kurztest (SKT) [21].

The board consists of 5×4 cells, on which ten/fifteen tokens are randomly located in the second, third, and fourth rows (see Fig. 2a). The goal of the exercises is to place five of the ten or fifteen tokens in the first line of the board, according to a given criterion (sorting ascending/descending order, only even/odd numbers).

The dynamics of the proposed cognitive task is simple. The patient waits for the robot's assistance at each turn (see Sect. 2.1). Next, the patient is requested to move the token. At this stage, only if SOCIABLE is enabled, the robot provides the backchannelling cue as soon as a token is picked. If the token is placed in the correct location, the robot congratulates the patient. On the contrary, if the patient moves the incorrect token, the robot reassures the patient and provide further assistance. After a predefined number of consecutive mistakes, the therapist moves the correct token on behalf of the patient, as a demonstration. Finally, in the case the patient does not move any tokens for more n secs, the therapist intervenes and offers additional assistance.

3.3 Participants

Sixteen PwDs (10 male and 6 female, with age distribution of $M = 75.9$ and $SD = 8.2$) were selected by the healthcare professionals. Seven of them were diagnosed with mild cognitive impairment, while the remaining nine had mild dementia. None of the patients had prior experience interacting with the robot.

3.4 Apparatus

The cognitive exercises were administered using an electronic board described in [5]. In order to detect when patients pick a token, the entire board is equipped with RFID antennas and each token with its unique RFID identifier (See Fig. 2a). We improved the previous implementation in [2], guaranteeing the triggering of the backchannelling behaviour in less than 0.2 sec. As a robotic platform, we employed the TIAGo[2] robot. The robot was customised with a new head including an LCD screen to provide affective responses as shown in Fig. 2b. These facial expressions were designed in collaboration with the care providers

---

[2] https://pal-robotics.com/robots/tiago/.

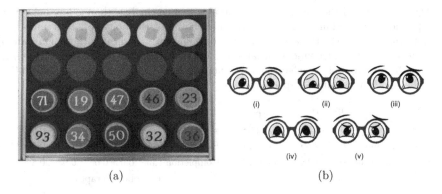

Fig. 2. Cognitive exercise (a), robot's facial expressions from [6] (b).

of Fundació ACE. Furthermore, the robot's gestures and speech were included as additional interaction modalities.

3.5 Evaluation Measures

At this stage of our work, we decided to employ only objective measures to assess our system in both the human-therapist and the robot-therapist studies. To do so, we measured patients' performance in terms of (i) completion time, i.e., the time they took to complete the task, (ii) number of mistakes, i.e., the number of times a wrong token was picked, or it was placed in the wrong location, (iii) ratio of SOCIABLE, i.e., the number of times SOCIABLE was grasped by patients normalised on the overall number of attempts, and finally, (iv) reaction time, i.e., the time they took to pick a token and place it in a given location after one of the levels of assistance was provided by the robot (see Sect. 2.1).

It should be noted that when the backchannelling behaviour was provided on a correct token, whether the patient detected it was not automatically recorded in our system because the robot was not able to infer if the social feedback was recognised. Therefore, the experimenter took note of whether the patient looked at the robot for getting confirmation feedback. On the contrary, detecting when patients picked a wrong token was done thanks to the electronic board as if SOCIABLE was recognised the patient would move the token back to its original position.

3.6 Protocol

The two user studies were carried out during a two-month period. In the first one, we conducted the human-therapist study and in the second one the robot-therapist one. Sessions were carried out once a week (4 patients) because of the COVID-19 restrictions.

Upon arrival, the experimenter greeted the patient and explained the purpose of the study together with the therapist. At this stage, members of the family

Table 1. Results of the linear regression analysis when the backchannelling behaviour was provided by the human therapist (a) and the robot therapist (b). It is important to note that R^2 defines the coefficient of determination, β indicates the magnitude of the effect that the independent variable has on the dependent variable, and the sign defines the direction of the effect, finally F and p-value are the value of the distribution and the significance value, respectively.

	R^2	F	β	p
# Mistakes	0.11	0.17	−0.26	0.68
Reaction time	0.08	2.69	−1.15	0.14
Completion time	0.09	1.18	−3.66	0.28

(a) human-therapist

	R^2	F	β	p
# Mistakes	0.26	10.98	2.56	0.002*
Reaction time	0.28	5.78	−2.64	0.006*
Completion time	0.02	0.6	0.93	0.8

(b) robot-therapist

were also allowed to attend. If the patient agreed to participate, the experimenter asked them to sign an informed consent form, which included the authorisation to collect data for scientific purposes. Next, a warm-up session was arranged for the patients in order to get accustomed to the board, the nature of the instructions and the kind of exercises.

The patients received instructions to play two test batteries of three trials. Between one trial and the other, a 5-min break was offered to the patients. After each trial, a new sequence of tokens was arranged by the experimenter. This is to avoid the patients memorising the tokens. After completing the first battery, patients were offered a break of 30 min in which they could relax a bit and have informal conversations with the therapist.

4   Evaluation

4.1   Human-Therapist Study

The objective of this first study was to evaluate the patients' performance when the social feedback was provided by the human therapist.

In order to validate whether the backchannelling behaviour of the human therapist had an impact on patients' performance, we formulate the following research hypothesis:

H1: When patients interact with the human therapist, their performance does not change whether the therapist provides them with SOCIABLE or not.

H1 was stated according to previous observational studies carried out with PwDs. From these studies, we noticed that patients when not provided with any backchannelling behaviour tried to solve the task anyway without altering their strategy.

To evaluate the impact of SOCIABLE on patients' number of mistakes, reaction time and completion time (dependent variables), we ran a simple linear regression. The results of the statistical analysis are reported in Table 1a. Overall, we did not find any statistical significance.

Specifically, with respect to the number of mistakes, findings showed that there was not a significant effect ($p = .68$) between when the human therapist provided patients with SOCIABLE ($M = 10.73$, $SD = 1.96$) and when the therapist did not offer it ($M = 11.04$, $SD = 1.63$).

Concerning the average reaction time, results suggested that the difference between patients' reaction time when interacting with the human therapist who provided SOCIABLE ($M = 4.86$, $SD = 2.66$) and when the therapist did not offer it ($M = 3.2$, $SD = 1.83$) was not significant ($p = .14$).

Finally, regarding the impact of SOCIABLE on patients' completion time, results showed that there was not a significant effect of SOCIABLE ($p = .28$) on patients' completion time (with $M = 48.8$, $SD = 9.5$; and without $M = 52.53$, $SD = 6.4$).

4.2   Robot-Therapist Study

The objective of the second study was to evaluate the legibility of the backchannelling behaviour and its impact on patients' performance when it was provided by the robot. We formulated the following research hypotheses:

H2: When patients interact with a TIAGo robot, capable of providing SOCIA-BLE, they recognise the social feedback and leverage it during the exercise.
H3: When patients interact with a TIAGo robot, their performance does not change whether the robot provides them with SOCIABLE or not.

With H2 we aimed at assessing the legibility of the backchannelling behaviour of the robot. On the other hand, we formulated H3, according to the main findings of the previous study, in which we expected that SOCIABLE would not alter patients' performance.

Concerning the legibility of SOCIABLE, we computed the percentage of times it was detected by the patients. It seems that, in average, patients leveraged the social feedback 78.4% of the time. We noticed that the remainder 21.6% of the time, they did not detect it for two main reasons: they were still discovering it (early stages of the first trial) or because they were at the end of the trial and did not need any confirmation from the robot.

Given those results, we then evaluated whether the social feedback had any impact on the patients' performance. To do so, we ran a simple linear regression, with SOCIABLE, as a predictor, controlling for patients' number of mistakes, reaction time and completion time. The results of the statistical analysis are reported in Table 1b.

Regarding the number of mistakes, results highlighted that the difference was significant ($p = .002$), indicating that patients when provided with SOCIABLE ($M = 10.43$, $SD = 1.67$) committed on average 2.56 mistakes more than when they were not provided with any social feedback ($M = 9.59$, $SD = 2.08$).

Similarly, we found a significant effect of SOCIABLE on patients' reaction time ($p = .006$). Indeed, when the robot was endowed with SOCIABLE participants took less time to pick up the next token to move ($M = 4.625$, $SD = 1.31$)

than when they interacted with a robot that did not provide any feedback ($M = 7.25$, $SD = 1.56$).

Finally, we did not discover any significant difference in patients' completion time ($p = .8$), that is the robot's backchannelling did not have any impact (with $M = 84.3$, $SD = 8.23$, without $M = 87.26$, $SD = 10.31$).

4.3   Discussion

The results from the human therapist study confirmed our research hypothesis H1. Indeed, patients' strategy and attitude toward the task were the same regardless of the social feedback provided by the therapist. On the other hand, from the robot therapist study, only H2 was supported by our findings, while H3 was only partially confirmed.

The 16 PwDs involved in the study were capable of detecting the backchannelling behaviour of the robot and leveraging it during the interactions (H2). Nonetheless, the impact of SOCIABLE on their performance (H3) was significant on some dimensions: the number of mistakes and reaction time.

Regarding our initial research question, we can conclude that when the backchannelling behaviour was detected by patients, it did impact their performance. We observed that when the robot replaced the human therapist, and it provided social feedback, patients' strategies to solve the task completely changed. Indeed, most of the patients started to pick up tokens randomly and very quickly without paying attention to the number of mistakes, but only waiting for the robot's social feedback to decide whether the token was the correct one or not. While not all of them implemented this strategy, by analysing the recording, we can conclude that it was a kind of pattern that we observed. This is also reflected in the significant differences we found in the number of mistakes and reaction time.

From this study, two important aspects of Human-Robot Interaction (HRI) emerged and merit comment: the role ascribed by patients to the robot and the cheating mechanism. We speculate that patients did not fully buy the legitimacy of the TIAGo robot as a therapist. Indeed, humans when interacting with other humans behave differently than when they interact with robots in the same context [4]. Such differences might be the result of applying different social [9] and moral norms [19] to humans and to robots. Another aspect related to the robot's role is its personality and communication style. Indeed, a human therapist would have lambasted the patient for having such behaviour by: (i) telling them to be more concentrated; (ii) gazing at them and making a negative facial expression; (iii) refusing to provide any feedback. In our context, the robot was endowed with an empathic and self-comparative personality, resulting in a very supportive and reassuring behaviour which was not programmed to tackle such lambasting behaviours. Considering switching to a more authoritarian personality might be a valid solution to face such situations. This idea is further supported by the findings of Maggi et al. [18] whereby a more authoritarian robot could be more suitable for tasks that require high cognitive demand than a polite one.

Concerning the "cheating" behaviour of patients when provided with SOCIA-BLE, we interpret it as a coping mechanism given the mental workload required by the task and to prevent negative feelings that they might experience during the session such as anxiety, pressure, or frustration for a negative evaluation [11,25]. We hypothesised that patients, by realising that the robot was not capable of detecting their behaviour, felt authorised to use it as a shortcut to solve the exercises. This interpretation is consistent with the findings of Petisca *et al.* [24] who found in their study that when participants were alone in the room with the robot (no other human was present) with no chance at all to get caught, participants were more keen to cheat.

5   Limitations and Future Work

Although the present results clearly support our research question, it is appropriate to recognise several potential limitations, both methodological and experimental. With respect to the methodological ones, we can include the limited sample size, which does limit the power of our findings. Given the promising preliminary results, in the future we aim at evaluating the system with a wider population. An additional limitation is the lack of subjective evaluation. It would be interesting to analyse the patients' perception in terms of cognitive workload, user experience and robot's capabilities. A follow-up study will be focused on this specific aspect.

Concerning the developmental limitations, we can mention the lack of adaptivity of the backchannelling. Indeed, we did not learn the "when", i.e., when to provide it, and the "what", i.e., what to say. Future work should explore the possibility to learn the backchannelling behaviour that best fits the patients' individual needs, similarly to [10]. A further limitation was the lack of detecting unexpected situations such the ones reported in this study. On the one hand, we could leave the final decision of reprimanding the patients to the human therapist. On the other hand, as mentioned before, we could integrate the current personality with a more authoritarian one that can tackle such edge situations and study whether the robot is better recognised as a reliable entity. The personalisation framework presented in [6] could be extended in a way to integrate both these two functionalities.

6   Conclusion

In this work, we aimed at evaluating the legibility of robot's backchannelling behaviour (SOCIABLE) and its impact on patients' performance during a cognitive training session. Towards such goal, we designed two within-subject studies: one in which the social feedback was offered by the human therapist and the other, in which it was provided by the robot. We found that patients were capable of detecting SOCIABLE. However, their behaviour and attitude towards the task in the two studies was quite different, leading us to speculate that patients (i) did not ascribe the robot the same authority they assigned to the human therapist, (ii) put in place cheating mechanisms without being worried to get caught when the backchannelling was provided by the robot.

Since robots in the near future are expected to be employed in sensitive roles, it is very important to be sure that they are prepared to tackle some of these situations. While these results are very preliminary, we believe that they can provide food for thought for the social robotics community about the implications that a given behaviour, designed for offering a better human-like experience, may trigger such unexpected behaviour.

References

1. Ali, S., Devasia, N., Park, H.W., Breazeal, C.: Social robots as creativity eliciting agents. Front. Robot. AI **8**, 275 (2021)
2. Andriella, A., Huertas-Garcia, R., Forgas-Coll, S., Torras, C., Alenya, G.: Discovering SOCIABLE: using a conceptual model to evaluate the legibility and effectiveness of backchannel cues in an entertainment scenario. In: Proceedings of the IEEE International Conference on Robot and Human Interactive Communication, pp. 752–759 (2020)
3. Andriella, A., Huertas-Garcia, R., Forgas-Coll, S., Torras, C., Alenyà, G.: I know how you feel: the importance of interaction style on users acceptance in an entertainment scenario. Interact. Stud. **23**(1), 21–57 (2022)
4. Andriella, A., Siqueira, H., Fu, D., Magg, S., Barros, P., Wermter, S., Torras, C., Alenyà, G.: Do I have a personality? endowing care robots with context-dependent personality traits. Int. J. Soc. Robot. **13**(8), 2081–2102 (2021)
5. Andriella, A., Suárez-Hernández, A., Segovia-Aguas, J., Torras, C., Alenyà, G.: Natural teaching of robot-assisted rearranging exercises for cognitive training. In: Proceedings of the International Conference on Social Robotics, pp. 611–621 (2019)
6. Andriella, A., Torras, C., Abdelnour, C., Alenyà, G.: Introducing CARESSER: a framework for in situ learning robot social assistance from expert knowledge and demonstrations. User Model User-Adap. Inter. 1–56 (2022)
7. Bonarini, A.: Communication in human-robot interaction. Curr. Robot. Rep. **1**(4), 279–285 (2020)
8. Clabaugh, C., et al.: Long-term personalization of an in-home socially assistive robot for children with autism spectrum disorders. Front. Robot. AI **1**, 110 (2019)
9. De Graaf, M.M.A., Malle, B.F.: People's judgments of human and robot behaviors: a robust set of behaviors and some discrepancies. In: Proceedings of the ACM/IEEE International Conference on Human-Robot Interaction, pp. 97–98 (2018)
10. Ding, Z., et al.: TalkTive: a conversational agent using backchannels to engage older adults in neurocognitive disorders screening. In: Proceedings of the Conference on Human Factors in Computing Systems, pp. 1–19 (2022)
11. Galil, A., Gidron, M., Yarmolovsky, J., Geva, R.: Cognitive strategies for managing cheating: the roles of cognitive abilities in managing moral shortcuts. Psychon. Bull. Rev. **28**(5), 1579–1591 (2021)
12. Gratch, J., Wang, N., Gerten, J., Fast, E., Duffy, R.: Creating rapport with virtual agents. In: Pelachaud, C., Martin, J.-C., André, E., Chollet, G., Karpouzis, K., Pelé, D. (eds.) IVA 2007. LNCS (LNAI), vol. 4722, pp. 125–138. Springer, Heidelberg (2007)

13. Hussain, N., Erzin, E., Metin Sezgin, T., Yemez, Y.: Speech driven backchannel generation using deep Q-network for enhancing engagement in human-robot interaction. In: Proceedings of the Annual Conference of the International Speech Communication Association, pp. 4445–4449 (2019)
14. Hussain, N., Erzin, E., Sezgin, T.M., Yemez, Y.: Training socially engaging robots: modeling backchannel behaviors with batch reinforcement learning. IEEE Trans. Affect. Comput. 1–14 (2022)
15. Iio, T., Yoshikawa, Y., Chiba, M., Asami, T., Isoda, Y., Ishiguro, H.: Twin-robot dialogue system with robustness against speech recognition failure in human-robot dialogue with elderly people. Appl. Sci. 10(4), 1522 (2020)
16. Inden, B., Malisz, Z., Wagner, P., Wachsmuth, I.: Timing and entrainment of multimodal backchanneling behavior for an embodied conversational agent. In: Proceedings of the ACM International Conference on Multimodal Interaction, pp. 181–188 (2013)
17. Iwasaki, S.: The Northridge earthquake conversations: the floor structure and the loop sequence in Japanese conversation. J. Pragmat. 28(6), 661–693 (1997)
18. Maggi, G., Dell'Aquila, E., Cucciniello, I., Rossi, S.: Don't get distracted!: the role of social robots interaction style on users cognitive performance, acceptance, and non-compliant behavior. Int. J. Soc. Robot. 1–13 (2020)
19. Malle, B.F., Scheutz, M., Arnold, T., Voiklis, J., Cusimano, C.: Sacrifice one for the good of many?: people apply different moral norms to human and robot agents. In: Proceedings of the ACM/IEEE International Conference on Human-Robot Interaction, pp. 117–124 (2015)
20. Murray, M., et al.: Learning backchanneling behaviors for a social robot via data augmentation from human-human conversations. In: Proceedings of the Conference on Robot Learning, pp. 1–13 (2021)
21. Overall, J.E., Schaltenbrand, R.: The SKT neuropsychological test battery. J. Geriatr. Psychiat. Neurol. 5(4), 220–227 (1992)
22. Park, H.W., Gelsomini, M., Lee, J.J., Breazeal, C.: Telling stories to robots: the effect of backchanneling on a child's storytelling. In: Proceedings of the ACM/IEEE International Conference on Human-Robot Interaction, pp. 100–108 (2017)
23. Perugia, G., Diaz-Boladeras, M., Catala-Mallofre, A., Barakova, E.I., Rauterberg, M.: ENGAGE-DEM: a model of engagement of people with dementia. IEEE Trans. Affect. Comput. 13(2), 926–943 (2022)
24. Petisca, S., Esteves, F., Paiva, A.: Cheating with robots: how at ease do they make us feel? In: IEEE International Conference on Intelligent Robots and Systems, pp. 2102–2107 (2019)
25. Wenzel, K., Reinhard, M.-A.: Tests and academic cheating: do learning tasks influence cheating by way of negative evaluations? Soc. Psychol. Educ. 23(3), 721–753 (2020)

Prototyping an Architecture of Affective Robotic Systems Based on the Theory of Constructed Emotion

Kuldar Taveter[1(✉)] and Alar Kirikal[1,2]

[1] Institute of Computer Science, University of Tartu, Narva mnt 18, 51009 Tartu, Estonia
kuldar.taveter@ut.ee
[2] Lightyear Europe Ltd., Volta 1, 10412 Tallinn, Estonia

Abstract. Recognizing emotions is one of the most difficult tasks for computers. Most emotion theories claim that basic emotions are genetically endowed, whereas the theory of constructed emotion states that our brain constantly uses past experiences to guide our actions and construct emotions and generates in each situation a new instance of emotion. This allows us to describe emotions in terms of multidimensional values – valence, arousal, and dominance. By describing emotion instances in terms of these dimensions, we can start comparing different emotional states based on the user input and reflect by a computational system on the emotional state of the user. This paper describes the design, implementation, and validation of a chatbot that can recognize the emotions of its human user and generates replies based on the current emotional state of the user perceived by it. The purpose of the chatbot is to prototype an emotion-aware social robot, which is based on the theory of constructed emotion.

Keywords: Emotion recognition · Neuroscience · Autonomous agent · Affective robot · Biologically inspired agent architecture

1 Introduction

The research problem to be tackled by this proposal is revising some foundations of designing autonomous software agents – both the ones embedded in hardware known as robots and those embedded in software known as software agents – with the emergence of the theory of predictive probabilistic processing in the brain [1], which is increasingly considered to be as important for neuroscience as the theory of evolution is for biology. According to the theory of predictive probabilistic processing, a human brain invisibly constructs everything one experiences by matching the given situation with the most similar situation from the past, which is found by very fast predictive simulations in the brain, and by "storing" each new situation. The identified closest situation from the past is then adapted to the current situation. As a part of each situation, also emotions are constructed in the brain, with the biological purpose to change the energetic body balance for dealing with the situation in concordance with the goals aimed to be achieved [2]. For example, if the goal is romantic love, the emotions *Passionate*, *Longing*, and

F. Cavallo et al. (Eds.): ICSR 2022, LNAI 13817, pp. 558–575, 2022.
https://doi.org/10.1007/978-3-031-24667-8_49

Lustful might be constructed which make this goal more attainable. Differently, if the goal to be attained is tough love or brotherly love, respective instances of the emotions *Disciplined* and *Bonded* might be constructed [3].

The theory of predictive probabilistic processing can fundamentally change the way software agents and chatbots are designed and implemented from traditional symbolic architectures towards probabilistic cognitive architectures for predictive processing [4]. However, computational implementation of predictive probabilistic processing is still faced with serious problems of intractability [5]. Different solutions have been proposed to overcome this challenge, such as sampling the environment by the agent [6] and heuristic solutions in the predictive architectures of software agents [7].

This paper describes the design and implementation of a chatbot which can be viewed as a prototype of affective robotic systems based on the theory of constructed emotion. Our assumption for prototyping is based on the work [32], according to which a working computational model of emotions can be included in the cognitive architecture underlying a software agent or a robot. Emotive robotic systems can be targeted at different areas, including interactions with older adults to overcome loneliness, which is a topic of the ongoing EU Innovation Action project "Pilots for Healthy and Active Ageing" (PHArA-ON).

2 Background

Emotion-aware chatbots have also been proposed before [2, 3] but differently from our work presented in this paper, they are not based on the theory of constructed emotion [36, 37], which is the up-to-date theory of emotion, based on the recent findings in cognitive psychology and neuroscience. From another perspective, we have represented and simulated situations for autonomous agents in [38–41].

2.1 Theory of Constructed Emotion

The theory of constructed emotion [2, 3] considers emotions as concepts that are based on situations. According to the theory of constructed emotion, human brain takes several types of input into account when creating a concept for the situation experienced by us [8].

Throughout life, we experience everything by our senses – sight, hearing, touch, smell, and taste. When we first feel something unique through our senses, we generate a concept of what it is and how we feel about it. For example, when we constantly feel cold little drops on our skin while walking outside, we associate it with rain. This means that next time we start sensing something similar, we do not need to process everything that is taking place, and our brain does not have to figure out on the spot that it is raining but instead can rely on prior experience. Once we have learned a concept, our brain memorizes the situation along with the emotions associated with it [8]. Next time we are in a similar situation, our brain retrieves and adapts the closest situation experienced in the past along with the emotions associated with it. Among other phenomena, this explains why we still feel strong emotions associated with simple memories from childhood.

Once we have learned a particular situation, sensory data matching with the similar situation experienced in the past can already give us information about the situation we are currently experiencing. This means that our brain is working in a predictive manner, which is important for the energetic efficiency of the brain, as the brain is the most energy-hungry part of our body [3]. Jointly with predicting situations from sensory input, we can also predict emotions associated with these situations [8]. Because of that, just talking about sad moments in our life can trigger the same emotion that we felt during the experience we are talking about because we are re-enacting the same situation. This also explains why some people can have difficulties with specific childhood memories shaping their lives and not being able to let go of some of the emotion concepts they formed as children. Predicting situations based on sensory input can also explain how our brain works as fast as it does – it does not have to process all the sensory input all the time [5]. This means our brain is constantly processing different possible interpretations of our current situation and retrieves the most similar situation from the past based on the current goal, motivation, and emotion.

For example, this explains how "muscle memory" works. Muscles do not have memory, but our nervous system does. Once we have learned a specific action or muscle movement based on certain input, we can predict it happening faster compared to processing the situation every time. In the same way that our nervous system helps us to predict an outcome of a muscle action, it can also predict and generate an instance of emotion.

In the same way as generating emotions based on the input received from our senses, our brain is actively thinking ahead of situations about to occur and creates emotions about situations that have not yet occurred. For example, while waiting for something good to happen, we often start feeling good already before it takes place because our brain is already living in the expectation of this situation which is accompanied by the emotion we are already feeling. This also means that the more we think about something about to happen, the more likely we are to experience it and the other way round. If we feel very much down and do not expect to feel better soon, it becomes more difficult to feel better as we are not expecting positive emotions to be constructed in our current emotional state.

Constructed emotions are not categorised in the same way as in simpler discrete models of emotion. Since emotions are always constructed from different inputs, the feeling in a similar emotional state, such as happiness, is never actually the same as it always differs in some aspects from the concrete situation we are experiencing. These differences can be expressed by means of the Valence-Arousal-Dominance (VAD) model [9], which enables us to characterise different emotions constructed along three dimensions, each represented as a numeric value. We will explain the VAD model in more detail in Sect. 2.3.

2.2 Relevance of Words

Words that we use in our daily language strongly shape the way our brain thinks and how we process the information about our environment [10]. Since birth humans are surrounded by language and words that shape our minds. In different linguistic environments and cultures, we are bound to learn to express ourselves in different ways as cultures have their own sets of words for describing different life situations. Once we start going through different situations in life, words help to associate these situations and feelings with previous experiences. A person develops emotion concepts through contextualized social interactions in which language plays a significant role [11]. For example, if we are told that what we see is "sad", it will connect in our mind to other episodes that are associated with that emotion. Words are also the key instruments in instantiating emotion concepts – i.e., constructing emotions [3]. Moreover, psychological theories also claim that emotional words are used in our brain as cues for identifying and retrieving situations [12, 13].

Associating words with emotions allows for flexibility and individual under- standing of similar situations. People can perceive similar situations with different emotions based on their previous experiences. This explains how people, especially from different cultural backgrounds, can easily react differently to a similar situation.

2.3 Emotion Categorisation

The Valence-Arousal-Dominance (VAD) model presents one way of describing emotions in a multidimensional format proposed by Russell and Mehrabian [9, 33]. Most dimensional models of emotions use valence and arousal as the main dimensions of describing constructed emotions [9] but there is no set limit of dimensions or agreed standard to be followed. However, the VAD model has been widely used in different studies [15–17] and it is compatible with the theory of constructed emotion [18]. Valence, arousal, and dominance are respectively used to describe positivity, engagement, and control over the affective state [14].

For example, happiness is an emotion that is very positive, engaging, and usually involves a strong dominating feeling. On the other end of the spectrum – sadness is not only negative in terms of valence, but also low in engagement and without a lot of control over the corresponding affective state. This can be compared to anger, which is also very negative, but also extremely engaging and dominant over the affective state. Comparison of VAD values of the six basic emotions, as hypothesized by Ekman [19], can be seen in Fig. 1.

However, this paper does not subscribe to the theory of basic emotions [19], which categorizes emotions into a fixed set of emotion types. The reason is that the theory of constructed emotion states that all emotions are instances created of concepts representing various situations. The theory of constructed emotion states that the brain is constantly interpreting the situations we perceive and thus calculating the expected actions to be performed. This means that every emotion we feel differs based on our current experience [8]. For example, when we feel happy in two different situations, it feels similar but there are always some differences in how we experience it [8]. A typical machine learning algorithm would classify both situations as "happiness", whereas the theory of constructed emotion enables to show by using multidimensional VAD models how the emotion was constructed and how it differs from other situations.

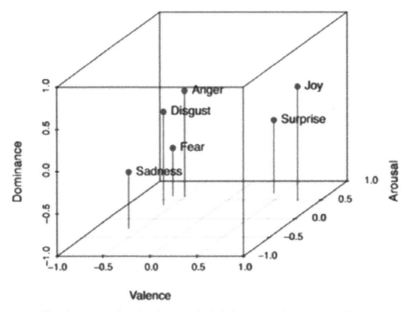

Fig. 1. VAD values for the so-called six basic emotions (source: [21])

3 Emotion-Aware Chatbot

3.1 Principles

In a dialog, both participants are engaging in predictions about each other's emotional states, which is also called emotion co-construction [8]. For that purpose, humans use verbal as well as non-verbal communication, such as facial expressions and body movements. When a human is interacting with a chatbot, the only form of information that a party can use for predicting emotions by the conversation partner is textual information. This means that a chatbot should be able to predict the emotional state of its human conversation partner based on the emotion-related words that the partner has used in the conversation. It can be shown that verbalizing as precisely as possible the emotion the partner has expressed may change the emotional state of the interaction partner by modifying its predictions about the partner [8].

The design and implementation of the emotion-aware chatbot described in this subsection is based on the mirror technique. In psychotherapy, the mirror technique is a conscious use of active listening by the therapist, accompanied by the reflection of the client's affective language to stimulate a sense of empathy [20]. In our case, the role of the therapist is played by the chatbot. For example, if the chatbot mirrors the textual input by the human by stating "you look sad", this impacts the next emotional state by the human conversation partner, which is rooted in emotion co-construction by the conversation partners [8], who are, in this case, the human and the emotion-aware chatbot with whom she or he is interacting.

3.2 Architecture

For the architecture of the emotion-aware chatbot called EmReflect, we have adapted and simplified the situation-based agent architecture for social simulations described in [7]. The EmReflect architecture consists of four kinds of modules: controller, memory, and representations of situations and expectations. These components and the relationships between them are represented in Fig. 2.

A situation instance is defined by all the input perceived by the agent about the situation represented by the instance, as well as the result of an action performed by the agent in that situation [34]. An expectation is defined through an action performed by an agent with some probability that will transfer the agent to a new situation [35]. Based on the perceived input, the chatbot performs an action based on the most probable expectation – prediction – associated with that situation. In our case, prediction is an emotionally reflective reply by which the EmReflect chatbot responds to its user.

Creating a situation instance also triggers the calculation of the motivation and emotion, while also updating the agent's memory. Motivation defines an agent's interest to perform one or another action and this way influences the choice of one or another expectation as a prediction.

Motivation and emotion calculations are done for every instance of a situation with the help by the memory. The memory module is used as a knowledge base for motivation and emotion calculations. Since memory stores situations and expectations that were predicted in the past, these knowledge base entries are helpful in creating expectations by finding similar situations that have already resulted in predictions in the past.

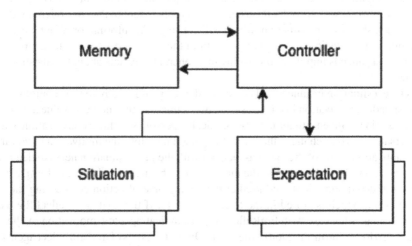

Fig. 2. The architecture of the emotion-aware chatbot EmReflect (adapted from [22])

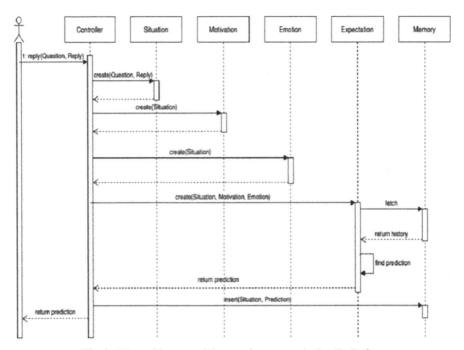

Fig. 3. The architecture of the emotion-aware chatbot EmReflect

Motivation, emotion, and their usage within the controller module are described in greater detail in the following paragraphs that are accompanied by Fig. 3.

The first step of the execution of the EmReflect agent is creating the situation. Within the agent architecture, the situation consists of a question that the chatbot asked the user and the reply that was given by the user. When a reply is sent to the controller, it will first create an instance of the situation, which will converge the information about the current situation – the question and the reply – both in the form of a freeform text. Creating a situation instance is important for storing in a coherent way data about the questions and replies.

Once a situation instance has been created, the agent is ready to start composing the corresponding motivation instance. Motivation represents by a numeric value the interest of the user in the given situation. For example, if a person is within a conversation and the conversation partner changes the topic, the person may lose the motivation to continue. The motivation value of the agent associated with the given situation helps to determine the prediction. By understanding the motivation of the user based on a freeform text, the agent can decide how it should predict the next course of action considering the goal of the agent, which is stored in the agent's memory. If the goal is to reflect the user's behaviour, as is the case with EmReflect, replies indicating a low motivation by the user would also lower the motivation of the agent. One of the goals of the EmReflect agent may be maximizing the motivation of the user to talk to the chatbot [23]. However, although motivation instances are implemented in the EmReflect chatbot, they are currently not used. The reason is that it was important to allow for step-by-step development and verification because the architecture of this kind of chatbot has multiple components that need tuning and validation.

In the EmReflect chatbot, the emotional state of the user is not categorized as belonging to a set of predefined emotions. Instead of that, the chatbot characterizes the emotional states of the user based on the dimensional approach described in Sect. 2.3. According to this approach, emotions are characterized according to their three dimensions – valence, arousal, and dominance. Utilizing this model for describing emotions facilitates computational comparison of emotional states because the values for different dimensions can be normalized and combined with the historic data of the same kind stored in the agent's memory. These values are calculated based on the textual input by the chatbot's user by means of the natural language processing (NLP) algorithm that is described in [24]. NLP consisted of the tokenization process performed by means of the Python NLTK library[1]. Since the usage of this library is common in NLP, we will not explain it further here. The tokenization results in a set of emotion-related words for which mean Valence-Arousal-Dominance (VAD) values are determined based on the datasets explained in Sect. 3.3. These VAD values characterizing the situation at hand represent the emotional state of the user necessary for calculating expectations and are stored within the corresponding emotion descriptor instance.

At the second step of the execution of the EmReflect agent, the VAD values of the emotion descriptor of the current situation instance are calculated. The emotional state of the user informs the agent on how it should reply, considering both the motivation associated with the given situation and the goal of the agent. For example, if the user is feeling sad, an emotional helper agent could make a prediction that it should be as emotionally supportive as possible by trying to increase the motivation of the user to write responses and talk about their problems. In case of the currently simpler EmReflect architecture, where the motivation of the agent is not considered, the emotion descriptor reflects the emotional state of the user, as it has been perceived by the chatbot, meaning that if the user is using words that indicate happiness, the agent will also reply happily. The emotion descriptor should describe the emotional state of the user based on the current situation that is represented by the given situation instance. This means that historic data from similar situations is not yet used for generating predictions, and the VAD values of the emotion descriptor are calculated solely based on the current text entered by the user. Calculation of the VAD values of the emotion descriptor is the most important part of EmReflect as the purpose of the application is to reflect the emotional state of the user based on their replies given while talking to the chatbot.

The final step of processing a single input from the user is creating instances of expectations. This is done as soon as the calculation of the VAD values to be stored in the emotion descriptor of the current situation is complete. As can be seen in Fig. 3, each expectation instance combines the knowledge obtained from the situation instance along with the associated motivation instance, if available, and the emotion descriptor, and the historic knowledge stored in the memory determining the probabilities of performing different actions by the agent according to the theory of constructed emotion. In EmReflect, the action chosen to be performed, which is known as a prediction, is a text reply given by the agent to the user. Prediction generation heavily depends on the

---

[1] https://www.nltk.org/

goal the agent is trying to achieve, together with other parameters used by the prediction algorithm, such as the historic knowledge. In the current version of EmReflect, possible replies given to the user are predetermined. The predefined replies were chosen to be generic enough so that they could be used as emotional replies in various contexts. VAD values for these replies were determined by the EmReflect chatbot in the same way how the VAD values for the user input were determined. For example, the predefined VAD values for the expression "Oh, that sounds bad!" were determined as V: 0.445, A: 0.624, D: 0.3855, and for the expression "That sounds good" as V: 0.8515, A: 0.442, D: 0.466. For generating a reply to the user, the EmReflect chatbot calculates the difference between the emotional VAD values of the user input and possible replies.

The difference is calculated by summing up the differences between the respective mean values of the valence, arousal and dominance of the user reply on one hand and predefined responses on the other hand. The reply with the lowest difference is used as the reply that is returned by the agent to the user.

In summary, the execution loop of the EmReflect agent, which is a simplified version of the agent architecture described in [7], consists of the following steps, where each step entails invoking the corresponding function with the given parameters:

1. Create an instance of situation: *Situation (Question, Reply)*.
2. Create an instance of motivation associated with the situation: *Motivation (Situation)*.
3. Create an instance of emotion associated with the situation: *Emotion (Situation)*.
4. Create instances of expectations about likely future situations: *Expectations (Situation, Motivation)*.
5. Generate prediction that defines the action performed by the agent by choosing one of the expectations: *Prediction (Expectations, History)*.

3.3 Datasets

The execution of the architecture of the EmReflect chatbot described in Sect. 3.2 requires data processing. Since the architecture of an emotion-aware chatbot only has a textual input by the user to work with, it requires rich corpora and previously stored data consisting of different words and phrases to interpret the textual input by the user. For dealing with motivation, the agent is required to know about the words and phrases that would indicate higher and lower motivational levels expressed by the user. Depending on the usage context, the need may also arise to express the motivation by the agent if the agent is capable of being motivational. A similar need exists for emotion calculation – a rich dataset is required for the agent to understand the emotional meaning of the input by the user. EmReflect does not yet use motivation as a part of expectation calculation but utilizes the emotional state of the user by finding the valence, arousal, and dominance values for the user input and replying with a prediction that has the most similar VAD values. Therefore, it was necessary to find a dataset that could be utilized by the EmReflect chatbot to interpret the emotional meaning of the freeform written text input by the human user.

Initially, the implementation of the EmReflect chatbot drew inspiration from the BayesACT project [25, 26]. This project used a similar approach for building emotional states but rather from the perspective of predicting the identities of the human participants. The BayesACT project has implemented algorithms that use VAD values for determining identities, behaviours, and actions, which are referred to as EPA values – evaluation, potency, and activeness. Datasets used by the BayesACT project [27] were initially chosen also for the EmReflect chatbot. However, soon it became clear that these datasets did not contain enough data for covering the VAD values for many popular emotion-related words and phrases – the dataset contained only about 1500 entries and originated in the dataset Indiana2002-04 [27] created for the Interact software [28]. Upon investigating different other datasets provided with the Interact software [28], it became visible that most of the datasets were around the same size as Indiana2002-04 [27].

Since the datasets of the Interact software [27, 28] were not sufficient for the EmReflect chatbot and the analysis of a freeform text is the main method of the VAD analysis, we started looking for and discovered other datasets of the same kind. We discovered that the most popular lexicon used so far in the research was the Bradley and Lang ANEW norms lexicon from 1999, which contained about 1000 words [29]. However, this dataset, while being innovative, was still too small to be utilized for our chatbot agent.

We found that newer lexicons with significantly higher numbers of included words and phrases had come out within the last 15 years with one of the biggest ones provided by Warriner, Kuperman, and Brysbaert, who extended their lexicon to nearly 14 000 English lemmas [30]. This dataset is also rich because for each included lemma it also contains information about the gender, age, and educational differences in its usage. This allows for better accuracy of VAD values when analysing a text in the given context because the agent is better aware of the user in terms of their gender, age, native language, and other characteristics, as VAD values can differ based on these parameters [30]. The dataset [30], which was introduced in 2013, was the largest dataset until 2018 when Mohammad introduced the NRC-VAD lexicon [10].

The EmReflect chatbot uses for processing the emotion words the NRC-VAD lexicon [10], which is currently the largest database of its kind, providing VAD values for 20 007 English words. Moreover, the NRC-VAD lexicon also includes translated values for over 100 languages [10, 31], where the translations are provided by Google Translate. Although the NRC-VAD lexicon also provides translations to other languages, the EmReflect chatbot currently makes use of only the English words. However, adding other languages to the EmReflect chatbot would require minimal changes, while preserving the current functionality. With the introduction of the NRC-VAD lexicon, the author also advanced research by comparing the new lexicon with the existing ones that indicated a higher reliability and accuracy of the NRC-VAD lexicon by Mohammad [10] in comparison with the previously largest lexicon by Warriner, et al. [30]. The size comparison of popular VAD-lexicons is presented in Table 1.

Table 1. Size comparison of different VAD-lexicons

Lexicon	Word count
Indiana2002–04	1 500
ANEW	2 477
Warriner et al.	13 915
NRC-VAD	20 007

4 Validation

Building a simulation that follows the theory of constructed emotion is an extremely difficult and time-consuming task. The theory of constructed emotion describes how the brain uses our memory to build an emotional state and considers input from various senses that feed our brain live information about our current situation. Representing all of this as a computer simulation in one go is not possible, as there are many possible routes for decision-making and several possible points of failure. Therefore, it was decided to narrow the validation experiment down to a chatbot application, which limits the sources of input for the simulation to only a textual input and generates the expectations based on just the emotion and motivation. While analysing and understanding a written text is still a difficult task for any software application to accomplish, our attempt helps to understand if constructing the emotional value from a freeform text can be accurate enough for generating a prediction in the form of an adequate reply by the emotion-aware chatbot.

While there are many possible solutions to design and implement this kind of chatbot and conduct an experiment on its usage, it was important from the beginning of the implementation to introduce a modular solution. Therefore, some architectural modules of the EmReflect chatbot were not used as a part of the research work reported in this paper but have still been implemented to demonstrate the possibility of further developing the application and complementing it with other aspects for improving the user experience.

4.1 Participants

The home page of the EmReflect chatbot with an introduction to the validation experiment was sent to 200 people in open chat rooms. Out of those, 17 persons registered for the experiment, who were instructed to access their unique URL every day for the duration of one week before going to bed to have a conversation with the EmReflect chatbot and fill in the questionnaire about their experiences thereafter. The participants were instructed to carry on daily conversations with the chatbot for the duration of one week.

Out of 17 participants, 2 participants did not provide any entries after the registration and were excluded from the results. The remaining 15 users interacted with the chatbot and filled in the questionnaire 3.5 times on average, whereas only 5 users had a conversation with the EmReflect chatbot for more than 5 times. Since the EmReflect chatbot did not include a reminder functionality, several users often forgot about initiating a daily conversation. Some of the participants also gave feedback during the experiment and expressed pity for missing out on one or two days. A reminder functionality would most likely have increased the number of results collected during the experiment.

4.2 Procedure

The home page of the application served as a source of information describing what the EmReflect application is about and how it works. A link to the registration page was provided after the informative introduction. For registration, the user had to insert their name and an e-mail address, which was later used to contact the participant for feedback. It was also possible to stay anonymous by providing a nickname and an e-mail address that would not reveal the identity of the user. For the EmReflect chatbot, it was not necessary to know any identifiable information about the user. After completing the registration, the user was presented with their unique web address that they were supposed to continue using daily to talk to the EmReflect chatbot – their emotional companion.

As soon as the user had been provided with the unique web address, the chatbot view was opened. Introductory comments were first shown to the user, which requested the user to write as thorough replies as possible. After that, the first question was asked from the user. Questions posed to the user were the same every day and they had been designed to ask the participant about their day – starting from the morning and finishing with how the user spent their evening. Each input by the user was processed by the EmReflect chatbot and an emotionally reflective response was predicted by the chatbot for the user after each reply to a question asked by the chatbot. Each participant could answer any question only once every day. The participants did not see any calculation values during the experiment and while they were aware of the idea of the validation experiment, the precise calculation results about their emotional state were purposefully left unknown to the user to stop people from trying to influence the chatbot by trying out different emotionally strong wordings to see how it changes judgement about the emotional state of the user by the chatbot. A conversation example is presented in Fig. 4.

One of the common feedback statements expressed by some of the participants during the experiment was that the same replies were repeatedly generated by the chatbot. This indicated that the emotion calculation from the input might be too generic, resulting in generic replies predicted by the EmReflect chatbot. This was probably caused by the fact that one of the main difficulties in emotion recognition based on natural language processing is the difficulty of understanding an emotional state based on a written text, which often requires fine-tuning to allow for better accuracy.

The reason is that if we look at all the words in a sentence, the mean VAD value of the whole sentence is often neutral because a sentence normally includes many keywords that have different emotional values associated with them. This can lead to a situation where specific keywords that should, for example, assign a strongly negative valence to the sentence, have as much of weight as any other words and therefore emotion recognition does not result in assigning a negative valence value to the sentence. Similarly, a sentence with one strong emotional keyword with a positive valence can easily become a neutral sentence, which will lead to a neutral response by the EmReflect chatbot.

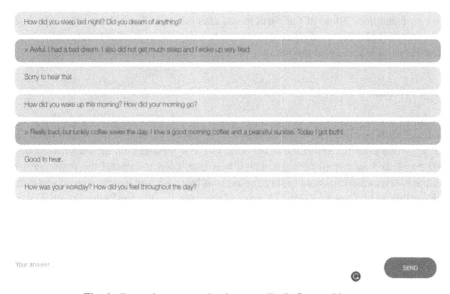

Fig. 4. Example conversation between EmReflect and its user

4.3   Results

Example data represented in Figs. 5 and 6 show the VAD values represented as two-dimensional data for valence, arousal, and dominance. The three dimensions of the data are represented on a two-dimensional scale by showing the same data three times along the dimensions of valence and arousal, valence and dominance, and arousal and dominance. Figure 5 represents the VAD values for the third question "How was your workday? How did you feel throughout the day?". Figure 6 shows the VAD values for the sixth question "How did you feel throughout the day in a few emotions? (Happy, sad, surprised, bad, fearful, angry, disgusted, …)." Figs. 5 and 6 represent the results from all collected entries by all participants. It can be seen from Figs. 5 and 6 that most of the results fall in the same area, the valence being mostly around 0.6, arousal around 0.4, and dominance near 0.5. However, Fig. 6 shows an interesting result concerned with the responses to the sixth question, which requests the user to describe their day in terms of six emotions. As we can see in Fig. 6, the replies to this question vary a lot between the participants, unlike the results to the other questions based on [24]. This most likely indicates that the emotion calculation for the first five questions resulted in a too generic emotional state and therefore the algorithm used for the emotional state calculation was not effective enough for accurate describing of the emotional states by the participants.

Figure 7 illustrates the feedback about the user experience of using the EmReflect chatbot. It visualizes the replies to the question about whether the chatbot helped the user to reflect on their day. As Fig. 7 shows, the majority of the 7 participants, who most actively interacted with the EmReflect chatbot, agreed that the chatbot helped them to reflect on their daily activities and emotional state. While this result does not directly connect to the success of simulating the theory of constructed emotion, which was another goal of the research work reported in this paper, it indicates that similar chatbots or social robots would possibly be used by people to help them to reflect on their emotional states.

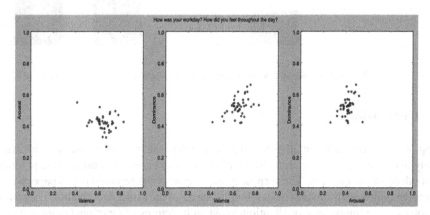

Fig. 5. VAD values for the third questions by the EMReflect chatbot.

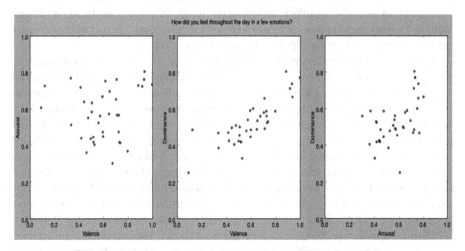

Fig. 6. VAD values for the sixth question by the EmReflect chatbot

EmReflect helped me reflect how my day went.

7 responses

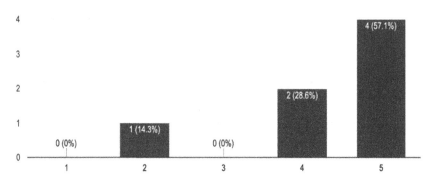

Fig. 7. Feedback summary about reflection accuracy. 1-Disagree; 5-Agree

5   Conclusions

Improving the emotional intelligence of the computer systems that we interact with in our daily lives is extremely important as it will make the experience of using these products smooth and more pleasant. The purpose of the research work reported in this paper was to prototype emotionally aware social robots by means of the EmReflect chatbot. The results emphasize the importance of situation-based architectures of emotional computational agents embedded in either hardware or software because according to the theory of constructed emotion, emotions are formed by the situations that we experience.

The importance of the results is underlined by the fact that many applications of computational agents are situation-based already by their nature, such as robots in healthcare and rehabilitation, robots for older adults, and domestic robots.

The project of the EmReflect chatbot has proven that there is a need for research on the topic of emotion-aware computational architectures and simulations. The theory of constructed emotion has a great potential for providing feasible theoretical foundations for designing and implementing simulation software that can construct emotional states from any input given, including the simulated emotional state of the computational agent itself. Many aspects, like normalized motivation scaling and the VAD model included by the theory of constructed emotion, can be represented in a tractable computational form, which allows engineers to build computational simulations and improve their accuracy over time to help researchers to find out how our brain works. Moreover, while computation simulations based on the theory of constructed emotion can help to solve the question of how our brain processes emotions, they can also improve our daily lives by solving important problems faced by the humankind. By introducing an accurate emotional mapping of the multimodal user input, it is possible to build applications that reduce stress, depression and anxiety and improve our mental health. This is crucial because it is widely known that people around the world fight with mental problems that are either not diagnosed or not even noticed until they require urgent attention and treatment that could have been prevented. An emotionally intelligent agent architecture can help to create solutions that help us in the form of a chatbot, journal analysis software, personal assistant, or an affective and social robot.

Acknowledgements. The research work reported in this article has received funding from the Pilots for Healthy and Active Ageing (Pharaon) project of the European Union's Horizon 2020 research and innovation programme under the grant agreement no. 857188 and from the European Social Fund via the IT Academy programme. The authors are expressing their gratitude to Syazwanie Filzah Zulkifli for her hard work in formatting the final version of this paper.

References

1. Clark, A.: Whatever next? Predictive brains, situated agents, and the future of cognitive science. Behav. Brain Sci. **36**(3), 181–204 (2013)
2. Barrett, L.F.: The theory of constructed emotion: an active inference account of interoception and categorization. Soc. Cogn. Affect. Neurosci. **12**(1), 1–23 (2017)
3. Barrett, L.F.: How Emotions Are Made: The Secret Life of the Brain. Houghton Mifflin Harcourt, Boston (2017)
4. Pfeffer, A., Lynn, S.K.: Scruff: a deep probabilistic cognitive architecture for predictive processing. In: Samsonovich, A.V. (ed.) BICA 2018. AISC, vol. 848, pp. 245–259. Springer, Cham (2019). https://doi.org/10.1007/978-3-319-99316-4_33
5. Kwisthout, J., Van Rooij, I.: Computational resource demands of a predictive Bayesian brain. Comput. Brain Behav. **3**(2), 174–188 (2020)
6. Friston, K., Adams, R.A., Perrinet, L., Breakspear, M.: Perceptions as hypotheses: saccades as experiments. Front. Psychol. **3**, 151 (2012)
7. Alt, J.K., Baez, F., Darken, C.J.: A practical situation-based agent architecture for social simulations. In: 2011 IEEE International Multi-disciplinary Conference on Cognitive Methods in Situation Awareness and Decision Support (CogSIMA), pp. 305–312. IEEE (2011)
8. Gendron, M., Barrett, L.F.: Emotion perception as conceptual synchrony. Emot. Rev. **10**(2), 101–110 (2018)
9. Russell, J.A., Mehrabian, A.: Evidence for a three-factor theory of emotions. J. Res. Pers. **11**(3), 273–294 (1977)
10. Mohammad, S.: Obtaining reliable human ratings of valence, arousal, and dominance for 20,000 English words. In: Proceedings of the 56th Annual Meeting of the Association for Computational Linguistics (Volume 1: Long Papers), pp. 174–184 (2018)
11. Hoemann, K., Xu, F., Barrett, L.F.: Emotion words, emotion concepts, and emotional development in children: a constructionist hypothesis. Dev. Psychol. **55**(9), 1830 (2019)
12. Best, J.B.: Cognitive Psychology, 5th edn. Wadsworth, Belmont (1999)
13. Tulving, E., Thomson, D.M.: Encoding specificity and retrieval processes in episodic memory. Psychol. Rev. **80**(5), 352 (1973)
14. Kensinger, E.A.: Remembering emotional experiences: the contribution of valence and arousal. Rev. Neurosci. **15**(4), 241–252 (2004)
15. Liu, Y., Sourina, O.: EEG-based dominance level recognition for emotion-enabled interaction. In: 2012 IEEE International Conference on Multimedia and Expo, pp. 1039–1044. IEEE (2012)
16. Reuderink, B., Mühl, C., Poel, M.: Valence, arousal and dominance in the EEG during game play. Int. J. Auton. Adapt. Commun. Syst. **6**(1), 45–62 (2013)
17. Mäntylä, M., Adams, B., Destefanis, G., Graziotin, D., Ortu, M.: Mining valence, arousal, and dominance: possibilities for detecting burnout and productivity? In: Proceedings of the 13th International Conference on Mining Software Repositories, pp. 247–258 (2016)

18. Wyczesany, M., Ligeza, T.S.: Towards a constructionist approach to emotions: verification of the three-dimensional model of affect with EEG-independent component analysis. Exp. Brain Res. **233**(3), 723–733 (2014). https://doi.org/10.1007/s00221-014-4149-9
19. Ekman, P.: Are there basic emotions? Psychol. Rev. **99**(3), 550–553 (1992)
20. Mirror technique. American Psychology Association (2021). https://dictionary.apa.org/mirror-technique. Accessed 1 July 2022
21. Balan, O., Moise, G., Petrescu, L., Moldoveanu, A., Leordeanu, M., Moldoveanu, F.: Emotion classification based on biophysical signals and machine learning techniques. Symmetry **12**(1), 21 (2019)
22. Sterling, L.S., Taveter, K.: The Art of Agent-Oriented Modeling. MIT Press, Cambridge (2009)
23. Shvo, M., Buhmann, J., Kapadia, M.: An interdependent model of personality, motivation, emotion, and mood for intelligent virtual agents. In: Proceedings of the 19th ACM International Conference on Intelligent Virtual Agents, pp. 65–72 (2019)
24. Kirikal, A.: Computational simulation of how emotions are processed in our brain according to the theory of constructed emotion. M.Sc. thesis, Institute of Computer Science, University of Tartu (2020)
25. Affect Control Processes (Bayesian Affect Control Theory). http://bayesact.ca. Accessed 29 July 2022
26. Hoey, J., Schroder, T., Alhothali, A.: Bayesian affect control theory. In: 2013 Humaine Association Conference on Affective Computing and Intelligent Interaction, pp. 166–172. IEEE (2013)
27. Affect Control Theory, Research and Teaching Resources for ACT. http://affectcontroltheory.org/resources-for-researchers/data-sets-for-simulation. Accessed 29 July 2022
28. Affect Control Theory, INTERACT 2.1 (Beta). https://affectcontroltheory.org/resources-for-researchers/tools-and-software/interact/. Accessed 29 July 2022
29. Bradley, M.M., Lang, P.J.: Affective norms for English words (ANEW): instruction manual and affective ratings. Technical report C-1, Center for Research in Psychophysiology, University of Florida, vol. 30, no. 1 (1999)
30. Warriner, A.B., Kuperman, V., Brysbaert, M.: Norms of valence, arousal, and dominance for 13,915 English lemmas. Behav. Res. Methods **45**(4), 1191–1207 (2013)
31. The NRC Valence, Arousal, and Dominance (NRC-VAD) Lexicon. https://saifmohammad.com/WebPages/nrc-vad.html. Accessed 29 July 2022
32. Osuna, E., Rodriguez, L.-F., Octavio Gutierrez-Garcia, J.: Toward integrating cognitive components with computational models of emotion using software design patterns. Cogn. Syst. Res. **65**, 138–150 (2021)
33. Russell, J.A.: Core affect and the psychological construction of emotion. Psychol. Rev. **110**(1), 145 (2003)
34. Russel, S., Norvig, P.: Artificial Intelligence: A Modern Approach. Prentice Hall, Upper Saddle River (2003)
35. Darken, C.: Towards learned anticipation in complex stochastic environments. In: Proceedings of the AAAI Conference on Artificial Intelligence and Interactive Digital Entertainment, vol. 1, no. 1, pp. 27–32 (2005)
36. Ghandeharioun, A., McDuff, D., Czerwinski, M., Rowan, K.: EMMA: an emotion-aware well-being chatbot. In: 2019 8th International Conference on Affective Computing and Intelligent Interaction (ACII), pp. 1–7. IEEE (2019)
37. Pamungkas, E.W.: Emotionally aware chatbots: a survey. arXiv preprint arXiv:1906.09774 (2019)
38. Shvartsman, I., Taveter, K., Parmak, M., Meriste, M.: Agent-oriented modelling for simulation of complex environments. In: Proceedings of the International Multiconference on Computer Science and Information Technology, pp. 209–216. IEEE (2010)

39. Taveter, K., Hongying, D., Huhns, M.N.: Engineering societal information systems by agent-oriented modeling. J. Amb. Intell. Smart Environ. **4**(3), 227–252 (2012)
40. Havlik, D., et al.: Training support for crisis managers with elements of serious gaming. In: Denzer, R., Argent, R.M., Schimak, G., Hřebíček, J. (eds.) ISESS 2015. IFIP AICT, vol. 448, pp. 217–225. Springer, Cham (2015). https://doi.org/10.1007/978-3-319-15994-2_21
41. Sulis, E., Taveter, K.: Agent-Based Business Process Simulation: A Primer with Applications and Examples. Springer, Cham (2022). https://doi.org/10.1007/978-3-030-98816-6

A Named Entity Recognition Model for Manufacturing Process Based on the BERT Language Model Scheme

Manu Shrivastava(✉) , Kota Seri , and Hiroaki Wagatsuma

Graduate School of Life Science and Systems Engineering Kyushu Institute
of Technology (KYUTECH), Kitakyushu, Japan
{shrivastava.manu712,seri.kouta100}@mail.kyutech.jp,
waga@brain.kyutech.ac.jp

Abstract. Industry 4.0 has put robotics on the forefront of manufacturing process, assistive healthcare etc. Robots are now involved in many
aspect of life and therefore it is very important to keep them working all
the time. Maintaining and repairing these robots requires highly skilled
manpower, to overcome the scarcity of skilled resources we aimed to
develop a knowledge base system/intelligent machine that are aware of
manufacturing process/machine and thus can help to overcome failure
causes or help in repairing. First step in this direction is to transform vast
knowledge present in Natural language to a form that is understandable
to machine. One way to achieve this goal is by representing language
using a logic formula that machines can interpret, like the Resource
Description Framework (RDF). The essential component for such representation is to identify entities and the relationship between them. This
research focuses on developing an artificial intelligent (AI) model for
identifying manufacturing entities from raw text using the Bidirectional
Encoder Representation from Transformer (BERT) language model. We
fine-tuned different pre-trained models of BERT to achieve improved
performance in identifying named entities.

Keywords: BERT · NER · Manufacturing process · Information
retrieval

1 Introduction

Language is one of the fundamental methods humans use to communicate their
thoughts, give a command, ask a question and express their emotions to each
other. Language evolution has taken millions of years to reach its current form.
There are a large number of languages available, each of which differs from the
others in various ways. Different words and sentence formation can be used to
convey the same intention, making language even more complex to understand,
sometimes even for humans. The recent industrial revolution has made human
and machine interaction a vital part of the day to day life. Such interaction can be

F. Cavallo et al. (Eds.): ICSR 2022, LNAI 13817, pp. 576–587, 2022.
https://doi.org/10.1007/978-3-031-24667-8_50

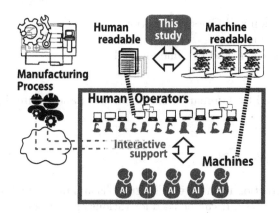

Fig. 1. The framework of the study

made easier if the machine can understand natural language. Various attempts have been made in this direction, but making machines understand language in its current complex form is very difficult. So another approach can be, to convert or represent language in a form that machines can easily understand.

As illustrated in Fig. 1, the target problem of the study is to provide a communicative support between human operators and machines to solve problems in the manufacturing process. In the preliminary step, the present study dealt with the fundamental issue to transform between human readable documents and machine-readable documents.

One way to represent natural language in a form understandable to the machine is by using logic formulae. One framework which uses logic to represent language is Resource Description Framework (RDF) triples or semantic triples. RDF is based on first-order logic, and is a set of three components, namely entities/subject, object and predicate (relation between subject and object). First-order logic, also known as predicate logic, is a way of knowledge representation that formalizes natural language into a computable format understandable to machines and robots. The basic requirements for constructing an RDF triple from natural language consist of two-part, the first is extracting or identifying named entities and the second is establishing a relationship between them.

The main contribution of this work is to take advantage of transfer learning used in language models for developing a Named entity recognition (NER) system. Identifying named entities is the foundation for creating knowledge base, better the model in identifying entities better the RDF. With the aim to attain state of the art performance in identifying named entity we proposed a model for NER in manufacturing domain by using the Bidirectional Encoder Representation from Transformer (BERT) pre-trained language model. The rest of the paper is organized as follows.

II. Related Work
III. BERT language model

IV. Data collection and Class Description
V. Implementation
VI. Evaluation metric and baseline method
VII. Result

This is followed by summarization of our work and future direction in Conclusion section.

2 Related Work

Information extraction from natural language is an important Natural Language Processing (NLP) task. It can be used for various applications such as Text summarization, Knowledge base generation, generating datasets for Machine learning algorithms, question answering systems etc. NER is a subtask of information extraction that aims to identify named entities like person name, organization name, location and date in unstructured text.

One can use NER to understand the context of a sentence by extracting entities from a sentence without prior knowledge. NER also plays a vital role in the development of a Knowledge Graph and is among the reasons why it has become quite popular [1].

NER has varied applications in every domain, and its potential use cases are being studied across diverse domains. Baigang et al. [2] used named entity recognition to extract knowledge from aeronautical data and applied it to understand, associate and manage the aeronautical data, making it understandable to machines. Hariharan et al. [3] used NER to extract knowledge from the financial domain and contribute toward building a system to generate questions and answers. The introduction of the BERT [4] language model has made a significant impact in the field of NLP. There are various NER models targeting specific domains based on BERT architecture. Such models include BioBERT [5]. BioBERT is a NER model adapted for biomedical corpora using the BERT language model and outperforms the previous state of the art model in biomedical named entity recognition, relation extraction and question answering. SciBERT [6] leverage the BERT language model to perform several NLP tasks such as sequence tagging, sentence classification and dependency parsing with the Dataset from a variety of scientific domain. SciBERT is trained in unsupervised mode on a large corpus from different scientific domains.

BERT model has also been used in other tasks, such as Syntactic analysis to determine the structure of input sentences. Kanerva et al. [7] use the BERT language model and CRAFT-SA dataset to generate the dependency structure of sentences which plays an important role in relation extraction. Another use of BERT for dependency parsing was proposed by [8]. They use the multilingual BERT model and outperform the best CoNLL 2018 language-specific systems in all of the shared task's six truly low-resource languages.

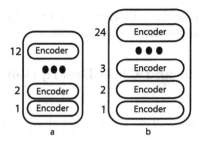

Fig. 2. BERT Model[1] (https://humboldt-wi.github.io/blog/research/information_syste ms_1920/bert_blog_post/) (a) BERTbase (b) BERTlarge

Several attempts were made for information extraction in different domains, but a little emphasis was made on building a NER model to automatically classify manufacturing processes in scientific text. One of the attempts for NER in the manufacturing domain is proposed by [9]. They proposed a NER model based on Bi-directional LSTM (BiLSTM) and Conditional random field (CRF) to extract entities belonging to 12 classes and achieve a promising result. Inspired by their work and the fact that the BERT model has provided state of the art result in many NLP tasks, we tried to explore the power of the BERT model for NER in the manufacturing process.

3   BERT Language Model

BERT stands for Bidirectional Encoder Representations from Transformer, developed by Google in 2018 [4]. BERT uses both the left and right context jointly to encode language because of which it has provided state of the art results on many NLP tasks. The BERT framework undergoes pre-training on unlabeled data and can then be fine-tuned for a specific task.

Different versions of the BERT model, which varies in training datasets and model parameters are available. Two standard sizes for the BERT model are BASE with 12 transformer layers and 110 million parameters and large with 24 layers and 340 million parameters approx. The architecture of $BERT_{base}$ and $BERT_{large}$ are shown in Fig. 2.

BERT is trained on a general Dataset, for two NLP tasks a) Masked Language Modeling (MLM) and b) Next Sentence Prediction (NSP). In MLM, the model needs to predict the hidden word in the input sentence based on the surrounding context, while in NSP, the model is given a pair of sentence and have to predict whether the sentence has a logical, sequential connection or have random relation. BERT learn word embedding by using context word and these embeddings can be used for downstream tasks such as NER, question and answering systems, and sentence classification. Downstream task performance can be improved when trained on domain-specific data. BioBert [5] and SciBERT [6] are some models finetuned/pretrained on domain specific scientific data.

4   Data Collection and Class Description

Table 1. Entity classes, tags and their description

S.No	Categories	Class tag	Description
1	Material	MATE	Dissimilar alloys, Ti alloy
2	Manufacturing process	MANP	Gas metal arc welding, Deposition process, Shaping, Joining
3	Machine/equipment	MACEQ	CNC machine, Thin-walled aluminium structure, Confocal sensor
4	Application	APPL	Industry-aerospace, Construction, Industrial, Plasma
5	Engineering features	FEAT	Slots, Notch, Loft, Surface finish, Fillet
6	Mechanical properties	CHAR	Corrosion resistance, Build rates
7	Process characterization	PRO	CT scan, x ray diffraction
8	Process parameters	PARA	Spindle speed, Temperature
9	Enabling technology	ENAT	Blockchain, laser
10	Concept/principles	CONPRI	Abrasion theory of friction, Smart Manufacturing
11	Manufacturing standards	MANS	STL format, DIN
12	Biomedical	BIOP	Trabecular bones, Scaffolds

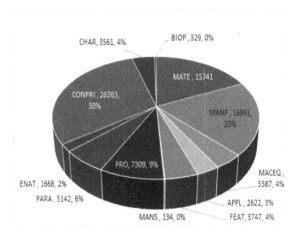

Fig. 3. Distribution of data

NER task is domain specific, and models trained on one specific domain's dataset may not perform well on other domain's tasks. We, therefore fine tuned the BERT model on manufacturing specific domain dataset. The Dataset [10] we used for fine-tuning our models is compiled using more than 500 thousand manufacturing process's scientific text abstracts. Kumar et al. [9] contain the details regarding annotation and data collection process. Entities are classified into 12 different classes, distribution of data among different classes is shown in Fig. 3.

Description of classes and tag assigned to classes are shown in Table 1 [9]. Data annotation follows the IOBES tagging scheme. IOBES is an extension of the BOI tagging scheme with two more tags, E and S. E marks the end of an entity span, and S is used for an entity having a span of a single word. Different tagging schemes may differ in performance, as shown by [11]. For the purpose of fine tuning BERT model for NER in manufacturing domain, we have divided the dataset into training, validation and test set in ratio of 80:10:10.

5   Implementation

In this research, we focused on NER task for the manufacturing domain. NER is a classification task which assigns different class labels to tokens. The classification layer of the model uses embeddings generated by BERT encoders as features to make a classification. BERT base and BERT large model are trained on data without targeting any specific domain and hence the embeddings generated are

Table 2. Hyper parameter space

Parameter	Value range
Learning rate	(1e–06, 1e–03]
Weight decay	(1e–12, 1e–1]
Per device train batch size	[4, 8, 16, 32]

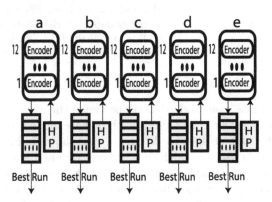

Fig. 4. Workflow a. Base-bert cased b. Bert-base uncased c. BioBert d. SciBert SCIVO-CAB cased e. SciBert SCIVOCAB uncased . HP stands for Hyper parameter space

Table 3. Hyper parameter for best run

Model name	Learning rate	Weight decay	Per device train batch size
Bert-base cased	3.0087755488011558e-05	7.368619378800244e-08	16
Bert-base uncased	0.00014482201184398306	1.5532997394307089e-06	4
BioBert	2.8098438430495002e-05	1.8058805195023753	4
SciBert SCIVOCAB cased	5.049550402691607e-05	3.8476163269415885e-06	8
SciBert SCIVOCAB uncased	1.8910884768041164e-05	0.010126886908969145	16

based on general context. However, as we are focused on manufacturing process scientific text, we used a Domain-specific model pretrained on the scientific text [6]. We also used the BERT base model [4] to compare the performance of the domain specific model against the model pretrained on a general domain. We fine-tuned these models with the Dataset [10] and observed promising performance.

Table 4. Base model and their description

Base model	Parameters	Data set
1. Bert base cased 2. Bert base uncased	12-layer, 768-hidden, 12-heads,	Unlabeled data containing 800 millions word from Books Corpus and 2500 millions words from English wikipedia
3. BioBert	110M parameters	Data extracted from different source, English Wikipedia (2.5 B words), BooksCorpus(0.8 B words), PubMed Abstracts (4.5 B words), PMC full-text articles (13.5 B words)
4. SciBert SCIVOCAB cased 5. SciBert SCIVOCAB uncased		Various dataset from different domains, some example are BC5CDR [13], JNLPBA [14], and SciERC [15]. Other details are available in [6]

We have used five base models[1] and fine tuned them for NER using manufacturing process scientific text. Details of those base models are shown in Table 4. Architecture for each of these model are same as shown in Fig. 2. Difference in these model is the dataset on which they are pre-train and how the data is used. Model 1 and 2 are pre-trained on data belonging to general domain. Model 3 is pre-trained on data specific to medical domain while model 4 and 5 is pre-trained on data belonging to scientific domain, majority of which belong to computer

---

[1] https://huggingface.co/models.

science domain. Other difference is how the data is used, in *cased model* data can contain both upper-case and lower-case letter where as in *uncased model* all letters are converted to lower-case.

We started with initializing the weight for all pre-trained models shown in Table 4. The next step is to find the values of different hyper parameters such as learning rate, batch size etc. Learning rate is a parameter in optimization algorithm that decide the step size with which weight of the network are modified with an objective to either maximize or minimize the cost function. Weight decay is a technique to avoid over-fitting and batch size is the number of sampled processed before updating the weights. For finding the optimal values of hyper parameters we used Optuna [12]. Optuna is an automatic hyper parameter optimization software framework that allows users to construct the parameter search space dynamically. The hyperspace used for hyper parameter tuning is shown in Table 2. Models are trained with values from hyperspace and the values which either minimize or maximize the objective depending on the task are returned as the best run. The details of our approach are shown in Fig. 4. After hyper parameter tuning, we obtain the values for the best run and train all five base models using these values. Details of these values are shown in Table 3. These values will be used for model training and generating the evaluation and training results.

6   Evaluation Metrics and Baseline Method

To evaluate the performance of BERT models, we use evaluation metrics like Precision (P), Recall (R) and F-score (F1). Precision is defined as the ratio of correctly identified positive label i.e., True Positive (TP), to all positive labels i.e., summation of TP and False Positive (FP). The equation is given in (1).

$$P = \frac{TP}{TP + FP} \tag{1}$$

Recall is defined as the ratio of TP, the correctly classified labels to summation of TP and incorrectly classified labels (False Negative (FN)) and is defined by Eq. (2).

$$R = \frac{TP}{TP + FN} \tag{2}$$

F-score is the harmonic means of Precision and recall as defined in Eq. (3).

$$F1 = 2 * \frac{P * R}{P + R} \tag{3}$$

We use seqeval[2], a python framework for calculating the evaluation metrics. Seqeval supports different tagging schemes, including IOBES tagging.

We have compared our models with FabNER [9] as a baseline model. FabNER is a NER recognition model using BiLSTM and Conditional random field. They have developed the dataset for NER in manufacturing domain from scratch and shown promising results.

---

[2] https://github.com/chakki-works/seqeval.

7 Result

Table 5. Class wise comparision with baseline model

Category	Precision		Recall		F1 Score	
	FABNER	$SciBERT_{MAN}$	FABNER	$SciBERT_{MAN}$	FABNER	$SciBERT_{MAN}$
APPL	0.84	**0.92**	0.80	**0.93**	0.82	**0.92**
BIOP	**0.88**	0.75	0.38	**0.86**	0.53	**0.80**
CHAR	**0.94**	0.88	0.81	**0.93**	0.84	**0.91**
CONPRI	**0.95**	0.92	0.87	**0.93**	0.90	**0.92**
ENAT	0.91	0.91	0.40	**0.90**	0.57	**0.91**
FEAT	0.91	**0.94**	0.80	**0.89**	0.85	**0.91**
MACEQ	**0.95**	0.92	0.71	**0.88**	0.82	**0.90**
MANP	0.90	**0.93**	0.83	**0.96**	0.87	**0.94**
MANS	**0.92**	0.88	0.35	**0.47**	0.52	**0.60**
MATE	**0.97**	0.91	0.90	**0.91**	**0.93**	0.91
PRO	0.93	0.93	0.82	**0.93**	0.89	**0.93**
PARA	0.91	**0.92**	0.87	**0.95**	0.87	**0.94**
OVERALL	**0.93**	0.92	0.84	**0.93**	0.88	**0.92**

Using the hyper parameter in Table 3 all models are trained for 32 epochs (epochs is the hyper-parameter that define the number of times entire dataset is processed by the model). Validation accuracy for different models along the epochs are shown in Fig. 5. Since this is the first attempt to identify entities in the manufacturing domain using the BERT language model to the best of our knowledge, therefore, we have used test accuracy of FabNER [9] as baseline model and is shown in Fig. 5 as a reference. We further evaluate the accuracy of the model on test dataset, test accuracy for different models is shown in Fig. 6. As it is clear from the comparison of F1 score for test dataset that SciBERT [6] cased model gives the best performance for named entity recognition in manufacturing domain among other models under consideration, therefore, we used this model for classwise comparision with baseline model. We will refer to SciBERT cased model fine tuned on [10] for NER task as $SciBERT_{MAN}$ in the rest of this paper.

A comparison of Class wise precision, recall and F1 score of $SciBERT_{MAN}$ and the baseline model are shown in Table 5. The overall F1 score for $SciBERT_{MAN}$ is 0.92, a 4.5% improvement from the baseline model. The highest F1 score are achieved in case of classes PARA (Process parameters) and MANP (Manufacturing Process), while the class with the lowest F1 score of 0.60 was MANS.

An example of NER for unseen text taken from abstract of Manufacturing process scientific text[3] is shown in Fig. 7. Entities from eight different classes are identified in the example, some words like 'as', 'be' is also identified as an entity for class MATE.

---

[3] DOI: 10.1109/EPTC.2009.5416556.

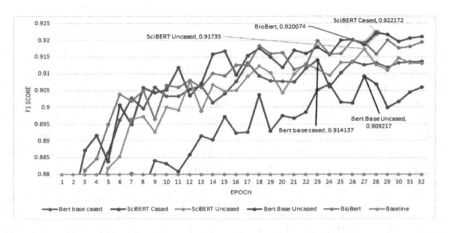

Fig. 5. F1 score comparison

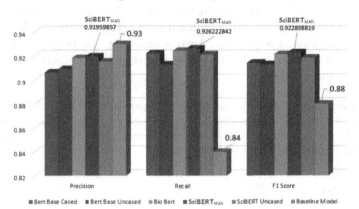

Fig. 6. F1 score comparison with baseline model

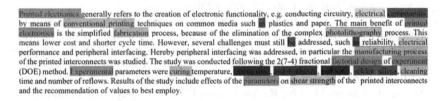

Printed electronics generally refers to the creation of electronic functionality, e.g. conducting circuitry, electrical components by means of conventional printing techniques on common media such as plastics and paper. The main benefit of printed electronics is the simplified fabrication process, because of the elimination of the complex photolithography process. This means lower cost and shorter cycle time. However, several challenges must still be addressed, such as reliability, electrical performance and peripheral interfacing. Hereby peripheral interfacing was addressed, in particular the manufacturing process of the printed interconnects was studied. The study was conducted following the 2(7-4) fractional factorial design of experiment (DOE) method. Experimental parameters were curing temperature, temperature, ..., ..., solder alloy, cleaning time and number of reflows. Results of the study include effects of the parameters on shear strength of the printed interconnects and the recommendation of values to best employ.

Class: Concept/principles: CONPRI, Application: APPL, Machine/equipment MACEQ, Manufacturing Process: MANP,
Material: MATE, Process parameter: PAPA, Engineering feature FEAT, Process characterization: PRO

Fig. 7. Example of NER for unseen text

8   Conclusion

In this research, we proposed a NER model for recognizing entities from manufacturing process scientific Text using the BERT language model. We fine-tuned different base models and our study shows that all of them achieve better F1 scores than the baseline model, which was based on BiLSTM and CRF. BERT architecture uses both the left and the right context for embedding because of which it can outperform many of the previous state of the art models. Our study was focused on BERT base architecture which has 110M parameters. Other versions of BERT, such as BERT large with 340M parameters are also available and may give a better result. Classes like MANS and BIOP, which have less percentage of data in the training set, has low F1 score. Data augmentation techniques can be used to generate more data for such classes in an attempt to improve their result. SciBERT [6] which is pretrained on the scientific text and evaluated on a suite of tasks from scientific domain, gives better results as compared to BERT-BASE trained on the general domain. A language model pretrained on text corpus of manufacturing domain may achieve better performance for manufacturing-related NLP tasks. Also, as shown by [11] tagging scheme effect the performance of the model, it will be interesting to compare our model for different tagging schemes.

Acknowledgment. This work was supported in part by JSPS KAKENHI (16H01616, 17H06383) and the New Energy and Industrial Technology Development Organization (NEDO), Project on Regional Revitalization Through Advanced Robotics (Kyushu Institute of Technology/Kitakyushu city, Japan)

References

1. Costa, R., Lima, C., Sarraipa, J., Jardim-Gonçalves, R.: Facilitating knowledge sharing and reuse in building and construction domain: an ontology-based approach. J. Intell. Manufact. **27**, 263–282 (2016)
2. Baigang, M., Yi, F.: A review: development of named entity recognition (NER) technology for aeronautical information intelligence. Artif. Intell. Rev. 1–28 (2022)
3. Jayakumar, H., Krishnakumar, M.S., Peddagopu, V.V.V., Sridhar, R.: RNN based question answer generation and ranking for financial documents using financial NER. Sādhanā **45**(1), 1–10 (2020). https://doi.org/10.1007/s12046-020-01501-3
4. Devlin, J., Chang, M., Lee, K., Toutanova, K.: Bert: pre-training of deep bidirectional transformers for language understanding. ArXiv Preprint ArXiv:1810.04805 (2018)
5. Lee, J., et al.: BioBERT: a pre-trained biomedical language representation model for biomedical text mining. Bioinformatics **36**, 1234–1240 (2020)
6. Beltagy, I., Lo, K., Cohan, A. SciBERT: a pretrained language model for scientific text. ArXiv Preprint ArXiv:1903.10676 (2019)
7. Kanerva, J., Ginter, F., Pyysalo, S.: Dependency parsing of biomedical text with BERT. BMC Bioinform. **21**, 1–12 (2020)
8. Tran, K., Bisazza, A. Zero-shot dependency parsing with pre-trained multilingual sentence representations. ArXiv Preprint ArXiv:1910.05479 (2019)

9. Kumar, S.B.: FabNER: information extraction from manufacturing process science domain literature using named entity recognition. J. Intell. Manufact. 1–15 (2021)
10. Kumar, A., Starly, B.: Dataset_NER_Manufacturing - FabNER: Information Extraction from Manufacturing Process Science Domain Literature Using Named Entity Recognition. (2021). https://figshare.com/articles/dataset/Dataset_NER_Manufacturing_-_FabNER_Information_Extraction_from_Manufacturing_Process_Science_Domain_Literature_Using_Named_Entity_Recognition/14782407
11. Lester, B.: iobes: a Library for Span-Level Processing. ArXiv Preprint ArXiv:2010.04373 (2020)
12. Akiba, T., Sano, S., Yanase, T., Ohta, T., Koyama, M.: Optuna: a next-generation hyperparameter optimization framework. In: Proceedings of the 25th ACM SIGKDD International Conference on Knowledge Discovery & Data Mining, pp. 2623–2631 (2019)
13. Li, J., et al.: BioCreative V CDR task corpus: a resource for chemical disease relation extraction. Database (2016)
14. Collier, N., Kim, J.: Introduction to the bio-entity recognition task at JNLPBA. In: Proceedings of the International Joint Workshop on Natural Language Processing in Biomedicine and its Applications (NLPBA/BioNLP), pp. 73–78 (2004)
15. Luan, Y., He, L., Ostendorf, M., Hajishirzi, H.: Multi-task identification of entities, relations, and coreference for scientific knowledge graph construction. ArXiv Preprint ArXiv:1808.09602 (2018)

Author Index

Abbasi, Nida Itrat II-23
Abubshait, Abdulaziz II-248
Ah Sen, Nick I-50
Aimysheva, Arna II-114, II-204
Al-Ali, Abdulaziz II-74
Alenyà, Guillem I-546
Alhaddad, Ahmad Yaser II-13, II-74
Aliasghari, Pourya II-160
Alimardani, Maryam II-135
Alonso-Martin, Fernando I-378
Alvarez-Benito, Gloria II-54
Amirabdollahian, Farshid II-85
Amirova, Aida II-114, II-204
Amores, J. Gabriel II-54
Anderson, Joanna II-23
Andriella, Antonio I-546
Angelopoulos, Georgios I-300
Anzalone, Salvatore M. II-124
Araujo, Hugo II-85
Arce, Diego II-518
Arıkan, Kutluk B. I-325
Arndt, Julia II-498
Assunção, Gustavo I-522
Aung, Phyo Thuta I-253
Avelino, João II-475
Azizi, Negin II-64, II-146, II-415

Baba, Jun II-194
Bachiller, Pilar II-462
Belgiovine, Giulia II-103
Belkaid, Marwen I-347
Bellotto, Nicola I-154
Belpaeme, Tony I-120
Bendel, Oliver II-689
Beraldo, Gloria I-198
Bernardino, Alexandre II-475
Bhattacharjee, Tapomayukh II-314
Biagiotti, Luigi I-143
Bian, Jianfeng I-417
Biswas, Pradipta II-452
Björling, Elin A. I-218
Blankenship, Cody II-381
Bodenhagen, Leon II-348
Bogliolo, Michela II-103

Boltz, Marie II-338, II-587
Boor, Latisha II-615
Boucher, Isabelle I-253
Bowland, Sharon II-338
Bray, Robert II-381, II-587
Breazeal, Cynthia I-89
Browne, Ryan II-550, II-574
Bruno, Barbara I-367
Buisine, Stéphanie II-701
Bürvenich, Berenike II-574
Bustos, Pablo II-462

Caballero, Fernando I-174
Cabibihan, John-John II-13, II-74
Cakmak, Maya I-218
Caleb-Solly, Praminda I-534
Camp, Nicola II-540
Cangelosi, Angelo I-61, I-241
Caramaschi, Marco I-143
Carfí, Alessandro I-267, II-508
Caro-Via, Selene II-171
Carrasco-Martínez, Sara I-378
Carreno-Medrano, Pamela I-50
Carros, Felix II-574
Casadio, Maura II-103, II-288
Casenhiser, Arowyn II-587
Casenhiser, Devin I-100
Castaneda, Gerardo Chavez II-299
Castaño-Ocaña, Mario II-54
Castillo, Jose Carlos I-130
Castri, Luca I-154
Castro-González, Álvaro I-208
Castro-Malet, Manuel II-54
Cavallo, Filippo I-511, I-522
Ceccato, Caterina II-135
Cerel-Suhl, Sylvia II-228, II-381
Cesta, Amedeo I-165, I-198
Chamilothori, Kynthia II-371
Chandra, Shruti II-146, II-299
Chang, Chin-Chen II-392
Charpentier, Samantha II-124
Charpillet, François II-36, II-45
Chen, Chih-Pu II-550
Chen, Dingfeng I-417

Chetouani, Mohamed II-124
Chi, Wenzheng I-417, I-427, I-496
Choi, JongSuk II-627
Ciardo, Francesca II-488
Ciccone, Filomena I-511
Cocchella, Francesca II-103
Cohen, David II-124
Cooper, Sara II-277
Cortellessa, Gabriella I-198
Cosgun, Akansel I-38
Crane, Monica II-587
Croft, Elizabeth I-38
Cruz-Garza, Jesus G. II-314
Cuellar, Francisco II-518

D'Onofrio, Grazia I-511
Dautenhahn, Kerstin II-64, II-146, II-160,
    II-299, II-415
De Benedictis, Riccardo I-198
Di Nuovo, Alessandro II-540
Ding, Zhiyu I-496
Dodge, Hiroko II-228
Dong, Lanfang I-440, I-475
Dossett, Benjamin II-560
Dragusanu, Mihai II-402
Du, Yegang II-550
Duarte, Nuno Ferreira I-267
Duncan, Brittany I-24
Dures, Emma I-534
Duzan, Joshua II-587

Effati, Meysam II-217
Elia, Tommaso II-508
Espuña, Marc II-171
Eyssel, Friederike II-601

Fan, Kevin II-415
Fane, Jennifer II-146
Feil-Seifer, David I-14
Feng, Shi II-550
Fernández-Rodicio, Enrique I-378
Fiorini, Laura I-511, I-522
Fitter, Naomi T. II-3, II-529, II-663
Foppen, Robin II-615
Ford, Tamsin II-23
Fracasso, Francesca I-198
Frei, Jonas II-359
Friebe, Kassandra I-388, I-402

Galizia, Giulia II-85
Gamboa-Montero, Juan José I-130, I-378
Garcia, Gonzalo A. II-54
Ge, Shuzhi Sam I-451, I-485
Ghafurian, Moojan II-160
Gibaja, Sareli II-518
Giuliani, Francesco I-511
Gómez, Randy I-174, II-54, II-427, II-439
Gou, Marina Sarda II-85
Gray, Mike II-146
Gu, Morris I-38
Guidi, Stefano II-615
Gunes, Hatice II-23

Hanheide, Marc I-154
Hao, Jiangshan II-427
Haring, Kerstin II-560
Havelka, Anina II-359
Hei, Xiaoxuan I-61
Heimann, Marc II-689
Helmi, Ameer II-3
Higgins, Angela I-534
Hoffmann, Matej I-388, I-402
Holm, Daniel G. II-348
Holthaus, Patrick I-228, II-85
Homma, Keiko II-574
Hong, Yang I-427
Hu, PuZhao I-475
Huanca, Dario II-518
Huang, Wenjie I-312
Hunter, Kirsty II-540

Iba, Soshi I-3
Ishiguro, Hiroshi II-194

Jang, Minsu I-188
Jao, Ying-Ling II-587
Ji, Xuejie I-440
Jiang, Wanyue I-451, I-485
Johnston, Julie II-540
Joly, Louis- Romain II-701
Jones, Peter B. II-23
Jouaiti, Melanie II-36, II-45, II-64, II-415
Jumela-Yedra, Cristina I-130
Junge, Rasmus P. II-348

Kalantari, Saleh II-314
Kamide, Hiroko II-194
Kang, Dahyun II-263, II-627
Kareem, Syed Yusha II-508

Karim, Raida   I-218
Katagiri, Masao   II-550
Katsanis, Ilias   II-13
Katz, Boris   I-89
Kawata, Megumi   II-194
Kaya, Mertcan   I-335
Kemeny, Betsy   II-338
Kerdvibulvech, Chutisant   II-392
Khavas, Zahra Rezaei   II-640
Kilina, Mariya   II-508
Killmann, Sophie   II-498
Kim, Jaehong   I-188
Kim, Jun San   II-627
Kirikal, Alar   I-558
Knaapen, Femke   II-371
Ko, Woo-Ri   I-188
Koay, Kheng Lee   I-228
Koenig, Kristen M.   II-3
Kong, Yuqi   I-427, I-496
Kotturu, Monish Reddy   II-640
Kühnlenz, Kolja   I-335
Kulić, Dana   I-50
Kumazaki, Hirokazu   II-194
Kunde, Siya   I-24
Kwak, Sonya S.   II-263, II-627

L'Arco, Gianluca   I-300
Lacroix, Dimitri   II-601
Laity, Weston   II-560
Lakatos, Gabriella   II-85
Lastrico, Linda   I-267, II-103
Lawrence, Steven   II-64
Lee, Jaeyeon   I-188
Lehmann, Hagen   I-388
Levinson, Leigh   II-54
Lewis, Martin   II-540
Li, Guangliang   II-427, II-439
Li, Guoming   I-440, I-475
Li, Jamy   I-75
Li, Tony   I-218
Lin, Jung-Kuan   II-248
Linden, Katharina   II-498
Liu, JeeLoo   II-674
Liu, Ziming   I-100
Llewellyn, Alison   I-534
Lohan, Katrin   II-359
Loizzo, Federica G. C.   I-511

Lopez, Edgar   I-218
Loucks, Torrey   II-299
Loureiro, Fernando   II-475

MacDougall, Luke   II-381
Maeda, Masashi   II-194
Maehigashi, Akihiro   II-652
Magistro, Daniele   II-540
Malfaz, María   I-208
Malinovská, Kristína   I-402
Malvezzi, Monica   II-402
Mamo, Robel   II-560
Manavi, Mehrbod   II-574
Mao, Meng   I-475
Marchesi, Serena   I-347, I-357
Maroto-Gómez, Marcos   I-208
Marques-Villarroya, Sara   I-130
Mastrogiovanni, Fulvio   I-267, II-508
Matsumoto, Yoshio   II-574
Matsuura, Naomi   II-194
Maura, Camila   II-518
Maure, Romain   I-367
McCallum, Kalvin   II-640
Menezes, Paulo   I-522
Merino, Luis   I-174
Mghames, Sariah   I-154
Miccio, Linda   I-290
Michler, Caroline   II-328
Mitchell, Kimberly   II-381
Mitchell, Scean   II-550
Moreno, Plinio   II-475
Morris, Tyler   II-228
Moulianitis, Vassilis   II-13
Mousavi, Mohammad Reza   II-85
Murthy, L. R. D.   II-452

Nakamura, Keisuke   I-174, II-427, II-439
Navare, Uma Prashant   I-357
Neef, Caterina   II-498
Nehaniv, Chrystopher L.   II-160
Nejat, Goldie   II-217
Norman, Utku   I-367
Núñez, Pedro   II-462

O'Reilly, Ziggy   I-357
Ocnarescu, Ioana   II-701
Ogawa, Toshimi   II-550, II-574
Okasha, Amr   I-325
Oleson, Katelynn   I-218
Onfiani, Dario   I-143

Oralbayeva, Nurziya   II-114, II-204
Orlandini, Andrea   I-165
Özdemir, Ozancan   I-325

Paek, Eun Jin   I-100
Páez, Álvaro   I-174
Palinko, Oskar   II-348
Pandey, Amit Kumar   II-74
Pantaleoni, Matteo   I-165
Paredes, Renato   II-518
Parenti, Lorenzo   I-347
Penaranda Valdivia, Karen   I-75
Pérez, Gerardo   II-462
Perez, Guillermo   II-54
Pérez-Zuniga, Gustavo   II-518
Perkins, Russell   II-640
Perugia, Giulia   II-371, II-615
Pini, Fabio   I-143
Pittman, Daniel   II-560
Ponce, Javier   I-174
Porta, Francesco   II-288
Prattichizzo, Domenico   II-402
Preston, Rhian C.   II-529
Prinsen, Jos   II-135
Pruss, Ethel   II-135
Pusceddu, Giulia   II-103

Qin, Yigang   I-100
Qu, Noah Zijie   I-75

Radic, Dubravko   II-238
Radic, Marija   II-238, II-328
Ragel, Ricardo   I-174
Raghunath, Nisha   II-529, II-663
Rea, Francesco   I-267, II-103
Recchiuto, Carmine Tommaso   II-288
Ren, Qiaoqiao   I-120
Rey, Rafael   I-174
Ricciardelli, Paola   II-488
Richert, Anja   II-498
Riches, Lewis   I-228
Rikmenspoel, Okke   II-615
Robinette, Paul   II-640
Robins, Ben   II-85
Rodríguez, Trinidad   II-462
Rojik, Adam   I-388
Ros, Raquel   II-171, II-277
Rossi, Alessandra   I-290, I-300

Rossi, Silvia   I-280, I-290, I-300
Ruiz Garate, Virginia   II-183
Russo, Sergio   I-511

Šabanović, Selma   II-54
Sager, Melissa   II-146
Salichs, Miguel Ángel   I-130, I-208, I-378
Samporová, Sabína   I-402
Sancarlo, Daniele   I-511
Sanchez, Christopher A.   II-529, II-663
Sandygulova, Anara   II-114, II-204
Santos-Victor, José   I-267
Sartore, Mégane   II-701
Schmidt-Wolf, Melanie   I-14
Schmitz, Alexander   II-550
Sciutti, Alessandra   I-267, II-103
Şengezer, Sabahat   I-325
Seri, Kota   I-576
Sgorbissa, Antonio   II-288
Shangguan, Zhegong   I-61
Sharma, Vinay Krishna   II-452
Shen, Zhihao   II-550
Shin, Soyeon   II-263
Shrivastava, Manu   I-576
Siddiqi, Aidan   II-587
Simms, Nathan   I-24
Sorrentino, Alessandra   I-511, I-522
Spitale, Micol   II-23
Su, Zewei   I-440
Sun, Lining   I-417, I-427, I-496
Sun, Zexuan   I-312
Suneesh, Shyamli   II-183

Taki, Yasuyuki   II-550
Tang, YingChao   I-475
Tapus, Adriana   I-61, I-110, I-312
Taveter, Kuldar   I-558
Tejwani, Ravi   I-89
Telisheva, Zhansaule   II-114, II-204
Toma, Marissa   II-248
Tomo, Tito P.   II-550
Torras, Carme   I-546
Tozadore, Daniel Carnieto   I-367
Trevejo, Franco Pariasca   II-550
Troisi, Danilo   II-402
Trovato, Gabriele   II-550, II-574
Truck, Isis   II-124
Tsumura, Takahiro   II-652
Turgut, Ali E.   I-325
Tuvo, Erika   II-488

Umbrico, Alessandro   I-165
Urano, Nanaka   II-550
Urbina, Fiorella   II-518
Uriarte, Gerson   I-24

van der Bij, Laura   II-615
Vigni, Francesco   I-280, I-290
Villani, Alberto   II-402
Vosen, Agnes   II-238, II-328
Vrins, Anita   II-135

Wagatsuma, Hiroaki   I-576
Wang, Hui   II-427, II-439
Wang, Wei   I-463
Wang, Yao   I-427, I-496
Wen, Yalun   I-3
Wengle, Erik A.   I-367
Weßels, Nathalie   II-498
Wick, Kristina   II-338
Wieching, Rainer   II-574
Wiese, Eva   II-248
Wilson, Jason R.   I-253
Wood, Luke   II-85
Wu, Xingwei   I-3
Wulf, Volker   II-574
Wullenkord, Ricarda   II-601
Wüst, Markus   II-359
Wykowska, Agnieszka   I-347, I-357

Xiao, Xiao   I-475
Xie, Yicen   II-248

Xu, Qingchuan   I-417
Xu, Tong   II-314

Yamada, Seiji   II-652
Yamane, Katsu   I-3
Yang, Wenjing   I-463
Ye, Rongguang   I-427
Yoshikawa, Yuichiro   II-194
Yozgatlıgil, Ceylan   I-325
Yu, Chuang   I-61, I-110, I-241, I-312
Yuan, Fengpei   II-338, II-381, II-587

Zecca, Massimiliano   II-540
Zehnder, Eloise   II-36, II-45
Zhanatkyzy, Aida   II-114, II-204
Zhang, Heng   I-61, I-110
Zhang, Lei   II-427, II-439
Zhang, Rui   I-451, I-485
Zhang, Zhonghao   I-451, I-485
Zhang, Ziyan   I-463
Zhao, Tianlin   II-314
Zhao, Xiaopeng   I-100, II-228, II-338,
   II-381, II-587
Zhegong, Shangguan   I-312
Zheng, Chuanxiong   II-427, II-439
Zheng, Yuhan   I-451, I-485
Zhou, Wenjun   I-100
Zhu, Hongbo   I-241
Zhu, Xierong   I-440
Ziltener, Andreas   II-359
Zou, Huiqi   I-100
Zou, Meiyuan   I-417

Printed in the United States
by Baker & Taylor Publisher Services

Printed in the United States
by Baker & Taylor Publisher Services